THE PLEASURES OF MEMORY

THE PLEASURES OF MEMORY

Learning to Read with Charles Dickens

Sarah Winter

Fordham University Press

New York 2011

Library of Congress Cataloging-in-Publication Data

Winter, Sarah.
    The pleasures of memory : learning to read with Charles Dickens / Sarah
Winter.—1st ed.
        p.   cm.
    Includes bibliographical references and index.
    ISBN 978-0-8232-3352-6 (cloth : alk. paper)
    ISBN 978-0-8232-3354-0 (ebook)
    1. Dickens, Charles, 1812–1870—Influence.   2. Collective memory and
literature.   3. Books and reading—Psychological aspects.   4. Books and
reading—History—19th century.   I. Title.
PR4588.W56   2011
823'.8—dc22

                                                        2010050791

Printed in the United States of America

13 12 11   5 4 3 2 1
First edition

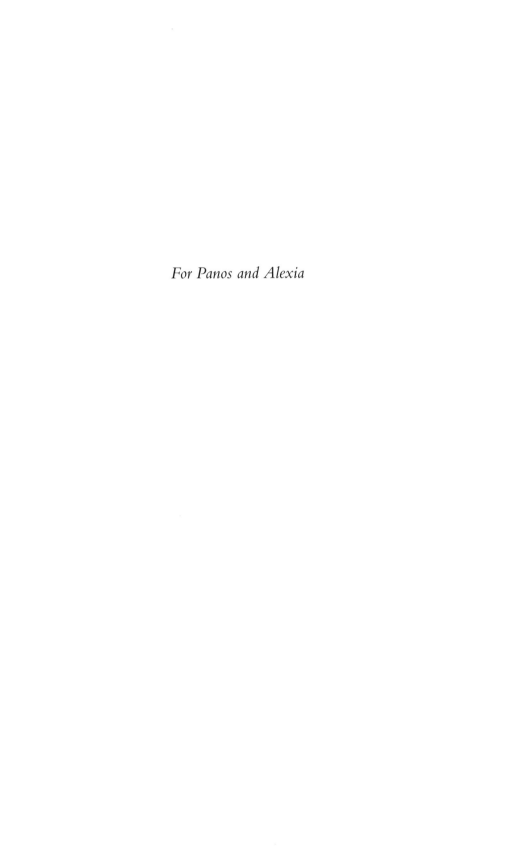

For Panos and Alexia

Contents

Figures

Preface

Opening her first collection of critical essays on English literature and culture, Virginia Woolf invokes an image of the common reader as her counterpart:

> The common reader, as Dr. Johnson implies, differs from the critic and the scholar. He is worse educated, and nature has not gifted him so generously. He reads for his own pleasure rather than to impart knowledge or correct the opinions of others. Above all, he is guided by an instinct to create for himself, out of whatever odds and ends he can come by, some kind of whole—a portrait of a man, a sketch of an age, a theory of the art of writing. He never ceases, as he reads, to run up some rickety and ramshackle fabric which shall give him the temporary satisfaction of looking sufficiently like the real object to allow of affection, laughter, and argument. Hasty, inaccurate, and superficial, snatching now this poem, now that scrap of old furniture, without caring where he finds it or of what nature it may be so long as it serves his purpose and rounds his structure, his deficiencies as a critic are too obvious to be pointed out; but if he has, as Dr. Johnson maintained, some say in the final distribution of poetical honours, then, perhaps, it may be worth while to write down a few of the ideas and opinions which, insignificant in themselves, yet contribute to so mighty a result.[1]

The common reader's tastes are both eclectic and holistic. Driven to create an entire structure of literary history out of the extraneous parts that he or she happens to encounter, the common reader engages the text as if it were a means of speaking to the author or a tableau offering access to a past era. While Woolf's essays in *The Common Reader* (1925) evince an uncommonly deep understanding of the tradition and works she analyzes, her alliance with the common reader's status, demonstrates her awareness that common reading has a history in which authors and critics have a very real stake, since they often rely on the intelligence of general readers. The question Woolf raises, then, is how did common reading come about? By invoking Johnson's characterization, Woolf implies a continuity in the practices of popular reading that spans at least three centuries and reaches into a fourth, if we include our own.

Woolf's characterization of the common reader's pleasures corresponds in very specific and perhaps surprising ways to estimations of Charles Dickens's influence offered shortly after his death. In a lecture delivered in 1871, A. W. Ward, professor of history and English at Owens College, Manchester, provided a culminating account for popular consumption of the intimate, causal relationship between Dickens's own original qualities of mind and the impact of his writings in shaping the experiences of the common reader. According to Ward,

> [Dickens's] imagination could call up at will those associations which, could
> we but summon them in full number, would bind together the human
> family, and make that expression no longer a name but a living reality. . . .
> Such associations sympathy alone can warm into life, and imagination alone
> can at times discern. The great humourist reveals them in every one of us.
> . . . But more than this. So marvelously has this earth become the inheritance
> of mankind, that there is not a thing upon it, animate or inanimate, with
> which, or with the likeness of which, man's mind has not come into contact;
> . . . with which human feelings, aspirations, thoughts, have not acquired an
> endless variety of single or subtle associations. . . . These also, which we
> imperfectly divine or carelessly pass by, the imagination of genius distinctly
> reveals to us, and powerfully impresses on us.[2]

Ward suggests that collective reading of Dickens's novels has created a common culture by revealing and amalgamating a general human stock of associations that is not normally accessible to the average person, while Dickens's mind becomes a wellspring of common aspirations through the associative power of his imagination. Common reading seems to be a form of participation in Dickens's encompassing mental powers, shared through his writings.

These sympathetic associations of both feeling and memory between author and reader that Ward describes do not seem to be mere figments; their "rickety and ramshackle fabric" is remarkably durable, as Woolf's account of common reading registers, in part because they gain their consistency, their provisional and ephemeral wholeness, in the form of a consensus purveyed by publishers, critics, schools, and readers on "the final distribution of poetical honours" within literary history and the literary curriculum. But such institutional structures, Woof insists, cannot fully account for the common reader's historical existence, or for his or her particular associations and pleasures. These seem to have a cultural life of their own.

Many years have passed in the writing of this book, and many persons have generously fostered my thinking and research, some of whom I may not have remembered to thank here. Elaine Hadley has been my principal intellectual interlocutor and resource in conceiving and completing this project; her suggestions have been timely and her friendship has been sustaining in multiple ways. Jann Matlock's meticulous reading of the entire revised manuscript and incisive feedback—representing only one of her many generous acts of friendship over the years—were extraordinarily helpful in the final stages of my writing. A crucial group of much-esteemed colleagues and friends on whom I have also relied extensively in bringing this project to fruition includes Nancy Armstrong, Jill Campbell, Eleni Coundouriotis, Ian Duncan, Langdon Hammer, Barbara Koziak, Linda Peterson, Joel Pfister, Thomas Recchio, and Irene Tucker. Thomas Recchio's support, both bibliographical and intellectual, for my interest in pedagogical materials was particularly valuable for my writing of chapter 6. James Eli Adams, Nigel Alderman, and Alexander Welsh provided answers to specific queries that confirmed or resituated my research questions at certain crucial points along the way. Students in graduate seminars at Yale University and the University of Connecticut helped me to clarify specific readings and methods. I am very grateful to the three reviewers for Fordham University Press: Audrey Jaffe, Eileen Gillooly, and Henry Sussman. Their criticisms and suggestions helped me greatly in restructuring the original manuscript. Helen Tartar has shown exceptional editorial support in making possible the publication of this book. Finally, I give heartfelt thanks to my parents for asking me regularly how the book was progressing, and to Panos and Alexia Zagouras for their patience, humor, and unflagging encouragement. I also thank Alexia Zagouras for her assistance in preparing the images for publication.

An earlier version of chapter 3 appeared as "Curiosity as Didacticism in *The Old Curiosity Shop*" in *Novel: A Forum on Fiction* 34, no. 1 (2000): 28–55. This material is included here by permission of the publisher, Duke University Press. I am also grateful for subvention support from the University of Connecticut College of Liberal Arts and Sciences for the publication of this book by Fordham University Press.

THE PLEASURES OF MEMORY

Introduction

Dickens and the Pleasures of Memory

> Much memory, or memory of many things, is called *experience*.
>
> Thomas Hobbes, *Leviathan* (1651)

> We recollect those relations only of which the registration is in-
> complete. No one remembers that the object at which he looks
> has an opposite side; or that a certain modification of the visual
> impression implies a certain distance; or that the thing he sees
> moving about is a live animal. To ask a man whether he remem-
> bers that the sun shines, that fire burns, that iron is hard, would
> be a misuse of language. Even the almost fortuitous connections
> among our experiences, cease to be classed as memories when
> they have become thoroughly familiar.
>
> Herbert Spencer, *The Principles of Psychology* (1855)

In the decades following Charles Dickens's sudden death on June 9, 1870, at the age of fifty-eight, Victorian critics and writers were divided in their judgments of his work. Eulogizing Dickens at Westminster Abbey on June 19, Benjamin Jowett, classical scholar, liberal educational reformer, and soon-to-be-elected master of Balliol College, Oxford, offered a positive summation: "Works of fiction would be intolerable if they attempted to be sermons directly to instruct us; but indirectly they are great instructors of this world, and we can hardly exaggerate the debt of gratitude which is due to a writer who has let us sympathize with these good, true, sincere, honest English characters of ordinary life, and to laugh at the egotism, the hypoc-risy, the false respectability of religious professors and others. . . . He whose loss we now mourn occupied a greater space than any other writer in the minds of Englishmen during the last thirty-five years."[1] In correlating Dick-ens's influence both with the educational effects of his popular fiction and

with his comic and satirical treatment of the hypocrisy of "religious professors," Jowett articulates a standard judgment among Victorians that Dickens's works offered a critical affirmation of English culture.[2] The terms of
Jowett's praise, as commonplace as they may seem, also provide a basis for
my account of the ways that Dickens's popularity became the vehicle for an
extra-institutional and nonpartisan literary reception that also produced an
accompanying cultural politics for literature. Jowett's seemingly generic observations about Dickens's influence in fact imply a coherent though not
highly technically articulated theory of literary reception that gained credi-
bility within an emerging international Anglophone market for serial fiction
in the nineteenth century, and that was ultimately adapted to explain how
the image of the author works within the literary curriculum to convey the
democratic values of a national and even global Anglo-American culture.[3]

Jowett's assumptions about the specifically educational impact of Dickens's writing raise a central set of questions for my project: What are the
sources of the popular belief that reading literature helps people become
better citizens by making them more socially aware, just, or humane? If they
exist, how would such effects of reading literature be manifested? And to
what extent have such expectations functioned not only as rationales for
the study of literature within the education system, where literary reading
practices and literary values are normally taught, but also as justifications of
the egalitarian potentials of modern mass culture? I contend that by establishing the literary value of popular serial fiction, Dickens's reception played
a central role in the way we have learned to read literature as an expression
of democratic values within the modern educational system.

Jowett's reference to the way Dickens's novels "occupied a greater space
than any other writer in the minds of Englishmen" draws on a widely accepted conception of the associative memory as a vehicle of collective reception. Jowett's distinction between the educational and the sermonic
registers of fiction also marks quite specifically how Dickens positioned his
writing as secular literature to contest the cultural politics of the evangelical
movement, particularly the Evangelicals' strategy to proselytize poor and
working-class readers by flooding the market with cheap religious tracts.[4]
By examining the operative psychological assumptions about the transmission of knowledge and pleasure through reading that underpin contemporary accounts of Dickens's authorial influence such as Jowett's, we can
understand the history of the popular reception of the serial novel in new
ways. In characterizing this associationist theory of the reception of serial

fiction—one that has often gone unrecognized in the history of literary crit-icism—I seek not only to illuminate the larger cultural effects of Dickens's consistent practice of serial publication but also to analyze in detail how his novels elicited certain kinds of reading practices that involved shaping read-ers' memories of reading in ways that also supported a social reformist agenda.

Jowett's view represents the tidal surge of a favorable Victorian critical consensus on Dickens's art and cultural influence that would ebb for several decades following Dickens's death. In reviews from the 1870s and 1880s, intellectuals such as G. H. Lewes and Mowbray Morris disparaged the "note of extravagance" in Dickens's style of writing and cast doubts on his artistic temperament.[5] Such doubts had also surfaced earlier in Dickens's career. In an 1856 review, Hippolyte Taine, the famous French critic, also emphasizes the indelible impression of Dickens's fictions on the reader's mind but views this effect in a more negative light:

> The imagination of Dickens is like that of monomaniacs. To plunge oneself into an idea, to be absorbed by it, to see nothing else, to repeat it under a hundred forms, to enlarge it, to carry it, thus enlarged, to the eye of the spectator, to dazzle and overwhelm him with it, to stamp it upon him so firmly and deeply that he can never again tear it from his memory—these are the great features of this imagination and style. In this, *David Copperfield* is a masterpiece. Never did objects remain more visible and present to the memory of the reader than those which he describes.[6]

While celebrating *David Copperfield* (1849–50) as an artistic achievement, Taine nevertheless pathologizes Dickens's imagination and influence, sug-gesting that both the novel's images and the reader's retention of their im-pression may be akin to monomania and obsession, and diagnosing the "inspiration" that produced them as a "feverish rapture" that fails to attain the higher unities of nature and art.[7] Attempting to forestall critics' misgiv-ings about Dickens's lack of control over his creativity, John Forster in his *Life of Charles Dickens* (1871–73) cautions in his friend's defense that "his literary work was so intensely one with his nature that he is not separable from it, and the man and the method throw singular light on each other."[8]

Much of the later nineteenth- and twentieth-century critical tradition on Dickens followed Forster's lead by incorporating this notion of a feedback loop between the author's life and his work, and between the formal aspects of the novels as representations of Dickens's idiosyncratic imagination and their effects on readers. This positing of a peculiar intimacy between Dickens's life and creative work has led to a vibrant tradition of biographical Dickens criticism. In the contexts of literary history, new media studies, and the history of reading and publishing, however, the feedback loop assumption can be newly interrogated as a relic of Dickens's Victorian reception.[9] As I show in subsequent chapters, one overlooked answer to the related question of why Dickens took up so much of his contemporaries' mental space, and why we still read his works today, involves certain specific features of Dickens's writing and critical reception that amount not just to memory effects but also to memory techniques. These techniques encompass a form of pedagogical cultural mnemonics embedded in Dickens's writing that also became a commonsense way of expressing the reader's taste in reading: what I characterize here as the pleasures of memory. These memory techniques were developed within an early nineteenth-century critical discourse that drew on both Enlightenment psychology and Romantic aesthetics to describe the impact of the new representational strategies developed in early Victorian serial fiction. In this respect, Victorian critical theories of the memory effects of Dickens's novels amount to a commentary on serial fiction as a new print medium of an emerging mass culture.

This sketch of the vicissitudes of Dickens's critical reception also suggests that Victorian definitions of the common reader, a common English culture, and Dickens's popularity were inextricably linked. Dickens's efforts to affect his readers *directly* through his writing—to teach them precisely how to read his novels, taking to heart and acting upon their precepts—deserve more detailed attention so that we may clarify how Dickens's fiction and celebrity author persona ended up playing such a salient role not only in shaping the nineteenth-century British literary field but also in providing a rationale for the emergent English literary canon. Dickens's popularity, I argue, provided a transitional model, both conceptually and historically, for linking and differentiating between the civic training afforded by school culture and the everyday pleasures of popular reading.[10]

In the course of this book's analysis, I take the terminology of Victorian literary criticism seriously as descriptive of nineteenth-century practices of literacy, writing, reading, and audience reception. By correlating such critical terminology with novelistic representations of the activities of memory, I show that Dickens's serial novels shaped a specific practice of popular reading as an educational transaction unfolding over time and within mental space between reader and writer. Such transactions entailed a guarantee central to Dickens's cultural politics: that popular literature's modeling of the social solidarity of the mass reading audience could bypass and resist both scholastic and religious forms of indoctrination in order to foster social justice outside the bounds of political and religious organizations. Dickens came to personify this guarantee—not a certification or a formal contract, but closer to a promise—and fleshed it out with qualities that we now recognize as the modern (sometimes dissident) writer's combination of political independence, artistic integrity, humanitarian concern, and inclusive cultural influence. Dickens's authorship also contributed to the emergence of modern celebrity, in the process creating a strategy for fame to be leveraged into humanitarian concern and social activism. Taine's negative response to Dickens's imagination could thus be read as resistance to the implicit terms of this promise—particularly its inclusiveness—characterizing it as undue influence, a kind of brainwashing. As I explore in greater detail in Chapter 6, one way for a literary critic invested in distinguishing between elite and popular genres to undermine the idea of reading as an informal, unsanctioned transaction of publicly shared intimacy among popular author, reader, and collective reading audience would be to diagnose it as delusional.

Dickens's type of personified guarantee of the public accessibility of reading also extended to a persuasive rationale for the social accountability of art and literature. This Dickensian notion that social responsibility and a duty to public service accrue equally to the popular writer and to his or her readers has played a pivotal role in articulating an alternative account of popular aesthetic choice as independent and not necessarily debased by proliferating forms of mass media. Dickens's defense of popular tastes in fiction both supported the marketing of serial fiction and called into question the equation of mass reading and reception with consumerism.[11] In place of primarily individualistic goals for literacy such as personal cultivation, social control, or self-help that were advocated by many Victorian social reformers, I argue, Dickens's serial novels taught reading as a collective transaction accomplished jointly by author and mass audience, leading, ideally, to the formation of an alternative social activist constituency. The serial medium of fiction also formed this independent constituency of readers around Dickens's celebrity authorship as itself serial, as open ended and non-hierarchical, shifting constantly over time, and thus as cutting across rather than assimilating the heterogeneity of readers' individual and social identities.[12] Persisting into the twentieth century both as an option linked to serial genres in popular culture and as a newly formalized technique of literary interpretation taught in elementary and secondary school English classes, such Dickensian-style participatory reading remains a viable alternative to the specialized reading practiced in academic literary criticism.

During the first half of the nineteenth century, the generic dimensions and physical appearance of popular serial fiction had not been fully distinguished from the similar design and marketing of broadsheets and tracts, whether their matter was journalistic, political, or religious (or any combination of these). The circulation of periodicals accelerated with the reduction and eventual elimination of the stamp taxes on newspapers and the duty on paper between 1833 and 1861. During this period the social value or legitimacy eventually accruing to serial fiction as a form of art, journalism, or propaganda was therefore an open question to be settled by readers, publishers, critics, and writers. Given these conditions of flux in determining which, if any, of the cheap publications might count as literature or worthwhile reading, Dickens's extra-institutional version of cultural politics constituted an intervention meant to establish the legitimacy of serial fiction as a literary genre.

In this book I characterize, from the perspective of cultural history, Dickens's project to shape the reception of popular serial fiction into a means of gathering readers into a new constituency with democratic, participatory potentials.[13] To call this a concerted or conscious project of cultural politics on Dickens's part would not be strictly accurate, but neither would it be correct to state that Dickens had no plan in instigating his readers' responses to his work, since he was often quite explicit in addressing his ambitions to please his readers and to improve social conditions through his writings. At this point in the history of Dickens scholarship, the myth of Dickens as a mostly untutored genius whose career developed in an opportunistic way can take its place as an artifact of the strangely prescient but quite effective auto-canonization of his work that I chart in subsequent chapters. Dickens's project for popularizing serial fiction as a mode of public education was not unprecedented—Evangelical organizing and publications provided a crucial precursor project and ongoing competing cultural politics.[14] Tactics such as the founding of new journals and the publication of serial fiction and tracts were also central to many overtly political movements that pursued specific political and legislative agendas, such as British abolitionism from the 1770s through the 1830s, Chartism in the 1830s and 1840s, the Anti–Corn Law League from 1839 to 1846, and the revived Reform League in the 1860s. As Elaine Hadley has noted in her study of the periodical publication venues of mid-Victorian liberals, "earlier generations of radical, romantic, and reactionary readers gave way to a public perceived to be rigidly partisan, with each 'serious' periodical, for instance, merely reflecting a clearly defined interest group, be it the Conservative Party, the temperance community, or little girls at home."[15] Dickens's writing and editing of novels and periodicals for a general readership throughout his career therefore manifests a distinctive strategy that would help to produce an important trend in Victorian publishing toward designing new periodicals to appeal to, and to define, a broad-based popular market.

Dickens began his writing career during the late 1820s and early 1830s in political journalism and parliamentary reporting, and he did not always avoid political controversy. But he did avoid joining particular political groups. However, in response to the *Times'* criticisms of incompetent government management of the Crimean War effort that contributed to heavy British casualties, Dickens made an exception to his general avoidance of political affiliation, joining the London-based Administrative Reform Association, "a movement formed in May of 1855 with the purpose of exerting pressure on the government to reorganize and reform its bureaucracy."[16] Dickens gave a speech at the Administrative Reform Association's third meeting in June 1855. He announced his support for its goals but also clarified his own role: "as one who lives by Literature, who is content to do his public service through Literature, and who is conscious that he cannot serve two masters—within my sphere of action I have, for some years, tried to understand the heavier social grievances and to help to set them right. [*Cheers*.]"[17] Dickens's speech ties together the investigative and reformist, as well as the epistemological and political, goals of his periodical writings as aspects of his efforts to perform "public service" by leveraging the cultural influence of literature and thus expanding the social impact of the author's intellectual labor. The excavator of ancient Assyrian and Babylonian palaces, Austen Henry Layard, who had served briefly as Liberal MP for Aylesbury in 1852 and was a principal organizer of the association, followed up by attempting to make Dickens's position—what I am calling his program for popular literature and cultural politics—more explicit: "He differed from his friend when he said he had not been engaged on political questions. It was true he [Dickens] had not made a trade of politics, but he had been engaged in true politics, in teaching how the feelings of all classes ought to be respected."[18] Layard emphasized that Dickens's specific task was "teaching" readers to recognize the concerns of all classes as legitimate. Dickens and Layard assign to literature the explicitly cultural role of shaping public opinion and individual sensibilities in the service of broad-based political and social reformist goals.[19] Layard's response also seems to presage the modern public schools' inclusive citizen-building goals, including training children to treat each other with respect as fellow classmates, whatever the differences in their backgrounds.

Dickens's influence was perceived by many of his contemporaries as broadly liberal and democratic, suggesting that the popular writer's "public service" could be more encompassing than a politician's or educator's, given the unevenness of educational provision and the growth of party politics during the 1850s and 1860s.[20] Such comments by Dickens himself and his contemporaries concerning the particular relationship between literature, social inclusiveness, and public service help to clarify why critics praised Dickens's novels for providing informal instruction without indoctrination. The notion of democracy identified with Dickens's authorship that I elucidate in this book was focused strenuously not on the extension of the franchise, as in Chartism, but rather on the full inclusion and participation of the poor in Victorian public and cultural life, to be made possible by the improvement of their living and working conditions.[21] Dickens's preoccupation with poverty in his fiction thus demonstrates another way that his message cuts across the class structure, as recognized both by Victorians and by historians of the Victorian period, by demonstrating that the poor do not really count as a politically recognized class and that as a result their social exclusion can end up being reinforced by categories of social analysis that emphasize social divisions.

Corresponding to this largely social and cultural definition of democratic participation, then, Dickens's serial novels define the democratic potentials of literature as emerging both in the transaction between reader and text, overseen by the author's cultural persona, and in the modes of the reader's taking part in a reading audience, rather than based in the strictly political content or resonance of a particular text. Democratically inclusive forms of reception could thus consist of shared predilections among readers for certain characters and shared investments in an ongoing serial narrative among others available in the marketplace. Such investments could happen by chance—Victorian readers with limited means would often have to settle for whatever kind of cheap print they could get hold of. But even chance reading could count as participation in a reading audience. Dickens's "public service" through literature does not suggest a liberal democracy of autonomous citizens, then, but rather it addresses the question of what kinds of

attachments and investments work across social classes to create a new experience of collectivity that could lend itself to political and social progress.
Such forms of investment could run counter to explicit party or religious
affiliations, but they could also coincide or coexist with them.

The line between popular authorship and politics was fluid, particularly
given the ongoing and vigorous development of politically radical popular
literature and journalism from the 1790s through the 1840s.[22] Dickens was
variously praised and attacked for dealing with political controversies in his
fiction. Yet Victorian novelists frequently viewed themselves as both educators and reformers of their readers. George Eliot commented that "man or
woman who publishes writings inevitably assumes the office of a teacher or
influencer of the public mind. Let him protest as he will that he only seeks
to amuse. . . . He can no more escape influencing the moral taste, and with
it the action of the intelligence, than a setter of fashions and furniture and
dress can fill the shops with his designs and leave the garniture of persons
and houses unaffected by his industry."[23] For Eliot, an author purveys moral
and intellectual influence almost inevitably as a new kind of intellectual
commodity meant to direct and refine the moral "taste" of both individual
readers and reading audiences.

The "office" of authorship, as Eliot terms it, thus implies an unavoidable
tendency to take on a program, whether intentionally or not, and the question remains whether popular authors affect their readers toward a specific
end or merely to increase sales. In a letter describing his speech at the Birmingham Banquet to Literature and Art in January 1853 to his friend the
actor W. C. Macready, Dickens describes his goals for a popular democratic
literature:

> I know you would have been full of sympathy and approval, if you had been
> present at Birmingham, and that you would have concurred in the tone I
> have tried to take about the eternal duties of the Arts to the People. I took
> the liberty of putting the Court and that kind of thing out of the question,
> and recognizing nothing but the Arts and the People. The more we see of
> Life and its brevity, and the World and its Vanities, the more we know that
> no exercise of our abilities in any Art, but the addressing of it to the great
> ocean of humanity in which we are drops, and not to bye-ponds (very
> stagnant) here and there, ever can or ever will lay the foundation of an
> endurable retrospect.[24]

Dickens imagines democratic art as partaking in the water cycle, so that individual artists and readers alike become "drops" who nevertheless converge in an "ocean of humanity" into which their efforts of both artistic

production and reception will eventually flow. The "bye-ponds" stand not simply for aristocratic or elite patronage of the arts and a resulting social exclusivity but also, and more significantly, for the cordoning off and separation of the arts from other everyday pursuits, a segmentation that effectively stagnates creativity of all kinds. By the end of Dickens's career, however, "the People" have quite explicitly become the mass reading public in the eyes of writers, editors, and publishers. Yet in the course of this transition, the mass reading public became a different kind of constituency from the one envisioned by early nineteenth-century radical publications.[25]

Such a fluid early to mid-Victorian constituency of readers offered new potentials for collective affiliation and organization and for social, cultural, and political participation. My contention is that Dickens's writing extended and reworked certain representational practices typical of radical publications precisely by *demarcating* the literary field and distinguishing it from the sphere of politics, while still allowing for readers' literary tastes and political allegiances to coexist, interpenetrate, and even change.[26] It is this openness to the potential coordination and realignment of affiliations, *without necessarily politicizing or depoliticizing readers*, that I delineate in Dickens's reception by showing how the specific reading practices and meanings assigned to serial reading's impact on the reader's mental space transformed Dickens's popular success into a cultural politics and ultimately a mission for literature within democratic education. Dickens's project for democratizing the arts represents not a reductive aestheticization of politics or, inversely, a general politicization of culture, but rather a wider extension of the arts into the Victorian public sphere to enable increased access to and recognition of creative and artistic work within everyday life. If the democratic arts are not conceived as strictly political, neither are they apolitical. In addition, in Dickens's case we can see that the "legitimate" print genres constituting literature were not always defined during the nineteenth century to exclude popular culture and its modes of reception.

Historians of British politics and English national identity have focused on the period between the 1832 and 1867 Reform Acts—encompassing most of Dickens's career—as one of significant turmoil and transition in English culture, particularly because of the extended working-class agitation for political reform expressed in Chartism, which one historian has described as "a mass movement unprecedented [in Europe] in scope and sustained militancy."[27] Prior to the consolidation of a two-party system after 1867, it was not clear what kind of organization, association, or affiliation would provide a dominant vehicle for political activity as the franchise was gradually extended. This is to say that during Dickens's lifetime, party membership was not a predominant or self-evident means of political expression or public participation.[28] Nor was it clear that popular literature or authorship would or should be nonpartisan, ecumenical, or even secular. In addition, the varied genres of print culture, whether periodicals, single or multivolume books, pamphlets, handbills, tracts, or advertisements, could mobilize multiple, simultaneous affiliations and interests—whether religious, educational, political, occupational, recreational, and so forth—fostering new tastes and demands among heterogeneous reading audiences. It seems conceivable, then, that reading audiences could form some kind of constituency, even if temporary, toward shared social and political goals that would not have to assimilate or express every aspect of any given reader's social or individual identity.

Dickens's serial novels also develop additional repertoires of representational strategies to supplement the popular melodramatic strategies of resistance to social and political hierarchies analyzed so astutely by Elaine Hadley and Sally Ledger.[29] I want to draw attention to the ways that Dickens's serial novels, in their form as new media that update and revise the conventions of existing media forms, *modernized* the inheritance of the rhetorical, satirical, and melodramatic forms of early Victorian radical writings. Dickens's serial novels enlisted a new kind of nonpartisan, extra-institutional, and often anti-institutional perspective by calling attention to the plight of the poor and advocating social solidarity across classes, a combined moral and social agenda that was widely recognized by Victorian reviewers as philanthropic or charitable, and that today we might be likely to term humanitarian.[30] I refer to the democratic and humanitarian rather than the radical cultural politics of Dickens's fiction, then, precisely because I want to delineate those forward-looking, participatory, and egalitarian elements of Dickens's writing that became transportable and were adapted to further new cultural and political uses beyond his immediate Victorian context. In the emerging twentieth-century literature curriculum, Dickens's authorial persona became associated with the cultural nationalism of an English literature curriculum in Britain, and an Anglo-American literary curriculum in the United States, along with a generic humanitarian ethic associated with a nascent concept of global citizenship suitable to the expansion and maintenance of colonies and empires.[31] This is an incipient version of cultural democracy, then, that prefigures the avowed values of a modern democratic society as articulated in, for example, the public schools, rather than in a party platform arguing directly for extension of the franchise.

Dickens's reputation as a tireless advocate of the poor within England became a central part of his canonical authorial persona. Dickens's trajectory from popular to canonical author, which I delineate in this book, also maps a broader history of the mass reading audience, from the religious and didactic motives for popular reading developed by writers of religious tracts for use in newly formed Sunday schools through popular serial fiction, with its heterogeneous readership and secularizing blend of political and moral interests, to the institutionalization of a civic and even humanitarian rationale for reading selections by newly canonical Anglo-American authors in school readers.[32] In tracing how Dickens's serial fiction both enacts this transition and illuminates its social and cultural history, I foreground the importance of *The Pickwick Papers* (1836–37) and *The Old Curiosity Shop* (1840–41)— two of Dickens's most popular novels among his contemporaries that are rarely read today, even in academic settings—to Dickens's version of a secular democratic cultural politics that would be adapted by the literature curriculum. I argue that *The Old Curiosity Shop* in particular, accused as it has been by critics of cheap and outdated sentimentality, should actually be understood as one of Dickens's most ambitious and innovative works for its modernization of Victorian pedagogy, reading practices, and the modes of reception that we have come to associate with mass media culture.

The perceived educational role of Dickens's serials also points to their role in addressing a deficiency in the early to mid-Victorian state's provision of both welfare and literacy to its populace, the majority of which was not made up of enfranchised citizens in 1870. Such widely disseminated fiction also affected national identity, as Jowett's emphasis on the Englishness of Dickens's characters attests. Historian Eugenio F. Biagini has written that unlike the rest of the nineteenth-century European countries, "The United Kingdom was neither a 'nation-state,' nor interested in becoming one. It was a rather archaic multinational state, held together by parliament, the monarchy, and the Protestant religion."[33] In his cultural history of Victorian intellectuals, Stefan Collini has argued in similar terms that "the complexity and ambiguities of the relation between the history of the 'British' state and the 'English' people may have increased the emphasis placed on the seemingly less problematic unity offered by the English language and its literature."[34] The modernizing Dickensian version of the reading audience, I argue, in effect updated the cultural nostalgia incorporated into a common Victorian conception of popular democracy shared by working-class radicals and many liberals that Biagini refers to as based in "face-to face relationships and virtually co-extensive with a local community." This notion of democracy as community that was also represented in Dickens's novels envisioned that "participation and debate would spontaneously arise from the awareness of common interests, and from the feeling of belonging to a sociocultural entity to which one felt a positive emotional commitment."[35]

The increasingly complex mid-Victorian reading audience not only crossed classes but included a mix of urban and provincial British readers as well as an international audience of Anglophone readers in the United States and Canada and across Britain's colonial possessions. Popular reading as incipient democratic participation, then, could no longer be conceived as local, yet the attachments that readers formed with characters and with the author could still be relayed into forms of "positive emotional commitment" to an image of English culture. Keeping in mind this history of conflict and ambiguity within British political identity, and both the elusive definition of and common prejudice against the idea of participatory democracy in the nineteenth century, I am interested in investigating what it would mean for citizens within and across nation-states to be defined collectively in their social identities, responsibilities, and experience of participation in national culture and public life as readers of popular serial fiction.

Associationism, Serial Memory, and Remediation

How would such a cultural politics for reading audiences become effective? As their pedagogical means toward shaping a participatory and independent reading audience, Dickens's novels provide an intellectual and affective method shared between author and readers and founded on the Victorian popular psychology of associationism, which achieved commonsense status through its implementation in reading instruction from the seventeenth century through the nineteenth. In charting the development of a wideranging discourse surrounding the associative memory's functions in both reading and socialization, I show how Dickens's serial novels incorporate associationist theories of memory both from Romantic aesthetics and from religious education and pious reading practices, in the process reshaping and secularizing the reading habit and reader reception. This new habit of serial reading does not culminate in religious conversion or necessarily support overtly spiritual or aesthetic values but rather replaces those aims with ecumenical and egalitarian social and political values. Such values, however, are still articulated as generically Christian both in Dickens's works and in the early twentieth-century English literature curriculum.

Memory plays a crucial mediating role in this development on multiple levels. Enlightenment empiricist psychological theories of the association of ideas conceive memory's operations as serial, with David Hume's writings, I argue, providing the most historically resonant notion of memory's role in supporting personal identity as virtual experience. The serial memory's function in linking the disparate experiences that make up personal identity creates crucial operative analogies between thinking, learning to read, and the practice of reading. These connections are doubly reinforced in practice when the text is itself serial in form, eliciting sequential as well as repeated events of reading over time. In this way, Dickens's serial fiction enlists memory as the medium where reading intersects with everyday life— doubling, in effect, the mediation of cheap serial fiction as a new print genre by mobilizing what was understood to be memory's crucial linking relation between sensory experience and personal identity, or between the world and the individual mind. By employing memory's own mediating functions, serial fiction achieves, conceivably, a perfect feedback loop of self-reflexive mediation, and thus of pedagogical communication.[36] The serial memory posited by associationism is thus also *remediated* and modernized through the socially formative and politically consolidating serial reading that Dickens's serial novels elicited.[37] I use the new media studies concept of remediation, describing the process through which new media revise the earlier forms from which they derive, to characterize this transition from an understanding of memory derived from Enlightenment associationist theory to a nineteenth-century notion of the memory's patterning role in reader reception that drew on popular associationism. Despite accounts of its obsolescence by Victorian intellectuals like George Eliot and G. H. Lewes in the 1860s and 1870s, Victorian uses of associationism, I argue, did not represent a theoretical throwback or a nostalgic return to an earlier mentality. Rather, through its empiricist genealogy, associationism was amenable to popularization and updating because of its equally generic and intimate common-sense model of reading as everyday experience.

Associationist psychology provided a lingua franca shared by Enlightenment moral philosophers, Romantic poets, Evangelical writers of didactic fiction, Utilitarian reformers, and pedagogical theorists and writers of spelling books from the seventeenth century through the 1880s.[38] Pedagogical methods common in Victorian schooling—including the pervasive so-called synthetic method of learning to read by memorizing sequences of syllables, which I discuss in Chapters 1 and 5—also feature the serial memory as a crucial vehicle for the pedagogical reproduction of ideas, social relationships, and attitudes. In order to account for the wide circulation of associationist concepts in various genres and texts, including pedagogical tracts, letters, autobiographies, rationales for publishing improving literature, treatises of psychology, and serial fiction, I have extended the period boundaries of my study to encompass relevant intellectual, cultural, and educational trends from the seventeenth century through the early twentieth. As indicated by the conceptual trajectory between my epigraphs from Thomas Hobbes and Herbert Spencer, associationist ideas about the serial functioning and registration of experience in the memory were so thoroughly familiar by the nineteenth century that they hardly had a theoretical status any longer. Yet Spencer's interest in those memories that no longer count as such, because they are in fact remnants of the organism's earliest perceptions, indicates the kind of conceptual work with associative memory that was still possible through the end of the nineteenth century.

The language of association psychology also provides a framework connecting what I characterize as Dickens's cultural politics to a social epistemology of novel reading that conceives the mental processes activated by reading as analogous to the shaping influence of a person's familial upbringing and education.[39] The English term typically employed to describe this process was ''experience,'' as the epigraph from Thomas Hobbes indicates. In the context of my study, *experience has the status of a technical term* designating the processes of both transmission and reception of knowledge, feeling, and understanding as well as their cumulative effects in the memory as wellsprings of invention. As an analogue of experience, reading, like memory, creates trains of thought or mental associations that can be implemented in various ways. For example, when memory functions primarily reproductively, reading for the sake of memorization may easily reinforce social conditioning, as utilitarian philosophers such as Jeremy Bentham and James Mill theorized. But associationist doctrines also assumed that by supplying an alternative source of associations and thus of reproducible memories—that is, by *supplementing* experience—reading could become a means to *revise* past associations, allowing the reader to correct or consciously to reappropriate what he or she has already learned in new ways. More obliquely, Dickens's satirical treatments of various sorts of Victorian hypocrisy remind the reader of the basic mental processes of habituation—conditioned responses that rely on ''rote learning'' and stereotype—that must come under pressure in order for connections that cut across class interests to find expression, even if such responses may themselves take newly revitalized conventional forms. This is a relation to knowledge as a product of the fundamentally social nature of personal experience—a social epistemology—that, I argue, Dickensian serial novels are capable of teaching readers, both at various moments within discrete texts and as a cumulative project when viewed from a cultural history perspective.[40]

How do I define a serial novel and its interaction with a theory of serial memory? A serial novel is a form of fiction, published either in weekly or monthly installments or as part of the contents of a periodical, that is much cheaper than the three-volume form of novel publication typical in the first two-thirds of the nineteenth century. This does not mean that serial fiction was affordable for all readers, but it was much more affordable for many readers than volume editions until cheap single-volume editions became more widely available toward the end of the century. (I discuss this publication history in detail in Chapter 2.) A serial memory is formed by interconnected verbal and visual elements, including sensations and ideas. Any element of such a chain of associated images, if it comes to mind through recollection or imagination, will unleash the entire series or cluster of associations. What I argue here is that an associationist conception of reading itself as functioning serially and cumulatively, and as laying down serial memories in the form of associations that are reinforced and reorchestrated by readers through repeated reading, comes to explain the effects on readers of the generic and material form of the serial novel, leading to an understanding of popular reception as also taking the form of shared and interlinked memories of reading. I show that this understanding of the coordination of serial fiction with serial memory provided the basis of an early Victorian theory of reception common among authors, critics, readers, and publishers. The serial novel and serial memory are therefore not identical but rather analogous forms of seriality that were conceived as operatively linked in a collective reception unfolding over time and varying in response to developing serial media. But this analogy depends on the relative cheapness of serial fiction as a form of publication that takes over from tracts and broadsides in also being widely disseminated and popular.

The nineteenth-century conception of the serial memory can be described, in Raymond Williams's terms, as a residual social formation that "has been effectively formed in the past, but [that] is still active in the cultural process, not only and often not at all as an element of the past, but as an effective element of the present."[41] Within Dickens's lifetime, associationism changed from a dominant to a residual psychological theory that nevertheless persisted in Victorian popular culture as a commonsense view about the relation between memory and both personal and social identity.[42] What I want to emphasize about the residual nature of associationism in relation to the development of scientific psychology and new media in the nineteenth century, however, is not its fading away, but rather its persistence as a crucial means for *modernizing* the new phenomenon of mass reading represented by Dickens's celebrity authorship. Another way of describing this book's project, then, would be to say that it shows how the residual forms of Enlightenment associationist psychology played an important role in specific attempts by Victorian writers, politicians, educators, publishers, and religious reformers to shape a mass reading audience as it emerged in the decades between 1830 and 1867.[43] Various curricular and institutional reforms inspired by Utilitarian theories of rational social planning in particular enlisted psychological ideas about the habit-forming nature of serial memory in order to shape a reading public, and ultimately a politically enfranchised electorate, according to the assumption that two intimately intertwined strands of the reading process—reading as socialization and reading as interpretation—could be separated. Such a separation could in turn leverage the educability of reading publics by channeling and controlling their capacity for political dissent. As I argue in Chapter 5, this is the liberal strategy of controlled access to democracy, running in parallel to and thus competing with his publicly articulated ideal of open public access to art, that Dickens would attempt to discredit in *Our Mutual Friend* (1864–65).

In associationism we can also find some of the deep conceptual and stylistic architecture of Dickens's reputation as an original and memorable writer. As I show in detail in subsequent chapters, Dickens's novelistic explorations of associationist memory have dimensions beyond the autobiographical shaping of his fiction in relation to his own memories and his development of the *Bildungsroman* tradition.[44] Dickens's novels are distinctive among other works of Victorian serial fiction because they explicitly teach serial reading as an associative practice, channeling the memories of reading they supply into a common experience as a basis for cultural politics. While I am not attempting to provide a key to unlock the meaning of all of Dickens's novels, I do argue that a crucial and heretofore overlooked reason why they became so popular and, later, canonical lies in the way that they *overtly thematize* the mode of their reception in associationist terms as collective or cultural memory. I show that associationism as a psychological theory, social aesthetic, and pedagogy provides a central element coordinating the narrative plots, educational aims, and rhetorical methods of a set of Dickens's most influential serial novels from *Pickwick* to *Our Mutual Friend*, encompassing what they represent, what they seek to enact in psychological and social realms, and even their theoretical self-description.

In addition to the larger Enlightenment intellectual tradition that affords the framework for Dickens's associationism, it can also be traced to his reading of Samuel Rogers's popular narrative poem *The Pleasures of Memory* (1792), from which I have borrowed the title of this book. Dickens refers to this poem in his dedication to Rogers of the separate-volume publication of *The Old Curiosity Shop* in 1841.[45] Rogers's treatise-like poem attempts simultaneously to convey and to explain the rational pleasure that the mind gleans from the associations evoked through recollection:

> Lull'd in the countless chambers of the brain,
> Our thoughts are link'd by many a hidden chain.
> Awake but one, and lo, what myriads rise!
> Each stamps its image as the other flies!
> Each, as the varied avenues of sense
> Delight or sorrow to the soul dispense,
> Brightens or fades: yet all, with magic art,
> Control the latent fibres of the heart.[46]

Invoking memory through its activity of association, the poem explains how an image from the past "awakens" and brings with it "myriads" of accompanying images and sensations. These memories are exact counterparts to thoughts: both are connected in series, and each revivified "chain" is also accompanied by the feelings originally associated with the "images" of the past as they reappear. Even when they involve painful thoughts, such recollections produce pleasurable and beneficial effects on the mind and feelings. As Rogers explains in his introductory "Analysis" of the first part of the poem, "The associating principle, as here employed, is no less conducive to virtue than to happiness; and, as such, it frequently discovers itself in the most tumultuous scenes of life. It addresses our finer feelings, and gives exercise to every mild and generous propensity."[47] Evidently, it is not so much the content as the ordering *connectivity* of the associative memory that produces its soothing and elevating influence on the mind. At stake in Rogers's notion of the associative memory's coherence, however, and in its role in discourse and innovation in poetic composition, is a larger eighteenth-century philosophical argument, still ongoing among writers whom we associate with Romantic aesthetics as well as among early Victorian writers, about the nature of the mind's participation in social bonds. The associative powers of memory extend outward from individual minds to social life through discourse, so that thinking and reading also function metonymically as forms of social connection.[48]

Associationism in Victorian popular psychology, pedagogy, and serial fiction also updates and secularizes the rhetorical topoi associated with both the reading of scripture and the inventive activity of memory.[49] As I show in detail in subsequent chapters, associationist pedagogy creates a particular relationship between learning to read and the trope of prosopopoeia. As the "trope of address" or apostrophe, Paul de Man has argued, prosopopoeia "is the very figure of the reader and of reading."[50] Prosopopoeia in Dickens's novels works as a figure of reading through which the author personifies the popular taste, legitimizing it as a simultaneously public and intimate form of address that has a posthumous existence in the reader's memory. Each reader's individual associations are linked in a network of common pleasures and interests to those of other readers through the relay point of the serial installment and the image of the author conjured up in the mind through prosopopoeia. Prosopopoeia also emerges in my analysis as the dominant trope for the effects of the study of literature on the student, and for the linkage between literature and public education, by figuring classroom reading as a medium of contact with the minds and humanizing influence of canonical authors. From the common nineteenth-century practice of instructing children to read in the churchyard to the educational idea that reading literature affords a connection with the thoughts and feelings of famous living and dead authors, associationist theories of pious Bible reading, serial novel reading, and classroom reading extend the pleasures of memory evoked through what I call "epitaphic reading" into a popular form of reception that can also be shared with other readers contemporaneously, or with future generations of readers, as cultural memory.

Novelistic Pedagogy and Universal Education

The pleasures of memory also invoke a tradition of critical and rhetorical thought on the educational value of literature dating to antiquity. Samuel Rogers's associationist poetics is in part an attempt to update the Roman poet Horace's classic recommendation in his *Ars Poetica* that poetry should both please and instruct. As Richard A. Barney has shown, eighteenth-century novels such as Lawrence Sterne's *The Life and Opinions of Tristram Shandy, Gentleman* (1759–67) also offered themselves as models for "how both successful socialization and coherent novelistic discourse depend on an effective organization of epistemology by pedagogy."[51] From the eighteenth century forward, justifications of fiction as a means of moral instruction for the young and ignorant frequently rely on the associationist pleasures of memory as a psychological explanation of how novel reading can function to inculcate particular attitudes and behaviors.

More specifically, Dickens's serial novels can also be read as responding to the anxiety demonstrated in Wordsworth's argument in the 1800 Preface to the second edition of *Lyrical Ballads* that both urbanization and rapid social change threaten "to blunt the discriminating powers of the mind," and that periodical publications instill in readers "a craving for extraordinary incident."[52] While developing what Jon Klancher has characterized as Wordsworth's project to reform the modern "reading habit," Dickens's serial fiction thematizes memory to help readers engage intelligently and responsibly with the emerging complexities and contradictions of modern urban life.[53] The Wordsworthian anxiety about the reading habit as a symptom of the psychological fragmentation caused by modernity resurfaces in a common justification offered by Victorian publishers and writers for the educational and moral effects of fiction, a rationale associated with liberalism that becomes much more complacent, confident, and disdainful of popular tastes by midcentury.[54] Anthony Trollope offers such a justification in his comparative 1879 review of Dickens and Thackeray: "Teaching to be efficacious must be popular. The birch has, no doubt, saved many from the uttermost depth of darkness, but it never yet made a scholar. I am inclined to think that the lessons inculcated by the novelists at present go deeper than most others."[55] Speaking of the influence of Dickens's novels more specifically, Trollope dismisses the question of whether their style or characters appeal to the reader or not: "Among the millions of those into whose hands these hundreds of thousands of volumes have fallen, there can hardly be one who has not received some lesson from what he has read." Trollope sums up that lesson as the ability "to recognize the fact that happiness is to be obtained by obeying, and not by running counter to the principles of morality."[56] Trollope's characterization of Dickens's influence reduces it to a mode of social control.[57] For Dickens's image of authorship, however, the popular pleasures of novel reading ultimately provide their own justification, in both aesthetic and market terms, in the various forms of readers' individual and collective engagements with the serial narrative.

In assessing Victorian commentaries such as Trollope's on the educational influence of fiction, it is also crucial to bear in mind that gradual expansion of governmental oversight of the local provision of education lagged noticeably behind other legislative efforts to effect social consolidation during the course of the nineteenth century. Basic literacy training was available to poor and working-class children during the Victorian period primarily on a "voluntary" basis and for a fee, with schools' standards stratified and curricula differentiated by income and social class, and availability of instruction highly uneven across both urban and rural areas.[58] The extensive educational projects implemented by both Anglican and dissenting religious organizations to extend literacy and religious instruction to workers and the poor from the late eighteenth century through 1870—including the founding, funding, and oversight of hundreds of schools and a significant number of teacher training colleges—were undertaken in the absence of a national mandate for universal schooling.[59] In fact, these efforts were in part expressions of resistance to such a mandate based on the sectarian nature of most schooling. Dissenters, Catholics, and Jews in particular did not want their children's education to be administered by the established Anglican Church, while Tory politicians also resisted legislative efforts in the 1840s to provide a secular and nondenominational education system.[60] Parliament partially funded these charitable voluntary schools at a rate that increased from £50,000 to £19.5 million in the period between 1750 and 1830.[61] Despite denominational differences, elementary schools provided a remarkably uniform type of instruction through 1870, extending to commonly used textbooks and a shared focus on imparting basic literacy and numeracy, religious instruction, and the inculcation of deference to "one's betters."[62] Gaps in local provision of elementary schooling were finally addressed by the Elementary Education Act of 1870, which created local school boards empowered to fund and build schools where they were lacking. School attendance was made compulsory up to age thirteen in 1880 but only became free of charge in 1891. The requirement to educate all children through secondary school finally passed into law in Britain, and with it the establishment of a national education system, through a series of acts between 1899 and 1902.[63]

As historian David Vincent has demonstrated, working-class Victorians nevertheless gained literacy in rapidly growing numbers, in part through their independent efforts to organize and run Sunday schools and also through the voluntary schools. As gauged from the marriage registrars for England circa 1833–70, "the average [literacy rate] for brides and grooms had passed 60 per cent before the State spent a farthing on education, and had reached almost 90 per cent before it entered into the field in its own right following Forster's Education Act of 1870."[64] Vincent concludes that "the foundation for the eventual victory [over illiteracy by the end of the nineteenth century] was laid not in the schoolroom but in the working-class family."[65] The spread of literacy and the growing range of publications that it fostered, along with extensive borrowing from the new free public libraries by working-class readers after 1850, thus functioned historically in lieu of a centralized national school system and curriculum to permit a varied, flexible, and socially uneven politics of literacy and culture.[66]

The institutionalization of the discipline of English also took place slowly in Britain over the course of the eighteenth and nineteenth centuries. English was first included as a subject in the curricula of provincial dissenting academies and the Scottish universities in the middle of the eighteenth century.[67] The first professors of English were appointed in 1828 at the non-denominational London University (founded in 1826, and later renamed University College London) and at the competing Anglican King's College, London, in 1831.[68] English literature was frequently designated as the poor man's (or any woman's or non-English person's) substitute for classical Latin and Greek; training in the classical languages was still reserved for elite education through the nineteenth century. Curricula for training working-class teachers began to include English literature in 1839, and the subject also became a mainstay of curricula and lectures at Mechanics' Institutes and Working Men's Colleges, as well as at the new colleges founded for women and for the training of women teachers, beginning with the establishment of Cheltenham Ladies' College in 1841; Queen's College, London, in 1848; and Bedford College in 1849.[69] In India, English studies was developed as an appropriate vehicle for extending British cultural influence, carrying out evangelical missions, and forming a cadre of Indian civil servants, beginning with the founding of Hindu College in 1816 in Calcutta and followed by Bentinck's English Education Act of 1835.[70] English literature was also included as a major subject in the Indian Civil Service examinations in 1855.[71]

The absence of a centralized educational system, however, meant that ideas about the educational influence of literature and the social and political influence of the literary field developed in distinctive ways in Britain.[72] During this extended time frame for the institutionalization of English literature as an academic subject, and prior to the organization of a system of universal elementary and secondary education, writers and publishers involved in producing reading material for the growing mass of readers could still envision their efforts as functioning independently from or as competing with the literacy initiatives of schools and the emerging professions as well as those sponsored by political and cultural organizations such as political parties and religious denominations. Dickens's popularity also emerged at a juncture in the larger extension of a worldwide Anglophone reading audience when the cultural authority of the modern author was not yet tightly intertwined with the institutional authority of any national school system and its specific distributions of cultural capital.[73] Thus, part of the independence from institutions that Dickens articulated as the modern author's democratic duty to perform a wide-ranging public service was contingent upon what, in hindsight, appears to be an opportunity to compensate for the absence of a national education system. Dickens's cultural politics, I argue, represented the possibility that popular literature could supply the cultural cohesion and democratic inclusiveness afforded by a system of universal public education.

Victorian Pedagogy, New Media Studies, and the History of Reading

The Pleasures of Memory contributes to the growing importance of the history of reading and the book within Victorian studies by bringing this already interdisciplinary field into dialogue with the history of education and new media studies.[74] While influential studies of the Victorian novel have often combined cultural and literary history with close interpretation of specific works, literature scholars more recently have both produced and made extensive use of scholarship in the history of reading and the book to investigate reader reception.[75] Some historians of the book, however, have pointed out the limitations of literary methods of textual exegesis or rhetorical analysis for understanding the histories of reading audiences, arguing that an accurate history of reception must study actual readers' access and responses to specific books.[76] For example, in the opening sentence of a recent manifesto for a new "political economy of reading," cultural historian William St Clair very publicly cautions that in assessing the cultural significance of particular works of literature, literary critics "should not lose sight of the sales figures."[77] The message is that if a certain book has not circulated widely, it cannot be endowed in retrospect with any clear cultural influence. Given the well-documented status of Dickens's novels as best sellers, this warning might be deflected by the Dickens critic, but St Clair's argument still seems to narrow the purview of literary criticism as an approach within the history of reading.

Examining the history of reading pedagogy, however, can permit us to locate outside the literary text the kind of reading practice and response that one can find both depicted and patterned within it, while the effects of such pedagogies on readers can also be substantiated by a range of contemporary sources. By paying attention to the history of education, we can more accurately determine how the effects of reading and literacy were conceived in the classroom and thus arrive at a more specific account of the processes of thought and moral agency that were commonly associated with the reading of fiction in the nineteenth century.[78] On this basis, my study also responds to Richard D. Altick's observation that many Victorian readers may have missed the "complexity" and "subtleties" of Dickens's art by extending the archive of sources relevant to understanding Victorian reading practices.[79] In this pedagogical context it becomes possible, for example, to see precisely how Dickens's serial novels incorporate reading strategies that undermine and revise methods of reading instruction and conventions of reception purveyed in Evangelical didactic literature.[80]

While the reading process has often been elucidated in educational terms as a hermeneutics, I focus here on reading as constitutively formative of the reader's understanding but also as a transitional activity within it.[81] My premise is that during periods of expanding literacy, reading may not always have a dominant role in mediating experience or shaping identity, but rather that it competes for attention with other everyday practices involving learning and the dissemination of knowledge. In this way, however, reading also becomes salient as an activity toward which literate Victorians devoted particular time and energy, in addition to functioning simply as a means toward another end such as self-improvement or obtaining information. If we think of the book as a variable medium in the context of new media studies, reading can also be understood as a constantly adaptable means of accessing many kinds of what we now call content, including images, advertising, and forms of knowledge explicitly labeled as information, through multiple and evolving technologies and genres, including serials. This means that reading and education had highly variable social profiles and effects beyond the major demarcations that were invoked across the Victorian political spectrum to divide the literate from the so-called illiterate.

In elucidating the specific psychological terms though which the effects of serial reading were characterized during the nineteenth century, this book also pays close attention to common associationist concepts articulated across various nineteenth-century fields of knowledge and textual genres, including serial fiction, conduct books, religious tracts, pedagogical treatises, works of moral philosophy, and spelling books.[82] The historical psychology of associationism that I offer here is geared toward examining the interplay between genre and reception.[83] In light of the renewed scholarly interest in serial fiction, reading audiences, and nineteenth-century psychological theories, it is also important to consider how the Dickensian cultural politics of popular reading that I delineate enters into Victorian debates about how (and whether) to distinguish between the psychological and social dimensions of experience, debates that, I argue, were still characterized by Enlightenment-era understandings of memory and experience.[84] To discern the epistemological, educational, and literary functioning of certain metaphors of mind and memory, and to understand more clearly how these changed in the course of the nineteenth century, it helps to read them as "literal" descriptions of how the mind works.[85] For example, when in the "Preliminary Word" of the opening number of *Household Words*, Dickens announces that the magazine aspires "to live in the Household affections, and to be numbered among the Household thoughts, of our readers," he not only is articulating metaphorically his intention to influence readers but also indicates that the magazine's stories are meant quite concretely to share in the reader's preoccupations and time, and its concerns to permeate their everyday domestic intercourse, just as the magazine itself will circulate materially among readers within the household and outside it.[86] Jowett's similar appreciation of Dickens as occupying the mental space of Englishmen conveys the unifying functions of national literary culture but also displays the assumption that reading can be a means to coordinate one's own personal, social, political, and cultural concerns. It is important, then, to take seriously the operative character of such formulations in order to achieve a more fine-grained understanding of how serial reading afforded and supported social connectivity in the nineteenth century through its emergence as a widespread practice and new medium of modern mass culture.

In Chapter 1, "Memory's Bonds: Associationism and the Freedom of Thought," I provide a cultural and intellectual history of the emergence of popular associationism in Victorian literary, critical, psychological, and pedagogical writings. Elucidating the sustained theoretical interest in the parallel, freely ranging functioning of memory, thinking, and imagination, I survey the history of associationist conceptions of mind, memory, and reading from the seventeenth century through the nineteenth in English and Scottish Enlightenment moral philosophy and pedagogical theory. Focusing on the writings of Francis Bacon, Thomas Hobbes, John Locke, David Hume, and David Hartley, I argue for the persistence into the nineteenth century of a strong philosophical tradition of interest in memory as a reliable, virtual medium linking mind and world. Utilitarian philosophers such as Jeremy Bentham and James Mill employed associationist theory to explain the interlocking theoretical and functional coherence among processes of associative memory, education and socialization, and projects for social and political reform. Hartley, I show, provided a crucial analogy between learning to read and the serial patterning of experience in the mind that was recycled repeatedly in popular didactic literature employing associationist principles in order to shape reader reception. Henry Mayhew's short pedagogical treatise *What to Teach and How to Teach It: So That the Child May Become a Wise and Good Man* (1842) demonstrates how Humean associationism, via the writings of Scottish Common Sense philosopher Thomas Brown, could be explicitly reformulated by Victorian writers and publishers, including Dickens, to provide a psychological rationale for Victorian instructional and periodical literature intended for a mass audience.

Chapter 2, "Dickens's Originality: Serial Fiction, Celebrity, and *The Pickwick Papers*," delineates the place of Dickens's serial fiction in the early Victorian literary field by charting the history of the critical reception of Dickens's first novel and his emergence as one of the earliest historical instances of the modern author as celebrity. I show how Victorian critics made repeated use of associationist conceptions of memory and rhetorical invention to characterize both the originality and the vivid impact on readers of Dickens's fictions, linking these effects to the author's humor, penchant for close observation, and retentive memory. The associationist jargon of critics and publishers of popular Victorian periodicals also informs the commonplace of Dickens criticism describing the feedback loop between the author's mind and the reader's memory. Dickens's own inventive associations become the sources of his moral influence, while his novels in turn produce the shared associations of his readers with the Humean-style "fictional realities" of such famous characters as Sam Weller and Sairy Gamp. I also show how *The Pickwick Papers* institutes Dickens's narrative technique of embedding associationist social epistemology and critique within his most famous characters' comedic dialogue. Characterizing Dickens's relationship to working-class readers, with particular attention to his acquaintance with cabinetmaker turned author John Overs, I argue that in his many charitable public appearances on behalf of universal education as a means of cultural inclusion of the poor, Dickens projected a model of popular reading as democratic participation in the arts. George Orwell's 1939 account of his own pleasures of memory in reading Dickens demonstrates that Dickens's celebrity authorship continued to personify a politically independent democratic mentality through the early decades of the twentieth century.

The following two chapters examine in detail the ways that Dickens's novels revise Victorian reading pedagogy by secularizing the protocols of pious reading employed by Evangelical writers of religious fiction for the poor. Chapter 3, "The Pleasures of Memory, Part I: Curiosity as Didacticism in *The Old Curiosity Shop*," examines one of Dickens's most popular serial novels alongside the religious tracts that were a hallmark of Evangelical propagandizing. Even as it shares with Evangelical tracts certain common associationist assumptions about the effects of reading on the memory, *The Old Curiosity Shop*, I argue, contests the cultural politics of the larger evangelical movement by subverting the rhetorical and ideological rationales behind didactic fictions, such as Hannah More's contributions to the Cheap Repository of Moral and Religious Tracts (1795–98) and Legh Richmond's *Annals of the Poor* (1814). Shaping an "anti-didactic" strategy for popular fiction, Dickens's moralizing tale about Little Nell's unjust death counteracts the cultural influence of evangelicalism by substituting a benevolent curiosity and activist sensibility in the place of Evangelical fiction's staging of pious deaths to motivate the reader's religious conversion and social deference.

Chapter 4, "The Pleasures of Memory, Part II: Epitaphic Reading and Cultural Memory," investigates Dickens's creation of narrative plots around the functions of the associative memory. Beginning with the stories collected in *Sketches by Boz* (1839), Dickens investigates memory disorders characteristic of urban life. *Nicholas Nickleby* (1838–39) not only dramatizes the effects of coercive pedagogies in its satire of the Yorkshire schools but also attributes Smike and Ralph Nickleby's failed familial relation to lapses of associative memory, leading to the impossibility of recognition or affection between father and son. Focusing on *Oliver Twist* (1837–39) and revisiting *The Old Curiosity Shop*, I show how these serials extend the associative powers of memory beyond the narrative itself, working out a technique to pattern the reader's own associations with the novel by creating memories of reading that become analogous to everyday experience through repeated and collective rereading. Each of these techniques also involves framing the facsimile experience generated by serial reading as "epitaphic": working through prosopopoeia by invoking either the character, a memory, or the figure of the author as its personification, reading becomes a means of connecting with absent others. By analogy, readers' shared memories of reading Dickens's serial novels leverage participation in a reading audience that could also function as a social activist constituency for solving the problem of poverty. In the chapter's conclusion, I analyze the further development in *Little Dorrit* (1855–57) of the self-reflexive epistemological dimensions of Dickens's novelistic thematization of memory as epitaphic reading. In this novel, Dickens's cultural politics of public service takes the form of Little Dorrit's vocation of domestic duty to her flawed family. In place of Mrs. Clennam's self-serving and repressive fundamentalist Bible reading, the narrative's associationist mnemonics positions Little Dorrit herself as a topos of memory standing for the novel reader's own linkage of social causes and conditions with human rather than divine responsibility. Paired as the alternatively positive and skeptical versions of a popularized Humean conception of memory's role in framing either duty toward or disdain for others, Amy Dorrit and Miss Wade guide the reader's virtual experience of dedicated and shared cultural memories as the basis of revitalized forms of social relation.

Chapter 5, "Learning by Heart in *Our Mutual Friend*," analyzes how Dickens's final completed serial novel actively includes the poor in Victorian cultural life by emphasizing the creative aspects of everyday labor and the independent thinking expressed even by the illiterate. As the opposing force to the impoverished person's inventiveness spurred by necessity, the rote uses of memory in both Victorian schooling and attitudes associated with social class come under attack in the novel. Jenny Wren, the doll's dressmaker, and Venus, the "articulator" of anatomical specimens, model memory's productive uses in entrepreneurial and artistic invention, thus enacting Victorian popular culture's democratic potential to provide cultural values bridging the social divisions of class. Situating the novel in the context of debates over franchise reform and parliamentary funding of popular education in the 1860s, I show that the schoolmaster Bradley Headstone's psychopathology not only correlates directly with his rote learning on the level of the novel's plot but also exposes the mid-Victorian state's role in the provision of false incentives for working-class literacy. The flawed Victorian liberal view of education as a vehicle for controlling the extension of the franchise threatens to derail Dickens's democratic project for literature by constraining memory's synthetic powers of mental coherence and social connection within the uneven distributions of culture provided by the emerging Victorian education system. *Our Mutual Friend* also builds on the critique of didactic religious literature in Dickens's earlier novels by redefining reading not as a scholastic routine or a strategy of "self-culture" geared toward a strictly limited social mobility, but rather as a critical performance medium: Twemlow's public rebuke to Podsnap in redefining the "feelings of a gentleman" to include the feelings of any man reinterprets and revivifies traditions, thus opening up cultural memory to public participation.

In the book's concluding chapter, "Dickens's Laughter: School Reading and Democratic Literature, 1870–1940," I analyze how Dickens's novelistic pedagogy and democratic project for popular fiction were institutionalized in the English literature curriculum. I begin by elucidating the stakes of the temporary collapse and recovery of Dickens's reputation in relation to the professionalization of the literary field in the final decades of the nineteenth century. George Eliot's negative criticisms of Dickens's sentimentalism about the poor in 1856 and G. H. Lewes's diagnosis in 1872 of Dickens's imagination as semi-deranged, I argue, both seek to marginalize Dickens's associationism and popularity in order to define both literature and psychology as distinct disciplinary forms of knowledge. During this same period, however, Dickens's status as a canonical author within the English literature curriculum was being consolidated. Examining literary histories, biographies, and British and American school readers and editions published between 1846 and 1919, I delineate the emergence of "the school Dickens," a standard image of Dickens's authorship that updates his humanitarian advocacy of the poor into an egalitarian ethic central to the English curriculum's role in training children for participation in democratic institutions. The twentieth-century English curriculum nevertheless excluded the distinctive serial form of the "historical Dickens's" popular fiction because it did not conform to the time and content coverage constraints of the English literature syllabus. In the final section of Chapter 6, I show that although they take different positions on mass culture's trajectory in the twentieth century, writers such as Henry James, G. K. Chesterton, George Orwell, and F. R. Leavis are able once again to celebrate Dickens on the basis of their own cherished childhood associations with reading his novels. Chesterton and Orwell revivify Dickens's independent democratic aesthetic—his very English ability, as Chesterton puts it, to "describe the democracy as consisting of free men, but yet funny men."[87] The pleasures of memory and the popular version of epitaphic reading that Dickens's early novels developed are also incorporated into elite literary reading practices in the form of a remainder of a "naive" relationship to reading as personal experience that the sophisticated critic cannot quite disavow, since it provides a significant basis for the academic distinction of professional literary reading and the division of reading into popular, classroom, and professional practices. Chesterton's and Orwell's image of Dickens's democratic laughter, however, not only confirms the linkage articulated in 1870 by Jowett between Dickens and English culture but also represents the self-subversion of this canonizing impulse by the historical Dickens's anti-institutional project.

In a brief afterword, I examine how the interconnection between forms of seriality manifested in associationist theories of memory and the print medium of serial fiction demonstrates an extended historical development of the reciprocal linkage between mode of reception and material form in modern media. This recursiveness in turn articulates a model for understanding how early twenty-first-century digital serial media may elicit new virtual and participatory forms of social relation.

1. *Memory's Bonds*

Associationism and the Freedom of Thought

> It is a dangerous attempt in any government to say to a Nation,
> *Thou shalt not read.*—Thought, by some means or other, is got
> abroad in the world, and cannot be restrained, though reading
> may.
>
> Thomas Paine (1792)

During one of his solitary walks to the Meagles family cottage at Twicken-
ham after Pet Meagles's marriage to Henry Gowan, Arthur Clennam learns
that Mrs. Tickit, the housekeeper who presides over the cottage in the
owners' absence, has caught a glimpse of Tattycoram, the orphan who lived
as companion and maid to Pet, until she ran away with Miss Wade. This
brief exchange, in Dickens's *Little Dorrit* (1855–57) bears an even greater
weight of meaning than the speculations Mrs. Tickit raises about Tattycoram's motives in her clandestine visit to the home of her former employers
and benefactors. Mrs. Tickit reports that when she saw Tattycoram she was
not exactly dozing but "I was more what a person would strictly call watching with my eyes closed." Clennam asks her to continue:

"Well, sir," proceeded Mrs Tickit, "I was thinking of one thing and thinking
of another. Just as you yourself might. Just as anybody might."
"Precisely so," said Clennam. "Well?"
"And when I do think of one thing and do think of another," pursued
Mrs Tickit, "I hardly need to tell you, Mr Clennam, that I think of the
family. Because, dear me! a person's thoughts," Mrs Tickit said this with an
argumentative and philosophic air, "however they may stray, will go more
or less on what is uppermost in their minds. They *will* do it, sir, and a person
can't prevent them."
Arthur subscribed to this discovery with a nod.

"You find it so yourself, sir, I'll be bold to say," said Mrs Tickit, "and we all find it so. It an't our stations in life that changes us, Mr Clennam; thoughts is free!"[1]

Mrs. Tickit's mind not only has been ranging over the Meagles family history but has also, simultaneously, been entertaining the problem of its own operations: Mrs. Tickit has been thinking about thinking. She is not only a housekeeper, it seems, but also a sort of amateur psychologist who has even developed a theory about a state of consciousness between waking and sleep.[2] Arthur initially dismisses the housekeeper's report, deciding that she had "clearly been started out of slumber" and therefore that Tattycoram's appearance must have been a dream, until he himself encounters both Tattycoram and her companion, Miss Wade, on the Strand in London shortly after this incident (509). If Mrs. Tickit's thoughts tend to stray freely, it is also no coincidence that they lead us directly to the stray girl who has rebelled against her servile condition in the Meagles's household, absconding to live domestically with another rebellious single woman.

Mrs. Tickit's argument about thinking carries significant social and political implications that require a whole novel to explore. The most challenging part of Mrs. Tickit's discourse is her assertion that "It an't our stations in life that changes us, Mr Clennam; thoughts is free!" What does she mean by this, and what does Dickens mean by making her the author of this quasi-philosophical argument? Mrs. Tickit's logic seems straightforward: she postulates that because her thoughts evade her control, they reveal a mental freedom that is common to everyone, as she indicates by drawing Arthur into her sense of a shared capacity for ranging thought—"You find it so yourself, sir, I'll be bold to say, . . . and we all find it so." This mental freedom consists of the ability to be carried away by one's own personal preoccupations; her thoughts, though they may stray, pursue recurrent themes related to her life. But her friendly assertion that she and Arthur are basically the same as far as the operation, if not the content, of their minds means that there is no economic or social criterion for the tendency to be lost in one's own thoughts.

Mrs. Tickit's statement also implies that, at a more autobiographical level, people become who they are through particular experiences. Her informal empiricist philosophy of mind posits a linkage between an individual's mental freedom to be carried away by his or her own concerns and a vision of equality based on common mental powers: while our social station "changes," or differentiates and shapes, us, our common freedom to think

makes each of us both alike and unique. Mrs. Tickit's thinking about thinking therefore does not show the same sort of independence from volition as
her thoughts. Her self-examination provokes the crucial turn in her logic
that translates her realization of the independence of mental processes from
complete conscious control—the freedom of thought—into a thinly veiled
political claim that "thoughts is free," also suggesting that Mrs. Tickit considers herself, in respectable liberal fashion, to be fully entitled to her own
opinions. Yet her claim extends beyond liberalism as a political philosophy
toward a more general defense of the mind as a space of freedom for persons
of all social conditions and levels of education in the Victorian society of
the 1850s.[3]

In the initial two chapters of this book, I investigate the widespread acceptance of this conception of the freedom of thought across the political
spectrum in Victorian society, as well as its psychological, philosophical, and
rhetorical bases. In doing so, I seek to clarify the implications of the assertion
of "mental freedom" for Dickens's associationist representations of memory
in his serial fiction and for what I am characterizing as his incipiently democratic cultural politics. The housekeeper's somewhat aggressive, somewhat
apologetic demeanor makes sense in light of the egalitarian, even democratic, implications of her ideas about the life of the mind.[4] It is significant
that in Dickens's novels a commonsense philosophy of mind, or what we
might call a popular psychology, is much more likely to emanate from a
housekeeper or a valet, a coachman or a doll's dressmaker, than from an
educated gentleman who might be supposed to possess a more systematic
knowledge of the world. In fact, the sharpness of a Dickensian character's
penetration of the connections between society and individual understanding tends to increase as his or her station in life is located at the lower end
of the social hierarchy.[5]

In their critical preoccupation with the dynamics of thinking, experience, and social change, Dickens's novels participate in long-standing debates that developed through the eighteenth and nineteenth centuries in
Britain connecting mind, education, economic principles, and social reform
accomplished through legislation. These debates engaged thinking men and
women from a range of backgrounds and political positions. From Utilitarians to Anglican Evangelicals, from political economists to socialist factory
owners and Chartist organizers, from pedagogical theorists and Sunday
school teachers to organizers of Mechanics' Institutes, from novelists to
members of Parliament—all were asking versions of the question that Mrs.
Tickit's theory attempts to address: what is the necessary relation, if such

exists, between the individual mind and social conditions? For many of these investigators, the solution to this question seemed most likely to stem in some way from access to education and the social impact of increased rates of literacy. Mrs. Tickit's discourse confirms the revolutionary social implications of Thomas Paine's assertion that "thought . . . is got abroad in the world," in ways related to the increase of literacy but not fully understandable in terms of the simple capacity to read.

In this chapter I delineate how thinking about thinking, particularly in the terms of the association of ideas, came to serve as a crucial means to articulate the relations among politics, social conditions, and human nature in the period from roughly 1714, ten years after philosopher John Locke's death, to circa 1870, when the physiological approach to psychology began to take hold as an institutionalized research program through the organization of university laboratories, professional associations, and journals.[6] During this period the philosophical theory of the association of ideas and its central conception of the serial and connective functioning of memory had a status as commonsense psychology among many educated Britons, much as the idea that individuals are inhabited by unconscious desires related to childhood experiences was often taken for granted among educated Europeans and Americans in the twentieth century.

A central contribution of empiricist associationism to nineteenth-century reform projects of various political persuasions lay in its function as a psychological basis for the optimistic notion that education could promote useful habits and beliefs leading to rational behavior, deference, social stability, and ultimately general human welfare. This optimism about the reformative power of education was supported by a commonly accepted analogy between reading and experience as activities relying on the associative memory for their coherence. Posed succinctly by eighteenth-century philosopher and physician David Hartley, who "spearheaded the establishment of [associationism] . . . as an explicit or definite school of psychology," this analogy supported a range of views attached to various political and aesthetic agendas about the role of education in cultivating the individual and in leveraging or managing social change.[7] The fundamental egalitarian notion that all minds can be located on a spectrum of similar capacities also meant that associationism supported "freedom of thought" in ways that were inherently (and perhaps surprisingly, in retrospect) destabilizing to attempts to naturalize and legitimize the existing social hierarchy based on psychological principles, whether by Evangelicals in their tracts teaching Christian faith and social deference to the poor or by Utilitarian philosophers such as Jeremy Bentham and James Mill, who attempted to rationalize social institutions based on basic psychological motives of pleasure and pain.

The epistemological writings of Bacon, Hobbes, and Locke formulate the empiricist psychology underpinning associationism's central theoretical role in eighteenth- and early nineteenth-century educational philosophy and pedagogy. I begin by examining Bacon's and Locke's conceptions of serial memory and turn later in the chapter to Hobbes's views of the role of the associative imagination in mental discourse, in order to make recognizable how subsequent associationist aesthetic, psychological, rhetorical, and pedagogical theories revise and recycle these earlier formulations within empiricist scientific methodologies and Enlightenment moral philosophy. This history of association psychology in British philosophical and educational thought illuminates the ways that Dickens's novels rely on the associative agencies of understanding, memory, and imagination—mental functions that were aligned in associationist theory—to shape reader reception. In the next chapter I show that Hobbes's and Bacon's seemingly historically remote metaphors for the memory's ranging search function in rhetorical invention reappear in *The Pickwick Papers* (1836–37). Here I examine how the associationist tradition of theorizing about mind as the product of experience endows memory with crucial epistemological functions. The mental coherence postulated by associationism also means that thought becomes highly formalized, a quality that nevertheless does not detract from the mind's ability to range freely. This chapter's analysis of the epistemological implications of associationist memory provides the groundwork for subsequent chapters to trace in detail how such associationist understandings of memory's serial support of personal identity lie behind the propensity of Dickens's novels to connect thinking to social life through serial reading.

Dickens's novelistic versions of associationism also draw on the rhetorical arts of memory and invention that eighteenth-century professors of rhetoric such as Adam Smith, Hugh Blair, and George Campbell had combined with an associationist faculty psychology, and that still formed the basis of training in rhetoric and elocution in Victorian grammar schools and universities.[8] This eighteenth-century empiricist New Rhetoric "cleave[d] to the essential worth of inventive language and, more broadly, the value of imaginative art."[9] In his *Analysis of the Phenomena of the Human Mind* (1829), James Mill provides an example of a mnemonic device: "Suppose I know that the idea of Socrates will be present to my mind at twelve o'clock this week: if I wish to remember at that time something which I have to do, my purpose will be gained, if I establish between the idea of Socrates, and the circumstance which I wish to remember, such an association that the one will call up the other."[10] Mill describes his version of a memory technique that was derived from classical Greek and Roman rhetorical pedagogies and still practiced by educated public men of his era.[11] Dickens also employed such memory techniques in his own public speaking. He was famous for the accuracy and astonishing capacity of his memory, and he gained a reputation as an outstanding public speaker of his day in company with such famous Victorian politician-orators as John Bright and William Gladstone.[12] Many who witnessed Dickens's speeches were amazed that he never consulted any notes.[13] George Dolby, manager of Dickens's public readings of his novels in the 1860s, recounts an occasion when he and Wilkie Collins learned of Dickens's use of memory techniques in composing and delivering speeches:

> He told us that, supposing the speech was to be delivered in the evening, his habit was to take a long walk in the morning, during which he would decide on the various heads to be dealt with. These being arranged in their proper order, he would in his "mind's eye," liken the whole subject to the tire of a cartwheel—he being the hub. From the hub to the tire he would run as many spokes as there were subjects to be treated, and during the progress of the speech he would deal with each spoke separately, elaborating them as he went round the wheel; and when all the spokes dropped out one by one, and nothing but the tire and space remained, he would know that he had accomplished his task, and that his speech was at an end.[14]

Dickens's use of a cartwheel with himself positioned in his "mind's eye" at the hub is an intriguing variation within a long tradition of cyclical and peripatetic mnemonic devices. These memory techniques involved both mental visualization and gesture. Dolby reports that after this conversation, he had various opportunities to witness Dickens speaking, and that each time, "I have been amused to observe him dismiss the spoke from his mind by a quick action of the finger as if he were knocking it away."[15] By the time Dickens finished his speech, then, he no longer occupied the hub of a wheel but rather was positioned imaginatively at the center of two concentric circles, perhaps representing his immediate audience surrounded by the wider sphere of his readership.

In addition, Dickens's description of his memory techniques indicates that he was familiar with another canon of classical rhetoric: *inventio*, or the art of discovering effective arguments for a particular occasion.[16] Such evidence suggests that Dickens received some formal rhetorical training during his schooling. During his stint as a shorthand reporter for the *Mirror of Parliament* and the *Morning Chronicle* from 1831 to 1836, Dickens also witnessed and recorded many speeches in the House of Commons, including memorable debates over the eventual Reform Act of 1832.[17] In speaking from memory without notes, Dickens was also following standard practice both in Parliament and at Cambridge Union Society and Oxford Union Society debates, where, historian Joseph S. Meisel explains, "even when speakers had prepared and memorized their whole speech in advance, it was nevertheless critical for success that the speech be delivered in such a way as to seem an extemporaneous flow and not a recitation from memory."[18] The most successful Victorian practitioner of the arts of memory would have been the speaker who, like Dickens, could most effectively mask his reliance on prior composition and memorization. Dickens's methods of composing speeches may also have translated to the writing of his novels, and vice versa. In an 1862 magazine interview, Dickens explained that "I never commit thoughts to paper until I am obliged to write, being better able to keep them in regular order, on different shelves of my brain, ready ticketed and labelled to be brought out when I want them."[19] The working notes that Dickens kept for his novels, within which he included certain reminders about plot and characterization listed under the abbreviation "Mems," or memoranda, seem also to have functioned as a kind of shorthand or scaffolding, and thus as another technique combining memory and invention.[20]

It is important to note that associationism is not synonymous with eighteenth-century sentimentalism, with its primary focus on sympathy as the vehicle of the social circulation of sentiments.[21] Insofar as Dickens's writings develop a specifically Victorian version of sentimentalism, I want to argue that they also take up philosophical sentimentalism's central epistemological question of the relation between reason and passion, or thought and feeling, as an unresolved problem requiring the mediating role of memory as a lynchpin between moral sentiments and epistemology. In the next three chapters, culminating in my discussion of Nell's scene of reading in *The Old Curiosity Shop* (1840–41) in Chapter 4, I show how Dickens's serial novels envision collective memories of reading as vehicles of a normative morality that avoids the Enlightenment theorists' grounding of sympathy in the individual's ability (or failure) to imagine the suffering of others. David Hume's discussion in *A Treatise of Human Nature* (1739–40) of the dependence of will on the passions rather than on reason has frequently been seen as one of the strongest arguments made in British Enlightenment moral philosophy for the importance of the moral sentiments. Hume's version of associationism was equally influential, if controversial, in placing a strong emphasis on the equivocal relations among memory, the self, and social life. This Humean focus on memory as the form of the self's consistency over time, I argue, brings us closer to the Dickensian novel's pedagogical conception of collective memory effects produced by reading serial fiction. In Chapter 4, I detail how the Humean and pedagogical associationist model of memory underpins representations of the effects of reading in *The Old Curiosity Shop*, the novel that critics have most often diagnosed as encouraging excessively sentimental responses to its representation of Little Nell's death.[22]

Dickens read Hume and owned an 1825 edition of Hume's *Essays and Treatises on Several Subjects*, which "was quite popular in the Victorian period."[23] Among the many figures surveyed in this chapter whose writings complicate the associationist tradition, I uncover a Humean associationist understanding of memory and fictionality as an element of the popular psychology purveyed by Dickens's serial fiction, subtly recognizable in Mrs. Tickit's discourse on thinking, for example. A pedagogical treatise by Dickens's contemporary, journalist and social investigator Henry Mayhew, helps me tease out the role of Humean epistemology within Victorian pedagogy's various applications of popular associationism. Dickens's serial novels, I argue, transform and update a Humean theory of the memory's role into a modern theory of serial reading as a vehicle of social relation and cohesion.

While most attractive to thinkers aligned with Enlightenment-era rationalism and materialism such as Joseph Priestley, associationist theory surfaces in works of evangelical piety by authors such as Isaac Watts and also informed theories of the mind's role in incorporating and influencing social change elaborated by philosophers and writers across the political spectrum, from William Wordsworth to Robert Owen, and from William Godwin to James and John Stuart Mill. Notable Romantic intellectuals including Samuel Taylor Coleridge and William Hazlitt offered incisive criticisms of associationist notions of mind that have frequently been taken as definitive by historians of psychology. Historians' retroactive endorsement of this critique of associationism positions the "Coleridgean orthodoxy" as a crucial turning point in a seemingly progressive theoretical trajectory that leads, in hindsight, toward modern scientific psychology. I conclude this chapter by showing that this assumption that associationist psychology must inevitably have been left behind in the course of the nineteenth century overlooks serial fiction's and Victorian popular pedagogy's roles in perpetuating and even extending associationism's status as a commonsense psychology informing early Victorian theories of reading and reception, which in turn provided early reviewers of Dickens's novels with their terminology for explaining both his popularity and the originality of his characters and narrative techniques.

Memory, Reflection, and Invention

Memory was the mental function most crucial from the seventeenth century to the nineteenth in empiricist philosophical, pedagogical, and political reformist theories and programs for reproducing and altering social conditions at the level of the individual mind. That memory could be conceived as creative and not merely reproductive is evident in Francis Bacon's treatise *Novum Organum*, or *The New Organon* (1620), an enormously influential work that sought to reinitiate scientific and philosophical inquiry on a rigorously empirical basis. In the context of providing numerous practical examples of inductive reasoning and experimentation, Bacon includes the functioning of memory in reference to his fifth "privileged instance"—or "types of experimental set-up which provide particularly powerful tools for investigating nature," as Lisa Jardine glosses the term—called "constitutive" or "bundled" instances (*instantiae constitutivae*).[24] Bacon explains that in the course of inductive investigation, the observer should be aware of "constitutive instances" as "particular forms which group certain bundles of instances (though by no means all) together into a common notion" (142). For Bacon, bundled instances include the use of "places" (*loci*) in mnemonics and in the composition or memorization of poetry. Such techniques involve what Bacon terms "*curtailment of the unlimited*": "For when one attempts to recall something or bring it to mind, if he has no prior notion or conception of what he is looking for, he is surely looking, struggling and running about here and there in seemingly *unlimited* space. But if he has a definite notion, the unlimited is immediately curtailed and the range of the memory is kept within bounds" (142–43).[25]

To elucidate this principle, Bacon provides one of his most revelatory metaphors for the role of memory in individual learning and scientific discovery:

> Those who have treated of the sciences have been either empiricists or dogmatists. Empiricists, like ants, simply accumulate and use; Rationalists, like spiders, spin webs from themselves; the way of the bee is in between: it

takes material from the flowers of the garden and the field; but it has the ability to convert and digest them. This is not unlike the true working of philosophy; which does not rely solely or mainly on mental power, and does not store the material provided by natural history and mechanical experiments in its memory untouched but altered and adapted in the intellect. Therefore much is to be hoped from a closer and more binding alliance (which has never yet been made) between these faculties (i.e. the experimental and the rational). (79)

Bacon illuminates the compromise he seeks to forge between a rationalism typically modeled too closely on introspection, and thus taking the mind for its compass, and an empiricism that cannot rise theoretically above the banal applications of its "useful" accumulated evidence in order to reach a more generally valid induction. The "way of the bee" creates an analogy between memory and philosophy, highlighting not only the cumulative but also the "in between"—mediating and transitional—inventive powers of memory when combined with intellect or understanding. The memory itself is like a beehive that, while storing, also categorizes, "converts," and transforms the evidence of experience and empirical investigation for fruitful future uses in both science and philosophy. Mind is not mere mechanism in this extended metaphor, but rather the bee, its hive and food sources, and the bee's work of retrieval, digestion, and storage represent what we could call a complete mental ecosystem of the productive as well as reproductive faculties of intellect and memory as they come into contact with the natural world.[26] This characterization of memory as synthetic as well as reproductive also gestures toward the kind of blended value- and fact-laden questioning of social conditions in which, as I show in subsequent chapters, Dickensian fiction engages its readers.

Relying extensively on metaphor like Bacon's epistemology, in his *Essay Concerning Human Understanding* (1689) John Locke emphasizes the role of memory in sustaining the sense of self, but he also dwells at some length on the vagaries of its functioning.[27] Locke begins with the metaphor of memory as "the Store-house of our *Ideas*" (150). Because the mind has no means to keep all ideas constantly under consideration, it needs a "Repository" that has the "Power . . . to revive Perceptions, which it has once had, with this additional Perception annexed to them, that it has had them before" (150). This additional "Power" to perceive the past existence of ideas is linked to Locke's crucial formulation of two fundamental mental faculties,

"Sensation" and "Reflection." Sensation provides ideas derived from sensory experience and observation, while reflection is "the *Perception of the Operations of our own Minds* within us, as it is employ'd about the *Ideas* it has got," or "that notice which the Mind takes of its own Operations, and the manner of them, by reason whereof, there come to be *Ideas* of these Operations in the Understanding" (105). Locke points out that there is no actual storehouse in the mind, but only the "ability" to retain and revive past impressions, which have greater or diminished strength based on the degree of pleasure or pain attached to the original "fixing" by the memory (150). For Locke, famously, memory is also implicated in the way the mind functions like a blank sheet of paper, impressed or etched by sensations represented as ideas. The larger "business" of memory is its function "to furnish to the Mind those dormant Ideas, which it has present occasion for, and in the having them ready at hand on all occasions, consists that which we call Invention, Fancy, and quickness of Parts" (153). Memory is essential to imagination because it supplies the ideas and impressions that these creative activities work upon. In the terms of classical rhetoric to which Locke alludes, memory is the wellspring of invention in discourse.

When ideas are strongly associated with pain or pleasure, they become firmly fixed in the memory, either through attention or repetition or because a person possesses a particularly retentive mind. Such fixed ideas, however, can become the kind of unreasoning mental habit, internalized custom, or preconceived judgment lacking evidence that Locke terms "prejudice"—a notion that later takes on the more familiar modern connotations relating to negative bias against particular persons or groups.[28] The topic of memory inspires some of Locke's most memorable figurative language in the *Essay*. Memories that are impressed without great strength, either because they are trivial or because the mental capacity itself is weak, can be fleeting, "leaving no more footsteps or remaining Characters of themselves, than Shadows do flying over Fields of Corn; and the Mind is as void of them, as if they never had been there" (151). Memories that are not frequently revived are necessarily evanescent, with the result that the vanishing of past ideas precedes and foreshadows the death of the self: "Thus the Ideas, as well as Children, of our Youth, often die before us: And our Minds represent to us those Tombs, to which we are approaching; where though the Brass and Marble remain, yet the Inscriptions are effaced by time, and the Imagery moulders away" (151–52). If for Bacon memory is an art and an ecosystem, for Locke memory contributes to epistemology by supporting the mind's capacity for reflection and self-reflection, providing the mental forms of materiality upon which both recollection and forgetting can be registered.

Mental Discourse and Social Thinking

Despite Locke's reservations about the reliability of memory, the empiricist epistemology that he helped inaugurate drew the activity of memory into its wake, and within the associationist strand of that tradition, memory's functioning often appears reassuringly automatic. Because memory has the status of both a functional and a fallible vehicle of social formation, however, its role in providing the groundwork for an epistemological theory is fraught with problems that would produce much new philosophical investigation, particularly by David Hume. In eighteenth- and nineteenth-century pedagogical theory, memory's relation to epistemology is also both central and ambivalent. If memory's functions support both the possibility of a coherent identity and the means of acquiring unthinking habits and inherited customs and prejudices, as Locke theorizes, it cannot be a completely reliable or sufficient source of scientific understanding or educational indoctrination.

The association of ideas can be understood most fundamentally as a theory about the mental processes of subject formation.[29] Association is conceived as a process automatically linking images and ideas based on contingencies of time and place, and also as a way that the memory makes seemingly accidental elements of an experience essential to the recollection of that experience. Associationist doctrine emphasized sensations produced by the immediate environment as the source of the mind's content and defined as associative processes such essential mental functions as the connection between sense impressions and ideas, the train of thought, volition, memory, and imagination. James Mill defines association most succinctly, if somewhat reductively: "Our ideas spring up, or exist, in the order in which the sensations existed, of which they are the copies. This is the general law of the 'Association of Ideas'; by which term, let it be remembered, nothing is here meant to be expressed, but the order of occurrence."[30] Mill's formulation brings out both the associative memory's serial functioning and its physiological aspects involving the brain and nervous system that support "chains" and interconnected networks of sensations and ideas. In addition, it is important to bear in mind that associations are just that—composites of sensations or of ideas—so they cannot be broken up into "prior" discrete bits or units of experience.[31] In his history of theories of memory, philosopher John Sutton argues that associationism offers a connectionist conception of memory according to which, very basically, memory traces consist of "patterned motions lack[ing] obvious boundaries" and are part of a "causal holism" dispersed across the entire mind conceived as a cognitive and affective system.[32]

Nevertheless, there were many different theories of how mental association attaches sense perceptions to particular representations, such as words and ideas. In 1775, Joseph Priestly, pioneering chemist, dissenting clergyman, radical political philosopher, pedagogical theorist, and one of the most assiduous popularizers of association psychology, characterized Hartley's influential associationist theories as a means "to deduce all the phenomena of thinking from the single principle of Association." Setting aside Hartley's theory of "vibrations" (a Newtonian physiological account of the way nerve impulses entering the white medullary substance of the brain are retained there and thus are transformed into associations or ideas), Priestley defines the association of ideas in psychological terms as follows: "When our minds are first exposed to the influence of external objects, all their parts and properties, and even accidental variable adjuncts, are presented to our view at the same time; so that the whole makes but one impression on our organs of sense, and consequently upon the mind. By this means all the parts of the simultaneous impression are so intimately associated together, that the idea of any one of them introduces the idea of the rest."[33] Whenever a similar object is perceived, all of its associated properties and the accidental circumstances surrounding the original impression are also recalled to mind. Sensations of pain and pleasure reinforce these associations, so that, in effect, one learns to experience habitual emotional responses based on past painful and pleasurable experiences.

Priestley explains how the associative process functions by uniting sense perceptions, including sensations of pain or pleasure, with ideas: "When we say that any idea or circumstance excites a particular passion, it is explained by observing that certain feelings and emotions have been formerly connected with that particular idea or circumstance, which it has the power of recalling by association." But in addition, other elements of a painful experience may also be invested with the same emotion, by association: "If a variety of painful emotions, and disagreeable feelings, have been associated with the idea of the same circumstance, they will all be excited by it, in one general *complex emotion*, the component parts of which will not be easily distinguishable; and by their mutual associations they will, at length, entirely coalesce, so as never to be separately perceived."[34] This tendency for complex emotions to conflate essential with accidental causes through association suggests a difficulty in reflecting upon and understanding the sources of one's feelings and ideas.[35] Even the operations of imagination can be explained through association: "In the wildest flights of fancy, it is probable that no single idea occurs to us but such as had a connexion with some other impression or idea, previously existing in the mind; and what we call new thoughts are only new combinations, of old simple ideas, or decompositions of complex ones."[36] For Priestley, associative memory is always grounded in the individual's "actual" experience and "the influence of circumstances."[37] Memory revives past associations; judgment assigns truth, by association, to propositions based on their concurrence or lack of concurrence with experience and with other propositions; and volition acts upon desires associated with particular pleasures, through means that have been associated with obtaining them. It was also a hallmark of associationist doctrine to separate the motivating states of feeling from intellectual processes, understood primarily as means for obtaining the ends dictated by feelings that lacked specific ideational content. Conceiving this associative process as not dependent on language, especially in the mind's earliest stages of development, Priestley asserts that "words are of great use in the business of thinking, but are not necessary to it."[38]

As we have begun to see in the writings of Bacon and Locke, the associationist concepts that became commonplace across many fields in the eighteenth century were formulated in seventeenth-century epistemological and psychological theorizing in both British and Continental philosophy.[39] Memory functions through association in the neurophysiology of René Descartes, while the theory of the association of ideas plays an even more prominent role in Thomas Hobbes's philosophy of language.[40] In *Leviathan* (1651), Hobbes's conception of "mental discourse," or the "Consequence or TRAIN of thoughts . . . that succession of one thought to another," understood as prior to or separable from discourse in language, seems to rest on the independence of memory as a neutral and innate function.[41] Memory ensures retrieval of the connections between particular past thoughts and the specific words that signify them, not only for an individual but also for an entire linguistic community. Hobbes often equates memory and imagination in associationist terms; both function serially and consist of connected trains or sequences of thought, the order of which depends on the temporal and spatial contiguity of the original sensations that produced them. He points to cause and effect as determining the sequences of ideas in the mind, and he differentiates the regulated and coherent trains of ideas created by waking perceptions from the random trains produced in dreams. Hobbes also links these associative processes to rhetorical invention; memory retrieves thoughts in association with the place and time of the original perception, while imaginative invention obeys associative cause and effect linkages.[42]

For Hobbes, as for Bacon and Locke, the functioning of memory is essential to language and discourse. Hobbes indicates that ideas or thoughts can exist separately from words: "the general use of speech is to transfer our mental discourse into verbal, or the train of our thoughts into a train of words." Words have two uses, the first of which defines language in terms of naming, a function that memory makes possible: "the registering of consequences of our thoughts, which being apt to slip out of our memory and put us to a new labour, may again be recalled by such words as they were marked by. So that the first use of names is to serve for *marks*, or *notes* of remembrance." When names or words become generalized into signs, memory preserves the connection between a particular member of a category and the sign that signifies them all, thus allowing for communication by creating the same connotation in the mind of speaker and listener: "One universal name is imposed on many things for their similitude in some quality or other accident; and whereas a proper name bringeth to mind one thing only, universals recall any one of those many."[43]

In addition to his discussions of memory in the *Essay*, Locke's theory of the association of ideas shows similarities to Hobbes's notion of the foundational nature of "mental discourse." Intellectual historian Hans Aarsleff calls Locke's chapter "Of the Association of *Ideas*" "the single most productive chapter in the *Essay*, right from the eighteenth century to the present."[44] Locke does not explicitly invoke memory in this chapter, which he added to the fourth edition of the *Essay* published in 1700. Nevertheless, it is clear from his description of the associations among ideas stemming from custom and habit that they either must be reactivated through the faculty of retention or can be activated automatically, as when a musician rehearses a well-known tune in his mind or on a keyboard, the notes occur in sequence "though his unattentive Thoughts be elsewhere awandering" (396). Locke distinguishes between the fortuitous association of ideas and those ideas that "have a natural Correspondence and Connexion with one another"; of these latter, he explains, "it is the Office and Excellency of our Reason to trace these, and hold them together." Association, however, forms ideas as a result of "Chance or Custom" (395). Locke warns that the irrational fixation on such contingent associated ideas can become a "sort of Madness" that is most often acquired at an early age. For this reason, "those who have

Children, or the charge of their Education, would think it worth their while diligently to watch, and carefully to prevent the undue Connexion of Ideas in the Minds of young People," for such "wrong Connexion[s]" pose such a threat to reasoning and moral action that "there is not any one thing that deserves more to be looked after" (395–97). Here Locke indicates a problem that instigates concerted efforts in Victorian reading pedagogy, as I discuss in Chapter 5, to train children habitually to make the correct association, or synthesis, between word and idea.

Locke introduces the problem of random associations with the example of the irrational "prejudices" that persist even in the most "sober and rational Minds": "*Ideas* that in themselves are not at all of kin, come to be so united in some Men's Minds, that 'tis very hard to separate them, they always keep company, and the one no sooner at any time comes into the Understanding but its Associate appears with it; and if they are more than two which are thus united, the whole gang always inseparable shew themselves together" (395–97). When not regulated according to reason, the association of ideas can provoke a kind of mental mob scene; in figuring contingent associations as a "gang always inseparable," Locke also suggests a connotation of political association and raises the specter of mob violence or revolution. Locke's reference to the negative epistemological effects of custom or randomly acquired associations also has a larger significance relating to prejudicial ideas one absorbs that are typical of one's companions and society.[45] I want to stress the way that Locke immediately references the social in describing mental associations, because this linkage occurs repeatedly in associationist theory. This emphasis is consistent with Locke's characterization of language in the *Essay* as "the great Instrument, and common Tye of Society" (402), and also demonstrates how Locke "expressly connected epistemology to semantic inquiry" in elaborating a semiotic notion of language as conventional.[46] Locke's equation of random associations of ideas with logical fallacy would suggest to eighteenth- and nineteenth-century educational theorists that prejudices resulting from mere customary socialization can be corrected through pedagogies that rationally and formally direct, or redirect, the formation of associations. Utilitarians such as Bentham and James Mill would develop the possibility of substituting generic, socially "beneficial" associations for habitual and customary "prejudicial" ones. Such a logic permitting the substitution of a new or revised set of mental habits for prior ones also appears in Dickens's novels, which substitute associationist "pleasures of memory" for the habits of piety and social deference presumed to be transmitted through the memorization of spelling books and catechisms in Victorian elementary schools.

David Hume's innovation in developing the theory of the association of ideas after Hobbes and Locke lies in the way he understands association as a fully subjective but nevertheless epistemologically operative synthetic activity of mind that guides the processes of thought, memory, and imagination. Thought must have some order and coherence, otherwise it would be a senseless and arbitrary jumble; so association works as a "gentle force" lending uniformity and regularity to the mind's operations.[47] To Locke's focus on the way that ideas are connected according to contiguity in space and time, Hume, following Hobbes, adds cause and effect, and he also recognizes resemblance and contrast or contrariety as forms of association (70). In *A Treatise of Human Nature*, Hume defines association as analogous to gravity: "a kind of ATTRACTION, which in the mental world will be found to have as extraordinary effects as in the natural, and to shew itself in as many and as various forms. Its effects are every where conspicuous; but as to its causes, they are mostly unknown, and must be resolv'd into *original* qualities of human nature, which I pretend not to explain" (12–13). In his later work, *An Enquiry Concerning Human Understanding* (1748), Hume terms the association of ideas a "general law, which takes place in all operations of the mind." The imagination inventively activates these associative connections and is thus able freely to reassemble trains of ideas and create new sequences and combinations: "Nothing is more free than the imagination; and though it cannot exceed that original stock of ideas, furnished by the internal and external senses, it has unlimited power of mixing, compounding, separating, and dividing these ideas, in all the varieties of fiction and vision."[48]

In the *Abstract of "A Treatise of Human Nature"* (1740), which Hume published to draw attention to the full-length *Treatise*, he contends that the imagination is not so free as to lack any coherence, for the association of ideas provides an underlying order even in the most extravagant fancies: "But notwithstanding the empire of the imagination, there is a secret tie or union among particular ideas, which causes the mind to conjoin them more frequently together, and makes the one, upon its appearance, introduce the other. Hence arises what we call the *apropos* of discourse: hence the connection of writing: and hence that thread, or chain of thought, which a man naturally supports even in the loosest *reverie*."[49] The importance of these formulations for my investigation of Dickens's uses of associationism lies in Hume's insistence on the structuring associative order of imagination. This is the kind of subtly regulated imagination, rendered also, as we saw earlier,

in Samuel Rogers's poem *The Pleasures of Memory* (1792), that Dickens's serial novels rely on as the basis for the perceived reality of the social connections that can emanate from shared experiences of reading. Such a finely
regulated imagination can both teach and be taught because of the way it
necessarily conveys a flexible order and a guiding thread both to the writer's
creative and rhetorical process of invention and to the reader's own reflec-
tive response to the fictional text.

Perhaps because of the *Abstract*'s function as a prospectus for the *Treatise*,
Hume also propagandizes for "the principles of association" as the basis of
his claim to the "glorious . . . name . . . of an *inventor*" in philosophy:

> 'Twill be easy to conceive of what vast consequence these principles must
> be in the science of human nature, if we consider, that so far as regards the
> mind, these are the only links that bind the parts of the universe together, or
> connect us with any person or object exterior to ourselves. For as it is by
> means of thought only that any thing operates upon our passions, and as
> these are the only ties of our thoughts, they are really to us the cement of
> the universe, and all the operations of the mind must, in a great measure,
> depend on them.[50]

Hume's emphasis on mental association as constituting the very bonds of
relation raises implications that I foreground throughout this study: connections among thoughts, relations between people, and even the "fabric of the
universe," insofar as they are accessible to human knowledge, come to depend on this pervasive "gentle force" connecting mind and world. As an
epistemology, associationism posits the train of thought, or the concept of
relation itself, as its principle of possibility and coherence, and its implications are so sweeping because it also affords a *common explanation* through a
theory of serial memory for both mental and social order and connection.
To rephrase Mrs. Tickit's assertion, if thoughts are free, then it is the associative "thread of thought," spun out through the activity of memory, that
simultaneously distinguishes one person from another and binds human beings together into an ordered society by ensuring shared meaning and sociability as well as innovation and renewal.[51]

The specific epistemological significance of the associative memory
emerges within Hume's famous argument in the *Treatise*'s chapter titled "Of
Personal Identity." For Hume, personal identity depends upon memory's
serial functioning: "As memory alone acquaints us with the continuance
and extent of this succession of perceptions, 'tis to be consider'd, upon that
account chiefly, as the source of personal identity. Had we no memory, we

never shou'd have any notion of causation, nor consequently of that chain of causes and effects, which constitute our self or person" (261–62). Since "every distinct perception, which enters into the composition of the mind, is a distinct existence, and is different, and distinguishable, and separable from every other perception, either contemporary or successive," then one must investigate whether "we observe some real bond" among the perceptions belonging to a given person or only "feel one among the ideas we form of them." Hume determines that personal identity is "merely a quality, which we attribute to [different perceptions], because of the union of their ideas in the imagination, when we reflect upon them" (259–60). In supporting this feeling of personal identity, memory provides *reliable fictions* for the philosophical skeptic and the imaginative writer.

Hume then focuses on resemblance and causation as the crucial forms of association that give rise to the idea of identity. The role of causation, in particular, allows Hume to create an analogy between mental and social order: "As to *causation*; we may observe, that the true idea of the human mind, is to consider it as a system of different perceptions or different existences, which are link'd together by the relation of cause and effect, and mutually produce, destroy, influence, and modify each other. Our impressions give rise to their correspondent ideas; and these ideas in their turn produce other impressions. One thought chaces another, and draws after it a third, by which it is expell'd in its turn" (261). Thinking in Humean epistemology functions associatively to attach one strand of the series of sensations to another as a relation of cause and effect. These causal series are shared across domains of experience. One might imagine that a mind in which "one idea chases another" would stage a chaotic drama of flight and pursuit, but instead these linked series produce an order in the "soul" resembling a "republic or commonwealth . . . in which the several members are united by the reciprocal ties of government and subordination, and give rise to other persons, who propagate the same republic in the incessant changes of its parts" (261).[52] For Hume, the "relation of causation" implied in the idea of identity serves the same ordering function as the republican form of government in supporting coherence through successive change: "And as the same individual republic may not only change its members, but also its laws and constitutions; in like manner the same person may vary his character and disposition, as well as his impressions and ideas, without losing his identity" (261). Thinking, within this analogy, is free to the extent that it reproduces formal but contingent, and ultimately historical, causal relations, even while the "constitution" of the person changes over time. The important legacy of Humean associationism for nineteenth-century political philosophers, writers, and pedagogues is to be found not in its republicanism but rather in the homology it posits among mental, social, and even political "relations" of resemblance and causation that will allow the Utilitarian philosopher, for example, to leverage reciprocal effects by intervening in either the mental "constitution" through education or the political "constitution" through legislation.[53]

Memory becomes the decisive associative function for Hume, then, not only because of its capacity to produce the sense of continuity but also because it provides a mental support of the conventionality of the social order. Memory allows the mind to project such identity both forward into the future and back into the past, even when recollection of specific memories is lacking: "But having once acquired this notion of causation from the memory, we can extend the same chain of causes, and consequently the identity of our persons beyond our memory, and can comprehend times, and circumstances, and actions, which we have entirely forgot, but suppose in general to have existed. For how few of our past actions are there, of which we have any memory?" (262). Hume's main purpose in this discussion is to deprive memory of its self-evidence as a source of identity within certain philosophical systems, in order to show how it works to "discover" the sense of self as the product of "a customary association of ideas" (260). In the course of his demonstration, Hume, like Hobbes and Locke, endows the associative memory with a crucial epistemological function: among other things, it allows one to think about thinking by sustaining the idea of the self upon the thread of mental discourse. There is also a certain epistemological pleasure in perceiving that the extension of thinking into places and times that one cannot fully remember or predict depends on the memory not as a faculty of recollection, though it is that, but rather as a *medium* that posits and supports the coherence of a multilayered and coordinated system persisting through constant, recursive serial change.[54]

An "Associationist Climate of Opinion"

Returning to Mrs. Tickit's theory of mind through our reading of Hume, we perceive that the movement of her thoughts according to her own preoccupations, despite the way it sometimes evades her conscious control, implies a "loose" kind of order that also serves to support her dual—psychological and sociopolitical—sense that her thoughts are "free," rather than merely random, chaotic, or determined by her circumstances. It seems, then, that in Dickens's novel, Mrs. Tickit is theorizing about thinking in the tradition of a Humean philosophy of mind, but how does this come about? By the mid–eighteenth century, both the Lockean and Humean notions of the association of ideas were widely known. In the fourth edition of his *Cyclopedia* (1741), Ephraim Chambers provides the following composite definition: "Association *of Ideas*, is where two or more ideas, constantly and immediately follow or succeed one another in the mind, so that the one shall almost infallibly produce the other; whether there be any natural relation between them, or not."[55] The associationist tradition developed a general description of two basic forms of association of ideas: (1) chance, or unnatural associations, derived from contiguity in time and place and (2) orderly, more natural associations depending on resemblance, contrariety, and cause and effect. Through the varied writings of such philosophers, pedagogues, poets, and critics as Joseph Addison, Erasmus Darwin, Richard and Maria Edgeworth, Francis Hutcheson, Hume, David Hartley, Priestley, Henry Home (Lord Kames), Isaac Watts, Alexander Gerard, James Beattie, Archibald Alison, William Wordsworth, Samuel Taylor Coleridge, William Hazlitt, Francis Jeffrey, and others, by the beginning of the nineteenth century, there had emerged what historian Martin Kallich calls an "associationist climate of opinion" according to which the association of ideas was widely "accepted as a psychological fact."[56] My point is not to assimilate the varied philosophical and aesthetic programs of these writers, but rather to highlight the role of a basic associationist understanding of memory as a psychological lingua franca for theorizing how the mind learns and retains knowledge so that it can take the form of experience or be transformed into oratory, science, or art.

In *Observations on Man, His Frame, His Duty, and His Expectations* (1749), the major philosophical treatise he produced over a period of eighteen years while practicing medicine, David Hartley provided an extensive elaboration of associationist psychology that was conceived independently of Hume's work but indebted to Locke.[57] To the repertoire of forms of association, Hartley added the distinction between synchronous and successive associations. Drawing on his training as a physician, Hartley elaborated a dualist mind-body theory that was more physiologically based than Hume's. He attempted to provide a basis in the nervous system and brain for the connections between thought and identity or causality that Hume believed were necessary and functional fictions. Hartley was also strongly interested in linking associationism with the practical and spiritual matters of education

and religious piety—the second half of his *Observations on Man* was a theological treatise defending scriptural authority. This applied associationism
made his ideas attractive to later eighteenth-century philosophers and writers such as Priestly, who sought to influence politics and society through
scientific research and education.[58]

Hartley's theory of association also envisioned the creation of a universal
philosophical language based on close observation of the mental processes
by which words are assigned to complex ideas, so that, in combination with
a common religion (Christianity), a universal progress in comprehension
toward complete uniformity and rational transparency of human communication could be attained. In *Observations on Man*, Hartley illustrates this possibility through an analogy describing two persons joining a crowd:

> Suppose two Persons, *A* and *B*, to go together into a Croud, and there each
> of them to see a Variety of persons whom he knew in different Degrees, as
> well as many utter Strangers. *A* would not have the same Ideas and Associa-
> tions raised in him from viewing the several Faces, Dresses, etc. of the
> Persons in the Croud, as *B*, partly from his having a different Knowledge of,
> and Acquaintance with them; partly from different Predispositions to
> approve and disapprove. But let *A* and *B* become equally acquainted with
> them, and acquire, by Education and Association, the same Predispositions
> of Mind, and then they will at last make the same Judgment of each of the
> Persons whom they see.[59]

As a seeming remedy for the problems located by Locke in the "mob"
of casual and fallacious associations that threatens to render the mind chaotic, Hartley puts forward an associationist view of education as a means to
organize and make sense of both minds and crowds. I have more to say
in Chapter 4 about the relation between mental associations and Dickens's
descriptions of the psychological effects of the crowded London streets, but
in this context Hartley's analogy suggests that society can be ordered, and
experiences and interests harmonized, based on the inculcation of shared
"predispositions" and standards of judgment. As he optimistically puts it,
"Association tends to make us all ultimately similar; so that if one be happy,
all must."[60] Formal similarity of human mental function produces the
grounds of social harmony.[61] Hartley extends the reformist implications of
this logic to argue that "the principle [*sic*] use of the doctrine of associations
must be considered to be the *amendment* of ethics and morals," and he proposes an educational application of the doctrine in determining how "the
tender minds of children can best be formed for virtue and piety."[62]

While his physiological "doctrine of vibrations" explaining how ideas connected with one another in the brain was not always embraced by subsequent theorists, Hartley's formulations of associationism, especially in the form given them by Priestley, became influential for the Utilitarian philosophers Jeremy Bentham and James Mill and the novelist and political philosopher William Godwin, as well as for Romantic poets such as Rogers, Coleridge, and Wordsworth. Hartley's recommendations for applying the association of ideas to morals and education were taken up most systematically by Bentham and Mill as the underlying psychological basis, along with Adam Smith's political economy, for their program of political and institutional reform. A systematic formulation of the progressive rationality of the associative memory appears in Bentham's *The Principles of Morals and Legislation* (1789) as the tenth item in a comprehensive list of the types of pleasures and pains that form the basis for a hedonistic calculus of the fundamental dynamics of human psychology upon which all moral instruction and governmental legislation should act: "The pleasures of memory are the pleasures which, after having enjoyed such and such pleasures, or even in some cases after having suffered such and such pains, a man will now and then experience, at recollecting them exactly in the order and in the circumstances in which they were actually enjoyed or suffered."[63] The pleasure seems to consist for Bentham not primarily in the content of the memory itself but rather in confirming the mind's capacity to recapture a past event accurately along with all its accompanying feelings. Recollection can sometimes transform a pain into a pleasure. The "pleasures of association," coming thirteenth in Bentham's list, are "the pleasures which certain objects or incidents may happen to afford, not of themselves, but merely in virtue of some association they have contracted in the mind with certain objects or incidents which are in themselves pleasurable."[64] This second formulation highlights the metonymic processes and displaced affect of the rational memory, as if certain pleasant things in life can only be experienced virtually, at secondhand, or in relation to some other activity or event.

The Utilitarians promoted a mental calculus based in the association of ideas that was designed to measure accurately and to predict the appearance of pleasures and pains, both as indexes of human behavior and foundations for appropriate legislation. In a note dated June 29, 1827, Bentham provides a shorthand version of the two central Utilitarian principles and their intellectual forebears: "Association Principle.—Hartley. The bond of connection between ideas and language: and between ideas and ideas. Greatest Happiness Principle.—Priestley. Applied to every branch of morals in detail, by Bentham: a part of the way previously by Helvetius."[65] According to the eighteenth-century French philosopher Claude-Adrien Helvétius, whose influential writings on education inspired Bentham, "the whole art of the legislator consists in forcing men, through their feeling of self-love, to be always just to one another."[66] The other essential element missing from Bentham's abstract was a theory of the identification of interests taken from political economy. Adam Smith had postulated in *An Inquiry Into the Nature and Causes of the Wealth of Nations* (1776) that market mechanisms of labor and exchange create a natural identity of interests allowing for the harmonizing of individuals' pursuit of self-interest. But given that the unequal distribution of wealth had made the conflict of interest between owners of capital and laborers readily apparent by the beginning of the nineteenth century, Bentham and James Mill also drew on Hartley's philosophy to develop a countervailing psychological account of the way that the mental functioning of association must ultimately support common interests if appropriate political structures could be devised to coordinate the uniform formation of all pleasures and pains so that pleasurable incentives would predominate.[67]

Politically radical writers also imagined how individuals could employ memory's ordering powers to resist tyranny. Autodidactic memory techniques are rendered concretely in an episode in Godwin's *Things as They Are; or, The Adventures of Caleb Williams* (1794) when Caleb, having been imprisoned as a result of his master Mr. Falkland's false accusation of theft, suddenly realizes that he can draw on his own mental resources in order to endure his solitary confinement: "Have I not been employed from my infancy in gratifying an insatiable curiosity? When should I derive benefit from these superior advantages, if not at present? Accordingly I tasked the stores of my memory and the powers of my invention."[68] After composing mentally in a series of genres including memoir, romance, and moral philosophy, Caleb re-creates and extends his education by rehearsing his past reading in mathematics, history, and oratory. Through this use of memory to "perfect the art of withdrawing my thoughts" from the unpleasant scenes of the prison, Caleb also claims to achieve mental liberty despite his unjust incarceration: "Mind appeared, to my untutored reflections, vague, airy, and unfettered, the susceptible perceiver of reasons, but never intended by nature to be the slave of force."[69] Godwin's novel suggests that his memory compensates Caleb both for the loss of company and freedom and for his lack of books—his skill in "withdrawing his thoughts" also resembles the silent reader's practiced withdrawal from the immediate stimuli of his or her surroundings into the interior discourse of interaction with a novel.

This kind of self-imposed ordering of mind as the result of training the memory appears in a commentary by John Jarndyce in *Bleak House* (1852–53), when Ada Clare asks her cousin why Harold Skimpole has turned out "such a child." Jarndyce's answer both employs an associationist pedagogical framework and emerges graphically on the page as a chain of associations linked by hyphens and double conjunctions that mimic paratactic dialogue, indicating simultaneously Jarndyce's tact and the unfolding of his train of thought: Skimpole "is all sentiment, and—and susceptibility, and—and sensibility—and—and imagination. And these qualities are not regulated in him, somehow. I suppose the people who admired him for them in his youth, attached too much importance to them, and too little to any training that would have balanced and adjusted them; and so he became what he is."[70] As many critics have noted, this series of qualities describes Skimpole as an excessive Romantic, but the diagnosis also relates Skimpole's state directly to his upbringing, suggesting that the "grown-up child" lacks the regulated pleasures of memory, the "balanced and adjusted" combination of rational and imaginative trains of thought described in Samuel Rogers's poem and demonstrated in Caleb Willams's heroic mental resistance to incarceration.[71]

Given the emphasis in this passage from *Bleak House* on Skimpole's lack of proper mental discipline, its associationism seems closer to the pedagogical applications of Hartley's theories that are also evident in Rogers's *The Pleasures of Memory*. Yet a Humean focus on identity and memory as coherent, conventional sources of identity also appears in Dickens's novels, as I show in greater detail in subsequent chapters. As evident in Godwin's and Samuel Rogers's writings, associationism was available to later writers directly through late eighteenth- and early nineteenth-century literary works as well as in philosophical treatises. In his history of the literature and print culture of Romantic-era Edinburgh, Ian Duncan has argued that Humean epistemology, in particular, "provides the philosophical basis for the fiction of the Scottish post-Enlightenment," particularly through the widely influential novels of Walter Scott: "Hume's case, that all representation is a fiction, a *poesis*, since all experience is mediated through the imagination, provides a stronger and more comprehensive theoretical base for fiction than any that had appeared hitherto, delivering it from the sentence of inauthenticity, of categorical opposition to reality. It licenses Scott's own fictional practice, with its deconstruction of the opposition between history and fiction and dialectical reconstitution of their difference in a suspension of empirical realism in the medium of romance."[72] Walter Scott's novels thus provided subsequent novelists such as Dickens with both a Humean framework for "fictionality as a more assured appropriation of the real rather than an evasion or denial of it" and a "Humean dialectic between reason and imagination, skeptical alienation and sympathetic absorption, that governs an enlightened relation to common life."[73] In associationist terms, the reading of fiction also takes on the qualities of this dialectic because of the relation Hume posits among memory, imagination, and identity as interconnected mental media, or bonds of thought, that nevertheless participate in the representational qualities of social and political life.[74]

Henry Mayhew's treatise on education, *What to Teach and How to Teach It: So That the Child May Become a Wise and Good Man* (1842), demonstrates how Humean epistemology enters nineteenth-century pedagogical and critical discussions about the moral effects of literature. Mayhew gets his Hume through revisions of his theories by Thomas Brown, a Scottish philosopher, poet, and one of the founders of the *Edinburgh Review*, from whose *Lectures on the Philosophy of Mind* (1820) Mayhew quotes liberally.[75] Mayhew's treatise functions as a somewhat reductive but nevertheless illuminating crib when juxtaposed with Dickens's novels, affording insight into the function of associationism within a theory of literary influence:

> But a knowledge of the relations of our thoughts and feelings is valuable, not only for the power it gives us over ourselves, but also for the influence it affords us over others. There is not a single communication that can be made from man to man that is not a metaphysical experiment. Certain feelings can be produced at will in the mind of another, only by the laws which regulate the succession of those feelings. The dramatist—the orator—the poet—the wit—the fop—are all practical metaphysicians—mental experimentalists— operators on the mind; and he who has the best acquaintance with the principles which regulate the suggestion [Brown's revised term for Humean association] of the thoughts and feelings he would inspire, must, it is evident, be the most successful in his art.[76]

One can see how Mayhew retraces the path of associationism's popularization in Victorian pedagogy and literature by incorporating a Humean version of mental causation, through Brown's notion of suggestion, into his own notion of intellectuals and artists as "mental experimentalists" who combine a scientific with an aesthetic and pedagogical influence.

In Chapter 4, I analyze further how Mayhew's treatise dovetails with the associationism of Dickens's narrator, who articulates the moral effects of reading on the memory. I make the case that Dickens's novels intervene in a competitive nineteenth-century literary field by encompassing the conflated forms of aesthetic and pedagogical influence that Mayhew's associationism articulates. I am not suggesting that Dickens was a self-styled Humean but rather that his novels draw their popular associationism and epistemology possibly from Dickens's own reading of Hume, but more probably from other literary works that develop a Humean notion of fictionality in the sense that Duncan has laid out, and, most important, from Samuel Rogers's *The Pleasures of Memory*. It should be noted that other Victorian intellectuals also took Hume seriously and attempted to update his ideas, including Thomas Henry Huxley, who in an 1894 essay endorsed both the essential correctness of Hume's psychological materialism and his role as the philosophical and scientific "protagonist of that more modern way of thinking, which has been called 'agnosticism.'"[77]

Associationism and Political Education

Writing in 1726, James Arbuckle asserted in a popularized Lockean vein, "And what is Education, for the most part, but a stocking of a Child's Brain with a Chain of Images?"[78] Association psychology also served as a theory of education during the period from the late seventeenth through the mid–nineteenth century that we have been examining. For example, rather than attempting to frighten children into piety or obedience with stories of children's transgressions and punishments, the successful early nineteenth-century writers Maria Edgeworth and Anna Laetitia Barbauld both drew on associationist doctrine to devise stories for young children that appealed to their nascent reason and facilitated learning by proceeding rationally from simple to complex ideas. The Philosophical Radicals' Utilitarian pedagogical schemes were salient instances of education as applied associationism. In 1815 James Mill wrote an article on "Education" for the fifth edition of the *Encyclopedia Britannica* in an attempt to promulgate Bentham's idea to found a nondenominational "Chrestomathic school," run according to the monitorial method of peer instruction, which would, as its name implies, be "conducive to useful learning."[79] For Mill, the larger social purpose of education is to provide "the best employment of all the means which can be made use of, by man, for rendering the human mind to the greatest possible degree the cause of human happiness." Following Hartley, Mill construes learning as a sequential process from simple to complex ideas: "the business of education is, to make certain feelings or thoughts take place instead of others . . . to work upon the mental successions." Mill concludes that if, as

Helvétius had argued, "the whole of th[e] great mass of mankind" may be regarded as "equally susceptible of mental excellence," then the role of education should be "to ascertain, what are the ends, the really ultimate objects of human desire; . . . what are the most beneficent means of attaining those objects," and "to accustom the mind to fill up the intermediate space between the present sensation and the ultimate object, with nothing but the ideas of those beneficent means."[80] Viewing education as the social instrument through which an artificial identity of interests can be produced in humanity at large, Mill posits that it can become the means to overcome differences of custom and class that have arisen through accidental and conventional associations of ideas.[81]

James Mill's advocacy of the ballot, in an article published in the *Westminster Review* in 1830 as a contribution to the debates over parliamentary reform that culminated in the Reform Act of 1832, envisions the independent elector as the end product of the strides that education would make in shaping the mental associations of the newly educated masses. The secret ballot would sanction an individual's ability to choose his representatives freely without external pressure or manipulation, while "the men of power and influence in the country," would be responsible "to watch over the instruction given to [the mass of the people]; to take them out of the hands of those who have an interest in giving them wrong opinions, to use the press with skill and activity, for the producing all sorts of salutary impressions, and obviating every impression of a different kind." The result of this energetic guidance of public associations, or opinion, would be that "We should then have a community through which wisdom and virtue would be universally diffused; and of which the different classes would be knit together by the ties of mutual benefaction."[82] As historian William Thomas points out, if for Bentham the ideal society should resemble a Panopticon, "with a governor-gaoler controlling the whole from his vantage point in the centre," James Mill's ideal model was "a large classroom, run on Lancasterian lines, in which those best qualified in morality and intellect, transmitted their teaching through subordinate monitors to numerous humble but eager pupils, until the whole room was a-murmur with diligence."[83]

Associationist psychology, whether in a more doctrinal or a commonsense form, was popular across the early nineteenth-century political spectrum, but particularly attractive to anti-establishment radical thinkers including Chartist and early socialist writers. As literary scholar Christopher Herbert has indicated, associationism was most often linked to a politics of "relativistic anti-absolutism": "its denial of the category of innate a priori ideas was directly continuous with the great Enlightenment critique of systems of society that justified themselves with reference to supposedly natural or divinely ordained and permanent principles of domination."[84] While Robert Owen pursued political goals that would come to be associated with socialism, he shared the Philosophical Radicals' (Utilitarians') focus on education and institutional reform as a means to both liberate and shape mental dispositions. In *A New View of Society* (1816), Owen argues that the rational application of the correlation between circumstances and habitual conduct to the education of children in "good habits" and charitable feelings should recommend itself without great difficulty to "the privileged," who may ensure in this way that "without domestic revolution—without war and bloodshed . . . the world will be prepared to receive principles which are alone calculated to build up a system of happiness, and to destroy those irritable feelings which have so long afflicted society."[85] Raymond Williams points out that by Dickens's time, Owen's views on the influence of environment had become commonsensical, but his vision of the social reform derived from associationist principles opened new possibilities for re-creating social institutions to foster an "alternative culture."[86]

Historian Gareth Stedman Jones has shown that Owenism focused on addressing the ideological rather than the political causes of social conditions; for the working-class followers of Owen, "in the absence of this moral revolution, political change would be in vain."[87] For example, in his will written in 1849, Henry Hetherington, a Chartist leader and publisher of Chartist tracts, expressed the hope that those attending his funeral would make an honest assessment of his life, so that "none may avow just and rational principles without endeavouring to purge themselves of those errors that result from bad habits, previously contracted, and which tarnish the lustre of their benign and glorious principles." Hetherington's comments sound almost Lockean in his adjuration that one should live according to rational principles rather than erroneous habits. Although he was no longer a member of the Owenite political movement at the time of his death, Hetherington also paid tribute to the importance of Owen's ideas: "These are my views and feelings in quitting an existence that has been chequered with the plagues and pleasures of a competitive, scrambling, selfish system by which the moral and social aspirations of the noblest human beings are nullified by incessant toil and physical deprivations; by which, indeed, all men are trained to be either slaves, hypocrites, or criminals. Hence my ardent attachment to the principles of that great and good man—Robert Owen."[88] In a similar vein to Victorian reviewers' accounts of the moral impress of Dickens's writings, which I study in detail in the next chapter, and bearing a tone resembling that of Dickens's own social criticism and early radical journalism, Hetherington's description of Owen's influence as taking the form of "principles" for which one can feel an "ardent attachment" demonstrates the blended nature of the intellectual pleasure featured in literary references to the pleasures of memory, and that seem also to be associated with the reading of early Victorian social reformist writing. Another Chartist, George Holyoake, commented in his autobiography that Owen's writings allowed "working men to reason on their conditions."[89] When read together, Hetherington's and Holyoake's understandings of their own new way of thinking in response to Owen's writings suggest that "reasoning on conditions" requires *overcoming* the habits of thought, often inculcated in religiously oriented schools for the poor, leading one to view these conditions as natural or ordained by Providence.

This kind of self-reflexive "reasoning on conditions," an issue that also forms one of the major preoccupations of Dickens's late novels, also seems to necessitate a consideration of the social conditions of thinking about thinking, in Mrs. Tickit's terms. Owen described his own change of perspective on religion in similar terms: "Thus was I forced through seeing the error of their foundation, to abandon all belief in every religion which has been taught to man. But my religious feelings were immediately replaced by the spirit of universal charity,—not for a sect or party, or for a country or a colour,—but for the human race, and with a real ardent desire to do them good."[90] Like Dickens, with his view of the author's duty to engage in "public service," Owen rhetorically distances himself from "sect or party," taking up instead the task to represent the interests of "humanity." "Reflection on conditions" plays a central role in Dickens's novels as well: it involves a correction, motivated by both reason and feeling, of a partial point of view or self-limiting "prejudice," and the substitution of a disposition to correct social injustices and benefit others, especially the poor. In Owen's case, not surprisingly, this change of heart resulted in the founding of schools at his factory in New Lanark, Scotland. The logic of associationism shared by Owen and Dickens exposes the psychological basis on which popular fiction could be conceived as acting directly and democratically outside political institutions, by drawing attention to and revising the reader's assumptions about the givenness of social conditions. In Chapter 3, I show that this logic was also shared by more conservative Evangelical writers, but with different assumptions about how the reader's associations could be channeled toward social deference and piety.

Dickens's novels link reflections on conditions to social change by imagining how the individual's free thought can exert a critical leverage on the entrenched and narrow interests embodied in existing institutions. For example, in *David Copperfield* (1849–50), David, during one of his visits to Doctor's Commons under the tutelage of Mr. Spenlow, an attorney and the father of his future wife, broaches the idea that "we might improve the Commons." Pointing to the example of the Prerogative Office, whose registrars accept exorbitant fees in return for stashing "all the original wills of all persons leaving effects within the immense province of Canterbury," in an unsafe "accidental building," David supposes that such a "mercenary speculation" has only escaped reform and modernization because it is "squeezed away in a corner of St. Paul's Churchyard, which few people knew." Mr. Spenlow, however, refutes David's criticisms with an amused seriousness:

> He said, what was it after all? It was a question of feeling. If the public felt that their wills were in safe keeping, and took it for granted that the office was not to be made better, who was the worse for it? Nobody. Who was the better for it? All the Sinecurists. Very well. Then the good predominated. It might not be a perfect system; nothing was perfect; but what he objected to was the insertion of the wedge. Under the Prerogative Office, the country had been glorious. Insert the wedge into the Prerogative Office, and the country would cease to be glorious. He considered it the principle of a gentleman to take things as he found them; and he had no doubt that the Prerogative Office would last our time.[91]

David reports that "I deferred to his opinion, though I had great doubts of it myself." Mr. Spenlow's own facade of affluence and professionalism is exposed as a fraud, however, after his accidental death, because he has failed to leave a will. The novel's satire shows that the wedge needs to be inserted into Mr. Spenlow's head, that is, into his conservative mentality—his justification of his own narrow interest as essential to the survival of the system as a whole. David's independent "doubts about the strict justice" of the existing legal system, by contrast, lead him to speculate that "we might even improve the world a little, if we got up early in the morning, and took off our coats to the work."[92] If Mr. Spenlow is against "the insertion of the wedge," then the Dickensian novel argues in favor of it, by suggesting that such systemic change requires an instigating doubt that the current conditions are just, accompanied by a fundamental belief in the possibility of improvement, to accomplish a moral revolution, overcoming the resistance of those who benefit from the "pernicious absurdity" of the way things are.[93]

Syllabic Reading and the Analogy with Experience

For the organizer of a religious curriculum or government-supported school in the 1830s and 1840s, the general associationist principle of human "plasticity" asserted by Owen formed the foundation of concrete practices in the classroom to instill attitudes and behaviors rather than to change society at large.[94] In a teaching manual published in 1837, Henry Dunn, a schoolmaster and secretary to the Lancasterian British and Foreign School Society (a nondenominational organization sponsoring schools for the poor and working class and supported by Dissenters), expressed a representative opinion among Victorian educators that "whatever others may think, the teacher must be satisfied, that any great moral change in the community, will be mainly effected by the instrumentality of schools."[95] Central to what I have been characterizing as Dickens's project of formulating a cultural politics for popular literature outside the school, then, was the development of an alternative model of learning. Serial fiction could form an additional or supplemental education for the reader, because reading was conceived as putting into play the same associative trains of thought as memory and experience. Both Victorian popular education and Dickens's novels rely on associationist theories of the coherence between mind and world, but in pursuit of contradictory goals: Victorian schooling was intended to produce social deference, while novel reading could become a means to exert leverage on social conditions by planting doubts in the reader's mind and simultaneously encouraging the belief not just in individual but in collective improvement.

We need to examine now in greater detail precisely what kind of transaction associationism posits between reading and experience. Hartley's formulation of the functional equivalence among memory, reading, and learning was particularly influential and became a guiding assumption about the psychological effects of literacy in nineteenth-century pedagogical theory. In *Observations on Man*, Hartley relies more specifically on an analogy between the syllabic method of teaching children to read and the process by which early associations attach pleasure and pain to particular ideas. He broaches this analogy with the supposition that simple sensations are imprinted in the child's mind in basic forms, the function of which can be equated with the letters of the alphabet. When these basic pains and pleasures are combined as the result of various experiences into more complex forms, they become like "the Words of a Language":

> Thus the reiterated Impressions of the simple sensible Pleasures and Pains
> made upon the Child, so as to leave their Miniatures, or Ideas, are denoted

by his learning the Alphabet; and his various Associations of these Ideas, and of the Pleasures and Pains themselves, by his putting Letters and Syllables together, in order to make Words: And when Association has so far cemented the component Parts of any Aggregate of Ideas, Pleasures and Pains, together, as that they appear one indivisible Idea, Pleasure or Pain, the Child must be supposed by analogous Association to have learnt to read without Spelling.[96]

Simple perceptions become cemented in the mind into ideas or concepts by repetition, and each idea carries with it a charge of pain or pleasure, depending upon the original affective context of the association. For Hartley, the associating mind not only creates a conceptual language of sense perceptions, but it also fashions experience more generally on the model of *learning to read*.

The syllabic, or "synthetic," method, common in Britain since the seventeenth century, taught reading through the spelling and memorization of syllables, which were then assembled to form words.[97] The guiding principle was that learning should proceed from the simple to the complex— from the letters of the alphabet, to a list of syllables, to complete words—and that the student's comprehension of words and sentences should follow (that is, quite literally come about subsequently to) his or her memorization, recognition, and repetition by spelling out of their component parts (Figure 1). The syllabic method was taught by means of spelling books authored by such famous eighteenth-century pedagogues as Lindley Murray and Sarah Trimmer, and it also gave rise to the publication of short didactic tales written in words of one syllable (Figure 2). According to Hartley's pedagogical analogy, then, the cognizance of complex ideas, which are the products of repeated and inextricable associations, is analogous to the child's ability, after much practice in combining discrete syllables, to read without spelling out loud. By implication, the intermediate stage of having to spell out syllables in order to put words together is equivalent to the forgotten early stages of the formation of mental associations.

Hartley's phrase "by analogous Association" indicates that he also classifies the figure of analogy itself as a type of association of ideas. The analogy meant to demonstrate the workings of mental association also creates an association linking the activity of reading, the process of learning to read, and the doctrine of the association of ideas. Hartley's theory thus gives an impetus to the prevalence of associationism in nineteenth-century pedagogy by conceptualizing reading as both an associationist metaphor for and a practical instance of the synthetic mental processes underlying experience through

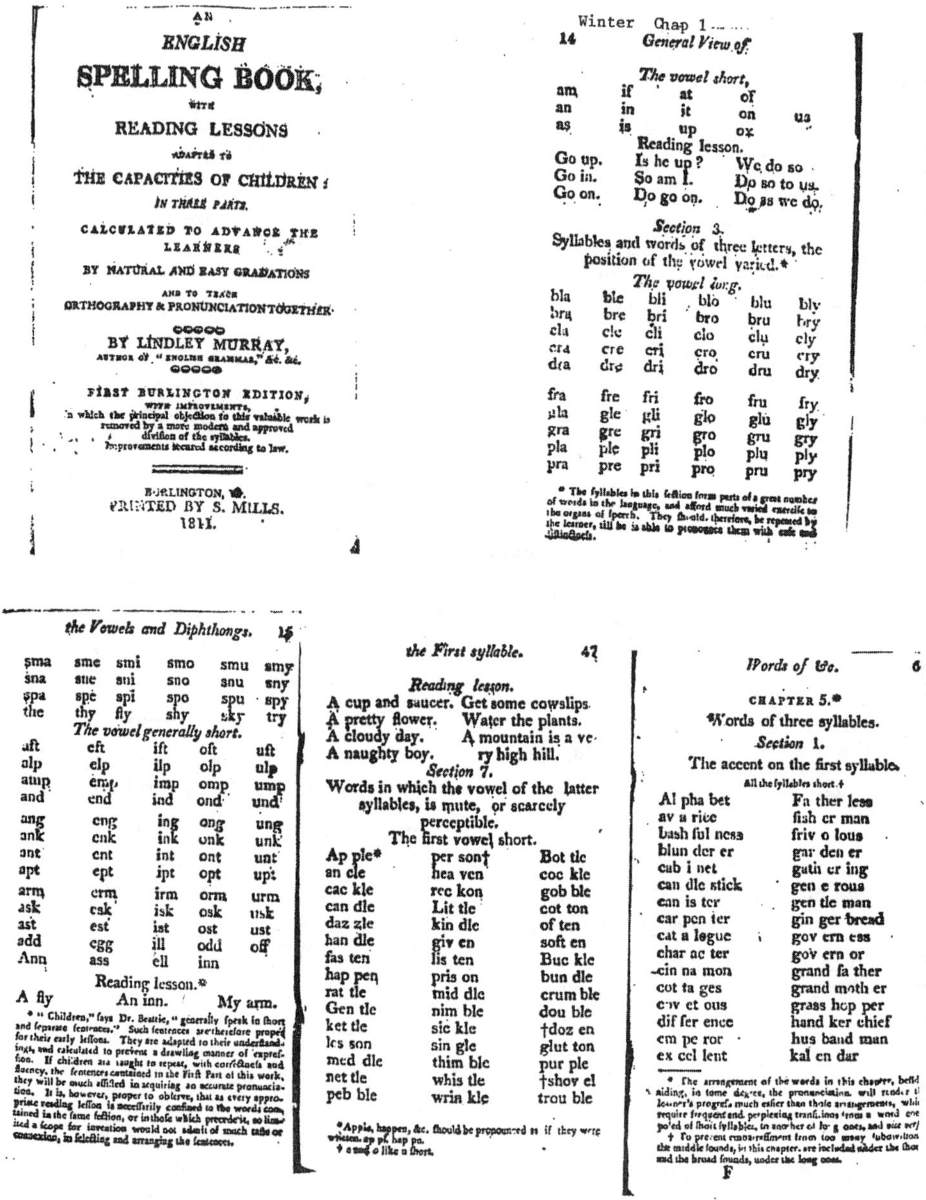

Title page (left)

AN

ENGLISH

SPELLING BOOK,

WITH

READING LESSONS

ADAPTED TO

THE CAPACITIES OF CHILDREN;

IN THREE PARTS.

CALCULATED TO ADVANCE THE
LEARNERS

BY NATURAL AND EASY GRADATIONS

AND TO TEACH
ORTHOGRAPHY & PRONUNCIATION TOGETHER·

BY LINDLEY MURRAY,
AUTHOR OF "ENGLISH GRAMMAR," &c. &c.

FIRST BURLINGTON EDITION,
WITH IMPROVEMENTS,
in which the principal objection to this valuable work is
removed by a more modern and approved
division of the syllables.
Improvements secured according to law.

BURLINGTON, Vt.
PRINTED BY S. MILLS.
1811.

Page 14

The vowel short,

am	if	at	of
an	in	it	on	us
as	is	up	ox

Reading lesson.

Go up.	Is he up?	We do so
Go in.	So am I.	Do so to us.
Go on.	Do go on.	Do as we do.

Section 3.

Syllables and words of three letters, the
position of the vowel varied.

The vowel long.

bla	ble	bli	blo	blu	bly
bra	bre	bri	bro	bru	bry
cla	cle	cli	clo	clu	cly
cra	cre	cri	cro	cru	cry
dra	dre	dri	dro	dru	dry
fra	fre	fri	fro	fru	fry
gla	gle	gli	glo	glu	gly
gra	gre	gri	gro	gru	gry
pla	ple	pli	plo	plu	ply
pra	pre	pri	pro	pru	pry

* The syllables in this section form parts of a great number
of words in the language, and afford much varied exercise to
the organs of speech. They should, therefore, be repeated by
the learner, till he is able to pronounce them with ease and
distinctness.

Page 15 — the Vowels and Diphthongs.

sma	sme	smi	smo	smu	smy
sna	sne	sni	sno	snu	sny
spa	spe	spi	spo	spu	spy
tha	thy	fly	shy	sky	try

The vowel generally short.

aft	eft	ift	oft	uft
alp	elp	ilp	olp	ulp
amp	emp	imp	omp	ump
and	end	ind	ond	und
ang	eng	ing	ong	ung
ank	enk	ink	onk	unk
ant	ent	int	ont	unt
apt	ept	ipt	opt	upt
arm	erm	irm	orm	urm
ask	esk	isk	osk	usk
ast	est	ist	ost	ust
add	egg	ill	odd	off
Ann	ass	ell	inn

Reading lesson.

A fly.   An inn.   My arm.

* "Children," says Dr. Beattie, "generally speak in short
and separate sentences." Such sentences are therefore proper
for their early lessons. They are adapted to their understandings, and calculated to prevent a drawling manner of expression. If children are taught to repeat, with correctness and
fluency, the sentences contained in the First Part of this work,
they will be much assisted in acquiring an accurate pronunciation. It is, however, proper to observe, that as every appropriate reading lesson is necessarily confined to the words com-
tained in the same section, or in those which precede it, no limited a scope for invention would not admit of much taste or
connexion, in selecting and arranging the sentences.

Page 47 — the First syllable.

Reading lesson.

A cup and saucer. Get some cowslips.
A pretty flower.   Water the plants.
A cloudy day.   A mountain is a ve-
A naughty boy.   ry high hill.

Section 7.

Words in which the vowel of the latter
syllables, is mute, or scarcely
perceptible.

The first vowel short.

Ap ple*	per son†	Bot tle
an cle	hea ven	coc kle
cac kle	rec kon	gob ble
can dle	Lit tle	cot ton
daz zle	kin dle	of ten
han dle	giv en	soft en
fas ten	lis ten	Buc kle
hap pen	pris on	bun dle
rat tle	mid dle	crum ble
Gen tle	nim ble	dou ble
ket tle	sic kle	†doz en
les son	sin gle	glut ton
med dle	thim ble	pur ple
net tle	whis tle	†shov el
peb ble	wrin kle	trou ble

* Apple, happen, &c. should be pronounced as if they were
written, ap pl, hap pn.
† o and o like a short.

Page 6 — Words of &c.

CHAPTER 5.*

Words of three syllables.

Section 1.

The accent on the first syllable.

All the syllables short.†

Al pha bet	Fa ther less
av a rice	fish er man
bash ful ness	friv o lous
blun der er	gar den er
cub i net	guth er ing
can dle stick	gen e rous
can is ter	gen tle man
car pen ter	gin ger bread
cat a logue	gov ern ess
char ac ter	gov ern or
cin na mon	grand fa ther
cot ta ges	grand moth er
cov et ous	grass hop per
dif fer ence	hand ker chief
em pe ror	hus band man
ex cel lent	kal en dar

* The arrangement of the words in this chapter, besid
aiding, in some degree, the pronunciation, will render t
learner's progress much easier than those arrangements, whi
require frequent and perplexing transitions from a word one
period of that syllable, to another of long ones, and vice vers†
† To prevent embarrassment from too many subdivision
the middle sounds, in this chapter, are included under the short
and the broad sounds, under the long ones.

F

Figure 1. Title page and sample pages from Lindley Murray, *An English Spelling
Book, With Reading Lessons Adapted to the Capacities of Children* (Burlington, Vt.:
S. Mills, 1811), showing syllabic reading exercises. Courtesy of the Yale
University Library.

Mary S. Bidwell's

JOHN MAY;

OR

The Life

OF

A GOOD BOY.

A TALE,

IN WORDS OF ONE SYLLABLE,

London:
PUBLISHED BY R. MILLER,
24, OLD FISH STREET, DOCTORS' COMMONS;
AND MAY BE HAD OF ALL BOOKSELLERS.

Figure 2. Title page of *John May; or The Life of a Good Boy. A Tale, In Words of One Syllable* (London: R. Miller, n.d.). Beinecke Rare Book and Manuscript Library, Yale University.

its serial recording in memory. As a metaphor for the mental process of association itself, analogy thus encompasses the sequential and potentially narrative form that shapes the associative "train of thought" into experience. Given that analogy itself is conceived as a fundamental associative process of mind, not only do reading and thinking resemble one another but they are also related, even homologous, mental functions—reading implies and requires thinking, while associative processes of thought proceed in an orderly, progressive fashion, like learning to read.[98] We can see in greater detail now that for Hartley, ideas are like Bacon's "bundled instances," having a status equivalent to that of words. Associative memory functions serially to "cement" the associations together to form both the complex ideas that provide the elements of experience and the memory of "spelling" that enables one to synthesize letters and syllables into words, and ultimately to read. The serial memory supports a set of functional homologies arranged in parallel series: between mental development and learning to read, between learning to read and the assimilation of experience, and finally between experience ordered by the memory and the social order. All these homologies ultimately depend upon the organizing concept of mind as coherent process and of memory as a *medium*—possessing, from our computer-age perspective, quasi-technological characteristics—that integrates multiple levels of seriality.

If reading is not just analogous but also mentally homologous to experience, it is not difficult to draw the converse, though not necessary, conclusion that complex thinking requires literacy. One can understand why Hartley's formulation would be useful to later Utilitarian reformers who wished to inculcate certain dispositions and ideas through education. Many nineteenth-century liberal reformers argued that certain types of complex thinking, such as participating in the franchise, flowed from literacy, so that the ability to read should also determine access not only to new ideas but to new social and political implementations of thinking.[99] Dickens's *Our Mutual Friend* (1864–65) encompasses a critique of Victorian popular education's focus on self-betterment and respectability and undermines any equation between literacy and higher-order cognition, as I show in Chapter 5. Nevertheless, Hartley's associationism implies a cognitive leverage in the activity of reading that would also apply to popular fiction: if chains of associations are analogous to syllables and words, and if experience is both analogous and homologous mentally to learning to read, then it does not require too great a leap to infer that reading fiction could be a source of new *virtual* experiences. Reading fiction, especially, could allow the mind access to new concepts and scenes, perhaps confirming new forms of as yet unarticulated experience—or provoking the reader to "insert the wedge" in accepted versions of social thinking. Moreover, serial fiction opportunistically takes direct advantage of how the mind learns, according to associationist doctrine. By reading serially, one presumably reinforces the serial processes by which the mind remembers what has been read. The pleasures of reading would be *precisely* the pleasures of memory.

In a discussion that is clearly indebted to Hume as well as to Hartley, James Mill in his *Analysis of the Phenomena of the Human Mind* also develops the associationist theoretical analogy among thinking, learning, and reading based on the common associative, serial functioning of memory, in all three activities. Mill argues that the difference between memory and imagination is very straightforward, though both faculties are similar in that they work through "ideas connected in trains by association."[100] Mill asserts that memory must function in the same way as imagination, but with an additional empirical quality, which we remember from Locke's definition: that "there is not only the idea of the thing remembered; there is also the idea of my having seen it" (329). Memory relies on two "important elements": "*the idea of my present self*, the remembering self; and *the idea of my past self*, the remembered or witnessing self. These two ideas stand at the two ends of a portion of my being; that is, of a series of my states of consciousness" (330–31). The memory "runs over the intervening states of consciousness called up by association," and this occurs "so rapidly and closely" that although the self's awareness of its own past existence emerges as a series, this is experienced as "a single point of consciousness" (331).

Mill also differentiates two types of remembering; the first, remembering of past sensations, "what we have seen, felt, heard, tasted, or smelt," and the second, remembering past ideas, or "what we have thought, without the intervention of the senses" (328). His example of the first type, as we might expect from his emphasis on the rhetorical arts of memory, is that of a public speech: "I remember to have seen and heard George III, when making a speech at the opening of his Parliament" (328). In contrast, his examples of the second type all refer to ideas retained from reading: "I remember my conceptions of the Emperor Napoleon and his audience, when I read the account of his first address to the French Chambers" (328). In distinguishing these two types of remembrance, Mill explains that his memory of sensation is inseparable from his own empirical knowledge of all the aspects of that past experience: "I cannot have the idea of George III; his person and attitude, the paper he held in his hand, the sound of his voice while reading from it, the throne, the apartment, the audience; without having the other idea along with it, that of my having been a witness of the scene" (330). By contrast, the memory of an idea is more complicated:

> I have a lively recollection of Polyphemus's cave, and the actions of Ulysses and the Cyclops, as described by Homer. In this recollection there is, first of all, the ideas, or simple conceptions of the objects and acts; and along with these ideas, and so closely combined as not to be separable, the idea of my having formerly had these same ideas. And this idea of my having formerly had those ideas, is a very complicated idea; including the idea of myself of the present moment remembering, and that of myself of the past moment conceiving; and the whole series of the states of consciousness, which intervened between myself remembering, and myself conceiving. (331)

So the very subtle and complex difference between the memory of a sensation and the memory of an idea emerges in the additional step of being conscious not only of the past self's presence at an event, in this case an instance of reading, but also of the past self's original conception of the complex ideas involved in reading Homer. The past self in the second instance is not a witness of an event but is rather a reader, someone who has assimilated ideas from a source other than the senses. This second instance also provides a theory of mediation: reading produces a mediated memory that also permits self-reflexivity and a Humean awareness of personal identity as a series of past states of consciousness leading up to the present. Mill's contrast between the kinds of memory involved in witnessing a speech by George III and reading about a speech by Napoleon, presumably in a newspaper, also suggests a preview of the historical transition mapped by sociologist of the modern media John B. Thompson from "the symbolic content exchanged in face-to-face interaction" to "networks of communication that were not face-to-face in character."[101]

Mill's account of the associationist analogy between reading and experience, based on the homologous functions of memory in each case, also views reading as inducing the mind to reflect upon the history of its own conceptualizations—or, as Mrs. Tickit demonstrates, to think about one's self thinking.[102] The associationist analogy between reading and experience was pivotal to nineteenth-century educational theory. In the comprehensive curriculum he outlines in *Chrestomathia* (1818), Bentham provides an application of associationist principles relying on the model of syllabic reading and implementing the serial memory for the purposes of mental training.

Bentham's complex tables of subjects are ordered according to the association of ideas so as to facilitate "general strength of mind": "Every part [of the course of instruction] having a natural connexion with every other, and every favourable occasion being embraced for bringing that connexion into view, every object will, by virtue of the principle of association, as often as it is presented, contribute more or less to fix every other in the memory, and thus to render the conception entertained of it so much the clearer." Bentham plans that the curriculum will develop from the more basic to the more complex subjects, just as the association of ideas proceeds by combining simpler perceptions and ideas into more complex ones, or syllabic reading proceeds from memorized syllables to words. The organization of the courses not only mirrors mental functioning but also takes advantage of it through repetition and elaboration, so that subjects are presented in "succeeding stages" that exercise (in order of complexity) sensation, memory, and judgment. Finally judgment will be implemented to ascertain "points of agreement and diversity"—that is, to recognize resemblance and distinguish contrast or contrariety.[103] In Bentham's pedagogy, associationist principles both determine the form and reinforce the effects of the curriculum. Bentham maps his Chrestomathic school (which was to be located in his garden but was never built) in a series of detailed instructional tables as one vast mnemonic topos—an architectural and curricular storehouse of knowledge to be reproduced as mental contents, procedures of thought, and system for the organization and transmission of knowledge.

Associationist principles in pedagogy remained current well into the nineteenth century. In his 1848 textbook on metaphysics for schoolchildren, Robert James Ballantyne both echoes Priestley's and James Mill's definitions of what he calls the two major "laws of association according to which the train of thought takes place" and seems to draw on the Hartleyan equation of syllabic reading methods with the association of ideas: "The second law of Association is this, that the tendency of one idea to recall another, is increased by their being repeatedly viewed together, or in immediate succession. It is by repetition that a boy gets the alphabet by heart. The sounds gradually become so associated in his mind in either successive order, that the first, when uttered, suggest the second, that the third, and so on."[104] The association of ideas could also be implemented in the classroom, as Dunn points out in his popular nonsectarian teaching manual in the 1830s:

> The chief point to be remembered by a teacher, in the cultivation of *all* virtue, and in the formation of every good habit, is, that *constant regard must*

be had to the principle of association. The power of ASSOCIATION is all but omnipotent in the minds of the young. Sympathy and pleasant associations, have far more influence in determining their habits and preferences, than either argument or persuasion. The great and difficult art is, *insensibly* to introduce into the mind pleasant associations with all that is good, and painful associations with all that is mean, degrading, or sinful. He who has accomplished this, has done much towards "*magnetizing* the mind anew, and calling it out into a fellowship and an existence of a higher order than it had previously owned."[105]

Here association not only describes the mental activity by which the children should learn habitually to attach the idea of virtues and vices to appropriate sensations, as James Mill had advised, but also explains the teacher's own influence, which must be subtle rather than overbearing or coercive. Thus, through association, teaching ideally becomes a kind of art, a practice of "insensible" inspiration and covert discipline.[106]

As media scholars David Thorburn and Henry Jenkins have argued, "the emergence of new media sets in motion a complicated, unpredictable process in which established and infant systems may co-exist for an extended period or in which older media may develop new functions and find new audiences as the emerging technology begins to occupy the cultural space of its ancestors."[107] This overlapping of old and new applies equally to the modes of reception of new print media such as the serial novel in the context of older reading pedagogies such as the syllabic method. The interlayering of the older syllabic method of learning to read by fragmenting language into syllables, words, and phrases, and finally building up to sentences and the new practice of reading fiction in installments, provides a particularly tight epistemological fit between the cognitive process of learning to read and subsequent reading habits.

All these kinds of associationist pedagogical influence—through environment, implicit and explicit training, and reading—appear in *Oliver Twist; or, The Parish Boy's Progress* (1837–39) in Fagin's repertoire of training techniques exercised upon Oliver during his seclusion with the juvenile gang of thieves. While Fagin also resorts to threats and physical violence, the novel stresses the more subtle moral and psychological effects of his scheme to force Oliver to join his criminal gang. Fagin's method of brainwashing begins with a period of isolating Oliver, during which he is locked up alone in the house all day, so that he is obliged "during long hours to commune with his own thoughts" (145). Then one day Oliver suddenly embarks on a period of constant association with his fellow pickpockets, who never leave him alone, and who encourage him to laugh "in spite of all his better feelings" at Fagin's "droll" stories of robberies committed in his youth: "Having prepared his mind, by solitude and gloom, to prefer any society to the companionship of his own sad thoughts in such a dreary place, [Fagin] was now slowly instilling into his soul the poison which he hoped would blacken it, and change its hue for ever" (152).

Fagin's ultimate tactic in assimilating Oliver to the gang will be to force him to commit a robbery with Bill Sikes, and thus to become a thief, but on the night prior to his being handed over to Sikes, Fagin also provides Oliver with an unnamed book of stories of great criminals (probably meant to suggest the *Newgate Calendar*) that has a dramatic effect on him: "The terrible descriptions were so real and vivid, that the sallow pages seemed to turn red with gore; and the words upon them, to be sounded in his ears, as if they were whispered, in hollow murmurs, by the spirits of the dead" (164). The telltale sign that the book's pages were "soiled and thumbed with use" indicates that it has been functioning as a textbook in crime for Fagin's "pupils," and Oliver can only drown out the insinuating voice it raises inside his head by praying out loud (164).[108] It is no accident that Oliver's religious training in literacy, presumably at a workhouse or pauper school but never narrated in the text, enables him to resist this attempt to impose a new training, a "catechism of [the] trade" in criminality (151). In its allusions to associationist theories of the effects of didactic reading, especially given the contrast with Oliver's prior experience of having been forced to "commune with his own thoughts" without company or book, the episode suggests that Fagin's primer in crime threatens to invade Oliver's mind and alter his thinking by displacing his earlier educational experiences and socialization and substituting a new form of schooling.

Nancy's reading reinforces the fatality of her criminal associations. During her clandestine meeting with Rose Maylie and Mr. Brownlow on London Bridge, Nancy complains of being almost overcome by fear during an attempt to distract herself by reading: " 'Horrible thoughts of death, and shrouds with blood upon them, and a fear that has made me burn as if I was on fire, have been upon me all day. I was reading a book tonight, to while the time away, and the same things came into the print.' " Mr. Brownlow answers that it is just "imagination," but Nancy contradicts him: " 'I'll swear I saw "coffin" written in every page of the book in large black letters,—ay, and they carried one close to me in the streets tonight' " (384). Nancy superstitiously but accurately foresees her own murder by her lover, Bill Sikes, in hallucinating the word "coffin" on the page. She also describes a reading effect in which the reader's thoughts invade the book—the complement to Oliver's experience of Fagin's manual of crime invading his thoughts. The novel implies that Nancy's fatal attachment to Bill derives not only from the nature of their sexual relationship and the cycle of violence that it has entailed, which Dickens stresses, but also from the emotional attachment and loyalty borne of longtime, habitual association. The genesis of the psychological necessity that restricts Nancy is demonstrated most analytically through the novel's scenes of reading as an experience where the boundaries between self and text loosen. Dickens's expansive figural and psychological use of reading in this novel parallels its role in associationist theory in conceptualizing the analogously serial mental processes involved in learning, cognition, memory, imagination, and the formation of the self. The cases of Oliver and Nancy suggest that associationism in Dickensian fiction also functions to chart the limitations both of social reform through education and of the capacity of unconscious pedagogical influences to penetrate the mind and shape the self.

Wordsworth's Poetics and the Persistence of Associationism

From its inception, associationist theory raised scientific, philosophical, and aesthetic objections. To the extent that the critics of associationism succeeded in undermining its scientific reputation, historians of nineteenth-century psychology have also tended to overlook the persistence of associationist conceptions of memory within scientific psychology, pedagogy, and literary criticism in the nineteenth and early twentieth centuries. Dickens's critique of Victorian pedagogy's reliance on rote learning in several of his novels draws on earlier criticisms of the more doctrinaire versions of associationism.

An early critic of the association of ideas and of Locke's epistemology was eighteenth-century Scottish philosopher Thomas Reid, founder of the Scottish Common Sense School of psychology based at Edinburgh University, which included Reid's student and successor Dugald Stewart, Thomas Brown, and Sir William Hamilton. Reid initiated this group's rethinking of the empiricism of Locke, Hume, and Hartley by questioning the basic assumption that "the impression on the brain continues, and is permanent," and doubting that any evidence of mental images could ever be found in the anatomical brain.[109] For Reid, associationist conceptions involve a circularity implying that, in order for a present experience to call up a past association, there must already be a means independent of the memory itself of gauging the resemblance between the original and the later instance.[110] Writing in opposition to both Hartley and Hume, Reid concludes that the self cannot sustain any reliable connection with its past, and thus it cannot be dependent on memory but rather must exist as a separate substance. But one should notice that in this critique, Reid insists on a strict separation between the epistemological and recall functions of memory that associationists did not recognize.

Political philosopher and aesthetician Edmund Burke was another critic of associationist theory. In his *Philosophical Enquiry Into the Origin of our Ideas of the Sublime and Beautiful* (1757), Burke, following Locke, indicates that association is responsible for certain unthinking responses to things, based on early forgotten experiences or the teaching of others. He takes pains, however, to distinguish between passions provoked by such associations and those that occur according to the "natural powers" of certain objects to evoke a particular emotional response: "it would be absurd . . . to say that all things affect us by association only; since some things must have been originally and naturally agreeable or disagreeable, from which the others derive their associated powers; and it would be, I fancy, to little purpose to look for the cause of our passions in association, until we fail of it in the natural properties of things."[111] Burke's aesthetic theory relies on a notion of innate responses and objective aesthetic criteria to found a uniform standard of taste based on a "stable emotional naturalism."[112]

William Hazlitt and Samuel Taylor Coleridge, despite their early interest in associationism and admiration for Hartley's writings (Coleridge named his first son David Hartley Coleridge), also became critics of the doctrine. In *An Essay on the Principles of Human Action* (1805), Hazlitt offered a detailed and systematic critique of Hartley's theory. Hazlitt objects in particular to Hartley's idea that people should be brought to think alike: "In short, to attempt accounting at all for the nature of consciousness from the proximity of different impressions, or of their fluxional parts to each other in the brain seems no less absurd than it would be to imagine that by placing a number of persons together in a line we should produce in them an immediate consciousness and perfect knowledge of what was passing in each other's minds."[113] For Hazlitt, Hartley's dispositionally coordinated social group becomes a series of monads posing as mind readers. However, elsewhere Hazlitt also refers to the cumulative impact of his own repeated reading of favorite classic books from his library in Humean associationist terms. Remembered books are "standard productions . . . links in the chain of our conscious being [that] bind together the different scattered divisions of our personal identity."[114] Notice that in order to undermine associationism, critics frequently attacked its fundamental notion of mental functioning as serial relation or connection.

While Coleridge paid tribute to Hartley in his *Religious Musings* (1794–96)—"and he of mortal kind/Wisest, he first who marked the ideal tribes/ Down the fine fibres from the sentient brain/Roll subtly surging"—he ultimately rejected the associationist version of imagination as a "mechanical fancy": "But equally with the ordinary memory the Fancy must receive all its materials ready made from the law of association."[115] Coleridge found it unacceptable to constrain the creative powers of imagination by understanding them as primarily synthetic. Furthermore, Coleridge believed he could see the disastrous consequences of adopting associationist psychology in the crass philosophical materialism of the French, with its catastrophic political consequences.[116] In the *Biographia Literaria* (1817), Coleridge follows the German idealist philosophers and Romantic writers, including Kant, Schiller, and Schelling, in insisting on the function of the will "to controul, determine, and modify the phantasmal chaos of association."[117] More famously, Coleridge also affiliates the associative memory with the Fancy, a lower-order combinatorial process that he attempts to cordon off from the more "idealizing and unifying" virtually ontological powers of the primary and secondary Imagination.[118] Coleridge ultimately abandoned the association of ideas circa 1801 as a part of his formal philosophy, but his attempt to inject feeling into a version of associationism that seemed to him overly rationalistic suggests a reading of the tradition that surfaces again in criticisms of Utilitarian programs of popular education, notably in Dickens's novel *Hard Times* (1854).[119]

In their formulations of the new pedagogical function of social institutions, however, many of the Romantics were closer to the empiricist theorists of association than some of their objections to associationist aesthetics and psychological doctrine would indicate.[120] In a now famous passage from his 1800 Preface to the second edition of *Lyrical Ballads*, Wordsworth offers his own reflections on the relevance of the association of ideas to the writing and reading of poetry:

> For all good poetry is the spontaneous overflow of powerful feelings; and though this be true, Poems to which any value can be attached were never produced on any variety of subjects but by a man who, being possessed of more than usual organic sensibility, had also thought long and deeply. For our continued influxes of feeling are modified and directed by our thoughts,

which are indeed the representatives of all our past feelings; and, as by contemplating the relation of these general representatives to each other, we discover what is really important to men, so, by the repetition and contin- uance of this act, our feelings will be connected with important subjects, till at length, if we be originally possessed of much sensibility, such habits of mind will be produced, that, by obeying blindly and mechanically the impulses of those habits, we shall describe objects, and utter sentiments, of such a nature, and in such connection with each other, that the under- standing of the Reader must necessarily be in some degree enlightened, and his affections strengthened and purified.[121]

In this passage, Wordsworth elaborates a pedagogical theory of the relation of thought and feeling in the experience of reading. In contrast to James Mill's more rationalist associationism, Wordsworth's formulation allows thoughts and feelings to have a reciprocal relationship through the mecha- nism of association: the poet's thoughts both represent his past feelings and modify or mediate new "influxes of feeling" on that basis. Wordsworth's view of the relation between memory and imagination resembles Bacon's metaphor of the philosophical memory as a beehive, both assimilating and transforming past experience. Because the poet's mind represents a height- ened instance of general human capabilities—through his enhanced sensi- tivity, his habit of thinking "long and deeply," and his resulting inductive ability to abstract and generalize in valid ways on the basis of these capacities and habits—his poetry also provides those common but unseen associations as deductions to be applied to experience. However, Wordsworth does not seem to envision teaching the reader of his poetry to practice the poet's own hard-won mental habits—his "blind and mechanical obedience" to the in- terplay between thoughts representing past thoughts and new influxes of feeling. Instead the poet should do all the hard mental work in composition so that the beneficial results can be extended indirectly through reading poetry. In contrast, Dickens's novels take Wordsworth's project a step fur- ther by attempting to teach readers of serial fiction a set of strategies allow- ing them to focus on and even to change their own habits of thought.[122]

If associationism became a popular psychology through its pedagogical applications in the late eighteenth century and through the middle decades of the nineteenth century, as a psychological doctrine it also raised a set of specifically scientific objections that would eventually lead to a new, more descriptive and less instrumental role for the associative memory within physiologically based psychological theories. In his discussion of Coleridge's "masterful demolition" of associationism in the *Biographia Literaria*, historian of Victorian psychology Rick Rylance concludes that associationism "crashed" during the mid–nineteenth century: "it fed the emergent psycho-physiology, but in so doing was comfortably swallowed."[123] This "Coleridgean" view of associationism's demise, however, has become a kind of orthodoxy in the historiography of British psychology.[124] Because of their primary focus on the development of psychology as a scientific discipline, historians of psychology have often overlooked the ways that associationism afforded a basic psychological vocabulary for Victorian pedagogy, literary criticism, and autobiographical writing through the end of the nineteenth century. Modified versions of associationist theories of memory circulated independently of the more doctrinaire and programmatic associationism propounded by Bentham and James Mill. Hartley's formulation of the analogy between reading and experience seems to have played an instrumental role in fostering Victorian pedagogues' optimism about the formative effects of classroom learning on individuals and the larger social effects of education.

Associationist understandings of memory in fact retained a significant conceptual role within many domains of nineteenth-century scientific psychological theory. In *The Principles of Psychology* (1855), for example, Herbert Spencer relies on the associative memory's fundamental assimilating and organizing role in structuring the interplay between the mind and its environment: "Memory then, pertains to all that class of psychical states which are in process of being organized. It continues so long as the organizing of them continues; and disappears when the organization of them is complete."[125] Spencer still constructs the organism's elaboration of experience into unconscious instinct through the sequences from simple to increasingly complex "bundles" of sensations and concepts that we recognize from earlier associationist theories.[126] Instincts thus become the forgotten experiences of a species.[127]

Associationist conceptions of mind and memory could also be translated into more physiologically based psychological theories. Writing in the 1870s, physician and physiologist William Benjamin Carpenter extrapolates associationist terminology directly into brain physiology in his theory of memory "traces," which are produced by the following causes: "(1) States of Consciousness as to places, persons, languages, &c., which are *habitual* in early life, and which are, therefore, likely to have directed the *growth* of the Brain; (2) Modes of Thought in which the formation of Associations largely participates, and which are likely to have modified the course of its *mainte-nance* by Nutrition after the attainment of maturity; or (3) Single experiences of peculiar force and vividness, such as are likely to have left very decided 'traces,' although the circumstances of their formation were so unusual as to keep them out of ordinary Associational remembrance."[128] Carpenter re-vises associationist concepts to articulate his physiological account of how the activities of the memory shape brain development, including both con-scious recollection and the unconscious traces of what seem to be traumatic experiences.

In his early writings, Charles Darwin also drew on associationism to modify the Lamarckian theory that habits developed by animals to satisfy needs could alter anatomy, producing anatomical changes that could be passed directly to offspring. Instead, Darwin theorized that habitual, uncon-scious associations based on sensory input could affect brain organization and become instinctive.[129] Associationist principles did not disappear from Darwin's writings after he had developed his theory of natural selection. In *The Descent of Man, and Selection in Relation to Sex* (1871), Darwin relies on association as a theory of learning to link animal and human cognition: "If we attribute this difference [in the ease of forming new habits based on ex-perience] between the monkey and the pike solely to the association of ideas being so much stronger and more persistent in the one than the other, . . . can we maintain in the case of man that a similar difference implies the pos-session of a fundamentally different mind?"[130] Darwin postulates that learn-ing must be a process of trial and error resulting in either painful failure or pleasurable success, and thus that it proceeds in equivalent ways but at differ-ent levels of complexity across species. In his discussion of the role of sexual selection in the evolution of human culture, Darwin also points explicitly to the role of the associative memory in the origins of conscience and mo-rality.[131] This salient instance of Darwinian evolutionary theory demon-strates that various concepts derived from associationism continued to play a significant if gradually attenuated role in Victorian scientific psychology, even though such usages cannot be viewed in retrospect as leading directly to a consolidated scientific discipline.

Associationist empiricism had formulated two fundamental questions that continued to interest and motivate many subsequent nineteenth-century approaches to psychological research, including those based in physiological investigation of the brain: What is the nature of the connection between mind and world? And what roles do language, literacy, and reading play in this relation? In subsequent chapters, I show that through self-aware characters like Mrs. Tickit, plots constructed around memory effects, and the framing of associationist principles in terms of chunks of moral teaching that can easily be remembered by the reader, Dickens's novels made multiple uses of associationist theory to shape serial reading for the purposes of entertainment, reasoning on conditions, "inserting the wedge" into entrenched institutions and mentalities, and fostering social connections among readers. In activating the pleasures of memory, Dickens's writings shaped serial reading as an occasion to exercise a freedom of thought orchestrated in the form of an exchange of common associations between author and readers.

2. Dickens's Originality

Serial Fiction, Celebrity, and *The Pickwick Papers*

> I was not, at any age, a person to sit still in her seat when others were looking out of windows, and my small nose was quickly flattened against one of the panes. There on the platform stood the Adored One! It was unbelievable, but there he was in the flesh; standing smiling, breathing, like ordinary human beings. There was no doubt, then, that "angels and ministers of grace," called authors, had bodies and could not only write David Copperfields, but could be seen with the naked eye. That face, known to me from many pictures, must have looked in some mysterious way into the face of Dora, of Agnes, of Paul Dombey, of Little Dorrit! My spirit gave a leap and entered a new, an unknown world.
>
> Kate Douglas Wiggin

In 1848, Charles Dickens performed in Glasgow with the Amateurs, a theater troupe that included Mark Lemon, John Forster, Henry Mayhew, and Douglas Jerrold. Outside the hotel where the troupe was staying, a crowd had gathered, hoping to catch a glimpse of the famous author as he exited the building. According to troupe member and amateur actress Mary Cowden Clark, who reported the incident in her memoirs, Dickens was dismayed at the throng he observed through a window and decided to let the others leave first to draw off the crowd. Meanwhile he and his friend Charles Knight, the publisher, waited behind and left together after most of the crowd had dispersed. As Dickens and Knight proceeded up the street, a woman approached Knight and asked, "Could you tell me, sir, which is Charles Dickens?" After Dickens pinched his friend's arm, Knight replied, "No, ma'am; unfortunately I couldn't." In Glasgow, at least, it was still possible for Charles Dickens to remain unrecognized in 1848, even when met face-to-face on the street by an admiring reader.[1]

We tend to think of modern celebrity as carrying with it an iconic status—it would be difficult for us to call a person whose face we could not recognize a celebrity, although certain radio personalities might constitute exceptions. Media studies scholar Fred Inglis has characterized twentieth-century celebrity as a combination of fame, consumerism, and technology. In terms of the reach of its representations, Inglis argues, celebrity super-sedes, though it does not entirely replace, such earlier forms of status as fame, honor, or renown, and it constitutes both a form and a symptom of the modern era's individualization of political and social values.[2] Dickens's status as a celebrity author emerged most fully during the 1850s and 1860s, when he undertook the public reading tours that brought him in person before large paying audiences as a performer of his own works, and when his image began to circulate more widely.[3] As a young girl, American author Kate Douglas Wiggin had easily recognized her idol, Charles Dickens, on the train platform after his public reading in Portland, Maine, in 1868. Would it be correct to say, then, that while Dickens was already famous in the 1840s, he was not yet a celebrity prior to the commodification of his image in the following two decades? Or could early Victorian celebrity take other forms, in addition to visual representation?

This chapter examines the central role of Dickens's writing in the emergence of serial fiction as a formative genre of the nineteenth-century British literary field. Instrumental to the particular success of Dickens's serial novels was his development of a new kind of authorial persona: the celebrity author who advocates the democratization of literature and galvanizes public concern around specific humanitarian causes that he or she has adopted. I argue that the emergence of Dickens's celebrity status involved the consolidation of a popular readership around a series of elements contributing to his critical reputation: the comedy of his characters, the idiomatic currency of his narrative style, and the specific memory and reality effects of his descriptions of everyday life. Early Victorian reviewers orchestrated the critical reception of Dickens's art and influence by applying associationist terminology that explained Dickens's originality as an effect of his direct impact on readers' understandings and sentiments.[4] Beginning with the reception of *The Pickwick Papers* (1836–37), readers and reviewers constructed Dickens's own mental attributes retroactively, through reflection on the experience of reading his novels, as the origin of both the effects that his novels seemed to produce upon individual readers and the common interests and attachments that readers developed in relation to his fictions. According to this account, which would become a canonical representation of Dickens's influence, the author's inventive memory produces the common repertoire of associations—the specific form of cultural memory—accessible to readers through his novels and his public persona.

Dickens's celebrity also provided a new justification for a common mode of reading and reception that was specifically designed to be accessible to all readers, rather than appealing to previously defined segments of the audience for cheap periodicals, such as working-class radicals or serious Christians. Dickens's celebrity, then, is one of the shapes taken by the widely circulated claim, which remained current throughout his career, that Victorian readers, regardless of age, sex, social background, or geographical location, became personally attached both to Dickens's characters and their specific styles of speech and to Dickens himself as an advocate of the poor. The circularity, or feedback loop, that I identify here is integral to celebrity as an emerging nineteenth-century media phenomenon of print, image, and performance.

I begin the chapter with a brief study of the term "celebrity" as a keyword, dating its appearance as a term for a person who achieves widespread popularity to the mid–nineteenth century.[5] Surveying the multiplication of publication formats for serial fiction from the 1830s through the 1850s, and analyzing the likely composition of Dickens's reading audience during this period, I position Dickens's development of celebrity authorship as a particular kind of intervention in the Victorian literary field. I show that Dickens elaborated a particular relationship to his working-class readers by supporting their social inclusion through his public appearances and speeches, while envisioning a more intimate role for his fiction in providing pleasurable and instructive reading. These goals align Dickens with liberal middle-class publishers such as Charles Knight, but I argue that Dickens was somewhat less interested than Knight in elevating working-class readers' tastes and more clearly focused on exposing readers across class lines to fiction that would clarify collective interests without appealing to partisan divisions.

In the second half of the Chapter, I analyze in detail the critical reception of Dickens's works, showing how Victorian reviewers' associationist terminology cuts across and coordinates their accounts of Dickens's originality, the reality effects of his descriptions of London life, and the reader's retention of his memorable scenes and characters. The psychological, epistemological, and pedagogical assumptions structuring Dickens's early novels correspond rather closely to the psychological terminology of many critical responses, so that it is appropriate to grant a measure of accuracy to accounts by Victorian critics of how Dickens's novels influenced reader reception. I show that Dickens's modern version of authorial celebrity circulated in the form of such associations, and that his preferred serial format of publication also served to reinforce such effects of serial memory, imputed to reading generally by associationist psychology and pedagogy, through the practice of reading fiction in installments. Dickens's novels also convey a particular relationship to the classical canons of rhetoric and mnemonics incorporated into the seventeenth- and eighteenth-century associationist writings that I surveyed in the previous chapter. Thus I also locate echoes of Baconian and Hobbesian formulations of memory's role in invention, inflected by Cockney wit, in *The Pickwick Papers*, and I bring to light a Humean version of the self's fictionality in the reception of Dickens's highly entertaining performances of Mrs. Gamp from *Martin Chuzzlewit* (1843–44).

Dickens's celebrity also came to represent a widely known repertoire of cultural associations and thus consolidated a set of common habits of thought and points of view conceived as effects of reading fiction more generally. In conclusion, I analyze how this understanding of Dickens's influence as the effect of his serial narratives on reader's memories became a vehicle of Dickens's status as an English cultural institution, as evidenced in George Orwell's 1939 evocation of Dickens as a canonical image of the Victorian liberal intellectual's resistance to partisanship and authoritarianism.

The Modern Author as Celebrity: A Brief History from Sources

The term "celebrity" was first used in relation to Dickens in the sense that he himself used it to describe Mr. Pickwick as a "gentleman . . . of celebrity."[6] The anonymous author of a series of notes found in the copy of the 1837 volume edition of *The Pickwick Papers* belonging to a self-styled "Circulating Book Society" (which met in the George and Vulture, the same pub where Dickens set the Pickwick Club meetings) suggests in one of his marginal comments that "With regard to the now boundless celebrity of 'Boz' I may well be excused saying a single word; his reputation is not European it is indeed mundane" and concludes that " 'Boz' is the Author of the Age."[7] This note is dated February 3, 1849, which suggests that by at least the late 1840s the term "celebrity" was in use to describe Dickens's fame and success as an author.[8] The *OED* records the earliest usage of "celebrity" as meaning "the condition of being much extolled or talked about; famousness, notoriety" as dating to 1600. But the earliest usage referring to "a person of celebrity; a celebrated person; a public character," credited to the author Miss Mulock, also dates to 1849 and seems to mark the term's novelty: "Did you see any of those 'celebrities' as you call them?"[9] Contemporaneous corroborating evidence for Dickens's "celebrity" under the earlier definition as worldwide fame is provided by an 1848 letter from one of Dickens's Russian translators, Trinarch Invansvich Wredenskii, from Saint Petersburg: "For the last eleven years your name has enjoyed a wide celebrity in Russia, and from the banks of the Neva to the remotest parts of Siberia you are read with avidity. Your *Dombey* continues to inspire with enthusiasm the whole of the literary Russia."[10] The transition from "celebrity" as fame or reputation to "celebrity" as a term for a famous person seems strongly associated with evolving understandings of the publicity and popularity surrounding authorship in the 1810s through the 1840s.[11]

A word search for "celebrity" on Google Books provides further preliminary evidence of a semantic shift in the use of the term from a high culture to a popular culture frame of reference. This randomly selected set of instances appearing in works dating from the late eighteenth century through the nineteenth suggests a pattern: in works published between 1780 and 1870, the term "celebrity" typically refers to the eminence of universities and university towns such as Paris, Edinburgh, and Cambridge; the fame of places associated with important historical events; the established authority of books and authors; or the renown earned by an individual in any highly respected field of endeavor, such as literature, science, medicine, politics, generalship, equestrian sports (horse racing), and the fine arts. For example, *The Public Characters of 1798* (1799) asserts that "the celebrity of Lord Nelson's name, has added another laurel to the honours of a county [Norfolk], already distinguished for the eminent characters it has produced."[12] As in Wredenskii's letter to Dickens, it is Nelson's "name" that has achieved celebrity, but Nelson himself is not yet referred to as "a celebrity." In an 1836 edition of his biography of Cowper, Robert Southey describes the poet's willingness to provide verses to the clerk of All Saints in Northampton to be used for epitaphs as "the most amusing proof both of his celebrity and his good nature."[13]

Moving into the mid–nineteenth century, in his mock biography of a self-promoting but obscure writer in "Cheap Celebrity" (1859), John Poole, a humorist and friend of Dickens, makes fun of late eighteenth-century village curates and apothecaries' tendencies to fancy themselves famous based simply upon their appearance in the provincial press: "Then was celebrity acquired upon very moderate terms; and a month's immortality in the columns of any one of the periodicals might be had for the asking."[14] Poole implies that with the expansion and greater sophistication of periodical literature in the nineteenth century, such literary celebrity is now reserved for writers, like Dickens, who have achieved much wider popularity among more sophisticated urban readers.[15] An 1854 work on Scottish universities uses the term to refer to the illustrious professors and medical school of Edinburgh: "We believe that the pride with which an intelligent Edinburgh tradesman regards his native city, has quite as much to do with its former and present literary celebrity, as with any other circumstance connected with it."[16]

In popular journalism, reviews, pedagogical works, and fiction published between 1880 and 1900, however, references to persons called "celebrities" begin to proliferate, with no apparent need to link their fame to any specific locale or institution. "Celebrity" is defined in an 1873 American primer as "the state of being famous; . . . fame, renown." No separate definition for "a celebrity" is included in this textbook.[17] By contrast, under the heading of "Slips Corrected," the author of an 1897 school book tries to stamp out the new popular connotation and enforce the earlier usage as the correct one: "Do not use *celebrity* for *celebrated person*. [Celebrity means renown, e.g., 'A man of celebrity in science.']"[18] The textbook may indicate anxiety about the leveling effects of popular culture in producing "celebrities" who may not have distinguished origins. Negative views of celebrities also entail a perception that their popularity is based on mere opportunism rather than on talent. In *The Theatres of Paris* (1880), critic J. Brander Matthews distinguishes between "artistry" and mere "celebrity" in acting, writing disparagingly of "Mlle. Sarah-Bernhardt" that "The trade of a celebrity, pure and simple, had been invented, I think, before she came to London; if it had not been, it is certain that she would have discovered it."[19]

By the end of the nineteenth century, references to "a celebrity" often deplore such persons as pandering to popular tastes. The young Winston Churchill published a satirical novel in 1898 entitled *The Celebrity: An Episode*, billed as "A story of the popular Celebrity, who is still writing books of high moral tone and unapproachable principle. A man prone to whim, a man with tactics worthy of a skilled diplomat and a man with the tendency to find himself in more than one tryst with a beautiful woman."[20] In a scene from the Anglo-Jewish writer Israel Zangwill's *The Mantle of Elijah* (1900), the president of the Young Men's Radical Association and the president of its Literary Section argue over who has the prerogative to introduce a visiting celebrity author: "Weeks of excited wrangling throughout the Club heralded the coming of the star, and even when he came, the point had not been decided. Broser and the President were still arguing it when the celebrity stood on the small stage behind the curtain. . . . 'Gentlemen, gentlemen,' appealed the celebrity, 'don't make me lose my reputation for punctuality.'"[21] The novel connects these struggles to garner the reflected grandeur of the unnamed celebrity author with the self-aggrandizing social and professional aspirations of its young male protagonist.

Early twentieth-century examples suggest that the phenomenon of celebrity had become as interesting to critics as the popularity of particular authors. "The Value of a Dead Celebrity," published in a 1900 issue of the *Cornhill Magazine*, satirizes the celebrity as a commodity. Offering to price the "relics" belonging to such deceased celebrities as Walter Scott, Charles I, Louis XVI, Napoleon, Rob Roy, and Sarah Siddons, the author surveys a series of recent purchases at auction of effects belonging to these deceased worthies as reported in the press. Totaling the catalog of the various items of hair, clothing, furnishings, jewelry, and so forth, he estimates that the average value of a dead celebrity is approximately £5,000.[22] A *North American Review* article from 1922 also suggests that the celebrity writer as cultural critic was initially an import from Britain. Discussing Matthew Arnold's views of the United States, the reviewer reports the general disappointment that this "celebrity" author, like Mrs. Trollope and Dickens, was critical of American culture, despite the fact that "The American magazines of 1883 and 1884 congratulated themselves that this visitor was really a celebrity, a celebrity who had studied our institutions, and who was likely to make more than insular comments on our *mores*."[23] Whether living or dead, by the early twentieth century the celebrity author has begun to circulate as a collectible commodity and exchangeable sign of cultural value.

A fuller treatment of the emergence of literary celebrity would need to consider the history of other related terms from the early nineteenth century, such as the "literary lion" or "to lionize," that also connoted the culture of literary salons and the particular social cachet of authors.[24] If the combined evidence from the *OED* and my Google Book word search is broadly accurate, however, it seems reasonable to conclude that authors were some of the first persons to be called "celebrities" because of their popularity, but that they also lost a certain elite cultural status by earning this denomination. Thus, Dickens must have been one of the earliest authors to become a modern celebrity.

The frequent presence of quotation marks around Dickens's pseudonym "Boz," as well as around Miss Mulock's term "celebrity" in the *OED* citation, reinforces the status of celebrity as a new social sign with both aural and visual dimensions. As they commented on his growing fame, Victorian reviewers often associated the power of Dickens's fictions to reveal the latent meanings and capture the characteristic voices of everyday London life with qualities of the author's mind, particularly his keen powers of observation and unusually retentive memory. The author and expert on Spanish art Richard Ford asserted in an unsigned review in 1839 that "Boz sketches localities, particularly in London, with marvelous effect; he concentrates with the power of a *camera lucida.*"[25] Dickens's narrative techniques seemed to function in powerfully visual and even documentary ways, in advance of photography's widespread practice and cultural impact.[26]

Dickens's celebrity became noticeable, and nameable, when a certain multiplicity of early readers began to carry around his novels' words inside their heads, particularly his characters' idiosyncratic styles of speech, and to use those words in their own speech, associating those quotations with distinctive features of the author's mind and perspective. A metaphorical treatment of such internalized influence occurs in *Master Humprey's Clock* (1840–41), when one of the small number of Dickens's overt authorial avatars, the crippled and solitary collector of old manuscripts, Master Humphrey, identifies the moral agency of the narratives he has been sharing, including the stories of Little Nell and Barnaby Rudge, with the tolling of the bells of St. Paul's: "Heart of London, there is a moral in thy every stroke! as I look on at thy indomitable working, which neither death, nor press of life, nor grief, nor gladness out of doors will influence one jot, I seem to hear a voice within thee which sinks into my heart, bidding me, as I elbow my way among the crowd, have some thought for the meanest wretch that passes, and, being a man, to turn away with scorn and pride from none that bear the human shape."[27] The chimes of St. Paul's, the heartbeat of London, echo the narrator's and the reader's own pulse, suggesting that the sensory effects of the narrative reverberating inside the reader's head provide the medium of mental connection between the narrative's encouragement of charity toward the poor and the reader's response, thus singling out the reader from the London crowd. Like London itself—the nation's capital, center of the book trade, and emerging information hub of Empire—Dickens's celebrity persona represents a circuit for a series of virtual sensory exchanges accomplished through the new medium of cheap serial fiction and linking readers into a virtual memory network.[28]

Serialization and the Market for Fiction

Dickens's fame emerged in the context of the rapid expansion of serial publications for newly literate as well as educated Victorian reading audiences from the 1830s through the 1860s. According to Richard D. Altick's seminal research, Victorian authors, publishers, and critics undertook the serialization of fiction as a means to achieve wide and profitable circulation of novels in periodical form.[29] Serial fiction quickly gained a reputation among Victorians as a genre fit in specific ways for forming, and possibly deforming, the reader's habits, opinions, and tastes. In a sermon delivered at Rugby Chapel in November 1839, for example, headmaster Thomas Arnold notes the increase in publication of popular fiction and delineates the effects of reading in installments on the schoolboy's mind: "The works of amusement published only a very few years since were comparatively few in number; they were less exciting, and therefore less attractive; they were dearer, and therefore less accessible; and, not being published periodically, did not occupy the mind for so long a time, nor keep alive so constant an expectation; nor, by thus dwelling upon the mind, and distilling themselves into it, as it were drop by drop, did they possess it so largely, colouring even, in many instances, its very language, and affording frequent matter for conversation."[30] Through his comparisons with expensive volume publication and serious academic reading, Arnold emphasizes that the serial's form and its cheapness are the most potentially injurious qualities of such literature, even aside from their possibly offensive, distracting, corrupting, or merely frivolous content. The habit of serial reading exerts a gradual and cumulative influence on both individuals and groups of readers, for whom the next installment becomes a source of common interest and anticipation. One can see in Arnold's pejorative account an anxiety about how serial reading takes up the mental space of English readers that is transformed into a general approbation forty-one years later in Benjamin Jowett's eulogy praising Dickens's educational influence.[31] To many Victorians, serial reading seemed capable of producing new social groupings that might overlay and reconfigure former relationships or even subvert them.

Reviewers of Dickens's early works often compared his rapid and expanding popularity to the earlier literary fame and success of Byron and Scott in the 1820s and 1830s. In an unsigned review in June 1839 of Dickens's novels through *Nicholas Nickleby* (1838–39), which was finishing its initial serial run, Richard Ford commented that "Like Byron, [Boz] awoke one morning and found himself famous, for, however dissimilar the men and their works, both were originals, and introduced a new style of writing."[32] If Scott, Byron, and Dickens represented both successive and competing types of literary originality leading to the emergence of the modern celebrity author, the distinctiveness of Dickens's version stemmed in crucial ways from his medium of publication. Within literary historiography and the history of publishing, Dickens's early popularity has been inseparably linked to Chapman and Hall's publication in April 1836 of *The Posthumous Papers of the Pickwick Club, Containing A Faithful Record of the Perambulations, Perils, Travels, Adventures, and Sporting Transactions of the Corresponding Members, Edited by "Boz,"* as the first serial novel in monthly installments.[33] Following on *Pickwick*'s success, the majority of Dickens's novels were published in a series of shilling monthly "parts" or "numbers," including three or four chapters totaling, on average, thirty-two pages of print and two plate illustrations. Interspersed were pages of advertisements and trade inserts sometimes so numerous that, in the case of *Bleak House*, for example, they surpassed the total pages of text.[34] Each number had a pale green paper cover with a title illustration that alluded to important characters and themes (Figure 3). The last of nineteen installments would be a two-shilling double number (bringing the total to twenty parts) including four plates, title page, frontispiece, preface, and other editorial matter.[35]

As John Sutherland has extensively documented, between 1839 and 1840 many publishers and authors attempted to copy and cash in on the *Pickwick* phenomenon by issuing a "cascade" of novels in monthly parts.[36] Sutherland argues that the novel in parts up to the 1860s "served a valuable transitional function in mobilizing a nationwide reading public before the full evolution of the fiction-carrying periodical."[37] The three novelists who succeeded most consistently with the form of monthly publication over the next three decades were Dickens, W. M. Thackeray, and Charles Lever: "For success [monthly part serialization] required an expensive 'name' author working in liaison with an expensive 'name' illustrator; lavish advertising; heavy and awkwardly recurrent production costs (up to £600 a month for a Dickens serial); and efficient kingdom-wide agency and co-publishing relations."[38] As late as the 1870s, novels in monthly installments were still appearing. George Eliot's *Middlemarch* (1871–72) and *Daniel Deronda* (January–September 1876), for example, were published initially in five-shilling parts, beginning with a bimonthly issue, and Anthony Trollope's *The Way We Live Now* (1874–75) also came out serially in the more typical twenty numbers. Although neither author's serializations reached the level of profits that had been garnered by Dickens's serials, these publications were still quite lucrative, since monthly payments to authors were based on sales. "Thackeray, Trollope, Ainsworth, and Lever had the greatest rewards of their writing lives from their novels in numbers," notes Sutherland, while Dickens himself was able to earn as much as £10,000 per novel.[39] Unlike Thackeray and Lever, Dickens stuck with his original monthly serial format

Figure 3. Cover of the original serial edition of *The Posthumous Papers of the Pickwick Club Containing a Faithful Record of the Perambulations, Perils, Travels, Adventures, and Sporting Transactions of the Corresponding Members, Edited by "Boz"* (London: Chapman and Hall, 1836–37), part 2 (May 1836). Beinecke Rare Book and Manuscript Library, Yale University.

for nine of his novels, including his last, the unfinished *Mystery of Edwin Drood* (1870). The monthly serial novel, therefore, constituted the print form that was most readily identified with Dickens's literary celebrity and that, combined with his periodical ventures, also produced his substantial personal fortune.

Other schemes for the part publication of fiction were also profitable. An earlier undertaking, Harriet Martineau's *Illustrations of Political Economy* (1832), appeared as a monthly series totaling twenty-five tales (rather than as a continuous serial narrative) and selling for one shilling and sixpence.[40] Reynolds's enormously popular *The Mysteries of London* (1844–46), modeled on the popularity in France of Eugène Sue's *Les mystères de Paris* (1842–43), was also published serially, but in weekly penny numbers rather than monthly numbers. The popular Victorian genre of weekly "penny dreadfuls" became a mainstay for consumers of cheap fiction through the nineteenth century and into the twentieth. Some of these serial gothic and adventure tales extended their run over a period of up to four years.[41] Graham Law has shown that "over the six decades of Victoria's reign, the dominant mode of serialization shifted unmistakably from the monthly to the weekly instalment. . . . The shift is from expensive, low-circulation formats produced for middle-class readers by book publishers, towards cheap, high-circulation formats produced for a mass audience by newspaper proprietors." The abolition of the "taxes on knowledge," in particular the newspaper stamp in 1855 and the paper duty in 1861, greatly encouraged this trend.[42] Dickens participated in these developments by editing, from January 1837 to February 1839, *Bentley's Miscellany*, where he published *Oliver Twist* (1837–39). He subsequently edited and wrote the contents of the threepenny weekly *Master Humphrey's Clock*, which carried some stories reprising the characters from *Pickwick*, as well as two of his serial novels: *The Old Curiosity Shop* (1840–41) and *Barnaby Rudge* (1841). Dickens also founded and edited two twopenny weeklies, *Household Words* (1850–59) and *All the Year Round* (1859–95; Dickens's role as editor ceased at his death), in which he also published three of his own novels—*Hard Times* (in *Household Words*, April–August 1854), *A Tale of Two Cities* (weekly in *All the Year Round*, April–November 1859, and concurrently as a stand-alone serial in eight monthly parts), and *Great Expectations* (in *All the Year Round*, 1860–61)—as well as novels by such successful authors as Wilkie Collins and Elizabeth Gaskell.[43] In addition to their publication in parts, Dickens's stories and early novels often appeared concurrently with their original publication as sometimes quite lengthy unauthorized fragments that were extracted and quoted in other periodicals.[44]

Dickens's early serial novels competed for readers' attention with the many new cheap publications geared specifically to working people and the lower ranks of the middle classes. This multiplication of cheap periodicals, made possible by continued technological advances in printing and the production of paper, added to the growing numbers and circulation of commercial newspapers and contributed to what many literary and book historians now view as the emergence in the 1840s of the mass circulation of periodical literature in Britain.[45] Many of these cheap periodicals began publication in the 1830s and 1840s, during the period that Dickens's career as a serial novelist for a socially diverse readership was consolidated. These included the *Penny Magazine* (1832–45); *Chambers's Edinburgh Journal* (1832–53); *Douglas Jerrold's Shilling Magazine* (1845–48) and the *Illuminated Magazine* (1843–45), also edited by Jerrold; the *Saturday Magazine* (1832–44), sponsored by the Society for Promoting Christian Knowledge; the *London Journal* (1845–1912); and *Reynolds' Miscellany of Romance, General Interest, Science and Art* (1845–69). Increasing numbers of such periodicals incorporating serial fiction and catering to particular niche audiences were undertaken from the 1850s through the 1870s. Exploiting mixed metaphors to convey the scope of this new phenomenon, one anonymous reviewer observed in 1859 that "More astonishing than Gas, or Steam, or the Telegraph, which are capable of explanation on scientific grounds, is that flood of Cheap Literature which, like the modern Babylon itself, no living man has ever been able completely to traverse, which has sprung up, and continues to spring up, with the mysterious fecundity of certain fungi, and which cannot be accounted for in its volume, variety, and universality by any ordinary laws of production."[46] The author's reference to new periodicals springing up like fungi alludes both to the capacity for mass production afforded by steam printing machines, which came into general use after 1840, and to the palpable emergence of a new phenomenon of mass literacy and consumption of print.[47]

These cheap periodicals featuring fiction, including both miscellanies and newspapers published weekly and monthly, were frequently addressed to a family audience and in some cases abundantly illustrated.[48] Sharing the goal of providing useful information as well as entertaining the reader of limited means, they also represented a variety of political and religious orientations. For example, some periodicals, such as those edited by Edward Lloyd, Jerrold, and G. W. M. Reynolds, announced their politically liberal and radical stances, while others were geared toward a pious Christian readership.[49] A series of eight different Chartist serials edited between 1847 and 1869 by

Ernest Charles Jones also published politically oriented serial fiction, including novels by Jones himself.[50] Influential and more costly literary reviews such as the *Athenaeum* (1828–1921), *Cornhill Magazine* (1867–1975), *Fortnightly Review* (1865–1954), *Blackwood's Edinburgh Magazine* (1817–1980), *Macmillan's Magazine* (1859–1907), and *Temple Bar* (1860–1906) also published fiction.[51]

Chapbooks, broadsides, temperance tracts, railway novels, and didactic religious tales constituted additional abundant reading matter for the literate lower-middle and working classes. They were typically sold very cheaply or distributed for free by such groups as the Society for the Diffusion of Useful Knowledge (SDUK); the Anglican Society for Promoting Christian Knowledge; the Religious Tract Society, run by Evangelicals; and the British Association for the Promotion of Temperance, founded in 1835, and its successor organization, the United Kingdom Alliance for the Suppression of the Traffic in All Intoxicating Liquors, founded in 1854, which also initiated a weekly penny newspaper, the *Alliance News*.[52] While I discuss the publishing initiatives of Anglican Evangelicals in greater detail in the next chapter, here it seems useful to emphasize that such tracts and broadsides could have circulations in the millions among a wide variety of readers. These numbers were only approached in Britain by the most successful, in terms of initial sales, of Dickens's serial novels, *The Old Curiosity Shop*, which reached a circulation of 100,000 per issue.[53] An 1882 estimate of Dickens's total sales figures in England after 1870 was 4,239,000 volumes.[54] When we include both the serials and Dickens's novels in volume form sold beyond the British Isles and in translation, however, we can estimate that Dickens's circulation figures must have been in the range of millions of copies by the time of his death. Numerous types of cheap and relatively cheap serial venues for fiction remained common through the 1890s, when monthly serial novels ceased to be published and the expensive (thirty-one shillings and sixpence) novel in three volumes, or "three-decker," also gave way to the six-shilling one-volume edition as the norm for the works of standard and popular English novelists.[55]

If Dickens's early serial novels were perceived as successful because of their originality, they also entered a literary field characterized by new cheap journals catering to readers' desires for intellectually sophisticated fare, such as the contents of Charles Knight's illustrated miscellany, the *Penny Magazine*, which began weekly publication in March 1832 under the sponsorship of the SDUK.[56] By December of that year, it had reached a circulation of 200,000, which Knight extrapolated to a likely readership of one million, given the pervasive Victorian practice of sharing newspapers, by either lending or mailing copies to friends and relatives, and reading aloud.[57] The *Penny Magazine* was not only revolutionary in terms of its low cost and the serious nature of its articles and illustrations, dealing with topics in science, literary criticism, history, geography, economics, and biography, but also unmatched during the course of the nineteenth century in its attempts to introduce lower-income readers to fine art engravings and authoritative art criticism. It set a precedent for the many illustrated cheap publications, including Dickens's own, that were popular as much for their pictorial matter as for their enlightening articles.[58] Knight's introduction to the first issue of the *Penny Magazine* also indicates a purpose that would link him with Dickens in a common endeavor to provide educational, high-quality, and morally uplifting periodical literature to the common reader; reading his "little Miscellany," Knight predicts, would "enlarge the range of observation [and] add to the store of facts" as well as "awaken the reason and lead the imagination into innocent and agreeable trains of thought."[59] Given that the *Penny Magazine* included intellectually challenging articles, we can interpret Knight's associationist terminology as indicating that the "agreeable trains of thought" induced by reading should amount to intellectual pleasure combining instruction and "enjoyment." Knight, however, was skeptical about the educational value of popular fiction.

Book historian Scott Bennett has delineated how the profitability and the commercial success of the *Penny Magazine* in creating a mass readership hinged on Knight and the SDUK's adoption of new publishing practices including "sharply increasing the number of copies printed to achieve a dramatically lower unit cost" and taking advantage of the ability that serials afforded the publisher "to forecast sales with some assurance."[60] Bennett argues that despite the SDUK's failure to persuade working-class readers to replace their reading of radical political periodicals with the *Penny Magazine*'s version of "useful knowledge," when the SDUK disbanded in 1846, twenty years after it was founded, "a mass market for cheap literature had clearly emerged."[61] The publication practices instituted for the *Penny Magazine* thus realized one of the SDUK's primary goals as articulated by Knight in a description of the effects of cheap publications on the new mass readership:

> They were making readers. They were raising up a new class, and a much larger class than previously existed, to be the purchasers of books. They were planting the commerce of books upon broader foundations than those upon

which it had been previously built. They were relegating the hole-and-corner literature of the days of exclusiveness to the rewards which the few could furnish; preparing the way for writers and booksellers to reap the abundant harvest when the "second rain" of knowledge should be descending "uninterrupted, unabated, unbounded; fertilizing some grounds and overflowing others; changing the whole form of social life."[62]

By bringing an end to the dearth of cheap reading, Knight sought both to democratize knowledge and to ensure the profitability of future publishing ventures. The success of the *Penny Magazine* forced other publishers to adopt the same practices, enlarging the range of cheap periodicals.

By the mid-1840s, however, the *Penny Magazine*'s readership had declined in response to what Bennett has called "the clear emergence of fiction as the most saleable commodity in that market."[63] Bennett suggests that one of the key factors in the *Penny Magazine*'s initial success was the SDUK's decision to avoid broaching any topics relating to religion or politics, a risky strategy since most successful periodicals were addressed to audiences identified with particular parties, political views, or religious sects. This strategy succeeded, however, despite the SDUK's demise, suggesting, according to Bennett, that political and religious controversy "was not to be the basis on which a mass reading market was to develop in the 1830s and 1840s." Instead, "the hunger for knowledge was . . . the pre-condition for the creation of a mass reading market."[64] To Bennett's conclusion, we must add that readers' hunger for *fiction* also drove the market for cheap serials during this period, as writers such as Dickens, Ainsworth, Jones, Jerrold, and Reynolds, in company with numerous editors and publishers, would perceive.

Among the recollections Charles Knight terms his "Pleasures of Memory" in his memoir, *Passages From the Life of Charles Knight* (1864–65), is an instance when Dickens wrote to him in 1844 praising the prospectus for a series of inexpensive books (encompassing chiefly works of history and biography and a few historical novels) called "Book-Clubs for all Readers." Dickens found "the scheme full of the highest interest" and added, "If I can ever be of the feeblest use in advancing a project so intimately connected with an end on which my heart is set—the liberal education of the people—I shall be sincerely glad."[65] Despite having published a total of 105 weekly volumes in this series, Knight did not consider it a great commercial success, as the average sale was only 5,000 copies.[66] He admits that "although very generally welcomed by many who were anxious for the enlightenment of the humbler classes, the humbler classes themselves did not find in them the mental aliment for which they hungered. They wanted fiction."[67] However, Knight explains that in 1854, "when I was inclined to think too harshly of the popular appetite for fiction," Dickens once again "remonstrated with me in the most earnest and affectionate spirit" in favor of working people's freedom to read what they like.[68]

Knight's association with the SDUK reflects a partisan orientation toward that group's overtly Whig principles of improving the working class through education. As an editor, Dickens seems to have attempted to succeed where the *Penny Magazine* failed by featuring fiction in his periodicals while avoiding an overt political affiliation. Tellingly, unlike Knight, Dickens was never an energetic participant in the campaign waged by publishers for the repeal of the "taxes on knowledge." He informed Knight that he "could hardly find the heart to press for justice in this respect, before the window-duty is removed. [The people] cannot read without light. They cannot have an average chance of life and health without it." While he joined publishers John Cassell and Thomas Crompton in a deputation to the chancellor of the Exchequer advocating repeal of the paper duty in February 1851, he informed the chancellor that he could "not honestly" support that measure "as against the soap duty, or any other pressing on the mass of the poor."[69]

Among liberal and radical Victorian publishers and writers, then, there existed significant differences in political, social, and educational rationales for providing working-class readers with "useful" or entertaining reading material. In 1853, John Cassell, a former lecturer for the National Temperance Society, founded both the highly successful *Cassell's Illustrated Family Paper* and the *Popular Educator*, a periodical including courses in a variety of subjects geared toward working-class self-education. Cassell, on the radical wing of the liberal spectrum, announced his ambitious educational agenda for publishing serial fiction in an 1858 letter to Lord Brougham: "Without professing to be a champion of Fiction, I may be allowed to state my opinion that novels may be rendered something more than mere books of amusement. That they may be made appropriate vehicles in the conveyance of useful lessons, inculcating good morals, cultivating the best affections of the heart, kindling the noblest aspirations, awakening inert ambition, inciting to enterprise and exertion, and thus advancing the Moral and intellectual welfare of the people at large."[70] Cassell's insistence on popular fiction's role in instilling an appropriate middle-class work ethic shows a different tendency from Dickens's championship of fiction, art, and literacy as affording working-class readers an opportunity for recreation and social and cultural participation.

As Ian Haywood has shown, Cassell's periodicals published explicitly anti-Chartist fiction, while Reynolds overtly aligned his career and writings with Chartism in 1848, even appearing on the platform at Chartist political rallies.[71] Reynolds also achieved huge popularity in the 1850s with serials geared toward the mass working-class audience, such as *The Mysteries of the Court of London* (1848–55), set in the eighteenth century and depicting "an unreformed society of extreme moral and political degradation which functioned as a 'shadow' of the Victorian present."[72] Dickens's consistent nonpartisanship both in his public role as a reformist author and in his fiction therefore seems more exceptional when analyzed in relation to the strategies of his immediate competitors for a mass readership. His stance was not so much apolitical as unaligned toward popular political movements and party politics, allowing him to address and assemble a heterogeneous reading audience that could also be mobilized toward nonpartisan causes.[73]

Serial publication also "made the novel into a valuable commodity," as Mary Poovey has argued, "by expanding the purchasing public beyond collective institutions (like circulating libraries) to a nation of individual buyers."[74] In his influential study of the impact of publishing practices on the Victorian novel, N. N. Feltes contends that the publication of *The Pickwick Papers* "marks the transition . . . from the petty-commodity production of books to the capitalist production of texts."[75] Furthering the consolidation of an inalienable property right in the text by the reform of copyright law through the Statute of Anne (1709) and the judgments in the *Donaldson v. Beckett* case of 1774, the trends toward commodification of literature and professionalization of authorship were intensified through the practice of serialization. This transformation, Feltes argues, combined with the greater consolidation of the publishing trade, drove authors toward the professionalization of their work and "militancy" in negotiating payment, the ownership of copyright, and other prerogatives.[76] Dickens's growing fame enabled him to bargain for more control over his work and higher percentages of his serials' revenues, and he also campaigned vigorously for the extension of international copyright laws.[77] According to Feltes, as the first cheap serial novel produced for mass distribution, *Pickwick*'s "originality" arose quite specifically from its "relations of production," so that "its format, and its literary form constituted the very commodity-text which could reach, as it produced, a mass audience."[78]

The commodity form of cheap publications may have shaped and fed the popular appetite for serial fiction, but it did not exclusively create it. In his analysis of the SDUK's publication efforts, Bennett concludes that "mass markets require some common ground, some common feeling, however partial or fleeting it may be in the day-to-day lives of the individuals who make up that market. . . . Surely it is possible for quite intense class feelings to coexist alongside an equally vivid sense of the commonalty in things that a mass market creates and on which it depends."[79] As Bennett's analysis shows, the mass audience itself is serial to the extent that it is continually reconstituted in relation to the publication of particular texts, and it can also *elicit* certain mass forms of publication such as serialized fiction by shifting away from less favored periodicals whose content, like that of the *Penny Magazine*, failed to provide the desired mix of fiction, entertainment, and instruction.

In his study of popular radical publications, Haywood draws attention to the comparative weekly average sales figures for cheap periodicals provided by bookseller Abel Heywood in 1851 to Parliament's Stamp Duty Commission: Cassell's *Working Man's Friend* sold 1,800 copies and Reynolds's *Mysteries of the Court of London* sold 1,500 copies, while Dickens's *Household Words* was achieving about half that rate at 600 copies per week.[80] Such figures indicate that Dickens's novels in installments sold better than his periodicals, but one would have to adjust that estimate to take into account those issues of *Household Words* and *All the Year Round* that serialized his novels. The question remains whether Reynolds's serial novels outsold Dickens's, at least in the 1850s. Sally Ledger states that "Dickens's popular reach was much greater than Reynolds's—his aim was to appeal to a cross-class readership, whilst Reynolds exclusively targeted readers from the working classes."[81] By comparing the bookseller Heywood's accounts, assuming they are accurate, with the sales figures of the original serial run of *Bleak House* (1852–53), we can estimate very roughly that Reynolds's weekly sales average of 1,500 copies of *The Mysteries of the Court of London* would have totaled approximately 78,000 copies per year *from just one bookseller*. Despite the difficulties of gauging the sales of a weekly versus a monthly serial, this rate of sales for Reynolds's serial novel, in direct competition with Dickens's concurrent novel, represents an approximate volume that compares favorably to (and may have exceeded) the total sales figures of 686,853 copies for *Bleak House* over nineteen months, as documented by Robert L. Patten.[82] If Reynolds had been reaching a broad-based audience of readers, his popularity should likely have remained as broad based as Dickens's. The fact that we still read

Dickens and not (or rarely) Reynolds, then, does seem to be related not only to the massive cumulative sales of Dickens's novels but also, in ways that the rest of this chapter and those that follow examine, to the cultural legitimacy forged through Dickens's cultivation of a cross-class and international Anglophone readership and his remediation of didactic genres that would be picked up later by the school curriculum. Dickens's management of his persona as a mainstream celebrity author who stayed out of party politics also inflected the self-identification of his audience as socially inclusive and participatory in its avowed appreciation of Dickens's serial novels.

Dickens's literary production and the serial publication of fiction more generally established the inextricability of literary, market, and social values in ways that contradicted not only the aims of religious instruction in Victorian popular education but, potentially, the high aesthetic value that Romantic writers accorded to literature. In her recent study of the conjoined conceptual histories of literary and economic value, Mary Poovey argues that Romantic aesthetics set out "to devise a model of value that could challenge the market evaluation registered by popularity or demand."[83] Romantic aesthetics defined literature as possessing "organic unity, linguistic connotation [vs. referential denotation, as in journalism or history], and textual [aesthetic] autonomy" from market value or use value.[84] Such an overt division of aesthetic and market rationales for literary writing contrasted, Poovey argues, with economic writers' relative lack of concern for original style in disseminating "useful information, which was also assumed to be more important than the way the information was presented."[85] Serial fiction, however, does not fit comfortably into a framework that distinguishes sharply between information-based and aesthetic values for writing. Early nineteenth-century writers, particularly novelists such as Dickens, relied on the income from sales and therefore had a considerable incentive *to articulate popularity and demand as sources of positive aesthetic values.* As a genre that by definition did not feature organic unity or claim aesthetic autonomy from the market, both in its material form and in its narrative conventions, serial fiction also resembled journalism quite closely. Periodical "miscellanies" that incorporated serial fiction among a variety of kinds of articles also approached readers directly as consumers choosing among a wide array of periodical literature. Whatever notion of aesthetics emerged from serial publication practices would have to coordinate literary value with an understanding of reception that mediated between the serial as commodity-text, as source of the reader's pleasure and edification, and as an expression of his or her taste in fiction.

Theories of literary reading and popular reception based in associationist principles, while combining assumptions about aesthetic appreciation from Enlightenment and Romantic aesthetics, are particularly useful in defining literary value without making a strict distinction between meaning and information, or between aesthetic value and commercial success. As I show in this chapter, early reviews of Dickens's novels linked attributes recognizable from Romantic aesthetic theory—such as the author's unique ability to convey his or her sustained deep train of thought and the reader's corresponding dependence on the mediation of the author's superior knowledge for aesthetic appreciation—to the reader's associative response to serial fiction. Associationist theories of reception also dealt with this developing fact-versus-fiction division, which Poovey identifies, by attributing aesthetic value to the pleasures derived from everyday reading through its formative effects on the reader's memory and individual knowledge base. Dickens's serials, I argue, thus *legitimized* readers' preferences for his version of referential novelistic representation by investing two forms of memory—both the author's invention and the reader's own associations with the text—with salutary moral and social values. When operating in tandem as cultural and artistic forms of influence, these explicitly shared forms of association merged both personal and public appreciation of literature into a collective reception and even a kind of cultural memory, rather than dividing reception into elite taste versus indiscriminate mass consumption.[86] Even Victorian reviewers writing in reputable literary journals could sanction such popular appreciation on the basis of the humane sentiments toward the poor, educational effects, and sense of belonging to a national culture that, it was presumed, could be reliably derived from Dickens's serial novels. Here we also begin to create a context, which I will elaborate in Chapter 6, for understanding why serial fiction's popularity seemed to subvert attempts by professionalizing Victorian writers, particularly after the 1860s, to define literary representation as affording a distinct kind of knowledge among the newly forming academic disciplines.[87]

Serial Reading and Dickens's Readers

Both historians of reading and literary critics have noted that Victorian periodical literature incited specific kinds of reading habits. Linda K. Hughes and Michael Lund have argued that the pervasiveness of serial publication during the nineteenth century was "an important cultural force" in consolidating central Victorian beliefs in the structuring influence of chronology and the irreversible linear sequence of the common stages of a human life.[88] They contend that serial reading also shared with nineteenth-century forms of capitalism "the assumption of continuing growth and the confidence that an investment (whether of time or money) in the present would reap greater rewards in the future."[89] In his survey of contexts for understanding Victorian readers' responses to *Dombey and Son* (1846–48), Richard D. Altick hypothesizes that readers' "powers of retention were strengthened . . . by the necessity of keeping the various characters and plots in mind across a span of nineteen months." Altick explains that Dickens's style "came to their assistance by proliferating the speech tags, physical idiosyncrasies, and other devices which refreshed the reader's memory," so that through this "dual kind of 'reinforcement' . . . the novel provided . . . a wonderfully lively and variegated world, a steadily growing store of permanently available memories."[90]

Such potentially widespread cultural effects of serial reading hinged on actual readers, and Dickens's novels garnered huge numbers of them. According to a much-cited 1837 review by G. H. Lewes, Dickens's audience was widely representative of Victorian society:

> "Boz" has perhaps a wider popularity than any man has enjoyed for many years. Nor alone are his delightful works confined to the young and old, the grave and gay, the witty, the intellectual, the moralist, and the thoughtless of both sexes in the reading circles, from the peer and judge to the merchant's clerk; but even the common people, both in town and country, are equally intense in their admiration. Frequently have we seen the butcher-boy, with his tray on his shoulder, reading with the greatest avidity the last *Pickwick*; the footman, (whose fopperies are so inimitably laid bare,) the maid servant, the chimney-sweep, all classes, in fact, read "*Boz*."[91]

Much evidence concerning Dickens's Victorian readers is anecdotal, but it tends to support Lewes's claim that readers of "all classes," to a greater or lesser extent, enjoyed his serials. Dickens's novels were certainly read by members of the Victorian bourgeoisie and aristocracy, including Queen Victoria.[92] Historians and critics generally agree that the majority of Dickens's readership through his lifetime was urban and middle class. The great variety of middle-class incomes, occupations, religious outlooks, and locations across Britain, however, complicates the seeming homogeneity of that designation. Altick documents a consensus among nineteenth-century observers of population statistics showing an increase in "the amorphous stratum between the old-established middle class (merchants and bankers, large employers of labor, superior members of professions) and the working class proper—the ranks of unskilled labor." The mass Victorian reading audience emerged from that entire middling social range, and particularly from "skilled workers, small shopkeepers, clerks, and the better grade of domestic servants," who are also likely to have made up the majority of Dickens's readers.[93] Dickens's novels also seem to have been popular among Victorian schoolboys and even at the universities, as evidenced by the parody exam on *Pickwick* written by a student at Christ's College, Cambridge, in 1857.[94]

It becomes possible to gauge the extent of Dickens's popularity among working-class readers by evaluating the audiences for his public readings, which began with a series of engagements at Birmingham at the end of December 1853 for the benefit of the Birmingham and Midland Institute. On December 30, Dickens performed a second reading of *A Christmas Carol* (1843) with the majority of seats set aside for working-class spectators at discounted prices.[95] Although their numbers are difficult to estimate, the enthusiasm of working-class and lower-middle-class audiences for Dickens's affordable public readings through the 1850s and 1860s suggests that they were also readers of his novels.[96] An editor for Cassell's publishing house, Thomas Frost, recorded in his 1880 memoir his view that Dickens did not become popular among the majority of working-class readers until the 1870s, as his works were still not widely available to them until then.[97] That estimate coincides with historian Jonathan Rose's findings concerning the frequency with which Dickens's novels were referenced by working-class autobiographers or borrowed from libraries and other collections patronized primarily by the laboring classes after the 1870s. Rose's extensive research leads him to conclude that Dickens was the only Victorian author "who ever matched the steady and overwhelming popularity of Defoe and Bunyan" among working-class readers.[98] Many late Victorian working-class readers as well as members of the Labour Party seem to have admired Dickens and cited his novels as favorite reading, even though they did not see him as a representative of working-class radicalism per se; sometimes they correlated the novels' messages with their own political affiliations and social experience, but not always.[99] A London leather-bag maker born in 1880 wrote, "Two names were held in great respect in our home, and were familiar in our mouths as household words, namely, Charles Dickens, and William Ewart Gladstone."[100] This juxtaposition also suggests that Dickens and Gladstone were viewed as counterparts in the related but distinct spheres of literature and politics. A 1906 survey of Labour MPs, which asked them to name the writers who had influenced them most, produced Dickens as the second-most-cited author (sixteen votes versus seventeen for Ruskin).[101]

Dickens's novels were commonly read out loud, either in the family circle or at public "penny readings."[102] Given that Dickens's serials could be borrowed or enjoyed through listening to others read them aloud, it seems likely that more working-class, servant, and rural readers than can currently be documented encountered Dickens's novels before the 1870s. Historian M. K. Ashby writes of the effects of both public "recitations" and private readings of Dickens's novels in her father's Warwickshire farming village in 1860s:

> People who were not at all literary, who had not read Fielding or Scott, needed no introduction to Dickens other than the infectious laughter and smiles of his readers. . . . Not to have your mind touched by Dickens was to remain a relic of the early nineteenth century, or maybe the eighteenth, as after all quite a number were. . . . All the tyrants and fools [of the village community] could be transmogrified into Dickens characters, and once you had smiled at your enemy you could think the better how to deal with him. . . . Thus Dickens affected the community life. The New Testament taught the principle of forbearance and Dickens supplied the technique of it.[103]

Various working-class autobiographers' accounts of their reading, as well as Ashby's and Rose's historical research, all seem to converge in suggesting that working-class readers perceived the influence of Dickens's novels as simultaneously ecumenical and critical, and as socially integrative across various social and regional groupings that nevertheless remained distinct. His stories could be adapted for the purposes of self-expression, satire, and social critique—a practical repertoire for a democratic cultural politics. If his novels taught "techniques" for sustaining the coexistence, if not the harmony, of the different segments and strands of Victorian society through mutual "forbearance," they also associated laughter with satire as indirect but satisfying means of "dealing with" the local "tyrants" and "fools" currently in charge of things.

According to his biographer John Forster, Dickens's editorial policies for *Household Words*, which began publication in March 1850, represented a project to provide recreation and imaginative reading for all readers:

> It was to be a weekly miscellany of general literature; and its stated objects were to be, to contribute to the entertainment and instruction of all classes

of readers, and to help in the discussion of the more important social questions of the time. . . . There was to be no mere utilitarian spirit; with all
familiar things, but especially those repellent on the surface, something was
to be connected that should be fanciful or kindly; and the hardest workers
were to be taught that their lot is not necessarily excluded from the sympathies and graces of imagination.[104]

Unlike the *Penny Magazine*, *Household Words* would not avoid controversial
topics with a political bearing, but it would follow the earlier periodical's
model of separating itself from sect or party. As is typical of Forster's literary
criticism, this account has associationist undertones, implying that reading
Household Words should "connect" even the most seemingly "repellant" or
painful social realities with some mediating image producing intellectual and
imaginative pleasure. The periodical would necessarily have wider, if indirect, political and social effects by addressing itself to large and inclusive
classes of readers, including working people, and by involving all such readers, and not just an exclusive audience of policy makers, in discussions of
"the more important social questions of the time."

Henry Morley, professor of English language and literature at University
College London and a former contributor to *Household Words*, confirms its
democratizing principles in his discussion of Dickens in an 1886 edition of
his history of English literature: "In 1850 Dickens established *Household
Words* as a weekly journal that was to join reason with imagination in support of every effort to improve society. There were to be tales, sketches,
poems, always designed in aid of right citizen-building. He would help one
half of the world really to know how the other half lived."[105] Drawing attention to Dickens's attack on Reynolds's journalism in the "Preliminary
Word" to *Household Words*, literary scholar Sally Ledger argues that "Dickens's cultural and political project in *Household Words* was to bridge—in a
manner more imaginative, if not more lucrative, than anything ever conceived by Reynolds—the incipient chasm that was opening up between
popular and radical culture from the 1840s onwards. By determinedly pursuing a broad popular readership at the same time as promoting a politics of
social reform, and by insisting on sustaining an inclusive conception of 'the
People,' Dickens's journalism persists with an older conception of 'popular'
culture (a culture 'of the people') that was gradually being superseded, from
the 1840s, by a commercial culture produced 'for' a mass-market populace."[106] Morley's account of Dickens's "citizen-building" agenda in *Household Words* indicates, however, that Dickens's cultural politics was not so

much an effort to salvage popular radical culture or to assimilate it to popular culture but rather it was transitional and innovative in the way that it
redeployed radical conceptions of popular reading toward new mainstream
and democratic uses.

What I wish to add to these evaluations, whether Morley's from the
1880s or Ledger's recent account, is a more detailed analysis of the practices
of reading that Dickens's serial publications developed. One of Dickens's
editorial directions to Morley, a frequent contributor of journalistic exposés
to *Household Words*, gives a pragmatic description of the strategies to vary
his narrative style in order to "get the publication down into the masses of
readers, and to displace the prodigious heaps of nonsense, which suffocate
their better sense":

> My confidence in the ability of such people to receive and relish a good
> thing, is so far from being the least shaken by this knowledge that I only feel
> the more strongly that the good thing must be done at its best . . . It is not
> enough to see a thing and go home and describe it, but . . . the necessity is,
> for ever upon us of patiently considering *how* to describe it, so as to give it
> some fanciful attraction or some new air. I have kept back the gold-refining
> paper, because it is exactly like a hundred other papers we might shake in a
> drawer together; merely shewing the reader what is to be seen as the Peep-
> Show man does.[107]

Disdaining voyeuristic, escapist, or sensationalistic appeals to readers, Dickens defines the format of *Household Words* as consisting in its accurate reporting imaginatively imbued with elements of literary style, allusions, and
familiar generic conventions. Within a competitive marketplace of print,
Dickens's goal is profitably to inform, reinforce, and shape the "better
sense" of the mass readership, thus also delivering what we can identify as
the associationist blending of intellectual and aesthetic pleasures of reading.

Such goals are also overtly progressive and educational. In his more direct
addresses to working-class audiences in his many speeches at banquets bene-
fiting Mechanics' Institutes and foundations in support of public funding for
the arts and public libraries, Dickens often praised laboring men's and wom-
en's diligence and sacrifices in obtaining an education. In a speech in 1853
at a dinner given in his honor by the Birmingham Society of Artists, he
asserts, "there are in Birmingham at this moment many working men infinitely better versed in Shakespeare and Milton than the average of fine gentlemen in the days of bought-and-sold dedications and dear books."
Dickens identifies himself directly with his writings and narrative persona,

promising that "what the working people have found me toward them in my books, I am throughout my life," and he reminds his primarily middle-class audience that "whenever I have tried to hold up to admiration [work-ing people's] fortitude, patience, gentleness, the reasonableness of their na-ture, so accessible to persuasion, and their extraordinary goodness toward one another, I have done so because I have first genuinely felt that admira-tion myself, and have been thoroughly imbued with the sentiment that I sought to communicate to others. [*Hear, hear.*]" A sign of his growing celeb-rity was Dickens's acceptance of silver-gilt salver and a diamond ring, which he said would wear as a "token" to remind him in case he should ever be "in danger of deserting the principles" that he had just articulated ("But I have not the least misgiving on that point").[108] On this occasion, which we can take as typical of many others, Dickens parlayed a celebration honoring his achievements as a "national writer" into an opportunity to praise and support working people and to win a recognition of their virtues from his primarily middle-class and bourgeois audience.[109] He pointedly indicates in the speech his awareness that some "working people" must be present in his audience, so that he does not speak over their heads, but also addresses them directly both as representatives of their class and, in effect, as a crucial constituency of his own cross-class cultural politics.

This speech demonstrates the ways that Dickens constantly attempted to exert control over the shape of his own celebrity and public influence, so that if he were praised extravagantly as a world benefactor (as he was at this dinner), he would inflect and redirect that praise to support and extend the legitimacy and literary value of popular fiction and to highlight how moti-vated working-class readers were in exercising their literacy and tastes. As the professionalization of authorship has been a direct result of the extension of literacy to "the people," Dickens argues, so their demand for "good" fiction has come to drive the market in "Literature": "Let a good book in these 'bad times' be made accessible—even upon an abstruse and difficult subject—and my life upon it, it shall be extensively bought, read, and well considered."[110] As much as Dickens attempted to shape the Victorian popu-lar taste, he also seems to have trusted it, relying on the intelligence of a general readership to recognize and, in effect, *to define literary value through demand* within a competitive market of popular serials. This stance also sug-gests that Dickens understood the professionalization of authorship as an el-evation of the social status of writers more generally, rather than as a segmentation of the literary field into more privileged versus hack produc-ers. As a result, the professional author within this field of cheap popular fiction and the democratization of taste could undermine the distinction between elite versus popular audiences.

Another frequent purpose of Dickens's public speeches was to ally his own influence as a popular author with the democratizing influence of institutions of higher education. Dickens also supported higher education as a means of eventually devolving class differences. During the Birmingham dinner, he enumerated and praised in turn a series of new educational institutions that had been founded at Birmingham to extend opportunities to working women, "poor inventors," and "juvenile delinquents": "where the words 'exclusion' and 'exclusiveness' shall be quite unknown [*great cheering*]; where all classes may assemble in common trust, respect and confidence."[111] Dickens's effectiveness in garnering funds for the many charitable educational efforts that he supported, as well as in fostering the positive public perception of such efforts, can be gauged from educationist Mary Carpenter's comments about his endorsement of the Ragged Schools in a letter to the *Daily News* (which Dickens edited at the time) published in February 1846: "The struggling efforts of a few individuals were brought into a striking and brilliant light by the magic pen of Charles Dickens who, by none of his writings, has reflected more true honor on himself, than by those simple but touching columns in the *Daily News*, in which he showed the world a glimpse of these children of misery, and of what was being done for them."[112] In their publications, charitable organizations frequently quoted passages from Dickens's writings demonstrating the suffering of the poor, as well as larger social dangers, such as epidemics, attendant upon widespread poverty in an effort to capitalize upon Dickens's fame—his newly emergent celebrity—and to raise support for causes that he had publicly endorsed or could be construed as approving through the tone of his writings.[113] We can see how Dickens's shaping of the role of the celebrity author or artist as humanitarian activist was an early version of the now-familiar early twenty-first-century cohort of humanitarian Hollywood actors, billionaire entrepreneurs, and rock stars.

Dickens's consistent and vehement defense of the laboring man, woman, and child's normal desire to enjoy imaginative escape and pursue intellectual improvement is represented most famously in *Hard Times*.[114] Dickens also voices his support for universal education as a means of advancing working-class contributions to literature in his preface to John Overs's *Evenings of a Working Man, Being the Occupation of His Scanty Leisure* (1844). The two men's six-year acquaintance began when Overs, a cabinetmaker by trade, sent Dickens some poems for publication in *Bentley's Magazine* in January

1839, just before Dickens's stint as editor ended, and thus too late for him to authorize their publication. The poetry was published elsewhere, however, and Dickens and Overs maintained their correspondence; Dickens lent Overs books, including Thomas Carlyle's *Chartism* (1839), and gave him suggestions on his writings without substantially editing them. The preface to Overs's book demonstrates that even in such a brief work as this one Dickens attempted to parlay his growing influence—what I am calling his emerging literary celebrity—into an argument on the political and cultural effects of literacy. Dickens argues that any "delicate" reader who feels "a genteel distaste to the principle of a working-man turning author at all" should instead support "the Universal Education of the people; for the enlightenment of the many will effectually swamp any interest that may now attach in vulgar minds, to the few among them who are enabled, in any degree, to overcome the great difficulties of their position." Resistance to the idea of universal education, Dickens asserts, can only be remedied by the presumably middle-class readers' witnessing the actual conditions of working-class life: "I earnestly entreat them to educate themselves in this neglected branch of their own learning without delay; promising them that it is the easiest in its acquisition of any: requiring only open eyes and ears, and six easy lessons of an hour each in a working town. Which will render them perfect for the rest of their lives."[115]

In a complex rhetorical construction, Dickens suggests that prejudice against the aspirations of a working-class writer is a sign of vulgar ignorance that can be overcome through a conjoint effort to change both mentalities and social conditions. Universal education will lead to social change so fundamental that working-class writers will no longer be unusual, and class bias against them will evaporate by such distinctions becoming obsolete. Dickens's recommendation of "six easy lessons" in an industrial town also suggests a parody of Victorian self-help literature that redirects the reader's motives of self-improvement toward social reform based in concrete knowledge of how working people are forced to live. Dickens thus shifts the burden of self-education rhetorically from the working-class writer to the middle-class reader. He implies that the educated classes must take the lead in extending education to the "people," but in suggesting that they can only do so by reeducating themselves, he voices an anti-elitist position, which I study further in Chapter 5, that is not typical of Victorian liberal middle-class educational reformers.

In *Chartism*, Carlyle also advocates universal education and emigration as two comprehensive solutions to the plight of the working classes. His rationale for universal education, "to impart the gift of thinking to those who

cannot think, and yet who could in that case think," creates a direct linkage
between literacy and awakened intellectual capacity.[116] Dickens's representations of the street smarts and enterprise of the poor in his novels, however,
generally contradict Carlyle's notion that education implants thought, since
they imagine a different sort of knowledge of everyday life equal and in
some ways superior in value to the knowledge provided by formal education. Universal education was also advocated in the 1840s both by Chartists
and by organizations such as the London Working Men's Association, the
Miners Association of Great Britain and Ireland, and the Metropolitan
Trades Delegates.[117] Dickens's conceptualization of democratic popular literature, however, falls somewhere between Carlyle's position and a radical
political platform. On the one hand, Dickens makes individual readers responsible for informing themselves about working-class conditions, but on
the other hand he argues for universal education, which requires political
action and state intervention. By adopting a position independent of party,
sect, or class interest, but without condemning such interests as if they were
simply sets of false values to be transcended by appropriate institutional reforms, Dickens articulates what I identify as a modern popular democratic
rather than a liberal program. As combined cultural forces, a democratic literature and universal education would contribute in crucial ways to creating
the specific social conditions for what we tend to associate with modern
democracies' stated (if unevenly achieved) educational goals of social inclusion—that is, within Dickens's immediate Victorian context, a form of "citizen-building" involving the working classes' equal participation in the
nation's collective political, social, and cultural life.

John Overs's views on universal education seem to have been in line
with a modified radical position informed by Dickens's novelistic interest in
democratic social inclusion of the poor. In an 1840 letter to Dickens, Overs
provides a detailed critique of Carlyle's *Chartism* as well as one of the very
few extant analyses by a working-class reader of the educational effects of
Dickens's serial novels. Commenting on Carlyle's recommendation of universal education as a solution for the political unrest of industrial laborers,
Overs argues that "it is [education] other than that of books which is
wanted; or, rather, it is that added to books, a knowledge of life which the
working man most requires, and which no school of the past or the present
attempts to give him." Implicitly questioning the value of the rote training
prevalent in Victorian elementary schools, Overs argues that Dickens's novels support the possibility of progressing beyond bare literacy toward the
ability to gain relevant, even revelatory, experience through reading: "Of

the thousands who delight in your labours, I am afraid there are very few who understand that their pleasure lies in the inculcation of this great and neglected Evangel, a knowledge of life: an Education which they have never had; which they never suspected the want of as an Education; but which, with ready soul and the instinct of nature, they comprehend at once, being set before them, and which they otherwise sluggishly, painfully, win by installments in their progress to the grave, and then understand not its characteristics."[118] Overs implies that reading Dickens's novels in install-ments can supplement the reader's unreflecting experience of everyday life, otherwise gained through painful trial and error "by installments in their progress to the grave." He theorizes that by revealing the latent coherence of experience as formed serially, recursively over time—that is, by teaching the pleasures of memory theorized by the associationist tradition—Dickens's serial fiction makes the world knowable by confirming the rele-vance of the working-class reader's hard-won experience.

Overs makes clear that this kind of educational reading does not substi-tute for experience, which can only be gained incrementally through strug-gle, nor does it implant knowledge in the reader, but rather it enlivens the reader's latent awareness and enhances his or her understanding. This is also a version of classical mimesis, by which the artistic representation provokes the recognition of a shared world that had been seen but not understood. But Overs's account offers a more specific response to the print forms of the 1840s by highlighting how the serial cumulative temporality of reading Dickens's novels in parts produces the particular reality effects lent by the reading of fiction to life itself. This everyday life, Overs emphasizes, nor-mally stints opportunities for self-reflection, especially for the working-class reader whose labor and economic survival take up all his time and efforts. Overs also defines Dickens's teaching as an alternative "Evangel"—a frame of reference that my next two chapters will elaborate by investigating the entry of Dickens's serials into competition with Evangelical didactic fiction for the poor. Setting aside Carlyle's framework for universal education as a tool toward social control, then, Overs explains how Dickens's novels could participate in reforming working-class culture of the 1840s: "But beside the Education of books, the mere Abode of learning and science; and beside your Education of social life and individual character, every individual has a right to be educated in Political economy with his natural, social, and na-tional rights, relations, and liabilities, with a knowledge of God and Nature; at his Country's expense, command and compulsion."[119] Dickens's novelis-tic education should function alongside a knowledge of political economy and universal free education as an element of an array of working-class civil rights. Overs's account of Dickens's influence demonstrates that its associationist framework came across as a consistent form of "inculcation" to at least one very astute and critical working-class reader who entered into dialogue with Dickens himself. As Overs stipulates, many readers and even periodical reviewers of Dickens works may overlook their central teaching, perhaps even while absorbing it: "I am afraid they see not the philosophy of your benevolent soul through the entertaining veil of your fictitious realities."[120] By registering such effects, Overs positions himself as the ideal reader envisioned by Dickens's early serial fiction and democratic cultural politics.

Pickwick*'s Currency and* "Boz's" *Originality*

While Overs's highly theoretical response to Dickens's influence was most likely exceptional among less affluent readers, his sense of readers' development of relationships to Dickens's narratives as supplements to experience, or "fictitious realities," seems to have cut across Victorian class demarcations. Numerous Victorian readers described their affectionate attachment to Dickens's novels and companionable friendship for Dickens's characters as personal ties developed through repeated readings and revisited in fond remembrance in later life. Victorian reviews, as well as the parodies, plagiarized "sequels," dramatic adaptations, and collections of popular scenes taken from Dickens's novels, show that the effects of attachment that Dickens's characters produced depended to a great extent on their distinctive kinds of discourse. The language of Dickens's characters became a kind of currency of his early celebrity. Commenting on the fifth number of *Pickwick* in 1837, a reviewer writes that "Boz marches on triumphantly, and has completely taken possession of the ear, and of the heart too, of his countrymen."[121] Whether read aloud or silently, Dickens's early fictions seem to have possessed some of the qualities of direct speech, including the capacity to elicit an oral response, as in stage melodrama. "Wellerisms," and saying something in the "'Pickwickian sense,' which removes offence from an offensive speech," became frequently repeated and imitated forms of humor that also identified the speaker as one of Dickens's many admirers.[122] Another 1837 review points to the word-of-mouth quality of "Boz's" popularity: "in less than six months from the appearance of the first number of the *Pickwick Papers*, the whole reading public were talking about them—the names of Winkle, Wardell, Weller, Snodgrass, Dodson and Fogg, had become familiar in our mouths as household words; and Mr Dickens was the grand object of interest to the whole tribe of 'Leo-hunters,' male and female, of the metropolis."[123] While such a statement probably exaggerates, it did not stray completely from the truth, since *Pickwick*'s sales were extensive and widespread, reaching most of the larger cities of Britain by the end of its run.[124] Altick lists *The Pickwick Papers* among the nineteenth century's "best-selling" novels, according to its early sales of 40,000 copies per installment by the fifteenth number, and its total sales in Britain of 140,000 in book form by 1863, and 800,000 by 1869.[125]

Reviewers quickly perceived this kind of conversational currency as having both positive and negative effects on the English vernacular. Commenting on *Oliver Twist* in an anonymous review in 1839, Richard Ford calls "Boz" "regius professor of slang, that expression of the mother-wit, the low humour of the lower classes, their Sanscrit, their hitherto unknown tongue, which, in the present phasis of society and politics, seems likely to become the idiom of England."[126] "Boz" renders street slang virtually classical, revivifying and legitimizing the dialect as if he were a philologist, even as he exposes "our ingenuous youth" to "such hidden depths of guilt" of which "they should not even suspect the possibility."[127] Two years later, an unsigned review pinpoints how Dickens "exhibits genius in embodying London character, and very remarkable skill in making use of peculiarities of expression, even to the current phrase of the day."[128] Such reviews suggest that Dickensian representation began to be embraced as realistic when readers recognized and accepted his characters' language as their own idiom. Describing the popularity of *Pickwick* in his biography of Dickens, Forster asserts that Sam Weller is "one of those people that take their place among the supreme successes of fiction, as one that nobody ever saw but everybody recognizes, at once perfectly natural and intensely original." But Sam's success as a literary creation also stems from his standing as a sign for a general experience of urban life: "Who is so amazed by [Sam's] inexhaustible resources, or so amused by his inextinguishable laughter, as to doubt of his being as ordinary and perfect a reality, nevertheless, as anything in the London streets?"[129]

Some reviewers, however, resisted Dickens's style as too close to lower-class speech. A particularly harsh anonymous review from the *Times* in 1846 attacks "the extraordinary style of composition which Mr Dickens is endeavouring to engraft upon the national literature . . . [which] may be

called, for want of a better term, the *literary ventriloquial,* for it aims at producing in words to the eye precisely the same effects as ventriloquism
achieves in sounds in the ear."[130] This critic's objections to Dickens's blending of the oral and the visual, even as he coins a term for the technique,
suggests that by "ventriloquizing" the "colloquial," Dickens was debasing
English literature, supplying an illicit voice from elsewhere (the streets, the
lower classes) to the effigy of national literature, which should instead be
the wellspring of correct usage.

One of the most important words launching Dickens's celebrity was his
early pseudonym, "Boz," often referred to as part of a quotation from direct
speech.[131] In an anonymous December 1837 review, drama critic and psychologist G. H. Lewes remarks that "When the *Sketches* came out, 'Have
you read Boz?' was the eternal question," admitting that "we were fairly
astonished at the rapidly increasing popularity of his name."[132] Dickens's
identity as the author behind the pseudonym had been revealed in July of
that year, the same month that the prominent *Literary Gazette* reprinted excerpts from *Pickwick.*[133] Thus Lewes is commenting not just on a name but
also on the emergence of Dickens's literary reputation. We could view the
pseudonym "Boz" as a precursor to the iconic image of the twentieth-century celebrity, since it seems to have functioned analogously as a kind of
verbal token or souvenir that could be exchanged among readers as a sign
of their participation in the young author's popularity. Writing to a friend
in Ireland on June 30, 1837, the novelist Mary Russell Mitford expresses her
amazement that her friend has not yet heard of "Boz" or *Pickwick*: "It is
fun—London life—but without anything unpleasant: a lady might read it
all *aloud*; and it is so graphic, so individual, and so true, that you could curt-
sey to all the people as you met them in the streets. I did think there had
not been a place where English was spoken to which 'Boz' had not yet
penetrated. All the boys and girls talk his fun—the boys in the streets; and
yet those who are of the highest taste like it the most."[134] Mitford also highlights the descriptive and journalistic, simultaneously visual and oral/aural
effects of Dickens's "graphic" scenes of London life. Like the early reviews,
Mitford's account shows the relay of connections among the currency of
the names "Pickwick" and "Boz," the "individuality" of the serial novel's
characters, and the accuracy, or imaginative "truth," of his representations.

If Dickens's celebrity initially emerged as his readers repeated and exchanged his characteristic words, then Dickens could be considered an
"original" in the same Pickwickian sense in which Mr. Pickwick, confiding

to the red-headed man, considers his manservant, Sam Weller: "I flatter myself he is an original, and I am rather proud of him" (381). Dickens's innovative language, characters, and stories reflect positively upon the Victorian reader, who enjoys and shares their popularity in the same way that Sam's clever and original sayings reflect positively on Mr. Pickwick, who has been both clever and original enough himself to appreciate the value of Sam's street smarts and acquire his services. Like Sam, the young Dickens as a novelty in print and conversation became collectable and exchangeable, and his early celebrity thus consisted in part in this traffic in his perceived originality. As Mitford's letter suggests, one did not need to feel awkward about being in the multitudinous company of Dickens's readers, whoever they might be, since even persons of the "highest taste" approved and enjoyed Pickwickian "talk" and "fun." In fact, Dickens's celebrity seems to have emerged, both in imagination and in sales figures, as readers joined this company with "Boz" and his audience, without having literally to step out of their familiar social circles.

All these elements of Dickens's early reception suggest a kind of tangibility to Dickens's celebrity, as if readers, in exchanging either his name or jokes, were also exchanging concrete sensory elements of the shared associations in speech and memory that they were forming with his works. In addition, the similar popularity of the acclaimed illustrations by Hablôt K. Browne, or "Phiz," further rendered the characters' appearances as well known as their exploits. As the anecdote that opens this chapter suggests, Dickens's early readers would have been more likely to recognize Mr. Pickwick on the streets of Glasgow or London than Dickens himself. Merchants also cashed in quickly on the serial's popularity: "Pickwick chintzes figured in linen drapers' windows, and Weller corduroys in breeches maker's advertisements."[135] Shops, meanwhile, began to stock "'Pickwick canes,' or 'Pickwick gaiters,' 'Pickwick Hats,' with narrow, curled brims; and even tobacco stoppers."[136] The circulation of sensory and linguistic experiences of Dickens's commodity-text quickly led to the profitable production, purchase, and marketing of more branded merchandise, as currency, later to become collectable memorabilia, of a reader's participation in the new social phenomenon of "Boz's" celebrity.

Memory and Invention

Dickens's characters' speeches and scenes may also have stayed in reader's memories, as Altick suggests, because their own associative qualities facilitated their memorability. Dickens seems to have devised the ultimate tactic for a successful commodity-text—to pattern his narration on the associative movement of thought so that it could be assimilated seamlessly by the reader, without any gap between representation and memory. But such seamlessness assumes that the associations garnered from reading are primarily reproductive ones, instead of also being generative of new associations within the context of the reader's own train of thought. The virtual status of shared associations as media consists in their adaptability to new contexts, or remediation. The status of associationism as a Victorian theory of reception means that serialization does not simply lend itself to repeated reading or recollection but can also allow the reader individually, and a self-identified audience of readers collectively, to generate new patterns and combinations of association with the widely perceived originality of a particular character, novel, or author who is quickly becoming a common mental and cultural possession and who, by the end of the1840s, would be referred to as a celebrity.

Dickens's novelistic comedy is clearly involved in this generative aspect of both his writing and his reception. In exploring this dimension of Dickens's originality as a mode of his reception, I want to focus especially on the associative thought and paratactic speech styles of some of his most popular and amusing characters. The first example that comes to mind from Dickens's early writings is Alfred Jingle:

> "My friend Mr Snodgrass has a strong poetic turn," said Mr Pickwick.
> "So have I," said the stranger. "Epic poem,—ten thousand lines—revolution of July—composed it on the spot—Mars by day, Apollo by night,—bang the field-piece, twang the lyre."
> "You were present at that glorious scene, sir?" said Mr Snodgrass.
> "Present! think I was; fired a musket,—fired with an idea, rushed into wine shop—wrote it down—back again—whiz, bang—another idea—wine shop again—pen and ink—back again—cut and slash—noble time, sir. Sportsman, sir?" abruptly turning to Mr. Winkle. (79)

The way that Dickens represents Jingle's discourse on the page makes it look disjointed, without design, but in fact any Victorian reader with some experience of poetry or the theater would perceive that it is highly structured and has the quality of an improvised performance: when read out loud, the dashes disappear, becoming hesitations or elided pauses for emphasis in delivery. Jingle's thinking also functions according to Bacon's inductive concept of "curtailment of the unlimited": he comically riffs around a particular idea, even as he seems to be "struggling and running about here and there in [the] seemingly unlimited space" of his imagination.[137] Jingle puns on the two meanings of "fired"—the gun and the poet's fancy—as he depicts himself composing his epic in the midst of the battle. Then the idea of the musket, and perhaps Mr. Winkle's attire, leads him to a new train of associations, relating war to hunting. Jingle's "presence" at the July Revolution is truly a matter of "thinking," or of imagination, but then, so is the reader's "presence" among the scenes of *Pickwick*.[138] As a famous Dickensian character, Jingle represents and reenacts Dickens's own associative faculty of invention that Victorian reviewers and critics would point to as the source of his originality and the reader's vivid imaginative experience of the narrative. If the reader finds him- or herself remembering Jingle or enjoying his jokes, then this remembrance also entails associating Jingle with Dickens's originality and, in virtual effect, participating in the kind of literary invention that produced Jingle.

But there is even more to Jingle's characterization than meets the eye and ear, since his joke offers an account of interrupted serial literary composition involving memory techniques that could be read as a figure for Dickens's own writing practice (minus the wine shop). Jingle's methods of impromptu composition display the kind of invention theorized in Hobbes's account of the relation between memory and imagination that, I have argued, provided a pivotal early formulation of memory's creative role in reading and invention for eighteenth-century associationist psychology. In his discussion in *Leviathan* (1651) of the "TRAIN *of Imagination*," Hobbes explains that in dreams, "The . . . [train] is unguided, without design, and inconstant; wherein there is no passionate thought, to govern and direct those that follow, to itself, as the end and scope of some desire or other passion: . . . And yet in this wild ranging of the mind, a man may oft-times perceive the way of it, and the dependence of one thought upon another."[139] When imagination is a waking function, however, Hobbes considers it to function according to cause and effect, while encompassing both memory and invention:

> In sum, the discourse of the mind, when it is governed by design, is nothing but *seeking*, or the faculty of invention, which the Latins called *sagicitas*, and *solertia*; a hunting out of the causes of some effect, present or past, or of the effects of some present or past cause. Sometimes a man seeks what he hath lost, and from that place and time wherein he misses it, his mind runs back, from place to place, and time to time, to find where and when he had it; that is to say, to find some certain and limited time and place in which to begin a method of seeking. Again, from thence his thoughts run over the

same places and times, to find what action or other occasion might make him lose it. This we call *remembrance*, or calling to mind; the Latins call it *reminiscentia*, as it were a *re-conning* of our former actions.[140]

Because invention and remembrance overlap, remembrance can furnish a constructively limiting order—"a train of regulated thoughts"—for imagination in rhetorical or poetic invention.[141] These activities of ranging and searching also become conscious memory techniques: "Sometimes a man knows a place determinate, within the compass whereof he is to seek; and then his thoughts run over all the parts thereof, in the same manner as one would sweep a room to find a jewel, or as a spaniel ranges the field till he find a scent, or as a man should run over the alphabet to start a rhyme."[142] As he unifies all these forms of searching and retrieving, Hobbes also provides a non-hierarchical theory of natural intelligence that we have noted appears repeatedly in the history of associationism's fundamental notion of the ranging freedom of thought.

Hobbes's account of memory's role in invention is close to Francis Bacon's earlier discussion of the relation between memory and invention in *The Advancement of Learning* (1605), where he translates the five canons of classical rhetoric (invention, arrangement, style, memory, and delivery) into his notion of the four "intellectual arts," the first of which is "the Art of Inquiry or Inuention." Bacon extends memory's role in invention beyond its function of recollecting past knowledge, showing that it helps to guide internal reasoning as well by providing signposts to inquiry and judgment, "For a facultie of wise interrogating is halfe a knowledge."[143] Bacon also employs the trope of seeking or chasing after an animal in flight within a limited space to describe the role of memory in invention: "So as to speake truely, it is no *Inuention*, but a *Remembrance* or *Suggestion*, with a Application: . . . Neuertheless, because wee doe account it a Chase as well of Deere in an inclosed Parke, as in a Forrest at large: and that it hath already obtayned the name: Let it bee called *Inuention*."[144] Bacon's differentiation between rhetorical invention of the kind used in speeches or arguments and scientific invention or the discovery of something new allows for the role of memory in retrieving knowledge in ways pertaining to the essential preliminary aspects of learning—those involving inquiry or the discovery of the appropriate questions to ask of a teacher or fellow investigator, or when one is perusing a learned author or book.

I return to these early formulations in Bacon and Hobbes as much to hear the echoes of their own uses of common tropes in Dickens's language as to chart the place of empiricist rhetoric in the history of his style.[145] This empiricist tradition conceiving of invention as a kind of inquiry implementing memory for the purposes of judgment and reflection, and not simply recollection, continued to inform later eighteenth- and nineteenth-century conceptions of the epistemological aspects of both literary invention and reception through the still-central role of classical rhetoric in Victorian grammar schools, provincial academies, and universities.[146] As I discuss later in this chapter, the sense articulated by Bacon and Hobbes that learning, reading, and composing are parallel and coordinated intellectual forms of *seeking* also reappears in figures used by reviewers to describe Dickens's originality.

Hobbes's image of memory as a ranging spaniel, perhaps chasing Bacon's deer in an enclosed park, may remind us that Alfred Jingle once had a Pointer that seemed able to read: "—surprising instinct—out shooting one day—entering enclosure—whistled—dog stopped—whistled again—Ponto—no go; stock still . . . dog transfixed—staring at a board—looked up, saw an inscription—'Gamekeeper has orders to shoot all dogs found in this enclosure'—wouldn't pass it—wonderful dog—valuable dog that—very" (79). Reading Dickens's joke as a reflection on Jingle's paratactic style, the literate hunting dog becomes an apt image for the associative memory itself. Like Jingle's Pointer, the associating mind functions in both automatic and purposeful ways, as if the borders between human and animal capacities, or between voluntary and involuntary memories, or between memory and "fictitious realities" are easily transgressed.

Dickens began writing at a time when a rich tradition of associationist, rhetorical, and empiricist theories of the coherence and copiousness of discourse and imagination was still available as a common currency of psychological, pedagogical, and aesthetic thought, and of novelistic representation.[147] More importantly, this tradition created analogies between scientific and aesthetic methods, so that empiricism and mimesis could be conceived and pursued in parallel. Even as early as *Pickwick*, Dickens's writing gives evidence of his creative participation in and transformation of rhetorical practices of invention, showing how serial narrative can provide the "half" of the reader's knowledge that involves training in both the empirical and the imaginative practices of fictional inquiry. Victorian reviewers recognized this rhetorical practice of invention in Dickens's works, and they describe it in the associationist language shared with belletristic rhetoric.

Dickens's early writings and growing celebrity also incorporated invention into *original topoi*, or exchangeable notions that readers could learn—*a new common sense* about the social, moral, and educative effects of popular literature that in turn became linked both to his new kind of celebrity authorship and a new understanding of the psychological impact of novelistic realism. Part of the way this comes about is through the novel's impressing the reader with what Bacon refers to as certain "marks or places," the loci or topoi of the arts of memory, which in novelistic terms become memorable characters and comic scenes.[148] For example, two thematically resonant transformations of spatial location into an account of cause and effect—akin to Jingle's improvisation on his rushing between battlefield and wine shop as spurs to poetic invention—occur close to one another in chapter 22, the second chapter of the eighth number of the original serial edition, when Mr. Pickwick, Mr. Peter Magnus, and Sam Weller are riding in a coach to Ipswich driven by Mr. Weller, senior. Sam points out to Mr. Pickwick that the "crowded and filthy street" in the part of London they are passing through on their way out of town is "Not a wery nice neighborhood" and then offers an initially puzzling observation that "poverty and oysters always seems to go together": "What I mean, sir, . . . is, that the poorer a place is, the greater call there seems to be for oysters. Look here, sir; here's a oyster stall to every half-dozen houses. The street's lined vith 'em. Blessed if I don't think that ven a man's wery poor, he rushes out of his lodgings, and eats oysters in reg'lar desperation" (383). Mr. Weller confirms his son's logic, commenting, "To be sure he does . . . and it's just the same vith pickled salmon!" (383). This joke provokes the reader to laugh out loud. Although this is perhaps an abstruse way to interpret it, in Hobbesian terms we could call this a jest resulting from the attempt to translate remembrance, or the way one's "mental discourse" metonymically provides associations related to spatial relations of contiguity, into invention or discovery of causal relations. Sam's parody of deductive logic suggests that because the poor live among many oyster shacks, eating oysters, or pickled salmon, must be a result of poverty.[149]

But just in case we might think that there is no valid logic or argument behind this comment other than fun, about two or three miles later Mr. Weller follows up Sam's conclusions with a similar observation, reflecting as he passes a turnpike, "Wery queer life is a pike-keeper's, sir":

> "They're all on 'em men as has met vith some disappointment in life," said Mr Weller senior.
>
> "Ay, ay?" said Mr Pickwick.
>
> "Yes. Consequence of vich, they retires from the world, and shuts themselves up in pikes; partly vith the view of being solitary, and partly to rewenge themselves on mankind, by takin' tolls."

"Dear me," said Mr Pickwick, "I never knew that before."

"Fact, sir," said Mr Weller; "if they was gen'lm'n you'd call 'em misanthropes, but as it is, they only takes to pike-keepin'."

With such conversation, possessing the inestimable charm of blending amusement with instruction, did Mr. Weller beguile the tediousness of the journey, during the greater part of the day. (383–84)

Mr. Weller turns the anti-logic of Sam's joke into a demonstration of a quasi-sociological and psychological method that also has the quality of a comic parable—"blessed are the pike-keepers." Mr. Weller also correlates spatial location with cause: the effect of being alone on a pike, collecting tolls, means that the pike-keeper must have experienced the prior cause of disappointment by his fellow human beings, resulting in his vocation of guarding and removing physical obstacles, but only for a fee. Mr. Weller's analysis, however, also dissects the social causes of the pike-keeper's isolation by highlighting the ways that language—naming and its social connotations—shapes our view of him. If he were a "gen'lm'n," he could be dignified by the title "misanthrope" and perhaps live in comfortable, if lonely, retirement, writing a bitter or humane memoir as his mood dictated. In this possibility, the pike-keeper foreshadows Mr. Pickwick's philosophical retirement at the end of the serial. But since he is a working man, he has to find an occupation, and not just a philosophy, that suits his temperament, outlook, and condition. Mr. Weller's lesson both teaches the reader to consider the social inequalities that contribute to the pike-keeper's "disappointment" and demonstrates the socially inflected and epistemological nature of human space and location.[150] The pike-keeper's job of monitoring roadblocks, whether to movement or to understanding, signifies both his epistemological function in Mr. Weller's anecdote and the coachman's own ability to traverse and explicate the underlying causal logic of social space. The coachman's movements also exhibit the serial circuit of the searching and inventive memory—a sort of shuttling back and forth on his route, noting both its changes and its familiar landmarks, that generates his intimate, analytical knowledge of social space.

Mr. Weller's lengthy and more overtly instructive analysis suggests that there may be a similar sociopolitical argument behind Sam's more condensed example of transforming place into cause. Perhaps there is a causal association besides contiguity explaining the connection between oyster shacks and poverty. Historically, oysters were a source of cheap and readily available protein; oyster shacks proliferated to serve the dietary requirements of the poor.[151] In addition, following Tony Weller's logic, Sam's observation suggests that the poor, like the pike-keeper, have been disappointed by their fellow humans' willingness to tolerate and condone social inequality, but instead of seeking to punish mankind or starting a revolution, they console themselves for this injustice by indulging in cheap delicacies. In this way, oyster eaters may also be stand-ins for the emerging mass readership for serial fiction—assuming that they have learned to read.

As evidenced in often-noted resemblances of *The Pickwick Papers* to Cervantes's *Don Quixote*, the retirement and disillusionment of the misanthropic gentleman is also the fate that would threaten Mr. Pickwick himself after his experience in the Fleet, if it weren't for Sam's "pike-keeping" guidance in lifting the temporary obstacles to his sympathy and understanding over the course of the novel. Sam clearly could have grown up a misanthrope, given his experiences of abandonment and homelessness, but he hasn't. This larger set of questions about the experiential nature of knowledge, and the removal of obstacles to knowledge, also structures the novel's impact on readers as they indulge in its serial form in "digestible" oyster-like segments over time—one never eats only one oyster. From its inception, the Dickensian serial's readership ostentatiously includes the common city people who might frequent oyster shacks—but oysters are also universally enjoyed by all classes. The novel thus stages its own reception by including a discussion of the compulsive consumption of a commodity, in this case oysters, as a commentary on the causes of poverty and social stratification. By contrast, however, through Sam's and Mr. Weller's anecdotes one learns to consume the novel not as a substitute for but rather *as a medium toward* questioning causes and linking them to social conditions. Perhaps most important, the narrator also connects the Wellers' humorous social analyses with the effects of Dickens's project to create cheap fiction meant, like the associationist pleasures of memory, to "blend" simultaneously "amusement and instruction." "Wellerisms" therefore become both a metaphor for and pedagogical technique of Dickens's novelistic epistemology and cultural politics. The serial novelist is a pike-keeper of sorts, except that his self-appointed task is to permit readers' sympathetic and enlightened passage from one social location to another, both in their imaginations and also through their participation in Dickens's own extensive and serial reading audience.[152]

Media scholars David Thorburn and Henry Jenkins have pointed out that "the introduction of a new technology always seems to provoke thoughtfulness, reflection, and self-examination in the culture seeking to assimilate it," often "tak[ing] the form of a reassessment of established media forms, whose basic elements may now achieve a new visibility, may become a source of historical research and renewed speculation." New media can also participate in this self-reflexivity: "Aware of their novelty, they engage in a process of self-discovery that seeks to define and foreground the apparently unique attributes that distinguish them from existing media forms. . . . As the example of [Cervantes's] *Don Quixote* implies, often the most powerful explorations of the features of a new medium occur in comedy."[153] We could also read *The Pickwick Papers* in this light as evidencing a comedic self-consciousness characteristic of the new medium of serial fiction, which was also defining itself in relation to earlier media of literary, theatrical, and oratorical invention, composition, and performance. In its larger cultural dimensions as a new print medium and development of memory's mediation among ranging imagination, searching invention, and integrated fictional and everyday forms of experience, Dickensian comic serial fiction claims as its hallmark a satirical social epistemology based on urban contiguities and metonymic invention—a self-reflexive practice of knowledge afforded to the reader in connected and cumulative parts.

Scenes and Figments

Another significant source of associative speech styles like Jingle's and the Wellers' that is contemporary with Dickens's early works is the Victorian popular theater. Louis James documents at least three theatrical plays based on *Pickwick* and believes that many more may have existed.[154] As literary scholar Deborah Vlock has shown, such theatrical adaptations played a major role in forming many Victorians' experiences of Dickens throughout his career, since many of his admirers would have known his characters through the theater without ever having read his books. Supporting the argument I have made that Dickens's celebrity was initially discursive—taking both textual and aural/oral forms—rather than directly mediated through his image is Vlock's observation that "The Victorian social, literary and theatrical establishments actively engaged in a semiotics of the voice, locating the signifiers of social place in speech."[155] The theatrical technique known as stage patter participated in this correlation of social position with speech as well as gender. Derived etymologically from "paternoster" and evolving from its medieval connotations as "rote delivery of the paternoster, a hypocritical devotion," Victorian stage patter, according to Vlock, was an "eccentric" style characterized by "logical discontinuities, and rapid, repetitive delivery." Associated with lower-class speakers, patter was "a language of form rather than content, in which words are deceptive because they deviate from conventional (elite) semantics, rhythms, and syntax." Patter was a performance of "the languages specific to socially marginalized groups" and "street culture," such as those reported in the journalism of Henry Mayhew, which surveyed the occupations of the urban poor.[156] The "female" patter of middle- or lower-middle-class women, particularly spinsters and widows, was "essentially comic, with its high-speed, run-on sentences, sparse punctuation, and logical circularity."[157] Male patter, by contrast, "typically belonged to lower working-class urban figures" such as costermongers and strolling entertainers: "less amusing than its feminine counterpart, [male patter] reinvents standard English, infusing the language with new words, new syntactic patterns, new (and generally subversive) ideas."[158] Among Dickens's female patterers would be characters (all widows) like Mrs. Nickleby, Sairy Gamp, the nurse from *Martin Chuzzlewit*, and Flora Finching from *Little Dorrit* (1855–57), while his male patterers would include Alfred Jingle and Sam Weller.

Drawing on Vlock's analysis of the social and linguistic politics of patter, I want to point out that when stage patter is incorporated to form the dialogue of some of Dickens's most popular characters, it also participates in the associationist conceptual framework of his serial fiction and its early critical reception. Sairy Gamp's monologues, for example, not only resemble patter but, in the context of her characterization as an originator of Mrs. Harris, her imaginary friend, also manifest the kind of metonymic and causal relations between memory and invention theorized by Bacon and Hobbes in the seventeenth century, and among memory, identity, and the witnessing of fictional versus live performance as theorized by Hume in the eighteenth century and James Mill in the nineteenth.

In his reminiscences of Dickens's public readings of excerpts from his novels in the 1850s and 1860s, Dickens's friend Charles Kent singled out the nurse as "perhaps the most intensely original and the most thoroughly individualized" of the characters that Dickens impersonated:

> She is not only a creation of character, she is herself a creator of character. To the Novelist we are indebted for Mrs. Gamp, but to Mrs. Gamp herself we are indebted for Mrs. Harris. That most mythical of all imaginary beings is certainly quite unique; she is strictly, as one may say, *sui generis* in the whole world of fiction. A figment born from a figment; one fancy evolved from another; the shadow of a shadow.[159]

Kent's analysis suggests that by impersonating Mrs. Gamp in his public read-ings, Dickens was in fact giving his audiences another multilayered image of his own inventive capacity to "evolve figments" of his own imagina-tion—characters that could in turn author another fictional character. Mrs. Gamp's creation of the "most mythical of imaginary beings," Mrs. Harris, personifies the ways that an individual's "fancy" can become, if only tem-porarily, the basis of a collective belief, just as Dickens mesmerized his audi-ences by personifying his own fictional characters.

In his detailed history of Dickens's public readings, Malcolm Andrews describes the "sympathetic kinship between author and reader" that Dick-ens's "charismatic presence" amplified in performance: "Dickens insinuated his presence into the experience of the story (powerfully so, since he was both narrator and creator of what he was reading), sometimes . . . sharing their enjoyment as if he were a detached spectator of the characters he pa-raded, at other times deliberately opening spaces for their responses and then, as it were, assimilating those responses into the ensuing recitation. . . . Thus he opened a kind of one-way dialogue with his audience, a kind of 'interpretation' of himself."[160] Dickens in performance, then, was even more like Sairy Gamp in his ability to double back and represent his own creative powers by impersonating his characters. Dickens's originality is manifested in the series of originations that proceeds from author to charac-ter (Mrs. Gamp) to the character's creation of an imaginary friend and inter-locutor (Mrs. Harris) to the reader's or spectator's memory of that fictional novelistic or authorial character.[161]

Dickens's public performances, then, give us insight into how his celeb-rity functioned even before he began to stage his public readings, as a rhe-torical effect of reading his serials, in the process of which the reader conjures up a mental image of the author as in prosopopoeia. If the charac-ter's associative speech patterns, or patter, were particularly memorable, then the memory of reading could become akin to a memory of a perform-ance. As we saw in Chapter 1, drawing on Humean empiricism in his asso-ciationist psychological theory, James Mill relies on a similar analogy between a memory of reading and a memory of witnessing a speech to dis-tinguish (incompletely) between the role of the self in memory and in imag-ination.[162] In both cases, for Mill, such memories involve a kind of virtual spectatorship where the self remembers its presence at a scene, whether witnessed or read. Dickens's performances, by analogy, could blur the dis-tinction between both author and character and the audience member's memories and imagination by highlighting the serial connection between the remembered self as reader and spectator. Every time an audience member witnessed a Dickens performance, then, he or she would experience self-recognition through memories of past serial reading.

John Stuart Mill clarifies his father's illustration of the congruity between memories of events and memories of imaginary ideas by arguing that "the imaginative emotion which an idea when vividly conceived excites in us, is not an illusion but a fact, as real as any of the other qualities of objects."[163] Likewise, Dickens's novels, whether read or in performance, seem to have produced memorable imaginative emotions that felt real. The reader, like the author or the fictional character who authors another even more explicitly fictional character, becomes the lynchpin in a series, anchoring the operative associationist analogies between memory and imagination, reading and witnessing a performance, and even the celebrity author and his fictional characters, both of which take on the qualities of publicity in performance. The audience member or reader thus bears the same relation to Dickens's authorial invention as Dickens does to Sairy Gamp's invention of Mrs. Harris—the spectator/reader, either by reading, seeing Dickens perform a reading, or remembering either event, virtually originates the image of Dickens as author.

The popular craze surrounding Dickens's performance of Mrs. Gamp's authorship of Mrs. Harris could also take on the dimensions of a philosophical debate. Novelist and potter William de Morgan recounts how on an excursion down the Thames in the summer of 1881, a party including the painter Edward Burne-Jones, the artist and author William Morris, and his friend the Oxford tutor Charles Faulkner engaged in a game of "Twenty Questions," which met a stumbling block when "Mrs. Harris" was proposed as an answer to be guessed at, and an argument ensued as to whether she was "abstract or concrete": "Charles Faulkner maintained that Mrs. Harris was just as concrete as any other character in fiction. Morris vigorously opposed this view; Mrs. Harris, he said, was simply a creature of Mrs. Gamp's imagination and did not appear in the story at all." Despite the "wild excitement" that ensued, the question remained unresolved.[164]

Perhaps this confusion arose because, within the novel itself, Mrs. Harris often appears in the context of Mrs. Gamp's associative patter concerning her professional experience presiding over births and sickbeds. Much of Mrs. Gamp's humorous discourse in fact consists of reminiscences, but of a confusing and fictive nature. Mrs. Gamp recounts her past dialogues with Mrs. Harris as what Kent terms "grotesque remembrances": she mixes memories of "real" events in her life with fictive "memories" involving

Mrs. Harris.[165] For example, she refers to the presumably actual day in her life "when [Mr.] Gamp was summonsed to his long home," alongside her past conversations with Mrs. Harris, which the reader learns are imaginary.[166] Mrs. Gamp's discourse itself works associatively, as in this example, where she is defending Mrs. Harris's actuality against Betsy Prig's insinuations of her unreality: "I have know'd that sweetest and best of women . . . ever since afore her First, which Mr Harris who was dreadful timid went and stopped his ears in a empty dog-kennel, and never took his hands away or come out once till he was showed the baby, wen bein' took with fits, the doctor collared him and laid him on his back upon the airy stones, and she was told to ease her mind, his owls was organs" (828). As James Mill's analogy between witnessing a scene and reading a scene describes, Mrs. Gamp's fictitious memory of Mr. Harris (or was it the baby?) falling into fits unleashes and incorporates metonymically what seem to be all the accompanying elements of the scene, including the "airy stones" and the almost incomprehensible (at least to me) simultaneously Cockney and surrealistic image, "his owls was organs."

As in the debate between Morris and Faulkner over whether Mrs. Harris possessed the "concrete" status of a literary character or the "abstract" status of a mere fancy belonging to a character, Mrs. Gamp herself is materialized by taking on an originating, authorial function. She becomes one of those "fictitious realities" that John Overs referred to as the principle attraction of Dickens's novels. In order to distinguish between Mrs. Gamp and Mrs. Harris, whom Kent calls a "figment born of a figment," however, some additional reality has to be lent to the original figment by calling her a character and consigning Mrs. Harris to the status of a fantasy. Accordingly, Dickens too as author and originator of Mrs. Gamp can occupy a more concrete space in the reader's memory than does Mrs. Gamp, who is merely a character he has invented or caused—except that if Mrs. Harris creates the effect of being "*sui generis,*" according to Kent, then she seems to exist beyond the author's origination and in the Humean epistemological realm of fictional effects without substantial causes. As we can see from Kent's account of Dickens's personifications of Mrs. Gamp in his readings, in her creation of Mrs. Harris and in her reality for the audience as a fictional author figure, Mrs. Gamp was just as much a celebrity as, or perhaps even more so than, Charles Dickens, who simply "ventriloquializes" her (borrowing the 1846 *Times* reviewer's neologism) in his public readings—or perhaps he channels her as a collective memory effect of his reading audience. Kent reports about the crowd's anticipation of a public reading by Dickens that "the words he was about to speak being so thoroughly well remembered by the majority before their utterance that, often, the rippling of a smile over a thousand faces simultaneously anticipated the laughter which an instant afterwards greeted the words themselves when they were articulated."[167] Here the audience seems collectively to manifest the pleasures of memory as a hallmark experience of reception in modern mass culture.

The associative proliferation of "remembered" detail in Mrs. Gamp's made-up recollections of Mrs. Harris also occurs in the novel's descriptive passages, amplifying the comedy. For example, this happens when, in preparation for their tea in Mrs. Gamp's lodgings, Betsy Prig "produced a handful of mustard and cress, a trifle of herb called dandelion, three bunches of radishes, an onion rather larger than an average turnip, three substantial slices of beetroot, and a short prong of antler of celery; the whole of this garden-stuff having been publicly exhibited, but a short time before, as a twopenny salad, and purchased by Mrs. Prig on condition that the vendor could get it all into her pocket. Which had been happily accomplished, in High Holborn, to the breathless interest of a hackney-coach stand" (829). This is a scene from comic theater, with the clown pulling an entire salad out of her pocket. The final sentence shows the associative power of the omniscient narrator's "memory" of this fictional observed event, the "reality" of which is established by the final detail of the inclusion of the crowd at the hackney-coach stand as witnesses or audience, and their fascination with the scene. The narrative thus transforms theater into fiction by incorporating the audience. Mrs. Gamp and the narrator play another dizzying, entertaining variation on the interplay of memory, invention, and imagination by showing how memories can be invented, and invention can be based on fictional memories that produce real emotions, which the audience or readers may in turn appropriate as their own.

Reality Effects

Dickens's early Victorian reviewers frequently noticed the visual and perceptual qualities of Dickens's descriptions. After the comment that Dickens's mind functions like a camera lucida, Ford's 1839 review extends his comparison by suggesting that Dickens is like a visual artist: "The identical landscape or occurrence, when reduced on one sheet, will interest and astonish those who had before seen with eyes that saw not, and heard with ears that heard not, on whom previously the general incident had produced no definite effect."[168] Ford suggests that the novels distill a complex reality into an iconic image that can also be easily remembered and mass produced because it appears "on one sheet." An 1838 review of *Nicholas Nickleby* in the *Spectator* claims that "The popularity of Boz . . . is one of the literary wonders of the day" and cites as one of the central "elements" of his influence his "perfect plainness, the common-life character of his subjects, and the art with which he imparts vitality to the literal and whatsoever lies on the surface."[169] For this reviewer, Dickens's fiction seems very close to journalism and is perhaps superficial for that reason. Dickens's own powers of observation were viewed as both striking and surreptitious; according to a newspaper description of Dickens in 1844, "he seemed to be scanning you, not obtrusively but unobservedly, from head to foot."[170] Here Dickens's originality becomes an effect of the ways that the empirical qualities of his fiction mirror and directly result from his exceptional capacity for unerring scrutiny. Such attributes could also seem a bit freakish and vulgar to some critics. While deploring the "bizarrerie of Mr Dickens's genius" in an 1858 review, journalist and editor Walter Bagehot nevertheless still reports, with an only slightly veiled intent to ridicule, Dickens's reputed "power of observation in detail": "We have heard,—we do not know whether correctly or incorrectly—that he can go down a crowded street, and tell you all that is in it, what each shop was, what the grocer's name was, how many scraps of orange-peel there were on the pavement. His works give you exactly the same idea."[171] For Bagehot, Dickens's eye is rather too indiscriminate in recording and transmitting everything he sees, yet he also praises Dickens for his ability to "comprehend the artistic material which is given by [London's] extent, its congregation of different elements, its mouldiness, its brilliancy."[172]

Dickens's serials as well as his imagination take on the ephemeral realism of a newspaper in recording the trivial events of everyday life; as Bagehot famously put it "He describes London like a special correspondent for posterity."[173] Emphasizing the connections between fictional realism and Dickens's practices as a journalist, John M. L. Drew points out that in his early articles and reviews for the *Morning Chronicle* from 1834 to 1836, Dickens typically "seizes on a background detail that has caught his attention, and dwells on it rather than on the main spectacle, in such a way as to undermine the ideological framework of the performance."[174] The critical or satirical edge of Dickens's early stories, ultimately collected as *Sketches by Boz* (1839), runs parallel to his early radical journalism, and thus the tales' realism cannot be viewed as simply a literary convention for self-referentiality.[175] An

1860 review of a volume of *Household Words* notes its pervasive but unob-
trusive editorial selection, so that the journal's organization encourages analysis and discussion, "because when facts are so wisely selected and
ingeniously put that they inevitably become for every intelligent hearer
starting points of valuable trains of thought, argument and discussion may
go on without semblance of didactic reasoning."[176] The positive educational
effects of Dickens's work as an editor seem to have dovetailed in some readers' minds with his novels' descriptive realism. Both kinds of periodical—
serial novel and journal—seem to have encouraged what we might call
critical thinking through metonymic juxtaposition, so that the reader is lead
to question and consider, pursuing an indicated "train of thought" or argument without sensing an overbearing didactic message. Such contemporary
responses also show how associationist jargon concerning "valuable trains of
thought" could be used to refer to differing interactions between instructive
and pleasurable reading in the Dickens-edited serial miscellany versus the
Dickensian serial novel.

Accounts of Dickens's descriptive realism by Victorian reviewers during
his lifetime tend to equate it, whether in positive or negative terms, with
the psychological complexity of the reader's reception of his serial narratives. Most reviewers assume that Dickens's serial fictions do not merely
transcribe what the author has seen. Instead a narrative technique mimick-
ing and incorporating an associative memory process comes into play to
make realistic details of character or city life become recognizable and
meaningful to the reader. In his earliest unsigned review of Dickens's work
in 1837, describing the impact on the reader of the scenes of Mr. Pickwick
in the Fleet prison, Forster writes that "All of it is real life and human nature.
It is not a collection of humorous or pathetic dialogues about people who
have no tangible existence in the mind; but it is a succession of actual scenes,
the actors of which take up a place in the memory."[177] Forster's account
demonstrates how the effects of reading were often couched in dramatic
terms, but he also seems to displace the theater as a merely "humorous or
pathetic" (a trivialization of the comic and tragic) medium of mere fictions,
or "intangible" characters, in favor of the novel's greater "actuality." This
account of realism recalls Jeremy Bentham's "Chrestomathic" curriculum,
in which subjects initially "exhibited in an isolated and quiescent state" will
later be reintroduced "as parts of a moving scene, acting upon one another."[178] There is an implied epistemological progression from the pictorial
to the dramatic that culminates in serial narrative forms whose scenes must
be enacted in the mental space constituted by private reading.

Developing this angle in a later unsigned review on the success of *Nicholas Nickleby*, which sold 50,000 copies throughout its serial run, Forster asserts in 1839 that "Thousands read the book because it places them in the midst of scenes and characters with which they are already themselves acquainted; and thousands read it with no less avidity because it introduces them to passages of nature and life of which they before knew nothing, but of the truth of which their own habits and senses suffice to assure them. This is a test which only a man of genius could bear."[179] Forster implies that Dickens's rendering of London life charts a common experience by making the known world recognizable and remarkable to the already initiated Londoner, while acquainting the rural or sequestered reader with unknown aspects of urban living. What makes this experience common and gives it the status of "truth" is precisely the reality and memorable quality invested in the mundane, familiar world through the practice of reading itself. Dickens's "genius" is proved by passing the "test" associated with classical Aristotelian mimesis: his novels provoke recognition because they conform to the reader's prior knowledge but, as truthful representations, they can also stand in for a lack of actual experience. Once again, Forster seems to downplay the theatrical, melodramatic, and conventional qualities of Dickens's fiction. Instead Forster implies that Dickens's novels produce their strong impact because they take up the same space in the memory as actual experiences. Memories of reading, however, have epistemological and pedagogical effects absent from everyday experience: when reading Dickens's novels, and in the process becoming newly aware of the familiar, one can also reflect upon everyday experience.

Forster concludes his review with fulsome praise of the novel as a source of morally instructive and pleasurable "recollections": "With what pleasant thoughts it has stocked our memory, with what true and tender sentiments enriched our hearts, with what a healthy and manly moral instructed our minds. With how much vivid distinctness each character takes its place before us, how plainly we see the individualities of each, the form of their faces, the accident of their habits, the nicer peculiarity of their minds. . . . The creative powers of the novelist, when properly directed and well sustained, take rank with history itself."[180] In his favorable comparisons of Dickens's fictions to history, Forster provides an updated Aristotelianism, putting it to use to distinguish Dickens's originality from the bulk of cheap popular literature. Reading Dickens's novels is not only an educational but also a mentally bracing exercise, producing "healthy and manly" sensations, and not the morbid imaginative excesses associated with the "penny dreadful" or the Newgate novel. Forster's approach to literary criticism also suggests that an experience of reading can become both memorable and generic if it is conveyed in the form of a unique (and exchangeable) "individuality"—through either the figures of Sam Weller and Mr. Pickwick or that of "Boz" or Charles Dickens. The author's "creative powers" take on causal force within the sphere of reading equivalent to history within the sphere of experience, and thus the novels seem to have the effect of collapsing Aristotle's famous distinction in the *Poetics* between poetry as universal and history as particular. Dickens as celebrity author, then, also comes to stand for and mediate a retrospective knowledge of social causality made possible by common experiences of reading fiction. Realism has its cognitive impact through the attributed authorial function, translated through the persona of a celebrity author whose retentive memory, empirical bent, and humanitarian outlook, as much as or even more than his books at this point in time, can become the common mental possession of his readers. Dickens's realism, then, is not so much about literal reality but about kinds of *virtual* reality mediated in parallel by the author's retentive memory, and his encompassing field of observation crystallized into a representative image or scene in his narrative fictions.[181]

Forster's formulations of how Dickens's novels affect readers are similar enough to Overs's account in his letter to Dickens to suggest that perhaps Overs read Forster's reviews and adapted them to convey the particular effects of Dickens's novels on working-class readers. Working-class autobiographer Norman Nicholson's account of his response to a Phiz illustration of *Dombey and Son*, which he read as a schoolboy in the 1920s, also indicates that even in the early decades of the twentieth century, readers could still view Dickens's novels, especially through their highly popular illustrations, as representing scenes corresponding closely to life:

> [The illustration shows] old Mrs. Pipchin, in her widow's weeds, sitting beside little Paul Dombey, and staring into the fire. I had never seen widow's weeds, of course, but everything else in that illustration, drawn in the 1840s, was as familiar to me, eighty years later, as the flags of my own back yard. The little, high, wooden chair, with rails like the rungs of a ladder, is the chair I sat in at mealtimes when I was Paul Dombey's age. The fireplace itself, the bars across the grate, the kettle on the coals, the bellows hanging at the side, the brass shovel on the curb, the mirrored over-mantel, the mat, the table swathed in plush, the aspidistra on the wall-bracket—all these I had

seen many times in my own house, or Grandpa Sobey's, or Grandma Nicholson's or Uncle Jim's. On a winter tea-time, before the gas was lit, the fitful firelight populated the room with fantasies as weird as any in Dickens. I would pick up my book sometimes and try to read by the glow from the coals, and the world I entered seemed not far removed from the world I had left. It was no more than walking from one room into the next.[182]

Nicholson finds a literal correspondence between the series of details in the Phiz illustration and his memories of the items included in the kitchens of his family and close relatives (Figure 4). He notes that even at the time of his initial reading of the novel, he immediately recognized and was struck by the correspondence between its scenes and his own childhood, so that his memory of reading Dickens also recalls the reality effect he experienced at the time, just as associationist criticism predicts. The novel's scenes reinforce and amplify the sense of reality that Nicholson attaches to his own experiences and memories, producing an effect of recognition. The correspondence between the illustration and Nicholson's memories also strengthens the impact of Dickens's novel on his awareness of both the familiarity and potential strangeness of his circumstances and sense of self, as both Overs's and Forster's accounts also describe in the obliquely Humean associationist framework recognizable in early Victorian criticism. The meaningfulness invested in the novel's scenes and descriptions, which the illustrations render even more fully visualized on the page, seems to confirm the coherence and reality of Nicholson's identity and memories.[183]

Reading the Author's Mind

Early reviewers also correlated Dickens's realistic descriptions with the epistemological applications of his sympathy for the poor, which they linked directly to the social reformist impact of his fictions on the individual reader and the reading public. As Ford puts it in his unsigned review of 1839, "Boz sets before us in a strong light the water-standing orphan's eye, the condemned prisoner, the iron entering into his soul. This individuality arrests, for our feelings for human suffering in the aggregate are vague, erratic, and undefined."[184] Poet and playwright R. H. (Richard Hengist) Horne's featured chapter on Dickens in his edited work *A New Spirit of the Age* (1844), a survey of the careers of important Victorian intellectuals of the 1840s, solidifies this reception of Dickens's humanitarian influence, pictured in the huge-eyed and youthful face, with its penetrating and fearless gaze, of the

Paul and Mrs. Pipchin

Figure 4. "Paul and Mrs. Pipchin," by H. K. Browne, from the original serial edition of Charles Dickens, *Dombey and Son* (London: Bradbury and Evans, 1846–48), part 3, December 1847. Beinecke Rare Book and Manuscript Library, Yale University.

engraved portrait by Margaret Gillies that appears as the frontispiece to the first volume (Figure 5).[185] Horne includes Dickens in a category of thinkers of "genial habit and maturity of mind" who, "having found out that the world is not 'all alike,' though like enough for the charities of real life, . . . identify themselves with other individualities, then search within for every actual and imaginary resemblance to the great majority of their fellow creatures, which may give them a more intimate knowledge of aggregate nature, and thus enlarge the bounds of unexclusive sympathy."[186] Horne imputes quasi-inductive and recognizably Wordsworthian methods to Dickens in his gathering of specific examples of humanity and relating them to his own experience to form a general representation of "aggregate [human] nature" (again, also like Bacon's "bundled instances"). The reader's corresponding mental stock of "representative individualities," gleaned from Dickens's texts, becomes in turn a repertoire of categories of persons with whom one should sympathize "unexclusively" in real life. The upshot is that Dickens's realist inductions produce a set of sympathetic deductive principles that his novels are actually able to teach to readers.

Like Ford, Forster, and Bageot, Horne focuses on Dickens's ability both to register individual differences and to seize on discrete, significant details of urban life in order to form them into a memorable scene:

> The materials of which the works under our present consideration are composed [Dickens's writings up to *Martin Chuzzlewit*], are evidently the product of a frequent way-faring in dark places, and among the most secret haunts where vice and misery hide their heads; this way-faring being undertaken by a most observing eye, and a mind exactly suited to the qualities of its external sight. . . . To several of the characters he has drawn, objections have often been made, that they were exaggerations, or otherwise not perfectly true to nature. It is a mistake to think them untrue; they are, for the most part, *fac-simile creations*, built up with materials from the life, as retained by a most tenacious memory. They are *not* mere realities, but the type and essence of real classes; while the personal and graphic touches render them at the same time individualized. (28–29)

Once again, Dickens's memory becomes the medium of a quasi-technological empiricism, a photographic and even, to our eyes, proto-cinematic reproduction of reality. Indicating Dickens's modernity, Horne distinguishes these generalizing and distilling qualities of Dickens's realism from Scott's historical documentary approach because, unlike Scott, "Mr. Dickens has no notes derived from books or records, but from a most retentive memory

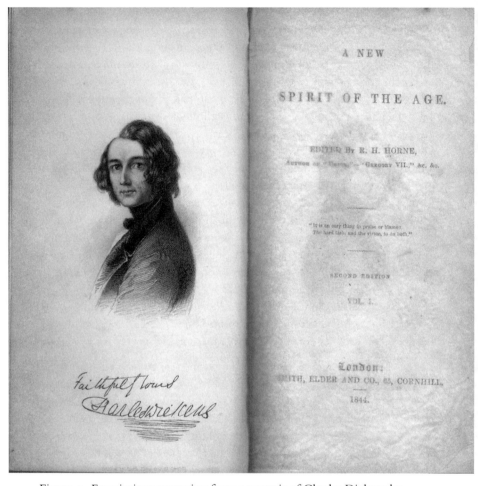

Figure 5. Frontispiece engraving from a portrait of Charles Dickens by Margaret Gillies and title page from *A New Spirit of the Age*, edited by R. H. Horne, 2nd ed., vol. 1 (London: Smith, Elder and Co., 1844). Courtesy of the Yale University Library.

and subtle associations; and all this he works up by aid of an inventive genius, and by genuine impulse rather than art" (71–72). Horne links Dickens's ability to evoke sympathy in his readers, then, directly to his ability to mask artifice and to foreground genuineness, based in his own powers of "fac-simile" memory and investigative methods. While Horne places Dickens on the spectrum of Romantic aesthetics, attributing his originality to spontaneous genius, he also insists on Dickens's objectivity: "The true

characteristics of Mr. Dickens's mind are strongly and definitively marked—
they are objective, and always have a practical tendency" (48). These effects
of authenticity and practicality are placed at the service of Dickens's readers,
causing them to recollect a common, individualized, and emblematic image
of human suffering, and to actualize their responses in relation to the feelings
they have invested in this recollected image: "It is this closeness to reality,
so that what he describes has the same effect upon the internal sense as *thinking of reality*, that renders Dickens very like De Foe" (74). Here we see again
the associationist idea, traceable to eighteenth-century writing, that thinking and reading are parallel processes, suggesting that the author's experiences can be transferred virtually as "fictitious realities" to other minds
through reading.

This chain of memory effects renders what many of Dickens's contemporaries claimed to have experienced as a common ethical response to reading his novels, particularly his Christmas books, as an impetus to charitable
sentiments and actions. Such feelings, I want to argue, should not be dis-
missed by the cultural historian or literary critic as epistemologically naive
or morally self-serving. Horne asserts that Dickens's influence in 1844, at
the age of thirty-two, "is extensive—pleasurable, instructive, healthy, refor-
matory" (74). Without corrupting the reader by a too close contact with
"depravity," Horne argues, Dickens's novels nevertheless "tend on the
whole to bring the poor into the fairest position for obtaining the sympathy
of the rich and powerful, by displaying the goodness and fortitude often
found amidst want and wretchedness, together with the intervals of joyousness and comic humour" (70–71). Horne's summation emphasizes the linkage between the epistemological, democratic, and social reform effects of
Dickens's novels that I have been investigating as specific elements of Dickens's shaping of serial reading into a medium of cultural politics. Dickens's
originality is involved not only in the rigorous documentation, distillation,
and communication of knowledge about social realities but in the rhetorical
fashioning of that knowledge in such a way as to most effectively advocate
for the poor. Again, what is noteworthy here is that the available framework
of associationist psychology, with its emphasis on memory's coherence,
allows Horne to articulate the congruence between Dickens's mental qualities—particularly his unusually retentive memory—and his representational
strategies. Horne points to the effects of Dickens's serial novels in reproducing in the reader's mind the very contours of the way that the author's own
thinking assimilates and orders reality. This coordination in turn produces

the larger educational and social reformist impact of Dickens's celebrity authorship on a reading public.

Like readers' attachments to his characters, their attachment to Dickens's public persona could function as a conduit through which to channel social sympathy toward individuals and classes of people. These are the aspects of the pleasures of memory that also became associated with Dickens's "Englishness" and later with his status as a canonical author within the English curriculum. A visual illustration of this connection between Dickens's mind and his authorial and social influence appears in Daniel Maclise's sketch of Dickens's first formal "performance" of one of his works, a reading of his forthcoming Christmas book *The Chimes*, at John Forster's rooms in December 1844 before an audience of friends, many of whom were also writers. The sketch shows Dickens with a starlike corona emanating from his head (Figure 6). Dickens is depicted not so much as a saint but rather as radiating the charisma associated with his power as celebrity author to change the world through the effects of his writings. The strong emotional reactions of his friends reported by Maclise—"shrieks of laughter" and "floods of tears"—also seem to have confirmed to Dickens that the story had succeeded in striking the "Sledge hammer" blow for the poor that he had intended.[187]

The visibility of Dickens's celebrity began to be more prominent as his career progressed. Because of his publishers' use of his image as a marketing tool, Dickens's portrait became increasingly available to readers as an icon of his authorial persona. Dickens himself used a line-drawing portrait for promotional purposes as early as 1837, in an advertisement of his new editorship of *Bentley's Miscellany*, and as part of a prospectus for *Master Humphrey's Clock*.[188] Two portraits that Gerard Curtis has documented as pivotal to the marketing of Dickens's image are the Daniel Maclise portrait commissioned by Chapman and Hall to be presented as a gift to Dickens at a banquet celebrating him, which also appeared as an engraved frontispiece to the final installment of *Nicholas Nickleby* in 1839, and the *New Spirit of the Age* frontispiece of 1844 (Figure 6). Since they held the copyright, Chapman and Hall could sell copies of the engraving of the Maclise portrait as a separate issue, and they also used it in advertisements of later Dickens publications. The mass production of Dickens's image seems to have taken off in the 1850s, particularly as a result of the wider availability of photographs, making Dickens's face more widely familiar by the 1860s. According to Curtis, Dickens sat "for over eighty photographs in his life," including "an exclusive sitting for the photographer Gurney in New York to promote his

AT 58, LINCOLNS INN FIELDS, MONDAY THE 2ⁿᵈ OF DECEMBER 1844.

Figure 6. "Dickens Reading *The Chimes* in John Forster's Rooms at Lincoln's Inn Fields, Monday, the 2nd of December, 1844," a sketch by Daniel Maclise. Mary Evans Picture Library. The other persons present were (clockwise from left) John Forster, Douglas Jerrold, Laman Blanchard, Thomas Carlyle, W. J. Fox, Alexander Dyce, William Harness, Clarkson Stanfield, Daniel Maclise, and Dickens's son Francis.

[second] American reading tour" in 1867.[189] One of these images produced for American consumption during Dickens's 1867–68 tour, a lithograph portrait of the author by Solomon Eytinge Jr., shows Dickens with his quill pen poised over the page and about to write, but also glancing sideways at the viewer with his famous penetrating look (Figure 7).[190]

Now we have a rich context in which to interpret Professor A. W. Ward's 1870 account of Dickens's influence on common reading, which I quoted in the preface: "[Dickens's] imagination could call up at will those associations which, could we but summon them in full number, would bind together the human family, and make that expression no longer a name but a living reality."[191] This affirmation of Dickens's mind as an image of cultural unification seems to have gelled in the weeks and months after his

"And so, as Tiny Tim observed, God bless us every one!"

Charles Dickens.

Figure 7. Lithograph portrait of Charles Dickens, 1867–68, by Solomon Eytinge Jr. Frontispiece to Frederic G. Kitton, *Dickens and His Illustrators* (London, 1899). Courtesy of Thomas Recchio.

sudden death in June 1870. Queen Victoria's immediate response to Dickens's decease, recorded in her diary, describes her impressions of a recent meeting during which Dickens chose to discuss with the monarch his hopes for "a much greater union of classes" in Victorian society: "He is a very great loss. He had a large loving mind and the strongest sympathy with the poorer classes."[192] The novelist's mind, accessible through his works, personifies not only the universalizing powers of literature but also the sympathetic (rather than consumerist or merely imitative) bonds of a mass readership. From its beginnings in the late 1830s, when "Boz's" name became "familiar" on everyone's lips, Dickens's celebrity had developed by the1870s into a marketable and canonical image of the modern author's originality and humanitarian influence.

Celebrity's Afterlife

By the time of Dickens's extensive public readings in Britain and the United States in the 1850s and 1860s, such practices as reading aloud, rereading and sharing installments, and exchanging phrases and jokes associated with popular scenes and characters, as well as theatrical adaptations and the marketing of "Pickwickiana" and other Dickens-themed images and goods, had made Dickens's novels and characters widely recognizable and familiar, even to persons who had not read them.[193] This chapter's history of Dickens's celebrity suggests that from the beginning, many readers probably learned to correlate whatever disparate effects they experienced from reading Dickens's novels with specific attributes of Dickens himself, as author and as public personality. This chapter's epigraph from American writer Kate Douglas Wiggin's autobiography indicates the growing cultural presence of literary celebrity in the nineteenth century, so that in looking back from the perspective of the early 1920s, Wiggin realizes that a child of her day might not be able to approach a famous author: "She would have heard of celebrity hunters, and autograph collectors, and be self-conscious, while I followed the dictates of my countrified little heart, and scraped acquaintance confidently with the magician who had glorified my childhood by his art."[194] By noticing how celebrity authorship as an image of national culture and mass reading as participation in a common culture started out as *linked and interdependent but not identical* phenomena, we can understand the sense of modernity and change marked by Jowett's idea of Dickens's influence as "occupy[ing] a greater space than any other writer in the minds of Englishmen during the last thirty-five years," that is, as consisting simultaneously of personal and cultural associations that have been shared and transmitted across a mass public in markedly new ways.[195] The idea of Dickens's authorship as standing for a common English culture was not a given in the early part of his career, but his style of authorship became associated with the institutionalization of English literature itself in the decades after his death—a development that I discuss in detail in Chapter 6.

Writing in 1939, George Orwell confirms the consolidation of this canonical image of Dickens's mind as both representative and culturally encompassing, but in a somewhat different sense. Orwell wonders, "Why does anyone care about Dickens? Why do I care about Dickens?" and then answers his question by referring to the common experience of reading Dickens's novels in childhood. Dickens's "familiarity," Orwell hypothesizes, hinges on "the memories they call up," so that "the same forces of association are at work" when one is thinking about Dickens as in thinking about a patriotic poem that one had to memorize in school and actively disagrees with in later life. But, Orwell asks, is Dickens then for the modern reader "merely an institution?" "If so, he is an institution that there is no getting away from. How often one really thinks about any writer, even a writer one cares for, is a difficult thing to decide; but I should doubt whether anyone who has actually read Dickens can go a week without remembering him in one context or another. . . . At any moment some scene or character, which may come from some book you cannot even remember the name of, is liable to drop into your mind."[196] Despite his distaste for what feel like compulsory aspects of Dickens's status as part of the literary establishment, Orwell still carries Dickens's characters around in his head and still thinks of his influence as acting through the reader's mental associations. Such associations no longer are pedagogically operative in themselves for Orwell but have rather become memories of childhood reading that attest to the role of Dickens's novels in transmitting a national culture through the schools. However, Orwell still asserts the peculiar quality that Dickens's fictions and characters seem to possess of being original and memorable, and thus remaining modern and relevant.

Echoing Ward, Orwell claims that the "central secret of his popularity" is Dickens's "generosity of mind" and his ability to represent "in a comic, simplified and therefore memorable form the native decency of the common man."[197] At the end of his long essay, Orwell draws a portrait of Dickens as his novels seem to conjure him up in the mind of the reader, based on the idea that "when one reads any strongly individual piece of writing, one has the impression of seeing a face somewhere behind the page":

Well, in the case of Dickens I see a face that is not quite the face of Dickens's photographs, though it resembles it. It is the face of a man of about forty, with a small beard and a high colour. He is laughing, with a touch of anger in his laughter, but no triumph, no malignity. It is the face of a man who is always fighting against something, but who fights in the open and is not frightened, the face of a man who is generously angry—in other words, of a nineteenth-century liberal, a free intelligence, a type hated with equal hatred by all the smelly little orthodoxies which are now contending for our souls.[198]

It is tempting to associate Orwell's portrait of Dickens from memory with an actual photograph of Dickens from 1859 showing him on the podium for one of his early public readings (Figure 8). In this photograph, Dickens is not laughing, but his expression seems to convey the kind of earnestness and open-mindedness that Orwell recalls in a politically heightened form in his composite image of Dickens's authorial persona and cultural impact. Given how readily Orwell can conjure up Dickens's animated face in his own mind, we can see that Dickens's image has garnered some of the strongly visual qualities of modern celebrity.

Writing during the ascendancy in Europe of both Communism and fascism, Orwell portrays Dickens as an anti-totalitarian figure—a representative of the "free intelligence" that Orwell associates with a nonpartisan but politically engaged version of Victorian liberalism. Corresponding to Ward's notion that Dickens's mind encompasses the history of human associations, Orwell argues that Dickens's persona stands for the possibility of derailing automatic thinking, along with the "smelly little orthodoxies" of dogmatic political ideologies. If Dickens is no longer a living celebrity, it seems that he still exists for Orwell as a viable historical mentality and as a figure of the modern intellectual. But both of these representative positions that Dickens occupies in modern culture and in Orwell's own mental space are still to be accessed and made newly relevant through the reading of his novels.

The question that remains for us to investigate in subsequent chapters is how idiosyncratic or typical Orwell's response to Dickens might have been: could such a view of Dickens come through the English curriculum, for example? My argument going forward is that Orwell's image of Dickens is a salient example of the blending of popular and elite cultural forms of reception, so that the intellectual's stance remains indebted to the serial pleasures of memory represented by Dickens's celebrity authorship that became available to a mass readership in the second half of the nineteenth century.

Figure 8. Charles Dickens giving a public reading, by (George) Herbert Watkins, albumen print, April 29, 1858. © National Portrait Gallery, London.

The next three chapters elucidate how the popular associationism that I have analyzed in Victorian reviewers' and critics' responses to the Dickens phenomenon underpins the pedagogical effects of Dickens's novels on readers. I show how Dickens's serial novels explicitly thematize the pleasures of memory, engage in contemporary debates over the emergence of a national education system, and teach readers to imagine themselves as participants in a democratic mass audience. The following chapter delineates the development of what I characterize as Dickens's anti-sectarian, democratic project in his fiction by investigating his competition in the 1840s with the evangelical movement's aggressive forays into the market for popular serial fiction.

3.   *The Pleasures of Memory, Part I*

Curiosity as Didacticism in *The Old Curiosity Shop*

> Curiosity is a vice that has been stigmatized in turn by Christianity, by philosophy, and even by a certain conception of science. Curiosity is seen as futility. However, I like the word; it suggests something quite different to me. It evokes "care"; it evokes the care one takes of what exists and what might exist; a sharpened sense of reality, but one that is never immobilized before it; a readiness to find what surrounds us strange and odd; a certain determination to throw off familiar ways of thought and to look at the same things in a different way; a passion for seizing what is happening now and what is disappearing; a lack of respect for the traditional hierarchies of what is important and fundamental.
>
>   Michel Foucault, "The Masked Philosopher"

In the previous two chapters, I have been investigating both how the associationist pleasures of memory imply a regulated freedom of thought activated and implemented in reading and how the figure of Dickens as celebrity author could channel the individual reader's attachment to the "fictitious realities" of Dickens's serial novels into larger group affiliations, such as a reading audience, a school, a democratic constituency, or a national culture. These circuits of linked associations create operative analogies and practical connections among the individual's train of thought, reading as a form of learning and experience, and the transacted commercial and social linkages of expanding nineteenth-century print culture. Such associations, however, also involved readers in competing forms of inculcation, whether religious, political, pedagogical, aesthetic, market based (as in advertising), or cultural. Religious messages were particularly pervasive in reading materials geared toward poor and working-class readers, who acquired their varying degrees of literacy within the voluntary schools sponsored by Anglicans and Dissenters. Like religious fiction, Dickensian serial novels also incorporated specific methods for communicating, interpreting, and even implementing their moral lessons.

While Dickens was a frequent critic of overbearing religious zeal in fiction, education, and politics, he was also widely perceived as exerting a strong moral influence over his popular readership. Writing in 1840 that Dickens "is now performing most efficaciously the office of a moral teacher," an anonymous reviewer related this impact to Dickens's provision of morally instructive fiction for the newly literate among the poor: "There are even millions who are just emerging from ignorance into what may be called good reading classes; all of whom Mr. Dickens is educating to honesty, good feeling, and all the finer impulses of humanity. He is the antidote, and a powerful one too, to the writers of the *Jack Sheppard* school [of popular Newgate crime fiction]."[1] Just after Dickens's death in 1870, another article in a working-class satirical periodical celebrated Dickens as "not only a romancer" but a "mighty preacher."[2] Dickens's close friend and biographer John Forster also attributes a reformative effect to *The Old Curiosity Shop* (1840–41), particularly in its depiction of Little Nell's death, describing its impact in personal terms as "a kind of discipline of feeling and emotion which would do me lasting good, and which I would not thank you for as an ordinary enjoyment of literature."[3] These accounts of the moral effects of Dickens's novels represent a common perception among Victorian critics that his authorship combined the kinds of influence exerted by the educator, clergyman, moral philosopher, and liberal parent.

Such assessments attribute to Dickens's novels a more forceful program to sway the reader than was commonly associated with literature, and that was closer to the type of didacticism typical of tracts published by religious societies for the conversion of the poor. In *Our Mutual Friend* (1864–65), Dickens satirizes didactic religious fiction for children, describing the kinds of stories read by Charley Hexam in a London Ragged School: "Young women old in the vices of the commonest and worst life, were expected to profess themselves enthralled by the good child's book, the Adventures of Little Margery, who resided in the village cottage by the mill; severely reproved and morally squashed the miller when she was five and he was fifty; divided her porridge with singing birds; denied herself a new nankeen bonnet, on the ground that the turnips did not wear nankeen bonnets, neither did the sheep who ate them; who plaited straw and delivered the dreariest orations to all comers, at all sorts of unseasonable times." This curriculum also conveys a motive for young readers to acquiesce in its moral schemes—as Dickens puts it, the message that "you were to do good, not because it *was* good, but because you were to make a good thing of it.''[4] Moral improvement is made potentially attractive to these precociously mature children when it is attached to the inducement of profit. In attacking this attempt to provide a self-serving incentive for goodness, however, Dickens does not imply that all kinds of fictional didacticism are similarly ineffective or hypocritical.

In his 1838 preface to *Oliver Twist* (1837–39), Dickens claims for his novel a similarly powerful impact that imagines how novel reading can affect society: "It appeared to me that to draw a knot of such associates in crime as really did exist; to paint them in all their deformity, in all their wretchedness, in all the squalid misery of their lives; to show them as they really are, . . . would be to attempt something which was needed, and which would be a service to society.''[5] Dickens describes his own technique as a realistic representation of the conditions that create a "knot" of criminal "associates," so that his narrative should duplicate these causal links and convey them in a form that could make such knowledge socially useful. Yet he also emphasizes the superior power of fiction to effect change in the reader. Of his own didactic and "realistic" depictions of lower-class crime, the young Dickens asks, "Have they no lesson, and do they not whisper something beyond the little-regarded warning of an abstract moral precept?''[6] This claim to "whisper something''—to insinuate a lesson—should be taken as only a preliminary figure for the more pervasive kinds of reformative and pedagogical effects of Dickens's version of popular literature.

In this chapter, I argue that the narrative strategies for promoting the reader's conversion developed by writers of religious tracts for the poor provide an important precursor to the more secular moral influence that reviewers attributed to Dickens's novels and that he claimed in the preface to *Oliver Twist*. In *The Old Curiosity Shop*, Dickens goes beyond an opposition between "abstract precepts" and surreptitious "lessons" to provide both the overt and subtle forms of instruction present in *Oliver Twist*, but this time in a generic opposition to religious fiction. Popular cheap fiction before Dickens's time often took the form of chapbooks and didactic religious tracts. *The Old Curiosity Shop* makes pointed reference to the influential didactic genre of Evangelical religious tracts by including an effigy of the famous Evangelical woman of letters, Hannah More, who became "the most successful propagandist of the 1790s" through her writing of short religious tales for the poor and anti-Jacobin political tracts.[7] In an attempt to "conciliate the favour" of the proprietresses and students of boarding schools for

young ladies in the vicinity of her waxwork exhibition, Mrs. Jarley transforms some of her wax figures to suit the academic taste: Mr. Grimaldi
dressed as a clown is redressed as Mr. Lindley Murray, the famous grammar-
ian, and "a murderess of great renown" is changed into Mrs. Hannah More,
while Mary Queen of Scots, "in a dark wig, white shirt-collar, and male
attire, was such a complete image of Lord Byron that the young ladies quite
screamed when they saw it."[8] More's inclusion in *The Old Curiosity Shop* as
a waxwork dummy alludes to her stock of characters and formulaic didactic
strategies.[9]

Although she began her career as a dramatist, after her conversion to "serious Christianity" More shaped her writing to carry out the Evangelical
goal of "converting the nation to vital religion," meaning an active life of a
serious Christian striving toward personal salvation and charitable works in
aid of the poor.[10] More became a widely read author through her contributions of didactic fiction to an early Evangelical publishing venture, the
Cheap Repository of Moral and Religious Tracts, a collection of short religious tales by various authors. Published anonymously between 1795 and
1798, the tracts included in the Cheap Repository were distributed at workhouses, hospitals, and prisons, and to the rural poor, charity children, and
students at Sunday schools, and sold by booksellers and itinerant hawkers
for between a halfpenny and one-and-one-half pennies per issue. During
the initial four-year period of their publication, several million copies were
put into circulation.[11] *The Old Curiosity Shop* positions Dickens's brand of
serial fiction to contest evangelical cultural politics both within the mid-
Victorian marketplace for cheap fiction and in the minds of readers. The
"consolation" that Nell's death should provide the reader, articulated most
concisely in the passage of the novel labeled "the schoolmaster's lesson," is
meant to challenge Evangelical didactic fiction's narrative transactions and
pedagogical access into the reader's moral life.[12]

In reconceiving the kind of moral lesson that a child heroine like Nell
could teach, *The Old Curiosity Shop* also disassociates the new medium of
serial fiction from an Evangelical providentialist epistemology, with its
view of literacy as a means of social control and of reading as a means
of conversion. Nell herself recalls the sanctified children of Evangelical
deathbed stories. Yet before her death, through her exposure to moralizing characters, poverty, and the suffering associated with the industrial
city, Nell also acts as a surrogate for the poor or working-class reader targeted by didactic religious tracts.[13] Through Nell's story, the novel reme-
diates the conventions of didactic religious fiction by undermining

Evangelical fiction's overt linkage of personal salvation to conservative politics and a calculus of economic self-interest and by substituting an alternative logic that I term "anti-didactic" because of its explicit critique of Evangelical didacticism.[14] At the same time, I analyze how *The Old Curiosity Shop* also constitutes a new self-reflexive form of novelistic didacticism based in curiosity as a secular inducement to reading that still has the potential to change the reader's mind and behavior.

The competition between early Dickensian serials and religious tracts becomes even more apparent in light of the associationist underpinnings of the highly popular stories of the deaths of pious children published at the beginning of the nineteenth century by the Evangelical clergyman Legh Richmond. Both *The Old Curiosity Shop* and Richmond's stories allude to Samuel Rogers's associationist poem *The Pleasures of Memory* (1792), and both theorize the associative serial memory as a source of the reader's engagement with and retention of the narrative's scenes and teachings. Dickens's novel does not simply provide a critique of Evangelical fiction's didacticism, but in its pervasive use of contrast as an organizing associative metaphoric and narrative principle, and as a spur to the reader's speculative interest, *The Old Curiosity Shop* devises a secular and novelistic epistemology based on curiosity. By assigning curiosity's pejorative, rapacious, and prurient connotations in the dwarf Quilp and his entourage, Dickens distinguishes an affirmative version of curiosity as "care," to adopt Michel Foucault's term for the equally epistemological and ethical desire to recognize the world's strangeness and thus to create an opening for novelty and change. Curiosity in *The Old Curiosity Shop* becomes a new kind of didacticism, affording a means to instruct the reader in an ethical investment in the narrative that is meant to lead directly to actions that benefit others through a commitment to social justice for the poor rather than personal salvation.[15]

In conclusion, I argue that by charting the transformation of the conventions of religious didacticism into curiosity in this novel, we can also perceive how it directly addresses and attempts to redirect a set of expectations that its readers would have carried over to serial fiction from their religious schooling. By studying how the novel itself anticipates and attempts to influence its own reception, therefore, we can also understand more clearly the specific reading practices that contributed to the lasting success of Dickens's serial novels.

Evangelical Publishing and Cultural Politics

As historian Ian Bradley has stated of the evangelicals' "cult of conduct," "If they could not convert the entire population of England to vital Christianity, the Evangelicals hoped at least to make sure that all should act as though they had been."[16] The evangelical religious revival from the mid–eighteenth century through the mid-nineteenth involved both Anglicans and dissenting denominations such as the Wesleyan Methodists. Beyond the specific activities of both of these large and varied denominations, the general effects of "permeation by filtration" of evangelical ways of life and thinking into Victorian culture were pervasive and widely recognized at the time by Victorian novelists and intellectuals.[17] Bradley estimates that "by 1850 there were probably between two and three million people in England who regarded themselves as Evangelical Christians," but the numbers of people in Britain and its colonies affected by evangelical missions, publications, schools, and charitable work were vastly greater.[18]

Numerous evangelical associations exerted pressure on the monarch and on Parliament to undertake specific kinds of reforms during the early decades of the nineteenth century. Evangelicals were convinced that the reform of British morals depended on strict observance of the Sabbath. This was a crucial platform of the Society for the Suppression of Vice reorganized in 1802, which also pursued legislation to crack down on prostitution, adultery, and the publication and sale of books that it considered indecent.[19] Evangelical politicians also exerted significant influence in major social reform causes between the 1780s and 1860s. William Wilberforce's piety led him to crusade in Parliament for the abolition of the slave trade, which took place in 1833 in Britain and its colonies. The devout Evangelical Anthony Ashley Cooper, Earl of Shaftesbury, assumed leadership in passing the Factory Act of 1847, which limited the working day of women and children to ten hours, and he also undertook significant responsibility for the reform of lunatic asylums.[20]

Evangelical efforts to reach and convert the growing audience of nineteenth-century readers were massive. For example, the Religious Tract Society, founded in 1799, could count a circulation by 1849 of "over 500 million copies of 5,000 separate publications," and at that date the society was also publishing tracts at a rate of twenty million per year.[21] Evangelical periodicals also proliferated from the end of the eighteenth century through the first half of the nineteenth, beginning with the dissenting *Evangelical*

Magazine (1793–1904), the Clapham Sect's influential *Christian Observer* (1802–72), the Calvinist *Christian Guardian* (1809–49), and the moderate Calvinist *Record* (1828–1923).[22] Evangelicals were also able to exercise a significant influence over Victorian readers' access to and selection of books. Charles Mudie was an evangelical and Dissenter who made sure that his network of Mudie's Select Circulating Libraries, initiated in 1842, lent only books that met appropriate standards of morality. Methodist W. H. Smith, who owned virtually all the railway station bookstalls, also restricted his offerings to publications that were deemed morally and religiously orthodox.[23] According to Bradley, by the 1860s "Evangelical standards of taste gradually came to predominate among publishers and authors."[24] Evangelicals were also responsible for founding, organizing, and administering hundreds of schools for the poor throughout Britain, including the Ragged Schools for the street children of London, which numbered more than one hundred and were educating over 100,000 children by 1850.[25]

Evangelical tracts and periodicals often appealed to readers through an analogy between spiritual and economic gains and stirred up readers' fears of damnation with a message about human depravity and original sin. The *Evangelical Magazine* celebrated the publication of religious literature as a defeat of "the novelists," who were imagined to be in league with the devil: "Because the enemy of mankind hath dressed Vice and Licentiousness in these engaging forms, must we therefore wholly surrender them to his service? By no means. Rather let us restore them to the cause of Virtue and Religion."[26] Given this anti-novel stance of many Evangelical publications, it makes sense that Dickens would turn the tables and assert the moral authority of his brand of popular novel. In his fiction and social commentary, Dickens could not overlook the mass influence of religious tracts, particularly those penned by Evangelicals, upon children and working-class readers. As Richard D. Altick points out, "it was through the publication of the Cheap Repository Tracts that influential middle-class Englishmen got their first experience in the mass production and distribution of reading matter," while "religious literature formed the largest single category of books published in Britain" during the nineteenth century.[27]

Dickens's satirical representations of evangelicals in his fiction target both Dissenters and Anglicans alike. Salient examples include Mr. Stiggins in *The Pickwick Papers* (1836–37), who is either a chapel-going Methodist or Low Church Evangelical Anglican; Evangelicals Mr. Chadband and Mrs. Pardiggle in *Bleak House* (1852–53); and strict Calvinist Anglican Evangelicals Mr. and Miss Murdstone in *David Copperfield* (1849–50) and Mrs. Clennam in

Little Dorrit (1855–57). It is also important to note, however, that Dickens publicly supported several reform efforts led by prominent Victorian Evangelicals, including the efforts of Lord Ashley (Shaftesbury) to reform child labor laws in the 1840s.[28] It was the Evangelicals' cultural politics, I argue, that Dickens attempted to undermine and displace in his serial fiction by personifying a critique of their judgmental mentality and interfering behavior toward the poor in individual characters, and in this way also criticizing evangelicals' proselytizing rationales for fiction. The Anglican Evangelicals, who held many positions in the church and government, were the most important organized middle-class cultural movement outside political parties to be reckoned with by a popular novelist such as Dickens who was establishing a nonsectarian and democratic influence for popular literature in shaping reading audiences. Considered in light of the absence of a national school system, the Evangelicals' work in founding schools for the poor and their extensive ventures into the mass production of religious publications can be understood within this book's framework of cultural history as a concerted attempt to shape a religiously based cultural politics that, like Dickens's own popularity, could cut across the social classes.

The Old Curiosity Shop *and Cheap Repository Logic*

Victorian estimations of Dickens's novels as exerting a positive moral influence also rehearsed a long-standing critical discussion about the moral impact of fiction that incorporated both secular and religious rationales.[29] Writing in 1750, Samuel Johnson singles out "the young, the ignorant, and the idle" as the intended audience of "familiar histories," "to whom they serve as lectures of conduct, and introductions into life." Yet the "knowledge of vice and virtue" that these novelistic examples impart comes with a surcharge of authority that derives not only from the youthful mind's unformed state but also, Johnson implies, from the fictional medium itself, because of the close cooperation of memory and imagination: "But if the power of example is so great, as to take possession of the memory by a kind of violence, and produce effects almost without the intervention of the will, care ought to be taken, that when the choice is unrestrained, the best examples only should be exhibited; and that which is likely to operate so strongly, should not be mischievous or uncertain in its effects."[30] Johnson imputes to fiction an impact on the youthful reader's memory that is at least equivalent to, and perhaps greater than, experience.

Related assumptions about the superiority of narrative example to the articulation of "axioms and definitions" in transmitting morality were shared by many late eighteenth- and early nineteenth-century writers, who turned to fiction in order to convey religious teachings and thus uphold the existing social and political order.[31] In her essay "On the Origin and Progress of Novel-Writing" (1810), Anna Laetitia Barbauld defended the reputation of the "humble novel" because of its "very strong effect in infusing principles and moral feelings," giving particular credit to Maria Edgeworth's works for children: "When works of fancy are thus made subservient to the improvement of the rising generation, they certainly stand on a higher ground than mere entertainment, and we revere what we admire."[32] Writing in the 1830s, Sarah Stickney Ellis, a Quaker-turned-Congregationalist author of temperance tales and popular conduct books for women, apologizes to her fellow Christians for her presumption in writing fiction by defending the greater effectiveness of a story in attracting the attention of resistant readers who lack a Christian perspective and knowledge of the Bible: "Fiction may be compared to a key, which opens many minds that would be closed against a sermon." She echoes Johnson's condemnation of "some writers [who] have confounded good and evil, making vice interesting and virtue insipid," but she stresses not so much fiction's ability to imprint patterns of understanding and behavior in the young as its capacity to provoke sympathy in mature readers: "by the contemplation of ideal characters . . . we are sometimes led on towards conviction; our feelings become softened in sympathy with theirs, we unconsciously pronounce our own condemnation, and conscience makes the application."[33] Thus didactic fiction appeals to the adult reader's conscience in order to instigate a moral and religious conversion through the unconscious "application" of its message to his or her own case.

In the preface to a collected edition of her *Repository Tales*, More argues that reading produces "a bias on the actings of the mind, though with a greater or less degree of inclination, according to the degree of impression made, by the nature of the subject, the ability of the writer, and the disposition of the reader." While the author cannot expect a "*general* effect" on the reader, she can hope that "some truth may be picked out from among many that are neglected; some single sentiment may be seized on for present use; some detached principle may be treasured up for future practice." More frames her sense of the necessary consonance between her prose style and the reader's intellectual capacities as a business relationship:

There must be, not merely that intelligibility which arises from the perspicu-
ousness of the author, but that also which depends on the capacity and
perception of the reader. Between him who writes, and him who reads,
there must be a kind of coalition of interests, something of a partnership
(however unequal the capital) in mental property; a sort of joint-stock of
tastes and ideas. The student must have been initiated into the same intellectual commerce with him whom he studies; for large bills are only negotiable among the mutually opulent.[34]

Imagining the relationship between author and reader in simultaneously
economic and pedagogical terms, More argues that a narrative should function as the reader's "initiation" into the intellectual level required to comprehend it. The educated author must supply the larger share of "capital"
for the "joint-stock of tastes and ideas," so that the ensuing "intellectual
commerce" does not greatly exceed the reader's intellectual preparation but
still invites his or her "partnership." To tax excessively the reader's mental
resources would be to present him or her with a bill too "large" to be repaid
in kind.

Such a transaction through the reading of fiction should instill a simultaneously moral and social or political "coalition of interests" that is the
ultimate aim of the didactic writer. More translates the notion of reading
as a business transaction into her larger understanding of the social contract that sustains the class hierarchy within British society. More grants
fiction a lesser power over the moral life of the reader than does Johnson
in order to emphasize the greater importance of Bible reading. Yet her
account of the business deal between the author and reader of her stories
posits both an analogy and a clear causal connection among spiritual, intellectual, and material "profits" that was a common feature of middle-class
English Protestantism.[35]

As More explained her moral and political motives, the stories distributed
under the imprint of the Cheap Repository were written "to improve the
habits, and raise the principles of the common people," and to satisfy the
"appetite for reading . . . among the inferior ranks in this country" with
"such wholesome aliment as might give a new direction to their taste, and
abate their relish for those corrupt and inflammatory publications which the
consequences of the French revolution have been so fatally pouring in upon
us."[36] The Cheap Repository was part of the Evangelicals' more general
undertaking of "managing public opinion,"[37] but More, who initiated and
oversaw the project, envisioned the tracts as a replacement for other forms

of popular cheap fiction such as chapbooks and ballads. "To teach the poor to *read*, without providing them with safe books," More warned, "is a dangerous measure."[38] In preparation for her writing, More purchased and consulted a variety of chapbooks, and her contributions to the Cheap Repository "made a point-by-point attack" on the popular songs, lewd verse, and sensational adventure and crime stories that chapbooks typically included.[39] Hannah's sister Martha (Patty) More's description of the system by which the sisters organized Sunday schools for the poor in the Mendip Hills of Somerset is also applicable to More's own views of her fiction: "Principles, not opinions, are what I labour to give them."[40]

More's tracts set the initial generic standard for nineteenth-century didactic religious fiction. One of her longest stories, *The Shepherd of Salisbury Plain*, displays the characteristic logic and repertoire of rhetorical figures that the reader was meant to acquire as a mental "joint-stock" of Evangelical habits and piety. As the story opens, a middle-class "gentleman," Mr. Johnson, encounters a shepherd whose piety piques his charitable interest. The shepherd and his family win the patronage of this traveling gentleman and the local clergyman not only because, upon inspection, their persons, dwelling, and food are found to be clean and modest but also because of the shepherd's ability to cite biblical verses and stories and to interpret them in simultaneously doctrinally appropriate and commonsensical ways. Even though the family has very little time to read, they have all memorized large parts of the Bible, which the shepherd considers "a kind of stock and trade for a Christian to set up with."[41] He explains that although he is too occupied with his sheep to read during the week, he still recalls biblical passages while he works, and this helps him "to keep out bad thoughts too" (197). In this memorized and habitual form, the Bible becomes a way and means of life, as the shepherd explains: "I have led but a lonely life, and have often had but little to eat; but my Bible has been meat, drink, and company to me, as I may say" (180). The shepherd displays the correlation between habitual piety and subsistence economy that ultimately gains him greater material rewards at the end of the story. The shepherd's rhetorical agility mirrors his didactic capacity to exemplify the blessings of poverty, so that his disregard for his material needs, based on their constant resignification as spiritual gains, makes him a representative of "true goodness" (187).

The shepherd's rhetoric also represents the intellectual maneuvers accompanying a spiritual change or conversion to serious Evangelical piety of the kind that the narrative hopes to inspire. When faced with an "actual want" such as hunger, the shepherd strives to "live upon the promises" of

faith (184). He supplies an analogy that, in displaying the limits of its application, permits the comprehension of the abstract concept of eternity: "There
is some comparison between a moment and a thousand years, because a
thousand years are made up of moments, all time being made up of the same
sort of stuff, as I may say; while there is no sort of comparison between
the longest portion of time and eternity" (185). The shepherd understands
privation as measurable, and thus finite and temporary, while his faith rests
on the corresponding, opposite conception of the infinite and eternal reward of salvation.[42] More's tale lends narrative form to this logic of abstraction and incommensurability, and the shepherd also teaches it as the product
both of his own Bible reading and of the reading of the tale in which he
figures. Such a logic, the tale implies, can be reproduced as a set of maxims
even when it is not fully understood, as in More's imagining of reading as
facilitating a "joint-stock" of interest between readers of "unequal" intellectual "capital." It is no coincidence, then, that in later editions of the story,
the visitors find among the meager stock of texts pasted on the "clean white
walls" of the shepherd's cottage the tale "Patient Joe, or the Newcastle Collier," one of More's other contributions to the Cheap Repository that recounts the patience under extremities of another pious working man (190).
The shepherd is not only an exemplary character in a tract but also an ideal
reader and emulator of didactic fiction whose thinking exemplifies the general Christian principles permitting the person of modest intellectual means
to abstract his wants from the material to the spiritual.

At the end of the tale, the shepherd does not have to live on the "meat
and drink" of faith and his memorized Bible. Instead, as a reward for his
piety, he is given an improved, subsidized cottage and nominated to the post
of parish clerk. Most important, he and his wife are also appointed as Sunday
school teachers. While the shepherd performs good actions for their own
sake, the story nevertheless shows him profiting materially as well as spiritually from his sincere professions of faith to the visiting gentry. In this way,
More provides a fictional demonstration of the economic principles that
supported Evangelical belief and practice. The Clapham Sect of Anglican
Evangelicals, with which More was affiliated, inaugurated "a tradition of
communicating the Gospel in commercial terms."[43] Evangelical writers and
preachers employed phrases such as "To close with the offer of God in
Christ" and "To acquire a saving interest in the Blood of Jesus."[44] This connection between religious and economic principles not only was rhetorical
but, as historian Boyd Hilton has argued, also supported the more general
evangelical defense of free trade according to the "psychological premise

[of] . . . the supremacy of economic conscience, the latter innate in man yet needing to be nurtured into a habitude through the mechanism of the free market, with its constant operation of temptation, trial, and exemplary suffering."[45] This economic and spiritual equation cut both ways, therefore, as it also gave a providential connotation to the operations of the free market. Critics of evangelical defenses of the personal ethics of capitalism, such as Dickens, however, would refuse to distinguish between enlightened economic interest, or "economic conscience," and selfish or exploitative self-interest.[46]

Another of More's more lengthy tales offers an even more explicit example of the economic logic employed to explain the spiritual benefits of faith. *The Two Wealthy Farmers; or, The History of Mr. Bragwell*, written in the form of a dialogue, recounts the downfall of Farmer Bragwell, whose religion rests on his sense of propriety and social obligation rather than sincere Christian belief. He represents the middle- and upper-class readers also targeted by the evangelical movement's attempts to turn nominal Christians away from their worldly ambitions and toward sincere piety and Christian mission. At one point in the story, Bragwell defends to his pious neighbor, Mr. Worthy, his exorbitant gains in an auction of some land that he purposely scheduled to take place immediately after all the bidders had eaten their fill and become drunk. Bragwell argues that as long as he has done nothing illegal and has added up his profits correctly, he has only followed the common "practice of people of credit." But Worthy refutes him:

> Sir, I am talking of final accounts, spiritual calculations, arithmetic in the long run. Now, in this your real Christian is the only true calculator: he has found out that we shall be richer in the end, by denying than by indulging ourselves. He knows, that when the balance comes to be struck, when profit and loss shall be summed up, and the final account adjusted, that whatever ease, prosperity, and delight we had in this world, yet if we have lost our souls in the end, we cannot reckon that we have made a good bargain. We cannot pretend that a few items of present pleasure make any great figure, set over against the sum total of eternal misery. So you see it is only for want of a good head at calculation, that men prefer time to eternity, pleasure to holiness, earth to heaven. (74)

Mr. Bragwell's later financial ruin and the deaths of his son and daughter (attributed to parental indulgence and novel reading, respectively) prove that he has calculated poorly, in terms of temporary worldly gain and vanity. While Mr. Worthy constantly attempts to expose the "false standard" (73) upon which Bragwell acts, he uses economic motives and logic to persuade him of the superior spiritual "bargain" of a Christian life that would ultimately win him the "sum total" of salvation and eternal reward in heaven. Describing Worthy's witnessing of Bragwell's downfall and confession of his sins, the narrator comments that "this moment of outward misery was the only joyful one [Worthy] had ever spent in the Bragwell family," since it signifies not only Bragwell's "real penitence" (93) but also the agency of providence in awakening his recognition of himself as a sinner in need of God's help (79).

In *Oliver Twist*, Dickens draws most overtly on the model of the didactic religious tracts by providing negative examples like that of Farmer Bragwell. Bad associations, in the case of Nancy, or crime and the corruption of children, in the case of Fagin, result in the characters' suffering and death. The transition from *Oliver Twist*'s didacticism to the anti-didacticism of *The Old Curiosity Shop*, however, involves the inclusion of a metacommentary on the fictional lesson, as if one of Dickens's purposes in creating Nell was to convey how it feels to be both the heroine and the object (intended reader) of a didactic tale. Nell's encounter with a school proprietress, Miss Monflathers, enacts this dual role, using formulas like those in More's tales. On an errand to the school to deliver a packet of handbills advertising the wax-works, Nell meets up with Miss Monflathers and her teachers and pupils, lined up, books open, about to take their morning walk. Contradicting her earlier approbation of the waxwork exhibit, Miss Monflathers seizes what seems to be an irresistible opportunity to turn Nell into a negative example and object lesson: "Don't you feel how naughty it is of you . . . to be a wax-work child, when you might have the proud consciousness of assisting, to the extent of your infant powers, the manufactures of your country; of improving your mind by the constant contemplation of the steam-engine; and of earning a comfortable and independent subsistence of from two-and-ninepence to three shillings per week? Don't you know, the harder you are at work, the happier you are?" (308). When one of the teachers begins helpfully to quote some verses authored by the Nonconformist clergyman and writer of famous hymns, Dr. Isaac Watts, Miss Monflathers interrupts her, saying, "The little busy bee . . . is applicable only to genteel children," while in the case of "poor people's children" like Nell, the verse should run, "In work, work, work. In work alway/Let my first years be past,/That I may give for ev'ry day/Some good account at last" (308–9).[47]

In attacking Nell as a naughty and idle waxwork child, the schoolmistress expresses the evangelical disapproval of popular entertainment that literary critics have frequently credited the novel, and Dickens's fiction in general, with attempting to contradict.[48] But the way that Miss Monflathers pedantically berates Nell, along with her connection with the effigy of Hannah More, emphasizes the anti-didactic purpose of the scene: to depict the effects on children and readers of a coercive pedagogy, delivered either by a teacher or by way of religious fiction or didactic poetry. By categorizing Nell as a poor child who should have been a factory girl, Miss Monflathers also leads the reader to imagine her as the heroine of a didactic industrial tale in which, given her physical weakness, she would suffer and die. By showing what it might feel like to become the object of a condescending lesson about one's low social origins, Nell represents the working-class reader targeted by didactic religious tracts. The scene suggests that the novel is willing to pursue its critique of didactic religious fiction to the length of creating a heroine "aware" of the narrative exigencies of her function.

But what does it mean to identify Nell as a figure for the Victorian factory child, if it is Miss Monflathers who teaches us to do so?[49] The narrative locus of Nell's interaction with the factory system occurs during chapters 44 and 45: she is carried bodily to rest inside a hellish metalworks (417–18) and, during a subsequent night of confused wandering, witnesses the destitution of unemployed workers, gazes on the corpses of their children who have died of want, and encounters a tumultuous melee of rioting, "when maddened men, armed with sword and firebrand, spurning the tears and prayers of women who would restrain them, rushed forth on errands of terror and destruction, to work no ruin half so surely as their own" (424–26). The narrator deplores the workers' misguided violence in tones that might have won More's approval, and the description seems to echo the antirevolutionary agenda of her tracts.[50]

Yet this episode also incorporates elements contesting a conservative representation of the discontent of factory workers as primarily self-destructive. When Nell visits one of the workers' hovels to beg for charity, she overhears a conversation between a woman and a "grave gentleman in black" who restores a deaf and dumb boy seized for theft to his mother. The gentleman explains his charitable action by confessing, "I had compassion on his infirmities, and thought he might have learned no better" (427). Another woman present, whose healthy son was transported for theft, responds to this gesture with outrage:

"If you save this boy because he may not know right from wrong, why did you not save mine who was never taught the difference? You gentlemen

have as good a right to punish her boy, that God has kept in ignorance of
sound and speech, as you have to punish mine, that you kept in ignorance
yourselves. . . . —Be a just man, sir, and give me back my son.''

   "You are desperate," said the gentleman, taking out his snuff-box, "and
I am sorry for you.''

   "I *am* desperate," returned the woman, "and you have made me so.''
(428)

Such a scene not only lends its weight to Nell's despair, but also seems to be
an encapsulated anti-didactic tract in which the gentleman who intrudes on
the working-class household is spurned for the ineffectual and hypocritical
nature of his intervention—as if a single act of charity could make up for
generalized neglect and the lack of schools that, in the view of Dickens and
many other supporters of popular education (including those evangelicals
involved in religious outreach through the education of the poor), could
contribute to the prevention of juvenile crime and improvement of the economic prospects of the poor.[51] Unlike More's shepherd, the working-class
woman talks back to the gentleman in black in order to refute the patronizing excuses for their destitution and ignorance offered by middle-class visitors to the poor.

   The disproportionateness of the industrial town's suffering also offers a
subtle criticism of the relation of privation to faith that More's shepherd
describes. In a passage relating Nell and her grandfather's entrance into the
town, the narrator exclaims, as if voicing their thoughts, "Why had they
ever come to this noisy town, when there were peaceful country places, in
which, at least, they might have hungered and thirsted, with less suffering
than in its squalid strife! They were but an atom, here, in a mountain heap
of misery, the very sight of which increased their hopelessness and suffering''
(414). The physical and moral threats of the urban slum makes the kind of
abstraction the shepherd practices impossible, while the spiritual calculus
that supplements subsistence by faith seems plausible only in the seemingly
more gentle conditions of the countryside.[52] Beyond communicating the
starving rioters' desperation and violence, which are terrifying to Nell,
Dickens responds to the Evangelical didactic project of keeping potentially
revolutionary workers in their places with the anti-didactic argument that
misery, agitation, and the potential for revolution persist as natural outcomes
of the harsh conditions of industrial slums. Unlike More's scenario for the
shepherd, who receives his improved housing (with a roof that doesn't leak)
only after he has demonstrated his piety and moral worth, *The Old Curiosity*

Shop argues that concerted measures to provide adequate housing must precede any accurate evaluation of working-class domesticity and morality.[53]

Nell's own anti-didactic role as a potential or surrogate factory child also accounts for the intensity of the narrator's rhetoric surrounding her response to the industrial town. The reader must not forget the anti-didactic lesson of Miss Monflathers's didacticism; it is this stand-in for Hannah More who wants to make Nell a scapegoat for class inequality and the factory system and be done with her.[54] The novel's reworking of the didactic conventions of religious fictions addressed to a readership including the laboring poor and working class suggests that it also targets this section of the growing mass audience for cheap fiction. For a working-class reader, then, the novel's industrial interlude might have seemed familiar in the ways it echoes didactic fiction's usual patronizing warning against "self-destructive" revolt. At the same time, the novel may be capable of provoking a more critical recognition of social injustices through its negative portrayal of paternalistic middle-class interventions into the working-class household.

The Schoolmaster's Consolation

In depicting Nell's suffering and death, *The Old Curiosity Shop* also reworks the focus of Evangelical religious fiction on the edifying deaths of pious children by incorporating social criticism. The Evangelical Reverend Legh Richmond's popular religious tales, including "The Dairyman's Daughter," "The Young Cottager," and "The Negro Servant," are particularly illuminating in relation to *The Old Curiosity Shop*'s anti-didacticism surrounding Nell's death. Richmond's stories were composed in 1809 and first published as serials in the *Christian Guardian* between 1809 and 1814.[55] Richmond was a chaplain to Queen Victoria's father, the Duke of Kent, and secretary of the Religious Tract Society, which reprinted the stories as a collection titled *Annals of the Poor* (1814). Later translated into French, Italian, German, Danish, and Swedish, *Annals of the Poor* reached a circulation by the end of Richmond's life approaching two million.[56] Even the future queen read Richmond's tales: "In 1833 a tourist in the Isle of Wight came across the Princess [Victoria], then aged fourteen, reading to her mother *The Dairyman's Daughter.* . . . She was seated on the grave of the young girl on whose life the story was based."[57] Reading in cemeteries, as we shall see in future chapters, was not just a figurative topos of nineteenth-century literature but an actual practice of literacy training and means of communing with the dead.

Two of Richmond's tales are autobiographical. Set on the Isle of Wight, they recount the deaths of a young girl or woman—Elizabeth, the thirty-one-year-old servant protagonist of "The Dairyman's Daughter" (in real life, a young parishioner named Elizabeth Wallbridge) and twelve-year-old Little Jane of "The Young Cottager." These stories correspond closely to Nell's plot in that, like Nell, Richmond's heroines patiently accept their demise.[58] Richmond's tales, however, represent his protagonists' conversions and also depict fervent discussions of faith between the narrator (Richmond himself) and the informally educated yet doctrinally sophisticated Elizabeth, or the precociously devout Jane. Like More in *The Shepherd of Salisbury Plain*, Richmond celebrates the piety of the poor: "How often is the poor man's cottage the palace of God! Many can truly declare, that they have learned the most valuable lessons of faith and hope, and there witnessed the most striking demonstrations of the wisdom, power, and goodness of God."[59] *The Old Curiosity Shop* differs ostentatiously from Richmond's narratives, however, by excluding the reader from participation in the moment of Nell's death. Instead, heightening the suspense built up in each serial installment, the revelation of Nell's death is delayed, taking place concurrently to the narration of the London scenes of chapters 56 through 70. Nell's death is only recounted in retrospect, after it is too late to save her, in chapter 71, which began the final serial installment of the novel, Richmond's goal, in contrast, is to provoke the reader's own conversion by allowing him or her to witness his heroines' piety during the final days and moments before their presumed salvation.

As Richmond describes them, his heroines' deathbed scenes occasion great grief but also afford significant spiritual benefit to the spectators. The pious death has a supremely important reformative function for the relatives and onlookers within the narrative and, it is implied, for the reader. During the final days of the consumptive Elizabeth's life, a devout soldier describes to Richmond the significance of his meetings with her: "I love to visit the sick; and hearing of her case from a person who lives close by our camp, I went to see her. I bless God that I ever did go. Her conversation has been very profitable to me." Richmond repeatedly evinces gratitude for the beneficial spiritual consequences of Elizabeth's death and funeral for her parents and himself. He declares his feeling that "each minute that was spent in this funeral chamber seemed to be valuable." Richmond employs the common evangelical terminology in ascribing spiritual "profit" and "value" to the ways that these unavoidable deaths instruct others to cherish faith above everything. As Elizabeth's aged father declares, "let us trust God with our child; and let us trust him with our own selves."[60]

Richmond addresses this most important final lesson to the reader in what seems intended as a kind rather than intimidating admonishment:

> My *poor* reader, the Dairyman's daughter was a *poor* girl, and the child of a *poor* man. Herein thou resemblest her: but dost thou resemble *her*, as she resembled Christ? Art thou made rich by faith? Hast thou a crown laid up for thee? Is thine heart set upon heavenly riches? If not, read this story once more, and then pray earnestly for like precious faith.[61]

Richmond does not threaten the reader living in poverty with damnation for failure to obey the story's moral injunctions but rather recommends repeated rereading in the hope of a resulting conversion, with the aid of divine grace, following upon the desire for redemption produced by the narrative. Here, then, is a variation on More's didactic logic, a gentler Evangelical didacticism, that nevertheless frames the response to a pious death as a spiritual gain prefiguring the reader's salvation, which is conceived as access to a "crown" and "heavenly riches." The Evangelical calculus attempts to console and convert grieving relatives and witnesses by redefining such loss as a means to obtain the measureless prize of eternal life.

In treating Nell's own exemplary death, *The Old Curiosity Shop* forecloses a spiritual calculus like the one that Richmond's text demonstrates. Dickens's serial novel makes a further anti-didactic move in relation to the genre of deathbed literature by depriving his readers of the ritual of "death-bed witness."[62] By foregoing a real-time narration of Nell's deathbed scene, and instead focusing on the reactions of Kit, the single gentleman, and the village schoolmaster to the vision of her grieving and confused grandfather, the novel refuses to pursue the possibility of edification through the witnessing of her death itself. There is nothing of spiritual "value," in Richmond's sense, in the helplessness of these men faced with the accomplished fact of Nell's death: "She was dead, and past all help, or need of it" (654). The schoolmaster's unanswered rhetorical question—"if one deliberate wish . . . could call her back to life, which of us would utter it!" (654)—articulates the novel's strong sense of the irony and injustice surrounding Nell's death in ways that Evangelical deathbed narratives could not condone. Nell's death, to the extent that it is infused with sentimentality, is framed as an accusation against unjust social conditions and as a series of associations in memory already rehearsed for the reader: "The ancient rooms she had seemed to fill with life, even while her own was waning fast—the garden she had tended—the eyes she had gladdened—the noiseless haunts of many a thoughtful hour—the paths she had trodden as it were but yesterday—

could know her no more" (654). In this way the novel also reverses the doctrinally motivated acquiescence implied by Richmond's narrator, who regrets the loss of his edifying conversations with Elizabeth, the dairyman's daughter: "But the rising murmur was checked by the animating thought; 'She is gone to eternal rest—could I wish her back again in this vale of tears?'"[63] Nell remains an anti-didactic heroine who "faded like the light upon a summer's evening" (655). Her death should neither frighten small children into a semblance of piety nor inspire a religious conversion. In this sense it is a resolutely stripped-down and ecumenical version of a long Christian literary tradition that Dickens's novel exploits and transforms. Critics who complained of Dickens's delectation and voyeurism in his staging of Nell's death also seem to have overlooked the novel's attempt to avoid the spiritual relishing of a pious death.[64]

The schoolmaster's response to Nell's death encapsulates the novel's anti-didactic project, articulating the absence of providence or any other overarching agency in Nell's loss. This shift, however, enables the novel to take on a providential momentum of its own, conveying a moral message that the narrator articulates to the reader as a stern consolation:

> Oh! it is hard to take to heart the lesson that such deaths will teach, but let no man reject it, for it is one that all must learn, and is a mighty, universal Truth. When Death strikes down the innocent and young, for every fragile form from which he lets the panting spirit free, a hundred virtues rise, in shapes of mercy, charity, and love, to walk the world, and bless it. Of every tear that sorrowing mortals shed on such green graves, some good is born, some gentler nature comes. In the Destroyer's steps there spring up bright creations that defy his power, and his dark path becomes a way of light to Heaven. (659)

Resurrection and heaven are still present in the novel as rewards for virtuous actions, but in addition to their nonsectarian Christian frame of reference they are also figures for the ways that lost loved ones, especially children, are to find a secularized afterlife in the memories and good deeds of the living.[65] The schoolmaster articulates this dictum in a much less ponderous fashion before Nell's death, when she confesses her grief over the sight of unvisited graves: "Nell, Nell there may be people busy in the world at this instant, in whose good actions and good thoughts these very graves—neglected as they look to us—are the chief instruments" (503). The dying girl is comforted by this reflection (503), and Kit provides an example of how such memories work, even before he knows that Nell is dying, when he explains to Barbara how remembering Nell inspires him to be better (631–32).

Some of Dickens's Victorian critics found fault with the "blank-verse" style (which Dickens claimed was inadvertent) of his moralizing paragraph, while others praised its sentiments and turned it into a self-contained poem.[66] Juxtaposing the passage with a parallel formulation in Richmond's "The Young Cottager," however, makes clear that the schoolmaster's consolation is an anti-didactic encapsulation that revises the logic of Evangelical fiction as a means of foregrounding how the reader should respond differently to Dickens's novel. Here is Richmond's account of the significance of twelve-year-old Little Jane's conversion, pious conversation, and deathbed for witnesses and his own readers:

> To *some*, I am persuaded, [Little Jane's] example and conversation were made a blessing. Memory reflects with gratitude, whilst I write, on the profit and consolation which I individually derived from her society. Nor I alone. The last day will, if I err not, disclose further fruits, resulting from the love of God to this little child; and, through her, to others that saw her. And may not hope indulge the prospect, that this simple memorial of her history shall be as one arrow drawn from the quiver of the Almighty to reach the heart of the young and the thoughtless? Direct its course, O my God! May the eye that reads, and the ear that hears, the record of little Jane, through the power of the Spirit of the Most Highest, each become a witness for the truth as it is in Jesus![67]

Little Jane's death and its narration achieve their cumulative impact first in Richmond's sermonic narrative memorialization, then through the reader's "witness" of the narrator's memory of Little Jane's conversion, and finally, "on the last day," in a retrospective vision that reveals all the souls whom Little Jane's story has benefited through their reading. Richmond indicates that the story may be read out loud as well as silently by appealing to both the reader's eye and ear as channels of reception and conversion. Ideally, the reading and repeated rereading of the tale should provoke repentance and reinforce piety.

These priorities shaped around conversion mark the persistence of that motive (and motif) in Dickens's moral message as well, but here the converting agency derives from a reorientation achieved through a view of death that is geared toward responding to the irreparable loss of a child through good deeds. Unlike the mercenary ethics of the story of "Little Margery" criticized in *Our Mutual Friend*, Dickens's "hard lesson" teaches that no charitable action should be motivated by any idea of gain for oneself, or it will fail both to commemorate the dead and to compensate for loss. *The Old Curiosity Shop* pursues its secularizing critique of the death of the child as an *unjust* loss, thus making an anti-didactic argument against the Evangelical interpretation of such deaths as a spiritual gain for the believer and as a manifestation of an overarching divine purpose.[68]

Richmond's and Dickens's didacticisms cross paths, however, not simply in their common theme of how to make sense of the death of the young and innocent but also in their narrative reliance on associative memory. Richmond articulates a practical technique, from which "the Christian may derive much profit," for perceiving and fixing in the memory typological associations between the natural world and the divine agency of creation.[69] Richmond explains that when the contemplation of nature or recollections of "past conversations and intercourse with deceased friends" become occasions for "religious meditation," "the memory becomes a sanctified instrument of spiritual improvement."[70] Richmond relies on the serial functioning of memory, which one can "greatly improve by exercise," to help him assemble his narratives of the exemplary deaths he has presided over: "one revived idea produces another, till the mind is most agreeably and usefully occupied with lively and holy imaginations." When employed for this purpose, the associative memory can provide "a series of welcome memorials."[71]

To illustrate the powers of the associative memory, Richmond quotes without attribution from *The Pleasures of Memory* by Samuel Rogers: "Lull'd in the countless chambers of the brain, / Our thoughts are link'd by many a hidden chain; / Awake but one, and lo, what myriads rise! / Each stamps its image as the other flies; / Each, as the varied avenues of sense / Delight or sorrow to the soul dispense, / Brightens or fades: yet all, with sacred art, / Control the latent fibres of the heart."[72] Memory's influence over the "heart" seems equivalent to the effects on the mind that Samuel Johnson attributes to fiction, but it is invested with a greater instrumentality in the "control" it exerts over the emotions. In the "Analysis" that explains the first part of the poem, Rogers outlines the moral usefulness of associative memory and, by implication, of his own poem as well: "The associating principle, as it is here employed, is no less conducive to virtue than to happiness; and, as such, it frequently discovers itself in the most tumultuous scenes of life. It addresses our finer feelings, and gives exercise to every mild and generous propensity."[73] In a similar way, Richmond explains the practical devotional uses for the serious Christian of the associative memory that also helps him write his tales. But he also adopts the moral effects of the pleasures of memory as the experience of mental order, regularity, and connection—qualities that Rogers explains in a primarily secular and philosophical sense, while Richmond adapts them to devotional purposes in constructing his religious narratives.[74]

The common link to Rogers makes clear that both Richmond in his Evangelical didacticism and Dickens, in what I have been calling his secularizing (nondenominational Christian) novelistic anti-didacticism, draw on associationist principles to formulate the effects of their narratives on the reader. Richmond's text provides striking evidence of the way that he also understood his own thinking and literary composition in associationist terms. At the end of "The Young Cottager," he reflects on little Jane's funeral and its effects on him in order to tie the strands of his narrative together:

> As I stood at the head of the grave, during the service, I connected past events, which had occurred in the churchyard, with the present. In this spot Jane first learned the value of the Gospel which saved her soul. Not many yards from her own burial-place, was the epitaph which has already been described as the first means of affecting her mind with serious and solemn conviction. It seemed to stand at *this* moment as a peculiar witness for those truths which its lines proclaimed to every passing reader. Such an association of objects produced a powerful effect on my soul.[75]

Richmond alludes to his having taught Jane to read by spelling out the epitaphs in the churchyard. Her acquisition of literacy becomes a demonstration of faith, while her Christian life begins and ends with examples of epitaphic reading, whether her own pious reading of the Bible or Richmond's own "epitaphic" tale of her demise and hoped-for redemption. For Richmond, the soul is the ultimate location for harboring the effects of the associative memory. In meditating on the pedagogical uses of the epitaph and cemetery, Richmond connects past and present, the meaning of Jane's conversion and his narrative, through an associationist logic that he clearly presumes will produce an equally "powerful" set of associations in the mind of the reader. Thus his text didactically asserts the serial connections and analogies among pious literacy and reading, the sanctifying experience of death, and the reader's salvation. Within Richmond's didactic framework, both reading and the Christian implementation of the associative memory become generically epitaphic.

Richmond's text also reminds us that Dickens's "schoolmaster's consolation" is epitaphic, particularly in its blank-verse form. Dickens's dedication of *The Old Curiosity Shop* to Rogers runs as follows: "To Samuel Rogers, Esquire, My Dear Sir, Let me have *my* Pleasures of Memory in connection with this book, by dedicating it to a Poet whose writings (as all the world knows) are replete with generous and earnest feelings; and to a Man whose daily life (as all the world does not know) is one of active sympathy with the poorest and humblest of his kind. Your faithful friend, Charles Dickens" (37).[76] The dedication and the novel itself, then, share the same epitaphic, commemorative function through prosopopoeia—conjuring up Rogers's influence for the reader—by ensuring the public memory of Rogers's good deeds of "active sympathy" that the schoolmaster's consolation envisions for Nell and for the other deceased children whom she represents. Nell herself becomes an emblem or personification of the transaction *The Old Curiosity Shop* teaches between personal loss, memorilization, and charitable social activism that the novel attempts to teach.[77]

The significant innovation in Dickens's reworking of the didactic uses of the associative memory from Evangelical fiction does not lie so much in its conception of reading as epitaphic commemoration, or even in the secular- izing tendencies of the schoolmaster's lesson, as in its revision and remedia- tion of didactic strategies from religious tract fiction to form a new set of anti-didactic but still morally uplifting incentives for reading of popular se- rial fiction. These new incentives come into focus at the end of the novel, when Kit tells "that story of good Miss Nell who died" at the request of his children. The narrator describes the children's reactions and the teller's manipulations of their associations: "when they cried to hear it, wishing it longer too, he would teach them how she had gone to Heaven, as all good people did; and how, if they were good like her, they might hope to be there too one day, and know her as he had done when he was quite a boy." Kit turns the children's tears into laughter by reminding them how Nell used to laugh at him (671). This formulation of Nell's life and death as a narrative lesson provoking both sadness and laughter resembles Richmond's sense of the mixture of feelings inspired by Christian "memorials": "The remembrance of former scenes and conversations with those, who, we be- lieve, are now enjoying the uninterrupted happiness of a better world, fills the heart with pleasing sadness, and animates the soul with the hopeful an- ticipation of a day when the glory of the Lord shall be revealed in the assem- bling of all his children together, never more to be separated."[78] The final illustration of Nell's ascent to heaven among the angels is positioned after the novel has closed so that it visualizes the associations provoked by Kit's storytelling, both within the narrative as the effect of Nell's story on Kit's children's minds and for the reader of Dickens's novel.

Yet Dickens's version of the memorialization of memory is much more retrospective than anticipatory. The novel's anti-didacticism also consists in its refusal of the eschatology implied in Richmond's account of the spiritually valuable associative functions of memory. There is as much forgetting as remembering in Kit's stories of Nell. Strong overarching historical tendencies of change and dissolution are constantly conjured up in the novel's gothic scenery. The past becomes irretrievable except through memory, and it is also cut off from a future eternity in which its meaning will be realized, becoming subject instead to the constant destruction, renovation, and flux that modernizing London itself represents. When Kit takes his children to visit the street where the curiosity shop used to stand, he can no longer find it: "new improvements had altered it so much, it was not like the same. . . . He soon became uncertain of the spot, and could only say it was thereabouts, he thought, and that these alterations were confusing" (671–72).

The Old Curiosity Shop culminates with a reference to the pervasiveness of change that even affects the narrative itself: "so do things pass away, like a tale that is told!" (672). Forster's observation that Nell's story provides a "discipline of feeling and emotion which would do me lasting good, and which I would not thank you for as an ordinary enjoyment of literature," can be read therefore as a paraphrase of the novel's anti-didactic formula. In its remediation of Evangelical tracts, *The Old Curiosity Shop* could therefore function as a practical way for the reader to mobilize painful feelings of loss as a spur to present corrective action in the world rather than future redemption in an afterlife, while loss itself remains unjustifiable in retrospect, and thus irrecuperable. The question remains, however, what further epistemological and ethical incentives the novel offers in place of Richmond's spiritual motives for reading, so that its impact can exceed "an ordinary enjoyment of literature."

Curiosity and Contrast

The most incisive anti-didactic element of *The Old Curiosity Shop*'s conceptual and metaphoric architecture is its use of curiosity as a basis for its revision and remediation of Evangelical narrative pedagogy. Curiosity, as another version of the pleasures of memory, affords an epistemological link between generous motivations and good deeds that also provides an alternative to the epitaphic logic of the schoolmaster's lesson. As a general term for natural inquisitiveness or the propensity to question reasons and causes, curiosity is also concerned with the role of human actions in bringing about a given situation. Within the novel's associationist didacticism more specifically, curiosity describes a state of associative self-consciousness, an epistemological desire to retrace in memory the past circumstances that have connected certain ideas and feelings in the mind, or certain scenes and persons in the world.

In her study of curiosity in the early modern period, Barbara Benedict points to the embrace of curiosity in empiricist epistemology, noting that both Thomas Hobbes and David Hume praise it as the source of the human institutions of science, language, and religion.[79] Benedict also draws attention to ambiguities in the literary representation of curiosity from the period from 1660 to 1830. Whether defined as inquiry, ambition, or "an object without a clear use" like the curiosities in Nell's grandfather's London shop, curiosity as attribute or thing seems to "stimulate contrary reactions of applause and horror."[80] *The Old Curiosity Shop* displays this ambivalent representational pattern by dividing curiosity into benevolent and predatory forms embodied in specific characters. Both of these kinds of curiosity are presented as alternative pedagogies. The novel ultimately emphasizes an ethical form of curiosity, expressed as inquisitive concern for others involving intellectual encouragement and care, rather than instruction or charity.[81]

It is no coincidence, then, that the characters in the novel who display lascivious or rapacious curiosity are also bad teachers. The dwarf Quilp shows overtly sexual interest in Nell, while persecuting Kit—even beating his effigy. Sally Brass attempts to perpetrate ingenious frauds through the notary office she shares with her brother, while abusing the "small servant" whom she keeps locked in the cellar. The novel depicts Quilp's and Sally's pedagogical influence as the attempted inculcation, through the threat of violence, of a false consciousness. Quilp resembles the sadistic boy of eighteenth-century children's fiction who torments birds and other small creatures. He delights in tricking others into admitting that he is hideous, thus forcing them to display their own hypocrisy in dealing with him. As Theodor Adorno observed, Quilp is an ugly embodiment of the capitalist profit motive.[82] In addition to the many rationales on the level of plot for Quilp's death by drowning, he also dies as a result of his rejection of any form of reasoning that is not attached to self-interest, "reprisal" (239), or profit; he ends up as a "deserted carcase" (620), tossed about by the river and deposited as refuse on its banks.[83] Quilp's reduction to detritus is represented as just, in contrast to the irony of Nell's innocence and death in the midst of her strange and incongruous associates. Like Quilp, Sally is a brutal pedagogue whose training consists of intimidation. She extorts false admissions from her "small servant" (and her illegitimate daughter with Quilp) when she questions the ravenous girl as to whether she would like more meat after serving her "two square inches" of mutton: "The hungry creature answered with a faint 'No.' They were evidently going through an established form" (351). Exhibiting grotesque and abusive versions of Miss Monflathers's browbeating of Nell, Quilp's and Sally's "established forms" betray the potential for abuse inherent in pedagogical and parental authority.

Dick Swiveller's relations with the Brasses' small servant, whom he nicknames the "Marchioness" to lend a more aristocratic atmosphere to their playing cribbage for a stake of "two sixpences" in the damp and filthy cellar kitchen (528), represent the novel's alternative comic version of curiosity as didacticism. Dick's positive difference as a teacher lies not only in his imaginative attempts to embellish the cellar, and his kindness in supplying the Marchioness with a generous portion of meat and beer, but also in his suspension of training through intimidation in favor of conversation and play. When the Marchioness refers to Sally as "such a one-er" for going out and leaving her locked in the kitchen, "after a moment's reflection," Dick tactfully decides, "to forego his responsibility of setting her right, and to suffer her to talk on; as it was evident that her tongue was loosened by the purl, and her opportunities for conversation were not so frequent as to render a momentary check of little consequence" (530). Dick plies the Marchioness with questions but waits for spontaneous answers, and instead of correcting her grammar and thus indirectly chiding her, he enables her, at this early moment of their unusual friendship, to speak freely. After her emancipation from the Brasses, Dick sponsors her educational "advancement" (668). Unlike the vain efforts to save little Nell from death, Dick's actions are efficacious. His curiosity exemplifies care—an open-ended educational influence and disinterested intervention in the life of another person.

Most important, there is nothing "systematic" about the way that Dick's and the Marchioness's fates ultimately coincide. In fact, Dick's interest in the Marchioness stems at first from his spontaneous wondering about her identity: "I'd give something—if I had it—to know how they use that child," Dick thinks to himself, "and where they keep her. . . . My mother must have been an inquisitive woman; I have no doubt I'm marked with a note of interrogation somewhere" (350). Instead of hoping to profit from his benevolent interest, Dick wishes that he could give something away in exchange for more knowledge about the Marchioness. Dick's curiosity, then, appears as an uneconomical and even extravagant form of interest that could replace the complex calculation of "self-interested" spiritual value offered as an incentive both for pious living and for the conversion provoked by the reading of Evangelical didactic fictions. This kind of glimpsing of a disadvantaged young women by a man wishing to do her well reappears in *Little Dorrit*, in Arthur Clennam's curiosity about the girl in the shadows of his mother's room, who turns out to be his future wife and the novel's heroine, Amy Dorrit. Unlike *Little Dorrit*'s focus on one obscure heroine, *The Old Curiosity Shop* constructs the happy, salvific plot of Dick and the Marchioness in parallel to Little Nell's decline into death, thus offering a diptych of rescue and loss.

The affirmative version of curiosity as care also connects the allegorical figuration of Nell's story and the novel's anti-didactic agenda through the figure of contrast. As we saw in Chapter 1, Hume added contrast or contrariety to the list of basic forms of mental association, pairing it with its opposite, resemblance.[84] Contrast, as one of the central functions for creating mental associations between ideas and feelings, also works to fix relations in the memory, to make them salient.[85] Thus the initial and overarching contrast between Nell and the strange relics, gothic settings, and decrepit companions surrounding her is both allegorical and didactic, with the didactic associationist element providing a secular logic for the popular religious connotations of the allegory. The instructive nature of the organizing element of contrast also requires that Nell be idealized: any taint would only blur the distinction between her and her associates. The use of contrast in the novel is not simply allegorical, however, since it frequently relates to basic modes of perception that instigate questioning, interpretation, and understanding, even before the contrasting elements can be correlated to their more abstract significations. The perception of a startling contrast spurs the associative functions of memory, leading to the equally epistemological and ethical problem of how to make sense of it.

To contest the confident interpretive strategies and conceptual patterns of didactic religious fiction, the novel also foregrounds the perception of contrast as a motive: "Everything in our lives, whether of good or evil, affects us most by contrast," Dickens's narrator asserts (493). This is an epistemological claim, based on an associationist logic, that meaning can be most powerfully accessed when objects, experiences, even words are juxtaposed with an element that differentiates them, makes them stand out from the often overwhelming and incoherent muddle of everyday life. Master Humphrey notes with some disapproval the "habit of allowing impressions to be made upon us by external objects," and claims that although the mind should depend on "reflection alone" for its understanding, it often would fail to note important evidence "without such visible aids" (55–56). Master Humphrey, the speculative observer, prefers not to trust his memory, which seems artificially to heighten the importance of certain visible signs. He surmises that he would never have been so "thoroughly possessed" by the image of Nell if it had not been "surrounded and beset by everything that was foreign to its nature, and furthest removed from the sympathies of her sex and age." This incongruity between Nell and her associates makes her a subject of such "interest" that Master Humphrey cannot stop thinking about her: "she seemed to exist in a kind of allegory." Yet such thinking engenders anxiety about Nell's fate. Humphrey enters on a "curious speculation," "to imagine her in her future life, holding her solitary way among a crowd of wild grotesque companions; the only pure, fresh, youthful object in the throng," but breaks off his train of thought, registering the likelihood that the incongruity instigating his speculations seems less than promising for Nell's future (56).

In his preface to the 1848 First Cheap Edition of the novel, Dickens also indicates, in an associationist vein, that this contrast between Nell and her surroundings was an original element of the scene as he was conceiving the story in his own mind, and that contrast, in effect, generated the narrative: "in writing the book, I had always in my fancy to surround the lonely figure of the child with grotesque and wild, but not impossible companions, and to gather about her innocent face and pure intentions, associates as strange and uncongenial as the grim objects that are about her bed when her history is first foreshadowed" (42). This description resonates with Bacon's and Hobbes's theories of memory's role in invention as a searching function that attempts to retrieve and reassemble knowledge according to certain characteristics that either align or differentiate specific ideas or things.[86] Whether the emphasis lies on strange objects or uncongenial companions, contrast works as the conceptual arrangement that provokes both the curiosity and care that in turn incite narrative. Nell is interesting and memorable because of her association with things that are incongruous but not impossible, since the effect produced by the novel involves the sort of curiosity that could provoke some kind of corrective action, and not prohibitive horror, resignation, or disbelief.

The anti-didactic tendency of the curiosity spurred by striking contrasts becomes apparent in light of the charitable visitor Mr. Johnson's methods of interrogating the shepherd in More's tale. Exercising a program of pious reflection that corresponds to Richmond's notion of the practical uses of associative memory, Mr. Johnson takes advantage of the occasion of his ride across Salisbury plain to recall a psalm illustrating how the visible world of nature reveals divine grace, "and he persuaded himself that the divine Spirit which dictated this fine hymn, had left it as a kind of general intimation to what use we were to convert our admiration of created things" (177). His thoughts are interrupted by a dog's barking, and on perceiving the shepherd and his cottage, he immediately begins to interpret the physical signs of the shepherd's spiritual worthiness: his repeatedly mended but intact and spotless clothing, his "open and honest countenance," and his "serious deportment and solid manner of speaking" (177–78). Mr. Johnson's interest in this pious shepherd involves decoding signs of preexisting criteria for correlating appearances with internal sanctification.

Master Humphrey's initial interest in Nell, however, arises from his general practice of wandering through London at night "speculating on the characters and occupations of those who fill the streets" (43). This is an exercise of the restless imagination (resembling Dickens's own habit of late-night roaming through the London slums), which Nell's situation invests with an anxiety beyond Master Humphrey's more typically detached curiosity. Master Humphrey, like Mr. Johnson, finds what he expects in the selfish old man who has irresponsibly sent his young granddaughter alone on an evening errand through the dangerous streets, and he adopts the same license to admonish Nell's grandfather that, in didactic tales, the middle-class visitors to the cottages of the "dissolute" poor typically demonstrate. Yet much of what Master Humphrey observes about the strange household is mysterious, and even his limited knowledge of Nell's unsuitable situation leads to no appropriate form of corrective action—his agency in affecting her is drastically limited in comparison with Mr. Johnson's charitable intervention.

In More's tale, the shepherd's analogies set up a hierarchy in which one of the terms, representing things of this world or of nature, is always superseded in favor of spiritual truths and providential intention. For a person of faith, such analogies exemplify epistemological certainty, and, like biblical parables, they are meant to be effective pedagogical tools. In contrast, *The Old Curiosity Shop* makes a spectacle of its lack of such epistemological certainty. But in its own anti-didactic fashion the novel argues for such uncertainty as a productive general condition—for narrative, certainly, but also for ethical deliberations. Think of Dick Swiveller's mock melodramatic curiosity about the possible effects of his intervention in the Marchioness's life:

"can these things be her destiny, or has some unknown person started an opposition to the decrees of fate?" (532). Unlike Miss Monflathers's catechistic attack on Nell, Swiveller's speculation about his agency in affecting the Marchioness's fate poses "a most inscrutable and unmitigated staggerer!" (532). The novel argues that it is precisely when you *do not already know the answer* or cannot easily recognize the type of person you are dealing with, but can begin to formulate a new kind of question or understanding, that the possibility of positive intervention emerges. Here we can see an instance of the technique that R. H. Horne attributed to Dickens: "[to] search within [individuals] for every actual and imaginary resemblance to the great majority of their fellow creatures, which may give them a more intimate knowledge of aggregate nature, and thus enlarge the bounds of unexclusive sympathy."[87]

Unlike typological analogy as deployed in the Evangelical stories we have examined, contrast does not permit the one set of concepts to supersede and replace another but instead keeps oppositions in play in ways that may both produce contradiction or admit a reconciling movement from one element to the other. Either outcome precludes the prejudicial imposition of preconceived hierarchies upon experience. This foreclosure of the possibility of escaping from temporality permits an anti-didactic tendency through which the novel, despite gesturing toward the consolations of heaven, refuses the transcendence of the past and the material world that the Evangelical writers' conceptions of conversion and salvation promise. Such a refusal, however, makes Dickens's serial novel even more dependent than Richmond's narratives on training the reader's memory by provoking his or her curiosity in order to sustain its didactic and social reform projects over the course of subsequent installments. This need to sustain interest exists precisely because the novel cannot count on the motive of conversion and the decisive break with the past that the deathbed scene seeks to accomplish, and which the pious reader is able to revisit constantly as a point of orientation in later life.

Changing Minds

What does it mean, then, for our understanding of the popularity of Dickens's novels that *The Old Curiosity Shop* redefines didacticism as curiosity in the ways I have been describing? Both Evangelical religious fiction and Dickens's novel attempt to teach the reader to rely on such fundamental figural and logical relations as analogy and contrast in order to create a complex correlation between a response to fiction and a social attitude or belief. Such correlations were presumed to work through the associative functions attributed to memory, which could record and make available to recollection ideas produced through reading in the same way that it facilitated the remembrance of experience. As basic associative principles, analogy and contrast could be employed in many kinds of discourses and for various purposes—they were part of the tool kit of psychological concepts adopted by writers who, for various reasons, were attempting to manage or intervene in social change by affecting the newly emerging mass readership.

The Old Curiosity Shop reconfigures the effects of novel reading in relation to authoritative popular genres designed to shape their readers' sensibilities, behaviors, and social expectations. Through these remediated didactic means, Dickens's novels do not simply persuade or instruct readers but rather provide new patterns of logic and emotion through which readers can form their judgments of society. As I show in subsequent chapters, Dickens serial novels continue to rework narrative strategies geared toward linking the acquisition of literacy to piety and social deference, which many of his readers would have encountered through their religious schooling. Through their inclusion of recognizably pedagogical conceptual and figurative patterns from other didactic and popular genres, the novels work to trigger and then modify habits of thought and forms of social explanation associated with familiar Victorian reading practices. In this context, "curiosity" describes the reader's own openness to influence by the text. But Dickens's associationist version of curiosity also draws an analogy between the reader's speculative interest in the narrative, that functions as an incitement toward continued reading of the serial novel, and the care that results in constructive intervention in the fate of another person. Curiosity thus links reading and effective action in an ethic of responsibility toward others. In this carefully targeted way, Dickensian fiction transforms reading as religious conversion into reading as a means to foster positive social change and social justice.

Tracing the incorporation of this anti-didactic protocol in *The Old Curiosity Shop* thus allows us to perceive how Dickens's novels may have constituted some of the conditions of their reception. The fact that Dickens attempted to put the conventions of Evangelical didactic fiction to new uses suggests his perception that such narrative strategies tended to be effective in forming readers' views. His own writings could therefore have a similar impact by communicating a different set of associations to readers than the transactions between reading and personal salvation promised by Evangelical fiction. In the following chapter, I read Dickens's early novels in a series, analyzing more fully how they sustain and refine the reader's curiosity about the strange juxtapositions and associations of modern urban life into the recognition of collective experience as entailing social responsibility and political accountability.

4. *The Pleasures of Memory, Part II*

Epitaphic Reading and Cultural Memory

> Miss Prism: . . . You must put away your diary, Cecily. I really don't see why you should keep a diary at all.
>
> Cecily: I keep a diary in order to enter the wonderful secrets of my life. If I didn't write them down, I should probably forget all about them.
>
> Miss Prism: Memory, my dear Cecily, is the diary that we all carry about with us.
>
> Cecily: Yes, but it usually chronicles the things that have never happened, and couldn't possibly have happened. I believe that Memory is responsible for nearly all the three-volume novels that Mudie sends us.
>
> Oscar Wilde, The Importance of Being Earnest (1895)

The previous chapter's account of the remediation of didactic literature and patterning of reception in *The Old Curiosity Shop* raises the question whether, for Dickens's contemporaries, the social reform effects of his writings were demonstrable. In the 1838 preface to *Oliver Twist* (1837–39), Dickens claims that the novel's representation of London's criminal underworld "attempted something which was needed, and which would be a service to society."[1] In his next novel, *Nicholas Nickleby* (1838–39), Dickens incorporated an exposé of the abuse of children at certain Yorkshire schools that he hoped would instigate both a governmental investigation and a boycott that would be fatal to the schools, or that at least would pressure them to reform. In his study of Dickens's views on education, John Manning describes the slow dissolution of the Yorkshire schools, which contemporaries attributed to the effect of *Nicholas Nickleby*, so that by the late 1840s they had virtually disappeared.[2] Dickens biographer Peter Ackroyd also reports the perception that Dickens's fictional attack on the Yorkshire schools had been effective: "Pupils were withdrawn; establishments closed and, within a year of the publication of *Nicholas Nickleby*, the *Quarterly Review* stated that '. . . the exposure has already put down many infant bastilles'—the reference to 'bastilles' linking them to the London workhouses which had the same nickname."[3] In the 1840s, then, Dickens gained a reputation as a writer whose novels had precipitated specific reforms.

In light of Dickens's avowed interest in popular education, it is not surprising that the type of institution he seems to have succeeded in uprooting was a school. In the preface to the 1848 First Cheap Edition of the novel, Dickens links the Yorkshire schools' existence to the government's failure to provide universal education: "Of the monstrous neglect of education in England, and the disregard of it by the State as a means of forming good or bad citizens, and miserable or happy men, this class of schools has long afforded a notable example."[4] Dickens implies that the potential social effects of his novel reach beyond the particular case it illustrates.[5] He also explains in detail how prior to writing the novel he obtained firsthand knowledge of the abuses perpetrated by the Yorkshire schoolmasters by personally investigating several schools during an information-gathering trip to Yorkshire in early 1838. Accompanied by the artist Hablôt Browne ("Phiz"), who later illustrated *Nicholas Nickleby*, Dickens went incognito, taking Browne's name as his own. He adopted the role of an agent for "a supposititious little boy who had been left with a widowed mother who didn't know what to do with him" (49). The trip demonstrates Dickens's practice of seeking an empirical basis for his social criticism and also links his early serial fiction directly with his initial career as a journalist.[6] John M. L. Drew has shown that Dickens's early journalism was significant in shaping "Boz's" authorial influence by "cultivat[ing] in the presence of . . . [his readers] the persona of an individual reporter with a wider than usual brief, who . . . roves from Parliament Square, through the Great Metropolis, and out into the provinces, indulging his faculty for detecting analogies between areas of the contemporary scene normally kept discrete in newspaper columns."[7] As Dickens asserted in the 1839 preface to the original edition, closer to the immediate effects of the novel's publication, "Mr. Squeers and his school are faint and feeble pictures of an existing reality, purposely subdued and kept down lest they should be deemed impossible" (45). By basing his novel in journalistic social investigation, Dickens can argue that its fictional treatment crystallizes the problem so that it becomes manageable.

Building on the previous chapter's analysis of Dickens's remediation of didactic religious tracts and revision of the Evangelical didactic calculus, I focus in this chapter on how his novels transmute plots about memory into memory techniques that become associated with the reading of Dickens's serial fiction. In *Nicholas Nickleby*, Dickens combines his journalistic investigation with a carefully constructed analogy between the collective neglect of glaring social problems and the failure of memory or its reduction to mere unthinking habit. This novel shows that the pleasures of memory are dependent upon particular relationships of kinship or friendship whose loss undermines both individual happiness and social ties. Dickens first developed this linkage in his early short narratives published in various newspapers between 1833 and 1837, collected in a two-volume work, *Sketches by "Boz," Illustrative of Every-Day Life and Every-Day People* (1836), and republished in parts (November 1837–June 1839), and in single-volume form (1839) as *Sketches by Boz*. One of these sketches, "Thoughts about People," first published in 1835, links the anonymity of city life with memory loss:

> 'Tis strange, with how little notice, good, bad, or indifferent, a man may live and die in London. He awakens no sympathy in the breast of any single person; his existence is a matter of interest to no one save himself, and he cannot be said to be forgotten when he dies, for no one remembered him when he was alive. There is a very numerous class of people in this great metropolis who seem not to possess a single friend, and whom nobody appears to care for. Urged by imperative necessity in the first instance, they have resorted to London in search of employment, and the means of subsistence. It is hard, we know, to break the ties which bind us to our home and friends, and harder still to efface the thousand recollections of happy days and old times, which have been slumbering in our bosoms for years, and only rush upon the mind to bring before it, with startling reality, associations connected with the friends we have left, the scenes we have beheld too probably for the last time, and the hopes we once cherished, but may entertain no more. These men, however, happily for themselves, have long since forgotten such thoughts. Old country friends have died or emigrated; former correspondents have become lost, like themselves, in the crowd and turmoil of some busy city, and they have gradually settled down into mere passive creatures of habit and endurance.[8]

Men belonging to this "class" of solitary Londoners, such as the middle-aged, unmarried office clerk living in a "little back room at Islington" observed by "Boz" at St. James's Park, have suffered a gradual lapse of function

of the associative memory because of their isolation. Not only do they fail
to recall the scenes of their youth, but they have also themselves been forgotten—or worse, have never become memorable at all—in the midst of
the "crowd and turmoil" of the city. This account suggests that the breaking
of past ties renders the forming of new ones difficult, or even impossible.
The failure of past associations to "rush upon the mind" is a precursor to
the loss of the capacity both to feel for others and to inspire reciprocal feelings: "Poor, harmless creatures these men are; contented but not happy;
broken-spirited and humbled, they may feel no pain, but they never know
pleasure."[9] To be unloved, one must be effectively uprooted. Yet if this is
so, then why does the narrative, accompanied by Cruickshank's humorous
but kind illustration of the clerk reading his newspaper at his dinner (Figure
9), render one such man memorable and thus significant? Through what
kinds of "thoughts about people" does this sketch seek to remedy the reader's ignorance of such solitary city dwellers? One hint that this illustration
offers is that a possible cure for such "passive creatures of habit and endurance" (in addition to dining out) lies in the development of a new habit of
reading periodicals.

"Thoughts About People" shows in an encapsulated form that later novels develop into full-fledged narratives how the chain of thoughts and memories may break down and thus require restoration. While *The Old Curiosity
Shop* (1840–41) can be viewed as both a culminating work in this early
phase and a transitional work that begins to conceive a cultural politics of
serial fiction more explicitly in opposition to evangelical didactic literature,
a series of early novels, including *Oliver Twist* and *Nicholas Nickleby*, along
with the Christmas books *A Christmas Carol* (1843) and *The Haunted Man
and the Ghost's Bargain* (1848), all treat the problem of lost associations and
displaced persons.[10] Focusing first on *Nicholas Nickleby*, I explore its version
of epitaphic reading as a means to counteract the memory lapses that represent the threat of isolation in the city. Dickens's novels also teach readers
what uses to make of such shared pleasures of memory associated specifically
with "fictitious realities." In the second half of the chapter, I revisit *The Old
Curiosity Shop* to delineate how that novel instructs the reader in a replicable
serial reading habit. The scene of Nell's repeated reading of the Bible in the
gothic chapel substitutes a secularized and literary style of reading for pious
reading. I argue that this recharacterization of reading, through its associationism, very subtly draws on a Humean skeptical epistemology about the
fictional nature of personal identity and experience. This popular Humean
framework provides support for the ways that Dickens's serials shape the

Figure 9. George Cruikshank, "The Poor Clerk," in *Sketches by "Boz,"*
Illustrative of Every-Day Life, and Every-Day People, vol. 1 (London: John
Macrone, 1836), 101. Beinecke Rare Book and Manuscript Library, Yale
University.

bonds of memory and reading into virtual relations within an emerging Victorian mass media culture. By making permeable the threshold between actual and fictional experience in memory, *The Old Curiosity Shop* encourages the reader, like Nell, to find a partial solace for death through a new reading habit that revises devotional reading to connect the reader's associations with Nell's story to common experiences of the loss of loved ones. Here epitaphic reading is generalized from the novel to the reading audience as a practice of social connection and participation. Two episodes from *Oliver Twist* further illustrate how memories of reading create associations in the reader's mind that can supplement actual experiences or supply fictional ones. The associationist analogy between experience and reading reinforces this sense that fictional memories, or memories of reading, take up the same kind of space in the reader's mind as experiences recollected from the past. On the basis of this interchangeability, readers' memories of reading Dickens's novels can conceivably serve as forms of personal and social relation to the extent that they take on the public status of experiences shared with other readers.

Tracing this development in one of Dickens's major novels from the 1850s, I show how in *Little Dorrit* (1855–57), memory once again plays a crucial role in the novel's social epistemology. In ways even more overt than the earlier novels, *Little Dorrit* invests the task of retracing the order of one's past associations with an ethical and social urgency. Memories become not only the ethical basis of social relations but also provide instigating causes to active duty in this novel. The problem of locating the source of Amy Dorrit's unstinting ethic of service to others provides a narrative "vanishing-point" (701) rendering all other social values relative to her devoted preservation of domestic ties and memories of her family's life in the Marshalsea prison. Yet by incorporating Miss Wade as a sexual dissident and anti-associationist skeptic whose negative memories of childhood lead her to view domestic life as essentially hypocritical and self-serving, *Little Dorrit* also self-reflexively questions the connection between memory and social reform forged in Dickens's earlier novels.

In conclusion, I consider Dickens's staging of his authorial intentions in his pronouncements about the epitaphic effects of *The Old Curiosity Shop*, in light of Henry Mayhew's contemporaneous educational treatise from 1842, *What to Teach and How to Teach It: So That the Child May Become a Wise and Good Man*. Mayhew defines the reading of English literature as a means of communing with dead authors across space and time that can be expanded to an international audience of readers through the mass production, transoceanic shipping and distribution, and increasing sales of books. Here "epitaphic" reading becomes a vehicle of mass communication that expands beyond literature's educational role of cultural consolidation within the nation-state. Mayhew's educational text enables us to perceive how the relaying function of Dickensian serial fiction in connecting individual readers into a self-conscious reading audience could be expanded to constitute an international network of readers. Readers across the world would receive English culture as represented by famous works of literature that, as in prosopopoeia, conjure up mental images of famous English authors. What readers do with such personifications is another question. Nevertheless, in this way the serial pleasures of memory become a characteristic form of reception within modern mass media culture.

Reading Crowds and Epitaphs: "Resurrectionist" Memory

Following the fortunes of a middle-class family forced by the death of a father and consequent economic hardship to move to London from their home in the country, *Nicholas Nickleby* retraces the narrative of dislocation sketched in "Thoughts about People." Extending the earlier sketch's attempt to draw attention to forgotten people, this novel asks readers to notice and revive the humanity of certain characters who have been reduced to "mere creatures of habit," and to condemn the inhumanity of certain "classes" of people whose memories have failed in both a functional and a moral sense. The Yorkshire schoolmaster Wackford Squeers exemplifies one such unreformed "class" that *Nicholas Nickleby* raised to noteworthy status and subjected to public condemnation.[11] In his 1848 preface, Dickens highlights the impetus that a vague childhood memory of his own associated with the Yorkshire schools gave to the writing of *Nicholas Nickleby*:

> I cannot call to mind, now, how I came to hear about Yorkshire schools when I was a not very robust child, sitting in bye-places, near Rochester Castle, with a head full of Partridge, Strap, Tom Pipes, and Sancho Panza; but I know that my first impressions of them were picked up at that time, and that they were, somehow or other, connected with a suppurated abscess that some boy had come home with, in consequence of his Yorkshire guide, philosopher, and friend, having ripped it open with an inky penknife. The impression made upon me, however made, never left me. I was always curious about them—fell, long afterwards, and at sundry times, into the way

of hearing more about them—at last, having an audience, resolved to write about them. (48)

Dickens marks the novel's thematic focus on education by the etymological gloss on the Greek origins of the word "pedagogue" as "guide, philosopher, and friend." He suggests that the origin of his ultimate decision to write a novel about the Yorkshire schools was an already close association in his memory between an incident in his own life related to the schools' terrible reputation and his early exposure to the novels of Fielding, Smollett, and Cervantes. *Nicholas Nickleby* itself would thus form another link in the chain of associations connecting Dickens's own reading of novels with his childhood memories of stories about the Yorkshire schools. In turn, *Nicholas Nickleby* extends Dickens's train of thought into a new series of associations in the minds of his readers that would connect the reading of his novel with the reform of the Yorkshire schools. The response of a receptive audience for his earlier serials made Dickens's own associations newly relevant, thus spurring his "resolution" to reshape them into the plot and characters of a new novel. As we saw in the case of Dick Swiveller's benevolent curiosity about the Marchioness in *The Old Curiosity Shop*, Dickens's curiosity about the Yorkshire schools also inspires him to undertake a benevolent public service by investigating and exposing their abuses in his novel.

Dickens's account of his recollection, however, conflates his own childhood memory and his research prior to writing the novel. One of Dickens's childhood friends, John Brooks, attempted to correct Dickens's recollection after the publication of *Nicholas Nickleby* by claiming that he was the Yorkshire schoolboy whom Dickens remembered, and by taking responsibility for foolishly operating on his own nose, thus exonerating his schoolmaster.[12] Dickens's research on newspaper reports of trials connected to cases of neglect at the schools before his trip to Yorkshire is likely to have been another source of his "inky penknife operation" memory. He turned up an account of two court cases from October 1823 related to a Mr. Shaw of Bowes Academy (often cited as the model for Squeers) who was convicted of allowing several boys to go blind from neglect and forced to pay two fines for damages of £300 each to the parents.[13] Dickens's account of his visit to Bowes village presents further evidence of this overlapping of recollections from his childhood and from his later research for the novel: "There is an old church near the school and the first grave-stone I stumbled on, that dreary winter afternoon, was placed above the grave of a boy, eighteen long years old. . . . I think his ghost put Smike into my head on the spot. . . .

The identical scoundrel you speak of I saw—curiously enough. His name is Shaw. . . . Another action was brought against him by the parents of a miserable child, a cancer in whose head he opened with an inky penknife, and so caused his death."[14] The gravestone in question read: "Here lie the remains of GEORGE ASHTON TAYLOR Son of John Taylor of Trowbridge, Wiltshire, who died suddenly at Mr William Shaw's Academy of this place, April 13th, 1822 aged 19 years. Young reader, thou must die, but after this the judgement."[15] This coincidence suggests that Dickens associated his own childhood memory with the story of the callous Mr. Shaw. Thus if the novel originates in a chain of Dickens's own associations, these associations also combine memories from different sources and periods, including Dickens's recollections of reading a variety of texts and genres, including novels, newspapers, and epitaphs.

Dickens himself was one of those "young readers" addressed by George Ashton Taylor's tombstone—he was just a few days short of his twenty-sixth birthday on February 7, 1838—so that the story of Smike in the novel becomes an alternative epitaph to the one Dickens himself had read. As an epitaphic novel, *Nicholas Nickleby*, like the young Yorkshire student's tombstone, both offers a "judgement" on those who harmed Smike and attempts to revivify memories of the forgotten dead by addressing a new and expanded audience of readers beyond the local churchyard. This connection of novels with epitaphs also recalls one of Dickens's early professional self-descriptions in 1836, when he left a calling card at an oyster house opposite the Strand offices of Vincent Dowling, the editor of *Bell's Life in London* (where a series of "Boz's" earliest sketches of London life called "Scenes and Characters" was published); the card read: "Charles Dickens, Resurrectionist, In Search of a Subject."[16] "Resurrectionists," or "resurrection men" were notorious but often tolerated criminals who exhumed corpses ("subjects") to sell as cadavers to anatomists.[17] By associating himself with such an unholy class of men, Dickens was of course joking, but perhaps he was also alluding to his journalistic ability to publicize abuses and even to "wake the dead" to clamor for justice.[18]

Dickens's self-description as a "resurrectionist" resembles John Locke's figures of memories in the *Essay Concerning Human Understanding* (1689) as inscriptions or epitaphs, or as reanimated corpses "roused and tumbled out of their dark Cells, into open Day-light, by some turbulent and tempestuous passion" like the biblical Lazarus or newly freed prisoners.[19] Such images of memory's revivifying effects point to the author's ability to evoke forceful associations with his novels in the reader's mind. One way of describing the set of early novels that I examine in this chapter would be to see them as explorations of the pedagogical logic of epitaphs, following William Wordsworth's observation that the generic "excellencies" of an epitaph "will be found to lie in a due proportion of the common or universal feeling of humanity to sensations excited by a distinct and clear conception, conveyed to the reader's mind, of the individual, whose death is deplored and whose memory is to be preserved."[20] These psychological effects of epitaphic reading can also be traced to a common early nineteenth-century practice, described by the Evangelical clergyman and writer of religious tracts Legh Richmond, of instructing children to read in the churchyard: "Sometimes, I sent the children to the various stones which stood at the head of the graves, and bid them learn the epitaphs inscribed upon them. I took pleasure in seeing the little ones thus dispersed in the church-yard, each committing to memory a few verses written in commemoration of the departed. They would soon accomplish the desired object, and eagerly return to me ambitious to repeat their task. Thus my churchyard became a book of instruction, and every grave-stone a leaf of edification for my young disciples."[21] *Nicholas Nickleby* takes up the epitaphic, instructional task to preserve the memory of a distinct but forgotten individual, like George Ashton Taylor or Smike, and yet also associates such figures with the reader's personal experiences of loss and morning. In this sense, the novel is also a rhetorical exercise in prosopopoeia, or giving a voice to the remembered dead.[22]

It is not a coincidence, therefore, that the "resurrected" Yorkshire schoolboy Smike suffers from a weak memory. First, he has been a victim of Squeers's brutal tutelage, which the novel portrays brilliantly as a grotesque and cruel parody of the syllabic method common in Victorian reading pedagogy. When Nicholas first arrives at Dotheboys Hall, Squeers attempts to locate the head boy so that he can give a demonstration of the school's "practical" methods:

"Please, sir, he's cleaning the back parlour window," said the temporary head of the philosophical class.

"So he is, to be sure," rejoined Squeers. "We go upon the practical mode of teaching, Nickleby; the regular education system. C-l-e-a-n, clean, verb active, to make bright, to scour. W-i-n, win, d-e-r, der, winder, a casement. When the boy knows this out of book, he goes and does it. It's just the same principle as the use of the globes. Where's the second boy?"

"Please, sir, he's weeding the garden," replied a small voice.

"To be sure," said Squeers, by no means disconcerted. "So he is. B-o-t, bot, t-i-n, tin, bottin, n-e-y, ney, bottinney, noun substantive, a knowledge of plants. When he has learned that bottinney means a knowledge of plants, he goes and knows 'em. That's our system, Nickleby: what do you think of it?"

"It's a very useful one, at any rate," answered Nicholas significantly. (155)

Squeers demolishes the goals of the syllabic method of learning to read by memorizing syllables; he is able to define the words and state their grammatical functions accurately, but he misspells the majority of them and incorrectly divides the syllables. His version of the method does not require memorization only but also encompasses what the narrator sarcastically calls "experiments in practical philosophy" (154). Squeers also takes the syllabic method one step further by requiring his students to "do" the words that they spell from memory. His "experiments" are not scientific but rather involve exploiting his students' labor: learning becomes "useful" for the taskmaster Squeers rather than for the pupils. The snows of a Yorkshire winter render gardening and washing windows particularly cruel instances of "practical" learning.

As the most cruelly used drudge of this system, Smike has suffered the virtual destruction of his intellectual capacities, including his abilities to memorize and recite. When Nicholas first becomes acquainted with Smike, he finds him incapable of learning his lessons:

The poor soul was poring hard over a tattered book with the traces of recent tears still upon his face, vainly endeavouring to master some task which a child of nine years old, possessed of ordinary powers, could have conquered with ease, but which to the addled brain of the crushed boy of nineteen was a sealed and hopeless mystery. Yet there he sat, patiently conning the page again and again, stimulated by no boyish ambition, for he was the common jest and scoff even of the uncouth objects that congregated about him, but inspired by the one eager desire to please his solitary friend. (210–11)

Smike's abjection exposes a culture of abuse behind the ethos of emulation—the competition among the boys for higher ranks in the school—that formed a fundamental rationale for boys in the lowest ranks of Victorian monitorial schools, in which the more advanced pupils taught larger groups of younger students, to strive to ascend to higher grades. Smike's inability to memorize is also linked to his fragmentary memories about his past, causing him to fear that he will not be able to die peacefully while recalling the faces of his family, as he saw another sick boy do: "What faces will smile on me when I die! . . . Who will talk to me in those long nights? They [memories of faces] cannot come from home; they would frighten me if they did, for I don't know what it is, and shouldn't know them. Pain and fear, pain and fear for me, alive or dead. No hope, no hope" (162). Like the forgotten London clerks of "Thoughts about People," Smike has become a creature of enforced "habit and endurance," lacking pleasant memories, whether of past happiness or sorrow. Without such associations to help him regulate his pain and fear, Smike is deprived of any possibility of recognizing either himself or others in the mirror of the past. In an almost perfect paraphrase of Samuel Rogers's analysis of the "pleasures of memory," and a precursor to the schoolmaster's consolation in *The Old Curiosity Shop*, one of the storytelling travelers on Nicholas's journey to Yorkshire explains that "If our affections be tried, our affections are our consolation and comfort; and memory, however sad, is the best and purest link between this world and a better" (129).

Despite these fears, Nicholas's compassion and patience begin to transform Smike and his capacity for memory revives: "He was an altered being; he had an object now, and that object was to show his attachment to the only person—that person a stranger—who had treated him, not to say with kindness, but like a human creature" (210). After Nicholas and Smike have escaped Dotheboys Hall and are journeying away from London to find employment, Nicholas gently examines Smike to see whether he can recollect the circumstances of his arrival at the school. By retaining Smike's gaze and asking leading questions, Nicholas manages to induce him to recall an early childhood memory of "a large lonesome room at the top of a house, where there was a trap-door in the ceiling" (348), a description that ultimately links Smike to his real identity as Ralph Nickleby's lost son and Nicholas's cousin. But in order for this identity to come to light, an intermediary mind is needed to retain this memory as evidence: "Nicholas marked him closely, and every word of this conversation remained indelibly fastened in his memory" (349). As a result of Nicholas's mediating influence, Smike's ability to remember is strengthened. In effect, Nicholas is able to supplement Smike's memories by reconnecting his chain of associations and then "indelibly fastening" them in his own memory.

Unlike the forgotten Londoners of "Thoughts about People," Smike has been befriended by a stranger (who turns out to be kin). Even though he still cannot remember his past home or family, he now can hope that he will not be forgotten after he dies, as he explains to Nicholas: "I could not part from you to go to any home on earth . . . except one, except one. I shall never be an old man; and if your hand placed me in the grave, and I could think before I died that you would come and look upon it sometimes with one of your kind smiles, and in the summer weather, when everything was alive—not dead like me—I could go to that home almost without a tear." When Nicholas chides him, "Why do you talk thus, poor boy, if your life is a happy one with me?" Smike expresses a shade of doubt: "Because *I* should change; not those about me. And if they forgot me, *I* should never know it. . . . In the churchyard we are all alike, but here there are none like me. I am a poor creature, but I know that well" (526). Smike fears that "others," including Nicholas and his family, will change in their regard for him after he dies—they may forget him. Therefore he prefers to think of himself as "changed" permanently in death, ignorant that he has been forgotten and perhaps taking all such mutability upon himself, while sparing others the ethical burdens of remembrance and forgetfulness.

Of course, the novel's final sentences assure us that Smike will be remembered daily in the conversations of his restored family: after his death Nicholas and Kate's children visit Smike's grave often and garland it with flowers. Similarly, Newman Noggs, the character who belongs to that class of lonely London clerks described in "Thoughts about People," is not forgotten and friendless either but instead retires in a small cottage close to the Nickleby family home. Yet Smike's visions of the churchyard as a place of nondiscrimination and equivalence, where a "poor creature" such as himself can finally achieve equality with all the other sleepers, also appear in the darker thoughts of Ralph Nickleby just before his suicide, as he passes a pauper cemetery:

> [Ralph] had to pass a poor, mean burial-ground—a dismal place raised a few
> feet above the level of the street, and parted from it by a low parapet wall
> and an iron railing; a rank, unwholesome, rotten spot, where the very grass
> and weeds seemed, in their frowsy growth, to tell that they had sprung from
> paupers' bodies, and struck their roots in the graves of men, sodden in
> streaming courts and drunken hungry dens. And here in truth they lay,
> parted from the living by a little earth and a board or two—lay thick and
> close—corrupting in body as they had in mind; a dense and squalid crowd.
> Here they lay cheek by jowl with life: no deeper down than the feet of the
> throng that passed there every day, and piled high as their throats. (902)[23]

Despite its potential familiarity to readers, this pauper burial ground can provide within the novel no setting to spur remembrance, for its leveling influence is not primarily that universal one of death but rather the social degeneration caused by neglect, disease, and squalor. By reducing the poor—both in their physical demise and also often in the eyes of those government officials and parliamentary commissions who treat them as statistics—to an indiscriminate heap of decaying corpses, the pauper burial ground precludes epitaphic reading. Its indiscriminate resting places fail as topoi of memory for both the mourner and the reader.

The scene leads Ralph to recall his service on a jury at an inquest over a suicide, and it suddenly occurs to him that the man in the case might be buried here, although he cannot locate his grave: there are no epitaphs for the unclaimed dead. Under the combined weight of the revelation of Smike's true identity, his own culpability in the history of his son's suffering and death, and the failure of all his own financial schemes and plots against Nicholas at the end of the novel, Ralph decides to join the crowd of the unremembered dead, cursing the tolling church bell just before he hangs himself in the attic room of Smike's revived memory: " 'Call men to prayers who are godly because not found out, and ring chimes for the coming in of every year that brings this cursed world nearer to its end. No bell or book for me; throw me on a dunghill, and let me rot there to infect the air!' " (906). Ralph construes suicide as vengeance on the living, a means "to spurn their mercy and compassion" by remaining unknown, unreconciled, and a source of moral pollution after his death (905). By embracing the anonymity of the pauper graveyard, Ralph refuses to participate in the epitaphic rituals of personification involved in remembering the dead. He rebels against memory's powers of association—its function in cementing the bonds of identity, kinship, and social connection—by choosing to remain disdainful of others and unloved.

Following the causality suggested in "Thoughts about People," which explains the lonely Londoner's condition as the result of economic pressures that require migration to the city, a further way to understand Ralph Nickleby's trajectory would be to link his resentment, as he does in his own mind, to his mercenary mentality. Ralph personifies the economic forces that drive country dwellers to seek urban employment. In addition to his money-lending concerns, he is a "capitalist" (69) and financial backer of the attempt by the United Metropolitan Improved Hot Muffin and Crumpet Baking and Punctual Delivery Company to monopolize the muffin and crumpet trade (72–73). Just after confirming his memories of the resemblance between Nicholas and his envied brother, Nicholas's father, Ralph continues his "unprofitable reflections" by planning his revenge: "Recollections like these,' pursued Ralph, with a bitter smile [speaking out loud to himself], 'flock upon me—when I resign myself to them—in crowds, and from countless quarters. As a portion of the world affect to despise the power of money, I must try and show them what it is" (525). Ralph is able to resist the persecutory "crowds" of memories by converting them into fuel for his revenge on Nicholas and self-vindication through "the power of money." As his fortunes decline toward the end of the novel, however, Ralph's ability to resist his memories begins to break down and he is unable to sleep. Once again in soliloquy he worries, "If I sleep, what rest is that which is disturbed by constant dreams of the same detested faces crowding round me—of the same detested people in every variety of action, mingling with all I say and do, and always to my defeat?" (865). In the novel's moral economy of memory, Ralph's "hot pursuit of his bad ends" (890) of gain and profit turns his memories into agents of judgment and punishment. The crowds of remembered faces that Smike longs for Ralph dreads; thus the son's and father's stories are linked by being the positive and negative versions of the conjoining bonds of association.

Toward the end of the novel, the London crowd becomes a metaphor for the ethical and epistemological problems involved in foregrounding any individual's distress amid the mass of human suffering and injustice.[24] Nicholas walks through the streets of London, this time considering how to prevent Ralph's plot to "sell" Madeline Bray in marriage to the old, lascivious moneylender and slum landlord Arthur Gride in exchange for his liquidating her father's debt to Ralph. I quote this mental catalog of injustices at length, and yet not even in its entirety, to show how a virtually unending series of linked examples of human misery threatens to engulf Nicholas's thoughts and the narrative as well:

> But now, when he thought how regularly things went on from day to day in the same unwavering round—how youth and beauty died, and ugly griping age lived tottering on—how crafty avarice grew rich, and manly honest hearts were poor and sad—how few they were who tenanted the stately houses, and how many those who lay in noisome pens, or rose each day and laid them down at night, and lived and died, father and son, mother and child, race upon race, and generation upon generation, without a home to shelter them or the energies of one single man directed to their aid—how in seeking, not a luxurious and splendid life, but the bare means of a most wretched and inadequate subsistence, there were women and children in that one town, divided into classes, numbered and estimated as regularly as the noble families and folks of great degree, and reared from infancy to drive most criminal and dreadful trades—how ignorance was punished and never

taught—how jail-door gaped and gallows loomed for thousands urged towards them by circumstances darkly curtaining their very cradles' heads, but for which they might have earned their honest bread and lived in peace . . . how much injustice, and misery, and wrong there was, and yet how the world rolled on from year to year, alike careless and indifferent, and no man seeking to remedy or redress it:—when he thought of all this and selected from the mass the one slight case on which his thoughts were bent, he felt indeed that there was little ground for hope, and little cause or reason why it should not form an atom in the huge aggregate of distress and sorrow, and add one small and unimportant unit to swell the great amount. (791)

My choice of what to elide from the longer passage is just as arbitrary as Nicholas's own and the narrative's stopping point, which is precisely the effect of amplification or *copia* that the seemingly infinite series of injustices and failures, cycling endlessly through time and human history, creates rhetorically.[25] Here is the inverse of Ralph's individualistic misanthropy: the threat of despair at the aggregate magnitude of human suffering. Such a litany—which includes a critique of the human penchant to divide and classify other human beings—verges on incomprehension because, like the "unwavering round" of everyday existence, it seems ineluctable. Here also is one of the possible drawbacks of the associating memory: instead of a strand or cluster of related, regulated ideas and images, it may produce an endless, repeating series that stymies constructive, synthetic thought with the weight and proliferation of its linked instances. The individual too becomes merely a link or "atom" within the forward spiraling movement of history. This possibility of the atomization of the individual mind recalls William Hazlitt's criticism of the "absurd" associationist notion that thinking could be regulated by "mere proximity," which, he argues, is tantamount "to imagin[ing] that by placing a number of persons together in a line we should produce in them an immediate consciousness and perfect knowledge of what was passing in each other's minds."[26] Nicholas's vision of the anonymous crowd of sufferers also provides the obverse of Wordsworth's definition of the epitaph's function as depending upon "the due proportion of the common or universal feeling of humanity to sensations excited by a distinct and clear conception, conveyed to the reader's mind, of the individual, whose death is deplored and whose memory is to be preserved."[27] Human suffering conceived in the aggregate precludes distinguishing the significant individual death from the mass of human mortality. It is this problem of the overwhelming incommensurability of injustice and the individual's reduction to anonymity or atomization within the aggregate, however, that the Dickensian novel's associationist memory techniques attempt to keep in check for the reader. In doing so, the novel also provides an alternative logic, grounded in both the material world and an empiricist theory of mind, to the competing logic of Evangelical providentialism, in which the meaning of an individual life is justified according to a notion of eternity and a divine plan.

Nicholas rebounds from these existential and cognitive threats, however, by virtue of his youth and his ability to collect his thoughts: "By dint of reflecting on what he had to do and reviving the train of thought which the night had interrupted, Nicholas gradually summoned up his utmost energy, and by the time the morning was sufficiently advanced for his purpose, had no thought but that of using it to his best advantage" (791). Regulating his thoughts by focusing on his goal of saving Madeline from the conspirators, Nicholas keeps the urban crowd's epistemological threat at bay. Though it verges on incoherence, the endless succession of human suffering and wrong is in fact coordinated with the novel's associative epistemological exploration of the mental and moral connections between the individual memory and social conditions. The solution to the threat of being a mere "unit" in a random series or set based in impersonal proximity is to find the common social causality within contiguity that supports both human relations and the chains of thought. By coordinating narrative description, plot, and memory effects, the novel teaches that the crowd can become a coherent object of knowledge—and an individual can pass through it without being reduced to an atom, an unprotesting "creature of habit," or a misanthrope—as long as relationships with others are initiated, sustained, and not forgotten. The pauper burial ground threatens literally and metaphorically to infect the living passers-by because the reason for its existence is social neglect and injustice. One can also recall the example of Nicholas as Smike's "solitary" friend: you only need to make one friend to begin a series, and then a nexus, of relationships. To think of oneself as a "mere unit," then, is to make a fundamental ethical and epistemological mistake: human relationships partially create and partially realize existing causal connections with others that exist in memory, in everyday proximity and contact, and in society conceived as a nexus of such concrete connections. We can also begin to see how the serial form of the novel extends this logic temporally and spatially to a network of readers who, through the new medium of cheap and mass-produced periodicals, become a self-consciously connected reading audience capable of forming a social or political constituency.

As perhaps most overtly associationist of Dickens's novels, *Nicholas Nickleby* exhibits the risk of endless seriality, or epistemological spiraling and its accompanying disorientation of the reader, entailed in the effort to coordinate theories of memory with a social epistemology. Serial novel reading itself becomes a solution to this threat. In keeping with its preoccupation with memory as a source of connection, *Nicholas Nickleby* also incorporates a salient counterexample of atomistic reading in Arthur Gride's private "contemplation" of "the entries in a dirty old vellum-book with rusty clasps":

> "Well-a-day!" he chuckled, as sinking on his knees before a strong chest screwed down to the floor, he thrust in his arm nearly up to the shoulder, and slowly drew forth this greasy volume, "Well-a-day now, this is all my library, but it's one of the most entertaining books that were ever written; it's a delightful book, and all true and real—that's the best of it—true as the Bank of England, and real as its gold and silver. Written by Arthur Gride—he, he, he! None of your story-book writers will ever make as good a book as this, I warrant me. It's composed for private circulation—for my own particular reading, and nobody else's. He, he!" (799)

Gride's pernicious perusal of the account book where he records his corrupt money-lending business exhibits all the negative effects of reading a text in "private circulation." Such exclusionary collapsing of authorship and reception claims to be self-warranting—"I warrant me"—and thus refuses an audience. Gride's monopolistic reading is the antithesis of the participatory reading that "story-book writers" elicit. As with Ralph Nickleby's soliloquies dwelling on his grievances, Gride's discourse is based on a desire to hoard and monopolize not only money but also information, to plot against others but not to involve oneself in any relationships that would entail obligation. However, Gride makes the mistake of equating his private account book with the sums it enumerates—believing its contents to be as "real" as gold in the "Bank of England," but without the susceptibility to circulation or theft of actual coins. Appropriately, Gride and Ralph are both undone when Gride's illiterate housekeeper, Peg Sliderskew, realizing the book's value because she has seen how her master prizes it, steals it as evidence revealing the scheme to defraud Madeline Bray through the withholding of a will. Even though she cannot read the account book, Peg still knows enough to use it for the purposes of blackmail by threatening to put it into circulation, causing the revelation of its secrets and the conviction of its author.

Explicitly opposed to the reading of fiction, Gride's "particular reading," with its analogies to the accumulation of capital and the exploitation of knowledge about others, becomes the inverse image of serial novel reading as a social practice. As a stiflingly private habit of consumption, such exclusive reading must be forcibly publicized, like the abuses of the Yorkshire schools, in the interests of justice. Like *The Old Curiosity Shop*'s critique of the Evangelical calculus as a hypocritical form of spiritual salesmanship, Gride's reading thus exemplifies how the Dickensian pleasures of memory seek to divest the collective experience of popular reading and its nascent versions of mass cultural participation from motives of rampant individualism or profit so that they can be invested with more communal purposes.

Reading as Experience

It is the quiet country-folks who read books, not we busy Londoners whose life is a scramble of clubs and parties. Books are aeras in these people's lives, and such as give them pleasure are remembered for years and years.

William Makepeace Thackeray (1857)

Nicholas's transformation in relation to Smike from stranger to friend to cousin suggests that the novel tries out each of these relations successively as a model for the reader's own connection to, or "kinship" with, the novel's characters. Dickens's next novel, *The Old Curiosity Shop*, incorporates further techniques for modeling the forms of social connection that serial reading encourages.[28] As I argued in the previous chapter, Little Nell's Victorian readers seem to have responded to her characterization as falling within the didactic genres of stories recounting the pious deaths of children or instructing children in the religious meaning of mortality. This kind of lesson was facilitated when the Sunday school classroom happened to be located, as it frequently was, near a churchyard. Legh Richmond takes the occasion of his epitaphic curriculum to warn his pupils quite sincerely that "young as they were, none of them were too young to die; and that probably more than half of the bodies which were buried there, were those of little children."[29] The memorization of epitaphs by Richmond's young "disciples" allows such churchyard associations to serve as a kind of supplement to the other texts they typically memorized in the course of their religious schooling, such as the Bible or a catechism.

This reading lesson in a churchyard was also common in early nineteenth-century children's literature. The young heroine of Charles and

Mary Lamb's *Mrs. Leicester's School* (1811) learns her alphabet from her mother's tombstone, and, in a Wordsworthian vein, comes to sense her mother's presence in the peaceful natural setting of the cemetery.[30] Dickens would return repeatedly to the reading of epitaphs both at the end of *Oliver Twist* and in Pip's visit to the grave of his parents in the opening chapter of *Great Expectations* (1860–61); such scenes become pivotal for forging thematic connections among death, kinship, and personal identity. In revisiting such Romantic topoi, *The Old Curiosity Shop* makes explicit the linkage between epitaphs and pedagogy by offering a new kind of exercise in novelistic reception. The novel's innovation within this tradition is to explicate Nell's own epitaphic reading practice, thus positioning it to perform the self-reflexive pedagogical function of associating the experience of reading Dickens's serial fiction with remembering and commemorating the dead.

Just as *The Old Curiosity Shop* revisits the theme of the unjust death of an exploited child from *Nicholas Nickleby*, so it also develops the connection between memories of the dead and moral agency. As we have seen, memory plays a crucial role in the schoolmaster's consolation, which he offers to Nell as a reassurance when she, like Smike, worries that the dead are often forgotten. He insists that the influence of the dead is present in the "good actions and good thoughts" of busy people, even when the dead themselves are not remembered.[31] The associationist framework of this logic is also significant: within the novel, the dead themselves, symbolized by "these very graves" that Nell tends in the cemetery, take on an abstract agency in thought through the process of association—they are the "chief instruments" in motivating good deeds, in part because they are no longer present as a potential source of selfish motives but instead promote (anti-didactic) "purified affection" (504).

The scene where Nell sits in the gothic baronial chapel among the tombs and teaches herself to imagine her own death shows her performing a similar set of substitutions that highlight the role of serial reading in this process of associating moral reformation with memories of the dead. This scene is introduced by the dictum about contrasts: "Everything in our lives, whether of good or evil, affects us most by contrast" (493). When Nell enters the old gothic church, she herself invites the contrast of youth and innocence with age, ruin, and decay, while the church becomes a setting in which all the opposing organizational and compositional elements of art and world tend toward a universal message about mortality and the inevitable passage of time: "the best work and the worst, the plainest and the richest, the stateliest and the least imposing—both of Heaven's work and Man's—all found one common level here, and told one common tale" (493–94). Much like Smike's fantasy of the equality he will finally achieve in death, both the setting of the old church and Nell's presence there suggest the existence of larger natural and temporal processes that either bring oppositions into harmonious relation with one another or dissolve distinctions into sameness.

Death is one such connecting and dissolving power. For David Hume, association is another non-hierarchical connecting power that also supports identity rather than indeterminacy: " 'Twill be easy to conceive of what vast consequence these principles [of association] must be in the science of human nature, if we consider, that so far as regards the mind, these are the only links that bind the parts of the universe together, or connect us with any person or object exterior to ourselves."[32] This conclusion about the formal rather than substantive characteristics of experience underpins Hume's epistemological skepticism. In *A Treatise of Human Nature* (1739–40), Hume determines that identity, whether of objects or of persons, involves the characteristics of constancy and coherence in time.[33] The relation of identity is not "something that really binds our several perceptions together" but rather "only associates their ideas in the imagination."[34] Thus personal identity too is "fictitious" as an effect of memory: "As memory alone acquaints us with the continuance and extent of this succession of perceptions, 'tis to be consider'd, upon that account chiefly, as the source of personal identity. Had we no memory, we never shou'd have any notion of causation, nor consequently of the chain of causes and effects, which constitute our self or person."[35] Hume concludes that the associative bonds of memory, identity, and causation cannot be seen or proved but only experienced: "We only *feel* a connexion or a determination of the thought, to pass from one object to another. It follows, therefore, that the thought alone finds personal identity, when reflecting on the train of past perceptions, that compose a mind, the ideas of them are felt to be connected together, and naturally introduce each other."[36] Hume's formulations of the epistemological functions of memory help elucidate the associationist assumptions about memory and identity that are at work in Nell's apprehension of her impending death.

The linked operations of association in the scene of Nell's chapel reading—both for Nell within the narrative and for the reader—suggest a subtly Humean epistemology, particularly in Nell's teaching herself to manipulate a transition from reading to thinking. When Nell first enters the chapel, she sits down among the tombs and, "gazing round with a feeling of awe, tempered with a calm delight, felt that now she was happy, and at rest" (494). Next she picks up a Bible, reads it, and then puts it down and begins to imagine the empty chapel in the coming spring—birds singing, shadows moving across the pavement, the breeze swaying the tattered banners hanging from the walls—when she will have died. These reflections are similar to Smike's imagining Nicholas visiting his grave in the summer. She reaches a conclusion, rendered in indirect discourse, having to do with mastering certain kinds of thoughts of death and *replacing them* with others: "What if the spot awakened thoughts of death! Die who would, it would still remain the same; these sights and sounds would still go on as happily as ever. It would be no pain to sleep amidst them" (494). If Hannah More's shepherd of Salisbury plain had been in Nell's situation, he would certainly have found consolation in thoughts of salvation by reading the Bible, and told us so. Legh Richmond's converted reader of his tales would be led to hope for her own salvation, and perhaps imagine herself among the blessed. But Nell picks up her Bible, reads it, and then puts it down again to initiate her own train of thought, not so much spurred by the content of her book, I would argue, although the fact of its being a Bible is no mere accident, as by the *process* of her repeated reading.

The episode seems to culminate in Nell's ascent to the top of the church's tower, where, as she emerges out into the sun, a "glory of the sudden burst of light" lifts her thoughts toward heaven.[37] This prefiguring of resurrection, however, is not a sufficient means for Nell to conceive and accept her own death, or for the novel to construct the reader's access to Nell's story as a collective consolation achieved through the reading of fiction. Instead, serial repetition ensues; Nell returns to the church two more times, not to revisit the transcendent view from the tower, but rather to repeat her interlude in the chapel:

> Again that day, yes, twice again, she stole back to the old chapel, and in her former seat read from the same book, or indulged the same quite train of thought. Even when it had grown dusk, and the shadows of coming night made it more solemn still, the child remained like one rooted to the spot, and had no fear, or thought of stirring.
>
> They found her there at last, and took her home. She looked pale but very happy, until they separated for the night; and then, as the poor schoolmaster stooped down to kiss her cheek, he thought he felt a tear upon his face. (496)

This repetition, which is only brought to a close by the intervention of others, signifies Nell's improvisation of a technique for accustoming herself to the thought of her own death. The technique involves the transition between reading and a specific train of thought envisioning in sensory terms her own eventual absence while the world carries on its usual rhythms without her. Nell's practice is based on associationist principles, not only because she is rehearsing a "train of thought" but also because she is creating an association both for herself and for the reader between the quiet, empty chapel and her own ceasing to exist—the vacant chapel becomes a topos for commemorating her death. The accompanying illustration shows Nell precisely during this repeated moment of the suspension of reading into her own train of thought (Figure 10).[38] Through Nell's new reading habit, then, the "pain" of anticipating her death dissipates because she is able to imagine the transition from life to death as analogous to the relationship between reading and looking up from the page to pursue her own thoughts. This analogy is epistemologically possible according to a Humean conception of memory's connective function in supporting personal identity simply as a feeling of continuity: the serial dimensions of the self in time can be captured by the serial nature of repeated reading, while to cease reading is, in effect, to temporarily pause and thus to perceive the self—to shift parallel serial processes, as it were, from reading to reflection. Nell's tears confirm that her improvised technique has allowed her to convert the pain of paradoxically "recollecting" her own death into the pleasures of memory. Through associationist and pedagogical means, Nell is represented as training *herself* to "remember" her own death, in the hope that others will remember her as well. She is a kind of "self-resurrectionist."

The novel connects the consolatory effect of Nell's chapel visit with the reading of the Bible, but it does so only obliquely. Hannah More describes the devotional influence of Bible reading, cautioning the pious reader not to misconstrue the intent of its teachings: "The Bible never warns us against imaginary evil, nor courts us to imaginary good. If, then, we refuse to yield to its guidance, if we reject its directions, if we submit not to its gentle persuasions—for such they are, and not arbitrary compulsions—we shall never attain to that peace and liberty which are the privilege, the promised reward, of sincere Christians."[39] Because it is not a work of fiction, according to More, the Bible does not attempt to reach the reader through his or her imagination or memory, like a novel does, but rather it addresses the reader directly, without any mediation or compulsion. The importance of the fact that Nell is reading the Bible, then, lies in the scene's revision of common Victorian habits of private devotional and church-sponsored classroom reading of scripture. Nell's reading does not directly respond to the Bible's

Figure 10. "Little Nell in the Gothic Church," by George Cattermole, in Charles Dickens, *The Old Curiosity Shop: A Tale*, vol. 2 (London: Chapman and Hall, 1841), 95. Beinecke Rare Book and Manuscript Library, Yale University.

own "gentle persuasion" in More's sense of devotional reading. Nor is this a scene that is meant to prepare Nell for salvation, or the reader for bearing witness to her salvation. Instead the repeated movement from reading to a train of thought envisions the aftermath of Nell's death as something like a memory of the empty, quiet church—an epitaphic marking of the absence of a specific person. This repetition—Nell's new reading habit—facilitates her ability to imagine her own absence because of the way her mind is operating in the associative space between, or combining, reading, remembering, and thinking. Nell's technique also demonstrates how the impress of sensations related to ideas of pleasure and pain creates associations in the memory. The specific *content* of Nell's train of thought consists in her imagining of her own absence through the sense impressions produced by the empty church. In this secularization of a practice of personal piety, the act of reading substitutes for the train of thought about her own death, allowing Nell temporarily to forget her own presence in the world. Then, when she puts the book down, she can invest her reveries about her own death with both the technical control and the partial suspension of self-awareness that reading permits. Nell's version of silent reading becomes a kind of suspended animation between life and death. The ability to read and then consider what one has read, to be aware of one's surroundings and then remove one's focus from them to peruse a text, permits a rehearsal of presence and absence of self-consciousness. This technique of oscillating between self-forgetfulness and self-reflection has the effect of making death conceivable and potentially less frightening. This is precisely not the droning repetition of syllables practiced in the Victorian classroom but instead provides an image of a quiet, inward teaching enacted for the reader of the novel. The novel foregrounds memory's role as a medium through which serial reading fosters a self-reflection that is not definitively anchored to piety.

The novel also offers Nell's reading as the positive pedagogical model for novel reading as a practice of connecting individual and social forms of memory. Nell's gaze away from the book in the accompanying illustration (Figure 10) captures precisely what the Dickensian cultural politics that I have been reconstructing aspires to effect through the new habit of popular serial reading: a transition or remediation from pious to secular reading that educates the reader to connect his or her own train of thought with the lessons in public service that the novel teaches.[40] Nell does not look down at her book but looks up, toward two gothic windows that invite a further layer of transitioning from reading to thinking to gazing outside at the world that persists beyond her consciousness. Showing the state of suspension between reading and thinking, the illustration of Nell's new reading habit captures that virtual ranging movement through mental space of the associative freedom of thought, where reading and one's own preoccupations blend together—a habit now so familiar in its further remediations as to go unnoticed when we make use of digital windows as portals to our web of virtual connections through the Internet, and engage in parallel associative processes of scanning, reading, and revisiting a series of Web sites, the contents of which are also updated serially.[41] Dickens's novel makes explicit in this scene how the new print medium of serial fiction alters earlier practices of devotional reading, with far-reaching implications, from our perspective, for further developments in our interactions with modern technological media. Associationist theories of memory as medium fostered Dickensian serial fiction's remediation of print technologies by framing reading as a virtual experience.

If Nell remains "rooted to the spot," then, this is because she has both perfected her new reading habit and become her own epitaph, for herself and for the reader—the "presence" of the reader in the scene, then, is crucial. It is significant that this scene takes place at the end of a serial issue, thus inviting the rereading of Nell's own featured practice of rereading.[42] Such rereading of the serial installment would likewise leave open a space for the Victorian reader's own speculations about Nell's fate between Nell's rehearsal of her death in thought and the narration of her death in a later weekly number of the novel.[43] Through investigating how Nell's reading habit works, however, we have also discovered another reason, in addition to the novel's rejection of the deathbed witness depicted in Evangelical fiction, why the reader is excluded diegetically from witnessing the moment of Nell's death: because Nell herself has already experienced it and rehearsed it for the reader through the scene of reading in the chapel. The novel leaves it for the reader to experience Nell's death in retrospect and in imagination—as Nell herself rehearsed her own death through reading in the chapel.

The reader of Dickens's novel thus encounters a layered exemplarity and complex form of instruction. First, one can learn that it is possible to remember the dead through the activity of reading Dickens's novel, which also takes on an epitaphic, "resurrectionist" function linked to prosopopoeia. On this level we are concerned with the implications of Nell's own reading for the reader's acceptance of the novel's epistemology of reading. Second, *The Old Curiosity Shop* offers a more ambitious response to Smike's and Nell's fear that the dead are often forgotten than is conveyed in the schoolmaster's consolation: it also demonstrates that serial novel reading affords a means both to preserve the memory of the dead and to recall and take notice of those living persons who, like the fictional characters Nell and Smike during their lifetimes, have been forgotten and overlooked—those city dwellers who are so anonymous that they don't even seem worth noticing or remembering. The transitional status of Nell's Bible reading—between a devotional and a secular practice—is also reinforced by its transitional pedagogy between classroom drill and popular reading. "No provision was made for silent reading" in the Victorian schoolroom, Richard D. Altick has emphasized.[44] Nell's silent reading in the chapel therefore replaces the Salisbury shepherd's memorization of the Bible, which conforms to the continued reliance on memorization in Victorian classrooms, providing an alternative model of silent reading that could supplement, and historically would eventually displace, Victorian practices of reading aloud in the classroom, before an audience, or at the family fireside.

In depicting this scene of Nell's reading that encompasses a more practical, pedagogical consolation in addition to the schoolmaster's overtly didactic one, Dickens develops the implications of some scenes from his earlier novel, *Oliver Twist*, that also posit a relationship between reading and remembering and thus elaborate a further crucial aspect of the way Dickens's novelistic pedagogy bridges private reading and cultural memory. In one scene, Oliver lies asleep, and Rose, Mrs. Maylie and Mr. Losberne are leaning over his bed, gazing at him, and trying to gauge his character from his features:

> The boy stirred, and smiled in his sleep, as though these marks of pity and compassion [Rose's tears, fallen upon his forehead] had awakened some pleasant dream of a love and affection he had never known. Thus, a strain of gentle music, or a rippling of water in a silent place, or the odour of a flower, or the mention of a familiar word, will sometimes call up sudden dim remembrances of scenes that never were, in this life; which vanish like a breath; which some brief memory of a happier existence, long gone by, would seem to have awakened; which no voluntary exertion of the mind can ever recall. (268)[45]

This is a moment in the text that we might pass over, since it seems to lack the prodigious originality that modern readers associate with Dickens. The passage implies that, like Smike, Oliver lacks memories of home. He is an orphan, raised in the workhouse, so he can only dream of a "love and affection he had never known." This passage compares dream thoughts to involuntary memories, and even to memories of forgotten dreams. But another possible explanation of these "remembrances of scenes that never were, in this life," is that they are recollections of books read in the past. These memories could belong to Oliver himself, given that he has never actually experienced such a "happier existence" except in his imagination. But they could also belong to the Victorian reader, for whom Oliver's latent happiness conjures up both her own experiences of the "rush" of past associations and *the imagined sensory effects evoked by reading*, perhaps in particular by her past reading of Wordsworth, whose poetry the passage seems to paraphrase.[46]

This kind of heightening of the associationist analogy between reading and experience is similarly evident in a later scene from the period of Oliver's convalesce from his gunshot wound with the Maylies in the country. In its imagery and rhetoric, this episode aligns with the rural scenes of *Nicholas Nickleby* and *The Old Curiosity Shop*. It begins with two of those characteristic exclamations by the narrator—like the one in *The Old Curiosity Shop* describing the devastating impact of Nell's journey through the industrial city—that invoke the impossibility of rendering an emotional effect adequately in words: "Who can describe the pleasure and delight, the peace of mind and soft tranquility, the sickly boy felt in the balmy air, and among the green hills and rich woods, of an inland village! Who can tell how scenes of peace and quietude sink into the minds of pain-worn dwellers in close and noisy places, and carry their own freshness deep into their jaded hearts!" (290). This figure is a kind of rhetorical question, a form of aporia or paradox called an *inopinatum*, a "faux wondering" that once again seems to paraphrase some unidentifiable but familiar earlier text or genre.[47] The reader of *Oliver Twist* seems to be invited to imagine these effects of the natural influences of the country on Oliver as being so profound that they defy description. But the rhetorical questions may also indicate that the evocation is already banal—even a cliché to be dispensed with quickly.

Yet there is a difference between what the reader is asked to imagine in the earlier passage from the novel describing Oliver asleep, and in the later one connecting Oliver's healing stay in the country with the city dweller's dreams of the countryside. In the first, we know that Oliver is "actually" situated in the country, so we are exhorted to approximate his "real" feelings. There is no indication in the rhetorical questions of the later passage, however, that the "pain-worn dwellers in close and noisy places" have been removed to the country. In fact, it seems much more likely that these city dwellers are among Dickens's readers, and therefore that *fictional* "scenes of peace and quietude" are meant to influence their "jaded hearts" just as Oliver's weariness and suffering are cured by his stay among kind friends in the country. The consoling effects of the novel's fictional rural scenes are substituted for actual jaunts to the country. It is also not necessary that the novel's urban readers have ever lived in the country in order to experience this effect, although some of them may have done so. Instead the novel evokes commonplace cultural memories reflecting the gradual urbanization of England that apply collectively to a mass readership that has also been formed not only in the context of larger nineteenth-century trends of social change, including economic dislocation and migration to the larger industrializing cities, but also through the reading of the many poems on pastoral themes included in popular eighteenth- and nineteenth-century anthologies of literature.[48]

Perhaps, paradoxically, the narrator's rhetorical questions address readers who resemble the lonely clerks of "Thoughts about People," those city dwellers who have become "mere passive creatures of habit and endurance" but who can still envision what it would be like to return to the country. A subsequent paragraph compares Oliver's convalescence to the lifelong city dwellers' attempts to "crawl forth" from their dwellings to catch a last glimpse of sunlight before they die, thus stocking their memories with consoling visions of "Nature's face":

> The memories which peaceful country scenes call up, are not of this world, nor of its thoughts and hopes. Their gentle influence may teach us how to weave fresh garlands for the graves of those we loved: may purify our thoughts, and bear down before it old enmity and hatred; but beneath all this, there lingers, in the least reflective mind, a vague and half-formed consciousness of having held such feelings long before, in some remote and distant time, which calls up solemn thoughts of distant times to come, and bends down pride and worldliness beneath it. (290)

This epitaphic passage from *Oliver Twist* forms a prelude to the effects of reading developed in *The Old Curiosity Shop*'s gothic church scene. The narrator does not refer to reading explicitly here. Instead, the consolation that *Oliver Twist* affords the urban reader through the narrator's rhetorically heightened supplying of fictional memories of rural scenes becomes associated in Nell's case *with the representation of consolatory reading itself.* As a precursor to the scene of Nell's chapel reading, then, this passage from *Oliver Twist* suggests that just as the memories created by reading are passed on to future generations who will read the same books, so more generalized epitaphic memories of the beloved dead can be shared through the reading of consolatory fictions, like the stories of Oliver and Little Nell. For example, the Victorian reader, reminded by Nell of his or her own child lost to illness, may pause or put down the novel, and then resume reading again. In that resumed reading, he or she can now imagine that the novel provides a shared and replicable means to relate these two activities—reading and remembering—in a generic form that can mediate a personal loss by generalizing it into a memory of reading shared with other readers.

If such shared reading takes the form of reading a serial novel, then the break and resumption within the reader's transitioning between reading and remembering also takes place repeatedly across installments. By staging these serial forms of transition between memory and reading within the narration, the text is rehearsing in advance the very forms that its own popular circulation—its status as a memory effect or topos of Victorian popular culture—will take. The Dickensian serial novel differs from religious didactic fiction by teaching the reader to treat memories derived from reading as *analogous but not equivalent to* memories derived from experience. A narrative of the pious deathbed inspires a mimetic response to an actual scene of salvation, while "fictitious realities" staged through Dickens's novelistic pedagogy are always virtual, just as is the Humean self, and thus inspire a response that is necessarily mediated at every level through the serial relay from reading to memory to experience. At the end of the century, Wilde captures this effect in his joke from *The Importance of Being Earnest*, which I have included as an epigraph, that memories have become the true sources of popular novels.

But such virtual relations are not without their effects in the real world. In a speech delivered in June of 1841, Dickens indicates that *The Old Curiosity Shop* has created a sense of mutual friendship between him and his readers based in shared memories connecting authorship intimately with reading: "I feel as if I stood among old friends, whom I have intimately known and highly valued. I feel as if the deaths of the fictitious creatures, in which you have been kind enough to express an interest, had endeared us to each other as real afflictions deepen friendships in actual life; I feel as if they had been real persons, whose fortunes we had pursued together in inseparable connection, and that I had never known them apart from you."[49] Dickens's speech helps make sense of the importance of death as both metaphor and experience across his early works. Shared memories of the dead provide both a thematic analogue and mental matrix for shared memories of reading. This analogy works particularly well, Dickens's speech implies, when shared memories of reading express a common interest in the deaths of fictional characters. In this way, readers also conceive of themselves as having shared a painful experience, turned into a pleasurable one through reading, registering their participation in a collective reading public.[50] Imagining the shared experience of a fictional death as a pleasure of memory would not need to be a morbid or even a particularly sentimental sort of indulgence. Instead, as a recognizable form of participation, such imagining could provide a means of "self-resurrection," recasting latent urban social relations as vital new metropolitan connections, relayed through Dickens's image of celebrity authorship. As a member of a modern reading audience, or of a subset of that growing mass audience made up of a particular author's readers, the reader's singular identity is not lost but rather confirmed as his or her associations are blended and joined with the memories of reading shared with other readers. The reader's life story as a form of the continuity of the self in memory becomes newly relevant when inflected through that common reading that the popular author personifies and elicits.

Nell's childlike nature also instills the reader's relation to her with a profoundly parental cast, thus suggesting Dickens's most general conception of his readership as a society of responsible adults who will be judged on the basis of their success or failure in their social and familial obligations. Dickens lamented after composing the death of Little Nell that "I can't preach to myself the schoolmaster's consolation, though I try."[51] Dickens described his conception of the book in a speech on June 25, 1841:

> When I first conceived the idea of conducting that simple story to its termination, I determined rigidly to adhere to it, and never to forsake the end I had in view. Not untried in the school of affliction, in the death of those we love, I thought what a good thing it would be if in my little work of pleasant amusement I could substitute a garland of fresh flowers for the sculptured horrors that disgrace the tomb. If I have put into my book anything which can fill the young mind with better thoughts of death, or soften the grief of older hearts; if I have written one word which could afford pleasure or consolation to old or young in time of trial, I shall consider it as something achieved—something which I shall be glad to look back upon in after life.[52]

Dickens positions his novel on the grieving Victorian reader's table next to the Bible. He emphasizes his unwavering self-discipline in executing the original plan of his tale (killing off Nell), so that he can achieve his larger goal to render Victorian mourning less morbid. This account of the novel's consolatory purpose also confirms that the scene of Nell's reading in the chapel has a self-referential function in relation to the novel's own pedagogy. Given Dickens's objections to the ostentatious display of wealth and sentiment in Victorian funerals, it seems clear that he further positions his novel as a means to reform Victorian mourning.[53] Dickens's articulation of his goals in relation to the reception of *The Old Curiosity Shop* suggests that, insofar as serial fiction influences Victorian popular culture, it does not encourage sentimental escapism or the indiscriminate consumption of commodities associated with modern critiques of mass culture but rather serves as a medium of shared consolation in relation to the common experience that death represented most emphatically for the Victorians. As Esther Schor points out, a member of a technologically advanced society where death is not an everyday occurrence may tend to "magnify the exquisite pain of bereavement while obscuring the calm commerce of condolence" that Dickens too seems to have been intent on providing to Victorian readers in *The Old Curiosity Shop*.[54]

Crucial to Dickens's own pleasures of memory connected with the novel is his belief that he has affected his readers *as he had intended*, an achievement that he can recollect as he grows older and that will act as a memorial after his death. In his will, Dickens "emphatically direct[ed]" that "my name be inscribed in plain English letters on my tomb, without the addition of 'Mr' or 'Esquire,'" and that his friends create "no monument, memorial, or testimonial whatever." Instead, he wrote, "I rest my claims to the remembrance of my country upon my published works, and to the remembrance of my friends upon their experience of me in addition thereto."[55] Eschewing monumental glory, Dickens conceived his posthumous, epitaphic existence as depending upon the bonds of cultural and personal memory embodied in his writings and personal friendships. These are also two complementary popular forms of the Humean theory of relations as "fictitious realities" that we now recognize as linked by a common inventive and mnemonic logic of association. Extending the sense of the author's cultural function in providing a shared cultural repertoire of epitaphs, in his final serial, *The Mystery of Edwin Drood* (1870), which remained unfinished at his death, Dickens seems to personify himself one final time as Stony Durdles, the stonemason and inscriber of gravestones and tombs, who ponders his existence while carving monuments and investigating crypts, "making his reflections here . . . surrounded by his works, like a pop[u]lar Author."[56]

The Dickensian popular novel recommended itself to the nineteenth-century reader, then, as a source of rational pleasure, instructive entertainment, and shared consolation. In its pedagogical features, serial fiction provides a narrative succession, whether in serial or volume form, that brings into play the cognitive routines we have come to recognize as the pleasures of memory: reasoning, reflection, recognition, learning, attachment, anticipation, curiosity. The Humean understanding of the fictionality inhabiting the formal bonds of thought, memory, and society takes on a "pop[u]lar" form in Dickens's fiction through the novel's invitation to the common reader to participate in fictional experiences, shared with others, as if they were his or her own. Novel reading conceived in this way thus becomes an everyday means to initiate and experience relation.

Memory as Duty

That the possible blending of fiction and the reader's own imaginative life may blur boundaries between reading and experience does not invalidate the existence of such transitions but rather supports the associationist conception of serial reading *as a practice or habit of transitioning*. In fact, the "self-resurrecting," reflexive qualities of reading as an activity of transitioning, in either direction, between the singular individual and the crowd, between thinking and reading, and between self-awareness and a sense of membership in a collectivity, may have provided readers with some of the greatest pleasure to be gained from serial novel reading as a new medium. Dickens's constructions of a solitary reading habit in *The Old Curiosity Shop* represented and rehearsed a type of reception that would come to be associated more generally with the reading of novels once the serial form had lost its viability.

The peak sales of 100,000 per issue attained by *The Old Curiosity Shop* during its initial serial run in 1840–41 seemed to guarantee that Dickens would have a reliable audience.[57] As a result, Dickens could address his readers as members of a mid-Victorian reading audience, which the positive response to his novels seemed to have consolidated as a new social and cultural phenomenon. The earlier novels' pedagogical shaping of the individual reader's pleasures of memory defined friendship and consolation as major modes of reception and *relation* capable of transforming Dickens's readership into a popular constituency. Once this new constituency emerged, however, it could be engaged to participate in more concerted actions, both as readers and as citizens or potential citizens. In this way, a reading audience could potentially enter into competition with the forms of engagement identified with other social institutions, such as churches, schools, or political parties, and popular reading could become another means for forming attitudes and behaviors in competition with the typical training that such institutions and organizations provided. Popular reading, like religion or politics, could itself become a source for new social attitudes by intervening in the way society is reproduced in individual minds.

Dickens's later novels, such as *David Copperfield* (1849–50), *Bleak House* (1852–53), *Hard Times* (1854), *Little Dorrit*, *Great Expectations*, and *Our Mutual Friend* (1864–65), move away from the remediation of earlier genres and formal pedagogical strategies common in the earlier works to offer a sustained investigation of the causal role of social institutions in shaping habits of thought that become characteristic mentalities dividing the social classes from one another. In this way, these works build on the earlier novels' pedagogical transactions with the individual reader in order to explore the social effects of serial novel reading as a generalized practice of everyday life. Extending *Nicholas Nickleby*'s exploration of the threat to the individual's pleasures of memory represented by the fear of becoming anonymous and unloved among a crowd of similarly unknown persons, *Little Dorrit* offers the metaphor of the prison as its dominant frame of reference for a knowledge of the mind's relations to society. Both the problem of knowledge and the metaphorical structure of incarceration thus also apply reflexively to the self, as critics have often noted.[58] How then does the symbolism of the prison in *Little Dorrit* interact with the pleasures of memory as a theory of thinking, reading, relation, and mediation? *Little Dorrit*, I argue, concerns itself with explaining the nature of mind as a form of causality that is capable of producing the prison as its institutional consequence. Because of memory's function connecting mind to world, thought to thought, self to its feeling of identity in time, and even one person to another within society, the prison as a figure for "the negation of the will," in critic Lionel Trilling's terms, must also imply a failure of memory.[59]

Within *Little Dorrit*'s pervasive atmosphere of restraint, surveillance, and threatened exposure of secrets, the characters' trajectories transfer them from enclosure to enclosure—from home to workplace, from government office to the stock exchange, from the streets to the Marshalsea debtors' prison—as if all space were ultimately institutionalized, and all modes of passage were simply temporary transits from one function to another.[60] One of the most disconcerting effects of reading *Little Dorrit* in sequence with Dickens's earlier works may be the extent to which certain characters have taken on the narrator's voice, as, for example, in Arthur Clennam's surprising confession to his new acquaintance and fellow traveler, the rather obtuse Mr. Meagles, while they are in quarantine in Marseilles, that "I have no will":

> I am the son, Mr. Meagles, of a hard father and mother. I am the only child of parents who weighed, measured, and priced everything: for whom what could not be weighed, measured, and priced had no existence. Strict people, as the phrase is, professors of a stern religion, their very religion was a gloomy sacrifice of tastes and sympathies that were never their own, offered up as a part of a bargain for the security of their possessions. Austere faces, inexorable discipline, penance in this world and terror in the next—nothing graceful or gentle anywhere, and the void in my cowed heart everywhere—this was my childhood, if I may so misuse the word as to apply it to such a beginning of life.[61]

If Arthur already knows about himself—and summarizes here for the reader—everything that Dickens's earlier novels argued about the self-justifying economic logic and emotional despotism of strict Calvinistic evangelicalism, what remains for him, or the reader, to learn from this story? As Miss Wade so stringently *concludes* at the beginning of the novel, "In our course through life we shall meet the people who are coming to meet us, from many strange places and by many strange roads . . . and what it is set to us to do to them, and what it is set to them to do to us, will all be done" (37). If Miss Wade, with her "unsubduable nature" (36) and disdainful reserve, can utter a fatalistic moral to the tale before it has even begun, how can the reader perceive its larger meaning, except through her deterministic retrospective gaze?

If determinism rules anywhere, its source is in the mind rather than in society, which the novel represents as unpredictable, random, and in flux. In fact, the plot hinges on an associative memory effect: Arthur's seemingly arbitrary connection between an unknown girl working in the shadows in his mother's room, whom he glimpses during his first visit to his home upon his return to London, and his father's incoherent dying wish that Arthur deliver to his mother an ornate gold watch with the letters "D. N. F.," "do not forget." It is Mrs. Clennam who first refers to the watch on the table next to her wheelchair "as a remembrance of your father" (47), but Arthur interprets the urgency with which his father pressed him to deliver it as meaning that it was to be considered not a keepsake but a portentous reminder of some "secret remembrance which caused him trouble of mind—remorse?" (58). The suspicion of his parents' guilt is formed as a "thought" that "flashed" upon him—an unwanted association between the watch and his father's distressed attempts to write to Mrs. Clennam before his death—while Arthur's accusation takes the form of provoking his mother to "remember" in her turn (58). He is almost certain that, because of the central role of avarice in his parents' lives, the wrong to be repaired must relate in some way to money: "For heaven's sake let us examine sacredly whether there is any wrong entrusted to us to set right. No one can help us towards it mother, but you" (58–59). But Mrs. Clennam repudiates his suspicions, pointing to her own invalidism as her "reparation" through confinement: "Let [Arthur] look at me, in prison, and in bonds here. I endure without murmuring, because it is appointed that I shall so make reparation for my sins" (60). Mrs. Clennam substitutes her crusading Calvinism for remembrance.

Arthur's strange association between his father's remorse and Amy Dorrit, called "Little Dorrit," seems at first to be a matter of mere contiguity— she happens to be in his mother's room on several occasions when Arthur first returns home:

> Sometimes Little Dorrit was employed at her needle, sometimes not, sometimes appeared as a humble visitor: which must have been her character on the occasion of his arrival. His original curiosity augmented every day, as he watched for her, saw or did not see her, and speculated about her. Influenced by his predominant idea, he even fell into a habit of discussing with himself the possibility of her being in some way associated with it. At last he resolved to watch Little Dorrit and know more of her story. (66)

Curiosity again plays its inductive and benevolent role in Arthur's postulating the significance of her presence and searching for its basis in a causal a relation. The real mystery about Little Dorrit, or rather the apparent mystery, involves her home, which, as Arthur discovers when he follows her "at a distance" (86) one evening, is the Marshalsea debtors' prison. Once his "original curiosity" and "predominant idea" lead him to focus on Little Dorrit, Arthur's will seems to revive through his desire to learn the history of Mr. Dorrit's insolvency and consequent residence in the Marshalsea.

Little Dorrit, perhaps most famously of all Dickens's works, is a novel about epistemological blockages and institutional paralysis. In fact, many Victorian critics disliked the critical tendency of *Little Dorrit*. "We don't want [Dickens] to be a politician, of whom there are plenty," complained one reviewer before the serial run was finished. "We want him to be a humourist, and painter of passion and life, where he stands almost without a peer."[62] The novel's harsh criticism of Victorian society across its governmental, religious, economic, entrepreneurial and even domestic sectors seemed to transgress the boundary between fiction and politics. The focus of this satirical critique, the Circumlocution Office, is the bastion of governmental obstructionism and incompetence, "beforehand with all the public departments in the art of perceiving—HOW NOT TO DO IT" (110). The witty young Ferdinand Barnacle frankly sums up the obfuscation that characterizes governmental functions: " '[The Circumlocution Office] is all right. We must have humbug, we all like humbug, we couldn't get on without humbug. A little humbug, and a groove, and everything goes on admirably, if you leave it alone' " (706). "Humbug," the novel shows, is always purveyed as its own justification; its "groove" is self-perpetuating and self-serving because it inheres in mental habits inculcated by the formative structures of class privilege, schools, churches, and government. Dickens's insistence in the preface to the 1857 volume edition, originally published as an afterword to the final serial installment of *Little Dorrit*, that the Circumlocution Office is not an exaggeration but simply represents "the common experience of an Englishman" (5) highlights the popularized empirical and journalistic frameworks of Dickens's satire.

Arthur's many "memorials," or petitions, to government in favor both of the Dorrits and of the engineer and inventor, Daniel Doyce, fall into the "groove" of the Circumlocution Office and disappear without a trace. Little Dorrit, however, provides a way of circumventing this bureaucratic cul-de-sac by opening a perspective on the present meaning of the past: she orients the novel's questions about knowledge and society as she transforms Arthur's confused memories into conscious experience, especially at the level of his own self-understanding. Like Arthur's father's watch, she is both a "token" meant to provoke recollection, and, as Arthur calls her in his despondent thoughts while in prison, a "vanishing-point": "Everything in its perspective led to her innocent figure. He had travelled thousands of miles towards it; previous unquiet hopes and doubts had worked themselves out before it; it was the centre of the interest of his life; it was the termination of everything that was good and pleasant in it; beyond there was nothing but mere waste, and darkened sky" (702). Her innocence counterbalances Miss Wade's fatalism. Little Dorrit does not affect only Arthur in this way; she also provokes Pancks's benevolent "curiosity" (393), which he pursues by revealing her connection to the fortune of the Dorrits of Dorsetshire (396).

Befitting her role as a "vanishing-point," Little Dorrit's own perspective on the world is "mysterious," having its origin in her early experiences in the Marshalsea prison:

> What her pitiful look saw, at that early time, in her father, in her sister, in her brother, in the jail; how much, or how little of the wretched truth it pleased God to make visible to her; lies hidden with many mysteries. It is enough that she was inspired to be something which was not what the rest were, and to be that something, different and laborious, for the sake of the rest. Inspired? Yes. Shall we speak of the inspiration of a poet or a priest, and not of the heart impelled by love and self-devotion to the lowliest work in the lowliest way of life?
>
> With no earthly friend to help her, or so much as to see her, but the one so strangely assorted [her friend and godfather, the turnkey at the Marshalsea

gate]; with no knowledge even of the common daily tone and habits of the
common members of the free community who are not shut up in prisons;
born and bred, in a social condition, false even with a reference to the falsest
condition outside the walls; drinking from infancy of a well whose waters
had their own peculiar stain, their own unwholesome and unnatural taste;
the Child of the Marshalsea began her womanly life. (80)

Little Dorrit's "inspiration" or vocation is equivalent to that of a poet or
priest but is explicitly gendered as "womanly," exemplifying self-denying,
motherly devotion to her family. She represents the possibility of converting
the "false" relations imposed by her existence in the prison—and by the
prison's own existence as an expression of morally "false" social conditions
and relations—into valid ones by restoring thwarted social connections
through her incessant service to others. In not posing a direct challenge to
political authority or gender hierarchies, then, Little Dorrit's vocation also
corresponds to Dickens's definition of his own "public service through Literature" in his 1855 speech before the Administrative Reform Association:
"to understand the heavier social grievances and to help to set them right."[63]
Hers is a feminine-gendered version of the novelist's own cultural politics,
and she becomes a vehicle for the pedagogical transmission of that cultural
politics to the reader.

But it is important to clarify that if understood in this way, this feminine
domestic service construed as a kind of public service does not simply involve the novel's inculcation of its own commitments to domestic ideology
along with a gendered division of labor. Rather, Little Dorrit herself represents the pedagogical identification of the novel's cultural politics with the
reader's potential experience of domestic life—that project, articulated in
Dickens's preface to *Household Words*, "to live in the Household affections,
and to be numbered among the Household thoughts, of our readers."[64] The
novel also connects Little Dorrit's service and the Dorrit family's dysfunc-
tions directly with the larger social injustices it represents. Mr. Dorrit's self-
deluding patronage of the other Marshalsea prisoners and his neglect of his
family form part of a series of bureaucratic and governmental failures associated with paternalism, cronyism, and the unbridled financial speculation and
corruption of Merdle's massive swindle. Given Amy Dorrit's propensity to
arrive at her view of the world independently of schools, we could also interpret her as a representation of an autodidact "with no knowledge even
of the common daily tone and habits of the common members of the free
community." It seems crucial to Dickens's larger project of claiming a cultural space for democratic literature that could compete with the influence

of churches and sectarian schools that a character like Amy be self-taught in her vocation of service and anomalous (that is, unselfish) vision of society.

The novel's lesson by way of the Dorrit family, then, would not be "If you fix the family then you can fix society," but rather "In order to fix the family, you must first address the larger social and political failures of which its deficiencies are a part and an effect."[65] *Little Dorrit* is not invested uncritically in domestic ideology, since it represents Amy's service as burdensome: "hav[ing] always upon her, the care of preserving the genteel fiction that [her family] were all idle beggars together" in the Marshalsea (82). As Arthur perceives, her own family overlooks her: "It was not that they stinted her praises, or were insensible to what she did for them; but that they were lazily habituated to her, as they were to the rest of their condition. . . . He fancied that they viewed her, not as having risen away from the prison atmosphere, but as appertaining to it; as being vaguely what they had a right to expect, and nothing more" (100–101). If readers, like Amy Dorrit's own family, view her vocation as "nothing more" than her feminine domestic role as preserver of the family, then they too have failed to separate Amy from the "prison atmosphere." If readers in turn rely on but overlook the exertion of feminine devotion and domestic labor, then they too belong to the category of those "lazily habituated" to their "condition." Thus the novel positions Little Dorrit as a "vanishing-point" not just for Arthur but also for the reader because she functions as a touchstone by which the value of all social discourses may be determined. Even domesticity itself becomes recognizable as "appertaining" to the "prison atmosphere" by being held up to Little Dorrit's "uncommon" example (396).

Amy Dorrit's characterization as an autodidact also reinforces the ways that the novel's views of causality and ethics dovetail in her perspective and also pertain to the transmission of knowledge within the evolving associationist pedagogical approach of Dickens's fiction. Throughout the novel, Little Dorrit's vocation is traceable to her inability to forget her original circumstances and transcend her past. During the family's tour of Europe after inheriting the Dorrit family fortune, Amy finds that she cannot easily adjust to their new life outside the prison: "Sitting opposite her father in the travelling-carriage, and recalling the old Marshalsea room, her present existence was a dream. All that she saw was new and wonderful, but it was not real; it seemed to her as if those visions of mountains and picturesque countries might melt away at any moment, and the carriage, turning some abrupt corner, bring up with a jolt at the old Marshalsea gate" (447). Even without saying anything, Little Dorrit has become a constant reminder, as her father complains ungratefully to her, of "a painful topic, a series of events," "that accursed experience" in the Marshalsea that Mr. Dorrit wishes to "obliterate," "eradicate," and "sweep off the face of the earth!" (460–61). Her presence unleashes memory effects that carry them back to the prison. Just as the affective architecture of her prison life formed her identity as the "Child of the Marshalsea" (80), so she herself becomes an unwelcome topos of memory for her family.

How is Little Dorrit's vocation of service linked to the novel's larger critique of ineffective Victorian bureaucracy and self-serving functionaries? According to the "airy young Barnacle," the mid-Victorian state functions primarily as "a politico diplomatico hocus pocus piece of machinery, for the assistance of the nobs in keeping off the snobs" (121). For the novel's reader, this means drawing the conclusion that government functions as a means of inter-class competition for positions and power between the aristocracy (the "nobs") and bourgeoisie (the "snobs"). Since the Circumlocution Office is impenetrable, however, responsibility for this circumstance seems to shift in the novel to the individual level. The working out of the characters' interconnected stories also represents another, more complex version of the social epistemology that connects individual minds to social causes and common social responsibility more generally. As a "vanishing-point" for Arthur's narrative and the mystery surrounding his parents' secret fault, Little Dorrit's inability to forget her past becomes pivotal to the novel's associationist epistemology and memory effects because only she is capable of tying together their larger significance.

At the end of the novel, Mr. Meagles and Daniel Doyce orchestrate the cancellation of Arthur's debts incurred during the Merdle stock swindle and his departure from the Marshalsea, which will be shortly followed by his marriage to Little Dorrit. Just prior to his departure, Mr. Meagles points out Little Dorrit crossing the Marshalsea yard as an object lesson for the repentant former runaway maid, Tattycoram, on the importance of self-sacrificing duty. Mr. Meagles points out that Little Dorrit has never resented the stigma of the Marshalsea, but instead, "her young life has been one of active resignation, goodness, and noble service." Mr. Meagles defines the guiding principle of Little Dorrit's vocation: "Duty, Tattycoram. Begin it early, and do it well; and there is no antecedent to it, in any origin or station, that will tell against us with the Almighty, or with ourselves" (774). Echoing the style of Hannah More's tracts, Mr. Meagles's tone is probably the most didactic that we hear in the novel, and because of his general obtuseness about foreign customs, conventionality, and want of tact, his lessons are suspect.

There is something disingenuous in placing this pronouncement in Mr. Meagles's mouth, as if the novel avows this lesson in its most doctrinaire rhetorical mode and disavows it at the same time in the shape of its messenger. For our purposes, Mr. Meagles's lesson on duty to the chastened maid reveals once again the popular serial novel's generic linkages with religious tracts for the poor, and is thus recognizable as part of Dickens's extended revision and updating of didactic conventions. In this respect, Mr. Meagles's lesson seems to provide the solution to the mysterious origin of Little Dorrit's knowledge: she learned on her own to construe necessity as "duty" because someone had to fill the void of parental responsibility left by her faded and self-absorbed father, or they would all have starved.[66] Here Dickens's novel also seems to invert the meaning of the moment in More's tale when the Salisbury shepherd claims to recite Bible passages in order to forget that he is hungry, implying that salvation is more important than nourishment. Amy Dorrit's vocation of familial "duty," undertaken because no one else will do it, does not make her service to her family any less essential, but it implies that the piety or kindness of the poor may also be born of exigency rather than acting as a means of compensating for want.

Within this novel's development and implementation of the arts of memory, then, Little Dorrit herself becomes a mnemonic device as well as an object lesson: what Amy *cannot* forget becomes what the reader *should not* forget. This dual association of duty with both responsibility and service provides the reader with a basis to evaluate individual ethical commitments and to demand the fulfillment of social obligations from those in power. Duty, in the didactic register of Mr. Meagles's instructions to Tattycoram, but also more broadly within the Dickensian novel's own pedagogy, lines up with memory, association, curiosity, pleasure, imagination, and the train of thought, as a series of terms designating those virtual, felt relations— Hume's "cement of the universe"—that render experience continuous and give the self a recognizable identity. Duty, like memory, seems to activate such virtuality into an ethics—a standard of moral behavior—that applies in the same way to everyone, and that could suit an egalitarian rather than a ranked and deferential society.

Through Little Dorrit's role as a "vanishing-point" for the narrative plot, the novel itself takes on a mnemonic function, leading the reader to recognize and remember the duties, responsibilities, and connections that Little Dorrit herself has understood and accepted. At the end of the novel, the narrator describes how Arthur and Little Dorrit "went quietly down into the roaring streets, inseparable and blessed; and as they passed along in sunshine and in shade, the noisy and the eager, and the arrogant and the forward and the vain, fretted, and chafed, and made their usual uproar" (787). Their "modest life of usefulness and happiness" (787) remains part of the "roaring streets," and thus they take their places without fear of isolation among the urban crowds that include the novel's own readers. That Arthur's and Little Dorrit's "usefulness" is immediately associated with their "happiness" suggests that their story also exemplifies the nineteenth-century pleasures of memory (787).

Skeptical Memory

The novel's solution to the causality behind Arthur's associations also leads to Mrs. Clennam's mind and, specifically, to her Bible reading. This causal association brings us once again to the contest between Dickens's democratic cultural politics and the evangelical cultural politics of spiritual reformation. [67] At her final interview with Little Dorrit before her own silencing and paralysis as a result of her house's collapse into ruins on top of the blackmailer, Rigaud-Blandois, Mrs. Clennam reveals the secret "cause in which, and the motives with which, I have worked out this work" (755). She admits that she has "sinned" by withholding the legacy that Little Dorrit should have received in her husband's uncle's will, and by punishing Arthur's real mother by taking her illegitimate child away and raising him as her own: "I have been an instrument of severity against sin. Have not mere sinners like myself been commissioned to lay it low in all time? . . . Even if my own wrong had prevailed with me, and my own vengeance had moved me, could I have found no justification? None in the old days when the innocent perished with the guilty, a thousand to one? When the wrath of the hater of the unrighteous was not slaked even in blood, and yet found favor?" (755–56). Mrs. Clennam's words reveal her exclusive reading of the Old Testament parts of the Bible, the nameless "book" found always on the table next to her chair in the novel's early scenes. As Little Dorrit gently reminds her, she has left out the New Testament message of forgiveness (756). Mrs. Clennam's "cause"—the source of her identity—is not just a mentality, then, but also a narrow and self-centered fundamentalist practice of literacy. In witnessing her self-justifying confession, Little Dorrit "recoiled with dread" (755) but then gently counters her with the example of the life of Christ: "We cannot but be right if we put all the rest away, and do everything in remembrance of Him. There is no vengeance and no in-fliction of suffering in His life, I am sure" (756). Mrs. Clennam takes literally the Victorian evangelical market incentives for piety, viewing her religion as a justification for her economic motives, while Little Dorrit corrects her through a formula of nonsectarian Christian "remembrance" that the Victorian reader should, in turn, bear in mind.

In characterizing "the notion of morality characteristic of dominant Victorian culture," historian Stefan Collini argues that "there was a tendency to extend the category of 'duty' as widely as possible," and that "the characterization of the alternative to performing one's duties stressed giving in to temptation or being seduced by one's inclinations, and these inclinations were regarded as inherently selfish."[68] If Mrs. Clennam's vindictive application of her Bible reading is a form of selfishness representing a Calvinistic mind-set more generally, then Little Dorrit's function as a reminder of duty also becomes recognizable as part of Dickens's *oppositional* cultural politics, formulated and disseminated by the serial novel itself through its associationist memory techniques. The novel contests evangelical propagandizing by positioning Little Dorrit's example as an alternative to a distorting fundamentalist reading of the Bible. This status of Little Dorrit's image of duty as representing a different, nonsectarian use of literacy, and not just a moral behavior, becomes clear when we remember how the novel in serial installments circulated like other cheap periodicals, including religious tracts, that were purchased at relatively low cost and produced for the mass readership. An important reason why Dickens stuck with the serial throughout his career, in addition to its profitability, may thus have been this very capacity of fiction issued in periodical installments to remediate the political and pedagogical connotations of the religious tract or pamphlet not just in its message but *in its physical form*. Thus the serial form works tactically within a cultural politics by supporting the perception that the novel could function like a tract in mobilizing readers as a potentially political constituency.

In light of *Little Dorrit*'s adoption of an oppositional stance toward evangelicalism, it becomes important to consider in turn what kind of position Miss Wade is taking when, in her first-person narrative contained in its own chapter and titled "The History of a Self-Tormentor," she declares, "I have the misfortune of not being a fool" (635). Miss Wade equates experience with cynicism and forgiveness with credulity. Hers are not the pleasures but the discontents of memory: "My experience . . . has been correcting my belief in many respects, for some years. It is our natural progress, I have heard" (35). However, though Miss Wade is a misanthrope, she is also enough of a philosopher that she takes pains to communicate her view of the world to at least one person. She writes a narrative of her life explaining to Arthur the reasons for her hatred of her former fiancé, now Pet Meagles's husband, the shallow artist Henry Gowan: "You don't know what I mean by hating, if you know me no better than that; you can't know, without knowing with what care I have studied myself, and people about me" (632). Miss Wade construes every event in her life as directly relevant to the stigma she carries as an illegitimate child: "From a very early age I have detected what those about me thought they hid from me. If I could have been habitually imposed upon, instead of habitually discerning the truth, I might have lived as smoothly as most fools do" (635). Her earliest memory involves her love for another little girl, whose affection she wishes to monopolize. She is angered, however, when she overhears her friend confess to her aunt that Miss Wade "has an unhappy temper; other girls at school, besides I, try hard to make it better" (636). Associating this "false and despicable" characterization with all further acts of kindness she receives from others, Miss Wade, perhaps correctly, deems them to arise from others' self-serving pity for her and condescension toward her inferior social status: "my first memorable experience was true to what I knew her to be, and to all my experience" (636).

Thus Miss Wade's experience becomes decisive in isolating her, both because she suspects all expressions of friendship as condescending and because she believes that all social conventions are necessarily deceptive and false. Miss Wade's ethic of resentment, even though it is based, like Little Dorrit's, on a refusal to let go of a series of constitutive memories, is anti-social because her experience is not cumulative. Despite Miss Wade's insistence that experience is merely a form of disillusionment, she cannot be disillusioned because she never learns anything to contradict or "correct" her earliest beliefs. Her portrait is so psychologically telling in associationist terms, however, because her prejudices are reasoned, originating in what Dickens's novels show to be common—though not universal—forms of middle-class Victorian behavior, including the tendency to patronize the poor and other social outsiders. In her narrative function in relation to memory, Miss Wade is thus the inverted mirror image of Amy Dorrit. Miss Wade's case illustrates how persistent associations in the memory may distort rather than reinforce human relationships. In these negative terms, however, she provides a further example of the novel's linkage of memory, identity, and social epistemology as analogous forms of causality.[69]

The novel shows paternalism and vested institutional interests both within the family and in social institutions to be void, hypocritical, and even exploitative, so the conservative social values associated with established authority and the liberal advocacy of educated elites are equally discredited. An alternative symbolic register and social leverage for acting upon an ethics of duty and service must therefore be found. I have argued that Amy Dorrit's function as a narrative, ethical, and epistemological "vanishing-point" allows the novel to convert what seems to be an arbitrary association between Arthur's memory of his father's remorse and Little Dorrit's contiguity to Mrs. Clennam into a causal relation that is borne out by the plot. This transformation of memory into cause involves a pedagogical implementation of the reader's comprehension of the plot (which is by no means guaranteed). By this means, the reader's own associations with the text should be linked through Little Dorrit's example to a generalized ethic of service to others existing independently of institutions that can be extended into social activism in response to the "understanding of the larger social grievances" promoted by the novel's critique of the Circumlocution Office. Thus the text should coordinate for the reader the same imperative toward "public service" that Dickens articulated for his own contributions to popular literature and editorial work in his 1855 speech, just before he began to write *Little Dorrit*. The novel makes its own claims on the reader's memory through a pedagogical transaction by which novel reading models a particular kind of social epistemology linking reading and social causality. This linkage should encourage corrective action rather than reinforce social determinism.

Mrs. Clennam and Miss Wade may also remind us of Francis Bacon's negative examples of "Rationalist spiders," who "spin webs" of causality "from themselves." Their epistemologies are flawed in being solipsistic, while their generalization of personal grievances into a punitive ethics is represented as an anti-social form of "self-torment."[70] The novel's teaching of a positive social ethic of memory, duty, and service nevertheless preserves an avenue toward skepticism as a viable epistemological stance for popular fiction, as Miss Wade's presence in *Little Dorrit* suggests.[71] Miss Wade's misanthropy supports the painful experience registered in Dickens's novels' repeated representations of violence and cruelty within families, that those closest to us are sometimes not very loving or loveable. Within the larger cultural politics represented by Little Dorrit's gendered mnemonics of duty, Miss Wade also appears as an acutely intelligent female dissident, both in her pessimistic nature and in her desire for intimacy with other women. Miss

Wade's embedded narrative thus also functions as another version of anti-didacticism, this time directed self-reflexively against the novel's own didactic prescription of duty: the suspicion is kept alive, through Miss Wade's skepticism, that Little Dorrit's domestic service to others is another particularly thankless species of "self-torment."

Epitaphic Literature

Developing and then moving beyond the moralized memory effects of *Oliver Twist* and *Nicholas Nickleby*, *The Old Curiosity Shop* and *Little Dorrit* ultimately elicit in different ways a self-reflexive reading practice by drawing attention to the transition between reading and being immersed in one's own straying thoughts—a transition that also constitutes the very mundane Victorian practice of reading fiction in parts as well as a secularized version of silent reading. This understanding of reading as an activity that crosses over into everyday life also affords a means of instigating the reader's "good deeds," as Dickens envisions them. Evangelical fiction seeks to provoke the reader's conversion toward salvation, while *The Old Curiosity Shop* envisions popular literature as competing with the Bible's influence. Popular serial fiction provides the reader both with a consolation for death and with a more inclusive form of cultural participation through the exchange of collective memories of reading that constitute new forms of cultural memory. *Little Dorrit* elevates a nondenominational Christian sense of familial and social obligation—"a modest life of usefulness and service" (787)—above both religious "causes" and profit motives by celebrating its autodidact heroine and her ethic of duty in the face of material necessity. This is not equivalent to Hannah More's substitution of the scriptures for bread, although we can now see the generic relation between More's and Dickens's didacticisms. Rather *Little Dorrit* imagines that a shared culture of everyday cares and duties, either in place of or supplementing other forms of social affiliation, can provide the common experience required for social and political consolidation that the evangelical movement's punitive and interfering methods, in Dickens's view, could never achieve. By channeling this ethic of social duty through the celebrity author's "public service through Literature," *Little Dorrit* begins to produce for the mid-Victorian reader an updated nonpartisan image of what historian E. P. Thompson refers to in the English Radical tradition as "the *active* duties of citizenship."[72] Through their attachment to such images, revisited in repeated serial readings, the popular reading audience could thus become a mobile and various alternative constituency for a participatory, and thus incipiently democratic, cultural politics.

Such a popular constituency of readers could also learn and practice epi-taphic reading on a global scale. In his short 1842 treatise on education, Henry Mayhew recasts the relationship between reading and experience posited by associationist theories of pedagogy and reception into the lan-guage of commodification. Mayhew conceives of the "resurrectionist" ef-fects of reading first in traditional terms as the way the reader gains access to the thoughts of dead authors:

> See! here is what we call a book: what is it in reality—in itself—physically, what but a collection of sundry scraps of paper, tattooed with curious char-acters? Has it soul, voice, intellect, imagination? No! it is a dull lump of senseless matter—barren as so much granite—thoughtless as the rags from which it sprang. What is it mentally? What, when looked upon by those skilled in its magic mysteries? The works of William Shakespere! the heart's historian! nature's evangelist! It is the sacred urn treasuring that part of him which could never die—the mausoleum of his immortal mind. To lift back the cover, is as it were to roll the stone from before the sepulchre, and to see him rise again in all his native glory. . . . His spirit shall be with yours, and yours with his, mingling like two rivers. . . . And yet what is there to connect us living with him dead? What but these mystic characters, and that wonderful little orb the eye?[73]

Referring this theory to Seneca, Mayhew emphasizes that it is the mind of the author that is transmitted through reading, and his or her thoughts that mingle sacramentally with the reader's own. But Mayhew also generalizes this process to any act of reading, which becomes a form of prosopopoeia, the art of communicating with the absent or dead: "In this [reading] the mother sees and listens to her absent child; in this, the lover gazes once more upon the darling features of her whom Fate has severed from his sight; in this, the lonely widow looks, and hears again the kindly counsellings of him whose voice the grave has hushed; and, poring into this, the student sits and communes with the glorious dead, while the long train of past events, in shadowy procession, sweep before his eyes" (3). Mayhew describes the kind of "epitaphic" reading that, I have argued, *The Old Curiosity Shop* is struc-tured to elicit. Beyond this personal contact with letters or books, which Mayhew also refers to as "literary communion" or "literary communica-tion," reading also constitutes a new medium of communication across vast distances, by which we can "transfer our sensations, thoughts, and emo-tions, to others, or to have theirs transferred to us, though there be the dis-tance of half the earth, or that more formidable barrier, the grave, existing between us" (3). Mass literacy and the mass production of books, Mayhew emphasizes, collapse the distances that other goods must travel by ship or railway: "*Steam only abridges space, whereas literature annihilates it altogether*" (3).

In mixing sacramental with commercial language, Mayhew is attempting to articulate education's role in shaping national identity within an emerging mass culture of print media, in advance of the terminology of mass media and communications that came into current use at the beginning of the twentieth century.[74] Mayhew's focus on reading as long-distance, virtually simultaneous communication in 1842 seems to foresee the technological developments following on the growing use of the telegraph in the later 1840s and 1850s. Still thinking in terms of shared kinship, Mayhew nevertheless stretches his ready-to-hand associationist framework to define mass reading as a practice of connectivity across distances, or modern mass communication: "By these simple, but glorious arts [of reading and writing], the whole civilized globe has been drawn as it were into one family circle, and a companionship created between those even whom seas divide" (3). The scope of such communication is potentially global due to the extension of commercial activity into Britain's colonies and the rest of the Anglophone world: "by the happy invention of literature [i.e., literacy], the very mind has become an article of commerce; and intellect as much a matter of merchandize as cotton and iron themselves" (3). Mayhew can already see in 1842 that the epitaphic function of English literature could be extended to consolidate a transnational and imperial form of English culture. Through literacy in English joined with literary reading as prosopopoeia, any reader of Shakespeare (or Dickens) all over the world could fill his or her mental space with an image of English "native glory" as embodied in its pantheon of dead authors.

In the next chapter I investigate how *Our Mutual Friend* engages with the social reproductive agency of the new education system that, in the course of the nineteenth century, was increasingly funded and overseen by Parliament. In contrast to Mayhew's celebration of education's links with the commodification of literature, *Our Mutual Friend* targets the commodification of mind as a negative effect of the developing mid-Victorian popular education system. Mayhew's vision for English literature as a new mass medium implies that any effective cultural politics for popular literature must also intervene in some way in the distribution of literacy. Providing a similar, more encompassing framework focusing on literacy in his final complete novel, Dickens also envisions the reading audience even more inclusively than in earlier works. *Our Mutual Friend* elucidates the status of reading not as consumption but as a kind of productive activity analogous to other kinds of work. Imagined in this way, the reading audience becomes a more diverse and more secular constituency made up of individuals who are also self-consciously involved in facing down material necessity, not only through their labor and service, but also by producing culture and art.

5.   *Learning by Heart in* Our Mutual Friend

Modern education is all cram—Latin cram, mathematical cram, literary cram, political cram, theological cram, moral cram. The world already knows everything, and has only to tell it to its children, who, on their part, have only to hear and lay it to rote (not to *heart*). Any purpose, any idea of training the mind itself, has gone out of the world. Nor can I yet perceive many symptoms of amendment. Those who dislike what is taught, mostly—if I may trust my own experience—dislike it not for being *cram*, but for being other people's cram, and not theirs. Were they the teachers, they would teach different doctrines, but they would teach them *as* doctrines, not as subjects for impartial inquiry.

John Stuart Mill, "On Genius" (1832)

Dickens's final completed novel, *Our Mutual Friend* (1864–65), could be described as a story about the repercussions of learning to read. I want to distinguish the novel's specific interest the experience of literacy from political arguments during the 1850s and 1860s about the role of education in enabling the Victorian laboring classes to exercise the franchise.[1] *Our Mutual Friend* counters the idea that literacy is requisite for citizenship by depicting illiteracy not simply as a form of deprivation but rather as an alternative, albeit marginalized, social experience.[2] The novel's exploration of the imaginative lives of illiterate people plays out the implications of the influential associationist analogy between experience and learning to read that I delineated in Chapter 1. In the wake of the repeated evocations of the pleasures of memory in Dickens's earlier novels as a framework for articulating popular literature's role in leading readers toward self-conscious participation in a reading audience, *Our Mutual Friend* investigates how thinking could be represented without making it dependent on a model of literacy. In the absence of literacy, how could memory act as a medium for the social inclusion and cultural participation of the poor?

Understood as a partial process with limited effects on individuals, learning to read is broached early on in the novel when Charley Hexam, the former mudlark turned Ragged School boy, visits the Veneerings' opulent mansion to deliver a message about the discovery of a drowned man. The narrator describes Charley as an unfinished production: "There was a curious mixture in the boy, of uncompleted savagery, and uncompleted civilisation. His voice was hoarse and coarse, and his face was coarse, and his stunted figure was coarse; but he was cleaner than other boys of his type; and his writing, though large and round, was good; and he glanced at the backs of the books, with an awakened curiosity that went below the binding. No one who can read, ever looks at a book even unopened on a shelf, like one who cannot."[3] Charley's newly acquired literacy has changed his capacity for knowledge and apprehension but has only partially improved his "coarse" manners and habits; still, he possesses skills and penetration that contradict his appearance. The paradox that Charley presents points to the novel's treatment of literacy's role in social change: is this half-educated pauper lad still a "savage" or has he been civilized by learning to read? Has the process of education created an individual or a "type"? The novel also develops Dickens's ongoing concern with the injustice of poverty by questioning how learning to read changes a person's prospects in life, and what the spread of literacy as a larger social phenomenon has to do with the everyday effects of reading.[4] If literacy becomes a requirement for political and cultural participation as a result of the spread of education and the growth of modern reading habits, and if money becomes the universal gauge of the value of all human activities, how can the everyday lives of the Victorian poor retain any larger significance, or their struggles remain visible as causes for public concern?

Our Mutual Friend conveys Dickens's "moral [and social] creed" that "nothing is high because it is in a high place; and nothing is low, because it is in a low one."[5] But it achieves a more axiomatic critique than this general refusal to map a moral onto a social hierarchy through its critical use of the metaphor of society as a school. *Our Mutual Friend* seems to share Henry Mayhew's "honest belief" that "a man may be utterly ignorant even of his A B C, and yet be not given to cutting throats, . . . that a man may be perfectly rational, and yet utterly illiterate." In his short treatise on education, Mayhew also objects strenuously to the notion that moral education can be conveyed through rote instruction: "There are many professed schools for the head, but none that I know for the heart."[6] Dickens's many novelistic treatments of education represent a sustained attempt to expose the ironies entailed for Victorian educators in the commonplace figure for memorization to which Mayhew refers, "learning by heart."[7]

Mayhew criticizes the separation between reason and emotion that Dickens's novels and cultural politics attempt to bridge by reshaping the associationist moralization of memory into the educational and democratizing effects of popular literature. *Nicholas Nickleby* (1838–39), *Dombey and Son* (1846–48), *David Copperfield* (1849–50), and *Hard Times* (1854) all depict the failure of schooling to convey useful knowledge or moral guidance to children, as well as the heartlessness, tyranny, and mercenary motives of an assortment of incompetent and cruel teachers.[8] *Hard Times* characterizes the psychological effects of the standardization of curricula and routinization of classroom teaching in schools supported by parliamentary grants after 1846. If popular education's role as a "factory system" becomes a central element of Dickens's larger critique of industrial society and the doctrines of political economy in *Hard Times*, the technique of rote learning itself takes on much broader significance in *Our Mutual Friend* as a figure for social reproduction—the transmission of patterns of thought and behavior from one generation to the next that John Stuart Mill criticized in 1832 as "cram." Rote learning in Victorian pedagogy was frequently criticized by liberal intellectuals like Mill and Matthew Arnold for reducing memory's inventive powers of association to mechanical repetition and mental storage of unrelated facts.

In order to understand how novel reading is entailed in *Our Mutual Friend*'s critique of the role of Victorian schooling in perpetuating a new set of social divisions based on the possession of literacy, it is helpful to recall the longevity of debates over rote learning as a pedagogical method. From the end of the seventeenth century, memorization as an individual practice and rote learning as a pedagogical technique were seen to present obstacles to learning. Both Thomas Hobbes and John Locke, for example, doubted the efficacy of improving the memory through exercises in rote memorization. In *Leviathan* (1651), Hobbes defines "absurdity" as an instance when "men speak such words as, put together, have in them no signification at all, but are fallen upon by some through misunderstanding of the words they have received and repeated by rote."[9] Hobbes suggests that rote learning of language can produce a "fault in discourse" which he considers "among the sorts of madness."[10] In his influential *Some Thoughts Concerning Education* (1693), Locke is particularly critical of the general practice of learning classical languages by memorizing grammar rules.[11] Like Hobbes, Locke asserts that the random acquisition of ideas can produce irrational and fallacious associations of ideas akin to madness.[12] Both philosophers deplore learning that seems to operate automatically, without requiring the student's comprehension of what is learned.

The rationalist educational theorists and followers of Locke Richard and Maria Edgeworth (father and daughter) in 1798 criticized the rote learning common in late eighteenth-century pedagogy and advocated in its place an individualized training of the memory:

> In accumulating facts, as in amassing riches, people often begin by believing that they value wealth only for the use they shall make of it; but it often happens, that during the course of their labours, they learn habitually to set a value upon the coin itself, and they grow avaricious of that which they are sensible has little intrinsic value. Young people who have accumulated a vast number of facts, and names, and dates, perhaps intended originally to make some good use of their treasure; but they frequently forget their laudable intentions, and conclude by contenting themselves with the display of their nominal wealth. Pedants and misers forget the real use of wealth and knowledge, and they accumulate without rendering what they acquire useful to themselves or to others.[13]

In rote learning, the retentive functions of memory take precedence over the more sophisticated synthetic functions, and as a result "the inventive and reasoning" faculties of children are also rendered "passive" when facts are not "associated with circumstances in real life."[14] The Edgeworths conclude that those who rely on mere memorization of lists of disassociated facts find that their minds are congested "with much knowledge baled up," and they become "an incumbrance to themselves and to their friends."[15]

The Edgeworths' metaphor of rote knowledge as "baled up" overvalued "treasure" reappears in the metaphorical structure of *Our Mutual Friend*, which is a story of both pedants and misers. Retaining the interconnectedness of mental and social forms of causality developed in Dickens's later works such as *Bleak House* (1852–53) and *Little Dorrit* (1855–57), *Our Mutual Friend* pursues the connections among memory, education, and social reproduction by drawing an analogy between the transmission of knowledge and the circulation of money and commodities. For example, Mr. Podsnap represents British cultural chauvinism, prudery, and the ostentatious display of wealth as forms of rote learning that the upper classes recycle and proclaim to justify their superior social position. *Our Mutual Friend* stages a development in Dickens's cultural politics that involves wresting the popular uses of literacy away from the emerging Victorian education system, with its logic of learning for the sake of bettering oneself. This contestation is staged most clearly in the novel's creation of Bradley Headstone, the street urchin turned schoolmaster whose thwarted pursuit of middle-class respectability represents the novel's critique of the misleading promises of class advancement extended by Parliament's funding of voluntary education for the poor and the training of working-class teachers from the 1840s through the 1850s. The syllabic method common in Victorian reading pedagogy, I argue in this chapter, also provides a specific instance of rote learning of unconnected facts that undermines the inventive uses of memory, literacy, and serial reading as media of social connection and participation modeled in Dickens's novels.

The novel's critical depiction of Bradley's mental "warehouse" (217), I show, also dovetails with midcentury Victorian educators' criticisms of the failure of rote learning to encourage students to synthesize disparate facts into useful knowledge. Paying close attention to the novel's engagement with political debates over cutbacks in government funding of popular education in the 1860s, I show that Bradley's thwarted disposition depicts the results of Parliament's disowning of the ambitions of working-class schoolmasters whose education at teacher training colleges had been funded by the government. In contrast to mid-Victorian liberals' advocacy of education as a means of training the working classes in loyalty to the state, however, Dickens in *Our Mutual Friend* represents the *extra-institutional* and independent uses of literacy as potentially democratic means of self-expression and social solidarity. As we saw in Chapter 1, through characters such as Mrs. Tickit in *Little Dorrit*, Dickens's novels insist that thought is free and independent of social origins. But through a figure like Jenny Wren, *Our Mutual Friend* also continues to make the argument that universal education is required to support the social recognition of human intelligence and creativity wherever it may exist in society. The novel also foregrounds the generalized cultural practice of invention as a source of productive work and personal identity, despite the limitations of what it diagnoses as a mid-Victorian political and moral economy of scarcity and waste.

Our Mutual Friend also moves away from the collective reading that the earlier novels envisioned as the result of readers' shared associations, which were also staged in Dickens's public readings of his novels. Through the confrontation between Mr. Twemlow and Mr. Podsnap over the meaning of the word "gentleman," Dickens's late serial novel suggests that reading, rather than being a means of rote learning, can express an idiosyncratic interpretation of a text or artifact. In this way, reading can be recognized—and taught—as a productive activity through which individuals fabricate and re-configure their social and economic viability within an increasingly perva-sive capitalist culture.

The Business of Literacy and the Failure of Mental Synthesis

Our Mutual Friend opens with a scene of social investigation reminiscent of Mayhew's journalism in which a father and daughter, Gaffer and Lizzie Hexam, ply their ramshackle boat on the refuse-ridden waters of the Thames. The narrator postpones the revelation that they are trolling for corpses in order to lead the reader to infer their occupation by process of elimination—they are not fishermen, bargemen, or river cargo-carriers but are nevertheless involved in an organized activity that, despite appearances, excludes them from the category of "half savage" and instead defines their habitual behavior as "business-like usage" (1–2). Allusions to cannibalism occur throughout this scene, however: through their salvage efforts, Gaffer reminds Lizzie, the river means "meat and drink to you!" (3), and moments later Rogue Riderhood asks Gaffer, "Arn't been eating nothing as has dis-agreed with you, have you, pardner?"(4). These allusions do not intensify the characters' potential savagery but rather underscore the unrelenting na-ture of an economic system that requires some people to make a living from the bodies of the dead. This opening chapter inaugurates the novel's con-cern with the marginal economic enterprises of the poor, which are often unpleasant but also demonstrate almost infinite human resourcefulness, de-spite a lack of capital: Gaffer's scavenging from the drowned, Jenny Wren's dressmaking for dolls from scraps of fabric, Venus's "articulation" (83) of scattered bones and taxidermic preservation of dead pets. Most prominently represented by Old Harmon's Dust Mounds, these enterprises involve gathering, recycling, reassembling, and reselling things cast off by others as waste.

Literacy initially appears antithetical to gleaning "meat and drink" from trash. The police Night-Inspector, with his "pen and ink, and ruler, posting up his books in a whitewashed office, as studiously as if he were in a monas-tery on top of a mountain, and no howling fury of a drunken woman were banging herself against a cell-door in the back-yard at his elbow" (24), seems to epitomize a necessary system of "civilized" social control that keeps everyone neatly in his or her place and provides the literate with a means of distraction from noisy protests or messy suffering. While such an equation of literacy with civilization becomes immediately suspect in the opening chapters of the novel, it cannot reinvest illiterate characters with moral and intellectual legitimacy without pointing out the pitfalls of ignorance. The illiterate Gaffer can only navigate his way across the handbills posted on the wall of his house in order to remember what is written on them—shift their relative positions, and he is lost in relation to print. Gaffer and his way of life are not resilient in the face of social change, and his rejection of his son Charley's education testifies to his own social and economic vulnerability. Yet the other illiterate characters are some of the novel's most proficient interpreters of other, nonlinguistic signifying systems: the Boffins are masters of indirect communication and dissimulation, Jenny Wren is an artist who translates what she perceives about social inequality into her dolls as "literal" personifications rather than texts, and Lizzie's fire gazing allows her imaginatively to re-create past events and envision the future.

Dickens's interest in the full spectrum of lower-class literacy in his fiction is reflected in the novel's representations of the various levels of partial literacy among the poor: Betty Higden's difficulties reading handwriting but "love" for "a newspaper" (198), Sloppy's theatrical ability to "do the Police in different voices" by reading the newspaper out loud (198), and Silas Wegg's accomplishments as a balladeer and "literary man—*with* a wooden leg" (49)—who can read Gibbon but doesn't know the difference between the "Rooshan" and Roman empires (58–59).[16] There is a striking difference between this range of literacy and the treatment in *Bleak House* of the street sweeper Jo's ignorance, which amounts to incomprehension of the world around him:

> "For *I* don't," says Jo, "*I* don't know nothink."
>
> It must be strange to be like Jo! To shuffle through the streets, unfamiliar with the shapes, and in utter darkness as to the meaning, of those mysterious symbols, so abundant over the shops, and at the corners of streets, and on the doors, and in the windows! To see people read, and to see people write, and to see the postmen deliver letters, and not to have the least idea of all that language—to be, to every scrap of it, stone blind and dumb! It must be very puzzling to see the good company going to the churches on Sundays, with their books in their hands, and to think (for perhaps Jo *does* think at odd times) what does it all mean, and if it means anything to anybody, how comes it that it means nothing to me? . . . His whole material and immaterial life is wonderfully strange; his death, the strangest thing of all.[17]

Jo's disorientation within the world of print becomes the reader's disorientation, as the narration moves inside and outside his limited awareness, much as Jo wanders through the streets of London driven from place to place by the police. Not the least part of the disorienting effect of the passage may be the middle-class reader's recognition that, despite his homelessness and illiteracy, "Jo *does* think." The narrator condemns the institutions that Jo does not understand for failing to take notice of his capacity for thought—his humanity—and to aid him as they should. Yet *Bleak House* consistently emphasizes Jo's passivity, victimization, and isolation by dwelling on his utter incomprehension of the world, while showing how educated society maintains its own form of ignorance as a generalized state of willed moral apathy.

In contrast to Jo, it is hard to imagine the Boffins, Jenny Wren, or even Gaffer Hexam as passive, isolated, "knowing nothink," and having "no business." The most ironic figure for *Our Mutual Friend*'s paradoxical moral transvaluation of illiteracy is Bradley Headstone—a former "Jo" who received a better share of schooling. Instead of illustrating how Parliament finally saw its responsibilities and instituted measures to begin to redress the ignorance of the uneducated, however, the novel depicts both Bradley and Charley as instances of the general condition of social reproduction as cram.[18] The novel traces the unfinished state of Charley's education and the defective state of Bradley's memories and affections directly to the specific effects of their schooling. The earliest technique of memorization that most Victorian schoolchildren encountered, no matter how rudimentary or formal their schooling might have been, was the syllabic or "synthetic method" of reading instruction embodied in many spelling books and dating at least to the seventeenth century, if not earlier.[19] The quasi-automatic learning associated with the "synthetic method" of memorizing syllables and then lists of words and postponing the reading of phrases and sentences also implied that various kinds of more subtle messages could be imparted along with words, rules, or facts.

Consider, for instance, the historian M. K. Ashby's account of the experiences of her father, Joseph Ashby, as a schoolboy in the village of Tysoe, Warwickshire, during the 1860s. Joseph had been a student at the new Anglican Church–affiliated National school in his village from the ages of five to eleven. The school had implemented a version of the monitorial method of teaching, according to which the schoolmaster taught the upper class while boy monitors taught the lower classes. The monitor, Charlie Reason, taught the youngest children to read using the syllabic method: "The chief business of the infants was to learn to chant the alphabet and the numbers to one hundred. In the next class they chanted tables and recited the even

numbers and the odd." A central element of the monitor's task seems to
have been simply to keep the youngest children awake, attentive, and in
their seats.[20] Similarly, the narrator describes the "atmosphere" of Charley
Hexam's Ragged School classroom as "oppressive and disagreeable; it was
crowded, noisy, and confusing; half the pupils dropped asleep, or fell into a
state of waking stupefaction; the other half kept them in either condition by
maintaining a monotonous droning noise, as if they were performing, out
of time and tune, on a ruder sort of bagpipe" (214). The "droning" bagpipe
noise represents the drone of oral recitation either off book or from memory.[21] Joseph Ashby recalled that the children in his class used to recite, "O-
n, on; b-o-n, bon; c-o-n, con;/L-o-n, lon; d-o-n, don; London," confirming how the syllabic method involved oral spelling, memorization, and
recitation of discrete and often meaningless syllables that were eventually
combined to form words.[22]

Joseph Ashby also recollected that "One didn't learn much but the place
was full of feeling," most frequently "frustration": "The air was filled with
little curses; little chests heaved over broken hearts," and then the children
would experience the "joy" of release when the bell rang, except that they
would have to control their impatience and march in strict order out the
door.[23] Ashby seems to have been most impressed by "the mystery" of the
Bible stories and catechism, but

> [t]he mystery slumped and vanished in the Duty towards my Neighbour, and
> it was upon this that the Vicar and his lady laid such stress. Boys and girls
> must never "pick and steal," nor lie, nor have any envy of folk luckier than
> themselves; they must learn to labour truly to get their own living and order
> themselves lowly and reverently to their betters. As to what was meant by
> all these phrases there was no mystery at all; the word "betters" was espe-
> cially firmly underlined and annotated. It meant the Vicar himself and the
> man who paid your father's wage.[24]

Ashby's schooling construed the Christian "duty towards my Neighbour"
as a lesson in accepting one's place in the social hierarchy.[25]

Methods relying on memorization were pervasive in Victorian elementary schools sponsored by both the Anglican National Society for Promoting
the Education of the Poor in the Principles of the Established Church in
England and Wales, organized from 1810 to 1811, and the British and Foreign School Society, a nonsectarian dissenting organization founded in 1808
and reorganized in 1810. As elementary schooling expanded from the 1830s
through the 1860s through both state-supported (though not mandated) and

independent schools, however, liberal Victorian educational reformers argued that learning by rote was failing to ensure both the student's grasp of
factual knowledge and acceptance of his or her place in society. Instruction
in reading through the syllabic method was, reformers feared, a system of
cram that forced young children to retain and "parrot" lists of "unmeaning
combinations."[26] From a cultural historian's perspective, teaching reading as
an exercise of the rote memory seems to assume that the mental synthesis
producing understanding is a process that needs to be formalized and that
the child must be trained to think in a rational fashion. The irony of the
"synthesis" named in the "synthetic" or "syllabic" method of reading pedagogy, then, was that it was premised on the necessity of first *disassociating* and
delaying the processes of mental synthesis involved in reading whole words
and phrases in order to teach the child to recognize discrete syllables by rote
memorization *before* forming them into words. This irony becomes particularly telling in light of David Hartley's authoritative 1749 analogy comparing
the various stages of experience to learning to read by means of the synthetic
method that I discussed in Chapter 1.[27] If the retention of experience by the
mind is, for Hartley, like learning to read, then by applying the synthetic
method to the actual teaching of reading, Victorian pedagogues were sending the process of learning into reverse, disaggregating the child's oral/aural
acquisition of language through associative processes in order to reformat
his or her mind for the purposes of formal literacy.

One observer of the synthetic system in use in mid-Victorian elementary
schools lamented the disconnect between learning to read through memorization of syllables and enjoyment of reading: "Spelling is still taught by
means of columns of long, hard, unconnected words, selected for their very
difficulty and rarity, to be learned by rote, or, as is said with unconscious
irony, 'by heart.' "[28] James Phillips Kay, later Sir James Kay-Shuttleworth,
the educational reformer and Victorian bureaucrat who played an instrumental role in directing Parliament's increasing involvement in popular education from the 1830s and 1840s, also viewed rote learning as an all-too-
frequent substitute for education and deplored what he called the "monitorial humbug."[29] In his history of reforms in Victorian education, Kay-Shuttleworth warns of the collapse of reference between word and thing that
can result from rote learning: "In book-learning there is always a danger
that the thing signified may not be discerned through the sign. The child
may acquire words instead of thoughts." He implies that those who are "satisfied with instruction by rote" are also dangerously self-satisfied in purvey-
ing all knowledge as dogma: "We are of opinion that to extend the province

of faith and implicit unreasoning obedience to those subjects which are the proper objects on which the perceptive faculties ought to be exercised, and on which the reason should be employed, is to undermine the basis of an unwavering faith in revelation, by provoking the rebellion of the human spirit against authority in matters in which reason is free."[30] Children take "nothing but words" from the rote teacher and will not become "earnest and truthful men," because their intelligence has not been engaged to make connections between experience and ideas: "the mind will refuse a lively confidence in general truths, when it has not been convinced of the existence of the particular facts from which they are derived."[31] Thus for Kay-Shuttleworth, rote learning not only leads to forgetting but also produces a gap in the child's understanding of linguistic signs that may undermine his or her belief in the interlocking symbolic systems upon which mainstream social and religious forms of authority are based.[32]

The narrator's descriptions of Bradley Headstone suggest that he has suffered the kind of cognitive dysfunction as a result of his rote learning that Kay-Shuttleworth feared. Bradley struggles to synthesize the various elements of the memorized knowledge in his mental "warehouse": "From his early childhood up, his mind had been a place of mechanical stowage. The arrangement of his wholesale warehouse, so that it might be always ready to meet the demands of retail dealers—history here, geography there, astronomy to the right, political economy to the left—natural history, the physical sciences, figures, music, the lower mathematics, and what not, all in their several places—this care had imparted to his countenance a look of care" (217). This "wholesale" knowledge seems to correspond to Karl Marx's contemporaneous definition of the commodity: such warehoused knowledge has lost its use value and instead consists merely of a "retail" or exchange value that qualifies Bradley to sell his services as a schoolmaster.[33] Commodified, compartmentalized knowledge like Bradley's is detached and inert rather than synthetic and therefore is inaccessible as intellectual capital because it resists the learner's recursive reinvestment in new knowledge. Thus the "owner" of such fragmented knowledge is also alienated from his own mental labor.

Our Mutual Friend also develops the powerful affective side to this pedagogy of rote memorization that Ashby's account highlighted. As in the Edgeworths' portrayal of the student who merely "bales up" knowledge, Bradley's excessive cramming tends toward a retention that always verges on forgetting: "There was a kind of settled trouble in his face. It was the face belonging to a naturally slow or inattentive intellect that has toiled hard to get what it had won, and that had to hold it now that it was gotten" (217). Despite being obliged to retail the mental products of his education through teaching children to learn by rote, Bradley's expression betrays that his real tendency is to hoard: his "suspicious manner that would be better described as one of lying in wait" is derived from his catechizing "habit of questioning and being questioned" (217). Thus his expression also resembles the "dark cloud of suspicion, covetousness, and conceit, overshadowing the once open face" of Mr. Boffin in his guise as a miser later in the novel (465). In the context of Victorian pedagogy, this resemblance between the pedant and the miser suggests that the question of education in the novel is not subordinate to its representation of a generally mercenary society but essential to it: a pedagogical system that commodifies knowledge has developed from the Victorian school's rigid institutionalization of the memory's retentive action, excluding its functions as a resource for imagination, inquiry, and invention.

The fact that the synthetic pedagogical method predates the factory system historically, as we saw in Chapter 1, also suggests that the mind forms a crucial connection, which the novel represents, between the histories of education and modern industrial society. The metaphors of acquisition and storage of knowledge, the figural quality of which John Locke had insisted upon, have nevertheless been marshaled as part of a rationale allying the functioning of mind with the manufacture of commodities and accumulation of wealth. Such a correlation of mental processes and economic interest, Dickens's novel demonstrates, forms a foundational conceptual prerequisite to, as well as a corollary of, capitalist culture.[34] In other words, the novel's critique of mercenary motives points to the problem of formal knowledge as a medium of exchange just as consistently as it points to the problem of the selfish accumulation of money.

As part of its critique of elementary schooling, the novel points to the causes of Bradley's failures of mental synthesis, his insecure possession of knowledge, and lack of self-possession, as inseparable from his *denial* of his lower-class origins. As Bradley's initial discussion with Charley about Lizzie demonstrates, the novel also suggests that the emulative culture of the elementary school, through which students are motivated to compete for a higher academic and social status, also requires that students begin to distance themselves from their families. "I hope your sister may be good company for you?" Bradley asks before he has met Lizzie (216), and so instructs Charley to doubt her respectability. Bradley's hard-won and carefully maintained "decency" (217) also masks his disavowal of his pauper past ("regarding that origin of his, he was proud, moody, and sullen, desiring it to be forgotten" [218]). As a result of his cramming, Bradley also seems to have lost access to his pre-literate knowledge of the streets, "the great Preparatory Establishment in which very much that is never unlearned is learned without and before book" (214). This suppression of his past leads to Bradley's most fatal error when he attempts to frame Rogue Riderhood, right in front of his own eyes, for Eugene's murder. Bradley assumes that because Riderhood is "a very ignorant man who could not write" (792), he also cannot detect the visible signs of the schoolmaster's plot against him.[35] Much as the Edgeworths predicted, Bradley has become an "incumbrance" to himself and his friends, and his burden of psychosocial contradiction is so heavy that it finally drags him (and Riderhood) down under the waters of the Thames to their deaths.

Podsnappery and Summary Knowledge

The representation of Bradley almost seems to make the case that illiteracy is preferable to becoming the product of the Victorian educational system. Illiterate poor characters such as the Boffins, Jenny, and Lizzie (with the notable exception of Wegg) seem to be the only members of society in *Our Mutual Friend* who engage in productive labor, even though "all print is shut" (50) to them. The novel's point, however, is not that the good illiterate characters gain a critical perspective on socialization "by rote" simply because of their escape from the discipline of schooling, or because of their social marginality. Rather, the crux of their moral influence lies in precisely *how* they substitute original arts of memory for the automatic uses that support social reproduction by rote.

In contrast, the novel's educated "Society" characters demonstrate that cram is pervasive across all social classes. They are either mercenary and vulgar, like the Veneering set, or, as in the case of Eugene and Mortimer, they seem to possess too much culture to participate productively in society. For example, making sophisticated use of a schoolroom dictionary analogy, Eugene can provide a critique of the presumption that success in the legal profession simply requires the individual to exert "energy": "If there is a word in the dictionary under any letter from A to Z that I abominate, it is energy. It is such a conventional superstition, such parrot gabble! What the deuce! Am I to rush out into the street, collar the first man of a wealthy appearance that I meet, shake him, and say 'Go to law upon the spot, you dog, and retain me, or I'll be the death of you?' Yet that would be energy" (20). An attack on both elite and popular versions of mid-Victorian individualism, the passage suggests a parody of both John Stuart Mill's defense in *On Liberty* (1859) of individual desires and "energy" as the "strong [natural] impulses" of those "whose cultivated feelings may be made the strongest" and of Samuel Smiles's popular rhetoric of self-empowerment in *Self-Help* (1859).[36] Eugene's ability to gloss "energy" as a "conventional superstition" "parroted" as if by rote, and to imagine actually exposing its logic as fraudulent by obeying its instructions to the letter, also suggests the novel's critique of the emergent ideologies of the Victorian professions. Yet Eugene's skepticism does not give him the "energy" or incentive either to abandon his professional expectations or to find work; as Mortimer puts it, "But show me a good opportunity, show me something really worth being energetic about, and I'll show you energy" (20). They articulate a sophisticated self-awareness typical of their role as intellectuals—the narrator observes that "it is likely enough that ten thousand other young men, within the limits of the London Post-office town-delivery, made the same hopeful remark in the course of the same evening" (20). Mortimer's qualification restores the face-saving possibility that only a lack of opportunity, and not an actual shortage of work or personal failure of initiative, prevents them from practicing their profession. But the satire reveals that a mere acknowledgment of one's rote socialization does not enable one to transcend it.

The reader may draw the conclusion that a highly educated intellectual like Eugene is liable to be paralyzed by his perception of the trap of "parrot gabble." It seems to take a superficial avatar of society like Lady Tippins, who excels at "taking cabs and going about" (250), to muster sufficient energy to execute a "piece of work" (246) by sending Veneering to Parliament. Veneering is a "representative man" (244) precisely because "nobody knows" him (249); he is recognizable as a product of the socioeconomic machine that runs politics by cranking out a series of "bran-new" wealthy men to buy seats in the House of Commons. But Eugene's position is more perplexing; he is capable of the most insightful ironies at his own expense and cuttingly critical sallies at the expense of others but cannot attain any understanding of "the troublesome conundrum long abandoned . . . Eugene Wrayburn" (295). Eugene's articulate detachment and self-criticism substitutes for his lack of self-knowledge, implying that it is the absence of connection between a cognizance of one's social role and the articulation of individual identity that causes the "chronic weariness" both he and Mortimer experience (88). Like the "great looking-glass" hung above the Veneerings' dinner table that figures the narrator's dissection of the "Society" characters' foibles (10–11), the novel exposes social hypocrisy but also represents the difficulties that even educated characters such as John Harmon, Bella Wilfer, Eugene, and Mr. Twemlow face in attempting to understand the relation between social complexities and their own predicaments. *Our Mutual Friend* questions the possibility of turning intellectual cultivation to socially critical account when it is accompanied by the incentive of class privilege. Such a fundamental change of perspective requires an acute crisis.

While Eugene is Bradley's self-chosen rival for Lizzie's love, the "eminently respectable" (129) Mr. Podsnap is Bradley's upper-class counterpart in mentality. The philistine lip service of Podsnappery presents another, more pervasive ideological form of rote learning producing the "self-satisfied" complacency of the bourgeoisie (128). Podsnap's identity consists of a memorized routine of "getting up at eight, shaving close at a quarter-past, breakfasting at nine, going to the City at ten, coming home at half-past five, and dining at seven" (128). Podsnappery, the "articles of a faith and school" (129), is so compact and easily replicable an attitude that it can be expressed in a characteristic "right-arm flourish" (133).[37] With this gesture, Podsnap "remove[s] from the face of the earth" everything not consisting of the routine, everything non-English, and anything "disagreeable" (141), such as "the circumstance that some half-dozen people had lately died in the streets of starvation" (140): "PRESTO with a flourish of the arm, and a flush of the face, they were swept away" (128). Podsnappery consists in a "summary" (133) knowledge without complexity or ambiguity; its effect is to telescope the world into a convenient perspective "confined within close bounds, as Mr. Podsnap's own head was confined by his shirt-collar" (129). Unlike Bradley's incoherence, Podsnap's narrow view relies on a habit of premature mental synthesis or stereotyping. His opinion of his daughter, Georgiana, for example, consists of categorizing her as "a certain institution in [his] mind, which he called 'the young person.'" Podsnap represents a middle-class prudery that amounts to prurience, since it cannot distinguish between "the young person's excessive innocence, and another person's guiltiest knowledge" (129), a conflation that encompasses suppressed knowledge of social injustice as well as sexuality.[38]

It is clearly no coincidence, then, that Podsnappery appears in its most comic and grotesque light in the form of a burlesque English lesson to a foreigner. When Podsnap quizzes a French-speaking guest at his dinner party, "Do You Find, Sir . . . Many Evidences that Strike You, of our British Constitution in the Streets Of The World's Metropolis, London, Londres, London?" and then restates his question: "Whether You Have Observed in our Streets as We should say, Upon our Pavvy as You would say, any To-kens— . . . Marks, . . . Signs, you know, Appearances—Traces," the con-fused foreigner, finally believing that he understands, blurts out, "Ah! Of a Orse?" (132). We get the joke, although Podsnap does not and immediately admonishes the gentleman for failing to "Aspirate the 'H' . . . Only our Lower Classes say 'Orse!'" (133). Podsnappery retails its own "syllabic" list of linguistic placeholders for understanding, or "Tokens," such as "British Constitution," "World's Metropolis," or "Providence," that signify an au-tomatic, ideological set of connotations, the primary functions of which are to take liberties for granted and to signal both class and national allegiance.

In order to clarify how *Our Mutual Friend* represents a change in tactics within Dickens's cultural politics, I want to point out that as the target of the novel's satire, it is significant that Podsnap is not an Evangelical or a religious hypocrite. In fact, Dickens's satire on religious hypocrisy is absent from this late novel, and instead he has shifted his attention to the growth of British nationalism and the extension of the state's influence over educa-tion and thus over the future of society. Podsnappery represents the mindset of a merchant-capitalist class whose "cultural" identity is a chauvinistic identification with the British Empire that claims the sanction of Providence for its own economic, social, and political interests (141). The symbolic equivalence of money, the British constitution, and manure makes clear how monetary exchange as an ultimate value taints the societal forms that are supposed to transcend commerce by representing historical continuity and cultural tradition. In the context of the novel, however, this exchangea-bility does not mean primarily that the constitution is a form of waste or a mere linguistic "token," but rather that its invocation by Podsnap displays a particular kind of rote social reproduction that operates like a dead lan-guage—such learning is only capable of replicating existing speech patterns, ideas, and social distinctions but cannot generate new meanings as the in-ventive memory does. The constitution as Podsnap uses it becomes not a marker of national identity but an alibi for shirking national responsibilities. Similarly, the sway of the "bran-new" in high "society" (6) indicates both the commodification of thinking extending to the privileged classes and a pseudo-novelty that lacks all originality. The replicability of the "bran-new" mindset that Podsnap embodies also sustains the novel's larger argu-ment that forms of literacy are directly related, for good or for ill, to the public imagination of British national culture.

Given the narrative's development of an associationist pedagogical focus on the visible and invisible forms of social reproduction in the mind, its depiction of habitual gestures, such as Podsnap's flourish, takes on an additional meaning as a form of acquired bodily automatism that seems to afflict most of the characters. Podsnap's habitual gesture of exclusion provides an exact counterpart to Bradley's excessively inclusive mind. Bradley has been required to learn a smattering of everything and "always seemed to be uneasy lest anything should be missing from his mental warehouse, and taking stock to assure himself" (217). Podsnap's flourishing of his arm represents the choice not to know unpleasant things that complacent and comfortable Victorians may allow themselves to forget, but these are precisely the things that Dickens's satirical treatment leads his readers to recognize and remember. In case we may be tempted to define Bradley's overstuffed mind as antithetical to Podsnap's favorite catchall, "oblivion," however, we should remember that even the schoolmaster's knowledge amounts to a form of social exclusion: he is only taught, and only imparts to his students, what Parliament and various religious authorities have deemed suitable to the education of the lower classes. If Bradley's and Podsnap's forms of rote learning—their inability or refusal to synthesize information and experience into morally relevant knowledge—are counterparts, then this means that the novel's plot is constructed precisely to link new forms of British nationalism directly to the growth of the school system as the coordinated vehicles of a moral blindness that afflicts all social classes.

The real antithesis to Podsnap's flourish is a much less dramatic, more commonplace gesture particularly characteristic of Mr. Twemlow, who, "with his hand to his forehead" (9), is perpetually at a loss to understand his own relation to Veneering and to penetrate the meaning of the "infectious" "Veneering fiction" (115) that marks Veneering's paradoxical status as simultaneously everyone's oldest and newest friend. Twemlow's hand-to-forehead gesture manifests the invisible mental activity of thinking and often indicates cognitive difficulties—not, like Podsnap's flourish, showing what one person feels he can dispense with knowing, but rather what someone else is conscientiously struggling to comprehend. Also unlike Bradley's "troubled" look, the hand-to-forehead gesture indicates not suspicion or insecurity but simply honest perplexity. It can also point to the seeming absence of willed intentions, as when Lizzie, "passing her hand across her forehead," explains to Charley that "it's no purpose of mine that I live by [the river] still" (228). The narrator even mocks it when practiced by Mrs. Veneering, who "presses her hand upon her brow, to arrange the throbbing intellect within" (244), before she attempts the "work" of "bringing in" her husband as an MP (244–54). This is a counterfeit gesture that simulates thinking, since Mrs. Veneering is only going to do the obvious, without any further consideration.

Instead of instantiating social connections, "Society" in *Our Mutual Friend* substitutes pseudo-relations as socially pervasive sources of counterfeit thought and discourse. "Tapping his forehead and breast," Eugene offers his own variation on Twemlow's gesture that includes heart and mind, and he follows it with another puzzle about identity: "Riddle-me, riddle-me-ree, perhaps you can't tell me what this may be?—No, upon my life I can't. I give it up!" (295). Eugene is dealing in his witty way with the same problem that plagues Twemlow, who is "stunned with the unvanquishable difficulty of his existence" (9). All these cognitive and existential problems surround the challenge of articulating one's own *complicity* in social "rote learning": it's simple enough to ridicule the Lady Tippinses of the world, to dismiss Podsnap in his turn, or even to puzzle out the Veneerings' "bran-newness," but quite another, for the reader, to conceive his or her own involvement in the chains of thought—to think about thinking—or to comprehend the forms of social transmission and value by which such mentalities sustain their currency. By returning to a fundamental epistemological question, which so interested empiricists such as Locke and Hume, of how the mind can reflect on its own operations, *Our Mutual Friend* in fact extends the Dickensian serial novel's work with associationist theory by exploring reading as an occasion for critical self-reflection.

The Schoolmaster's Culture

The novel dissects the pedagogical theory behind social rote learning most systematically through its critique of the Victorian schoolmaster's culture. As Philip Collins has pointed out, in *Our Mutual Friend*, Dickens's focus on "the sociology of the new race of trained teachers" presents in Bradley Headstone a character new to fiction who was also "the best available example of the social difficulties in rising from the lower to the middle class."[39] In representing not only a student of the popular education system but also a "highly certificated stipendiary schoolmaster" (216), Bradley would have been a recognizable figure to any reader who had sent a child to a school supported by parliamentary grants or who had followed recent debates surrounding the government's funding of elementary education. His characterization also indicates Dickens's familiarity with the arrangements by which the training of "stipendiary" schoolmasters was supported by government grants. I return to Bradley to determine why the novel analyzes the school-master's culture so minutely, among so many other possible examples of the phenomenon of social mobility. The publication of the novel from May 1864 through December 1865 coincided with the beginnings of organized pressure for another round of electoral reforms that would enfranchise a greater percentage of middle-and skilled working-class male voters. The middle-class Reform Union was founded in Manchester in March 1864, and the working-class Reform League was founded in February 1865.[40] By the time of this agitation, Dickens had become quite sympathetic to a major increase in working-class enfranchisement. Responding to a peaceful march and mass meeting of the Trades Societies at Beaufort House, Kensington, on December 3, 1866, in which between 22,000 and 25,000 persons partici-pated, Dickens wrote in a letter:

> As to the Reform question, it should have been, and could have been, perfectly known to any honest man in England that the more intelligent part of the great masses were deeply dissatisfied with the state of the represen-tation, but were in a very moderate and patient condition, awaiting the better intellectual cultivation of numbers of their fellows. The old insolent resource of assailing them and making the most audaciously hardy statements that they were politically indifferent has borne the inevitable fruit. The perpetual taunt "Where are they?" has called them out with the answer, "Well, then; if you *must* know, here we are." . . . I have a very small opinion of what the great-genteel have done for us, that I am very philosophical indeed concerning what the great vulgar may do: having a decided opinion that they can't do worse.[41]

Dickens points to the pursuit of education by the working classes as their deliberate effort to extend democracy by preparing for their own enfran-chisement, so that when they are addressed as a tardy constituency for re-form, they confound their critics by having already constituted themselves as such. In the period prior to the Second Reform Act of 1867, parliamen-tary debates in the early 1860s over the funding and oversight of popular education reveal ambivalence among both politicians and educational re-formers about working-class social mobility and political enfranchisement but also suggest a significant staging ground for the growing political accep-tance of the idea of a more extensive democracy. These debates provide a specific political and even legislative context for *Our Mutual Friend*.

In July of 1861, Robert Lowe, the vice president of the Committee of the Privy-Council on Education for Palmerston's Liberal coalition govern-ment, presented a minute or bill containing a "Revised Code" governing parliamentary support of elementary schools for the poor and working classes.[42] The Revised Code was based upon the recommendations of a royal commission known as the Newcastle Commission, appointed in 1858 to evaluate the state of popular education. In calling for a commission, Parliament wished first to investigate how rising public expenditure on education for the poor could be contained and, second, in apparent contradiction, to respond to concerns that Britain was falling behind other European nations such as France and Prussia in its educational efforts. The Newcastle Commission's mandate was to propose how more children could be educated for less public money. According to the Minute of 1846, which had put in place the government's sponsorship of popular education, Parliament provided approximately one-third of the income, in the form of various kinds of grants, for elementary schools and teacher training colleges founded and financed by voluntary associations affiliated primarily with the Church of England as well as with various dissenting groups.[43] Schools received grants based on government inspectors' evaluations of religious instruction, acceptable building and sanitary standards, level of attendance, and overall quality of instruction. Parliament also replaced the unsatisfactory monitorial method of teaching with a system of certificated teachers, trained in colleges under government inspection in a curriculum set by the Education Department, and pupil-teachers, who, after fulfilling a five-year apprenticeship under certificated teachers, matriculated upon examination to the training colleges.

Reviewing this system, the Newcastle Commission's report, issued in 1861, found that an insufficient number of children who passed through the state-supported schools could read, write, and cipher. It recommended that half of the capitation grant given for each child who attended the school should be based on the results of individual examinations in reading, writing, and arithmetic administered by government inspectors, and the other half simply on adequate attendance, and, as before, on the school's passing government inspection.[44] Lowe's Revised Code, however, went beyond the commission's recommendations by making the entire capitation grant contingent upon each child's success in passing the examination. As he put it in speech before the House of Commons on February 13, 1862, "I cannot promise the House that this system will be an economical one, and I cannot promise that it will be an efficient one, but I can promise that it will be one or the other. If it is not cheap it shall be efficient; if it is not efficient it shall be cheap."[45] Critics of the Revised Code, such as Kay-Shuttleworth and Matthew Arnold, who was a government inspector of schools, found fault not only with its new system of "payment-by-results," but also with its radical revision of Parliament's relationship with certificated teachers and pupil-teachers, and thus with the teacher training colleges. This payment-by-results plan was not only intended to make sure that "the public will get value for its money."[46] It was also framed to supply an inducement to teachers to produce the desired results by abolishing the salary augmentation grants that they had been receiving from the government based on their rank in taking their certificate and years of attendance at the training college. The Revised Code made the teacher's salary entirely contingent on how many students passed the examination, thus encouraging teachers to make sure students memorized the book on which they would be tested by the inspector.[47] The Revised Code also removed financial incentives for teachers to train pupil-teachers by cutting their remuneration for instructing them and removed all pecuniary value from the training college certificate, making it merely honorary.

In sum, the Revised Code applied free-market principles to popular education in an effort to impose a shift from the primarily qualitative standards that the inspectors had previously applied to a system of quantitative measurements of a teacher's and school's performance. In a more complicated sense, however, the Revised Code was also a response to the social effects that legislation in the arena of popular education had produced on the "class" of elementary school teachers, who were recruited from among poor and working-class pupils.[48] A letter of instructions of the secretary of the Committee of the Privy Council on Education (often referred to as the Committee of Council) establishing the certificate examination for elementary school teachers in 1848 explicitly articulated the government's "determination . . . to elevate the position of the elementary school teacher, by qualifying him to occupy a higher station, and by rewarding his more efficient services by superior endowments."[49] It was not surprising, then, that the schoolmasters and pupil-teachers began to see themselves as virtual civil servants, since they received their grants directly by post from London, their hours of work were fixed by the government, and the Committee of Council, by its power to apprentice pupil-teachers, determined which of them would hold teaching positions and gain advancement in their occupation.[50]

The 1861 commission report, in contrast, refers to the teachers as "almost creations of the Committee of Council" but also specifically refutes any assumption that there exists a "moral right" on the part of teachers to continue to receive grants from the state.[51] In his defense of the Revised Code before the House of Commons, Lowe declared it his duty to put a stop to "the fearful increase of . . . pretensions" on the part of teachers, who may become "an army of stipendiaries" and "a dangerous organization for attacks on the Treasury."[52] In order to justify the government's desire to insulate financial decisions about elementary education from the influence of "the persons working that educational system,"[53] Lowe quotes in evidence part of a report to the commission by one inspector of training colleges, who concludes that the teachers "naturally think more of what education has made them than of what it first found them." The inspector further complains that these working-class teachers "easily lose sight of the fact that they have risen from a very humble social position, and they crave for that status which education seems generally to secure. I think too that in some cases they are too apt to forget that they owe the culture they have to the public provision made for them."[54] Functioning as a disavowal of the social reformist goals of the 1846 Minute, the Revised Code reminded schoolmasters that they owed their "culture" to the state while denying that Parliament had ever held out a promise of their substantial recognition as a cadre of civil servants.[55] The Revised Code thus represented a concerted effort by Parliament to rein in the social and political "pretensions" of schoolmasters, who in the 1850s and 1860s were forming professional associations, organizing as a voting bloc, and demanding public recognition of their contributions to the public good.[56] Within the terms offered by *Our Mutual Friend*, the Revised Code becomes a version of Podsnap's flourish, sweeping away the schoolmasters' claims on the state.

The Newcastle Commission's investigation of popular education also produced a psychosocial profile of the schoolmaster that parallels Dickens's characterization of Bradley Headstone. The report observed that whatever pedagogical training and general education working-class schoolmasters received, these cannot compensate for the lack of "general cultivation of mind" typical of a middle- or upper-class upbringing: "A person who has been accustomed through life to refined and intelligent society will express himself with greater simplicity and liveliness than another possessed of equal natural abilities and equal acquired information who has had fewer social advantages."[57] While the commissioners imply that the schoolmaster's training should operate to confirm existing social divisions, much evidence exists to indicate that it had the effect of creating a socially ambiguous class. Teachers themselves felt that their education left them in an "anomalous" position because they "fail in the good manners which would facilitate their rising to a better."[58] As Mr. Snell, a schoolmaster from East Coker, complained to the Newcastle Commission, "The man who studies human laws, he who understands the human frame and the healing art, the artist who can produce a picture, each has a recognized position, and is esteemed; but the man who labours for the elevation of his fellow, who deals with the human intellect, who is entrusted to cut and polish the most precious jewel in creation, is a mere social nonentity."[59]

Bradley represents the schoolmaster's "anomalous" social identity as a "wild energy" (396) sparked by his attraction to Lizzie and enflamed by his jealousy of Eugene. The narrator describes Bradley as precisely one of those ambitious types of boys who, the commissioners warn, should avoid the schoolmaster's occupation: "there was enough of what was animal, and of what was fiery (though smouldering), still visible in him, to suggest that if young Bradley Headstone, when a pauper lad, had chanced to be told off for the sea, he would not have been the last man in a ship's crew" (218). Once Bradley has met and become attracted to Lizzie, she begins to function as an alibi for his social insecurities. When she refuses his marriage proposal, Bradley's fury and his convoluted reasoning about Eugene's role in her decision typify his social as much as his sexual jealousy: "I have stood before him face to face, and he crushed me down in the dirt of his contempt, and walked over me. Why? Because he knew with triumph what was in store for me tonight" (400). The education that Bradley has acquired only by chance and enormous effort Eugene possesses as one of the "social advantages" of his upper-class background and public school education, to borrow the Newcastle Commission's terms. This social privilege also functions as a kind of cognitive entitlement that seems to enable Eugene to penetrate and thus forestall the schoolmaster's ambitions and desires. Because of his disavowal of his past, Bradley also lacks independent experiential grounds for questioning his schoolmaster's culture.

The novel represents Bradley as incapable of any objective criticism of the education system that has produced him, and thus his severely felt resentment of Eugene can only emerge as paranoid hatred.[60] When Bradley insists to Eugene, "Do you suppose that a man, in forming himself for the duties I discharge, and in watching and repressing himself daily to discharge them well, dismisses a man's nature?" (291), he implies that his social climb toward respectability has forced him to smother his masculinity.[61] It breaks out in his attraction to Lizzie, but his ambiguous social status provides him with a defective version of masculinity that puts him at particular disadvantage in relation to the model of cigar-smoking, urbane masculine privilege that Eugene represents. Bradley's personal breakdown thus figures the social impossibility of his position—his rage points to the ideological contradictions of educational reforms that hold out the meritocratic promise of an elevation in class status that the working-class schoolmaster's limited "culture" cannot deliver.

Given how much Bradley Headstone resembles the schoolmaster as that figure was represented in parliamentary commissions, reports by normal school principals, conduct books, and even letters of complaint written to occupational journals by schoolmasters themselves, we might wonder what Dickens's novelistic treatment adds to this discourse of social and psychological diagnosis and classification, and how it may differ from it. If we happen to be teachers ourselves, we are likely to sympathize with the Victorian schoolmasters' claims both to social recognition and to political expression as a voting constituency. Yet Dickens's narrator shows no particular sympathy for Bradley—certainly not the brand of spirited liberal defense that Kay-Shuttleworth offered when he castigated the undercutting of teachers by the Revised Code as "an unexampled breach of public faith with a most meritorious class."[62] Through Bradley, the novel furthermore attacks one of the most basic rationales for popular education that Dickens himself had shared throughout the 1840s and 1850s—that the education of the masses would prevent crime and replace or forestall punitive disciplinary measures such as imprisonment or deportation. In his condemnation of the Revised Code, Kay-Shuttleworth warns that any "Statesman who refuses to make an immediate outlay on the religious education of the people, in order to humanise their manners, correct their habits, increase their intelligence, and raise their moral condition, or prefers to cripple such an outlay for the sake of some immediate paltry economy, is not only shortsighted, but he must in his heart disbelieve the efficacy of moral and religious agencies as antidotes to pauperism."[63] *Our Mutual Friend* exemplifies this criticism but reverses Kay-Shuttleworth's thesis. Instead of preventing crime, in the representative case of Bradley Headstone the popular education system has *produced* a criminal through the psychological effects of allowing the schoolmaster to attain a certain level of culture but keeping him firmly in his class and crimping his mind through a mechanical pedagogy of cram. Bradley Headstone's characterization, I would argue, radicalizes the Newcastle Commission's findings by turning its analysis of the schoolmaster's defective culture into a demonstration of the specific injustice perpetrated by Parliament's own disavowal of the aspirant social group that it had helped to constitute.[64]

Our Mutual Friend also depicts in psychological terms a set of political consequences through Bradley's characterization. As one proponent of the pupil training system put it, a central purpose of the entire effort to train working-class teachers was to "loyalise" this particular segment of the working-class population.[65] Kay-Shuttleworth believed so strongly in this initiative that he personally funded the early operating expenses of the Battersea normal college.[66] In his attack on the Revised Code, Kay-Shuttleworth argues that the middle classes must devise "the means of sifting out the best representatives of the classes supported by manual labour from the mass, and conferring the franchise on them." He insists that "The effect of a steady perseverance in a system of national education, such as is at present in operation, would be to raise such men within the pale of the constitution. The 23,000 teachers and pupil-teachers will certainly all possess the franchise."[67] *Our Mutual Friend* depicts the consequences of withholding social recognition from a subaltern class that has been formed quite purposefully to identify itself with the legitimacy of the state: if the natural ambitions of members of this class are thwarted, they may turn on the ruling classes, who, by their very nature, always receive concrete and symbolic marks of status along with their perhaps equally flawed elite education.

We are now in a position to understand more clearly why Dickens focused on the popular education system in this novel published between May 1864 and November 1865. Given the ferment leading up to the Second Reform Act of 1867, there were many pressing issues involving the aspirations of members of the working classes to greater political participation that the novel could have taken up and developed. An 1855 *Household Words* article, "The Great Baby," further illustrates how Dickens's critique of doctrinaire religion and party politics shifted focus over the subsequent decade to a critique of the hypocrisy of the tutelary state in *Our Mutual Friend*:

> There are two public bodies remarkable for knowing nothing of the people, and for perpetually interfering to put them right. The one is the House of Commons; the other the Monomaniacs. Between the Members and the Monomaniacs, the devoted People, quite unheard, get harried and worried to the last extremity. . . . Now, the Monomaniacs, being by their disease impelled to clamber upon platforms, and there squint horribly under the strong possession of an unbalanced idea, will of course be out of reason and go wrong. But, why the Members should yield to the Monomaniacs is another question. And why do they? Is it because the People is altogether an abstraction to them; a Great Baby, to be coaxed and chucked under the chin at elections, and frowned upon at quarter sessions, and stood in the corner on Sundays, and taken out to stare at the Queen's coach on holidays, and

kept in school under the rod, generally speaking, from Monday morning to Saturday night? Is it because they have no other idea of the People than a big-headed Baby, now to be flattered and now to be scolded, now to be sung to and now to be denounced to old Boguey, now to be kissed and now to be whipped, but always to be kept in long clothes, and never under any circumstances to feel its legs and go about of itself? We take the liberty of replying, Yes.[68]

Written in the wake of riots in London's Hyde Park in early July 1855 by working-class demonstrators against the proposal of new sabbatarian laws restricting trade on Sundays, Dickens's diatribe targets the platform-hogging "Monomaniacs," or the evangelicals, whose Sabbatarianism, for Dickens, constituted their "unbalanced idea."[69] We can see further evidence here that evangelical "monomania" constitutes the antithesis of the pleasures of memory afforded by Dickens's serial fiction. *Our Mutual Friend*, however, moves beyond the evangelical movement as the ongoing antagonist of Dickens's cultural politics, following up on the other party to his earlier critique of what we might call a mid-Victorian version of special interest politics: the "Members." Dickens blames MPs for responding to narrow sectarian pressures, warning them that their condescension to the working classes has been widely noticed: "And do the Members and the Monomani-acs suppose that this is *our* discovery? Do they live in the shady belief that the object of their capricious dandling and punishing does not resentfully perceive that it is made a Great Baby of, and may not begin to kick thereat with legs that may do mischief?"[70]

Our Mutual Friend frames the Revised Code as just one more version of such "dandling and punishing" by showing how the schoolmaster has been constructed as a social type embodying the "abstraction" that the working classes remain for the governing classes.[71] However, Bradley does not repre-sent the threat that the working classes will rebel against this infantilizing treatment. Instead Bradley's drive to disavow his low origins through a rise in social status represents the government-bred "Baby" produced by Victo-rian popular education's attempt to form the working class into a tractable electorate, just as the Evangelicals had attempted to do in the 1790s through their publishing and educational initiatives. As a response to the relationship between the liberal mid-Victorian state and the working classes envisioned by the Revised Code, *Our Mutual Friend* represents the current state of pop-ular education just prior to the Second Reform Bill of 1867 as the takeover by the Members of the Monomaniacs' project of moral tutelage, with the

same class restrictions still in place. This is not the kind of universal education that Dickens, as well as the Chartists and other working-class political
and labor organizations, had advocated in the 1840s.

Raymond Williams has pointed out that in relation to social ideas Dickens's fiction places a "characteristic emphasis on the consequences of an
idea, rather than on the idea itself," so that "what [Dickens] is then refuting
is not so much an idea as a whole social formation."[72] *Our Mutual Friend* is as
harsh in its exposure of the false promises and coercive effects of the popular
education system as *Nicholas Nickleby* was in its expose of the Yorkshire
schools. But the later novel goes beyond a critique of institutions to dissect
the most fundamental mental operations that make possible the reception
and propagation of social formations by individuals. Pursuing the associationist framework developed in the earlier novels for representing thinking,
memory, and reading as equally psychological and social forms of relation,
Our Mutual Friend represents rote learning and the commodification of
memory as procedures by which the various ideological supports of capitalist society are reproduced as forms of common knowledge. The schoolmaster's culture represents not simply the penetration of the market logic to
which Dickens objected in the Evangelicals' economic rationales for conversion and salvation, as well as in institutional mechanisms advocated by
Utilitarians for extending literacy to the masses as a means of implanting
reason. What *Our Mutual Friend* finally opposes symbolically is *the larger cultural and political logic of reducing all forms of socialization and democratization to
versions of schooling.* The novel rejects a version of schooling that, like the
synthetic method, *restarts* the processes of learning as if the child, or the
worker, were a "Big Baby." It rejects a formalization of experience that excludes the world outside the school and that assumes there are no political
uses of memory other than loyalization or cram.

Without a role for art and culture that is at once independent of the state
but also not transcendent over or separate from civil society, literature loses
its ability to carve out an extra-institutional influence, and thus its potentially democratizing agency. Dickens made this position on the role of democratic education explicit in a speech delivered in September 1869 to the
Birmingham and Midland Institute, of which he had been elected president
for that year. As in his 1853 speech to the Birmingham Society of Artists
that I analyzed in Chapter 2, Dickens once again praises in minute detail the
individual accomplishments of the institute's industrial students in fields
such as chemistry, engineering, and factory production, and he also notes
the increased enrollments of working-class students over the sixteen years

of the Institute's existence, pointedly welcoming the participation of female students.[73] Dickens reiterates his vision for the nonpartisan, independent, and inclusive democratic functioning of educational institutions: "I hope and believe that [the Institute] will always be expansive and elastic; for ever seeking to devise new means of enlarging the circle of its members, . . . and never more evincing any more disposition to stand still than time does, or life does, or the seasons do. And above all this, I hope, and I feel confident from its antecedents, that it will never allow any consideration on the face of the earth to induce it to patronize or be patronized [*applause*], for I verily believe that the bestowal and receipt of patronage in such wise has been a curse on England."[74] Dickens concludes his speech by repeating in public what he stated in his letter about the effects of the 1867 Reform Act: "I will now discharge my conscience of my political creed, which is contained in two articles, and has no reference to any party or persons. My faith in the people governing, is, on the whole, infinitesimal; my faith in the People governed, is, on the whole, illimitable."[75] Because this statement caused some confusion, as the listeners could not discern the absence of the capital *P* in the first case, and its presence in the second, Dickens made sure that the proofs of his speech that were published by the institute showed the correct capitalization.[76]

I am not suggesting that this speech summed up Dickens's personal position on all the issues taken up by Gladstone's Liberal government; many in the Victorian press as a result of this speech called him "unsatisfactory as a political philosopher."[77] Instead I want to emphasize how he publicly linked his support for democratic education quite specifically to his nonpartisan, popular democratic "political creed" in his capacity as an author. On January 6, 1870, just a few months before his unexpected death, Dickens returned to the Institute to fulfill his role as president by personally handing out prizes and certificates to all the students. Joking about the perceived gaffe during his previous visit involving his "confession of political faith [*applause*], or perhaps I should better say, want of faith. [*Laughter.*]," Dickens once again clarified his intended capitalization and restated his view, by quoting historian H. T. Buckle, that the legislators should always be the "mere servants of the people, to whose wishes they are bound to give a public and legal sanction."[78] Dickens here underlines his belief in modern electoral democracy as a widely participatory form of government.

As I show in the rest of the chapter, *Our Mutual Friend* provides an alternative to cram. Through its implicit arguments with the mid-Victorian state's usurpation of an exclusive pedagogical role, *Our Mutual Friend* also frames a critique of the associationist tradition to the extent that it relies on a model of mind as infinitely adaptable or revisable. In place of the reproductive function of the school, *Our Mutual Friend* also presents a series of inventive and socially inclusive uses of both knowledge and memory. By investigating them, we can also discover a link between the Bradley-Eugene-Lizzie plot and the Boffins–John Harmon–Bella plot, as well as make sense of Mortimer's return to "Society" at the end of the novel.

Learning by Heart

> We are disposed to think that those must be naturally slow and stupid, who do not perceive the resemblances between objects which strike us, we say, at the first glance. But what we call the first glance is frequently the fiftieth: we have got the things completely by heart; all the parts are known to us, and we are at leisure to compare and judge.
>
> Richard and Maria Edgeworth, *Practical Education* (1798)

While their education of cram has induced Bradley and Charley to renounce their experience outside the school, Lizzie Hexam, like Amy Dorrit, clings to her old associations as the framework of her identity. The novel emphasizes her imaginative and autobiographical uses of memory through her habit of fire gazing into the "the hollow down by the flare" and recalling "pictures" of their childhood for Charley (28–29). Lizzie reminds Charley, through a string of associated terms, that she has a moral purpose in retaining their past ties: "Any compensation—restitution—never mind the word—you know my meaning. Father's grave" (227). But Charley (like the Dorrit family in relation to Amy) only feels frustration with Lizzie's continuation of their past life: "Why can't you let bygones be bygones? Why can't you . . . leave well alone? . . . What we have got to do is turn our faces full in our new direction, and keep straight on" (227–28), meaning they should "leave behind" (712) old affections. When Charley "drops" Bradley after he suspects him of Eugene's attempted murder, he does so "as if there was no softening old time behind him . . . in his hollow empty heart" (712). Lacking the Veneerings' nouveau-riche capacity to appear always "brannew," Charley must aggressively and blatantly pursue the scholastic ethic of emulation—he seeks to attain a "perfect respectability" merely for the sake of "self" and by himself (712).

Lizzie, in contrast, wishes to "make some amends" for her father's "business-like usage" of stealing from the dead, which she considers a crime, although Gaffer himself attempts to distinguish between his "living" and theft by denying that the dead have any claim to or use for money (4–5). Eugene not only reads her guilty knowledge on the first night of their meeting by the river over the anonymous corpse of a drowned man thought to be John Harmon but takes advantage of his penetration to convince her to accept his help in arranging for reading lessons: "True pride wouldn't have schoolmasters brought here, like doctors, to look at a bad case. True pride would go to work and do it. . . . Your false pride does wrong to yourself and wrong to your father" (236). The narrator, in describing Lizzie's efforts to resist Bradley's attempts to coerce and shame her into marrying him, defines this pride as independence: "With much of the dignity of courage, as she recalled her self-reliant life and her right to be free from accountability to this man, she released her arm from [the schoolmaster's] grasp and stood looking full at him" (398). *Our Mutual Friend* thus invests Lizzie with its positive messages about learning by heart as an alternative to cram, presenting her moral excellence as deriving from her life experiences as well as from the way her memories fuel her imagination, affections, and self-reliance. Of course, it is also Lizzie's retention of her physical strength and waterside character that enables her to row "down the stream as never other woman rowed on English water" and rescue Eugene from murder and drowning (700).

Lizzie Hexam is not the only character in the novel who sees "pictures" from the past. The Boffins make a duty of preserving the traces of the Harmon household; after they inherit and rename Harmon's dust mounds, they plan to "keep [the Bower] as it stands" and make it into a memorial to "our old master, our old master's children, and our old service" (185). While they are somewhat naively proud of their conscientious duty to an unworthy master, they also show a healthy willingness to "act up to" (99) their new fortune and spend their time "daily cruising about, to look at shops" (811)—forays into conspicuous consumption that the narrator refuses to condemn in people who have been deprived of luxuries and enjoyments. The Boffins resist the seemingly indiscriminate and universal processes of dissolution of value, so that, as Mortimer puts it, "everything wears to rags." Mr. Boffin refutes him, insisting, "I won't go so far as to say everything . . . because there's some things that I never found among the dust" (91).

Mrs. Boffin even more than her husband keeps past attachments alive, particularly her recollections of the miser Old Harmon's two children: "'I've only to shut my eyes . . .' said Mrs. Boffin, speaking with her eyes closed, and her left hand thoughtfully touching her brow, 'then, there they are! The old man's face, and it gets younger. The two children's faces, and

they get older. A face that I don't know. And then all the faces!'" (191–92).
Mrs. Boffin also makes the hand-to-forehead gesture, which for her signifies
the tenuous act of remembrance. Although she does not fully understand
why, the faces of the unhappy Harmon family appear, age, and persist in her
mind. In fact, Mrs. Boffin's retentive memory and kind heart function to
tie two major strands of the narrative together. Only at the end of the novel
does the reader learn that halfway through its action, Mrs. Boffin actually
saved John Harmon from a second "drowning"—the renunciation of his
true name and identity that he contemplates in book 2, chapter 13—that
would have meant his permanent disappearance, and the derailment of the
plot. When John Harmon and the Boffins reveal their concealment of
John's identity to Bella at the end of the novel, Mrs. Boffin discloses that a
fateful recognition scene took place the night after Bella refused John
Rokesmith's initial marriage proposal:

> I tapped at his door, and he didn't hear me. I looked in, and saw him a-
> sitting lonely by his fire, brooding over it. He chanced to look up with a
> pleased kind of smile in my company when he saw me, and then in a single
> moment every grain of the gunpowder, that had been lying sprinkled thick
> about him ever since I first set eyes upon him as a man at the Bower, took
> fire! Too many a time had I seen him sitting lonely, when he was a poor
> child, to be pitied, heart and hand! Too many a time had I seen him in need
> of being brightened up with a comforting word! Too many and too many a
> time to be mistaken, when that glimpse of him come at last! No! no! I just
> makes out to cry, "I know you now! You're John!" And he catches me as I
> drops. (770)

Mrs. Boffin's rendition of this classic recognition scene blended with melodrama also counterbalances in specific terms the negative aspects of memorization associated with the novel's focus on rote learning. [79] Her repetitive
descriptions of her sympathetic encounters with the lonely boy convey how
his features were imprinted in her memory over time. Mrs. Boffin exhibits
a form of knowledge that cannot become mere "mental stowage" because
it is personal and unique: the recognition of a well-known face. In his
working notes for the fifth number, Dickens sketched out this recognition
scene, writing, "Her memory awakened without her knowing how.—By
Rokesmith's face," next to the phrase "Mrs Boffin and the faces." [80]

Once again a "resurrectionist" plot element can be understood as involving memory as a means of reviving past connections metaphorically associated with death. The possibility of such a recognition marks Dickensian

fiction's consistent moral message in relation to learning by heart, for unlike the novel's social climbing characters, the Boffins are mindful of their friends, and "forgetful" of themselves (777). They stand against the mercenary didactic logic of the children's stories, embodied in the story of "Little Margery" that Charley read in his Ragged School, which encourage charitable actions for the sake of pious self-justification (214). This recognition also represents an alternative form of knowledge that links the Harmon plot to the preoccupation with rote learning and profiting from concealed knowledge of others represented most strongly in the Bradley-Eugene-Lizzie and the Lammles-Fledgeby-"Society" plots, as well as in the figure of the mercenary literary man, Wegg.

The sentimental domestic resolution of the Harmon plot, however, creates an interpretive difficulty in relation to the novel's positive representations of recognition as the revival of memory's powers of connection. The birth of John and Bella's baby before the end of the novel, a rare event in Dickens's works, seems to hold out the promise of further renewal through biological reproduction, thus counterbalancing the mechanical cram that has threatened to cancel the past only to create a simulated present. But the novel's treatment of the general social preoccupation with position and money, especially through Mr. Boffin's playing the part of a "hard-hearted" miser (775) in order to convert Bella, also stages a "pious fraud" (771), a kind of misdirection on the level of the plot that cannot fully explain away the enjoyment of their superior power and knowledge by the authors of Bella's reform. Mr. Boffin's adoption of the "Miser's school" (586) to "correct and amend" (776) Bella thus fails to insert the wedge to derail the larger social inculcation of selfish motives and market values because it proceeds without Bella's knowledge. The deception produces her domestic happiness, but it undercuts her conscious agency and therefore cannot be generalized as an alternative to Podsnap's and Bradley's versions of rote learning in order to affect society as a whole.

In a similar fashion, Eugene and Lizzie's unconventional marriage relegates them to the private sphere, providing only a partial solution to the larger problem of class antagonism and social exclusion that the schoolmaster's plot details. It suggests Eugene's image of an isolated "lighthouse" existence consisting of "a defined and limited monotony" that is more "endurable" than "the unlimited monotony of one's fellow-creatures" in "Society" (145). Should the reader believe Eugene's acceptance of the word "wife" as the proper name for his recognition of his relation to Lizzie (741–42), or the self-serving implications of his claim early in the novel that he cannot reform his ways as "a bad idle dog" because "there's nobody who makes it worth my while" (235)? Eugene's deathbed conversion to making some sort of decision about his life neither demonstrates nor refutes the possibility that he has finally found reform "worth [his] while"; in fact, Eugene confesses to Lizzie his fear that he will "disappoint your good opinion and my own—and that I ought to die, my dear!" (754). The novel does not point, then, like Mr. Boffin's "dearest and kindest finger-post" (775), to these marriages themselves as the means to resolve the questions it has raised about the mental mechanisms of socialization but rather redirects attention to the reactions they provoke in witnesses, and potentially in readers.

Culture as Invention

In a world where all things are reworked and resold, and only human beings are allowed to go to waste, loving memories like Lizzie's and Mrs. Boffin's seem to have the power to resist profit motives and the rote habit of "words without thoughts," and thus to sustain identities through the associative connections that function as "the cement of the universe" in the Humean causal sense. But their recollections cannot do the countervailing work of invention that is required to reform social relations by linking private dreams and attachments to the public sphere, where such "learning by heart" may have some effect on the standardization of thinking implied in socialized "rote learning." This countervailing work is instead figured through another instance of the remediation of the pleasures of memory that I have been tracing throughout this study.

In censuring the Revised Code's attempt to apply market logic to popular education, Kay-Shuttleworth argues that learning cannot be viewed as a "natural want," "otherwise an ignorant man's appetite for knowledge, a savage man's desire for civilization, a heathen's thirst for revealed truth, ought to be in proportion to their destitution; whereas mental, moral, and religious destitution have no appetite—they have no desire—they make no demand." Instead, he asserts, "The desire for knowledge has been implanted in the population by founding schools."[81] In contrast to this top-down liberal view of culture, in *Our Mutual Friend*, none of the "artists," or practitioners of invention, are from the cultured classes. Instead, one is a "Preserver of Animals and Birds and Articulator of Human Bones" and the other is a crippled girl who has devised a career as a "doll's dressmaker." The narrative also attributes to these lower-class inventors, Venus and Jenny

Wren, the entrepreneurial "energy" that Eugene and Mortimer lack because they don't need to work to survive. Like Lizzie, Venus bases his sense of "right" on his "pride" in "his calling" and desire to "live by" it, so that he breaks his temporary alliance with "Weggery" and informs Mr. Boffin about Old Harmon's hidden will that Wegg has discovered (578). Blending science and art, Venus has studied and practiced until he is "perfect" in his knowledge of anatomy (83), so that he can both remain faithful to nature in articulating skeletons and, when required, as in the case of ribs "because every man has his own ribs, and no other man's will go with them," be "miscellaneous" and original in his reconstructions (79–80). In other words, he is able to satisfy the aesthetic requirements of verisimilitude while working experimentally with particular specimens in order to render "a perfect Beauty" (80).

Unlike Victorian schooling, such transformative cultural work also disrupts "rote learning" through its inventive reconstitution of the past through the arts of memory. Venus's work also links up thematically to the associative memory's function in Dickens's novels of "resurrecting" the dead to cater to his customers' pleasures of memory. The "hydrocephalic babies" (583) in jars and other anatomical specimens in Venus's shop provide instructive pleasures by enlightening the curious as to the internal architecture of the human form, while the deceased pets preserved taxidermically become keepsakes and decorations (81). Not only do Venus's "articulations," then, evoke the novelist's originality in his use of language, but his fashioning of man-made constructions based on nature resembles the mimetic capacity of Dickens's fiction, celebrated by Victorian critics, to represent an alternative "fictitious" world that nevertheless creates an effect of reality.

Like Venus, Jenny Wren, as many critics have recognized, is also a figure for the novelist.[82] But because of her illiteracy, she provides an almost ethnographic account of human invention and the making of art as universal activities of human culture. Jenny's doll's dressmaking exemplifies Dickens's novelistic epistemology because it both relies on the innovative use of memory and acts as social criticism. In an overtly instructive exchange with Riah, the elderly Jewish servant of the hypocritical moneylender Fascination Fledgeby, Jenny explains that while attending her father's funeral, she conceived a new idea for a doll:

> "Cinderella, dear child," the old man expostulated, "will you never rest?"
>
> "Oh! It's not work, cutting out a pattern isn't," said Miss Jenny with her busy little scissors already snipping at some paper. "The truth is, godmother, I want to fix it while I have it correct in my mind."

"Have you seen it to-day, then?" asked Riah.

"Yes, godmother. Saw it just now. It's a surplice, that's what it is. Thing our clergymen wear, you know," explained Miss Jenny, in consideration of his professing another faith.

"And what have you to do with that, Jenny?"

"Why, godmother," replied the dressmaker, "you must know that we Professors, who live upon our taste and invention, are obliged to keep our eyes always open. And you know already that I have many extra expenses to meet just now. So it came into my head while I was weeping at my poor boy's grave, that something in my way might be done with a clergyman." (734)

This exchange teaches the reader just how Jenny Wren can lay claim to the title of "Professor" of "taste and invention." She relies on her recollection of things observed, but her "cutting out" of shapes functions to "fix" the mental image in a *new* form so that, unlike the practice of syllabic reading, she does synthesize a new conception. This whole procedure has an associationist and rhetorical resonance, since Jenny's imaginative uses of memory draw on remembered images and scenes to spur a new combination of conventional topoi or commonplaces.

Jenny's art also converts private experience—her mourning at her alcoholic father's grave—into a more typical "pattern." She creates both a figure (the clergyman) and a happy ending (marriage) out of her loss and Cinderella-like, lonely and persecuted past. She knows that she can most easily turn a profit by turning a "melancholy" scene into a happy one—another version of Samuel Rogers's pleasures of memory that transform even sad thoughts into "mild and generous" ones.[83] There is a kind of euphemism here, but it is self-conscious rather than sentimental. "Taste" in Jenny's own popular culture definition requires understanding one's audience, as the writer and publisher of serial fiction must do, while "invention" consists of recasting a personal experience as something public and familiar. Her "expert ways" (734) entitle Jenny to "profess" her craft, not only because she is consummately skilled and diligent in her work, but also because the novel wishes to invest such original and practical knowledge as hers with a cultural authority equivalent to the professional's. Significant to her awareness of audience is her tolerant consideration of the beliefs of others, including those like Riah, who "profess another faith." Jenny's art and her claims to a kind of expertise exhibit democratic and commercial inclusiveness.

Jenny's inventive proficiency and creativity allow the novel to suggest both that educated citizens and the institutions of the state have no monopoly on culture, and that the sphere and effects of art are coextensive with society, as implied by Dickens's democratic cultural politics. As an alternative to social reproduction as cram, inventive cultural production has a potentially generalizing and formative influence if it can gain access to an audience, such as the readers of serial popular fiction. This influence, like that of new media that recast traditional elements into a new form, is based upon the creative recycling of social figures that have been reinterpreted with critical insight and reinvested with individual meaning by both artists and readers.[84] In this way, Jenny's doll's dressmaking is also a figure for serial novel reading as a creative recontextualization in the reader's own everyday preoccupations of Dickens's fictions in parts.

Jenny's satirical humor also demonstrates popular Victorian art's critical edge. Riding on the omnibus on her way home from punishing the money-lender Fascination Fledgeby with a pepper plaster, she practices the kind of trenchant observation that feeds her creative process by "pressing on the road all the gaily-dressed ladies whom she could see from the window, and making them unconsciously layfigures for dolls, while she mentally cut them out and basted them" (724). Seen in psychological terms, she might seem punitive, the daughter of abusive alcoholic parents. Seen in political and historical terms, or in the generic terms of stage melodrama, however, she is a carnivalesque or revolutionary figure, ready to execute popular justice through painful physical punishment and the public disgrace of hypocrites. Unlike Jo's illiterate relation to the world as "scraps" of inassimilable experience, Jenny's *culturally literate but unlettered* mental "cutting out" disassembles social symbols and reconstitutes them in scraps of fabric. She also makes the "gaily-dressed ladies," whom she herself will never resemble, into "unconscious" participants in her art. Jenny is just as resentful and in many ways as violent as Bradley, but her mimetic work of invention enables her, for the most part, to carry out her revenge in imagination.[85] If Jenny is a figure for the novelist, then she also expresses the cutting edge of the "generous anger" that George Orwell, for one, would impute to Dickens as a form of political expression.[86] Despite her marginalization, Jenny's dolls come to circulate freely in a hierarchical society that would happily exclude the impoverished cripple if it even knew of her existence.

Jenny is also self-taught: "Never was taught a stich, young man!" she insists to Sloppy at the end of the novel. "Just gobbled and gobbled, till I found out how to do it" (809). *Our Mutual Friend* inverts a liberal theory of knowledge diffusion from the cultural elites down to the masses; the Boffins, Lizzie, Betty Higden, Sloppy, and Jenny Wren represent a resurgence of moral influence, originality, and productive economic activity—learning by heart from the "bottom" up.[87] Since Venus and Jenny have independently fabricated "business-like" professions by opening up their own niches in a vastly varied and extensive market for recycled goods, in representing their work as both entrepreneurial and lower class, Dickens's novel moves toward an expansive notion of what counts as both productive labor and cultural participation. Jenny's and Venus's entrepreneurship indicates that they are more mainstream than their idiosyncratic trades and personalities might indicate at first glance. *Our Mutual Friend* shows that economic innovation occurs among the poor in ways unauthorized by banks and factories.

If Jenny and Venus represent ways of thinking that question stereotypes about the lack of culture among the poor or uneducated but still depend on shared forms of evaluation such as taste and profitability, they are nevertheless isolated from high "Society," and this sphere must not remain untouched by the synthetic, productive, and recuperative activities of memory that they represent. This is why at the end of the novel Mortimer Lightwood returns to the Veneerings' dinner table to hear the "Voice of Society" (817) respond to Eugene's marriage to Lizzie. It is telling for my reconstruction of Dickens's cultural politics that the decision whether Eugene and Lizzie's marriage can be deemed acceptable is made by a "vote" (819) taken by the self-appointed "Committee" (817), which represents, as in Dickens's earlier anti-didacticism, both a satirical treatment and a revision of what counts as parliamentary procedure, and as political activity more generally. Before the vote, however, there is a general desire to pin down Lizzie's occupation as a "female waterman, turned factory girl" (817). Mortimer repeatedly contradicts this Miss Monflathers–like or parliamentary-bluebook-style attempt at categorization, however, causing an effect of a parodic anticatechism (817). All the diners vote to condemn the marriage as a "*mésalliance*" (818) because of Lizzie's low origins and lack of money, until Lady Tippins "perceives Twemlow with his hand to his forehead" and realizes that in their canvassing of opinions, he has been "forgotten" (819).

At the end of the novel, Twemlow finally reaches a moment of clarity; while he "has the air of being ill at ease as he takes his hand from his forehead," for once his discomfort is not cognitive—he has understood the social causes of his struggle to grasp the "unvanquishable difficulty of his existence." Twemlow removes his hand from his forehead because he has finally made up his mind both about Eugene and Lizzie's case and about his own:

> "I am disposed to think," says he, "that this is a question of the feelings of a gentleman."
>
> "A gentleman can have no feelings who contracts such a marriage," flushes Podsnap.
>
> "Pardon me, sir," says Twemlow, rather less mildly than usual, "I don't agree with you. If this gentleman's feelings of gratitude, of respect, of admiration, and affection, induced him (as I presume they did) to marry this lady—"
>
> "This lady!" echoes Podsnap.
>
> "Sir," returns Twemlow, with his wristbands bristling a little, "*you* repeat the word; *I* repeat the word. This lady. What else would you call her, if the gentleman were present?"
>
> This being something in the nature of a poser for Podsnap, he merely waves it away with a speechless wave.
>
> "I say," returns Twemlow, "if such feelings on the part of this gentleman induced this gentleman to marry this lady, I think he is the greater gentleman for the action, and makes her the greater lady. I beg to say that when I use the word gentleman, I use it in the sense in which the degree may be attained by any man. The feelings of a gentleman I hold sacred, and I confess I am not comfortable when they are made the subject of sport or general discussion." (819–20)

In silencing Podsnap, Twemlow also solves the problem of his own relationship to Veneering: it no longer matters who Veneering's oldest friend is, because Twemlow's identity cannot be summed up in that connection. Not only has he recovered from his confusion over his own "poser" about the meaning of his existence, but his final removal of his hand from his forehead also signifies that he has in fact remembered his feelings as a gentleman, by his own expansive definition.

Twemlow extends the connotations of the word "gentleman," making it a title awarded on the basis of generous behavior rather than social origin. We recall that in his resistance to David Copperfield's idea that Doctor's Commons could be improved, Mr. Spenlow had recourse to "the principle of a gentleman to take things as he found them." In redefining the "feelings of a gentleman," then, Twemlow has succeeded in "inserting the wedge" into the version of Victorian cram represented by Podsnappery.[88] Twemlow's dispute with Podsnap also demonstrates more generally the pedagogic aims of Dickens's brand of popular fiction: to inspire a kind of reading in which learning that contradicts and revises both received opinions and the reader's previous education can take place, even if its effects are limited. In order to be effective, such innovation requires a grounding in a recognizable past—like Twemlow himself, a gentleman is almost an eighteenth-century figure with associations of a status rather than class-based social order.[89] Twemlow's revivifies tradition *with a difference* represented by its opposition to Podsnappery, so that it becomes newly relevant to the present and manages to avoid both nostalgia and anachronism. Analogously, the new or original in Twemlow's intervention in rote learning cannot be the "bran-new," which is always false because it pretends to have no origins, but rather must be the product of a new understanding of the "common experience of an Englishman" that Dickens pointed to in justifying his satire of the Circumlocution Office in *Little Dorrit*.[90] The political significance of Twemlow's argument therefore goes beyond his specific justification of Eugene and Lizzie and lies in the *mode* of his defense. Twemlow's conjuring of the figure of the democratic gentleman takes place as part of an exchange with Podsnap that subverts the form of rote learning or catechism: the answers are not supplied in advance, and the definition of the word under examination is open to interpretation, even as Twemlow's removal of his hand from his forehead suggests that he already knows it by heart. Mortimer too makes a deliberate choice in detecting in Twemlow the "Voice of Society" that he has been seeking and, after seeing Twemlow home, "fares to the Temple, gaily" (820).

The novel does not hand its only "rearticulation" of social values to a rather quaint, if democratic, gentleman, however; both Mrs. Boffin in her sentimental recognition scene and the self-reliant "female waterman," Lizzie Hexam, also offer further examples of revisionary learning by heart. Lizzie's version emerges in the novel's narration of her thoughts as she races to rescue a seemingly unknown person from drowning:

> Following the current with her eyes, she saw a bloody face turned up towards the moon, and drifting away.
>
> Now, merciful Heaven be thanked for that old time, and grant, O Blessed Lord, that through thy wonderful workings it may turn to good at last! To whomsoever the drifting face belongs, be it man's or woman's, help my humble hands, Lord God, to raise it from death and restore it to some one to whom it must be dear!

It was thought, fervently thought, but not for a moment did the prayer check her. She was away before it welled up in her mind, away, swift and true, yet steady above all—for without steadiness it could never be done—to the landing place under the willow-tree, where she had seen the boat lying moored among the stakes.

A sure touch of her old practiced hand, a sure step of her old practiced foot, a sure light balance of her body, and she was in the boat. A quick glance of her practiced eye showed her, even through the deep dark shadow, the sculls in a rack against the red-brick garden-wall. Another moment, and she had cast off (taking the line with her), and the boat had shot out into the moonlight, and she was rowing down the stream as never other woman rowed on English water. (699–700)

Detailing Lizzie's every "practiced" movement as "sure," "steady," and "true," this climactic scene of rescue enacts Lizzie's redemption of her father's memory. In their trajectory toward a larger, representative status, Lizzie's actions of rescue raise the same implications as Twemlow's redefinition of "gentleman." While Lizzie does not publicly defeat that symbol of bourgeois complacency, Podsnap, the narrative frames her act for the reader in terms that register a larger *national* relevance through their reference to the British navy—she rows as if she were a sailor on "English water." Lizzie's androgynous character as a "female waterman, turned factory girl" suggests a recognition of an active and independent resourcefulness in working-class femininity different from, but not inferior to, the self-sacrificing middle-class version of domestic duty represented by heroines of Dickens's earlier novels such as Florence Dombey, Esther Summerson, or Amy Dorrit.

In contrast to Bradley, Lizzie also represents the model working-class reader envisioned by Dickens's late novel: newly literate, but with her street smarts still intact. Lizzie's internal utterance of a prayer as she launches into action connects her characterization to the remodeling and remediation of conventions from religious fiction undertaken in Dickens's earlier serial novels. Lizzie's category-blurring heroism, too, is an instance of the novel's staging of invention as a generalized cultural practice common to all social classes, whether literate or illiterate. Both through her characterization and through the pattern embodied in her practical wisdom and activity, she serves as a prototype for popular literature's ability to reshape social rote learning about the limitations and exclusions associated with gender and social class in the context of a democratic cultural politics.

Reading as Performance

Lizzie's thoughts and actions during her rescue of Eugene delineate the precise bodily, affective, and cognitive combination through which the novel
also envisions serial reading as an activity of social renewal—a tacit, highly
skilled practice put to innovative uses. At stake in Lizzie's rescue is also a
consciousness of crisis that leads to a positive intervention. Contradicting
midcentury Victorian liberal common sense, the novel's representation of
the literate characters' cram versus the illiterate characters' retained ability
to "learn by heart" and act upon their experience also implies that there is
no automatic correlation between literacy and cognitive control, or between the acquisition of literacy and either personal improvement or beneficial social change. Given that the reader, like Mortimer, may heed
Twemlow as the new "Voice of Society," replacing Podsnappery, the possibility also exists that the novel itself can produce an effect more substantive
than the disturbance and ill humor evinced by the other diners after Twemlow's pronouncement. Precisely how should such a pedagogical effect
work? What kind of new synthetic knowledge should the reader take from
the novel, in opposition to rote learning? Mr. Boffin demonstrates one possible answer to these questions in his response to the domestic fiction of the
restored Harmon household after he and Mrs. Boffin have been peeking
through the door at Bella as she nurses the baby:

> "It looks as if the old man's spirit had found rest at last; don't it?" said Mrs.
> Boffin.
>   "Yes, old lady."
>   "And as if his money had turned bright again, after a long, long rust in
> the dark, and was at last beginning to sparkle in the sunlight?"
>   "Yes, old lady."
>   "And it makes a pretty and promising picter; don't it?"
>   "Yes, old lady."
>   But, aware at that instant of a fine opening for a point, Mr. Boffin
> quenched that observation in this—delivered in the grisliest growling of the
> regular brown bear. "A pretty and a hopeful picter? Mew, Quack-quack,
> Bow-wow!" And then trotted silently down-stairs, with his shoulders in the
> state of the liveliest commotion. (778)

Mr. Boffin repeats his own staging of the miser's deepest sarcasm about the
possibility of human happiness within the family—a sarcasm that itself was
a parody of baby talk—as if to insinuate that a mature person could never

really believe in the truth of such a clichéd domestic "picter." Mr. Boffin's response provides a comedic counterpart to Twemlow's more serious interventions and Lizzie's habitual moral action, as it also consists of a citation of a type familiar from didactic literature—in this case, the innocent child instead of Twemlow's gentleman or Lizzie's good Samaritan—for the purposes of distancing the reader from an oversimplified sentimental reaction. By making fun of his and Mrs. Boffin's own conventional sentimentality, Mr. Boffin gives the reader permission to enjoy the redemptive scene of mother and child. But such parody also conveys the novelistic epistemology that forms the hallmark of Dickens's cultural politics based in conceiving popular reading as a kind of relation: not defining knowledge as a commodified "mental stowage," or even as Mr. Boffin's benevolent "finger-post" omniscience, but instead as a self-critical thinking about thinking, involving an often comic questioning of the reader's own habitual responses and trains of thought.

Performative reading as depicted within the text provides another reliable, though not certain, occasion for a lesson in open-ended revision of conventional responses. Early in the novel Mr. Boffin describes the effect he believes reading out loud will have on him to Silas Wegg: " 'I want some reading—some fine bold reading, some splendid book in a gorging Lord-Mayor's show of wollumes' (probably meaning gorgeous, but misled by association of ideas); 'as'll reach right down your pint of view, and take time to go by you' " (50). Mr. Boffin imagines that reading can be purchased as a service, on the one hand, but that its effects can also change one's orientation, attitudes, and habits of perception—one's point of view. By interrupting him and correcting his diction, the narrator suggests that Mr. Boffin's attitude is naive and mistaken on this first point, since his hiring of Wegg participates in the larger flawed view of literacy as a commodity. The fact that Mr. Boffin's malapropism resembles a Lockean accidental association of ideas recalls the comic improvisation of earlier characters like the Wellers and Sairy Gamp. Furthermore, the idea of "gorging" on reading is relevant in the contexts of both educational cram and the pleasures of memory. Again contesting the notion articulated by Kay-Shuttleworth that the state must implant the desire for knowledge in the poor, Mr. Boffin implies that the illiterate, especially within a larger culture of print, actively hunger for reading and knowledge, and not simply in order to improve their social standing, but to alter and enhance their understanding of the world.

When Eugene embarks on one of his typical witty, digressive glosses of the word "reading," he extends its dimensions toward performative interpretation: "(By-the-bye, that very word, Reading, in its critical use, always charms me. An actress's Reading of a chambermaid, a dancer's Reading of a hornpipe, a singer's Reading of a song, a marine painter's Reading of the sea, the kettle-drum's Reading of an instrumental passage, are phrases ever youthful and delightful)" (542). A "reading" is not only an individual interpretation of a given repertoire or text, but it is also fundamentally conceived as improvisational and serial, producing multiple variations on an original, like Dickens's own dramatic readings of his novels. In this way, such performative reading is fundamentally public. The equally "critical" and "delightful" effect that Eugene associates with the fact that words have multiple meanings correlates with the originality of an individual interpretation, such as Jenny Wren's or Venus's forms of invention. Such "readings" as interpretive practices of everyday life are also directed toward pleasing multiple and heterogeneous audiences. Reading in Mr. Boffin's or Eugene's senses thus takes on the status of a decentralized activity of critical interpretation or lively performance undertaken at will by individuals or groups. It can just as easily be practiced on the puzzle of common people's predilection for oysters, or on the sources of a mania for financial speculation, as on a written text, a piece of music, or a work of art. The performed aspect of both Mr. Boffin's and Eugene's ideas of interpretive reading, much like the structure of the classroom or the theater, blurs the distinction between public and private spheres, and between individual thoughts or memories and collective reception.

Interpretive reading brings to light Dickens's reader's own version of Mr. Boffin's "chief literary difficulty" concerning "what to believe, in the course of his reading": "he was divided in his mind between half, all, or none; at length, when he decided, as a moderate man, to compound with half, the question still remained, which half? And that stumbling-block he never got over" (476). Are we to believe in Boffin's homely genuineness or his seeming omniscience while in his guise as a miser, in Eugene's reform or his perpetual laxity, in Twemlow's democratic extension of the status of a gentleman or Bradley's failure to become one? The highly developed narrative techniques required to render these alternatives explicit as questions of interpretation also transmit the novel's pedagogical and critical effects. If a more inventive form of learning to read and taking part in public life is to take the place of cram, it must, like the narrative, be self-reflexive enough to call into question the opposition between experience and formal knowledge imposed by rote learning, and thus to begin to undo the irony implied in learning by heart within Dickens's late novels' darkening representations of modern capitalist culture.

Our Mutual Friend, as I have read it, offers a different approach to memory as medium of popular reception in its direct attack on the commodification of memory in the Victorian school system. In revised associationist terms, it calls for reading as the practice of a *general capacity* for learning, interpretation, and the rearticulation of culturally authoritative words in ways that adapt them to individual insights and new meanings arising from changing social circumstances.[91] The anti-didactic pedagogical modes of the memory effects in Dickens's earlier novels find their limitations in the inadequacy of the school as a metaphor for society and of schooling as a framework for human experience. In exposing these limitations, *Our Mutual Friend* provides a culminating rationale within Dickens's career for conceiving popular literature as a form of cultural participation independent of the school.

This fundamental critique of school culture, however, got lost as Dickens's celebrity authorship after his death became a phenomenon of massmarket publishing, including the anthologizing of works of literature for school use. In the final chapter, I investigate the inclusion of Dickens's works in the English literature curriculum in Britain and the United States. This process of canonization produces the historical irony that Dickens's humanitarian authorial persona as defender of the poor, minus his critique of modern institutional culture, were enlisted to exemplify English literature's educational mission of citizen-building in the early decades of the twentieth century. The resistance to institutionalization, sectarianism, and party politics that I have associated with what I call the "historical Dickens's" democratic cultural politics for popular literature breaks down with the emergence of the "school Dickens," I argue, in part due to the success of Dickens's own anti-didactic narrative strategies in his early works. I conclude the book in the following chapter, then, by delineating the implications of this mutation of Dickens's cultural politics from an oppositional to an institutionalized form for our understanding of how reading literature came officially to be invested with a democratizing influence.

6.   *Dickens's Laughter*

School Reading and Democratic Literature, 1870–1940

> With only occasional exceptions, democracy, in the records that
> we have, was until [the nineteenth century] a strongly unfavor-
> able term, and it is only since [the period from the last third of
> the nineteenth century to the first third of the twentieth] that a
> majority of the political parties and tendencies have united in
> declaring their belief in it. This is the most striking historical fact.
> . . . It would sometimes be easier to believe in democracy, or to
> stand for it, if the [nineteenth-century] change had not hap-
> pened and it were still an unfavorable or factional term. But that
> history has occurred, and the range of contemporary sense is its
> confused and still active record.
>
> Raymond Williams, *Keywords*

Through his lifetime, Dickens's celebrity authorship projected an image of
popular democratic literature as a means for readers to generate and share
lasting social and aesthetic values that could cut across other social divisions.
By featuring characters whose prodigious flights of verbal invention (Sam
Weller or Sairy Gamp) or creative entrepreneurship (Venus and Jenny
Wren) represent the author's own powers of invention, Dickens's serials
figure the reading of fiction as a generative reshaping of experience involving a legitimate popular taste as well as individual powers of selection and
retention in the memory. By aligning reading and authorship with the everyday work of the poor, popular serial fiction redefines literacy and education as practices of cultural production from the ground up, rather than as
vehicles of an undiscriminating mass consumption that needs to be directed
by the influence of liberal publications and state schools. Conceived in this
way, public art such as Dickens's novels could directly sponsor the social
inclusion of the poor.

Many of the qualities that early readers and critics seem to have found most engaging and original in Dickens's novels through the 1840s and 1850s, however, would cease to appeal to certain Victorian intellectuals in the decade just before and after his death in 1870—for these critics, the popular appeal of Dickens's novels and characters indicates their deficiency of intellectual and aesthetic values. I begin this chapter by analyzing how George Eliot and G. H. Lewes attempted to discredit both Dickens's artistic competence and his modes of appeal to readers by criticizing both the associationism underlying the celebrated "reality" of Dickens's characters and scenes and his attribution of virtue and sophistication to the poor. By derailing the Dickensian cultural association of popular serial fiction with the egalitarian pleasures of memory, Eliot and Lewes also articulate new scientifically based formal protocols for realism that could give literature an authoritative standing among emergent disciplines such as psychology and cultural history and distinguish between high and low cultural modes of reception. Eliot's and Lewes's objections to Dickens's influence on readers indicate how closely Dickens's literary reputation was linked to what I have been characterizing as the democratic cultural politics associated with his version of celebrity authorship. They advocate indirectly for individualized silent reading and marginalize the popular Victorian forms of reception associated with serial fiction, thus helping to launch the modernist critique of mass culture.

In the middle section of the chapter, I trace the inclusion of Dickens's works in British and American school readers and the publication of certain of his novels as stand-alone school texts, showing how, from the 1880s through the 1920s, Dickens's brand of celebrity authorship and his humanitarian posture were adapted into a canonical version of Dickens's authorship that personified the English literature curriculum's function of cultural consolidation. In this way, English as a school subject becomes "Dickensian," since Dickens's canonical image seems to personify not just the effects of reading his own novels in the literature classroom but also the effects of the English curriculum more generally within a system of public education meant to train children to practice classroom cooperation and consideration for less fortunate others as models for civic participation.

By investigating the selections from Dickens's works along with prefaces and apparatus that appear in these textbooks designed for use in public schools, I also illuminate the relationship between what I call the "historical Dickens" and the "school Dickens." The historical Dickens is a recognizably Victorian version constructed by academic scholarship, a category in which I include my own account of Dickens's cultural politics, involving his celebrity authorship and pedagogical shaping of serial fiction as a vehicle of popular democratic culture. The school Dickens is an equally historical personification of this same Dickensian democratizing project, but put to specific uses in the schools to support the uses of English literature to teach humane and inclusive social values and sophisticated aesthetic tastes. The historical Dickens thus also represents the shifting figure of the canonical author who (like the "historical Shakespeare" or the "historical Milton") emanates from scholarly or biographical efforts to contextualize literature in its historical moment, while the school Dickens takes over and transforms the Victorian reception of Dickens. Both of these versions, I argue, have contributed to forming the image of Dickens still in circulation in global popular culture today.

The political impact of the historical Dickens's project to shape serial reading into a democratic form of cultural participation in support of the goals of universal education becomes especially challenging to define in light of Raymond Williams's diagnosis of the ambiguous consensus about democracy as a political value that emerged in the course of the nineteenth century. I argue, nevertheless, that Dickens's democratic cultural politics succeeded by being incorporated into the school system, even though his particular "political creed" of nonpartisanship mutated into a generic form of civics training that also feeds into academic freedom. Because Dickens's cultural politics shaped serial reading as a means to form a mass reading audience and legitimize the popular taste, the incorporation of Dickens into the English literature curriculum suggests both the institutionalization of that legitimization and its reconfiguration into newly formalized classroom routines of reading. The story of Dickens's canonization, then, shows us how an initially extra-institutional—even at times anti-institutional—and nonpartisan version of democratic art became a vehicle for converting literacy training into a civics lesson through its dominant trope of prosopopoeia, or personification.

Ironically, then, in light of Dickens's ultimate critique in *Our Mutual Friend* (1864–65) of the "cram" involved in mid-Victorian schooling for the lower classes, the late-nineteenth-century literary histories and textbooks that formulate the school Dickens seize upon the anti-didactic secularizing strategies developed in Dickens's earlier novels to create new standard models for classroom reading. During the early period of consolidation of English literature in the United States public schools that I consider here, the school Dickens thus seems to overtake the historical Dickens in reshaping reading as an institutionalized form of training for democratic participation. In this transition from Dickens as a Victorian public intellectual to Dickens as a canonical author, the school Dickens continues to personify the pleasures of memory, but this time his image conveys a form of epitaphic reading that puts students in touch with the canonical author's civilizing influence through classroom reading.

In the chapter's conclusion, I trace how the associationist pleasures of memory become part of a division by which academic criticism distinguishes a sophisticated response to literature from a popular or middlebrow one. Eliot and Lewes do not have the last word in arguing for the cognitive seriousness that should restrain the "hallucinatory" pleasures of reading Dickens's popular serial fiction. Writing during the early to middle decades of the twentieth century, Henry James, George Gissing, and F. R. Leavis still refer to their associations with childhood reading of Dickens's novels, describing these recollections as intrinsic to their vocations as writers and critics, while setting such memories apart from serious critical engagement. The modern writer or critic's unwillingness to demystify his or her own associations with Dickens's novels does not indicate simply that the pleasures of memory have been intellectually discredited, as in Eliot's and Lewes's critiques. Rather, I argue that the *preservation* of such associations with childhood reading precisely as responses untouchable by criticism facilitates the distinction between reading for pleasure and reading critically that would define the disciplinary identity of literary studies, differentiating its academic forms of reading from the participatory, democratic ethos of popular reception. In contrast to this group of critics for whom a reconsideration of Dickens provides an occasion to redefine literary values, G. K. Chesterton and George Orwell find new uses for the image of Dickens as a nonpartisan advocate of popular democracy. They offer an image of Dickens's laughter to represent democracy's capacity for autocritique, in this way reconstituting Dickens's cultural politics as an alternative to the school Dickens's linkage of modern citizenship with cultural nationalism.

Both the school Dickens and the historical Dickens as equally powerful reconstructions point to Dickens's popularity as a historical phenomenon of reading and publishing history that resists a definitive political diagnosis or institutionalization in the curriculum. Typically existing outside the curriculum, modern serial media constitute the cultural afterlife of nineteenth-century styles of popular reading that the literature syllabus could not assimilate. If the English literature curriculum is Dickensian in its announced function as a repertoire of humane associations, the new serial genres, in their constant renewal of changing forms of association and relation, extend and remobilize Dickens's inclusive and exuberant vision of modern mass culture.

Dickens as Mass Hallucination

> The number of those who read novels has become millions in England during the last twenty-five years. In our factories, behind our counters, in third-class railway carriages, in our kitchens and stables, novels are now read unceasingly. . . . There has grown up a custom of late, especially among tea dealers, to give away a certain number of books among their poorer customers. When so much tea has been consumed, then shall be a book given. It came to my ears the other day that eighteen thousand volumes of Dickens's works had just been ordered for this purpose. The bookseller suggested that a little novelty might be expedient. Would the benevolent tea-dealer like to vary his presents? But no! The tradesman, knowing his business and being anxious above all things to attract, declared that Dickens was what he wanted. He had found that the tea-consuming world preferred their Dickens.
>
> Anthony Trollope (1879)

As we saw at the end of Chapter 1, versions of memory's associative functioning persisted in nineteenth-century psychology as a commonsense framework for explaining the evolution of instinct and the neural connectivity underlying thought in a brain-based theory of mind. However, the moralization of memory characteristic of Dickens's serial fiction became more strictly associated with popular reading, while scientific psychology was increasingly recognized in the course of the nineteenth century as a specialized area of scientific study distinct from moral philosophy, education, and aesthetics. As Rick Rylance explains in his history of Victorian psychology, 1850–1880 was a period of consolidation and professionalization during which a physiologically and biologically oriented psychology gradually developed. This emerging scientific psychology was an "open discourse, . . . crossing wide disciplinary interests," and engaging "economists, imaginative writers, philosophers, clerics, literary critics, policy-makers, as well as biomedical scientists," among them George Eliot and George Henry Lewes.[1] Both famous in their own right as psychologists, Eliot and Lewes criticize Dickens's fictional techniques on psychological grounds, evincing a concerted effort to displace the authority of his brand of popular fiction and celebrity authorship.

Eliot took the opportunity of addressing Dickens's novelistic psychology in "The Natural History of German Life," a review of two works by the German cultural historian Wilhelm Heinrich von Riehl that came out in the *Westminster Review* of July 1856, during the initial run of *Little Dorrit* in monthly parts from December 1855 through June 1857. Eliot begins her review by gesturing toward an associationist framework: "It is an interesting branch of psychological observation to note the images that are habitually associated with abstract or collective terms—what may be called the picture-writing of the mind, which it carries on concurrently with the more subtle symbolism of language. Perhaps the fixity or variety of these associated images would furnish a tolerably fair test of the amount of concrete knowledge and experience which a given word represents, in the minds of two persons who use it with equal familiarity."[2] Eliot seems to take up the Hobbesian problem of "words without thoughts," and Hartley's ambition to coordinate trains of thought in crowds, by proposing an experimental means to verify psychologically that different speakers are thinking of the same image when using the same word. As it develops, however, her analysis pursues the issue of the epistemological grounds of language more obliquely, in order to focus on the question of what counts as an adequate method for relating human psychology to the "natural history" of a nation, a project with affinities to the emerging modern disciplines of cultural history, anthropology, and ethnography.[3]

To elucidate this new model of research, Eliot seems to concretize the metaphor of "trains of thought," constructing a hypothetical common traveler who vaguely associates trains with images of a "Bradshaw" or of "the station house with which he is most familiar, or of an indefinite length of tram-road." She contrasts this train passenger's ad hoc experience with the layered forms of knowledge possessed by a man who has had "successively the experience of a 'navvy,' an engineer, a traveller, a railway director and shareholder, and a landed proprietor in treaty with a railway company," whose mental images "would include all the essential facts in the existence and relations of the *thing*" (107). Like the common traveler, Eliot argues, most persons who speak of "'the people,' 'the masses,' 'the proletariat,' or 'the peasantry'" have very few concrete images associated with these terms because their experience, like the traveler's, is simply that incidental kind, lacking in both detail and organization. Yet despite a lack of concrete knowledge of the masses, the majority of liberal Victorian reformers and politicians do not hesitate "to theorize on those bodies with eloquence," or "to legislate for them without eloquence" (108). Her initial analogy, how-ever, reveals that she does not recommend consulting the peasants or work-ers themselves for corrective accounts of "the complex facts summed up in the collective term" (108), nor does she advocate investigative journalism in the style of Dickens and his collaborators on *Household Words*, or of Henry Mayhew. Instead Eliot observes that "the landholder, the clergyman, the mill-owner, the mining-agent have each an opportunity for making pre-cious observations on different sections of the working classes, but unfortu-nately their experience is too often not registered at all, or its results are too scattered to be available as a source of information and stimulus to the public mind generally" (112).[4] What is needed, she argues, is a detailed study en-compassing a "natural history of our social classes" based on careful "obser-vations" by "a man of sufficient moral and intellectual breadth, whose observations would not be vitiated by a foregone conclusion, or by a profes-sional point of view" (112). That this expertise is not fully professionalized, which for Eliot would detract from its breadth and disinterestedness, seems to point to the comprehensive perspective of the novelist.

Eliot emphasizes the contrast between the managerial oversight exercised by the various candidates she proposes for the role of natural historian, and the abstract and ideologically preconceived views of the partisan legislative reformer. This displacement of the politician also alerts us to Eliot's formula-tion of a new cultural politics for literature based on both a positive view of managerial expertise and the development of a rigorous realist method. Such a method produces objective knowledge in direct opposition to the "common experience of an Englishman," for example, to which Dickens referred in his defense of his satire on the Circumlocution Office in *Little Dorrit*.[5] Eliot's new model of expert knowledge requires a detached liberal perspective provided either by the objective social scientist or by the novel-ist as sympathetic observer.[6] Criticizing the idealization of "jocund" peas-ants (109) purveyed by certain artists and novelists who sentimentalize the poor and agricultural laborers "under the influence of traditions and prepos-sessions rather than of direct observation" (108), she provides a strong de-fense of scientific empiricism joined to her famous statement of her own realist aesthetic: "Art is the nearest thing to life; it is a mode of amplifying experience and extending our contact with our fellow-men beyond the bounds of our personal lot" (110). In order to realize this more expansive kind of experience for the reader, Eliot asserts, novelists and other social investigators must demystify idealized pastoral images of the poor: "The thing for mankind to know is, not what are the motives and influences which the moralist thinks *ought* to act on the labourer or the artisan, but what are the motives and influences which *do* act on him. We want to be taught to feel, not for the heroic artisan or the sentimental peasant, but for the peasant in all his coarse apathy, and the artisan in all his suspicious selfishness" (111). Eliot's elegant chiasmus reinforces the impact of her own pedagogical assertion that readers must be "taught to feel" more objectively about the poor; they must not be afraid to diagnose "the people" as morally flawed or intellectually limited in order to be able to sympathize with them as they "truly" are.

Referring to Dickens, without naming him, as "one great novelist who is gifted with the utmost power of rendering the external traits of our town population," Eliot regrets his failure to render their "psychological character—their conceptions of life, and their emotions—with the same truth as their idiom and manners" (111). Eliot's objections to the "unreality" of Dickens's plebian characters are couched in a rhetoric of high and low art, repeatedly assigning to Dickens the ability "to reproduce external traits" or the "humorous and external," as in the genre of popular melodrama, but not the more complex responses to the deeply "emotional and tragic" (111). Eliot finally pinpoints her reservations about Dickens's art as related to his "frequently false psychology . . . in encouraging the miserable fallacy that high morality and refined sentiment can grow out of harsh social relations, ignorance, and want; or that the working classes are in a condition to enter at once into a millennial state of *altruism*, wherein everyone is caring for everyone else, and no one for himself" (111). Eliot's criticisms of Dickens in this context, then, afford perhaps one of the most telling pieces of evidence that his celebrity authorship had come to be identified by the 1850s with his championing of social reform efforts geared toward improving living conditions and education for workers and the poor, regardless of his support for working-class political goals.

Dickens also personifies the generic conventions associated with popular stage melodrama, religious fiction, and both Radical and Evangelical didactic literature that Eliot attempts to relegate to the status of anachronisms. In this way, she also discredits their various accompanying versions of cultural politics that had, up to the midcentury, articulated concrete and instrumental connections among sentiments, knowledge, popular reading of serial publications, and political action and that were associated explicitly with writings about the poor and working classes and sometimes authored by working-class writers. In place of these popular genres that tended either to pursue political aims directly through literature, or to shape popular literacy as another means toward greater democratic participation, as I have been arguing was the thrust of Dickens's cultural politics, Eliot offers to bridge novelistic realism and social scientific expertise. She proposes that *clarifying the divisions of knowledge* will permit the eventual transcendence of social divisions within the natural unfolding of national history, understood as the growth of national self-consciousness. Eliot thus seeks to displace Dickens's unsystematic approach with a more discriminating authorial perspective and narrative art that, instead of attributing the same "motives and influences" to the laborer and artisan as to any other human being, would differentiate the psychological motives of the various social classes based on a more comprehensive range of expert knowledge of their actual conditions.

In falsifying the "psychological character" of Dickens's representations, Eliot supplies a subtly altered pedagogical role for fiction that correlates art's enlargement of the reader's sympathy and "amplification" of the reader's experience with a psychological expertise resting on the notion of subjective interiority as separable from one's social identity. According to this logic, Little Dorrit becomes a "false" character because she is psychologically impossible within the conditions in which she has grown up. *Little Dorrit*'s depiction of the laboring classes of Bleeding Heart Yard as caught up in the larger ideological mystifications of the Merdle swindle and the Circumlocution Office—the same traps that imprison and thwart the reforming middle classes—would also be false according to Eliot's argument that the author should delineate a class-specific psychology for each social division, so that the realist novel could function as "a valuable aid to the social and political reformer" (112). This alliance of scientific psychology, social scientific investigation, and the novel also accomplishes a division of labor by which the novel works on the individual reader's sympathies while the social scientist's "Natural History" informs social policies. Both the pressure-group politics of the evangelicals and Dickens's celebrity model of the reading audience as a popular constituency are to give way to Eliot's insertion of the expert as a necessary intermediary between political institutions and the public.

Returning at the end of the essay to her initial interest in understanding the relation between language and nonlinguistic thought, Eliot modifies that connection as well. She views social change as both evolutionary and historical, as she explains through an analogy between "the historical conditions of society" and language: "Language must be left to grow in precision, completeness, and unity, as minds grow in clearness, comprehensiveness, and sympathy. And there is an analogous relation between the moral tendencies of men and the social conditions they have inherited. The nature of European men has its roots intertwined with the past, and can only be developed by allowing those roots to remain undisturbed while the process of development is going on, until that perfect ripeness of the seed which carries with it a life independent of the root" (128–29). In this organic metaphor drawn from nineteenth-century comparative philology, history produces a "seed" of moral and national consciousness that becomes "independent" of the past and social conditions only through a long process of development. At the culmination or "perfect ripeness" of this process, humanity will no longer need language to function as a kind of cultural memory because words will have caught up with current conceptions of human needs. Within this essay's programmatic formulation of a cross-disciplinary realist method, the direct political leverage through "reasoning on conditions" that was conceived feasible in Utilitarian reformist writing, Owenism, Chartist publications, or Dickens's early serial fiction appears as a naive or crude method at best.[7]

The logical next step in discrediting Dickens's uses of associationist psychology, novelistic pedagogy, and style of cultural politics seems to have been to attack his celebrity authorship, a task that G. H. Lewes carries out postmortem in his 1872 review of the first volume of John Forster's *Life of Dickens* (1871–73). Packaged as an attempt to explain the frequent disdain for Dickens's novels voiced by critics despite his enormous popularity, Lewes's review systematically dismantles the associationist representational strategies of Dickens's works. Lewes discredits as a kind of mass delusion the pedagogical transaction between Dickens's mind and the reader's associations that early Victorian critics had analyzed: Dickens "was a seer of visions; and his visions were of objects at once familiar and potent. Psychologists will understand both the extent and the limitation of the remark, when I say that in no other perfectly sane mind (Blake, I believe, was not perfectly sane) have I observed vividness of imagination approaching hallucination."[8] The comparison with Blake shifts Dickens's imagination into the categories of both Romantic genius and insanity. In Lewes's only thinly disguised polemic for a form of fiction based on scientific psychology, imagination and memory are no longer aspects of the Baconian philosophical mind as "beehive," conceived as inventive functions for retaining, recombining, and recreating experience.

The interplay between memory and imagination that allows the reader's memories of reading to become analogous to memories of real events in

Dickens's associationist model of reading becomes for Lewes a symptom of disorder and confusion that turns reading into the source of a generalized fantasy:

> To [Dickens] also *revived* images have the vividness of sensations; to him also *created* images have the coercive force of realities, excluding all control, all contradiction. What seems preposterous, impossible to us, seemed to him simple fact of observation. When he imagined a street, a house, a room, a figure, he saw it not in the vague schematic way of ordinary imagination, but in the sharp definition of actual perception, all the salient details obtruding themselves on his attention. He, seeing it thus vividly, made us also see it; and believing in its reality however fantastic, he communicated something of his belief to us. He presented it in such relief that we ceased to think of it as a picture. So definite and insistent was the image, that even while knowing it was false we could not help, for a moment, being affected, as it were, by his hallucination. (571)

Lewes's insistence on the "vividness" of Dickens's imagination reinforces in order to undermine the connection developed in earlier Victorian criticism between the reading of serial fiction and a popular Humean epistemology. For Hume, we recall, imagination reinforces belief in the constitutive fictions of consciousness: "The memory, senses, and understanding, are therefore, all of them founded on the imagination, or the vivacity of our ideas."[9] For Lewes, however, these "vivid" qualities of Dickens's "definite and insistent" images transgress the distinction between imagination and reality in ways that disqualify their empirical qualities and psychological resemblance to experience.

If Dickens's images and scenes are "mere" hallucinations, then readers' associations with Dickens's novels must be debunked by the modern critic as pseudo-effects that cannot attain the status of real memories: "the image [his characters presented] was so suggestive that it seemed to *express* all that it was found to *recall*, and Dickens was held to have depicted what his readers supplied" (572). Here Lewes breaks the feedback loop between the author's mind and the reader's memory, reducing the associationist analogy between reading and experience into the reader's mundane, physiological "recall" of an incident of reading. By clearly differentiating memories of reading from memories of real life, Lewes here invalidates the interplay between experience and reading that, I have argued, Dickens's serials taught Victorian readers to rehearse as a kind of epitaphic personification, based in the common experiences of death and loss, through which serial reading mediates a form of shared experience. Literary theorist Paul de Man clarifies that "prosopo-poeia is hallucinatory," since, as "the visual shape of something that has no sensory existence," it enacts the impossibility of distinguishing between hal-lucination and perception.[10] This effect of personification produced by Dickens's writing, then, for Lewes must be shown to be *merely* figurative.

Lewes also diagnoses a credulous Victorian readership's unwillingness to accept that Dickens's characters were "merely masks" as a sign of their lack of sophistication: "Unreal and impossible as these types were, speaking a language never heard in life, moving like pieces of simple mechanism always in one way (instead of moving with the infinite fluctuations of organisms, incalculable yet intelligible, surprising yet familiar), these unreal figures af-fected the uncritical reader with the force of reality; and they did so in virtue of their embodiment of some real characteristic vividly presented" (572). Drawing on an evolutionary psychology to heighten the contrast between Dickens's characters and real biological organisms, Lewes forcefully miscon-strues Dickens's associationist rhetoric by implying that Dickens's personi-fications fail because they are inaccurate. His "uncritical" readers, by believing in Dickens's characters as truthful representations of human na-ture, were therefore tricked into accepting "masks" in place of realistic people. After calling him "perfectly sane," Lewes portrays Dickens as sur-prisingly delusional. One era's psychology becomes a later era's psychopa-thology.[11] For Lewes, then, Dickens no longer can be viewed as the originator of Mrs. Gamp's originality but has instead become another ver-sion of Mrs. Gamp, and thus his characters correspond to a debunked Mrs. Harris—they are not personifications of the inventive imagination itself, but mere fakes and illusions that their author takes for real and passes off as such. Lewes undercuts the cultural persuasiveness of the Dickensian version of prosopopoeia as the trope both of reading as a form of thinking, and of the reader's relation to other readers. He, in effect, condemns the lack of proper distinction manifested by Dickens's characters, not only between fiction and reality, but, as de Man puts it, "between reference and signification on which all semiotic systems . . . depend," including later novelistic and psy-chological forms of realism.[12]

Lewes suggests even more damagingly that Dickens's art undermines the critical powers of the reader, as well as the authority of the critic to establish aesthetic value and the canons of realism in art, by infecting the reader with Dickens's own artistic confusion. Rendered obsolescent by Lewes, then, are not only the Enlightenment intellectual tradition behind Dickens's associa-tionism, whether in moral philosophy or in education, but also the Dicken-sian serial novel's claim to literary value as a phenomenon of popular reception and vehicle of cultural memory. When Lewes unmasks Mrs. Gamp as Dickens himself, his readers' attachments to him and his characters are equally unmasked, no longer seeming to involve ties of domestic friendship within the anonymity of urban life or the intimacy of private thoughts and memories. Such personal attachments, it seems, should be reserved for real people rather than for fictional characters—there is a kind of aesthetic austerity operating here. Otherwise, as in Eliot's earlier insistence on the need to see "rustics" and "mechanics" as the creatures distorted by their social conditions that they "really" are, we risk mistaking the ideal for the real when we seek to take appropriate action in the real world. Just as Dickens himself cannot control his hallucinations, and the reader cannot readily evade the vivid memories that his novels create in both the public and individual mind, Dickensian novelistic pedagogy becomes coercive and infectious rather than instructive or reformative—much as Eliot had also implied, Dickens offers readers not a parallel reality, as popular Humean associationism would have it, but a pseudo-reality that undermines their grasp of the real.

Lewes concludes his attack, in ways that have stuck in subsequent Dickens criticism, by pointing out that Dickens was never an intellectual:

> [Dickens] presents an almost unique example of a mind of singular force in which, so to speak, sensations never passed into ideas. Dickens sees and feels, but the logic of feeling seems to be the only logic he can manage. Thought is strangely absent from his works. I do not suppose a single thoughtful remark on life or character could be found throughout the twenty volumes. Not only is there a marked absence of the reflective tendency, but one sees no indication of the past life of humanity having ever occupied him; keenly as he observes the objects before him, he never connects his observations into a general expression, never seems interested in the general relations of things. (576)

The implicit, unfavorable comparison with George Eliot's fiction is apparent here. There is no "Natural History," it seems, in Dickens's works—seeking to mirror experience, they fail to elevate literature to the status of knowledge, and thus they cannot be credited with realism. In a tour de force of psychological reductionism, the associationist social epistemology conveyed in Dickens's serial novels—precisely geared, I have argued, to establish the "general relations of things" concretely in experience through the reader's everyday participation in popular serial reading—becomes inverted into Lewes's diagnosis of Dickens's intellectual defects. Lewes's criticisms of Dickens imply that the fully epistemologically adequate and mature realist novel does not simply teach us how to read and think but instead *thinks for us in its own right* by including numerous "thoughts" and "reflections" that are recognizable not as didactic lessons or rhetorical address but as full-fledged "ideas" equivalent to the analytical concepts of social science or philosophy. Lacking such formal ideas, Dickens's imagination takes the literal form of mechanical reproduction, while his novels become the medium of an emerging mass culture characterized by an absence of thought and an acceptance of the trumped-up facsimile in place of the real.

Lewes provides a relatively early version of the elite modernist critic's dismay at "uncritical" popular tastes that sets the tone for later attacks by academic literary critics on Dickens's art. In her influential 1932 study of the British reading public, for example, Q. D. Leavis echoes Lewes's view that Dickens's novels lack thought, explaining that he was aiming for a merely emotional response: "Dickens stands primarily for a set of crude emotional exercises . . . for instance, the formula 'laughter and tears' that has been the foundation of every popular success ever since (Hollywood's as well as the bestseller's). Far from requiring an intellectual stimulus, there are the tears that rise in the heart and gather to the eyes involuntarily or even in spite of the reader, though an alert critical mind may cut them off at the source in a revulsion of disgust."[13] The fact that Dickens so clearly stands in for the "lowbrow" reader and mass-market genres that are the more immediate targets of Leavis's own "revulsion" suggests that Lewes too, in his hyperbolic rendering of the hallucinating popular author and his deluded audience, was in fact formulating the stereotype that Leavis inherited, and that one can also see in Trollope's tongue-in-cheek observation in 1879 that "the tea-consuming world preferred their Dickens."

When Lewes turns the accusation of "distortions of human nature" (572) against Dickensian characters, therefore, like Eliot, he conducts a disciplinary reorientation that supplies new scientific, historical, and aesthetic grounds for relegating Dickens's associationist social epistemology and overtly didactic art to obsolescence. The Dickensian serial novel becomes an epistemologically retrograde genre within the framework that Eliot and Lewes establish for the realist novel among the modern disciplines, and thus its audience also takes on a more specific social character as "uncultivated" (i.e., the mass audience). What I wish to emphasize is the way that Eliot and Lewes set out to recharacterize a whole way of thinking about the progressive social effects of mass literacy and the reading of serial fiction by personifying an entire early Victorian social formation as Dickens and relegating it to the past. To this end, the novelistic pedagogy of memory that Dickensian fiction affords, with its now embarrassing and naive democratic rhetoric about uplifting the poor, social harmony among classes, and social (not just individual) improvement achieved through the reading of literature, should be replaced by a novelistic *psychology* with respectable, rigorous, and up-to-date disciplinary affiliations. The radical political enlightenment envisioned by Chartists and Owenites, or the repentance and conversion hoped for by Evangelicals and Methodists, or the social connection through shared memories of reading attempted in Dickensian fiction were all conceived as transformative, galvanizing forms of response that, Eliot and Lewes imply, may continue to sway the uninformed but can no longer inspire belief in sophisticated modern readers. Dickens's influence becomes both not quite secular enough and too politically radical (i.e., crudely instrumental) for the educated literary culture that Eliot and Lewes envision.

Literature scholar Nicholas Dames has charted how physiological novel theory developed from the late 1850s through the 1890s in the writings of a group of intellectuals whose work crossed several disciplinary domains, including Lewes, as well as the professional academic psychologist and pedagogical theorist Alexander Bain and critics Geraldine Jewsbury and E. S. Dallas. Dames shows that these later Victorian writers formalized the individual's practice of silent reading as the standard model for novel reading in general. Dames argues that for Lewes, "an act (silent reading) that takes us close to the constant inner workings of the mind (a wavelike consciousness) is best studied with reference to a form (the novel) that asks of us nothing but a submission to the rhythms of that wave."[14] Similarly, in Bain's theorizing, "the novel's place in modern life is cemented by its rhythmic signature of brain waves in the modern individual confronted with a ramifying set of stimuli: constant 'periodicity' between minor shocks, or 'discharges,' and moments of lassitude, or 'relaxed intermissions'" mark the initiation and suspension of silent reading. For both Lewes and Bain, "These wave theories are theories of the novel as sequence, and more particularly as a sequence that effectively mirrors the functioning of everyday solitary consciousness."[15] Dames suggests that these theories fit "the rhythm of 'discharge' and 'quiescence' necessarily built into an intrinsically interrupted form of publication" such as the serial novel.[16] When we take into account Lewes's specific criticisms of Dickens, Dames's argument that physiological understandings of reading offered "a theory of silent, individual reading's impact upon genre" also implies that the earlier associationist model of serial reading as a *participatory* activity involving shared, even noisy, forms of sociability was displaced when a brain-based theory of silent reading became dominant.[17] In this process, serial novel reading was not just *described* but also *construed* in new ways by the physiological theorists as primarily silent, cognitively wavelike, and individualized.

This shift within novel criticism into a scientific understanding of reading as an individualized and silent practice occurred during the same mid- to late-nineteenth-century period when the system of compulsory and universal state-supported education was slowly developing in Britain. The physiological critics' theories of silent reading, however, assume uses of literacy that were quite different from those envisioned for classrooms, where oral recitation was still common. During the same period that the serial novel's role in representing common reading practices came under the purview of expert psychological knowledge, therefore, its model of sociability and participation was also being adapted into the consolidating social functions of the school.[18]

The School Dickens and Democratic Literature

Given Lewes's consignment of the Dickensian pleasures of memory to readers of uncultivated tastes, it should not surprise us that the very qualities that Eliot and Lewes criticized in Dickens's novels became grounds for Dickens's inclusion in the English literature curriculum for primary and secondary schools in the late nineteenth and early twentieth centuries. Here I provide a history both of Dickens's emergence as a worldwide best-selling author from the late nineteenth through the early decades of the twentieth century and of the shaping of his identity as a canonical author during this same period in school readers (textbooks), literary histories, and curricula. We have seen how Dickens's cultural influence was celebrated just after his death by academics like Benjamin Jowett of Oxford and Adolphus William Ward of Owens College, Manchester, in terms that institutionalize the image of Dickens's originality articulated by the earliest reviewers of his serials in the 1830s and 1840s. Discussing Dickens's claim to future fame in his short critical biography of 1882, for example, Ward consolidates this early reception as the standard account of Dickens's art and personality for the purposes of literary history. Praising "the mental and moral vigour" of Dickens's style, Ward concludes that "in him there were accordingly united with rare completeness a swift responsiveness to the impulses of humour and pathos, an inexhaustible fertility in discovering and inventing materials for their exercise, and the constant creative desire to give to these newly created materials a vivid plastic form."[19]

Counting positively for Ward is precisely the inventive "vividness" of imagination that Lewes found false and deceptive. Echoing John Forster's anonymous 1837 review of *The Pickwick Papers* (1836–37), Ward emphasizes the mimetic qualities of Dickens's narrative style, his "faculty of converting into a scene—putting, as it were, into a frame—personages that came under his notice, and the background on which he saw them."[20] Unlike Lewes, Ward credits Dickens with knowing that his creations were fictitious: "his imaginative power and dramatic instinct combining to produce an endless succession of effective scenes and situations, ranging through almost every variety of the pathetic and humourous."[21] Quoting, and thus rendering canonical as self-description, Dickens's 1853 letter to Macready describing his desire to address his art to the "great ocean of humanity in which we are drops,"[22] Ward both publicizes and institutionalizes it as Dickens's creed of democratic art. Ward links Dickens's popularity to his focus on "domestic life," and his empirical depiction of "types of character . . . which are accordingly those which most of us have opportunities enough of comparing with the realities around us; and this test, a sound one within reasonable limits, was the test he demanded."[23] For Ward, Dickens's novels evince respect for his readers' critical intelligence—a crucial criterion for popular literature to count as educational rather than escapist.

Like Benjamin Jowett's eulogy of Dickens, Ward's biography also commends Dickens for embodying in his characters powerful negative examples of the typical moral failings of Englishmen: "To be sure, unless it be Mr. Chadband and those of his tribe, we shall find the hypocrite and the man-out-at-elbows in real life less endurable than their representatives in fiction."[24] Dickens's satire, then, enables a more general self-criticism of Englishness beyond simply blaming individuals. Ward concludes his biography by defending both Dickens's style and his appeal to posterity as expressions of his humanitarian vocation: "He conscientiously addressed himself, as to the task of his life, to endeavour to knit humanity together. The method which he, by instinct and by choice, more especially pursued was that of seeking to show the 'good in everything.' This it is that made him, unreasonably sometimes, ignobly never, the champion of the poor, the helpless, the outcast. He was often tempted into a rhetoric too loud and too shrill, into a satire neither fine nor fair; for he was impatient, but not impatient of what he thought true and good."[25] This view of Dickens as a sympathetic humanitarian intellectual and social crusader would become the standard image of his authorship in the school curriculum. Dickens's humanitarian influence nevertheless took on new roles as his creed for democratic art came to characterize English literature's role in imparting civic values.

The resurgence in Dickens's reputation in the 1880s and 1890s was a phenomenon both of the expansion of publishing for a mass audience and of the growth of a national education system in Britain, and of the standardization of curricula for public education supported at the local and state levels in the United States. Despite trenchant critiques of his art by leading late Victorian literary intellectuals, including Margaret Oliphant, the brothers Leslie and James Fitzjames Stephen, and Mowbray Walter Morris, the sales figures for Dickens's novels continued to grow after his death.[26] Crucial vehicles for the emergence of Dickens as an English cultural institution were the cheap editions of his works that burgeoned in number between 1871 and 1920.[27] Dickens's novels were reissued during his lifetime in a variety of formats, from the lavishly half- or full-morocco-bound editions in one or two volumes, costing between twenty-one and twenty-six shillings, to the Cheap edition in onepence-halfpenny weekly numbers. Only after his death, however, did a series of very cheap editions appear that would reach significantly larger numbers of poorer readers. Chapman and Hall issued the Household edition in 1871 in penny numbers, as well as in somewhat more expensive monthly parts and small quarto volume editions. Chapman and Hall and Routledge entered into agreements in 1878 for bulk sales and distribution of Dickens's works in both Britain and the United States, including the two-shilling People's edition of Dickens's works and the twenty-one-volume Charles Dickens edition costing eighteen shillings for the collection. In his study of Dickens's relations with his publishers, Robert L. Patten documents that within "twelve years after his death no fewer than 4,239,000 volumes had been purchased in England alone," while others were offered as free gifts by merchants, including those given gratis to purchasers of tea, as noted by Trollope in 1879.[28]

In the early decades of the twentieth century, Dickens's novels remained very popular: Chapman and Hall's sales were 2,000,000 from 1900 to 1906, while the Everyman's Library editions of *David Copperfield* (1849–50) published by J. M. Dent in the 1920s became best-sellers.[29] Estimates of sales in the United States through the 1940s, especially in light of the wide circulation of paperback editions, gave Dickens the status of "the best-selling author in the history of American publishing," while translations of his novels also sold widely across Europe.[30] One of these new late nineteenth-century cheap editions, Routledge's World Library of the "works of great writers," sold for threepence in paper and sixpence in cloth. In his preface, series editor the Rev. Hugh Reginald Haweis proclaims his hope for the fifty-two volumes that "if not a complete cure for indolence and vice, [they] may at least prove a powerful counter-charm." In provisioning the "reading world beneath the surface [of society]," Haweis also imagines affecting the culture of an enlarged electorate: "I hope that, with a wide extension of the franchise, the time has arrived for the best books to be offered to a large class hitherto almost untouched by such literature."[31] In his 1886 introduction to the series imprint of *A Christmas Carol and The Chimes* (which were originally published as separate works in 1843 and 1844), Haweis is more explicit about how reading Dickens should build citizenship: "No mere 'jokist' ever got the hold which Dickens has acquired over a thoughtful and intelligent public. To his broad wit and pungent humour he adds a photographic minuteness of observation, and accurate acquaintance with out-of-the-way-life, chiefly town life; a graphic fitness of expression, a powerful dash of melodrama; and last, but not least, a broad sympathy with human suffering and an ineradicable belief in human goodness. There have been many preachers of original sin: it remained for Dickens to preach us the homely but more genial gospel of original righteousness."[32] Haweis condenses the now standard mainstream view of Dickens into a kind of marketing recipe—throw in a "dash" of generic Christian teachings, sympathy with the poor, and optimism about human improvement and you can produce direct moral effects on the mass readership. Summing up the Dickens's "gospel" in an updated form that savors of temperance societies, self-help literature, and social science, Haweis pronounces that "There is good in everybody, if you can get at it; and the wicked are mostly the victims of a diseased organization or a defective social environment."[33]

Alluding to the recent 1884 Representation of the People Act, under which the majority of (male) voters now qualified by occupation rather than by ownership of property, Haweis implies that the newly enfranchised "factory worker" or the "commercial and uncommercial travellers" may confirm their membership in "a thoughtful and intelligent public" of readers who can demonstrate that they are "righteous" and "good" citizens by buying this Routledge edition of *A Christmas Carol and The Chimes*.[34] Despite the perception by some conservatives that the 1884 Act had created "unmoderated democracy," Haweis's preface takes advantage of the legislative trend toward growing political representation for working people to open up a convenient marketing niche for popular editions of classic literature.[35] Within this marketing rationale, Dickens's message of respect for all classes supports commercial literature's self-appointed role in transmitting English civic pride, tolerance, and self-esteem to the newly enfranchised. In other words, the selection process for repackaging Victorian popular serial fiction as "classic" literature in cheap editions involves stamping Dickens's advocacy of the poor as an appropriate humanitarian sensibility for the modern citizen. Haweis's pitch supplies the kind of all-purpose citizen-building approach articulated by the English critic and university extension lecturer, John Churton Collins, who argued in *The Study of English Literature* (1891) that "the people" "need political culture, instruction, that is to say, in what pertains to their relation to the State, to their duties as citizens; and they also need to be impressed sentimentally by having the presentation in legend and history of heroic and patriotic example brought vividly and attractively before them."[36] Here "vividness" no longer marks the Humean connectivity of thought, or the author's imagination as a vehicle for a mass hallucination, as in Lewes's critique of Dickens, but rather it indicates the pedagogical success of a work of literature in conveying an image of national identity that entails a relationship of duty to the nation-state.

Haweis's packaging of cheap classics as recipes for citizenship training is thus also consistent with historian Stephen Heathorn's analysis of the cultural nationalist conceptual framework in history textbooks published in Britain between 1880 and 1914. Heathorn documents a consensus view among British educationists across the political spectrum that the primary function of schooling for the working-class student was to teach "the responsibilities of citizenship and national loyalty" through "encouragement of a shared national culture."[37] Heathorn argues that "instruction in basic literacy was, for the great majority of the English population between 1880 and 1914, the means by which an understanding of the 'nation' and one's 'place' within it, as well as one's place in the world, was first discursively formed."[38] Among educators developing English as a school subject in Britain during this period, there was also a growing sense that literary education should improve students' taste in reading and insulate them from the pernicious influences of penny-dreadfuls. In her study of British English teachers, Margaret Mathieson points out, "By 1921 it seemed very obvious to the subject's supporters that if the [English] teacher succeeded in creating enthusiasm for good books in his pupils, he was achieving far more than the stimulation of new interests—he was improving characters."[39]

Throughout the nineteenth century in Britain, school readers were a crucial vehicle for shaping the relationship between literature and national identity through education. Beginning with Evangelical tracts and spelling books published at the end of the eighteenth century, messages about the duties of the poor to their betters were purveyed in religious terms through explicitly didactic and educational reading material designed for use in elementary schools. As textbooks became more readily available during the nineteenth century, most schools did not have sufficient funds to purchase separate subject readers, so compendium readers and spelling books were by far the most common means for teaching reading.[40] In the earlier nineteenth century, these general readers focused on instilling social deference, orthodox religious belief in conformity with the religious affiliation of the particular voluntary school, and a basic knowledge of reading, writing, and arithmetic. After the 1862 Revised Code, such readers became the basis of mandatory testing by school Inspectors, fostering a rigid curriculum based in memorization of the textbook's contents. As historian of education J. M. Goldstrom has shown, after the 1850s, some secular readers became available that included instruction in basic principles of political economy, geography, and natural history.[41] By the end of the 1850s, the numbers of schoolbooks in use had increased substantially; Goldstrom estimates that there were approximately 2,225,000 readers in use in 1859.[42]

Growing numbers of schools and students as a result of the various waves of educational reform, from the Revised Code through the series of acts expanding educational provision through the end of the century, made the textbook industry more and more profitable. Standards developed for examination at all levels of the new national curriculum between 1875 and 1882 required the child to demonstrate "intelligent" and "expressive" reading. As a result, the educational codes of 1880 and 1882 stipulated the use of specialized readers providing instruction in basic geography, English literature, and history.[43] These mandates, as Heathorn indicates, provoked the expansion of educational publishing by both well-established and new firms, including the English and Scottish publishers A. & C. Black, Blackie, Cassell, Chambers, Longman, Macmillan, Nelson, Pittman, and Thomas Nelson and Sons.[44] Edward Arnold, a new publishing firm founded in 1890 and geared toward supplying the textbook market, initiated its textbook line with Arnold's English Literature Series, featuring abridgements of Dickens's novels for the child reader edited by J. H. Yoxhall, MP and author.[45] An advertisement for this series in an 1891 issue of the *Journal of Education* offers *David Copperfield*, *The Old Curiosity Shop* (1840–41), and *Dombey and Son* (1846–48) in an inexpensive one-shilling-twopence imprint, or a prize edition with gilt edges costing two shillings, while an advertisement in a 1907 issue of the *Educational Times* lists an expanded series including *Pickwick* and

A Tale of Two Cities (1859).[46] This grouping begins to indicate which works by Dickens were presumed most suitable for young readers in abridged form.

Developing in parallel with these British textbook publishing ventures were such projects for the consolidation of English literature and language as subjects of scholarly study as that "great monument to Englishness," the *New* (later the *Oxford*) *English Dictionary*.[47] The original *OED* without the supplements (1888–1928) cites 5,553 words and 7,512 quotations from Dickens's works, by far the largest number from a group of prolific Victorian authors including Robert Browning (2,682 words, 2,965 quotations), Charles Darwin (1,523 and 1,658), George Eliot (2,430 and 2,618), Ruskin (2,879 and 3,231) and Thackeray (3,412 and 4,348). Victorian authors with quantities of *OED* citations comparable to those of Dickens are Carlyle (5,258 and 6,376) and Tennyson (4,537 and 6,832).[48]

In addition to the philological approaches to literature afforded by the *OED*, literary history became profitable in this same period both in the form of textbooks and in biographical series devoted to great English writers. We have already reviewed Ward's contribution on Dickens to Macmillan's popular series English Men of Letters, initiated in 1877 and edited by John Morley, the politician and editor of the *Fortnightly Review*.[49] Many other similar biographical series followed in subsequent decades, with contributions from leading literary critics such as Leslie Stephen and Edmund Gosse. Such biographies often conveyed the "conviction that familiarity with the lives of outstanding individuals tended to have an inspirational effect, above all a morally elevating effect, as an incitement to the development of 'character.'"[50] In the context of this wave of books exploring exemplary lives, Dickens represents another inspiring case of individual success under difficulties.

Biographical sketches and critical assessments of Dickens appearing in British and American biographies and literary histories between the 1870s and 1920s further illustrate how the early Victorian critical reception of Dickens was encapsulated and adapted as a rationale for the pedagogical uses of his works within the English literature curriculum. The earliest literary history referring to Dickens seems to have been Thomas Budd Shaw's 1846 textbook *Outlines of English Literature*; published in London by Murray, it was also republished in later American editions.[51] Shaw's discussion of Dickens, "the greatest name in the contemporary literature of Great Britain," appears in a chapter on "The Modern Novelists" including both eighteenth- and nineteenth-century authors.[52] As Dickens's contemporary,

Shaw does not yet know how his career will turn out, but he offers an assessment that will become standard after Dickens's death:

> Even should he write no more he has done enough to deserve the love and admiration of posterity; his works possess the highest and rarest of merits—that of complete originality both of matter and of form; his view of life is generous elevating genial; he sympathises with what is good and noble in all classes and conditions alike; he makes us love our kind; he makes us love the exercise of the humbler and more modest virtues; he chronicles the minor accidents and impressions of life; his writings, though describing the manners of the poorest and lowest classes of mankind, contain nothing which can shock the most fastidious taste; and the only things he has held up to ridicule or detestation are vice hypocrisy or the pretensions of imbecile vulgarity. He is an author of whom England may be proud.[53]

Later literary histories and textbooks stay remarkably close to Shaw's 1846 account of Dickens's influence. Dickens's canonical identity thus seems to have crystallized from the 1880s through the 1930s in the form of a portrait taken in the 1840s during the first phases of his career, as if the subsequent two decades of his literary and editorial output made no difference for the purposes of his curricular role in personifying English authorship.[54]

One of the most successful literary histories for advanced students, Henry Morely's *A First Sketch of English Literature* (1873), mentions Dickens in the twelfth edition of 1886—the first to include Victorian authors—providing a short biography and survey of Dickens's works and career. In the context of a comparison between Dickens and Thackeray, Morley fits Dickens's life into a standard Victorian self-help narrative featuring the overcoming of his childhood disadvantages: "Dickens, with little aid of school education in his early years, and in much contact with the lower forms of life, had the energy of genius strengthened, and its sympathy deepened, by a youth of battle against adverse circumstances. . . . A vigour impatient of all check set itself face to face with the ills of life, and spent the gifts of rare genius in service to humanity." Defending Dickens's art against certain critics' charges of "extravagance" and "vulgarity," Morley emphasizes that Dickens's early struggles provided him with "a more vivid sense of social needs, and keener sympathies with those who are forced to fight the battle with less strength to overcome." Morley also works to generalize the specifically Victorian context of Dickens's novels toward a more symbolic meaning suitable for classroom use, arguing, for example, that the Court of Chancery in *Bleak House* (1852–53) stands for "the something outside a man's life that may at any day bring fortune to him without labour of his own. Such hope is a blight upon the life that trusts to it."[55] While retaining the now standard focus on Dickens's personal "vigour," prolific and "vivid" imagination, and sympathy with social outcasts that Ward's extended critical biography also supplies, Morley's textbook version of Dickens's life story conveys the idea that a good work ethic and social sympathies are directly linked criteria for personal advancement and literary achievement.

This shaping of Dickens's life story into a self-help narrative reappears in a slightly different form in Irish-born American journalist R. Shelton Mackenzie's detailed and extensively documented biography, which he evidently succeeded in rushing to press within two months of Dickens's demise. The book's dedication celebrates Dickens as "a Man of the People," in contrast to Scott, Bulwer, Macaulay, and Thackeray, who "either were of high family descent or had received the best education that money could bestow." Mackenzie grants Dickens the honorary status of a product of American public education, pointing out that "Dickens, son of an obscure Government clerk, whose pedigree no one has cared to trace, received only such an education as, free of cost, every State in our Union bestows upon its children."[56] Commenting on Dickens's politics, Mackenzie writes that "it is universally known that his political opinions were strongly liberal" and insists that, given his universal popularity, "any of the London boroughs would have been proud and glad if he had consented to be its representative." Pointing out that he "had resolved, at the beginning of his career, to devote himself to literature, wholly and solely," Mackenzie suggests that Dickens would have lost his distinctive form of authorial influence if he had entered the House of Commons rather than relying "on the Press, to work out all his public purposes."[57] Mackenzie thus endorses Dickens's version of modern authorship as separated from formal politics but bridging political, journalistic, and literary forms of influence. Commenting on the outpouring of grief in the United States when news of Dickens's sudden death was received, Mackenzie proudly asserts that "Mr. Dickens knew—none better—that for every one reader he had at home, he had fifty in this country, and that he was more thoroughly understood here than even on his own soil."[58] Mackenzie's Dickens becomes an adopted American citizen so that he may exemplify how to build a successful life on the basis of a public school education.

These standard elements of Dickens's canonical image appear repeatedly in the popular critical and curricular reception during the period from 1870

to 1900: man of originality and genius, successful despite early family struggles, possessing a photographic mind of incomparable imaginative power
that reproduces "vivid" images and scenes that become memorable for the
reader; unique qualities of physical and mental "vigour"; compassionate
crusader for the poor who was inspired by his early experiences of London's
poverty and street life; preeminent humorist; critic of religious hypocrisy
and class prejudices; politically liberal or even radical, but eschewing politics
in service of literature; lover of the theater and actor in amateur theatricals.
Other widely used literary histories, such as American Reuben Post Halleck's 1900 *History of English Literature*, provide slightly revised or embel-
lished versions of this standard narrative, seemingly recycled from either
Henry Morley's or A. W. Ward's books.[59] The Lewesian critique of Dickens's "fantasized" characters as mere caricatures also appears as a leitmotif in
literary histories from this period. Halleck writes that "Dickens is a master
of caricature. The heroes and heroines of his books are usually colorless and
lifeless but certain characters possessing some exaggerated mannerism live
forever in the memory."[60] Yet Halleck's rationale for teaching literary
history through the biographies of exemplary authors is still overtly
associationist:

> Various masterpieces seem like unconnected islands in an unexplored ocean.
> There is no way of making these masterpieces seem otherwise except by
> teaching the history and development of the literature of which they form a
> part. Mental association is based primarily on contiguity. Ideas must be
> grasped by the mind at the same time before they can be known to be
> related. It is difficult for young minds to knit into one fabric ideas which are
> presented at considerable intervals and under associations so different as
> occur in the study of various masterpieces.[61]

For Halleck, the literary canon (like the author's mind for Ward) embodies
an authoritative chain of cultural associations to be passed on by the textbook's organization as a chronological anthology. Viewed as vehicles of association, such anthologies seemingly teach themselves: each time the
student works with the textbook he or she should also form ordered mental
associations with the book's selections. Yet Halleck insists on the required
contextualization of the anthologized selections within literary history so
that they create an effect of continuity.

   In assembling the following account of Dickens's canonical image in
American school readers, I have not attempted a systematic study of textbooks by publisher or region of adoption within the United States but instead have opted to analyze in detail several readers that provide the most

explicit directions for their organization, pedagogical use, and presentation of selections. Historians of education, literary historians, and book historians alike have dated the emergence of the formal study of English literature, viewed as a subject distinct from rhetoric and oratory, in the United States roughly to the second half of the nineteenth century.[62] Jean Ferguson Carr, Stephen L. Carr, and Lucille M. Schultz note that earlier nineteenth-century American school readers frame reading "as a crucial national project, one that will shape citizens, unite a diffuse geographical space, and help negotiate differences in language, background, and class."[63] Educational publications in the United States during the period from 1880 to 1940 contributed to the emergence of a national "culture of print" characterized by "the extension and rapid circulation of print technologies and forms" in combination with "the extension of schooling to previously excluded populations."[64] Published in the United States from the 1890s through 1919, this sample set of textbooks that I examine here represents a burgeoning and lucrative market in educational materials. Book historians Carl F. Kaestle and Janice A. Radway note that the growing culture of print contributed to "the consolidation of nationalism," but that such developments also produced a "tension between centralization, concentration, and standardization on the one hand, and specialization, small-scale production, and the diversification of published reading material on the other."[65]

Schoolbooks necessarily tend toward the standardizing end of this spectrum, given their curricular role, but even here a variety of educational philosophies and methods are apparent. Richard L. Venezky and Kaestle note a crucial shift in American reading pedagogy during this period from instruction in phonics, involving memorization of syllables and words and reading aloud in the classroom (a version of the earlier syllabic method), to silent reading, a "'whole word' method of reading rather than phonics," and "a gradual softening of the moral messages of reading texts." The "whole word" method stressed the new reader's recognition of entire words, "emphasiz[ing] comprehension and context" rather than memorization. These pedagogical shifts were part of a new "child-centered progressive education movement" that featured competing strands, including both "close attention to the child's interests and motivations," and a counterbalancing " need for efficiency to prepare children for jobs in American industries." Those educators who favored public education as a means toward employment also saw silent reading as superior to "the often slow and clumsy method of recitation" because it saved classroom time, particularly in the larger public schools, and thus "promoted both efficiency and comprehension" as well as facilitating evaluation of reading skills by written rather than oral examination.⁶⁶ Nevertheless, several literature textbooks that I examine here promote group discussion, guided by the teacher, of the meaning of literary texts as the basis for the student's understanding, suggesting that silent reading was only one mode of classroom engagement, and not necessarily a dominant one.

In order to respond to a plethora of different state curricular requirements, American textbook publishers produced "reading texts [that] tended to be bland and homogeneous because they were designed for broad acceptance."⁶⁷ Venezky and Kaestle detect an "Anglo-American bias" represented by textbook authors themselves and evident in the forms of "identities and perspectives" conveyed by the textbooks. Reading instructors increasingly saw their role as facilitators of literacy skills that would lead naturally to the "aesthetic appreciation" of Anglo-American literature as "the basis for an assimilative school culture."⁶⁸ Unlike single-author school texts, anthologies represent the literary canon in serial form and through multiple genres. Advanced literature readers suitable for secondary school and college students make up an important part of the sample of English literature readers that I have surveyed. Such works were targeted to the growth in high school attendance in the United States: fewer than 5 percent of students continued to high school in 1880, while over 50 percent achieved a high school education in 1940.⁶⁹ English literature readers typically include a varied selection of short readings across historical periods and genres by both American and English authors.

What is striking about the way these school readers frame Dickens's authorship is their consistency with the Victorian critical reception of Dickens's early serials. The school Dickens as I reconstruct it here suggests a delayed or latent effect of auto-canonization within Dickens's novels prior to the emergence of the English literature curriculum. As personified by Dickens, the English literature canon itself might also be viewed as projecting a capacity for self-selection prior to any specific classroom use. Further research would be needed to determine whether such an effect of auto-canonization was unique to Dickens's canonical image or might be typical of modern authors whose school profiles seem to correspond to the ways that they marketed their own authorial image during their lifetimes. Nevertheless, given Dickens's status as one of the first modern literary celebrities, it is not surprising that he would also come to personify what literature itself should do in the public or national school classroom.

The standard account of Dickens's life and moral influence that we have seen in the early literary histories reappears in literature readers as a capsule biography preceding excerpted selections from his novels or shorter works reprinted in full. Accompanied by a portrait of the author and often by a picture of Gad's Hill Place, the large house in Kent that Dickens purchased in 1856 with the proceeds of his fame and the location of his early death, these brief accounts geared toward young readers emphasize the financial troubles of Dickens's parents during his childhood and typically refer to his childhood dream to purchase the Gad's Hill house, thus encompassing Dickens's life in a classic American "rags to riches" story. As an effect of the inclusion of his writings, often excerpted, among the selections anthologized in these readers, however, the originality so emphasized by the Victorian reviewers and standardized in the 1870s-era textbooks and biographies is set in a new context: Dickens becomes one more name in a series of great authors listed in the table of contents. A frontispiece illustration from an 1890s-era American textbook, *The Normal Course in Reading: Fifth Reader*, portrays this effect of the textbook canon as an illustrious company in a set of cameo portraits, or emblems, each captioned with a quotation, forming an Anglo-American literary pantheon and representing the four genres of poetry, fiction, history, and drama (Figure 11). Grouped in a diagonal with emblems of Tennyson and Shakespeare, and surrounded by the American authors William Cullen Bryant, Henry Wadsworth Longfellow, Washington Irving, and Oliver Wendell Holmes Sr., Dickens's emblem is captioned with the phrase "The ties which link the poor man to his humble hearth . . . bear the stamp of heaven."

The caption is taken from chapter 38 of *The Old Curiosity Shop*, where the narrator draws a strong contrast between the sense of possession with which the wealthy regard their land and the sentimental attachment that the poor feel for their temporary lodgings:

> The ties that bind the wealthy and the proud to home may be forged on earth, but those which link the poor man to his humble hearth are of the true metal and bear the stamp of Heaven. The man of high descent may love the halls and lands of his inheritance as a part of himself, as trophies of his birth and power; his associations with them are associations of pride and wealth and triumph; the poor man's attachment to the tenement he holds, which strangers have held before, and may to-morrow occupy again, has a worthier root, struck deep into purer soil. His household gods are of flesh and blood, with no alloy of silver, gold, or precious stone; he has no property

Figure 11. Frontispiece to *The Normal Course in Reading, Fifth Reader*, by Emma J. Todd and W. B. Powell (New York: Silver, Burdett, and Co., 1895). Courtesy of Stanford University Library/Google Books.

but in the affections of his own heart; and when they endear bare floors and walls, despite of rags and toil and scanty meals, that man has his love of home from God, and his rude hut becomes a solemn place.[70]

The new context of the textbook selectively illuminates the simultaneously pedagogical and political goals of the passage as it originally appeared in the novel, where it serves an argument for the necessity of improving affordable housing in order to foster the patriotism of the poor: "In the love of home, the love of country has its rise; and who are truer patriots or the best in time of need—those who venerate the land, owning its wood, and stream, and earth, and all that they produce? or those who love their country, boasting not a foot of ground in all its wide domain?"[71] As Heathorn explains, many authors of late nineteenth-century British school readers found that "the image of 'home'" worked to "capture the unique sense of belonging that they wanted to convey" in their lessons on citizenship as a feeling of belonging within the modern nation-state.[72] In the American textbook illustration, the model of democratic citizenship as based in a shared attachment to the idea of home has come to function so well since the 1840s as an image of patriotism, newly enshrined within the democratic public school curriculum, that *The Old Curiosity Shop*'s contestation of the landowning aristocracy's social and political ascendancy can be omitted. This affiliation of the poor man's associations with home and nation with the image of Dickens is also forward-looking in the way it exemplifies the democratic sentiments and civic participation of renters and apartment dwellers, as well as owners of homes, businesses, and small farms, rather than associating citizenship with the ownership of estates or capital.

The caption to Dickens's portrait, then, conveys his canonical image as a crusader for the poor, connecting his works as presented by the textbook with a democratic populism suited to American readers. The illustration also arranges the cameos in a way suitable for provoking the young reader's own associations with the textbook's contents. A mention of each writer by the teacher, for example, will invoke in the student's memory the illustration's image of each author, along with its characteristic phrase, each arranged into a self-contained and linked network by the anthology form. The illustration's clustered cameos also represent the English literature textbook as a successor to the serial novel in its function of "linking" a continually growing audience of readers together into a transatlantic reading public now supported by an Anglo-American English literature curriculum. An inspirational caption to the entire set of portraits appeals to the young reader's own aspirations toward achievement as a product of democratic public schooling: "Lives of great men all remind us, we can make our lives sublime, and departing leave behind us, footprints on the sands of time." The inclusion of Holmes and Bryant, both associated with progressive causes such as abolitionism and immigrant rights, conveys the egalitarian associations of this group of authors. Lane Stiles's research on pedagogies related to post-1920 high school readers shows that such anthologies were typically used by teachers as supplements to the reading of a series of "individually packaged classics" by single authors. The effect of canonicity as itself a serial form arranging literary works chronologically was, then as today, most fully embodied in the course syllabus.[73]

The particular selections from Dickens's works included in the random set of American readers that I surveyed further indicate how his authorial influence was condensed and made emblematic for the purposes of the curriculum. These selections include "A Child's Dream of a Star" (from *Household Words*, April 6, 1840) and "The Death of the Little Scholar" (from *The Old Curiosity Shop*, chapter 24) in *The Fifth Reader, for the Use of Public and Private Schools* (Brewer and Tileston, 1863); "Lying Awake" (first published in *Household Words*, October 30, 1852), "A Christmas Tree" (from *Household Words*, extra Christmas number, 1850), and "The United States" (from *A Child's History of England* [1851–53]) in *The Normal Course in Reading: Fifth Reader* (Silver, Burdett, 1895); "The Doll's Dressmaker" (from *Our Mutual Friend*) in *Cyr's Fourth Reader* (Ginn, 1898); "David Copperfield Finds His Aunt" (from *David Copperfield*, chapter 13) and "A Christmas Goose" (from *A Christmas Carol*) in *The Eaton Readers: Fourth Reader* (Eaton, 1906); "Mr. Winkle on Skates" (from *The Pickwick Papers*, chapter 30) in *The Eaton Readers, Fifth Reader* (Eaton, 1906); "The Cratchits' Christmas Dinner" (from *A Christmas Carol*), "The Ivy Green" (from *The Pickwick Papers*), and "Little Nell I" and "Little Nell II" (from *The Old Curiosity Shop*, both excerpts recounting Old Humphrey's initial meeting with Nell and her grandfather in London, chapters 1–3) in *The Language Readers: Fifth Reader* (Ginn, 1906); "The Child's Story" (from *Household Words*, extra Christmas number, 1852) in *The American School Readers, The Literary Reader for Higher Grades* (Macmillan, 1912); and the abridged "A Christmas Carol" in *Wheeler's Graded Literary Readers, with Interpretations: An Eighth Reader* (W. H. Wheeler, 1919).[74] From this sampling, we can draw the preliminary conclusion that the editors selected stories by Dickens meant to appeal to young readers, focusing on Christmas, child characters, and fantastic or fairytale-like themes. Each of these textbooks includes a short biography of

Dickens, many are illustrated, and several include lists of vocabulary words and questions on the reading.

Excluding George S. Hillard's 1863 *Fifth Reader*, the time span of the rest of this group of readers published between 1890 and 1919 also charts text-book publishers' anticipation of and response to work by committees of the National Education Association, which studied the role of English literature in relation to rhetoric, composition, and reading instruction. A report was issued in 1894 that formalized the status of English studies as equivalent to classical studies and advised that four years of English should be required in the high school, with curricular attention focused on learning about authors and reading works of literature, and de-emphasizing instruction in literary history.[75] *Wheeler's Graded Literary Readers, with Interpretations: An Eighth Reader* shows ample evidence that textbook writers and publishers implemented these requirements. It is a lavishly produced textbook including black and white reproductions of famous paintings by European artists as illustrations. Most revealing of the curricular uses of its contents are the interpretive introductions to each selection clearly directing students to a specific way of reading the text.

The short introduction to "A Christmas Carol" describes a class discussion meant to elicit the central meaning of Dickens's tale. Students were asked to "name what they considered the very noblest quality that any person can possess," and allowed "a day and a night in which to think it over." Each of the forty-two children described in turn the quality he or she had chosen, including "courage, honesty, honor, truthfulness, sincerity, modesty, sympathy, innocence, charity, pity, frankness, mercifulness and kindness." One girl proposed "*well-wishing*" because "if *everybody* wished well to all others, there could be no evil in the world," and it was this quality that was selected as "the very noblest" by a class vote. Dickens's text in turn confirms the appropriateness of this vote, according to the textbook writers:

> In the story of "A Christmas Carol," you will see that Charles Dickens thought so, too. . . . The great heart of Charles Dickens "wished well" to everybody on earth, especially the poor. He saw that *not* wishing well left thousands in hunger and misery at Christmas time, . . . So he wrote this beautiful story of poor old Scrooge, the evil-wisher, and of Tiny Tim who wished, "God bless us, *every one*," in the hope that it might be read before Christmas and transform all poor old Scrooges into well-wishers. . . . Few stories have ever been written that have made more people really happy than this. Probably it has turned millions of sour-tempered Scrooges into well-wishers and transformed many a bleak Christmas into a joyous time of feasting and loving.[76]

Tiny Tim's blessing is not italicized in the original novel, so the textbook's authors have added emphasis here, showing students how to include "*every one*" both in their own moral compass and, as practice for such generalized feelings, in their classroom interactions. This textbook formulation also seems to translate for a young reader's comprehension the kind of reading effect channeling Dickens's moral influence described by R. H. Horne in 1844: "the [novels] tend on the whole to bring the poor into the fairest position for obtaining the sympathy of the rich and powerful, by displaying the goodness and fortitude often found amidst want and wretchedness, together with the intervals of joyousness and comic humour."[77] Horne imagines a more rhetorical effect in the advocacy directed vertically toward "the rich and powerful," while the textbook imagines "well-wishing" as extending horizontally, so that the studied ignorance of social distinctions operating in the classroom can function as a principle of political equality among citizens. This particular American textbook seems dedicated to adapting the kind of generic humanitarian influence that Horne ascribed to Dickens's works decades earlier into a central justification of literature's role in the school curriculum.

Remembering Mr. Weller senior's parable in *The Pickwick Papers* of the pike-keeper's occupation as the working man's alternative to the gentleman's philosophical misanthropy, we could say that the early twentieth-century literature classroom works to move children across the pike of social stratification that they experience outside the school into democratic citizenship as a collective and egalitarian identity inculcated by the literature curriculum's teaching of humane moral values. The textbook's introduction to "A Christmas Carol" also ties such moral lessons to the democratic procedures—giving equal representative value to the opinions of both boys and girls—of the public school classroom. This textbook was published in 1919, the same year that the United States Congress passed the Woman Suffrage Amendment, while the Nineteenth Amendment to the United States Constitution granting women the right to vote was passed into law the following year.[78] Thus the vote on the meaning of "A Christmas Carol," through which one girl's interpretation was endorsed by all, also positions co-education as preparation for women's participation in the franchise.

In their general introduction, the editors explain that "the Purpose of Teaching Reading is unquestionably to enable the child to get from the printed page the *Images*, the *Thoughts*, and the *Emotions* of the author who wrote the page." They lay out the precise process by which the poet receives inspiration from a perception, evoking an emotion, which is "crystallized into words" that make up a poem: "THE FOUR STEPS: 1. An emotion.

2. An abstract relation to life. 3. The concrete forms of the relation to life. 4. The words of the poem." All the student reader has to do to grasp the poet's original emotion is to repeat this process through which the poet composed the poem, "but in exactly the reverse order." Here we see another formula for epitaphic reading that also marks an important transition from memorization to paraphrase as the central modern technique of literary pedagogy.[79] The novice interpreter's goal, however, is not simply repetition or absorption of the author's ideas: "The child can interpret only by his own experiences. No matter how simple or primitive such introductions may look in a series of readers, the only introductory helps that are of value are the ones that recall to the child his own personal experiences and not some far-away literary information with which the child's mind cannot possibly function."[80] We can conclude that the classroom vignette illustrating how to "interpret" Dickens's "A Christmas Carol" as a story of "well-wishing" is meant to function as a kind of surrogate experience, or as a vehicle for modeling the connection between individual experience and the classroom reading of literature, in specific ways. We also recognize the popular associationist underpinnings of this pedagogy as it evolved from Victorian classroom practices of memorization, and the Dickensian pleasures of memory instituted by the reading of serial fiction, to produce new modes of interpretive paraphrase still with us today that invite children to make literature relevant to their own lives. The incentives for reading that Dickensian serial fiction designed for the often newly literate Victorian reader in competition with evangelical practices of pious reading have been newly revised and readapted for the English literature curriculum. The particular kind of experience that formal literary reading in its turn "recalls," however, is *classroom* practice. In the instance of the framing interpretation of "A Christmas Carol," this classroom reading involves the exercise of choosing among possible interpretations of the text by popular vote—a choice framed and ratified by the curriculum. In this way, the textbook elicits a kind of consent to its own procedures of selection and interpretation.

Such classroom exercises also form the participatory matrix through which the child's own experiences become *relevant* in relation to the literary text's evocation of the author's original emotion—the English literature canon aims to function for each child quite intimately as prosopopoeia. The classroom becomes an echo chamber for dead authors as they have been interpreted by the democratic protocols of school reading, where both students as a class and each individual student all take their places in a chain of connections leading, ultimately, to the national author as representative of a specifically democratic form of national belonging. The textbook stages such belonging as democratic because it is ostensibly based in free and inclusive group choices confirmed by the curriculum. This does not mean that Dickens's works or any other piece of literature could not be read differently outside the classroom, but the curriculum does not factor such independent reading into its insistence that literature must have an individualized meaning for the student that is generalized within the context of the class.

The particular introduction in the *Wheeler's* reader to Dickens's "A Christmas Carol" gains wider relevance as an account of the epitaphic reading framed by the curriculum if we compare it with the introductions preceding the textbook's selection of Byron's "The Eve before Waterloo" (taken, as the editors scrupulously inform the student, from the third Canto of "Childe Harold's Pilgrimage") and "Antony's Oration over Caesar," from Shakespeare's *Julius Caesar*. The introductory "interpretations" to these excerpts provide a brief historical background to Napoleon's rise and fall and to the assassination of Caesar by the conspirators. In each introduction, the editors point out that Caesar and Napoleon are, together with Alexander the Great, "the three most remarkable men who ever lived."[81] By analogy, then, the most "remarkable" trait about Dickens for the purposes of this textbook turns out to be something relatively equivalent in scale, but measured in cultural terms, to an imperial conquest: the extensive reach of Dickens's humanitarian authorial influence in turning "millions of sour-tempered Scrooges into well-wishers." In literary histories and for early twentieth-century textbook writers and publishers, the direct moral effects of Dickens's fiction seem to have become generally accepted as historically demonstrable by correlating Dickens's sales figures with his celebrity authorship and humane message about helping the poor.

Within this particular textbook's selections, therefore, Dickens's inclusion stands out as an incomplete instance of the historical deracination accompanying canonization analyzed by John Guillory in his study of the transmission of cultural capital through literary education: "By suppressing the context of a cultural work's production and consumption, the school produces the illusion that 'our' culture (or the culture of the 'other') is transmitted simply by contact with the works themselves. But a text tradition is not sufficient in itself either to constitute or to transmit a culture, and thus school culture can never be more than a part of a total process of acculturation which, for societies with schools, is always complex and has many other institutional sites."[82] *Wheeler's* treatment of Dickens as a defender of the poor seems, by this account, significantly dependent upon the historical

Dickens as a recognizably Victorian construct. The kind of "contact" with the author that the textbook offers seems to have been facilitated by Dickens's own self-representation as a popular author for whom literature was a form of public service that was equivalent in its effects to his support for universal education. The textbook's identification of the curriculum with an image of authorship constructed through the Victorian critical reception of Dickens's originality and techniques of descriptive realism also appears as an elaboration of the historical Dickens's democratic cultural politics, suggesting that the early-twentieth-century English literature curriculum for schoolchildren could be accurately characterized more generally as a Dickensian project.

An abridged 1892 English Classic Series edition of *A Christmas Carol*, published in New York and "edited for school and home use," conveys a similar set of messages about the worldwide reach of Dickens's humanitarian influence. The text opens with a short biography followed by brief appreciative quotations about Dickens by Carlyle and from the sermon and eulogy delivered at Dickens's funeral, along with a list of the author's works. The text also includes a list of recommended secondary works, including Ward's *Dickens* and Mackenzie's biography. The prefatory note to the text informs the reader of the "hundreds of letters written to [Dickens] by people in humble circumstances telling him amid many confidences about their homes, how the *Carol* was read there aloud, and was kept upon a little shelf by itself, and did them no end of good." The *Carol* on a little shelf by itself seems to have taken the place of or been positioned next to the Bible. The late nineteenth-century reader is assured, according to the formula we now recognize, that "When we remember the *Carol* and other Christmas stories by Dickens have been sold by the hundreds of thousands, how shall we estimate the effect they have had in teaching lessons of fellowship and charity, in making the happy season of Christmas time more sacred and more cherished, and in furnishing examples of courage, patience, generosity, and noble feeling?"[83] Most intriguing for our study of Dickens's personification of the English literature curriculum, however, are the final two pages of the textbook, including "Dickens's Golden Rules" consisting of the passage from chapter 42 of *David Copperfield* where the narrator/author describes his habits of diligence and earnest commitment to all he undertakes, and a one-page list of "Selections from Dickens to Commit to Memory." These selections from *A Christmas Carol*, *Dombey and Son*, *David Copperfield*, and *The Old Curiosity Shop* refer either to Christmas, to the rewards of diligent effort, to the power of "dreams" and imagination, or to consoling thoughts of death, including Scrooge's "I will honor Christmas in my heart and try to keep it all the year," and the schoolmaster's lesson from *The Old Curiosity Shop*: "When death strikes down the innocent and young, for every fragile form from which he sets the panting sprit free, a hundred virtues rise, in shapes of mercy, charity, and love, to walk the world and bless it."[84] The textbook's editors respond to the original maxim-like form of the school-master's lesson by extracting it from the novel, for catechism-like moral training in the English literature classroom. The prominent placement of *The Old Curiosity Shop*'s teachings in these school readers provides further evidence of that novel's influence in secularizing and modernizing devotional reading practices that I analyzed in Chapter 4.

This textbook extends in its turn the pedagogical work of Dickens's serial fiction in transforming and displacing Victorian didactic classroom genres, in the process writing the reading lessons of future English literature students. Epitaphic reading seems to have lived on, then, in the earliest versions of the institutionalized school Dickens, now newly "resurrected" from the archives of educational history and available in full-text, digitized form on Google Books, which becomes in its turn a virtual classroom with aspirations to universal access to knowledge.[85] The convenient length of *A Christmas Carol* (like Hannah More's *The Shepherd of Salisbury Plain*, long enough to be a substantial text, but not so long as to cause tedium or excessive difficulty for the newly proficient reader), and its shaping of a nonsectarian Christian conversion story, makes it the closest in its generic dimensions to the popular religious tracts that it replaces as Victorian literacy training evolved into the English curriculum. This seemingly ephemeral English Classics school edition from 1892 thus provides additional material evidence for the importance of Dickens's serial fiction as a significant transitional medium for learning to read in the nineteenth century—generically positioned between tracts and textbooks and socially positioned between evangelical proselytizing and the national school system.

Along with *A Christmas Carol* and *The Old Curiosity Shop*, *David Copper-field* and *A Tale of Two Cities* appear frequently within this inaugural phase of the institutionalization of the school Dickens.[86] In a detailed survey of high school English curricula commissioned by the United States secretary of the Interior and published in 1932, Dora V. Smith, associate professor of education at the University of Minnesota, documents that *A Tale of Two Cities* ranked fifth among the thirty most commonly taught works in high school English classes, with its most frequent appearance in grades eight through eleven being in tenth-grade classrooms. *A Christmas Carol* also came in twentieth on the list, showing up slightly more often as eighth-grade reading.[87] Smith also notes that the nineteenth-century novel begins to make its appearance in American curricula after 1900.[88] In a study of New York state secondary school English curricula published in 1941, Smith includes data gathered from seven different New York towns representing a variety of demographics on the popularity of books among boys and girls grouped by age. These lists include many now canonical authors of both adult and young adult literature, but also many popular authors as well. Smith reports that "Shakespeare, George Eliot, and Dickens were the standard authors most read by girls in the tenth grade."[89] Dickens's novels tend to rank in the top to middle ranges of these lists of approximately forty-five to fifty-five works, with middle and high school girls and boys listing *A Tale of Two Cities* and *David Copperfield* as favorite works by Dickens. Garnering the highest number of votes among authors preferred by tenth-grade boys, Dickens was also ranked fifth most popular (after Margaret Mitchell, George Eliot, James N. Hall, and William Shakespeare) among tenth-grade girls.[90] On the basis of Smith's reports, as well as the sample of textbooks and cheap editions surveyed, we can conclude that British and American publishers, teachers, and textbook writers between 1870 and 1940 responded to Dickens's popular fiction as a means to learn how to read literature as a source of humanitarian sentiments and democratic principles and behaviors.

By comparing the conventions of textbooks for advanced student readers with the packaging of works of literature for an educated adult audience, we can further elucidate the close relationship between the critical reception and marketing of Dickens's novels as standard literary classics and nonacademic forms of popular appreciation for Dickens's writings and characters during this period. Both the academic and popular forms of reception retain traces of the associationist terminology employed by early Victorian reviewers. From the late 1870s, volume editions of Dickens's novels produced both for the educated reader and for use in university courses begin to include lengthy biographical and critical introductions as well as critical apparatus. The Riverside Press series editions of Dickens's novels in two volumes, first published by the Boston publisher Houghton Mifflin in the 1870s and reissued in the 1890s, include a substantial biographical and critical introductory essay by Edwin Percy Whipple, an American essayist and literary critic who died in 1886.[91] Whipple concludes his introductory essay on *David Copperfield* by drawing the reader's attention to the "vitality" that Dickens invested in his imaginative creations as the reason why his works have outlasted the productions of other writers. Quoting (via Forster's biography) Dickens's self-description to Forster of his emotional exhaustion after completing *David Copperfield*, reproduced in the novel's preface—"*I seem to be sending some part of myself into the Shadowy World*"—Whipple shifts Dickens's imaginative burden of authorship onto the reader's response, which in turn constitutes a confirmation of the novelist's greatness:

> In this statement we recognize a truth, too much overlooked, that such complete absorption in beings of the imagination, is a terrible drain on the very substance,—on the reserved force of the mind. Hundreds of novelists tell their stories without much exhaustion of body or soul; but to Dickens the writing of a romance was a very serious affair, involving an expenditure of physical and mental vitality, of which fluent narrators of pleasing tales, superficial both in incident and character, have no conception. The compensation is that one of Dickens's romances outvalues a hundred of theirs, and that he is the more appreciated and enjoyed the more he is *re*read. The advantage which the man of genius thus obtains is shown in the permanency of his works, outliving, as they do, all books which make no call on the interior sources and springs of spiritual life.[92]

While sounding notes similar to Lewes's argument that Dickens's extravagant imagination was unhealthy, Whipple's appreciation reasserts a Romantic aesthetic centered on self-sacrificing artistic genius as an appropriate mode for a general readership to appreciate Dickens. For Whipple, it is this very expenditure of energy, sacrificial in nature, that ensures Dickens's permanence, while other popular authors of his day are "hardly remembered by a reader of the present generation."[93] Incurring the kind of indebtedness that the living owe to the dead, the modern reader also accesses the author's canonical image epitaphically as part of the virtual "Shadowy World" emitted by Dickens's imagination and accessible through the text. Whipple even alludes to the possibility that such "expenditures" of Dickens's imagination killed him in the end. In "compensation" for the author's sacrifice of "vitality," much as the evangelical model of pious reading for conversion instructed, the late nineteenth-century reader can experience Dickens's salvific gift of "serious" engagement with his readership *by rereading*, thus returning his debt for the dead author's imaginative expenditure of "vitality" in the form of an apostrophe, an internal tribute drawn from the reader's own "interior sources and springs of spiritual life."[94] Whipple's formulation of the literary classic's influence on the life of the educated American reader is also akin to the way Henry

Mayhew in his 1842 educational treatise assimilates literary reading as a virtually sacramental communion with the thoughts of dead authors with the unifying cultural effects of new technologies of mass communication.[95]

The "literary classic" edition also updates and standardizes the pleasures of memory for common readers who need some coaching on how to "appreciate" and "enjoy" literature. One commentator on Whipple's critical introductions and literary histories reports that they "satisfied conveniently and effectively the general desire for information, and . . . doubtless furnished opinions ready-made for many ingenuous readers who did not discriminate nicely between what they thought and what they remembered."[96] When read outside the classroom, introductions to literary classics can insert authoritative "furnished opinions" between readers' remembered associations and their understanding of the text on literary grounds, thus differentiating the critical from the personal meanings of literature.[97]Such edited editions of literary classics suggest that the nineteenth-century popular forms of appreciation associated with Dickens's early works were transformed into what Janice A. Radway has analyzed in detail as the protocols of "middlebrow reading," embodied, for example, in the selection criteria of the Book-of-the-Month Club, founded in 1926: "What made the [reading] experience most profoundly transformative was the act of experiencing something with greater force and fervor than one might be permitted in ordinary daily life. Accordingly the judges sought out books that would enable their readers to identify passionately with either fictional or historical characters, just as they promoted writers who could capture the attentions of their readers and prompt them to respond intensely to the peculiarities of the author's vision. A sense of absorption or connection, I think, was the state to be achieved through middlebrow reading."[98] In contrast to the social epistemology that, I have argued, Dickens's serial fiction conveyed as a form of social connection with other members of the Victorian reading audience, the "middlebrow" response, according to Radway, constituted an "individualist personalism" providing forms of social connection through reading specific to the highly differentiated social world of the mid-twentieth-century professional-managerial class. Such "personalism also functioned to counter the singularity of individuals and to meliorate their separation from one another by insisting always on their capacity for identification."[99] Identification with books and participation in a national "book club" that consisted of a process of editorial selection, then, becomes the twentieth-century American reader's version of that feeling of friendship for the author, his characters, and other readers that Dickens's celebrity authorship transacted for his Victorian readers.

By the first decade of the twentieth century, Dickens, along with many other "classic" authors, had also become a subject of academic study in colleges and universities in both Britain and the United States. College-level textbooks from this era, such as the 1908 Booklovers Edition of *The Works of Charles Dickens*, a two-volume series published by the University Society of New York, offer an increasing bulk of scholarly apparatus. Resembling a present-day Norton Critical Edition, the text includes a "Life of Dickens" section consisting of pieces by Forster, Mamie Dickens, and A. W. Ward, along with a series of critical introductions and contemporary and nineteenth-century reviews of the novel accompanied by textual notes. Here the novice academic reader finds the materials for a scholarly, contextualized understanding of Dickens's work in place of the "ready-made" responses proffered to the middle-brow reader by the editors of the "literary classic." Like the disciplinary consolidation of English literary studies, the canonization of Dickens's novels in British universities seems to have taken place later than in the United States, and in a more piecemeal fashion, depending upon the type of institution. Adoption of works by Dickens and other Victorian writers into higher education English curricula may well have occurred first in Britain in the teacher training schools and colleges geared toward working- and middle-class students. A 1906 issue of the *Education Outlook*, a professional journal for teachers, includes an advertisement for Black's School Editions of *Barnaby Rudge* and *A Tale of Two Cities*, both edited by the head mistress of Braintree Pupil-Teachers Centre and costing two shillings, sixpence, including "ample introductions, brief notes. Good type."[100] Such textbooks remind us that English literature was from the beginning also a subject for training working-class teachers.

Other organizations besides schools played a role in institutionalizing Dickens's authorship in the early decades of the twentieth century. In 1902 the Dickens Fellowship was founded in London as "a worldwide association of people who share an interest in the life and works of Charles Dickens," with the initiation of its affiliated journal, the *Dickensian*, following in 1905. The Fellowship's objectives were " 'to knit together in a common bond of friendship lovers of the great master of humour and pathos, Charles Dickens,' to spread the love of humanity, to campaign against those 'social evils' that most concerned Dickens, and 'to assist in the preservation and purchase of buildings and objects associated with his name or mentioned in his works.' "[101] The Fellowship self-consciously constructs continuities with the terminology of positive Victorian responses to Dickens, including the appeal to the "common bond of friendship" forged among readers by Dickens's works and its humanitarian ethos, combined with its more focused commitment to those causes singled out for attention by Dickens, all tied up with a new project of preserving Dickens as a monument of world cultural heritage.[102] The Dickens Fellowship thus seems to have preserved the pleasures of memory as an organizational rationale for the collective self-identification and even possible social activism of Dickens's modern readership.

Noting that Dickens's works went out of copyright in 1921, fifty years after Dickens's death, under the 1911 British Copyright Act, Paul K. Saint-Amour analyzes James Joyce's parodic "near-verbatim" lifting of material from *David Copperfield* in chapter 14 (the "Oxen of the Sun" episode) of *Ulysses* (1922) as a move that "tips its hat thematically to the birth of a literary corpus into the public domain with the termination of copyright, the author's second death."[103] Fortunately for at least some dead authors like Dickens, the curriculum sustains the afterlife of authorship within the public domain, as if the reader approaching a literary classic were entering simultaneously into a mausoleum, museum, archive, and auditorium, all echoing with past students' and readers' many voices and memories.

Dickensian School Culture and the Exclusion of the Serial

This chapter's history of Dickens's canonization in Britain and the United States from 1870 to 1920 uncovers another of those critical feedback loops with which I began this study. Like the mirroring effect between Dickens's mind and his works posited by early Victorian reviewers and approved by Forster's biography in the 1870s, Dickens as a cultural institution seems to realize in specific ways the project of democratic cultural politics that I have been tracing in parallel through Dickens's novels, his competition with evangelical propagandizing, and his performance of celebrity authorship. The school Dickens and the historical Dickens are competing historical constructions based on very similar evidence of Dickens's popular reception. Dickens's early novels' seeming prescience about their curricular destiny—their pre-programming as if specifically for school use because of the role didactic fiction played in shaping the Victorian market in popular serial fiction—makes the school Dickens appear to be the historical Dickens's own creation. The extent of overlap between these two versions of Dickens, therefore, must become one of the methodologically self-conscious findings of this book.

In identifying the major elements of the historical Dickens's cultural politics, I have argued that this project entailed legitimizing the social value of popular literature and implementing the growing cultural influence of his celebrity authorship toward the ends of humanitarian public service and universal education. Dickens's serial novels develop a new pedagogical rationale for the moral influence of fiction based on egalitarian associationist psychological principles, which permit a blending of reading and experience in the reader's memory. Memory functions almost technologically, I have shown, as a medium within the new forms of reception that take shape in response to, and then elicit, the publication of serial fiction. Targeting the apparently hypocritical, self-serving economic logic of salvation offered to readers of evangelical didactic fiction, Dickens's early novels entered into competition with the evangelical movement's tactics of mass publication and explicit propagandizing of newly literate readers. In this way, I have argued, Dickens's authorship shaped the new reading audience for serial fiction as a constituency independent of party, school, or sect, to be mobilized for grassroots activism in solving urgent social problems associated with poverty. Moreover, this new mass constituency of readers could develop into a self-aware body of democratic citizens if their attachment to the celebrity author and his works could be channeled into a sense of greater solidarity of concern across class lines, without ignoring or homogenizing evident class differences.

The school Dickens seems to assimilate this cultural politics wholesale, not in the extra-institutional and independent form that Dickens himself insisted on, but rather as an accomplished fact proved by Dickens's international popularity and the massive sales figures of his books. The humanitarian rationale that the historical Dickens attempted to substitute for evangelical incentives toward pious reading now authorizes the school Dickens's canonical image as a defender of the poor, inculcated within the curriculum as a personification of a "well-wishing" sensibility for youth that also serves as a qualification for adult political participation. The positioning of the historical Dickens's cultural politics in opposition to evangelical cultural politics, however, disappears from view within the classroom. The school system also effectively subsumes and standardizes the independent and heterogeneous constituency of readers that the historical Dickens mobilized through his writing as outside the political system *because this independent readership was at that point lacking the coordination of a universal system of education.*

The classroom space also restages the transitional cognitive and imaginative space between reading and thinking posited by associationist psychology and Dickens's serial fiction—the undifferentiated mental space and ranging activity of parallel processes of memory, imagination, and thinking that Eliot and Lewes attempted to differentiate qualitatively into the diverging but cognate disciplines of literature and scientific psychology. The English curriculum reshapes the associationist pedagogical analogy between experience and reading toward a new technique of citizen formation involving the identification of literature and literary reading with civic principles of equality and political participation anchored in the student's personal experiences. This transaction between reading and experience must now take place in the national or state public school system for the very reason that its function as a gateway to political participation was still not fully accessible to all persons within the respective nation-states, the British Empire, or the United States' overseas territories in the early twentieth century. Thus the historical Dickens's pointed nonpartisanship also seems to provide a model for the generic nonpartisanship required as the basis for the school-child's formal training to exercise citizenship, necessarily presumed by the public schools as "prior" to the adoption of any political affiliation and as suspending particular cultural identities attached to ethnic, racial, or religious differences. In the process, however, the historical Dickens's external stance of institutional critique finds no role in the early-twentieth-century English curriculum but will reemerge after the social activism of the 1960s.

I have noticed that the school canonizes Dickens's anti-didacticism as the new democratic didacticism, so that during the period from 1870 to 1900 his early works are most commonly selected for young readers.[104] The historical Dickens's criticisms of the state's sponsorship of Victorian schooling as a limited means of social advancement and his exploration of what culture would look like if the poor gained greater access to education, but also if their everyday inventiveness were included in the wider sphere of democratic art, also fall outside of school culture because the democratic classroom of the early twentieth century claims to have solved the problem of access by mandating universal education. It is precisely this claim that the school system as a vehicle of the state can provide an avenue of access to and inclusion of the masses within democratic culture that *Our Mutual Friend* directly contests. Viewed not just in pedagogical terms but also as a nascent rationale for a public system of education, the historical Dickens's cultural politics attempted to shape the goals of that education system as explicitly inclusive and democratic in advance of its eventual appearance.

The case of Dickens also suggests that such an auto-canonizing effect may in fact be present in any work of literature—may in fact help to define a piece of writing as literary—insofar as it projects to posterity through prosopopoeia the task of perpetuating the dead author's fame. If the historical Dickens appears complicit, in advance, with the dehistoricizing trajectory of the school Dickens's institutionalization, Dickens's novels also provide an antidote to this effect in the forms of epitaphic reading and the educational pleasures of memory they afford as remnants of early Victorian reception. But if the school Dickens also emerges in relation to the historical Dickens in ways similar to Sairy Gamp's creation of Mrs. Harris—the figment of a figment, the school's standardized personification of a Victorian authorial persona—on what terms does it make sense to differentiate between these levels of personification and historical reconstruction, whether by academic criticism or within the curriculum? Discovering the school Dickens should not lend a retroactive effect of originality to the historical Dickens by implying that it might be possible to avoid the curriculum's reliance on personification or deracination altogether.

In order to step outside this methodological feedback loop in which I seem to have become entangled before reentering it willingly, I want to point out that it was precisely the genre of popular Victorian serial fiction that the English literature curriculum did *not* assimilate. Reading a novel in multiple parts does not lend itself to the syllabus's dominant historical coverage model. It is in precisely such generic terms, then, that we can distinguish between the school Dickens and the historical Dickens as both representing fully historical versions of modern authorship and reading with different implications for learning to read literature. While the school Dickens personifies the institution of literature within the school curriculum and academic literary criticism, the historical Dickens lives on outside the school, perhaps less recognizably but more unexpectedly, in the proliferation of twentieth- and twenty-first-century popular serial genres, such as comic books, dime novels, radio, television sitcoms, cinema sequels, fan fiction, and hypertexts.[105] The serial medium of Dickens's novels and their reception resisted assimilation into early-twentieth-century school culture simply because of an inconvenient format, and perhaps also because of the association of serial genres with popular culture. What persists, then, of the historical Dickens, despite the early objections of Eliot and Lewes, are the perennially contemporary and fresh pleasures of memory—the psychological and generic forms of popularity, celebrity, and popular reception—associated with serialization.

Dickens's Laughter

A further complication within the emerging twentieth-century division between secondary school and college-level literature curricula, or academic
and lay reading, emerges, however, when we look at several critical recon-
siderations of Dickens and his work dating between 1900 and 1970 that represent the personal significance for a writer of a memory of reading
Dickens's novels in childhood. Unlike Whipple's middle-brow readers,
who should discharge their cultural debt to Dickens through rereading, serious modern writers and academic critics must *avoid* tainting their early associations by rereading Dickens. Despite his criticisms in 1865 of *Our Mutual
Friend*'s "lifeless, forced, mechanical" characters,[106] in an autobiographical
text of 1913, Henry James describes the impossibility of approaching Dickens with any critical equanimity:

> He did too much for us surely ever to leave us free—free of judgment, free
> of reaction, even should we care to be, which heaven forbid: he laid his hand
> on us in a way to undermine as in no other case the power of detached
> appraisement. . . . His own taste is easily impugned, but he entered so early
> into the blood and bone of our intelligence that it always remained better
> than the taste of overhauling him. When I take him up to-day and find
> myself holding off, I simply stop: not holding off, that is, but holding on,
> and from the very fear to do so; which sounds, I recognise, like perusal, like
> renewal, of the scantest. I don't renew, I wouldn't renew for the world;
> wouldn't, that is, with one's treasure so hoarded in the dusty chamber of
> youth, let in the intellectual air. Happy the house of life in which such
> chambers still hold out, even with the draught of the intellect whistling
> through its passages. We were practically contemporary, contemporary with
> the issues, the fluttering monthly numbers—that was the point; it made for
> us a good fortune, constituted for us in itself romance, on which nothing, to
> the end, succeeds in laying its hands.

James goes on to describe his childhood reading of *David Copperfield* after
the hours when his light should have been put out, when he couldn't keep
quiet because of "the strain of the Murdstones and I broke into the sobs of
sympathy that disclosed my subterfuge."[107] Dickens *can't be reread* in any
proper way by the adult James because his image must not be threatened by
the "intellectual draught" of critique, lest those childhood memories of
reading be swept away as well, and the childhood self with which they are
intimately connected brought into the skeptical light of adult judgment.

But this is not the only reason for James's reluctance to "renew" his contact with Dickens's works—perhaps risking the sacramental sense that Dickens "laid his hand" on the next generation of writers by laying his own critical hands, in return, unkindly, on Dickens. There are also debts of literary intelligence and a certain shared taste owed to Dickens that partake of that "good fortune" and "romance" associated with the sense of contemporaneity created by the serial medium, those "fluttering monthly numbers" and that world where one's participation in a collective culture of periodical reading was palpable: "For these appearances, these strong time-marks in such stretches of production as that of Dickens, that of Thackeray, that of George Eliot, had in the first place simply a genial weight and force, a direct importance, and in the second a command of the permeable air and the collective sensibility, with which nothing since has begun to deserve comparison." James attributes much of that "genial weight" to the high intellectual tone of what he calls "the more sovereign periodical appearances," but we need to remember that by including Dickens's novels in parts in this broader phenomenon of serial publication, James also incorporates their broad-based readership in the "permeable air" of that moment and thus reveals his own participation in the collective Victorian reading audience.[108]

James's recollections separate themselves from the historical crowd of such memories of childhood reading, however, through his felt privilege of having met Dickens in person, in Boston in 1867 at the age of twenty-four, when he experienced the profoundly inaugural and transformative effect of Dickens's authorial celebrity: "How tremendously it had been laid upon young persons of our generation to feel Dickens, down to the soles of our shoes, no more modern instance that I might try to muster would give, I think, the least measure of; I can imagine no actual young person of my then age, and however like myself, so ineffably agitated, so mystically moved, in the presence of the exhibited idol of the mind who should be in that character at all conceivably 'like' the author of *Pickwick* and *Copperfield*." Dickens is unequalled, for James, in "the long, the purely 'Victorian' pressure of that obligation" that his influence created.[109] Dickens was *the* world-famous author, and, at that historical moment, no other modern version "conceivably" more "moving" could be imagined. For someone who met Dickens, James says very little about him, focusing instead on the transfer of Dickens's aura within his own emotions. James's reluctance to revisit Dickens's novels later in life, then, also reflects the impossibility of discharging the debt of that shared "good fortune" that Dickens's success brought to the whole enterprise of modern literature.

Despite James's historical closeness to Dickens, his physical proximity even, the "idol of the mind" that he created through his reading, when it appeared in front of him, was less real than his own memories of reading. In other words, as much as James knows himself to be an elite critic and preeminent practitioner of a form of modern fiction "beyond" Dickens's Victorian taste and artistic capacities, he still participates in the pleasures of memory that have been, by this time, associated with childhood reading and the school subject of English. Because Dickens's authorial image has come to represent literature's shaping influence on human development from youth to adulthood, James implies that it is acceptable to cherish memories of reading Dickens as part of one's identity, both as an individual and as a fellow novelist, as long as they do not become confused with his own operative critical and aesthetic criteria for modern literary writing.

Like James's commemoration, recollections of reading Dickens by George Gissing, George Orwell, and F. R. Leavis also blend definitions of professional literary criticism with the pleasures of nonacademic reading associated with childhood. In a 1901 essay titled "Dickens in Memory," Gissing recollects "finger[ing] the pages" of a "thin, green" number part of *Our Mutual Friend* as a child, and handling a "bound volume" of *Little Dorrit* (1855–57) while focusing primarily on the illustrations. Naming *The Old Curiosity Shop* as "the first real, substantial book" that he "read through," Gissing admits that while "Dickens's sentiment, . . . may distress the mature mind of our later day, [it] is not unwholesome, and, at all events in this story, addresses itself naturally enough to feelings unsubdued by criticism." Like James, Gissing seems to imply that a mature view of Dickens's work must inevitably be critical, threatening to draw one's childish love for Dickens into its wake. As a young writer, however, Gissing did use Dickens's novels as a guide to London, while he also relied on Forster's biography to teach himself how to emulate Dickens's "regular" "punctual" practice as "a man of method" and to cope with the disappointment of rejection letters from editors. His goal was "not to imitate Dickens as a novelist, but to follow afar off his example as a worker. From this point of view, the debt I owe him is incalculable. Among the best of my memories are those moments under a lowering sky when I sought light in the pages of his biographer, and rarely sought in vain."[110] Gissing remains silent about any inspiration that he may have derived from Dickens's art but acknowledges Dickens's career as his model in professional authorship. Like James, he seems to cloister the feelings associated with memories of this personal recourse to Dickens, keeping them separate from both a critical assessment of Dickens's fiction and from his own writing and aesthetic values.

I can now add a more contemporary context for George Orwell's estimation of Dickens's influence that I discussed in Chapter 2. In contrast to Gissing, Orwell is frank about his distaste for the school Dickens, "ladled down everyone's throat in childhood," and skeptical about the mere legitimacy of Dickens's image as an English cultural institution: "And then the thought arises, when I say I like Dickens, do I simply mean that I like thinking about my childhood? Is Dickens merely an institution?"[111] Seeing the implications of the relationship that I have been investigating between the historical Dickens and the school Dickens, Orwell answers this question in 1939 once again through prosopopoeia, summoning up Dickens's Victorian persona in the reader's mind: "He is laughing, with a touch of anger in his laughter, but no triumph, no malignity. It is the face of a man . . . who is *generously angry*—in other words, of a nineteenth-century liberal, a free intelligence, a type hated with equal hatred by all the smelly little orthodoxies which are now contending for our souls."[112] Orwell's version of Dickens's laughter seems positioned to contend directly with the school Dickens as national heritage and humanitarian vehicle of citizenship training constructed by the textbook. Orwell's image of Dickens's "free intelligence" also updates the popular pleasures of memory and associationist freedom of thought that underpin Dickens's novelistic epistemology and pedagogy. Rather than rendering Dickens a sacred relic, Orwell makes a renewed claim to his democratic cultural politics by elaborating the social, aesthetic, and political implications of his own memories of reading Dickens's novels.

In a move now familiar to us, F. R. Leavis begins *Dickens the Novelist*, a revisionist 1970 book written with Q. D. Leavis, by admitting his "resistances and reluctances" in undertaking to reread *Dombey and Son*: "The book was vividly in my mind; I had heard it read out, and read admirably, by my father, for family reading was still an institution in those days, and Dickens of course was before all others the classic for such use." Such family reading, however, causes Dickens "a consequent disadvantage in one's later experience," unlike Shakespeare, who "could never be thought of as a writer qualified for fullest appreciation in one's less mature and sophisticated days." But Dickens could not easily be reread, Leavis explains, not only for lack of time but also because "one remembered Dickens as a classic, it was perhaps on the whole best to leave, piously and affectionately, to the memory and associations of the early acquaintance. When one dipped one found very readily the kind of thing one had recalled, though divested now, where some of the most cherished manifestations of the Dickensian genius were concerned, of some of the magic. And one could too easily light on places where the wonderful vitality clearly ran too much to repetitiveness or to the cheapnesses and banalities of Victorian popular art."[113] Again, the academic critic must keep at arm's length certain aesthetically unreliable early Victorian qualities of Dickens's novels—their sentimentality, "cheapness," popularity, and "magic"—while still expressing a willingness to indulge in a certain nostalgia about childhood reading, and making an effort to recuperate that tarnished reputation of "Victorian popular art" for the serious business of literary criticism. Nevertheless, the pleasures of memory instigate Leavis's ultimately admiring critical reconsideration of Dickens's art as a novelist, even though, after the thorough discrediting by Eliot, Lewes, and subsequent sophisticated critics, such pleasures do not seem to merit critical reflection.

I conclude this account of critical strategies for balancing serious academic versus "uncritical" popular modes of reception surrounding Dickens's canonical image by backtracking a bit in time to G. K. Chesterton's 1906 critical biography, *Charles Dickens*, a homage to Dickens's novels that stands out as a parting but also particularly penetrating reassessment of Dickens's cultural politics. Chesterton's take on Dickens is illuminating because he sidesteps both Lewes's critique of Dickens's retrograde psychology and hallucinatory art and the school's adoption of the generically Christian and humanitarian Dickens, even as he grasps the historical rationales behind both. Chesterton begins by indicating his own awareness of the critical commonplace that consigns Dickens's novels to childhood reading, followed by mature admiration from afar: "He is treated as a classic; that is, as a king who may now be deserted, but who cannot now be dethroned" (3). Chesterton's often humorous formulations, constructed on the model of a chiasmus, closely and self-consciously track the critical circle or associationist feedback loop that I have been tracing between Dickens's mind and the effects of his works, as well as the seeming collusion between the school Dickens and the historical Dickens: "A definite school regarded Dickens as a great man from the first days of his fame: Dickens certainly belonged to this school."[114] This self-canonizing self-attribution of greatness was not a conceit but arose from an attitude that Chesterton attributes to the early-nineteenth-century "Dickens Period" as an "age under the shadow of the French Revolution" (5) whose "main idea was the idea of human equality" (8). The "humanitarianism" of this age was both "rough and rowdy" but "addressed toward encouraging the greatness in everyone" (7–8). Confessing his identity as a member of the Liberal party (12) while labeling Dickens a "good Radical" (226), Chesterton nevertheless chides the Liberals of his day for waiting for another great man like Gladstone instead of looking in Dickensian democratic fashion beyond the Carlylean ideology of "great men": "Every man was waiting for a leader. Every man ought to be waiting for a chance to lead" (12).

Chesterton brilliantly sums up Dickens's contestation of evangelicalism in one sentence: "Christianity said that any man could be a saint if he chose; democracy, that any man could be a citizen if he chose" (13–14). Just as happens implicitly in the English literature textbooks, religion overtly for Chesterton becomes subordinate to democracy, which in turn becomes the unifying explanation of Dickens's life and art: "It is useless for us to attempt to imagine Dickens and his life unless we are able at least to imagine this old atmosphere of a democratic optimism—a confidence in common men" (15). Summing up the two waves of critical reaction against Dickens represented by "realists" (with whom we may include Eliot and Lewes) who found his characters impossible, and followed by the fin-de-siècle "decadents," who conversely admired his exaggeration but concluded that "Dickens exaggerated the wrong thing" by constantly inflating the feeling of joy instead of melancholy, Chesterton observes that "few now walk far enough along the street of Dickens to find a place where the cockney villas grow so comic that they become poetical" (20). Yet, Chesterton insists, "this braver world of his will certainly return; for I believe that it is bound up with realities, like morning and the spring" (22). So the jaded modernist reader of Chesterton's life of Dickens should imagine, if only for a moment, his neo-Dantean world transformed back into Dickens's revolutionary comic world: "If democracy has disappointed you, do not think of it as a burst bubble, but at least as a broken heart, an old love-affair. . . . Surrender the very flower of your culture; give up the very jewel of your pride; abandon hopelessness, all ye who enter here" (223). There is something vaguely juvenile and embarrassing for the sophisticated critic about an avowed love for popular democracy, even in the guise of Dickens's genius, so that Chesterton has to brazen it out rhetorically against the modernist skepticism that he anticipates.

Chesterton concedes to critics like George Eliot that "it hardly cost [Dickens] any artistic pang to make out human beings as much happier than they are" (271). But he follows with an extended defense of Dickens as a follower of Christ (279), a singularly effective humanitarian reformer relying on a "mystical contradiction" (273) or "central paradox" (274): "If we are to save the oppressed, we must have two apparently antagonistic emotions in us at the same time. We must think the oppressed man intensely miserable, and at the same time, intensely attractive and important. We must insist with violence upon his degradation; we must insist with the same violence upon his dignity. For if we relax by one inch the one assertion, men will say he does not need saving. And if we relax by one inch the other assertion, men will say he is not worth saving" (273). As if defending Dickens directly against Eliot's charges, Chesterton asserts that a certain idealization of the oppressed is rhetorically necessary to anyone who adopts the humanitarian cause of social justice. Chesterton systematically associates the democratic Dickens with the resonant principles of the French Declaration of the Rights of Man and Citizen (1789): dignity, humanity, brotherhood. Thus Chesterton's account situates Dickens historically only to universalize once again his particular kind of democratic humanitarianism as the continued possibility not so much of a political revolution but of a cultural one, a lasting reformation of sensibility that could outlive limited critical, literary, and even political fashions.

As an antidote, then, to the embarrassment that modern critics and sophisticated readers may feel toward the "vulgar optimism" commonly associated with Dickens's democratic sentiments, Chesterton (like Orwell, who must have read his predecessor's text closely) provides his own reading lesson, conjuring up an image of both Dickens's Englishness and his satirical democratic laughter:

> No one but an Englishman could have filled his books at once with a furious caricature and with a positively furious kindness. In more central countries, full of cruel memories of political change, caricature is always inhumane. No one but an Englishman could have described the democracy as consisting of free men, but yet of funny men. In other countries where a democratic issue has been more bitterly fought, it is felt that unless you describe a man as dignified you are describing him as a slave. This is the only final greatness of a man; that he does for all the world what all the world cannot do for itself. Dickens, I believe, did it. (299)

According to Chesterton, Dickens's unique cultural contribution to the world was to make democracy funny, thus desacralizing it and rendering it once again the unruly rule of the poor, or the *demos*, as the ancients defined it.[115] For Chesterton, the Rights of Man, if they are to remain current, can be extended only through laughter, because democracy must be hopeful and lighthearted rather than militant, or it loses its egalitarian identity. We recognize Chesterton's mobilization of cultural nationalism in attaching to Dickens England's "special status" as having "escaped" a popular revolution in the nineteenth century; this idealized image of British uniqueness would collapse after World War I. But Chesterton also provides a rationale for blending rather than differentiating the historical and the school versions of Dickens: if the historical Dickens personifies an egalitarian and humane, and even radical, democracy, then his self-critical "laughter" also infects the uses of the school Dickens for citizen-building. Within school culture, Dickens's democratic laughter may enact a self-subverting, anti-institutional political potential. Yet Chesterton's celebration of Dickens's ability to laugh at democracy also reveals itself as potentially a more subtle and sophisticated version of the school Dickens, in associating Dickens's uniquely "humane" caricatures with English political history and institutions.

In his own satirical turn, Chesterton concludes his study by proposing that the "insane humour" and "beatific buffoonery" represented by Mrs. Sapsea's "wild epitaph" (written by Mr. Sapsea) from *The Mystery of Edwin Drood* (1870) should stand in for "the serious epitaph of Dickens" (243). Mrs. Sapsea's tombstone reads as follows (with variable capitalization roughly preserved):

ETHELINDA
Reverential Wife of
MR THOMAS SAPSEA,
AUCTIONEER, VALUER, ESTATE AGENT, &c.,
OF THIS CITY,
Whose Knowledge of the World,
Though somewhat extensive,
Never brought him acquainted with
A SPIRIT
More capable of
LOOKING UP TO HIM.
STRANGER, PAUSE
And ask thyself the Question.
CANST THOU DO LIKEWISE
If Not,
WITH A BLUSH RETIRE.[116]

Mrs. Sapsea's epitaph praising a wife's (potentially hypocritical) subservience in fact memorializes Mr. Sapsea's own conceit in rendering her gravestone into his own monument. Taking such an epitaph both comically and seriously in turn as Dickens's own, as Chesterton recommends, requires recognizing it as the auto-satire planted in Dickens's novels that undercuts their serious anti-didactic lessons. If we venerate Dickens, we step back into the feedback loop within which we risk the self-memorialization and conceit of Mr. Sapsea. Reading Mrs. Sapsea's epitaph in this way, we realize that the school Dickens has missed the joke unleashed proactively in Dickens's novels against just such an eventuality as the English literature curriculum. Like Dickens's performances of Sairy Gamp performing Mrs. Harris, Mrs. Sapsea's epitaph also figures Dickens's originality as both self-authorizing and self-subverting by initiating the series of substitutions interchanging the reader of the epitaph/novel, with Mr. Sapsea as author, with Mrs. Sapsea as the character created to self-reflexively represent and mock the "original" invention of the novelist. Thus the epitaph provides another instance of Dickens's novelistic and authorial uses of prosopopoeia, but one that spoofs the persona of the canonical author as the self-promoting representative of the English literature curriculum with its obligatory, self-congratulating invocations of a national literary tradition.

The association of reading literature with the history of popular democracy, both in what I have characterized as the historical Dickens's cultural politics and in the literature curriculum's reading lessons in humanitarian citizenship represented by the school Dickens, calls into question the divisions between academic and popular practices of reading that began to govern the distinctions of publishers, critics, and teachers between sophisticated and uncritical reading audiences in the final decades of the nineteenth century and the early decades of the twentieth. As an irreverent personification of democratic literature and its historical reception, the anti-canonical image of Dickens's laughter takes on its critical role in unmasking such distinctions between high and low culture as hypocritical. Bearing the brunt of this self-reflexive laughter, we critics in turn can readily admit that academic reading has always conjured up the popular pleasures of memory as a precursor form of reception in the evolution of specialized literary analysis, and one that may be especially closely related to those critical approaches that claim popular anti-establishment intellectual credentials. In addition, the pleasures of memory form a positive motive shared between common readers and professional scholars for the public support of the arts as cultural and national institutions within modern societies.

The historical Dickens and the school Dickens turn out to be two sides of one canonical emblem of authorship that personifies the rare, long-lasting, and highly lucrative capacity of Dickens's work to bridge elite and popular tastes across local, national, and global reading audiences.[117] Do the school Dickens and the historical Dickens both appear, then, as equally historically valid accounts of learning to read with Charles Dickens, especially given the doubly motivated (both authorizing and subversive) prosopopoeia of Dickens's laughter at the epitaphic ambitions of the modern author, and at epitaphic reading as the outcome of the literary curriculum? Quoting a favorite author, "We take the liberty of replying, Yes," and "with a blush retire."

Afterword

By paying attention to associationist theories of reception in Victorian literary criticism and pedagogical theory, my study has specified how the reading lessons provided by Dickens's serials could have contributed to the novel's central role, along with the newspaper, in constituting the nation as an imagined political community of readers, according to Benedict Anderson's influential formulation.[1] Dickens's serials signpost the "homogeneous, empty time" that for Anderson characterizes the reading nation, by inviting readers to associate individual and shared memories of his serial novels with their own experiences, and encouraging them to exercise preferences for specific books and characters.[2] This is not simply consumption but the active appropriation of culture that philosopher Michel de Certeau includes among the literate practices of everyday life.[3]

The collective epistemology of reading based on associationist principles that Dickens's novels elaborate also amounts, in effect, to a theory of the ideological reproduction of society, but one that allows for the possible interruption and rerouting of seemingly automatic and unconscious processes of internalization because of the regular, though sometimes fragile, logic of the parallel mental functions of learning, reading, remembering, and inventing that support them. From the perspective of the cultural history of reading, studying such historically specific theories of reading as associationism supplied to Victorian readers and critics permits a more detailed and reflexive approach than theories of ideology or interpellation have typically afforded to analyze specific cognitive and material transactions between new media and readers. Understanding the associationist conception of the serial memory as a *synthetic* and not simply retentive mental function within the context of the history of reading has also enabled me to pinpoint how a psychological theory intersected with the generic features of serial fiction and extended into a popular practice of reading as an exercise in social relation. Through this kind of correlation, therefore, it becomes possible to specify how a genre's or a particular literary work's self-definitions can cue without predetermining readers' memories and thus form a part of their preoccupations.

The methods of the history of reading can seem "associationist" in their turn to the extent that they pay attention to a similar meshing between the formal features of texts and readers' tastes and contingent encounters with print. Guglielmo Cavallo and Roger Chartier have recently outlined an approach to the history of reading that, by conjoining the methods of literary history and "a social history of the uses of writing," enables an analysis of not just "the constraints that limit the [reader's] frequenting of books" but also "the resources that can be mobilized by the reader's liberty": "This dialectic of constraint and invention implies a meeting place between a history of the conventions that regulate the hierarchy of genres and define the modalities and levels of discourse, on the one hand, and, on the other, a history of the schemes of perception and judgement inherent in each community of readers. One of the major objectives of the history of reading thus necessarily resides in identifying the fault lines that, over the long term, separate the readers or readings imagined, designated or targeted in specific works from the plural and successive publics those works actually had."[4] By focusing on the role of associationist theories of serial memory in this study of Victorian reading, I have emphasized the interplay between the reader's formal acquisition of literacy and his or her previous uses of language or contact with texts, as well as points of incoherence or overlapping among uses of literacy or strategies for gleaning meaning from a text that nineteenth-century readers acquired in different institutional contexts such as schools, or associated with different types of texts and media. Experience is a helpful technical term more generally within the history of reading and new media studies, I would argue, because it invites interrogation of the zones of indeterminacy between constraint and invention that reading often involves, permitting a more precise investigation of the cognitive and practical transitions between the format of texts and the reader's "schemes of perception." Experience, in effect, points to the intermediate or partial nature of historical "fault lines" between specific media and changing audiences.

For these equally methodological and historical reasons, I have been interested in the ways that reading and learning to read, as transitional practices meshing mind and world, register in subtly different ways as experience, particularly in the reading of serial fiction as a medium that encourages such transitioning. Serialization lends itself to investigating reading as a transitional practice across media, given its tendency toward suspension, repetition, anticipations, openness to interruption, and changes in format (such as advertising and illustration), and because of its generic frequency within new forms of mass publication. Modern and contemporary media such as radio, cinema, television, the Internet, and the World Wide Web have also remediated the seriality associated with Dickensian fiction for a mass audience. Fictional serials become particularly interesting for their encouragement of the reader's, writer's, viewer's, or fan's engagement with the intermittent and virtual bonds in memory between personal experience and representation across media. People tend to care about and retain associations with fictional characters and plots that have unfolded in serial formats over time; these meanings associated with serial media become embedded in recollections of other significant events, both individual and collective, not just because of their significance to the individual but because of their capacity for accruing a shared cultural relevance over time. This is probably one reason why many people still like to watch new television serials and revisit older "classics," despite the many alternative kinds of digital content that are available through the Internet but not yet so widely shared on a cultural basis.

In addition to the continuing development of serial media, the kind of independent and heterogeneous constituency of readers that Dickens's novels addressed and that his public readings manifested in person also seems to have reappeared at the beginning of the twenty-first century.[5] In the cultural afterlife of the early nineteenth century's print media breakthroughs, this new version of a Dickensian-style egalitarian popular reading audience manifests itself now as a digitally interfaced web of "netizens." Comically Dickensian, such a neologism and the creature it identifies combine the orchestrated freedom of human invention with a machine mechanism. According to media critic Mark Poster, "the netizen might be the formative figure in a new kind of political relation, one that shares allegiance to the nation with allegiance to the Internet and to the planetary political spaces it inaugurates."[6] Poster argues that global information technologies based in the "human-machine interface," because they are not controlled by nation-states and are multidirectional, may encourage "a new cultural practice of resignification."[7] As an inaugural instance of the spread into everyday life of modern communication technologies, the serial novel appears as a crucial early medium for the modern interface involving virtual communication and connectivity across mental and spatial distances. As it was possible to conceive mental associations and memories of reading in a Humean sense as forms of identity and social relation, now the human-machine interface projects virtual selves and relations instantaneously in digital form across continents and oceans—as if twenty-first-century technology had finally realized David Hartley's eighteenth-century image of coordinated mental communication among a random crowd of people, or Henry Mayhew's nineteenth-century affirmation that mass publishing and global transportation could allow people to "transfer our sensations, thoughts, and emotions, to others" across the globe.[8]

It is tempting to imagine that Charles Dickens would have welcomed the new possibilities for communication, public performance, and political affiliation beyond the nation-state that "netizenship" seems to promise. Much as Dickens wandered through the streets of Victorian London, purportedly scanning and recording scenes in his photographic memory, modern netizens wander obsessively through the world of digitized media, scanning and downloading digital content. Netizens may exercise mental freedom and freedom of speech across national borders—even under unfree political conditions—in multitudinous, spontaneous, and often unauthorized associations. In the midst of all this mental, physiological, commercial, and technological connectivity, a Dickensian democratic attitude of humorous and stringent self-satire remains vital (if not sufficient) to sustaining a generously critical perspective while safeguarding and extending the egalitarian potentials of global communication. As we encounter others' words and images posted and archived virtually in the World Wide Web (the latest version of Bacon's beehive of memory), modern "netizens" may also catch a glimpse of ourselves not only as technologically enhanced but as historical beings, still ranging, searching, and retracing our tracks across seemingly unlimited digital networks framed within the formally bounded space of a window—and, recognizing the continuities of our serial pleasures and desires to communicate with and even change the lives of distant others, we may, like *Pickwick*'s original readers, laugh out loud!

Notes

Preface

   1. Virginia Woolf, "The Common Reader," in *The Common Reader: First Series*, eBooks@Adelaide, http://ebooks.adelaide.edu.au/w/woolf/virginia/w91c (accessed June 12, 2010).

   2. "Charles Dickens. A Lecture by Professor Ward. Delivered in Manchester, 30th November, 1870," quoted in John Forster, *The Life of Charles Dickens*, ed. J. W. T. Ley (London: Cecil Palmer, 1928), 727. All quotations in this book preserve the spelling and emphases of the original text.

Introduction: Dickens and the Pleasures of Memory

   1. Benjamin Jowett, *Times*, June 20, 1870, in George H. Ford, *Dickens and His Readers: Aspects of Novel-Criticism since 1836* (Princeton, N.J.: Princeton University Press, 1955), 109. Jowett's election as master of Balliol College occurred on September 7, 1870 (my thanks to Anna Sander, archivist of Balliol College, for providing the exact date).

   2. Jowett also aligns Dickens with his own rational Christianity and critical views on ecclesiastical doctrines. See Peter Hinchliff and John Prest, "Jowett, Benjamin (1817–1893)," in *Oxford Dictionary of National Biography* (Oxford: Oxford University Press, 2004–10), http://www.oxforddnb.com/view/article/15143 (accessed December 1, 2008).

   3. On the translation of Dickens's novels into Chinese and the appropriation of his criticisms of Victorian society by Chinese writers critical of British and Western imperialism, see Eva Hung, "The Introduction of Dickens into China (1906–1960): A Case Study in Target Culture Reception," *Perspectives* 4, no. 1 (1996): 29–41. I am grateful to Lorraine Paterson for calling my attention to the reception of Dickens's novels in China.

   4. In keeping with the conventions of much scholarship on the evangelical movement in Britain, I will capitalize the appellation "Evangelical" when referring to Evangelical members of the established Church of England and use the lowercase "evangelical" to refer to the larger movement including Anglicans, Methodists, and other evangelically minded, proselytizing dissenting denominations. According to the same logic, I will refer to "dissenting" denominations and to persons as "Dissenters."

5. Mowbray Morris, "Charles Dickens," *Fortnightly Review,* December 1, 1882, xxxii, 762–79, in Philip Collins, ed., *Dickens: The Critical Heritage* (New York: Barnes & Noble, 1971), 602.

6. Hippolyte Taine, "Charles Dickens: Son talent et ses oeuvres," in Collins, *Dickens: The Critical Heritage,* 337–38.

7. Ibid., 339. Publication dates provided after the first reference to a Dickens novel indicate the time span of the original serial publication, either in parts or in a periodical.

8. John Forster, *The Life of Charles Dickens* (London: J. M. Dent, 1966), 2:263.

9. For recent collections focusing on new media studies, see Lisa Gitelman and Geoffrey B. Pingree, eds., *New Media, 1740–1915* (Cambridge, Mass.: MIT Press, 2003); Clifford Siskin and William Warner, eds., *This Is Enlightenment* (Chicago: University of Chicago Press, 2010); and David Thorburn and Henry Jenkins, eds., *Rethinking Media Change: The Aesthetics of Transition* (Cambridge, Mass.: MIT Press, 2003). For a seminal early study, see also Marshall McLuhan, *Understanding Media: The Extensions of Man* (New York: McGraw-Hill, 1964), and for a mechanism- and artist-centered view of the history of media, see Friedrich A. Kittler in *Discourse Networks 1800/1900,* trans. Michael Metteer with Chris Cullins (Stanford, Calif.: Stanford University Press, 1990), and *Gramophone, Film, Typewriter,* trans. Geoffrey Winthrop-Young and Michael Wutz (Stanford, Calif.: Stanford University Press, 1999).

10. Illuminating studies of Dickens's imagination and the critical reception of his work from which I have benefited include Rosemarie Bodenheimer, *Knowing Dickens* (Ithaca, N.Y.: Cornell University Press, 2007); Ford, *Dickens and His Readers*; Garrett Stewart, *Dickens and the Trials of Imagination* (Cambridge, Mass.: Harvard University Press, 1974); and Alexander Welsh, *The City of Dickens* (Oxford: Clarendon Press, 1971).

11. As Michel de Certeau points out in his study of literacy as a practice of everyday life, "To assume that [the public is moulded by the products imposed on it] is to misunderstand the act of 'consumption.' This misunderstanding assumes that 'assimilating' necessarily means 'becoming similar to' what one absorbs, and not 'making something similar' to what one is, making it one's own, appropriating or reappropriating it." *The Practice of Everyday Life,* trans. Steven Rendall (Berkeley: University of California Press, 1984), 166.

12. See John Guillory's critique of the common assumption among cultural theorists "that epistemological positions have a *necessary* relation to political positions." "The Sokal Affair and the History of Criticism," *Critical Inquiry* 28 (Winter 2002): 475.

13. For a brief account informed by Walter Benjamin's theories of how cultural history both reconstructs and transforms the past in relation to present concerns, see Jonathan Crary, *Techniques of the Observer: On Vision and Modernity in the Nineteenth Century* (Cambridge, Mass.: MIT Press, 1990), 6–7. Also pertinent to my approach is Roger Chartier's comment that cultural history "takes into account the specific nature of the field of cultural practices, which is not immediately congruent with

that of hierarchies and social divisions." *Cultural History: Between Practices and Representations*, translated by Lydia G. Cochrane (Ithaca, N.Y.: Cornell University Press, 1988), 14.

14. Two important early studies of Dickens's views on education and educational reform are Philip Collins, *Dickens and Education* (London: Macmillan, 1963), and John Manning, *Dickens on Education* (Toronto: University of Toronto Press, 1959). For a challenging analysis of Dickens's novelistic revisions of the languages of political economy, mathematics, and science toward a new theory of mimetic language, see John Schad, *The Reader in the Dickensian Mirrors: Some New Language* (London: Macmillan, 1992).

15. Elaine Hadley, *Living Liberalism: Practical Citizenship in Mid-Victorian Britain* (Chicago: University of Chicago Press, 2010), 44.

16. Olive Anderson, "The Janus Face of Mid-Nineteenth-Century English Radicalism: The Administrative Reform Association of 1855," *Victorian Studies* 8, no. 3 (1965): 232. This group of "successful business and professional men who prided themselves on their own modernity" directed their most pointed criticisms toward the mismanagement of ministries resulting from aristocratic monopoly of these functions. In addition, the group sought measures to broaden the electorate and guarantee the independence of members of Parliament by reducing the influence of party organizations and clubs, and of party agents (238). Michael Slater points out that Dickens's participation in the Administrative Reform Association was "the only time in his life that he ever joined a political movement," *Charles Dickens* (New Haven and London: Yale University Press), 390. This observation depends in part on how one defines a political movement, however, since Dickens also lent his support to the Eyre Defense Committee in 1866. See note 31.

17. Charles Dickens, speech to the Administrative Reform Association, June 27, 1855, in K. J. Fielding, ed., *The Speeches of Charles Dickens* (Oxford: Clarendon Press, 1960), 200–201.

18. Ibid., 207.

19. In the month following this meeting, Dickens began writing *Little Dorrit*, with its satirical attack on the nepotism and inefficient bureaucracy of the "Circumlocution Office." It would be an oversimplification simply to diagnose Dickens and Layard's position as indicative of a middle-class, meliorist liberal reformism with no real agenda for social or political change. Both Dickens's and Layard's formulations of the popular author's "true" political influence in fact sound quite close to the language of Edmond Beales's speech, in his role as president, at the inaugural meeting of the Reform League, formed in 1865 and representing the aspirations of the skilled working class to further extension of the franchise: "I verily believe that it is most unwise and most perilous to the best interests of England to perpetuate grossly unjust distinctions, and consequently dangerous animosities, amongst the different classes in the state, and that he is the truest and best friend of his country who seeks to put an end to these distinctions and animosities, and to weld all classes together by unity of interest into one harmonious whole. (*Applause.*) That harmony, that unity of interest which every patriot, every true statesman, every earnest Christian

ought to long for can never exist whilst forty-nine-fiftieth of the working classes and thousands of other English men are excluded from the franchise." In Catherine Hall, Keith McClelland, and Jane Rendall, *Defining the Victorian Nation: Class, Race, Gender and the British Reform Act of 1867* (Cambridge: Cambridge University Press, 2000), 95.

20. For my understanding of the mid-Victorian public sphere, I draw on Hadley, *Living Liberalism*; Hall, McClelland, and Rendall, *Defining the Victorian Nation*; and Mary Poovey, *Making a Social Body: British Cultural Formation, 1830–1864* (Chicago: University of Chicago Press, 1995).

21. In its inability to address poverty as a still-massive human problem of economic inequality, modern democracy as a social system is still an unfinished project. I have found philosopher Jacques Rancière's theories on poverty, politics, and democracy helpful in formulating this account of the democratic potentials of the Victorian reading audience. Rancière draws attention to the disdain for mass culture that has permitted certain intellectuals of both the Right and the Left to criticize democracy by equating it with the debased and unruly preferences of the masses: "The equation democracy = limitlessness = society, on which the denunciation of the 'crimes' of democracy is based, presupposes, then, a threefold operation: it is imperative, first, to reduce democracy to a form of society; second, to make this form of society identical to the reign of the egalitarian individual by grouping under the latter all sorts of disparate properties, everything from mass consumption to the claims of special minority rights, not to forget union battles; and finally, to charge 'mass individualist society,' henceforth identical to democracy, with pursuing the limitless growth that is inherent to the logic of the capitalist economy." *Hatred of Democracy*, trans. Steve Corcoran (London: Verso, 2006), 19–20. The tendentious identification of democracy with society itself also leads to "the firmly fixed identity between democratic man and the individual consumer" (23). Instead, for Rancière, democracy is "where politics begins . . . the drawing of lots, the democratic procedure by which a people of equals decides the distribution of places," and thus "the disjoining of entitlements to govern from any analogy between human convention and the order of nature" (40–41).

22. For a recent study of this trend, see Ian Haywood, *The Revolution in Popular Literature: Print, Politics and the People, 1790–1860* (Cambridge: Cambridge University Press, 2004).

23. George Eliot, "Leaves from a Note-Book," in *Essays of George Eliot*, ed. Thomas Pinney (New York: Columbia University Press, 1963), 440.

24. Charles Dickens, *The Letters of Charles Dickens*, ed. Madeline House, Graham Storey, and Kathleen Tillotson, Pilgrim Edition (Oxford: Clarendon Press, 1965–2002), 7:10. In an earlier letter of September 2, 1852, to his friend the philanthropist Angela Burdett-Coutts describing his attendance at a celebration of the opening of the Manchester Free Library "for the people," Dickens writes in similar terms of his authorial vocation of public service: "With that gallant people at my back—as they always are—I have a more fervent hope than ever, of setting right at last what is very wrong in my calling. I have the object so deeply at heart, and so

strongly feel the advantage I have in my present power in such matters (which involves a great duty) that I am in a desperate earnestness that I think I must produce something." Charles Dickens, *The Heart of Charles Dickens: As Revealed in His Letters to Angela Burdett-Coutts*, ed. Edgar Johnson (New York: Duell, Sloan and Pierce, 1952), 205. What is "very wrong in my calling" seems likely to be what Dickens refers to in the Birmingham speech as class exclusivity and patronage in the arts. For Dickens's Birmingham speech, see Presentation to Dickens and Banquet to Literature and Art: Birmingham, January 6, 1853, in Fielding, ed., *The Speeches of Charles Dickens*, 154–63.

25. For a detailed analysis of radical publications in the 1840s, with a particular focus on the work of Edward Lloyd and George W. M. Reynolds, see Haywood, *The Revolution in Popular Literature.*

26. Literary historian Sally Ledger has argued persuasively that "as an inheritor of the popular radical cultural networks of the early nineteenth century Dickens acted as a cultural bridge between, on the one hand, an older, eighteenth-century political conception of 'the People' and, on the other hand, a distinctly mid-nineteenth-century modern conception of a mass-market 'populace' that had been created by the rise of the commercial newspaper press during Dickens's formative years as a journalist and novelist. Moving between these twin conceptions of 'the People' (a political entity) and the (mass-market) 'populace' (a commercial entity), the extent of Dickens's attempt to politicize the latter was unrivalled in the second half of the nineteenth century." *Dickens and the Popular Radical Imagination* (Cambridge: Cambridge University Press, 2007), 2–3. Extending and modifying Ledger's argument in a more forward-looking way, I contend that for the audience of common readers envisioned by Dickens as "the People," novel reading could foster a new kind of cultural participation that was amenable to political affiliation but less overtly political than the forms of social solidarity geared toward extension of the franchise envisioned in early Victorian radicalism.

27. Trygve R. Tholfsen, "The Intellectual Origins of Mid-Victorian Stability," *Political Science Quarterly* 86, no. 1 (1971): 59.

28. On the cultural politics of political parties and associations during this period, and the subsequent organization of the two major Conservative and Liberal parties after 1867, see James Epstein, *In Practice: Studies in the Language and Culture of Popular Politics in Modern Britain* (Stanford, Calif.: Stanford University Press, 2003); Hadley, *Living Liberalism*; James Vernon, *Politics and the People: A Study in English Political Culture, c. 1815–1867* (Cambridge: Cambridge University Press, 1993); and John Belchem, *Class, Party and the Political System in Britain, 1867–1914* (Oxford: Basil Blackwell, 1990).

29. Elaine Hadley, *Melodramatic Tactics: Theatricalized Dissent in the English Marketplace, 1800–1885* (Stanford, Calif.: Stanford University Press, 1995); Ledger, *Dickens and the Popular Radical Imagination.* See also Peter Brooks, *The Melodramatic Imagination: Balzac, Henry James, Melodrama, and the Mode of Excess* (New Haven, Conn.: Yale University Press, 1976).

30. In their discussion of the history of new media, Lisa Gitelman and Geoffrey
B. Pingree note that "There is a moment, before the material means and the conceptual modes of new media have become fixed, when such media are not yet
accepted as natural, when their own meanings are in flux. At such a moment, we
might say that new media briefly acknowledge and question the mythic character
and the ritualized conventions of existing media, while they are themselves defined
within a perceptual and semiotic economy that they then help to transform" (*New
Media, 1740–1915*, xii). Historian Thomas L. Haskell has also posited that "new
technologies . . . supply us with new ways of acting at a distance and new ways of
influencing future events and thereby impose on us new occasions for the attribution of responsibility and guilt. In short, new techniques, or ways of intervening in
the course of events, can change the conventional limits within which we feel
responsible enough to act." "Capitalism and the Origins of the Humanitarian Sensibility, Part I," *American Historical Review* 90, no. 2 (1985): 356. Haskell makes this
point in the context of linking abolitionism with the rise of capitalism, arguing that
the accountability for promises and the long-range foresight accompanying capitalist
notions of contract fostered not only the historically new general acceptance of the
idea that slavery is morally reprehensible but also the specific sense of urgency that
dictated its abolition.

31. Humanitarian motives conceived as sources of political, social, and religious
activism, particularly in relation to the movements to abolish slavery and the slave
trade and to improve working conditions in mines and factories, gained significant
legitimacy and widespread public support in Britain in the 1830s and 1840s. But the
humanitarianism associated with abolitionism in particular suffered a loss of legitimacy and popularity, resulting in part from the rise of anthropological theories of
the hierarchy of the races during the 1850s and 1860s. Dickens himself was not
immune either to mid-Victorian racialist arguments or to racist sentiments, as evidenced in his 1853 *Household Words* essay "The Noble Savage," in Dickens, *Gone
Astray and Other Papers from "Household Words," 1851–59*, ed. Michael Slater, Dent
Uniform Edition of Dickens' Journalism (London: J. M. Dent, 1999), 141–48; his
inflammatory reaction to the Indian "Mutiny" of 1857; and his support for the pro-
Eyre forces in the controversy following Governor Edward Eyre's violent suppression of the uprising in Morant Bay, Jamaica, in 1865. In reference to Dickens's written responses to these events, see Grace Moore, "Swarmery and Bloodbaths: A
Reconsideration of Dickens on Class and Race in the 1860s," *Dickens Studies Annual*
31 (2002): 175–202. Moore argues that Dickens was better able to separate issues of
class and race in relation to colonial conflicts by the 1860s, thus showing greater
"moderation" in his views than Thomas Carlyle, for example. Nevertheless, from
an historical perspective on the limitations of Dickens's humanitarian claims, it
seems that he could have chosen to side with John Stuart Mill and Charles Darwin
in finding Eyre's recourse to martial law excessive and criminally liable, but he did
not. For histories of the Governor Eyre controversy see, Bernard Semmel, *Jamaican
Blood and Victorian Conscience: The Governor Eyre Controversy* (Boston: Houghton

Mifflin, 1963), and the more recent study by R. W. Kostal, *A Jurisprudence of Power: Victorian Empire and the Rule of Law* (Oxford: Oxford University Press, 2005).

32. Humanitarianism is not an unambiguously positive social ethic. Its history as a form of both independent philanthropic benevolence and of state-sponsored policy is tied up in the histories of the Atlantic slave trade, finance capitalism, European colonialism and imperialism, the international law of human rights, and decolonization. Important works investigating the nineteenth-century discourse of humanitarianism in these complex contexts include Ian Baucom, *Specters of the Atlantic: Finance Capital, Slavery, and the Philosophy of History* (Durham, N.C.: Duke University Press, 2005); David Brion Davis, *The Problem of Slavery in the Age of Revolution, 1770–1823* (New York: Oxford University Press, 1999); Adrian Desmond and James Moore, *Darwin's Sacred Cause: How a Hatred of Slavery Shaped Darwin's Views on Human Evolution* (Boston: Houghton Mifflin Harcourt, 2009); Catherine Hall, *Civilizing Subjects: Metropole and Colony in the English Imagination, 1830–1867* (Chicago: University of Chicago Press, 2002); Haskell, "Capitalism and the Origins of the Humanitarian Sensibility, Part I," and "Capitalism and the Origins of the Humanitarian Sensibility, Part II," *American Historical Review* 90, no. 3 (1985): 547–66; Douglas A. Lorimer, *Colour, Class, and the Victorians: English Attitudes to the Negro in the Mid–Nineteenth Century* (New York: Holmes & Meier, 1978); Nancy Stepan, *The Idea of Race in Science: Great Britain, 1800–1960* (London: Macmillan, 1982); and George W. Stocking Jr., *Victorian Anthropology* (New York: Free Press, 1987). For an overview, see also Patrick Brantlinger, "A Short History of (Imperial) Benevolence," in *Burden or Benefit: Imperial Benevolence and Its Legacies*, ed. Helen Gilbert and Chris Tiffin (Bloomington: Indiana University Press, 2008), 13–28.

33. Eugenio F. Biagini, "Introduction: Citizenship, Liberty and Community," in *Citizenship and Community: Liberals, Radicals and Collective Identities in the British Isles, 1865–1931*, ed. Eugenio F. Biagini (Cambridge: Cambridge University Press, 1996), 13.

34. Stefan Collini, *Public Moralists: Political Thought and Intellectual Life in Britain, 1850–1930* (Oxford: Clarendon Press, 1991), 352–53.

35. Eugenio F. Biagini, "Liberalism and Direct Democracy: John Stuart Mill and the Model of Ancient Athens," in Biagini, *Citizenship and Community*, 23.

36. My thinking about memory's mediation has been confirmed and advanced by Clifford Siskin and William Warner's recent formulations of Enlightenment and the history of mediation in their introductory essay to *This Is Enlightenment* (Chicago: University of Chicago Press, 2010), 1–33.

37. David Thorburn and Henry Jenkins have argued that new media "engage in a complex and ongoing process of 'remediation,' in which the tactics, styles and content of rival media are rehearsed, displayed, mimicked, extended, critiqued. . . . Self-reflexivity and imitation are contrasting aspects of the same process by which the new medium maps its emergent properties and defines a space for itself in relation to its ancestors" (*Rethinking Media Change*, 7, 10). In focusing on memory as a medium, I shift more strongly toward psychological theories of reception than do Thorburn and Jenkins with their notion of remediation in media technologies. On

the technological aspects of remediation, see also Jay David Bolter and Richard Grusin, *Remediation: Understanding New Media* (Cambridge, Mass.: MIT Press, 2000).

38. Associationist terminology still does a good job describing what thinking and remembering feel like intuitively. In a recent analysis of the relation between cognitive science and the history of reading, Andrew Elfenbein indicates that contemporary psychological studies of reading still rely on the lingua franca of the association of ideas. "Cognitive Science and the History of Reading," *PMLA* 121, no. 2 (2006): 484–502. In this book I use the term "Utilitarian" to refer to persons and ideas associated with the late eighteenth- and early nineteenth century utilitarian philosophy of Jeremy Bentham and James Mill. The lower-case term "utilitarian" is a more generic designation of ideas and policies, and it applies more broadly beyond the followers of Bentham. As a political movement, Bentham's and Mill's followers were also called "Philosophic Radicals" or "Philosophical Radicals."

39. On the epistemological dimensions of the novel, see J. Paul Hunter, *Before Novels: The Cultural Contexts of Eighteenth-Century Fiction* (New York: Norton, 1990); Michael McKeon, *The Origins of the English Novel, 1600–1740* (Baltimore: Johns Hopkins University Press, 1987); Ian Watt, *The Rise of the Novel: Studies in Defoe, Richardson, and Fielding* (Berkeley: University of California Press, 1957); and, most recently, George Levine, *Dying to Know: Scientific Epistemology and Narrative in Victorian England* (Chicago: University of Chicago Press, 2002).

40. For important recent studies of Victorian psychology and the psychology of reading, see Rick Rylance, *Victorian Psychology and British Culture, 1850–1880* (Oxford: Oxford University Press, 2000), and Nicholas Dames, *The Physiology of the Novel: Reading, Neural Science, and the Form of Victorian Fiction* (Oxford: Oxford University Press, 2007). On Victorian memory and nostalgia more generally, see Ann C. Colley, *Nostalgia and Recollection in Victorian Culture* (Basingstoke, UK: Macmillan, 1998), and Nicholas Dames, *Amnesiac Selves: Nostalgia, Forgetting, and British Fiction, 1818–1870* (Oxford: Oxford University Press, 2001).

41. Raymond Williams, *Marxism and Literature* (Oxford: Oxford University Press, 1977), 122–23. John B. Thompson's account of the way an individual's encounter with new media changes but does not "uproot" tradition is similar to Williams's definition of residual formations: "As individuals gained access to media products, they were able to take some distance from the symbolic content of face-to-face interaction and from the forms of authority which prevailed in the locales of everyday life. . . . The mediazation of tradition endowed it with a new life: tradition was increasingly freed from the constraints of face-to-face interaction and took on a range of new traits." *The Media and Modernity: A Social Theory of the Media* (Stanford, Calif.: Stanford University Press, 1995), 180.

42. Richard Terdiman has defined the "memory crisis" of the nineteenth century as the "pervasive perception," based on both the political ruptures of revolutions and the repeated migrations of populations to the cities, that the past was inaccessible, that representation too had become deeply problematic, and that "the

mnemonic faculty had *itself* undergone mysterious and unsettling mutations." *Present Past: Modernity and the Memory Crisis* (Ithaca, N.Y.: Cornell University Press, 1993), 6–7. The persistence of Enlightenment associationism in the nineteenth century, however, supported countervailing attempts to sustain or repair a relation to the past through a residual notion of the memory as a common ground of both subjective and social coherence. Such attempts were not necessarily nostalgic— Dickens, for one, saw much of England's past history as a chronicle of titled barbarism.

43. On the emergence of mass culture in Britain during this period, see Richard D. Altick, *Writers, Readers, and Occasions: Selected Essays on Victorian Literature and Life* (Columbus: Ohio State University Press, 1989), 141–73; Pam Morris, *Imagining Inclusive Society in Nineteenth-Century Novels: The Code of Sincerity in the Public Sphere* (Baltimore: Johns Hopkins University Press, 2004); John Plotz, *The Crowd: British Literature and Public Politics* (Berkeley: University of California Press, 2000); and Poovey, *Making a Social Body*.

44. In this book, I develop in new directions an important ongoing literary critical analysis of memory effects in Dickens's novels. Rosemarie Bodenheimer has eloquently explored Dickens's autobiographical invocations of memory and his novelistic treatments of the manifestation of painful and involuntary memories in chapter 3 of *Knowing Dickens*. Nicholas Dames has analyzed Dickens's associationism, focusing in particular on the centrality of associationist principles in *David Copperfield* (1849–50), as a means of constructing a coherent autobiographical version of the self through narrative (*Amnesiac Selves*, 125–48). Michael S. Kearns argues that "although Dickens never declared his allegiance to association psychology, both the language and the concepts of this psychology are so prominent in his character portrayals that he can fairly be termed an association novelist." *Metaphors of Mind in Fiction and Psychology* (Lexington: University Press of Kentucky, 1987), 158–59. Historian Rick Rylance also confirms Dickens's consistent reliance on associationism despite his attacks on utilitarian-inspired educational programs and politics, which were informed by associationist doctrine (*Victorian Psychology*, 56).

45. Charles Dickens, *The Old Curiosity Shop*, ed. Angus Easson (London: Penguin, 1972), 37. Dickens dedicates the book to Rogers in recognition of both the "generous and earnest feelings" conveyed by his poetry and his lesser-known philanthropy, his "active sympathy with the poorest and humblest of his kind." *The Pleasures of Memory* was very well received by critics and particularly admired by Byron. Fifteen editions of the poem were published by 1806, most of which were runs of 1,000–2,000 copies. Richard Garnett, "Rogers, Samuel (1763–1855)," rev. Paul Baines, in *Oxford Dictionary of National Biography* (Oxford: Oxford University Press, 2004–10), http://www.oxforddnb.com/view/article/23997 (accessed January 14, 2009). For a useful short account of Rogers's relation to Dickens, see Philip V. Allingham, "Samuel Rogers (1763–1855), Survivor from 'the Age of Sentiment,'" http://www.victorianweb.org/authors/rogers/bio.html (accessed May 21, 2008). Allingham notes that a successful edition of *The Pleasures of Memory*, lavishly illustrated with 114 plates by J. M. W. Turner and T. Stothard, was published in

1834. William St Clair provides a detailed publishing history of *The Pleasures of Memory*, documenting the sale of more than 50,000 copies of the poem by 1850. St Clair notes that Rogers's "works remained widely available throughout most of the nineteenth century." *The Reading Nation in the Romantic Period* (Cambridge: Cambridge University Press, 2004), Appendix 9, 632. St Clair also includes Rogers in a group of "literary authors of the romantic period . . . most respected at the time," in company with Byron, Campbell, Coleridge, Moore, Scott, Southey, and Wordsworth (ibid., 210).

46. Samuel Rogers, *The Pleasures of Memory with Other Poems* (Paris: Baudry's European Library, 1852), 20–21.

47. Ibid., vii–viii.

48. Literature scholars have been used to thinking of the memory and narrative as organized metonymically because of salient theorizing in psychoanalysis as well as foundational texts in narratology, such as Sigmund Freud, *The Standard Edition of the Complete Psychological Works of Sigmund Freud*, vols. 4–5, *The Interpretation of Dreams*, edited by James Strachey in collaboration with Anna Freud, assisted by Alix Strachey and Alan Tyson, and translated by James Strachey (London: Hogarth Press and Institute of Psycho-analysis, 1953–74); Jacques Lacan, *Écrits: A Selection*, trans. Alan Sheridan, 2nd ed. (New York: Norton, 1977); Gérard Genette, *Figures of Literary Discourse*, trans. Alan Sheridan (New York: Columbia University Press, 1982); and Paul de Man, *Allegories of Reading: Figural Language in Rousseau, Nietzsche, Rilke and Proust* (New Haven, Conn.: Yale University Press, 1979). A study of associationist conceptions of memory leads, however, to a different consideration of the ways these metonymic processes could be put to voluntary, regular, and familiar uses, through rhetorical techniques of memory, everyday scholastic routines of memorization, the pious reading of scripture, or the habitual reading of serial fiction.

49. The continued use of rhetorical memory techniques by nineteenth-century writers also suggests that we need to revise the story of the nineteenth-century "demise" of rhetoric. John Bender and David E. Wellbery, for example, argue that "the evacuation from cultural memory of the topoi—those dense and finely branched semantic clusters that had since antiquity governed discursive invention— coincided exactly with the emergence of Romanticism. The Romantic destruction of rhetoric altered the temporal framework of literary production, replacing rememorative conservation (*traditio*) with an insistence on originality." "Rhetoricality: On the Modernist Return of Rhetoric," in *The Ends of Rhetoric: History, Theory, Practice*, ed. John Bender and David E. Wellbery (Stanford, Calif.: Stanford University Press, 1990), 15–16. Yet Romantic writers did not abandon rhetoric or associationism as a theory of mind that, in effect, psychologized rhetorical principles. See the specific arguments to this effect collected in Don H. Bialostosky and Lawrence D. Needham, eds., *Rhetorical Traditions and British Romantic Literature* (Bloomington: Indiana University Press, 1995). See also Jules David Law, *The Rhetoric of Empiricism: Language and Perception from Locke to I. A. Richards* (Ithaca, N.Y.: Cornell University Press, 1993).

50. Paul de Man, "Hypogram and Inscription," in *The Resistance to Theory* (Minneapolis: University of Minnesota Press, 1986), 45.

51. Richard A. Barney, *Plots of Enlightenment: Education and the Novel in Eighteenth-Century England* (Stanford, Calif.: Stanford University Press, 1999), 3.

52. William Wordsworth, *Selected Poems and Prefaces*, ed. Jack Stillinger (Boston: Houghton Mifflin, 1965), 449.

53. Jon P. Klancher, *The Making of English Reading Audiences, 1790–1832* (Madison: University of Wisconsin Press, 1987), 37.

54. See, for example, [Wilkie Collins], "The Unknown Public," *Household Words*, August 12, 1858, 217–22, and Margaret Oliphant's "The Byways of Literature: Reading for the Million," *Blackwood's Edinburgh Magazine*, August 1858, 200–216, discussed by Mary Poovey in *Genres of the Credit Economy: Mediating Value in Eighteenth-and Nineteenth-Century Britain* (Chicago: University of Chicago Press, 2008), 310–12, 324–28.

55. Anthony Trollope, "Novel-Reading. The Works of Charles Dickens. The Works of W. Makepeace Thackeray," *Nineteenth Century* 5, no. 3 (1879): 25.

56. Ibid., 33.

57. See Elaine Hadley's *Living Liberalism*, chapters 1 and 5, on the ambivalence of Trollope's elaboration of Liberal politics in own his novels—a complexity that belies his simplistic and rather dismissive account of Dickens's influence.

58. The extension of education in the nineteenth century was accompanied by increased stratification of types of schools. Historian Brian Simon shows how, in addition to organizational and curricular changes, midcentury reforms of the grammar schools and the prestigious public schools by a series of parliamentary commissions resulted in the reallocation of their ancient foundations, endowed for the purpose of funding impoverished and local scholars, to other uses, causing the grammar schools to admit primarily middle-class, and the public schools almost exclusively upper-class, scholars. As a result, Simon argues, "by the 1890s, the middle classes enjoyed a subsidized system of education" while "the vast majority of working-class children were consciously debarred from receiving an education above their station." *Studies in the History of Education, 1780–1870* (London: Lawrence & Wisehart, 1960), 335.

59. For a history of the training colleges, see R. W. Rich, *The Training of Teachers in England and Wales During the Nineteenth Century* (Cambridge: Cambridge University Press, 1933), and Asher Tropp, *The School Teachers: The Growth of the Teaching Profession in England and Wales from 1800 to the Present Day* (London: William Heinemann, 1957).

60. On Anglican-Tory resistance to secular education, see Simon, *Studies in the History of Education*, 338–39.

61. David Vincent, *Literacy and Popular Culture: England, 1750–1914* (Cambridge: Cambridge University Press, 1989), 53–54.

62. For an account of this cross-denominational curricular uniformity, see the classic study by J. M. Goldstrom, *The Social Content of Education, 1808–1870: A Study*

of the Working Class School Reader in England and Ireland (Shannon, Ireland: Irish University Press, 1972).

63. For the details of this history, see H. C. Barnard, *A Short History of English Education, from 1760 to 1944* (London: University of London Press, 1947), and Simon, *Studies in the History of Education.*

64. Vincent, *Literacy and Popular Culture*, 53–54. Vincent draws his statistics from the registrars of marriages and reports from the Registrar General. On working-class initiatives in organizing schools during the nineteenth century, see also Thomas Laqueur, *Religion and Respectability: Sunday Schools and Working Class Culture, 1780–1850* (New Haven, Conn.: Yale University Press, 1976); Richard Johnson, "'Really Useful Knowledge': Radical Education and Working-Class Culture, 1790–1848," in *Working-Class Culture: Studies in History and Theory*, ed. J. Clarke, C. Crichter, and R. Johnson (New York: St. Martin's Press, 1970), 75–102; E. P. Thompson, *The Making of the English Working Class* (New York: Vintage, 1966); and Raymond Williams, *The Long Revolution* (Harmondsworth, UK: Penguin, 1965).

65. Vincent, *Literacy and Popular Culture*, 54.

66. On the importance of public free libraries in increasing access to books after Ewart's Act in 1850, and their large percentage of working-class patrons—81 percent, according to one parliamentary survey of thirty-seven libraries in 1876–77— see Philip Waller, *Writers, Readers, and Reputations: Literary Life in Britain, 1870–1918* (Oxford: Oxford University Press, 2006), 49–56.

67. On this earliest period of the formal study of English, see Thomas P. Miller, *The Formation of College English: Rhetoric and Belles Lettres in the British Cultural Provinces* (Pittsburgh: University of Pittsburgh Press, 1997).

68. See Alan Bacon, "English Literature Becomes a University Subject: King's College, London as Pioneer," *Victorian Studies* 29, no. 4 (1986): 591–612. On the history of English literary studies, see also Chris Baldick, *The Social Mission of English Criticism, 1848–1932* (Oxford: Clarendon Press, 1983); John Guillory, "Literary Study and the Modern System of the Disciplines," in *Disciplinarity at the Fin de Siècle*, ed. Amanda Anderson and Joseph Valente (Princeton, N.J.: Princeton University Press, 2002), 19–43; Ian Hunter, *Culture and Government: The Emergence of Literary Education* (Basingstoke, UK: Macmillan, 1988); Gerald Graff, *Professing Literature: An Institutional History* (Chicago: University of Chicago Press, 2007); Margaret Mathieson, *The Preachers of Culture: A Study of English and Its Teachers* (Totowa, N.J.: Rowman and Littlefield, 1975); and D. J. Palmer, *The Rise of English Studies* (London: Oxford University Press, 1965).

69. See R. W. Rich, *The Training of Teachers in English and Wales During the Nineteenth Century*, chaps. 2–4; Baldick, *The Social Mission of English Criticism*, chap. 3.

70. Gauri Viswanathan, *Masks of Conquest: Literary Study and British Rule in India* (New York: Columbia University Press, 1989), 43.

71. Palmer, *The Rise of English Studies*, 46–47.

72. The case of Scotland, however, was somewhat different from those of Wales and England; on the distinctive aspects of the educational history of Scotland, see

Robert Crawford, *The Scottish Invention of English Literature* (Cambridge: Cambridge University Press, 1998).

73. For a sociological analysis of the school and cultural capital, see Pierre Bourdieu, "Systems of Education and Systems of Thought," in *Schooling and Capitalism: A Sociological Reader*, ed. Roger Dale, Geoff Esland, and Madeleine MacDonald (London: Routledge & Kegan Paul and Open University Press, 1976), 192–200; "The Forms of Capital," trans. Richard Nice, in *Handbook of Theory and Research for the Sociology of Education*, ed. John G. Richardson (New York: Greenwood Press, 1986), 241–58; and *Distinction: A Social Critique of the Judgement of Taste*, trans. Richard Nice (Cambridge, Mass.: Harvard University Press, 1984). See also John Guillory, *Cultural Capital: The Problem of Literary Canon Formation* (Chicago: University of Chicago Press, 1993).

74. The history of the book has focused on archival, demographic, and material culture research, including the assessment of various social groups' access to print; the history of literacy and education; the economics of publishing and bookselling; the book as material object and commodity; the circulation of print genres through purchase or borrowing by individuals; the history of libraries and other collections; and the gathering of evidence for the ways readers have typically used periodicals, books, textbooks, chapbooks, religious tracts, and other forms of print publication. Among the important works in this field that focus on British developments in the eighteenth and nineteenth centuries are Richard D. Altick, *The English Common Reader: A Social History of the Mass Reading Public, 1800–1900*, 2nd ed. (Chicago: University of Chicago Press, 1957); Kate Flint, *The Woman Reader, 1837–1914* (Oxford: Clarendon Press, 1993); Klancher, *The Making of English Reading Audiences*; Jacqueline Pearson, *Women's Reading in Britain, 1750–1835: A Dangerous Recreation* (Cambridge: Cambridge University Press, 1999); Alan Richardson, *Literature, Education, and Romanticism: Reading as Social Practice, 1780–1832* (Cambridge: Cambridge University Press, 1994); Vincent, *Literacy and Popular Culture*; and Viswanathan, *Masks of Conquest*.

75. Much recent literary scholarship on the history of the nineteenth-century novel has focused on its role in transmitting middle-class mentalities, gendered identities, and psychological interiority. See, for example, Nancy Armstrong, *Desire and Domestic Fiction: A Political History of the Novel* (New York: Oxford University Press, 1987), and *How Novels Think: The Limits of Individualism from 1719–1900* (New York: Columbia University Press, 2006); Deidre Shauna Lynch, *The Economy of Character: Novels, Market Culture, and the Business of Inner Meaning* (Chicago: University of Chicago Press, 1998); D. A. Miller, *The Novel and the Police* (Berkeley: University of California Press, 1988); and Garrett Stewart, *Dear Reader: The Conscripted Audience in Nineteenth-Century British Fiction* (Baltimore: Johns Hopkins University Press, 1996).

76. Responding to Richard D. Altick's groundbreaking work in *The English Common Reader*, historian Jonathan Rose argues that while "the old book history studied what people read and whether they could read and the new book history studies how they read, neither has really explored mass intellectual responses to

342 Notes to pages 23–24

reading," as Altick had recommended, and that both of these approaches have yet to fully grapple with the question "How do texts change the minds and lives of common (i.e., nonprofessional) readers?" Rose outlines a "history of reading audiences" that would "define a mass audience, then determine its cultural diet, and ultimately measure the collective response of that audience not only to particular works of literature, but also to education, religion, art, and any other cultural activity." Rose is particularly critical, however, of attempts by literary critics to uncover the effects of reading within literary texts because "for the most part they have only speculated about the reactions of hypothetical readers." "Rereading the English Common Reader: A Preface to a History of Audiences," *Journal of the History of Ideas* 53 (1992): 48, 51, 49. By contrast, in his analysis of the interpolated reader in Victorian literature, literary critic Garrett Stewart attempts to bridge the gap between reader and text by pursuing the reader as a rhetorical figure "conscripted" by the literary text, arguing that such rhetorical figures as the novel supplies to encode the reader's reception are constitutive, though not exclusively so, of the particular kind of reading that the text rehearses (*Dear Reader*, 11–12). Both Rose and Stewart criticize theories of reception oriented toward the critique of ideology. See also Rose's *The Intellectual Life of the British Working Classes* (New Haven, Conn.: Yale University Press, 2001).

77. William St Clair, "But What Did We Actually Read?" *Times Literary Supplement*, May 12, 2006. In his comprehensive study of publishing practices during the Romantic period, St Clair proposes that "if we could trace print, and understand how certain texts came to be made available in printed form to certain constituencies of buyers and readers, we would have made a good start in narrowing the questions to be addressed in tracing ideas." *The Reading Nation in the Romantic Period* (Cambridge: Cambridge University Press, 2004), 6–7.

78. Important recent collections of essays in the field of the history of reading practices are Jonathan Boyarin, ed., *The Ethnography of Reading* (Berkeley: University of California Press, 1993); Guglielmo Cavallo and Roger Chartier, eds., *A History of Reading in the West*, trans. Lydia G. Cochrane (Amherst: University of Massachusetts Press, 1999); Cathy N. Davidson, ed., *Reading in America: Literature and Social History* (Baltimore: Johns Hopkins University Press, 1989); John O. Jordan and Robert L. Patten, eds., *Literature in the Marketplace: Nineteenth-Century British Publishing and Reading Practices* (Cambridge: Cambridge University Press, 1995); and James Raven, Helen Small, and Naomi Tadmor, eds., *The Practice and Representation of Reading in England* (Cambridge: Cambridge University Press, 1996). On the history of reading pedagogy and rhetoric in England and the United States, see two studies by David Bartine: *Early English Reading Theory: Origins of Current Debates* (Columbia: University of South Carolina Press, 1989), and *Reading, Criticism, and Culture: Theory and Teaching in the United States and England, 1820–1950* (Columbia: University of South Carolina Press, 1992).

79. Victorian readers "did not analyze their experience of literature in any really penetrating manner, and so they did not leave any psychological documents (as, for

example, Coleridge had done) to aid us in our effort to discover how they read."
Altick, *Writers, Readers, and Occasions*, 139.

80. Serial fiction has garnered growing interest among literary historians in recent years. Valuable recent studies of serial fiction include Mary Hamer, *Writing by Numbers: Trollope's Serial Fiction* (Cambridge: Cambridge University Press, 1987); Linda K. Hughes and Michael Lund, *The Victorian Serial* (Charlottesville: University Press of Virginia, 1991); Graham Law, *Serializing Fiction in the Victorian Press* (New York: Palgrave Macmillan, 2000); Laurie Langbauer, *Novels of Everyday Life: The Series in English Fiction, 1850–1930* (Ithaca, N.Y.: Cornell University Press, 1999); Michael Lund, *Reading Thackeray* (Detroit: Wayne State University Press, 1988); Richard Maxwell, *The Mysteries of Paris and London* (Charlottesville: University Press of Virginia, 1992); Kevin McLaughlin, *Writing in Parts: Imitation and Exchange in Nineteenth-Century Literature* (Stanford, Calif.: Stanford University Press, 1995); David Payne, *The Reenchantment of Nineteenth-Century Fiction: Dickens, Thackeray, George Eliot, and Serialization* (Basingstoke, UK: Palgrave Macmillan, 2005); Mark W. Turner, *Trollope and the Magazines: Gendered Issues in Mid-Victorian Britain* (Basingstoke, UK: Macmillan, 2000); and Deborah Wynne, *The Sensation Novel and the Victorian Family Magazine* (New York: Palgrave Macmillan, 2001). Also useful for understanding the reception of serial fiction is new research that combines the publication history of Victorian periodicals with the methods of media studies, as represented in Laurel Brake, Bill Bell, and David Finkelstein, eds., *Nineteenth-Century Media and the Construction of Identities* (Basingstoke, UK: Palgrave Macmillan, 2000). For comparative contexts with the history of serial fiction in France, see James Smith Allen, *In the Public Eye: A History of Reading in Modern France, 1800–1940* (Princeton, N.J.: Princeton University Press, 1991), and *Popular French Romanticism: Authors, Readers, and Books in the 19th Century* (Syracuse, N.Y.: Syracuse University Press, 1981); Martyn Lyons, *Readers and Society in Nineteenth-Century France: Workers, Women, Peasants* (Basingstoke, UK: Palgrave Macmillan, 2001), and *Reading Culture and Writing Practices in Nineteenth-Century France* (Toronto: University of Toronto Press, 2008); Jann Matlock, *Scenes of Seduction: Prostitution, Hysteria, and Reading Difference in Nineteenth-Century France* (New York: Columbia University Press, 1994); and Maxwell, *The Mysteries of Paris and London.*

81. For a seminal discussion of reading as a hermeneutics, see Hans-Georg Gadamer, *Truth and Method*, trans. Joel Weinsheimer and Donald G. Marshall, 2nd rev. ed. (New York: Continuum, 1989), 383–405. Other important works on narrative and the theory of reading include Roland Barthes, *The Pleasure of the Text*, trans. Richard Miller (New York: Hill and Wang, 1975); Wayne Booth, *The Rhetoric of Fiction*, 2nd ed. (Chicago: University of Chicago Press, 1983); Umberto Eco, *The Role of the Reader: Explorations in the Semiotics of Texts* (Bloomington: Indiana University Press, 1979); Norman N. Holland, *The Dynamics of Literary Response* (New York: Oxford University Press, 1968); Wolfgang Iser, *The Act of Reading: A Theory of Aesthetic Response* (Baltimore: Johns Hopkins University Press, 1978); Hans Robert Jauss, *Aesthetic Experience and Literary Hermeneutics* (Minneapolis: University of Minnesota Press, 1982); and Jane P. Tompkins, ed., *Reader-Response Criticism: From*

Formalism to Post-structuralism (Baltimore: Johns Hopkins University Press, 1980). Iser points out that serial fiction instigates "a special kind of reading" because "the reader is forced by the pauses imposed on him to imagine more than he could have if his reading were continuous" (*The Act of Reading*, 138–39).

82. I draw on classicist Jean-Pierre Vernant's understanding of the methods of historical psychology: "For the historian of today, the psychological no longer constitutes a principle of intelligibility, a self-evident norm to be imposed. Rather it has become one aspect among others of historical material, one of the dimensions of the subject, a problem that needs to be accounted for in the same way as all the rest of the data." Vernant also observes that in different cultures and historical periods there are "many forms of memory, linked to particular techniques of remembering, practiced in social milieus for well-defined purposes." "History and Psychology," in *Mortals and Immortals: Collected Essays*, ed. Froma I. Zeitlin (Princeton, N.J.: Princeton University Press, 1991), 262, 265. Similarly, in his recent exploration of associationist psychology as a precursor to current theories of distributed memory in neurology and cognitive science, John Sutton notes that scholars across many disciplines "feel the need again to connect cognition and culture, to question the boundaries which keep apart not just neuroscience and philosophy of mind, but also psychology and history," in order to retain the ability to question the "current consensus" on the relation between mind and brain. *Philosophy and Memory Traces: Descartes to Connectionism* (Cambridge: Cambridge University Press, 1998), 30.

83. Other recent approaches to the history of novel reading understand reader response through linguistic, psychoanalytic, or cognitive theories. On the new research in literary studies and cognitive science, see F. Elizabeth Hart, "The Epistemology of Cognitive Literary Studies," *Philosophy and Literature* 25, no. 2 (2001): 314–34, and Alan Richardson, "Cognitive Science and the Future of Literary Studies," *Philosophy and Literature* 23 (1999): 157–73. Hart describes the field of cognitive literary studies as seeking to develop a "cognitive historicism" that investigates "the discourses on brain and mind science through the literary and philosophical texts of earlier periods" (316). Hans Adler and Sabine Gross offer a cautionary evaluation of this new approach in "Adjusting the Frame: Comments on Cognitivism and Literature," *Poetics Today* 23, no. 2 (2002): 195–220. For recent examples of novel criticism that blend psychoanalytic concepts with cultural history, see Armstrong, *How Novels Think*, and John Kucich, *Imperial Masochism: British Fiction, Fantasy, and Social Class* (Princeton, N.J.: Princeton University Press, 2006).

84. For recent studies of the history of nineteenth-century psychological theories, and of Victorian literature's relations to Victorian psychology, see Rylance, *Victorian Psychology*, and Jenny Bourne Taylor and Sally Shuttleworth, eds., *Embodied Selves: An Anthology of Psychological Texts, 1830–1890* (Oxford: Clarendon Press, 1998); Maureen N. McLane, *Romanticism and the Human Sciences: Poetry, Population, and the Discourse of the Species* (Cambridge: Cambridge University Press, 2000); Laura Otis, *Organic Memory: History and the Body in the Late Nineteenth and Early Twentieth Centuries* (Lincoln: University of Nebraska Press, 1994); Edward S. Reed, *From Soul to Mind: The Emergence of Psychology from Erasmus Darwin to William James* (New

Haven, Conn.: Yale University Press, 1997); Graham Richards, *Mental Machinery: The Origins and Consequences of Psychological Ideas, Part 1: 1600–1850* (Baltimore: Johns Hopkins University Press, 1992); Alan Richardson, *British Romanticism and the Science of Mind* (Cambridge: Cambridge University Press, 2001); Sally Shuttleworth, *Charlotte Brontë and Victorian Psychology* (Cambridge: Cambridge University Press, 1996); Helen Small, *Love's Madness: Medicine, the Novel, and Female Insanity, 1800–1865* (Oxford: Oxford University Press, 1996); and Alison Winter, *Mesmerized: Powers of Mind in Victorian Britain* (Chicago: University of Chicago Press, 1998). On the representation of physiology in Dickens's writings, see also John Gordon, *Physiology and the Literary Imagination: Romantic to Modern* (Gainesville: University Press of Florida, 2003), 57–113.

85. Sutton observes that reading past theories of mind and memory requires a certain kind of literalization: "History encourages distrust of judgements which praise certain 'theories' of memory for their sober freedom from metaphor, denigrating the overly metaphorical nature of others. The point is not just that metaphor is generative rather than inevitably obstructive to the pursuit of truth, or that psychology in particular must necessarily adopt and adapt familiar terms: it is that memory is a domain in which there are particular problems in drawing even provisional lines between metaphorical and literal descriptions" (*Philosophy and Memory Traces*, 13).

86. Charles Dickens, "A Preliminary Word," in *Household Words*, March 30, 1850, in *The Amusements of the People and Other Papers: Reports, Essays, and Reviews, 1834–51*, ed. Michael Slater, Dent Uniform Edition of Dickens' Journalism (Columbus: Ohio State University, 1996), 177.

87. G. K. Chesterton, *Charles Dickens: A Critical Study* (New York: Dodd, Mead, 1911), 299.

1. Memory's Bonds: Associationism and the Freedom of Thought

1. Charles Dickens, *Little Dorrit*, ed. Stephen Wall and Helen Small (London: Penguin, 1998), 507–8. All further references will appear in the text.

2. An earlier description of this phenomenon by Dickens's narrator appears in *Oliver Twist*: "There is a kind of sleep that steals upon us sometimes which, while it holds the body prisoner, does not free the mind from a sense of things about it, and enable [*sic*] it to ramble as it pleases" (Charles Dickens, *Oliver Twist*, ed. Philip Horne (London: Penguin, 2002), 281; this edition reproduces the text of the original serial publication. All further references will appear in the text. For a discussion of Dickens's interest in such unusual mental states, see Rosemarie Bodenheimer, *Knowing Dickens* (Ithaca, N.Y.: Cornell University Press, 2007), 11–14. The fact that Dickens puts one of his own psychological theories in the mouth of Mrs. Tickit gives even more weight to her pronouncements about "free thoughts."

3. Mrs. Tickit's generic conception of mental freedom as common to all does not coincide with mid-Victorian liberalism's cultivation of an "abstract embodiment," characterized by Elaine Hadley as "strikingly formalized mental attitudes . . .

346 Notes to pages 33–35

such as disinterestedness, objectivity, reticence, conviction, impersonality, sincerity, all of which carried with them a moral valence." *Living Liberalism: Practical Citizenship in Mid-Victorian Britain* (Chicago: University of Chicago Press, 2010), 9. Dickens's cultural politics seems to be distinct from this formalized, highly intellectual liberalism.

4. A similar exchange occurs in *Nicholas Nickleby* (1838–39), ed. Michael Slater (London: Penguin, 1986) between Ralph Nickleby's clerk, Newman Noggs, and Mrs. Nickleby on the subject of whether the clerk has thought to order a cab to transport Kate Nickleby to her uncle's house:

> "I can't suffer you to think of such a thing," said Mrs. Nickleby.
> "You can't help it," said Newman.
> "Not help it!"
> "No. I thought of it as I came along; but didn't get one, thinking you mightn't be ready. I think of a great many things. Nobody can prevent that."
> "Oh yes, I understand you, Mr. Noggs," said Mrs. Nickleby. "Our thoughts are free, of course. Everybody's thoughts are their own, clearly."
> "They wouldn't be if some people had their way," muttered Newman. (196)

Newman Noggs's reference to "some people" probably refers both to his master, Ralph Nickleby, who represents the "capitalist" class (69) exploiting Noggs's labor and presuming to own his loyalty, and the moral/political category of those who attempt to exert a tyrannical personal dominance over others.

5. Of course, there is a lower limit to this correlation, as a figure like Jo the crossing sweeper in *Bleak House* (1852–53) demonstrates.

6. Hans Aarsleff dates the beginnings of Locke's widespread influence to within ten years after his death, citing among other evidence Addison and Steele's regular references to Locke's writings in the *Spectator*. "Locke's Influence," in *The Cambridge Companion to Locke*, ed. Vere Chappell (Cambridge: Cambridge University Press, 1994), 252. For the Harvard psychologist and philosopher William James's dating of the emergence of physiological psychology to 1870, see his *Principles of Psychology* (New York: Henry Holt and Company, 1890), 1:4; discussed in Rick Rylance, *Victorian Psychology and British Culture, 1850–1880* (Oxford: Oxford University Press, 2000), 70–71.

7. D. B. Klein, *A History of Scientific Psychology: Its Origins and Philosophical Backgrounds* (New York: Basic Books, 1970), 615.

8. John Guillory lays out the trajectory from the belletristic rhetoric of Blair and Campbell to modern English studies in the university in "Literary Study and the Modern System of the Disciplines," in *Disciplinarity at the Fin de Siècle*, ed. Amanda Anderson and Joseph Valente (Princeton, N.J.: Princeton University Press, 2002), 19–43.

9. James Engell, "The New Rhetoricians: Psychology, Semiotics, and Critical Theory," in *Psychology and Literature in the Eighteenth Century*, ed. Christopher Fox (New York: AMS Press, 1987), 208. Among the "New Rhetoricians," many of whom were active in the Scottish Enlightenment, Engell includes Adam Smith,

George Campbell, Joseph Priestley, Hugh Blair, James Beattie, Thomas Gibbons, Lord Kames, Thomas Sheridan, and Robert Lowth (278). The history of reading as a field would benefit from a new rapprochement with the history of rhetoric, which is also explicitly oriented toward a theory of audiences.

10. James Mill, *Analysis of the Phenomena of the Human Mind*, ed. Alexander Bain, Andrew Findlater, and George Grote, 2nd ed. (New York: Augustus M. Kelley, 1967), 1:324.

11. For a history of the development of classical "arts of memory" in Western Europe, see Francis A. Yates, *The Art of Memory* (London: Pimlico, 1992), and Mary J. Carruthers, *The Book of Memory: A Study of Memory in Medieval Culture* (Cambridge: Cambridge University Press, 1992).

12. For an analysis of the centrality of William Gladstone's oratorical persona on the hustings to his version of Victorian liberalism, see Hadley, *Living Liberalism*, chap. 6.

13. K. J. Fielding, "Dickens as a Speaker," in *The Speeches of Charles Dickens: A Complete Edition*, ed. K. J. Fielding (Oxford: Clarendon Press, 1960), xix–xx.

14. George Dolby, *Charles Dickens as I Knew Him: The Story of the Reading Tours in Great Britain and America (1866–1870)* (Philadelphia: J. B. Lippincott, 1885), 275–76.

15. Ibid., 274. Two recent studies of Dickens as a performer of his own novels and as a public speaker are Malcolm Andrews, *Charles Dickens and His Performing Selves: Dickens and the Public Readings* (Oxford: Oxford University Press, 2006), and Matthew Bevis, *The Art of Eloquence: Byron, Dickens, Tennyson, Joyce* (Oxford: Oxford University Press, 2007).

16. The five canons of classical rhetoric are invention, arrangement, style, memory, and delivery. For a useful and brief discussion of the history of the canons of memory and invention, see Sharon Crowley, *The Methodical Memory: Invention in Current-Traditional Rhetoric* (Carbondale: Southern Illinois University Press, 1990), 1–11.

17. John M. L. Drew outlines the rhetorical influences on and development of Dickens's style in *Dickens the Journalist* (London: Palgrave Macmillan, 2003), 160–68.

18. Joseph S. Meisel, *Public Speech and the Culture of Public Life in the Age of Gladstone* (New York: Columbia University Press, 2001), 21–22.

19. *Harper's New Monthly Magazine*, June–November 1862, 379, quoted in John Butt and Kathleen Tillotson, *Dickens at Work* (London: Methuen, 1957), 28. Butt and Tillotson also discuss in detail Dickens's use of very brief notes as compositional and presumably memory aids in planning his serialized novels.

20. See Harry Stone, ed., *Dickens' Working Notes for His Novels* (Chicago: University of Chicago Press, 1987).

21. Esther Schor identifies the importance of sympathy for Enlightenment moral philosophers such as Hume, Francis Hutcheson, and Adam Smith as a vehicle for the circulation of moral sentiments and "a necessary link between the affections of individuals and the normative morals of a society." *Bearing the Dead: The British*

Culture of Mourning from the Enlightenment to Victoria (Princeton, N.J.: Princeton University Press, 1994), 7. Fred Kaplan defines the Victorian version of sentimentalism as the "popularly cherished . . . belief that human beings are innately good, that the source of evil is malignant social conditioning, and that the spontaneous, uninhibited expression of the natural feelings (good because they are natural, good because we are by nature good) is admirable and the basis for successful human relationships." *Sacred Tears: Sentimentality in Victorian Literature* (Princeton, N.J.: Princeton University Press, 1987), 7.

22. Similarly, while the sentimental social novel's focus on the suffering of individual characters within plots about social injustice may also work as a generic model for Dickens's representational strategies, this model does not tell us enough about the specific ways that Dickensian novels conceive the effects of serial reading in pedagogical terms and in relation to earlier genres of cheap fiction. For an analysis of the subgenre of the sentimental social novel in France, see Margaret Cohen, *The Sentimental Education of the Novel* (Princeton, N.J.: Princeton University Press, 1999), 135–50.

23. Kaplan, *Sacred Tears*, 7, 146 n. 5.

24. Lisa Jardine, introduction to Francis Bacon, *The New Organon*, ed. Lisa Jardine and Michael Silverthorne (Cambridge: Cambridge University Press, 2000), xxi. Further references will appear parenthetically in the text. I focus here on part 2 of Bacon's treatise.

25. Francis Yates argues that while it is unclear exactly how Bacon intended to revise the arts of memory, he did apply them for scientific purposes: "Amongst the new uses to which [the normal art of memory] was to be put was the memorizing of matters in order so as to hold them in the mind for investigation. This would help scientific inquiry, for by drawing particulars out of the mass of natural history, and ranging them in order, the judgement could be more easily brought to bear upon them. Here the art of memory is being used for the investigation of natural science, and its principles of order and arrangement are turning into something like classification" (*The Art of Memory*, 258). As might be expected from Bacon's project to launch a "Great Renewal" of scientific method, he also proposed to revise and improve the arts of memory in the *Advancement of Learning* (1623); see Yates's discussion, 357–59. For a recent study of the influence of Baconian science in Victorian literature and culture, see Jonathan Smith, *Fact and Feeling: Baconian Science and the Nineteenth-Century Literary Imagination* (Madison: University of Wisconsin Press, 1994).

26. Julie Robin Solomon writes that "although Bacon's self-distancing obscures the role that the self and its interests play in the act of knowing, his emphasis upon the exchangeability of knowledge makes evident its socially interdependent character. . . . In Bacon's schema, the communally organized discovery and reassembly of bits and pieces of the universe allow at least some humans to realize the social character of their existence through the act of transforming it, together." *Objectivity in the Making: Francis Bacon and the Politics of Inquiry* (Baltimore: Johns Hopkins University Press, 1998), 226.

27. In *An Essay Concerning Human Understanding*, ed. Peter H. Nidditch (Oxford: Clarendon Press, 1975), John Locke discusses the function of memory in book 1, chapter 10: "Of Retention," and its essential role in consciousness and personal identity in book 2, chapter 27, "Identity and Diversity." All further references will appear in the text. For a history of metaphors associated with memory, including memory as writing, see Douwe Draaisma, *Metaphors of Memory: A History of Ideas About the Mind*, trans. Paul Vincent (Cambridge: Cambridge University Press, 2000).

28. For an analysis of Lockean formulations of prejudice and toleration as they affected the history of the novel and the emergence of modern conceptions of human rights, see Sarah Winter, "The Novel and Prejudice," *Comparative Literature Studies* 46, no. 1 (2009): 76–102.

29. In this sense, empiricist associationism describes processes of inculcation implied in the modern sociological understanding of the habitus as, in Pierre Bourdieu's words, "systems of durable, transposable dispositions" making up the "embodied history" that provides an "infinite yet strictly limited generative capacity," an "art of inventing" of human beings in society. *The Logic of Practice*, trans. Richard Nice (Stanford, Calif.: Stanford University Press, 1990), 55–57. Associationism would describe the psychological acquisition of a particular habitus by the individual mind.

30. Mill, *Analysis*, 1:78.

31. See John Sutton's explanation of the strange physiological dimensions of early associationist views of mental connections offered by Descartes and Hartley: "What are called associationist 'atoms' are psychological or psychophysiological and supervene on a physical base, and thus are not really atoms at all. . . . There's no initial stage at which bare impressions float round the mind before they are hooked up with others: traces are always already complex. . . . With no part of the system ever inactive, it often makes no sense to ask what items in memory *were* before they were associated with others." Thus, "reconstructing the history of associationism . . . suggests the dispensability of both atomism and sensationalism." *Philosophy and Memory Traces: Descartes to Connectionism* (Cambridge: Cambridge University Press, 1998), 243–44.

32. Ibid., 202, 19–20.

33. Joseph Priestly, *Priestley's Writings on Philosophy, Science, and Politics*, ed. John A. Passmore (New York: Collier Books, 1965), 43. For a detailed discussion of Hartley's theory of vibrations as a connectionist theory of distributed memory, see Sutton, *Philosophy and Memory Traces*, chaps. 12–14.

34. Joseph Priestley, *Introductory Essays to Hartley's Theory of the Human Mind, on the Principle of the Association of Ideas* (London, 1817), 186.

35. In keeping with his experimental approach to scientific research, and akin to Bacon's discussion of "curtailment of the unlimited," Priestly argues that repeated impressions of similar objects or experiences of analogous events allow the mind to distinguish essential from incidental elements of complex ideas, because "the necessary parts and properties will occur more often than the variable adjuncts

... and thus we shall be able to distinguish between those parts or properties that have been found separate, and those that have never been observed asunder." *Priestley's Writings*, 43.

36. Priestley, *Introductory Essays*, 183–87.

37. Ibid.

38. Priestly, *Priestley's Writings*, 47–48.

39. See the useful history by Howard C. Warren, *A History of the Association Psychology* (New York: Charles Scribner's Sons, 1967). Other helpful discussions can also be found in Rylance, *Victorian Psychology*, 55–69, and Nicholas Dames, *Amnesiac Selves: Nostalgia, Forgetting, and British Fiction, 1818–1870* (Oxford: Oxford University Press, 2001), 127–38. For a detailed history of the associationist bases of English aesthetics and literary theory, see Martin Kallich, *The Association of Ideas and Critical Theory in Eighteenth-Century England: A History of a Psychological Method in English Criticism* (Paris: Mouton, 1970). Adela Pinch provides illuminating readings of the role of associationist ideas in "the eighteenth century revolution in epistemology, which both gave feelings empirical origins and declared their social benefits," producing a conception of feeling as both "personal" and "impersonal," in *Strange Fits of Passion: Epistemologies of Emotion, Hume to Austen* (Stanford, Calif.: Stanford University Press, 1996), 7.

40. For Hobbes's associationism, I also rely on Kallich's summary in *The Association of Ideas and Critical Theory*, 18–30. For a detailed study of associationism and connectionism in Descartes neurophysiology, see Sutton, *Philosophy and Memory Traces*, chap. 3.

41. Thomas Hobbes, *Leviathan, with Selected Variants from the Latin Edition of 1668*, ed. Edwin Curley (Indianapolis: Hackett, 1994), 12.

42. Ibid., 16–17.

43. Ibid.

44. Aarsleff, "Locke's Influence," 268.

45. The second nature of custom and habit, as Sutton observes, provokes some of Locke's most pessimistic observations about the limitations of human cognition: "There are no inevitable cultural implications of associationism: but then as now it focused urgent debates about the sources, justification, order, and integrity of cognitive processes" (*Philosophy and Memory Traces*, 198–99). According to Sutton, in framing his understanding of the dependence of the sense of identity on memory in the context of the "animal spirits" theory of nerve function, Locke also follows on and revises Descartes, who posited the existence of an invisible vital fluid or spirit coursing through the nerves as a conductor of action from the will to the muscles (see *Philosophy and Memory Traces*, 157–76).

46. Michael Losonsky, *Linguistic Turns in Modern Philosophy* (Cambridge: Cambridge University Press, 2006), 5.

47. David Hume, *A Treatise of Human Nature*, ed. P. H. Nidditch, 2nd ed. (Oxford: Oxford University Press, 1978), 10. All further references will appear in the text.

48. David Hume, *Enquiries Concerning Human Understanding and Concerning the Principles of Morals*, ed. L. A. Selby-Bigge and P. H. Nidditch, 3rd ed. (Oxford: Clarendon Press, 1975), 51, 47.

49. David Hume, "Abstract of A Treatise of Human Nature," in *A Treatise of Human Nature*, ed. L. A. Selby-Bigge and P. H. Nidditch, 662.

50. Ibid., 661–62.

51. In the preface to the English-language edition of his *Empiricism and Subjectivity: An Essay on Hume's Theory of Human Nature*, trans. Constantin V. Boundas (New York: Columbia University Press, 1991), Gilles Deleuze argues that Hume's "most essential and creative contribution[s]" to philosophy include the following aspects: "He gave the *association* of ideas its real meaning, making it a practice of cultural and *conventional* formations (conventional instead of contractual), rather than a theory of the human mind. Hence, the association of ideas exists for the sake of law, political economy, aesthetics, and so on. . . . He created the first great logic of *relations*, showing in it that all relations (not only 'matters of fact' but also relations among ideas) are external to their terms. As a result, he constituted a multifarious world of experience based upon the principle of the exteriority of relations. We start with atomic parts, but these atomic parts have transitions, passages, 'tendencies,' which circulate from one to another. These tendencies give rise to *habits*. . . . We are habits, nothing but habits—the habit of saying 'I.' Perhaps, there is no more striking answer to the problem of the Self" (ix–x). I would add that Hume's understanding of the association of ideas encompasses a theory of mind as itself "external" in its constitutive sociality.

52. Because of its relation of exteriority or permeability to social life, Hume's associating mind should not be identified as the seat of the autonomous, property-owning individual, whom philosopher Jürgen Habermas associates with the rise of the bourgeois public sphere. Indeed, Hume does not figure in Habermas's *The Structural Transformation of the Public Sphere: An Inquiry Into a Category of Bourgeois Society*, trans. Thomas Burger and Frederick Lawrence (Cambridge, Mass.: MIT Press, 1989).

53. Such a conception of the fit between psychology and social order forms an integral part of the seventeenth- and eighteenth-century development of "liberal governmentality," a modern form of administration of market society that, according to literary scholar Mary Poovey, "involved understanding human motivations, including the desire to consume, rather than simply measuring productivity or overseeing obedience." Poovey notes that "the knowledge that increasingly seemed essential to liberal governmentality was the kind cultivated by moral philosophers: an account of subjectivity that helped explain desire, propensities, and aversions as being universal to humans as a group." *A History of the Modern Fact: Problems of Knowledge in the Sciences of Wealth and Society* (Chicago: University of Chicago Press, 1995), 147. The concept of liberal governmentality is based on Michel Foucault's theories included in *The Foucault Effect: Studies in Governmentality*, ed. Graham Burchell, Coline Gordon, and Peter Miller (Chicago: University of Chicago Press, 1991).

54. It is beyond the scope of this chapter to take on the issue of how Hume's theory of association could resolve or exists in tension with or fails to resolve his famous stance of epistemological skepticism or the problem of induction. The section of book 1 of the *Treatise* in which Hume discusses memory's function in "discovering" personal identity is followed immediately by the concluding section 7, in which he describes his "philosophical melancholy" on realizing that this notion of a connection from cause to effect and thus the belief in the "continued existence of matter" is all a product of the imagination, which is responsible for the "vivacity of our ideas" that alone produces our "assent to any argument" or belief in the external existence of any object or of the self (264–66). I will discuss this epistemological crisis further in Chapter 5. For an illuminating discussion of the epistemological contexts of Hume's skepticism, see Poovey, *A History of the Modern Fact*, 197–213. For a seminal philosophical analysis of Hume's theory of causation, see J. L. Mackie, *The Cement of the Universe: A Study of Causation* (Oxford: Clarendon Press, 1974).

55. Quoted in Kallich, *The Association of Ideas and Critical Theory*, 9.

56. Ibid., 70–71, 66.

57. Klein, *A History of Scientific Psychology*, 613–37.

58. Hartley's physiologically based view of memory also allowed him to theorize the *interlaying*, rather than the atomistic connection, of memory traces (these were hypothetical entities composed of minute particles in a medium of Newtonian ether flowing through neural channels) in the medullary substance of the brain. As Sutton points out in his analysis of how associationism prefigures connectionism in modern cognitive science, Hartley's speculative neurophysiology implies that the traces left behind by earlier "vibrations" can be "modified and altered" by subsequent ones and also tend to coalesce with them, so that the "storage [of memories] is not separate from ongoing processing" (*Philosophy and Memory Traces*, 252–55).

59. David Hartley, *Observations on Man, His Frame, His Duty, and His Expectations* (Gainesville, Fla.: Scholars' Facsimiles and Reprints, 1966), 1:333–34.

60. Ibid., 84.

61. Correspondingly, if rational association is a source of order, then aberrant associations may cause madness. In his 1786 treatise on the classification and treatment of insanity, physician and mad doctor Thomas Arnold affirms in Hartleyan terms that "when the mind can regulate properly all its operations, it is then in a sound and rational state: but in proportion as the reverse takes place, in such proportion is it in a state of unsoundness and insanity." *Observations on the Nature, Kinds, Causes and Prevention of Insanity, Lunacy, or Madness* (London: G. Ireland, 1786), 2:284, quoted in Sutton, *Philosophy and Memory Traces*, 228.

62. David Hartley, *Various Conjectures on Perception, Motion, and Generation of Ideas* (Los Angeles: Augustan Reprint Society, 1959), 54–55, quoted in Richard Olsen, *The Emergence of the Social Sciences, 1642–1792* (New York: Twayne, 1993), 101.

63. Jeremy Bentham, *The Principles of Morals and Legislation* (New York: Hafner Press, 1948), 36.

64. Ibid., 37.

65. Jeremy Bentham, *The Works of Jeremy Bentham*, ed. J. Bowring (Edinburgh: 1838–48), 10:561, cited in Elie Halévy, *The Growth of Philosophic Radicalism*, trans. Mary Morris (Boston: Beacon Press, 1955), 433.

66. Halévy, *The Growth of Philosophic Radicalism*, 20.

67. For in-depth analyses of the Utilitarian program, see ibid., and William Thomas, *The Philosophic Radicals: Nine Studies in Theory and Practice, 1817–1841* (Oxford: Clarendon Press, 1979).

68. William Godwin, *Caleb Williams*, ed. Maurice Hindle (London: Penguin, 1988), 192.

69. Ibid., 194–95.

70. Charles Dickens, *Bleak House*, ed. Nicola Bradbury (London: Penguin, 1996), 671.

71. On this theme, see also Malcolm Andrews, *Dickens and the Grown-Up Child* (Iowa City: University of Iowa Press, 1994).

72. Ian Duncan, *Scott's Shadow: The Novel in Romantic Edinburgh* (Princeton, N.J.: Princeton University Press, 2007), 133.

73. Ibid., 124, 137.

74. Hume's philosophy as received through the eighteenth-century novelistic tradition also provides another point of access to understanding how Dickens's novels extend an empiricist perspective on everyday life as part of their pedagogical effects on readers. Ian Duncan explains that "Humean empiricism generates a 'novelistic' model of the imagination that will pose a fertile alternative to the Kantian-Coleridgean 'lyric' model, associated (in modern academic criticism) with English Romantic poetry, which casts the imagination as trace of an alienated transcendental cognition. Hume's philosophical legitimation of the fictive as an 'authentic' representation of common life, since common life is a consensually reproduced fiction, coincides chronologically with the affirmation of fictionality in a cluster of major English novels, from *Tom Jones* to *Tristram Shandy*" (*Scott's Shadow*, 124–25). For a valuable extended discussion of Humean associationist psychology and aesthetics in relation to the novels of Walter Scott, see also Catherine Jones, *Literary Memory: Scott's Waverly Novels and the Psychology of Narrative* (Lewisburg, Pa.: Bucknell University Press, 2003).

75. Graham Richards situates Brown as a student of Reid and Dugald Stewart, who were critics of Locke, but notes that Brown carefully worked through, revised, and thus extended Hume's philosophy. *Mental Machinery: The Origins and Consequences of Psychological Ideas, Part 1: 1600–1850* (Baltimore: Johns Hopkins University Press, 1992), 332–39.

76. Henry Mayhew, *What to Teach and How to Teach It: So That the Child May Become a Wise and Good Man* (London: William Smith, 1842), 12.

77. Thomas Henry Huxley, *Collected Essays*, vol. 6, *Hume: With Helps to the Study of Berkeley* (London: Macmillan, 1894), 70–71. Huxley defines Hume's agnosticism not in its religious sense (though that is clearly implied) but in terms of "its profession of an incapacity to discover the indispensable conditions of either positive or negative knowledge, in many propositions, respecting which, not only the vulgar

but philosophers of the more sanguine sort, revel in the luxury of unqualified assurance" (70–71).

78. James Arbuckle, *Hibernicus's Letters*, vol. 2 (London, 1734), 191.

79. M. J. Smith and W. H. Burston, editorial introduction to Jeremy Bentham, *Chrestomathia*, ed. M. J. Smith and W. H. Burston (Oxford: Clarendon Press, 1983), xiv. In his plan for a rationally organized secondary school for middle-class children, Bentham proposed to implement the monitorial method, in which older pupils instructed large, ranked classrooms of younger pupils. This method was developed at the turn of the nineteenth century by the Anglican clergyman Andrew Bell and the Dissenter Joseph Lancaster. Smith and Burston also chart the history of the failure of Bentham's school project.

80. James Mill, "Education," in *Political Writings*, ed. Terence Ball (Cambridge: Cambridge University Press, 1992), 159–60, 139, 147, 159, 153.

81. For a detailed analysis of Mill's explanation of cultural differences as products of education, see Sarah Winter, "Mental Culture: Liberal Pedagogy and the Emergence of Ethnographic Knowledge," *Victorian Studies* 41, no. 3 (1998): 427–54. See also W. H. Burston, *James Mill on Philosophy and Education* (London: University of London and Athlone Press, 1973).

82. James Mill, "The Ballot," in *Political Writings*, 266–67. For a detailed analysis of the secret ballot as a vehicle of the "individuated privacy" conceived by Victorian liberalism as a formalist abstraction of politics, see Hadley, *Living Liberalism*, chap. 5.

83. Thomas, *The Philosophic Radicals*, 143.

84. Christopher Herbert, *Victorian Relativity: Radical Thought and Scientific Discovery* (Chicago: University of Chicago Press, 2001), 42–43.

85. Robert Owen, *Robert Owen on Education*, ed. Harold Silver (Cambridge: Cambridge University Press, 1969), 76. As Harold Silver explains, this kind of "rationalist position" in the field of education had broad political implications: it "is concerned, then, with the concept of justice, because it is unjust for society to deprive the individual of his equal right to the fullest development. It is concerned with the concept of truth, because it is only by diffusing an awareness of the true nature of society and man that the unjust structure of society can be rectified. It is concerned with happiness, because happiness lies not in fettering the individual to his artificial status in an artificially organised society, but precisely in releasing him from such fetters and enabling him to participate on a footing of equality in areas of human experience which have been withheld from him." *The Concept of Popular Education: A Study in Ideas and Social Movements in the Early Nineteenth Century* (London: MacGibbon & Kee, 1965), 56.

86. Raymond Williams, "Dickens and Social Ideas," in *Dickens, 1970*, ed. Michael Slater (New York: Stein and May, 1970), 93–94.

87. Gareth Stedman Jones, "Rethinking Chartism," in *Languages of Class: Studies in English Working Class History, 1832–1982* (Cambridge: Cambridge University Press, 1983), 124. This stance meant that although the Owenites shared with the Philosophical Radicals (later known as Utilitarians) a basic political orientation

toward utility, or a "natural human capacity to pursue happiness," rather than toward rights as a means to secure human betterment, they attempted not to distinguish among or oppose class interests, while Bentham and Mill singled out the middle class to realize the rational progress of society (124–25).

88. Henry Hetherington, *Democratic Review*, September 1849, 159, quoted in ibid., 127. On Dickens's early radical journalism, see Drew, *Dickens the Journalist*, and Sally Ledger, *Dickens and the Popular Radical Imagination* (Cambridge: Cambridge University Press, 2007). Hetherington had an oblique connection to Dickens: he evidently published a pirated version of thirty-two of Dickens's "Sketches by Boz" in the journal *The Odd Fellow* in 1839; he was subsequently threatened with legal action, presumably by Dickens's publishers, Chapman and Hall, and had to issue a written apology. Louis James, *Fiction for the Working Man, 1830–50* (London: Oxford University Press, 1963), 46.

89. G. J. Holyoake, *Sixty Years of an Agitator's Life* (1893), 1:19, quoted in Jones, "Rethinking Chartism," 127.

90. Robert Owen, *The Life of Robert Owen by Himself*, in *Robert Owen on Education*, ed. Harold Silver (Cambridge: Cambridge University Press, 1969), 67.

91. Charles Dickens, *David Copperfield*, ed. Trevor Blount (London: Penguin, 1966), 540–41.

92. Ibid., 540.

93. Ibid., 541.

94. Owen, *The Life of Robert Owen*, 132.

95. Henry Dunn, *Popular Education; or, The Normal School Manual* (London, 1837), 14, quoted in David Vincent, *Literacy and Popular Culture: England, 1750–1914* (Cambridge: Cambridge University Press, 1989), 85.

96. David Hartley, *Observations on Man*, 1:318–19.

97. For an account of this method and the most commonly used textbooks, see Victor E. Neuburg, *Popular Education in Eighteenth Century England* (London: Woburn Press, 1971), chap. 3.

98. Gillian Beer has explained in reference to Charles Darwin's uses of analogy in his theory of natural selection that "There is always a sense of *story*—of sequence—in analogy, in a way that there need not be in other forms of metaphor. . . . Analogy is predictive metaphor." Furthermore, as Beer points out, "analogies may turn out to be homologies." *Darwin's Plots: Evolutionary Narrative in Darwin, George Eliot and Nineteenth-Century Fiction*, 2nd ed. (Cambridge: Cambridge University Press, 2000), 74.

99. On the issue of literacy as a criterion for working-class political participation, see Hadley, *Living Liberalism*, 87–88, and Vincent, *Literacy and Popular Culture*, chap. 7.

100. Mill, *Analysis*, 1:328–31. All further references from vol. 1 will be included in the text.

101. John B. Thompson, *The Media and Modernity: A Social Theory of the Media* (Stanford, Calif.: Stanford University Press, 1995), 180–81.

102. The 1869 edition of James Mill's *Analysis* is a virtual palimpsest of the history of associationist theory, including John Stuart Mill's footnote expressing strong skepticism about his father's confidence that he can easily distinguish between memory and imagination: "The only difficulty about Memory, when once the laws of Association are understood, is the difference between it and Imagination; but this is a difference which will probably long continue to perplex philosophers. . . . But (apart from the question whether we really do repeat in thought, however summarily, all this series) explaining memory by Self seems very like explaining a thing by a thing. For what notion of Self can we have, apart from Memory?" (*Analysis*, 1:339–40).

103. Bentham, *Chrestomathia*, 26.

104. James Robert Ballantyne, *An Outline of Metaphysical Enquiry with Special Reference to the Phenomena of the Human Mind* (Benares School Book Society, 1848), quoted in N. W. Saffin, *Science, Religion, and Education in Britain, 1804–1904* (Victoria, Australia: Lowden, 1973), 315.

105. Henry Dunn, *Principles of Teaching; or, The Normal School Manual: Containing Practical Suggestions on the Government and Instruction of Children*, 10th ed. (London, n.d.), 179. As secretary of the British and Foreign School Society after 1830, Dunn was in charge of editing the society's report and appointing inspectors of all the society's affiliated schools. He was also superintendent of the society's training school at Borough Road, Southwark. His manual was published in its first edition in 1800 and was reprinted through eleven editions. G. F. Bartle, "Dunn, Henry (1801–1878)," in *Oxford Dictionary of National Biography* (Oxford: Oxford University Press, 2004–10), http://www.oxforddnb.com/view/article/38813 (accessed July 23, 2009).

106. Dunn's further idea of "magnetizing the mind" probably alludes to mesmerism. For a detailed treatment of Victorian views and applications of mesmerism, see Alison Winter, *Mesmerized: Powers of Mind in Victorian Britain* (Chicago: University of Chicago Press, 1998).

107. David Thorburn and Henry Jenkins, eds., *Rethinking Media Change: The Aesthetics of Transition* (Cambridge, Mass.: MIT Press, 2003), 2.

108. Elaine Hadley has argued that the scene of Oliver's reading represents a shift in the register of melodrama from a theatrical, performed cultural mode to a psychological, subjective one that nevertheless invokes melodramatic stage conventions (Oliver's kneeling down to pray) in order to undo the primarily psychological interiority posited by a Utilitarian model of discipline and social classification. *Melodramatic Tactics: Theatricalized Dissent in the English Marketplace, 1800–1885* (Stanford, Calif.: Stanford University Press, 1995), 119–30. Patrick Brantlinger understands the scene of Oliver's reading in reference to the debate taking place in the 1830s and 1840s about the relation between crime and education, and as crucial to creating a distinction between criminal reading and the respectable middle-class reading that Dickens was seeking to associate with the novel. *The Reading Lesson: The Threat of Mass Literacy in Nineteenth-Century British Fiction* (Bloomington: Indiana University Press, 1998), 69–92.

109. Thomas Reid, *The Works of Thomas Reid*, vol. 3, *Essays on the Intellectual Powers of Man*, ed. W. Hamilton (Edinburgh: MachLachlan, Stewart, 1849), 3354a–b, quoted in Sutton, *Philosophy and Memory Traces*, 262, 266. On the Scottish Common Sense School, see also Klein, *A History of Scientific Psychology*, 638–98.

110. See Sutton, *Philosophy and Memory Traces*, 267.

111. Edmund Burke, *A Philosophical Enquiry into the Origin of Our Ideas of the Sublime and Beautiful*, ed. David Womersley (London: Penguin, 1998), 160–61.

112. Kallich, *The Association of Ideas and Critical Theory*, 135.

113. William Hazlitt, "Remarks on the Systems of Hartley and Helvetius," in *An Essay on the Principles of Human Action, on the Systems of Hartley and Helvetius, and on Abstract Ideas* (Bristol, UK: Thoemmes, 1990), 81. For a detailed account of Hazlitt's views of Hartleyan associationism, see David Bromwich, *Hazlitt: The Mind of a Critic* (New Haven, Conn.: Yale University Press, 1999), 58–103.

114. William Hazlitt, "On Reading Old Books," in *The Plain Speaker* (1826), quoted in Willliam St Clair, *The Reading Nation in the Romantic Period* (Cambridge: Cambridge University Press, 2004), 395.

115. Kallich, *The Association of Ideas and Critical Theory*, 130; Samuel Taylor Coleridge, *Biographia Literaria*, ed. J. Shawcross (Oxford, 1907), 1:202, quoted in Kallich, *The Association of Ideas and Critical Theory*, 271.

116. Sutton, *Philosophy and Memory Traces*, 231–32.

117. Samuel Taylor Coleridge, *Biographia Literaria; or, Biographical Sketches of My Literary Life and Opinions*, ed. James Engell and W. Jackson Bate (Princeton, N.J.: Princeton University Press and Routledge and Kegan Paul, 1983), 116–17. On the German philosophical response to associationism, see also Gary Hatfield, *The Natural and the Normative: Theories of Spatial Perception from Kant to Helmholtz* (Cambridge, Mass.: MIT Press, 1990).

118. See Coleridge, *Biographia Literaria*, 83–88, 304. For Coleridge's critique of Hartley's associationism, see 89–128.

119. On the question of dating and a detailed account of this change in Coleridge's views, see Jerome Christensen, *Coleridge's Blessed Machine of Language* (Ithaca, N.Y.: Cornell University Press, 1981), especially chap. 2.

120. Alan Richardson has argued that despite attacks by Coleridge and Wordsworth on the rationalist educators who relied on associationist psychology, the Romantics were part of a late eighteenth- and early nineteenth-century "consensus" on education: "one stressing not traditional skills, 'accomplishments' and factual knowledge but rather, intellectual preparedness and the ability to quickly assimilate new information and learn new tasks. . . . With its emphasis on 'habit,' 'association,' and internalized discipline, this new mode of thinking (perhaps one should say this new set of conditions for educational thought) reflects a shift in educational practice from the instilling of formal precepts to the imposition of 'living rules,' marking part of a more general cultural shift which saw social power take less coercive and more consensual, individualistic forms." *Literature, Education, and Romanticism: Reading as Social Practice, 1780–1832* (Cambridge: Cambridge University Press, 1994), 60.

121. William Wordsworth, *Selected Poems and Prefaces*, ed. Jack Stillinger (Boston: Houghton Mifflin, 1965), 448.

122. Dirk den Hartog mentions Dickens's associationism but focuses on Dickens's elaboration of Wordsworthian psychology for the purposes of representing "the self's continuity." *Dickens and Romantic Psychology: The Self in Time in Nineteenth-Century Literature* (London: Macmillan, 1987), 2.

123. Rylance, *Victorian Psychology*, 65, 67–68, 63, 55. For an analysis of Coleridge's indebtedness to a Humean associationist view of imagination, see Cairns Craig, "Coleridge, Hume, and the Chains of the Romantic Imagination," in *Scotland and the Borders of Romanticism*, ed. Leith Davis, Ian Duncan, and Janet Sorenson (Cambridge: Cambridge University Press, 2004), 20–37.

124. For historian Graham Richards, "regardless of their philosophical greatness, from Psychology's point of view the Associationists remained sidetracked in the rather futile quest of trying to figure out how atomistic sensations can be cobbled together into what we actually experience. . . . Berkeley, the critic might claim, drifts off into mystic reverie, Hume terrifies the life out of himself and switches to writing history, and Hartley is, to be honest, a historical curiosity with no direct legacy. . . . The Associationist tradition . . . played a rather minor part in founding Psychology" (*Mental Machinery*, 237). Richards instead makes the contributions of the writers of the Scottish Common Sense School, particularly Reid, central to his account of psychology's progress as a discipline.

125. Herbert Spencer, *The Principles of Psychology* (London: Longman, Brown, Green, and Longmans, 1855; repr., Westmead, UK: Gregg International, 1970), 563.

126. Ibid.

127. Ibid., 556.

128. William Benjamin Carpenter, *Principles of Mental Physiology*, 2nd ed. (London: Henry S. King, 1875), 436–37, in Jenny Bourne Taylor and Sally Shuttleworth, eds., *Embodied Selves: An Anthology of Psychological Texts, 1830–1890* (Oxford: Clarendon Press, 1998), 154–57.

129. On the development of Darwin's ideas about instinct, see Robert J. Richards, *Darwin and the Emergence of Evolutionary Theories of Mind and Behavior* (Chicago: University of Chicago Press, 1987).

130. Charles Darwin, *The Descent of Man, and Selection in Relation to Sex*, 2nd ed. (New York: Prometheus Books, 1998), 78.

131. Ibid., 634–35.

2. Dickens's Originality: Serial Fiction, Celebrity, and The Pickwick Papers

1. Peter Ackroyd narrates this incident in *Dickens* (New York: HarperCollins, 1990), 547.

2. Fred Inglis, "The Performance of Celebrity," lecture delivered at the Humanities Institute, University of Connecticut, Storrs, April 3, 2003.

3. For a discussion of the circulation of Dickens's portraits and growing public familiarity with his appearance subsequent to the beginning of his public readings,

see Malcolm Andrews, *Charles Dickens and His Performing Selves: Dickens and the Public Readings* (Oxford: Oxford University Press, 2006), 152–69. Gerard Curtis delineates the history of the dissemination of Dickens's image in "Dickens in the Visual Market," in *Literature in the Marketplace: Nineteenth-Century British Publishing and Reading Practices*, ed. John O. Jordan and Robert L. Patten (Cambridge: Cambridge University Press, 1995), 213–49, and *Visual Words: Art and the Material Book in Victorian England* (Aldershot, UK: Ashgate, 2002), 143–95.

4. In *The Physiology of the Novel: Reading, Neural Science, and the Form of Victorian Fiction* (Oxford: Oxford University Press, 2007), Nicholas Dames points out that contemporary critics have often neglected Victorian theories of the novel and of novel reading (2).

5. I refer to Raymond Williams's *Keywords: A Vocabulary of Culture and Society*, rev. ed. (New York: Oxford University Press, 1983).

6. Charles Dickens, *The Pickwick Papers*, ed. Robert L. Patten (London: Penguin, 1972), 276. All further references will appear in the text. All quotations from this edition of *The Pickwick Papers* have been compared with the Clarendon edition of the novel, edited by James Kinsley (Oxford: Clarendon Press, 1986).

7. Anonymous note, quoted in Joseph Grego, ed., *Pictorial Pickwickiana: Charles Dickens and His Illustrators* (London: Chapman and Hall, 1899), 1:51. This annotated copy of *The Pickwick Papers* is held in the Library of the British Museum.

8. Some of the earliest connotations of authorial celebrity were linked to the new practice among early nineteenth-century reviewers of "puffing," or extravagantly praising, a forthcoming book in periodicals belonging to the book's publisher. One of the pioneers of this kind of advertising disguised as reviewing, the publisher of the *New Monthly Magazine* and of silver-fork novels, Henry Colburn, is referred to by Robert Montgomery in 1827: "Let but the smile of Colburn suavity illuminate the MS. and your forthcoming prodigy will meander through all the papers in the full tide of paragraphic celebrity." In Lee Erickson, *The Economy of Literary Form: English Literature and the Industrialization of Publishing* (Baltimore: Johns Hopkins University Press, 1996), 152, and Andrew Elfenbein, "Silver-Fork Byron and the Image of Regency England," in *Byromania: Portraits of the Artist in Nineteenth-and Twentieth-Century Culture*, ed. Frances Wilson (London: Macmillan, 1999), 79. On Byron's reputation and celebrity during the Victorian period, see also Andrew Elfenbein, *Byron and the Victorians* (Cambridge: Cambridge University Press, 1995); Ghislaine McDayter, "Conjuring Byron: Byromania, Literary Commodification and the Birth of Celebrity," in Wilson, *Byromania*, 43–62; and Tom Mole, *Byron's Romantic Celebrity: Industrial Culture and the Hermeneutic of Intimacy* (Basingstoke, UK: Palgrave Macmillan, 2007).

9. *Oxford English Dictionary*, 2nd ed., s.v. "celebrity."

10. John Forster, *The Life of Charles Dickens* (London: J. M. Dent, 1966), 2:62. The slightly unidiomatic use of articles and syntax suggests that Forster is quoting verbatim from the letter. Wredenskii's usage of the relatively new term "celebrity" suggests that it came into English and was available to an educated Russian via the French term *célébrité*, which also seems to have come into currency in the early

1840s according to the *Petit Robert* 1: *Dictionnaire Alphabétique et Analogique de la Langue Française*, 2nd ed. (Paris: Le Robert, 1982), 271.

11. In his study of Byron's Romantic celebrity, Tom Mole dates the emergence of modern celebrity culture to the late eighteenth-century craze surrounding actors such as David Garrick, Sarah Siddons, and Edmund Kean, and the popularity of poets such as Mary Robinson, Ann Yearsley, and Letitia Landon (*Byron's Romantic Celebrity*, chap. 1).

12. *The Public Characters of 1798* (Dublin: J. Moore, 1799), 370. Two advanced, full-text-only Google Book searches for "celebrity" using slightly different parameters (the first applying a time frame between 1790 and 1930, and the second without such date restrictions) on March 11, 2009, generated 8,200–8,500 hits, including texts dated to the present. I reviewed approximately 140 full-text works dating between 1799 and 1930. Certain hits repeated between the two searches, so my approximate total of hits reviewed was about 35 percent of the relevant references to "celebrity" under my parameters on the day of my detailed search.

13. William Cowper and Robert Southey, *The Works of William Cowper, Esq.: Comprising His Poems, Correspondence and Translations. With a Life of the Author by the Editor, Robert Southey*, vol. 2 (London: Baldwin and Cradock, 1836), 282.

14. John Poole, *The Comic Sketch-Book; or, Sketches and Recollections* (London: Routledge, Warne, and Routledge, 1859), 88.

15. Ibid.

16. James Lorimer, *The Universities of Scotland: Past, Present, and Possible* (Edinburgh: W. P. Kennedy, 1854), 59, 67, 84.

17. William Swinton, *Word-Analysis: A Graded Class-Book of English Derivative Words, with Practical Exercises in Spelling, Analyzing, Defining, Synonyms, and the Use of Words* (New York: Ivison, Blakeman, Taylor, 1873), 65–66.

18. Asa Hollister Craig, *New Common School Question Book: Comprising Questions and Answers on All Common School Studies* (New York: Hinds and Noble, 1897), 8. The first edition of this American textbook was published in 1872. I do not know whether the entry on "celebrity" was in that edition or was added later.

19. J. Brander Matthews, *The Theatres of Paris* (London: Sampson Low, Marston, Searle, & Rivington, 1880), 100.

20. Bookcover blurb, Winston Churchill, *The Celebrity: An Episode* (London: Macmillan, 1898; repr., Kessinger, 2003). Churchill's celebrity author sounds like a precursor to Ian Fleming's James Bond character.

21. I. Zangwill, *The Mantle of Elijah* (New York: Harper and Brothers, 1900), 198.

22. Harold MacFarlane, "The Value of a Dead Celebrity," *Cornhill Magazine*, March 1900, 367–71.

23. Stanley T. Williams, "The Founding of Main Street—IV: The Letters of Matthew Arnold," *North American Review* 216 (1922): 411.

24. Dickens spoofs the phenomenon of lionization in the figure of the society hostess Mrs. Leo Hunter, author of the "Ode to an Expiring Frog," "who is proud

to number among her acquaintance all those who have rendered themselves celebrated by their words and talents," and hosts a dinner party featuring a "literary
lion" in *The Pickwick Papers* (274–76).

25. [Richard Ford], review, *Quarterly Review*, June 1839, 38–102, in Phillip
Collins, ed., *Dickens: The Critical Heritage* (New York: Barnes & Noble, 1971), 82.

26. On the relationship of the new medium of photography to the novel's role
in capturing everyday life, see Nancy Armstrong, *Fiction in the Age of Photography:
The Legacy of British Realism* (Cambridge, Mass.: Harvard University Press, 1999).

27. Charles Dickens, *Master Humphrey's Clock and A Child's History of England*
(Oxford: Oxford University Press, 1991), 109. One of Dickens's least studied publishing ventures, *Master Humphrey's Clock*, was begun under the auspices of Chapman and Hall in April 1840 as a weekly, and later monthly, miscellany written solely
by Dickens. Including narratives of visits by Mr. Pickwick and the Wellers, father
and son, to the aged antiquarian Master Humphrey, and with illustrations by both
George Cattermole and Hablôt K. Browne ("Phiz"), it initially consisted of a series
of short narratives presented by Old Master Humphrey as manuscripts stored in the
case of his grandfather clock and shared with a group of friends at a weekly meeting.
When sales began to flag because of readers' expectations of a longer narrative,
Dickens began *The Old Curiosity Shop* in the fourth number and continued that
novel in installments after that. *Master Humphrey's Clock* ceased publication in
November 1841, after the completion of *Barnaby Rudge*. It closed with Master
Humphrey's death (Derek Hudson, introduction to *Master Humphrey's Clock and A
Child's History of England*, v–vii).

28. For an analysis of the emergence of nineteenth-century information culture, see Alexander Welsh, *George Eliot and Blackmail* (Cambridge, Mass.: Harvard
University Press, 1985), and for an account of the historical complexity of the emergence of various forms of print culture, see Adrian Johns, *The Nature of the Book:
Print and Knowledge in the Making* (Chicago: University of Chicago Press, 1998).

29. Richard D. Altick, *The English Common Reader: A Social History of the Mass
Reading Public, 1800–1900*, 2nd ed. (Chicago: University of Chicago Press, 1957),
279–80.

30. Thomas Arnold, *Christian Life, Its Course, Its Hindrances, and Its Helps: Sermons, Preached Mostly in the Chapel of Rugby School*, 4th ed. (London: B. Fellowes,
1845), 39, 41, quoted in Linda K. Hughes and Michael Lund, *The Victorian Serial*
(Charlottesville: University Press of Virginia, 1991), 2–3.

31. See Benjamin Jowett, *Times*, June 20, 1870, quoted in George H. Ford,
Dickens and His Readers: Aspects of Novel-Criticism since 1836 (Princeton, N.J.:
Princeton University Press, 1955), 109.

32. [Ford], review, *Quarterly Review*, June 1839, 38–102, in Collins, *Dickens: The
Critical Heritage*, 81. According to Ian Duncan, Dickens's references to Scott during
the period when he was establishing his own status as a famous and best-selling
author from 1838 to 1842 were "addressed less to matters of literary technique than
to Sir Walter as representative of the profession of novelist. The context of these
references is almost always discussions of publication, reader-reception, sales, and

contracts." *Modern Romance and Transformations of the Novel: The Gothic, Scott, Dickens* (Cambridge: Cambridge University Press, 1992), 190.

33. John Sutherland, *Victorian Fiction: Writers, Publishers, Readers* (New York: St. Martin's Press, 1995), 89. It was also the first work that appeared under the name "Charles Dickens" rather than the pseudonym "Boz," but this did not take place until the first volume edition was published in 1837. As a serial fiction, *Pickwick*'s authorship was still associated with "Boz," the author of numerous short fictional "sketches" first published in several newspapers, and even these began as anonymous publications. Dickens began signing his stories as "Boz" with "The Boarding-House—No. II" in *Monthly Magazine*, August 1934, but had been publishing anonymously since December 1833. For a complete chronology of the publication history of Dickens's early sketches, see Duane DeVries, *Dickens's Apprentice Years: The Making of a Novelist* (New York: Harvester, 1976), 147–57. J. Don Vann provides complete chronologies of the publication of Dickens's serial novels in *Victorian Novels in Serial* (New York: Modern Language Association of America, 1985), 61–75.

34. Robert L. Patten, *Charles Dickens and His Publishers* (Oxford: Clarendon Press, 1978), 219–21. For a complete facsimile edition of one of Dickens's novels in its original serial installments, including advertisements, see Charles Dickens, *The Life and Adventures of Nicholas Nickleby*, edited by Michael Slater, 2 vols. (Philadelphia: University of Pennsylvania Press, 1982).

35. John Butt and Kathleen Tillotson, *Dickens at Work* (London: Methuen, 1957), 14. On the publication history of *Pickwick*, see also J. Don Vann, "The Early Success of *Pickwick*," *Publishing History* 2 (1977): 51–55; Robert L. Patten, "*Pickwick Papers* and the Development of Serial Fiction," *Rice University Studies* 61 (Winter 1975): 51–74.

36. Sutherland, *Victorian Fiction*, 87–106.

37. Ibid., 103.

38. Ibid., 87, 93.

39. Ibid., 104, 106.

40. Ibid., 89.

41. Simon Eliot, "The Business of Victorian Publishing," in *The Cambridge Companion to the Victorian Novel*, ed. Deirdre David (Cambridge: Cambridge University Press, 2000), 42.

42. Graham Law, *Indexes to Fiction in the "Illustrated London News" (1842–1901) and the "Graphic" (1869–1901)*, Victorian Fiction Research Guides, 1–3, http://www.canterbury.ac.uk/arts-humanities/Media/victorian-researchfiction/Home.aspx (accessed December 2008).

43. See John M. L. Drew's *Dickens the Journalist* (London: Palgrave Macmillan, 2003) for a valuable and detailed account of Dickens's editorial work.

44. Kathryn Chittick, *Dickens in the 1830s* (Cambridge: Cambridge University Press, 1990), 114, 126. Such publication practices could be included under Inglis's category of "the technology of celebrity" to the extent that they supported the dissemination of Dickens's textual presence ("The Performance of Celebrity").

45. Sally Ledger, *Dickens and the Popular Radical Imagination* (Cambridge: Cambridge University Press, 2007), 142. For the dating of this dramatic growth of serial publication to the 1840s, see also Altick, *English Common Reader*, 277–93; Eliot, "The Business of Victorian Publishing"; and Ian Haywood, *The Revolution in Popular Literature: Print, Politics and the People, 1790–1860* (Cambridge: Cambridge University Press, 2004), 2.

46. Anon., "Article I," *British Quarterly Review*, April 1, 1859, 316.

47. Altick, *English Common Reader*, 262.

48. Periodicals publishing serial fiction include *Bentley's Miscellany* (1837–68), which published William Harrison Ainsworth's *Jack Sheppard* (1839–40); two periodicals owned or edited by Ainsworth, *Ainsworth's Magazine* (1842–54) and the *New Monthly Magazine* (1814–84); *Fraser's Magazine* (1830–82); the *Family Herald* (1844–1940); *Cassell's Illustrated Family Paper*, initiated in 1853, and its successor, *Cassell's Family Magazine* (1867–1910); *Chambers's Journal of Literature, Science and Arts* (est. 1856 as the successor to *Chambers's Edinburgh Journal*); *Welcome Guest* (est. 1858), which published Mary Elizabeth Braddon's serial fiction; the *Illustrated London News* (1842–1901), a fivepence weekly; the *Graphic* (1869–1932), an illustrated weekly costing sixpence that serialized novels by Trollope and Margaret Oliphant; the *Sunday Times* (1822–), which included serial fiction from the 1840s through the early 1850s; *Bow Bells: A Weekly Magazine of General Literature and Art, for Family Reading* (1862–97); *Boy's Journal* (1863–71); *Boy's Own Paper* (1879–1967); *Beeton's Boy's Own Magazine* (1855–71); and *Sharpe's London Magazine* (1845–52). This list is gleaned from Altick, *English Common Reader*, chaps. 12 and 13; Sutherland, *Victorian Fiction*, 87–106; Law, *Indexes to Fiction*, 3–5; and Margaret K. Powell and Susanne F. Roberts, "Imperial Views, Colonial Subjects: Victorian Periodicals and the Empire: Images from an Exhibition, Sterling Memorial Library, Yale University, August–October 1999."

49. This group includes *Leisure Hour* (1852–1903), *Sunday at Home: A Family Magazine for Sabbath Reading* (1854–1900), *Home Friend* (1852–54), *Once a Week* (1859–80), *Good Words* (1860–1906), the *Monthly Packet* (1851–99), and the *Quiver* (1861–1926), which was published by Cassell's and included serials by Mrs. Henry Wood.

50. For a detailed listing of these publications and analysis of Jones's career and writings, see Ledger, *Dickens and the Popular Radical Imagination*, 152–67.

51. Eliot, "The Business of Victorian Publishing," 49.

52. For contemporary sources on these organizations, see William Jones's *The Jubilee Memorial of the Religious Tract Society* (London, 1850); S. G. Green's *The Story of the Religious Tract Society* (London, 1899); and G. Hewitt's *Let the People Read* (London, 1949), all cited in "Historical resources for UK temperance movement at Institute of Alcohol Studies, Alliance House Foundation, London." *Alcohol and Drugs History Society* http://historyofalcoholanddrugs.typepad.com/alcohol_and_drugs_history/2007/08/historical-reso.html (accessed October 11, 2010).

53. Eliot, "The Business of Victorian Publishing," 44.

54. In Altick, *English Common Reader*, 384.

55. Eliot, "The Business of Victorian Publishing," 38–40. For an account of the numerous works of Victorian fiction originally published as serials in periodicals, see Hughes and Lund, *The Victorian Serial*.

56. On the educative functions of periodical literature, see Walter E. Houghton, "Periodical Literature and the Articulate Classes," in *The Victorian Periodical Press: Samplings and Soundings*, ed. Joanne Shattock and Michael Wolff (Leicester, UK: Leicester University Press and University of Toronto Press, 1982), 3–27. See also Alan Rauch's analysis of the SDUK's role in the Victorian "knowledge industry" in *Useful Knowledge: Victorians, Morality, and the March of Intellect* (Durham, N.C.: Duke University Press, 2001), 24–59.

57. Patricia Anderson, *The Printed Image and the Transformation of Popular Culture, 1790–1860* (Oxford: Clarendon Press, 1991), 51–52.

58. See Anderson's discussion of the *Penny Magazine*'s innovations in the publication of fine art illustrations in ibid., chap. 2.

59. Charles Knight, "Reading for All," *Penny Magazine* 1 (1832): 1,in ibid., 53.

60. Scott Bennett, "Revolutions in Thought: Serial Publication and the Mass Market for Reading," in Shattock and Wolff, *The Victorian Periodical Press*, 228, 234. See also Scott Bennett, "John Murray's Family Library and the Cheapening of Books in Early Nineteenth Century Britain," *Studies in Bibliography* 29 (1976): 139–66.

61. Bennett, "Revolutions in Thought," 227.

62. Charles Knight, *Passages from the Life of Charles Knight* (New York: G. P. Putnam's Sons, 1874), 329–30, in ibid., 227. Knight quotes *Quentin Durward*, by Walter Scott.

63. Bennett, "Revolutions in Thought," 246.

64. Ibid., 248–51.

65. Charles Knight, *Passages from the Life of Charles Knight*, 400, 404–6.

66. Ibid., 406.

67. Ibid., 410. For a discussion of Knight's attempts to establish book clubs, see Victor E. Neuburg, *Popular Literature: A History and Guide* (London: Woburn Press, 1977), 195–200.

68. Knight quotes Dickens's letter as follows: "The English are, so far as I know, the hardest worked people on whom the sun shines. Be content if in their wretched intervals of leisure they read for amusement and do no worse. They are born at the oar, and they live and die at it. Good God, what would we have of them!" (*Passages from the Life of Charles Knight*, 426–27).

69. Dickens's position on the "taxes on knowledge," including the quotations from his letters, is detailed in Patten, *Charles Dickens and His Publishers*, 222–23 n. 16.

70. Cassell to Brougham, September 29, 1858, Brougham correspondence, University College London Library, in Anderson, *The Printed Image*, 121.

71. Louis James, "Reynolds, George William MacArthur (1814–1879)," ed. H. C. G. Matthew and Brian Harrison, in *Oxford Dictionary of National Biography* (Oxford: Oxford University Press, 2004–10), http://www.oxforddnb.com/view/

article/23414 (accessed December 18, 2008). See the detailed discussion of Lloyd's and Reynolds's publications in Haywood, *Revolution in Popular Literature*, chap. 7.

72. Haywood, *Revolution in Popular Literature*, 231–36, 218–19.

73. Elaine Hadley explains that the burgeoning of mostly sectarian newspapers and the expansion of both electors and readers by midcentury created a new dynamic in the understanding of public opinion by Victorian liberals as "utterly unmediated mass publicity": "the mid-Victorian public sphere is by no means the object or organ of valued public discourse [for liberals] but rather a phantasmagoric threat to the given realities of liberal status." *Living Liberalism: Practical Citizenship in Mid-Victorian Britain* (Chicago: University of Chicago Press, 2010), 44–45. This liberal anxiety about mass publicity is therefore distinct from the views of publishers and writers such as Knight, Reynolds, Chambers, and Dickens, all of whom were much more enthusiastic, in different ways, about the new mass readership.

74. Mary Poovey, *Uneven Developments: The Ideological Work of Gender in Mid-Victorian England* (Chicago: University of Chicago Press, 1988), 104.

75. N. N. Feltes, *Modes of Production of Victorian Novels* (Chicago: University of Chicago Press, 1986), 3.

76. Ibid., 6. Feltes cites Karl Marx, *Capital* (Harmondsworth: Penguin, 1976), 1:558. For studies of the professionalization of authorship in nineteenth-century Britain, see Poovey, *Uneven Developments*, chap. 4; Cathy Shuman, *Pedagogical Economies: The Examination and the Victorian Literary Man* (Stanford, Calif.: Stanford University Press, 2000); Jennifer Ruth, *Making Professions: Labor, Value, and the Mid-Victorian Novel* (Columbus: Ohio State University Press, 2006); Paul K. Saint-Amour, *The Copywrights: Intellectual Property and The Literary Imagination* (Ithaca, N.Y.: Cornell University Press, 2003); Peter L. Shillingsburg, *Pegasus in Harness: Victorian Publishing and W. M. Thackeray* (Charlottesville: University of Virginia Press, 1992); and Martha Woodmansee, *The Author, Art, and the Market: Rereading the History of Aesthetics* (New York: Columbia University Press, 1994).

77. For a detailed history of Dickens's financial arrangements with his publishers, see Patten, *Charles Dickens and His Publishers*. On Dickens's advocacy of international copyright, see Alexander Welsh, *From Copyright to Copperfield: The Identity of Dickens* (Cambridge, Mass.: Harvard University Press, 1987).

78. Feltes, *Modes of Production of Victorian Novels*, 12–13.

79. Bennett, "Revolutions in Print," 251.

80. Haywood, *Revolution in Popular Literature*, 238–39.

81. Ledger, *Dickens and the Popular Radical Imagination*, 169.

82. Patten reproduces these figures in *Charles Dickens and His Publishers*, 355. Haywood estimates the combined total sales of Reynolds's *The Mysteries of London* (1844–48) and *The Mysteries of the Court of London* (1848–55) as greater than one million copies (*Revolution in Popular Literature*, 170). Neuburg reports that *The Mysteries of London* "sold at a rate of nearly 40,000 copies per week" (*Popular Literature*, 157).

83. Mary Poovey, *Genres of the Credit Economy: Mediating Value in Eighteenth- and Nineteenth-Century Britain* (Chicago: University of Chicago Press, 2008), 286.

84. Ibid., 290–91.

85. Ibid., 300, 306.

86. This development of a mainstream theory of popular reception to explain the popularity of serial fiction also predates the dispute between "generalist" and research-based models of literary studies characterizing the university-based discipline of literary studies in the last decades of the nineteenth century, as analyzed by literary scholars Gerald Graff in *Professing Literature: An Institutional History* (Chicago: University of Chicago Press, 2007) and John Guillory in *Cultural Capital: The Problem of Literary Canon Formation* (Chicago: University of Chicago Press, 1993).

87. Pierre Bourdieu dates the emergence of the modern literary field as a sphere of relative autonomy from the market to the second half of the nineteenth century in France. *The Rules of Art: Genesis and Structure of the Literary Field*, trans. Susan Emanuel (Stanford, Calif.: Stanford University Press, 1996), 47–112.

88. Hughes and Lund, *The Victorian Serial*, 2, 16.

89. Ibid., 71.

90. Richard. D. Altick, *Writers, Readers, and Occasions: Selected Essays on Victorian Literature and Life* (Columbus: Ohio State University Press, 1989), 124–25. In relation specifically to "retrospective" narrative in *The Pickwick Papers*, Patten also argues that not only is Dickens's first serial novel notable for its "suffusion of pastness" and "nostalgia for previous modes of discursive practice, feeling, and social organization," but it also establishes "looking backward" as a "way of reading" that fosters learning by allowing characters and readers alike to find "alternative explanations more consonant with outcomes and experience." "Serialized Retrospection in *The Pickwick Papers*," in Jordan and Patten, *Literature in the Marketplace*, 131.

91. [G. H. Lewes], review of *Sketches, Pickwick*, and *Oliver Twist*, *National Magazine and Monthly Critic*, December 1837, 445–49, in Collins, *Dickens: The Critical Heritage*, 64.

92. On the young Queen Victoria's exchange with Lord Melbourne, then prime minister for the Whigs, on the depictions of poverty and crime in *Oliver Twist* in 1848–49, see the extracts from Victoria's diaries included in Collins, *Dickens: The Critical Heritage*, 44.

93. Altick, *English Common Reader*, 82–83. Altick notes that "the unknown factors relating to the distribution of Dickens's first readers . . . make confident generalizations almost impossible" (*Writers, Readers, and Occasions*, 119). For a more recent account of who was included in the midcentury Victorian middle classes and how many they were in terms of total numbers and percentages of the population, see K. Theodore Hoppen, *The Mid-Victorian Generation, 1846–1886* (Oxford: Clarendon Press, 1998), 31–55.

94. For public schoolboys' readings of Dickens, see Altick, *English Common Reader*, 182. The exam on *Pickwick*, written by parodist C. S. Calverley, appears in Collins, *Dickens: The Critical Heritage*, 39–40. Collins records that "*Pickwick* was, clearly, already a cult book: and swopping [*sic*] arcane Dickens tags was something of an undergraduate fashion" (39).

95. Helen Small questions how many of the spectators of Dickens's perform-ances over the years really were from the working classes, since most of the readings did not offer special free tickets for them, and few could have afforded even the cheapest shilling tickets. "A Pulse of 124: Charles Dickens and a Pathology of the Mid-Victorian Reading Public," in *The Practice and Representation of Reading in England*, ed. James Raven, Helen Small, and Naomi Tadmor (Cambridge: Cam-bridge University Press, 1996), 273. Matthew Bevis provides more documentation of working-class attendance at Dickens's lectures, however, as well as of workers' participation during the 1850s and 1860s in "penny readings" staged by associations that rivaled the Mechanics' Institutes and were organized by working-class members who also performed as readers. At these readings, Bevis notes, a popular recitation text was the trial scene from *The Pickwick Papers*. "Dickens in Public," *Essays in Criticism* 51, no. 3 (2001): 331–32.

96. For critical assessments of Dickens's attitudes toward working-class audi-ences of his public readings, see Janice Carlisle, "Spectacle as Government: Dickens and the Working-Class Audience," in *The Performance of Power: Theatrical Discourse and Politics*, ed. Sue-Ellen Case and Janelle Reinelt (Iowa City: University of Iowa Press, 1991), 163–80, and Small, "A Pulse of 124."

97. Thomas Frost, *Forty Years' Recollections* (London, 1880), 323, in Anderson, *The Printed Image*, 161–62.

98. Jonathan Rose, *The Intellectual Life of the British Working Classes* (New Haven, Conn.: Yale University Press, 2001), 111.

99. In *The Intellectual Life of the British Working Classes*, Jonathan Rose cites numerous instances of working-class readers' preference for Dickens's works, with most of his evidence dating from the 1870s through the early twentieth century. On working-class readers' tastes in the first half of the twentieth century, see also Joseph McAleer, *Popular Reading and Publishing in Britain, 1914–1950* (Oxford: Clarendon Press, 1992).

100. Charles H. Welch, *An Autobiography* (Banstead: Berean Publishing Trust, 1960), 33, quoted in Rose, *The Intellectual Life*, 111.

101. Jonathan Rose, "Rereading the English Common Reader: A Preface to a History of Audiences," *Journal of the History of Ideas* 53 (1992): 56.

102. Ibid., 113–14.

103. M. K. Ashby, *Joseph Ashby of Tysoe, 1859–1919: A Study of English Village Life* (Cambridge: Cambridge University Press, 1961), 94.

104. Forster, *The Life of Charles Dickens*, 2:65.

105. Henry Morley, *A First Sketch of English Literature*, 26th ed. (London: Cassell, 1890), 1059. The first edition of Morley's text was published in 1873; he added an extensive discussion of literature "in the reign of Victoria" (excluding living authors) to the twelfth edition of 1886.

106. Charles Dickens, "A Preliminary Word," *Household Words*, March 30, 1850, in *The Amusements of the People and Other Papers: Reports, Essays, and Reviews, 1834–51*, ed. Michael Slater, Dent Uniform Edition of Dickens' Journalism (Columbus: Ohio State University Press, 1996), 178; Ledger, *Dickens and the Popular Radical*

Imagination, 171–72. Ledger offers a detailed analysis of the contents of the early issues of *Household Words* as representing Dickens's systematic "embrace of both high and low culture" (172–92). For a more critical view of periodicals edited by such figures as Knight, Dickens, and Chambers as participating in a "counter-revolutionary" project, see Haywood, *Revolution in Popular Literature*, 218–42.

107. Charles Dickens, letter to Henry Morley, October 31, 1852, in Drew, *Dickens the Journalist*, 112–15; The complete letter can be found in *The Letters of Charles Dickens*, ed. Madeline House, Graham Storey, and Kathleen Tillotson, Pilgrim Edition (Oxford: Clarendon Press, 1965–2002), 6:790–91.

108. K. J. Fielding, ed., *The Speeches of Charles Dickens: A Complete Edition* (Oxford: Clarendon Press, 1960), 154–55.

109. Ibid., 154.

110. Ibid., 157.

111. Ibid., 159–60.

112. [Mary Carpenter], *Ragged Schools: Their Principles and Modes of Operation, by a Worker* (London, 1850), 4, in Norris Pope, *Dickens and Charity* (New York: Columbia University Press, 1978), 162.

113. Pope, *Dickens and Charity*, 162.

114. For an intriguing argument that *Hard Times* targets representations of the working classes in parliamentary Blue Books, rather than seeking to fathom working-class experience, see Carolyn Vellenga Berman, "'Awful Unknown Quantities': Addressing the Readers in *Hard Times*, *Victorian Literature and Culture* 37.2 (September 2009): 561–82.

115. Charles Dickens, preface to *Evenings of a Working Man, Being the Occupation of His Scanty Leisure: By John Overs. With a Preface relative to the Author by Charles Dickens* (London: T.C. Newby, 1844), in *The Uncommercial Traveller and Other Papers, 1859–70*, ed. Michael Slater and John Drew Dent, Uniform Edition of Dickens' Journalism (Columbus: Ohio State University Press, 2000), 419.

116. Thomas Carlyle, *Chartism*, in *Selected Writings*, edited by Alan Shelston (London: Penguin, 1971), 222.

117. Brian Simon, *Studies in the History of Education, 1780–1870* (London: Lawrence & Wisehart, 1960), 340–46.

118. John Overs to Charles Dickens, July 20, 1840, in Sheila M. Smith, "John Overs to Charles Dickens: A Working-Man's Letter and Its Implications," *Victorian Studies* 18, no. 2 (December 1974), 208–9.

119. Ibid.

120. Ibid.

121. Anon. review, *Metropolitan Magazine*, September 1836, 13, in Collins, *Dickens: The Critical Heritage*, 31.

122. Percy Fitzgerald, *The History of Pickwick* (London: Chapman and Hall, 1891), 4.

123. [Abraham Hayward], *Quarterly Review*, October 1837, 484–518, in Collins, *Dickens: The Critical Heritage*, 57.

124. Patten, "*Pickwick Papers* and the Development of Serial Fiction," 64–65.

125. Altick, *English Common Reader*, 383.

126. [Richard Ford], *Quarterly Review*, June 1839, 83–102, in Collins, *Dickens: The Critical Heritage*, 83.

127. Ibid.

128. Anon. review of *Oliver Twist, Spectator*, November 1838, 1114–16, in Collins, *Dickens: The Critical Heritage*, 42.

129. Forster, *The Life of Charles Dickens*, 1:74.

130. Anon. review of *Pictures from Italy, Times*, June 1, 1846, in Collins, *Dickens: The Critical Heritage*, 140.

131. John Forster explains the pseudonym's origin: "This was the nickname of a pet child, [Dickens's] youngest brother Augustus, whom in honour of [Smollet's] Vicar of Wakefield he had dubbed Moses, which being facetiously pronounced through the nose became Boses, and being shortened became Boz. 'Boz was a very familiar household word to me, long before I was an author, and so I came to adopt it'" (*The Life of Charles Dickens*, 1:55).

132. [G. H. Lewes], review of *Sketches by Boz, Pickwick*, and *Oliver Twist, National Monthly Magazine and Monthly Critic*, December 1837, 455–59, in Collins, *Dickens: The Critical Heritage*, 64.

133. Ackroyd, *Dickens*, 196.

134. From A. G. L'Estrange, *Life of Mary Russell Mitford* (1870), 3:78, in Collins, *Dickens: The Critical Heritage*, 35–36.

135. [Abraham Hayward], *Quarterly Review*, October 1837, in Collins, *Dickens: The Critical Heritage*, 57. On the phenomenon of commodity culture surrounding Victorian periodicals, see Catherine Waters, *Commodity Culture in Dickens's "Household Words": The Social Life of Goods* (Farnham, Surrey, UK: Ashgate, 2008).

136. Fitzgerald, *The History of Pickwick*, 24–25.

137. Francis Bacon, *The New Organon*, ed. Lisa Jardine and Michael Silverthorne (Cambridge: Cambridge University Press, 2000), 143.

138. Describing his own composition of an epic, Jingle adds the seemingly random occasion of the July Revolution in France. This random element is, in this case, produced by the author's own associations and his momentary forgetfulness of the year in which the novel was set; Dickens adds a footnote to the 1847 Cheap Edition of the novel noting that this was "A remarkable instance of the prophetic force of Mr Jingle's imagination; this dialogue occurring in the year 1827, and the Revolution in 1830" (79).

139. Thomas Hobbes, *Leviathan, with Selected Variants from the Latin Edition of 1668*, ed. Edwin Curley (Indianapolis: Hackett, 1994), 12.

140. Ibid., 12–13.

141. Ibid.

142. Ibid., 13.

143. Francis Bacon, *The Advancement of Learning*, ed. Michael Kiernan (Oxford: Clarendon Press, 2000), 2:112–13.

144. Ibid., 111–12.

145. Hobbes's notions of invention in mental discourse seem to align particularly well with Dickens's improvisational comedic style. Similar and more historically proximate conceptions of the relation between memory and imagination would have been available to Dickens through his reading of eighteenth-century novels by Oliver Goldsmith and Laurence Sterne, or the poetry of Samuel Rogers and William Wordsworth.

146. On the history of rhetorical education in the nineteenth century as a precursor to and competitor of the emergent discipline of English literary studies, see John Guillory, "Literary Study and the Modern System of the Disciplines," in *Disciplinarity at the Fin de Siècle*, ed. Amanda Anderson and Joseph Valente (Princeton, N.J.: Princeton University Press, 2002), 19–43, and Thomas P. Miller, *The Formation of College English: Rhetoric and Belles Lettres in the British Cultural Provinces* (Pittsburgh: University of Pittsburgh Press, 1997).

147. For a recent detailed study of rhetoric and public speaking in Victorian and modernist literature, see Matthew Bevis, *The Art of Eloquence: Byron, Dickens, Tennyson, Joyce* (Oxford: Oxford University Press, 2007).

148. Bacon, *The Advancement of Learning*, 112–13.

149. For an illuminating analysis of Sam Weller's parodies of deduction and the origins of "Wellerisms" in Cervantes and Shakespeare, see Garrett Stewart, *Dickens and the Trials of Imagination* (Cambridge, Mass.: Harvard University Press, 1974), 73–75.

150. For a psychoanalytically inflected reading of Jingle's and the Wellers' speech patterns as reflecting unconscious linguistic energies, see Steven Marcus, "Language Into Structure: *Pickwick* Revisited," *Daedalus* 101, no. 1 (1972): 183–202. On the evolution of Dickens's early novels, see also Marcus's *Dickens: From Pickwick to Dombey* (New York: Basic Books, 1965). Kevin McLaughlin analyzes Sam Weller's similes as exhibiting a kind of "fetishism," an "almost complete disregard for contextual origin or indeed similarity itself," indicative of the novel's general interest in "collection" as a strategy of "false equilibrium," or an attempt to organize in narrative form the arbitrary connections of urban life. *Writing in Parts: Imitation and Exchange in Nineteenth-Century Literature* (Stanford, Calif.: Stanford University Press, 1995), 114, 116. Such divergent readings are not so much contradictory as demonstrative of the suggestiveness of Dickens's invention.

151. My thanks to Ian Duncan for explaining the factual basis of the joke to me.

152. Here we also see a foreshadowing of the biting social satire that some Victorian reviewers from the mid-1850s through the 1860s, such as James Fitzjames Stephen, Margaret Oliphant, E. S. Dallas, and G. H. Lewes, criticized in Dickens's later novels, *Bleak House*, *Little Dorrit*, and *Our Mutual Friend* (1864–65). See the reviews by these critics collected in Collins, *Dickens: The Critical Heritage*.

153. David Thorburn and Henry Jenkins, eds., *Rethinking Media Change: The Aesthetics of Transition* (Cambridge, Mass.: MIT Press, 2003), 4–5.

154. Louis James, *Fiction for the Working Man, 1830–50* (London: Oxford University Press, 1963), 49.

155. Deborah Vlock, *Dickens, Novel Reading, and the Victorian Popular Theatre* (Cambridge: Cambridge University Press, 1998), 81.

156. Ibid., 40, 94–95. Vlock criticizes Dickens's use of patter as an instance of pervasive Victorian techniques for the social containment of the speech of subversive males and "redundant" females, such as spinsters. For a detailed analysis of gender and humor in the nineteenth-century novel, see also Eileen Gillooly, *Smile of Discontent: Humor, Gender, and Nineteenth-Century British Fiction* (New York: Columbia University Press, 1999).

157. Vlock argues that Dickens's female patterer characters in particular were inspired by the stage patter of the famous Victorian comedian and impersonator Charles Matthews, whose repertoire included several loquacious female characters (*Dickens, Novel Reading*, 129). Dickens biographers John Forster and Peter Ackroyd also identify the importance of Matthews as a model for Dickens's novelistic use of patter.

158. Ibid., 40.

159. Charles Kent, *Charles Dickens as a Reader* (London: Chapman and Hall, 1872; rpt. New York: Haskell House, 1973), 208.

160. Andrews, *Charles Dickens and His Performing Selves*, 250–51.

161. Richard Maxwell has argued persuasively that Mrs. Gamp also exemplifies the related quality of "singularity," which, as part of a repeated series of verbal tags, gestures, and scenes, signifies an organizational structure shared by the narrative and a society that lacks consensus. *The Mysteries of Paris and London* (Charlottesville: University Press of Virginia, 1992), 126–49. It is the creation of a pleasurable consensus in readers' memories around such characters as Mrs. Gamp that I want to foreground as a phenomenon of Dickens's reception carrying larger implications for democratic participation.

162. James Mill, *Analysis of the Phenomena of the Human Mind*, ed. Alexander Bain, Andrew Findlater, and George Grote, 2nd ed. (New York: Augustus M. Kelley, 1967), 1:328, 331.

163. John Stuart Mill, *Autobiography*, ed. John Robson (London: Penguin, 1989), 123.

164. This incident is reported without reference to source in Amy Cruse, *The Victorians and Their Reading* (Boston: Houghton Mifflin, 1936), 168–69. I am grateful to Thomas Recchio for pointing out this anecdote to me.

165. Kent, *Charles Dickens as a Reader*, 215.

166. Charles Dickens, *Martin Chuzzlewit*, ed. P. N. Furbank (London: Penguin, 1968), 828. All further references will be included in the text.

167. Kent, *Charles Dickens as a Reader*, 20.

168. [Ford], review, *Quarterly Review*, June 1839, 38–102, in Collins, *Dickens: The Critical Heritage*, 82.

169. Anon., "Boz and His *Nicholas Nickleby*," *Spectator*, March 31, 1938, 304, in Collins, *Dickens: The Critical Heritage*, 69.

170. Anon., *Pictorial Times*, April 20, 1844, in Ackroyd, *Dickens*, 200.

171. Walter Bagehot, "Charles Dickens," review of the Library Edition of Dickens's Works, *National Review*, October 1858, 459–86, in Stephen Wall, ed., *Charles Dickens: A Critical Anthology* (Harmondsworth, UK: Penguin, 1970), 126.

172. Ibid, 126–27.

173. Ibid.

174. Drew, *Dickens the Journalist*, 24.

175. Questioning the purported referentiality of Dickens's realism, J. Hillis Miller argues that Dickens's narrator's adoption of the journalistic "we" in *Sketches by Boz* "depersonalizes him, reduces him to a function, and at the same time suggests that he is divided into two [public and private] consciousnesses." "The Fiction of Realism: *Sketches by Boz, Oliver Twist*, and Cruikshank's Illustrations," in *Dickens Centennial Essays*, ed. Ada Nisbet and Blake Nevius (Berkeley: University of California Press, 1971), 88.

176. Anon. review of William Henry Wills, "Old Leaves, Gathered from *Household Words*," *Examiner*, January 21, 1860, in Drew, *Dickens the Journalist*, 182.

177. [John Forster], review of *The Pickwick Papers*, *Examiner*, July 2, 1837, 421–22, in Collins, *Dickens: The Critical Heritage*, 37.

178. Jeremy Bentham, *Chrestomathia*, ed. M. J. Smith and W. H. Burston (Oxford: Clarendon Press, 1983), 26.

179. [John Forster], review of *Nicholas Nickleby*, *Examiner*, October 27, 1839, in Collins, *Dickens: The Critical Heritage*, 48–51. Publication figures are from Altick, *English Common Reader*, 383.

180. Ibid., 51.

181. Benjamin Jowett, *Times*, June 20, 1870, 14, in Ford, *Dickens and His Readers*, 109.

182. Norman Nicholson, *Wednesday Early Closing* (London: Faber and Faber, 1975), 142–45, in Rose, *The Intellectual Life*, 113. Similarly, Neville Cardus, the son of Manchester launderers, found that "David Copperfield so often behaved and thought as I behaved and thought that I frequently lost my own sense of identity in him." *Second Innings* (London: Collins, 1950), 45–47, in Rose, *The Intellectual Life*, 113. Rose notes that many working-class autobiographers adopted the narrative style of *David Copperfield* (1849–50) while also attesting to their personal experience of the "reality" of Dickens's characters and settings: "While the first wave of modernist critics was dismissing Dickens as a melodramatic caricaturist, working people were reading his novels as documentaries, employing the same frame that their grandparents had applied to Bunyan" (113, 114).

183. Nicholson's reading, then, also implies that mass reception of popular fiction could involve appropriation, incorporation, and modification of the novel's schemes of representation as part of the reader's own experience rather than ideological inculcation, as philosopher Michel de Certeau's understanding of mass reading as a practice of everyday life also theorizes. *The Practice of Everyday Life*, trans. Steven Rendall (Berkeley: University of California Press, 1984), 82–90.

184. [Richard Ford], review, *Quarterly Review*, June 1839, 83–102, in Collins, *Dickens: The Critical Heritage*, 82.

185. Margaret Gillies was a successful painter and portraitist whose works were widely shown at prestigious exhibitions. She "received early and vital support from the radical Unitarian and feminist entourage of *The Monthly Repository*—specifically from Richard Hengist Horne, Leigh Hunt, Thomas Powell and in particular Thomas Southwood Smith," the physician and sanitary reformer with whom she lived for twenty years (he was already married). Charlotte Yeldham, *Margaret Gillies RWS, Unitarian Painter of Mind and Emotion 1803–1887* (Lewiston, N.Y.: Edwin Mellen Press, 1997), 3.

186. R. H. Horne, *A New Spirit of the Age*, 2nd ed., vol. 1 (London: Smith, Elder, 1844), 4. All further references are included in the text.

187. For Maclise's account of this event, see Ackroyd, *Dickens*, 447.

188. Curtis, "Dickens in the Visual Market," 235–36.

189. Ibid., 238.

190. Curtis argues that this type of image of the author with pen in hand takes its place in a long iconographic tradition dating from the Middle Ages (*Visual Words*, 172–95).

191. "Charles Dickens. A Lecture by Professor Ward. Delivered in Manchester, 30th November, 1870," in John Forster, *The Life of Charles Dickens*, ed. J. W. T. Ley (London: Cecil Palmer, 1928), 727.

192. Diary entry for June 11, 1870, in *Letters, 1862–78*, ed. G. E. Buckle (1906), 2:21, in Collins, *Dickens: The Critical Heritage*, 502.

193. Small, "A Pulse of 124," 266. Small argues that Dickens's public readings "form an important cultural extension of the contemporary political debate about franchise reform," and that "the political ideals of liberal reform have their cultural realization in these Readings, for, in listening to Dickens, his reading public was encouraged to develop and demonstrate that capacity for rational appreciation, critical discernment and moral sensibility desired in the voting public." Particularly in the case of working-class audience members, "under Dickens's active management the idea of the reading public became the means to a liberal celebration of reading as the forum in which all classes could come together, united in the enjoyment of a common sensibility" (267–69). This chapter's analysis suggests that self-conscious participation in Dickens's reading audience was orchestrated in various ways by the structure of Dickens's texts and registered in the language of his critical reception before the period of Dickens's public readings.

194. Kate Douglas Wiggin, *My Garden of Memory: An Autobiography* (Boston and New York: Houghton Mifflin, 1923), 42.

195. Benjamin Jowett, *Times*, June 20, 1870, quoted in Ford, *Dickens and His Readers*, 109.

196. George Orwell, *Dickens, Dali, and Others* (New York: Harcourt, Brace, 1963), 57–58.

197. Ibid., 73–74.
198. Ibid., 75.

3. The Pleasures of Memory, Part I: Curiosity as Didacticism in The Old Curiosity Shop

1. Anon. review, *Metropolitan Magazine*, December 1840, 111, in Philip Collins, ed., *Dickens: The Critical Heritage* (New York: Barnes & Noble, 1971), 93–94. Jack Sheppard was an eighteenth-century robber famous for breaking out of Newgate prison, and also the eponymous hero of a novel by William Harrison Ainsworth that began its serial run in 1839 in *Bentley's Miscellany*, coinciding with the final installments of *Oliver Twist*.

2. *Tomahawk: A Saturday Journal of Satire*, June 25, 1870, 245–46, quoted in George H. Ford, *Dickens and His Readers: Aspects of Novel-Criticism since 1836* (Princeton, N.J.: Princeton University Press, 1955), 80.

3. John Forster to Charles Dickens, January 16, 1841, in Dickens, *The Letters of Charles Dickens*, ed. Madeline House, Graham Storey, and Kathleen Tillotson, Pilgrim Edition (Oxford: Clarendon Press, 1965–2002), 2:187 n.

4. Charles Dickens, *Our Mutual Friend*, ed. Michael Cotsell (Oxford: Oxford University Press, 1989), 214. Philip Collins has identified Charley Hexam's school with the Ragged Schools for the poor street children of London, begun in the early 1840s; Dickens was both a supporter of these schools and critic of some of their methods. "Dickens and the Ragged Schools," *Dickensian* 55 [May 1959]: 94–109. Dickens describes a visit to such a school in "A Sleep to Startle Us," *Household Words*, March 13, 1852, reprinted in Charles Dickens, *Gone Astray and Other Papers from "Household Words," 1851–59*, ed. Michael Slater, Dent Uniform Edition of Dickens' Journalism (London: J. M. Dent, 1999), 49–57.

5. Charles Dickens, *Oliver Twist*, ed. Peter Fairclough (London: Penguin, 1966), 34–35.

6. Ibid., 35.

7. Mitzi Myers, "Hannah More's Tracts for the Times: Social Fiction and Female Ideology," in *Fetter'd or Free? British Women Novelists, 1670–1815*, ed. Mary Anne Scholfield and Cecilia Macheski (Athens: Ohio University Press, 1986), 267. For an excellent recent critical biography of More, see Anne Stott, *Hannah More: The First Victorian* (Oxford: Oxford University Press, 2003).

8. Charles Dickens, *The Old Curiosity Shop*, ed. Angus Easson (London: Penguin, 1972), 288. All further references will appear in the text. The text of this edition is from the 1841 first volume publication by Chapman and Hall and is identical with the text of the original serial in *Master Humphrey's Clock*. For a meticulous publication history of *The Old Curiosity Shop*, see Elizabeth M. Brennan's introduction to the Clarendon edition (Oxford: Clarendon Press, 1997), xiii–ciii.

9. On More's didacticism in the context of Victorian industrial fiction, see Catherine Gallagher, *The Industrial Reformation of English Fiction, 1832–1867* (Chicago: University of Chicago Press, 1985), 37–41.

10. Ian Bradley, *The Call to Seriousness: The Evangelical Impact on the Victorians* (London: Jonathan Cape, 1976), 34.

11. On the production and circulation of the Cheap Repository Tracts, see G. H. Spinney, "Cheap Repository Tracts: Hazard and Marshall Edition," *Library*, 4th ser., 20, no. 3 (1939): 295–340, and Ford K. Brown, *Fathers of the Victorians: The Age of Wilberforce* (Cambridge: Cambridge University Press, 1961), 123–55. Historian Owen Chadwick details that "the distribution of tracts took no account of seasons. They were handed out in pleasure boats and omnibuses, left open on the tops of hedges, proffered on sticks to galloping horsemen, sent to criminals awaiting the rope, given to cabmen with their fare." *The Victorian Church, Part 1, 1829–48* (New York: Oxford University Press, 1966), 443.

12. Charles Dickens to John Forster, January [17?], 1841, in Dickens, *The Letters of Charles Dickens*: "When I first began (on your valued suggestion) to keep my thoughts upon this ending of the tale, I resolved to try and do something which might be read by people about whom Death had been, —with a softened feeling, and with consolation" (2:188).

13. Samuel F. Pickering Jr. argues that, like didactic religious fiction, Dickens's novels appealed to lower-class readers educated in Sunday schools, whose curricula would have been likely to include didactic tales; his novels were published in parts, as were religious tracts; and his characters, like those of didactic fiction, were often viewed as recognizable social and moral types. *The Moral Tradition in English Fiction, 1785–1850* (Hanover, N.H.: University Press of New England, 1976), 107–22.

14. On remediation, see David Thorburn and Henry Jenkins, eds., *Rethinking Media Change: The Aesthetics of Transition* (Cambridge, Mass.: MIT Press, 2003), 7, 10.

15. Such uses suggest an evolution in the eighteenth-century views of curiosity as a socially transgressive form of ambition investigated by Barbara M. Benedict in *Curiosity: A Cultural History of Early Modern Inquiry* (Chicago: University of Chicago Press, 2001).

16. Bradley, *The Call to Seriousness*, 145. Norris Pope argues that despite their religious doctrine of providentialism, in their charitable efforts many Victorian evangelicals ultimately came to endorse in practice the environmental explanation that the "crime and immorality" of the poor most frequently resulted directly from poverty, lack of proper sanitary and living conditions, unemployment, and lack of education. *Dickens and Charity* (New York: Columbia University Press, 1978), 200.

17. Boyd Hilton, *The Age of Atonement: The Influence of Evangelicalism on Social and Economic Thought* (Oxford: Clarendon Press, 1988), 26.

18. Bradley, *The Call to Seriousness*, 52.

19. Ibid.

20. Ibid., 128–29.

21. Ibid., 42. William St Clair estimates the distribution of Religious Tract Society publications between 1840 and 1850 at 23 million. *The Reading Nation in the Romantic Period* (Cambridge: Cambridge University Press), Appendix 7, 569.

22. Hilton, *The Age of Atonement*, 9–10.

23. Richard D. Altick, *The English Common Reader A Social History of the Mass Reading Public, 1800–1900*, 2nd ed. (Chicago: University of Chicago Press, 1957), 300–302.

24. Bradley, *The Call to Seriousness*, 98.

25. Ibid., 46.

26. *Evangelical Magazine*, 1st ser., no. 13 (1805): 515, in Doreen M. Rosman, *The Evangelicals and Culture* (London: Croom Helm, 1984), 189. Evangelicals condemned novel reading as a waste of time and a source of corrupting influences and unrealistic expectations, especially for young girls. On the other hand, many Evangelicals, like William Wilberforce, found themselves "extremely interested" in the novels of Walter Scott (Rosman, *The Evangelicals and Culture*, 184–93). For a thorough discussion of Evangelical and Methodist publications condemning novel reading, see Altick, *The English Common Reader*, chap. 5.

27. Altick, *The English Common Reader*, 76, 108.

28. Peter Ackroyd, *Dickens* (New York: HarperCollins, 1990), 273, 373.

29. J. Paul Hunter's *Before Novels: The Cultural Contexts of Eighteenth-Century Fiction* (New York: Norton, 1990) traces the relation of the novel to earlier didactic genres in chaps. 9–11.

30. Samuel Johnson, *Rambler*, March 31, 1750, in Ioan Williams, ed., *Novel and Romance, 1700–1800: A Documentary Record* (London: Routledge, 1970), 143–44.

31. Ibid., 144.

32. Anna Laetitia Barbauld, "On the Origin and Progress of Novel-Writing," from *The British Novelists* (1810), in *Early Women Critics, 1660–1820: An Anthology*, edited by the Folger Collective on Early Women Critics (Bloomington: Indiana University Press, 1995), 180–81.

33. Sarah Stickney [Ellis], "An Apology for Fiction," in *Pictures of Private Life* (Philadelphia: Carey, Lea, and Blanchard, 1833), ix, vii, vi, x. See Amanda Claybaugh's astute analysis of the contradictions within the domestic ideology of Ellis's temperance tales in *The Novel of Purpose: Literature and Social Reform in the Anglo-American World* (Ithaca, N.Y.: Cornell University Press, 2007), 95–99.

34. Hannah More, *The Works of Hannah More, Complete in Seven Volumes*, vol. 1, *The Repository Tales* (New York: Harper and Brothers, 1855), viii.

35. On the cultural pervasiveness of the economic logic of Evangelicalism through the middle decades of the nineteenth century, see Hilton, *The Age of Atonement*.

36. More, "Advertisement," in *The Works of Hannah More*, n.p.

37. David Spring, "The Clapham Sect: Some Social and Political Aspects," *Victorian Studies* 5 (September 1961): 39.

38. Hannah More, *Evangelical Magazine* 2 (1795): 388, in Samuel F. Pickering Jr., *John Locke and Children's Books in Eighteenth-Century England* (Knoxville: University of Tennessee Press, 1981), 121.

39. Pedersen argues that the *Tracts* functioned as "a concerted attempt to change people's minds." The stories were intended to undermine not only the "content of popular literature but also the very existence of a popular culture autonomous from

dominant society" by "outlining the norms of a single Christian culture and differ-
entiat[ing] the godly from the ungodly of all classes by their adherence to these standards." "Hannah More Meets Simple Simon: Tracts, Chapbooks, and Popular
Culture in Late Eighteenth-Century England," *Journal of British Studies* 25 (1986):
107–8.

40. More is quoted in Martha More, *Mendip Annals*, 9, in Bradley, *The Call to
Seriousness*, 147–48. More's tireless work and donation of substantial sums from her
own earnings from her writing to found and maintain schools for the poor in the
coal-mining towns of the Mendip Hills suggest a more complex personal commitment to social improvement than her doctrinaire pronouncements in her published
works indicate. See Jane Nardin, "Hannah More and the Problem of Poverty,"
Texas Studies in Literature and Language 43, no. 3 (2001): 267–84.

41. Hannah More, *The Shepherd of Salisbury Plain*, in *The Works of Hannah More*,
197. All further references to this work will appear in the text.

42. More's shepherd transforms his experience of poverty into an intellectual
problem or rhetorical figure, in this case, an analogy leading to an antithesis. More
thus makes her shepherd "naturally" eloquent. In another of the *Tracts*, a well-to-
do young woman who unknowingly marries into a poor family articulates the connection More's fiction posits between piety and intelligence, especially among the
poor: "I was surprised to find they [her in-laws] had very good sense, which I never
had thought poor people could have; but, indeed, worldly persons do not know
how much religion, while it mends the heart, enlightens the understanding also"
(*The Two Wealthy Farmers*, in *The Works of Hannah More*, 97).

43. Michael Hennel, *John Venn and the Clapham Sect* (London, 1958), 207–8,
cited in Spring, "The Clapham Sect," 39.

44. Spring, "The Clapham Sect," 39. He cites G. W. E. Russell, *A Short History
of the Evangelical Movement* (London, 1951), 130.

45. Hilton, *The Age of Atonement*, 69.

46. See Albert O. Hirschman, *The Passions and the Interests: Political Arguments
for Capitalism Before Its Triumph* (Princeton, N.J: Princeton University Press, 1977),
for an authoritative account of the way the concept of interest became invested
historically with economic motives during the seventeenth and eighteenth centuries. Anthony Ashley Cooper, Lord Shaftesbury, in his *Inquiry Concerning Virtue, or
Merit* (1711), criticized as a form of "Self-Love" the Christian moral calculus that
counts on eternal happiness through salvation; see Esther Schor's discussion in *Bearing the Dead: The British Culture of Mourning from the Enlightenment to Victoria*
(Princeton, N.J.: Princeton University Press, 1994), 27–29. For a recent philosophical meditation on the difficulty of conceiving the possibility of a "gift outside any
economy" in both Western philosophy and Christian theology, see Jacques Derrida,
The Gift of Death, trans. David Wills (Chicago: University of Chicago Press, 1995),
94–115.

47. Isaac Watts's original, "Against Idleness and Mischief," from *Cheap Repository. Divine songs attempted in easy language for the use of children by I. Watts, D.D. To
which are added, prayers for children*_[Bath], [between ca. 1795 and 1798?], 17–18, Gale

Eighteenth Century Collections Online (accessed Oct. 15, 2010), goes: "How doth the little busy bee / Improve each shining hour, / And gather honey all the day / From every opening flower!—In works of labour or of skill, / I would be busy too; / For Satan finds some mischief still / For idle hands to do.—In books, or work, or health- ful play, / Let my first years be past, / That I may give for ev'ry day / Some good account at last" (second verse omitted).

48. On Dickens's defense of popular entertainment, see Paul Schlicke, *Dickens and Popular Entertainment* (London: Allen and Unwin, 1985).

49. George Gissing articulates the link between Nell and factory children as problematically allegorical: "Heaven forbid that I should attribute to Dickens a deliberate allegory; but, having in mind those hapless children who were then being tortured in England's mines and factories, I like to see in Little Nell a type of their sufferings; she, the victim of avarice, dragged with bleeding feet along the hard roads, everywhere pursued by heartless self-interest and finding her one safe refuge in the grave." *Charles Dickens: A Critical Study* (London, 1898), 211.

50. Paul Schlicke interprets industrial interlude in *The Old Curiosity Shop* as referring to the Chartist uprisings contemporary with the novel's publication, while Theodor Adorno views the novel as a simultaneously mythological, historical, and social image of the "crisis" of the industrial order for which Nell atones through her death. Schlicke, "The True Pathos of *The Old Curiosity Shop*," *Dickens Quarterly* 7, no. 1 (1990): 189–99; Adorno, "Rede über den *Raritätenladen* von Charles Dick- ens," *Gesammelte Schriften*, vol. 11, *Noten zur Literatur*, ed. Gretel Adorno and Rolf Tiedemann (Frankfurt am Main: Suhrkamp, 1973), 515–22, translated by Michael Hollington as "An Address on Charles Dickens's *The Old Curiosity Shop*," *Dickens Quarterly* 6 (1989): 95–101. See also Hollington's "Adorno, Benjamin, and *The Old Curiosity Shop*," *Dickens Quarterly* 6, no. 3 (1989): 87–95.

51. For an example of Dickens's opinions on the connection between educa- tion and the prevention of crime, see "Boys to Mend," *Household Words*, September 11, 1852, 597. See also Sir James Kay-Shuttleworth's influential account of the ways that the influence of educational institutions can substitute for the punitive measures of law in *Four Periods of Public Education* (London: Longman, Green, Longman, and Roberts, 1862), 197–206, 453–56.

52. In the manuscript there follows a passage, which Dickens chose to delete for reasons of space, that echoes the findings and rhetoric of such pamphlets as James Phillips Kay's (later Kay-Shuttleworth) *The Moral and Physical Condition of the Work- ing Classes Employed in the Cotton Manufacture in Manchester* of 1832 and parallels Edwin Chadwick's influential and virtually contemporary *Report on the Sanitary Condition of the Labouring Population of Great Britain*, begun in 1839 and published in 1842. Dickens's narrator describes with heavy sarcasm and in the strongest terms of cause and effect the moral consequences of the squalid streets and alleys of the indus- trial town—"places where, let men disguise it as they please! no human beings can be clean, or good, or sober, or contented"—on the inhabitants, "whose irreligion, improvidence, drunkenness, degeneracy, and most unaccountable of all, whose dis- content, good gentlemen reprobate in Parliament tide, till they are hoarse" (705 n.

1). In a speech on the first anniversary of the Metropolitan Sanitary Association on May 10, 1851, Dickens made the similar point that "Searching Sanitary Reform must precede all other social remedies, and that even Education and Religion can do nothing where they are most needed, until the way is paved for their ministrations by Cleanliness and Decency"; thus his reformist and novelistic rhetoric are consistent. In K. J. Fielding, ed., *The Speeches of Charles Dickens: A Complete Edition* (Oxford: Clarendon Press, 1960), 129. The deleted paragraph from *The Old Curiosity Shop* concludes with a sarcastic summation of futile and pernicious efforts to address these environmental ills by "devising for [the workers'] reformation Sabbath bills without end . . . and building up new churches with a zeal whose sacred fervour knows no limits" (705 n. 1). Undermining More's illustration of the incommensurability of a single human life and eternity, Dickens emphasizes the ironic contrast between the material and physical causes of the problem of poverty and the abstract, spiritual solution offered by those he views as religious zealots. While they would not have agreed to postpone their urban missionary work, many evangelicals nevertheless demonstrated a similar "practical environmentalism" in their charitable involvements in education and sanitary reform, which Dickens downplays by focusing on Sabbath bills. See Pope, *Dickens and Charity*, chap. 5. See also Donald M. Lewis, *Lighten Their Darkness: The Evangelical Mission to Working-Class London, 1828–1860* (New York: Greenwood Press, 1986).

53. For a history of the emergence of domesticity as an evaluative and administrative category in relation to Victorian legislative supervision of the working classes, see Mary Poovey, *Making a Social Body: British Cultural Formation, 1830–1864* (Chicago: University of Chicago Press, 1995), chap. 6.

54. In reading *The Old Curiosity Shop*'s industrial scenes, Garrett Stewart has concluded that Nell functions as a surrogate for the middle-class reader, who gains his or her knowledge of the "suffering masses" and learns to empathize with them through Nell's own suffering, while remaining safely ensconced at the domestic fireside. Stewart categorizes the riot scene, with its invocations of working-class violence, as typical of Dickens's "reactionary social diagnosis." *Dear Reader: The Conscripted Audience in Nineteenth-Century British Fiction* (Baltimore: Johns Hopkins University Press, 1996), 187–92, 190.

55. G. F. W. Munby, "Richmond, Legh (1772–1827)," rev. Clare L. Taylor, in *Oxford Dictionary of National Biography* (Oxford: Oxford University Press, 2004–10), http://www.oxforddnb.com/view/article/23595 (accessed January 14, 2009).

56. Elisabeth Jay, *Religion of the Heart: Anglican Evangelicalism and the Nineteenth-Century Novel* (Oxford: Clarendon Press, 1979), 151; Munby, "Richmond, Legh (1772–1827)."

57. Bradley, *The Call to Seriousness*, 36.

58. Marilyn Georgas traces the relation of *The Old Curiosity Shop* to the *ars moriendi* tradition represented by such popular devotional texts as Jeremy Taylor's *The Rule and Exercises of Holy Living and Dying*, first published in 1651. "Little Nell and the Art of Holy Dying: Dickens and Jeremy Taylor," *Dickens Studies Annual* 20 (1991): 35–56. Samuel F. Pickering Jr. also discusses the didactic aspects of the dying

child in Evangelical fiction in *The Moral Tradition in English Fiction*, 122–23. Dennis Walder mentions Richmond's tales as models for Nell's story, but without entering into a detailed comparison, in *Dickens and Religion* (London: Allen and Unwin, 1981), 84.

59. Legh Richmond, *Annals of the Poor* (London, 1828), 32.

60. Ibid., 117, 132, 130–31.

61. Ibid., 135.

62. As Elisabeth Jay points out in her study of Anglican Evangelicalism and the novel, "the emphasis on death as a centre for teaching" was understood to be a "typically Evangelical concern." The ritual of the "death-bed witness" was crucial to reassure "a circle of attendants that their departing friend had truly been saved," and she points out that Richmond's "conversation" with the dying girls of his tracts "provides the prototype for the variety of catechetical exchange to establish the dying person's frame of mind" (*Religion of the Heart*, 157, 160).

63. Richmond, *Annals of the Poor*, 125.

64. In the absence of a sense of the novel's critique of Evangelical literature, Nell's death appeared to later readers either as simply maudlin in its sentimentality or as incompletely secularized, leaving the novel open to the accusation that it presents a false set of conventions. James Fitzjames Stephen seems to have reacted in this way, writing in 1855 that the author "gloats over the girl's death as if it delighted him; he looks at it . . . touches, tastes, smells and handles it as if it was some savoury dainty which could not be too fully appreciated." *Cambridge Essays*, 154, 175, quoted in Loralee MacPike, " 'The Old Curiosity Shape': Changing Views of Little Nell, Part I," *Dickens Studies Newsletter* 12, no. 2 (1981): 36.

65. According to what literature scholar Alexander Welsh has called Dickens's "special doctrine of the function of memory in moral life," active goodness in the world works as a surrogate memory of the dead. *The City of Dickens* (Oxford: Clarendon Press, 1971), 101. Walder also defines Dickens's view of Christianity as drawing on "feelings [that] by definition transcend sectarian barriers, and offer a unifying rather than divisive faith" (*Dickens and Religion*, 91).

66. R. H. Horne praised the blank verse of the passage and reconfigured it in verse form in *A New Spirit of the Age*, 2nd ed., vol. 1 (London: Smith, Elder, 1844), 65–70. Responding to Horne's detection of his penchant for blank verse, Dickens explained that "I *cannot* help it, when I am very much in earnest." *The Letters of Charles Dickens*, ed. Walter Dexter (London: Nonesuch Press, 1937–38), 1:808, quoted in Ford, *Dickens and His Readers*, 70 n.

67. Richmond, *Annals of the Poor*, 261–62.

68. For an account of the Wordsworthian influence behind this opposition to selfishness and idea of childhood as a time when the self is innocent of egotism, see David Bromwich, *Hazlitt: The Mind of a Critic* (New Haven, Conn.: Yale University Press, 1999), 58–59.

69. Richmond, *Annals of the Poor*, 59, 126–27.

70. Ibid., 58–59.

71. Ibid.

72. Samuel Rogers, *The Pleasures of Memory with Other Poems* (Paris: Baudry's European Library, 1852), 20–21, ll. 169–74, quoted in Richmond, "Dairyman's Daughter," 59. Richmond does not cite the poem's title or author, presumably because it was so well known, or possibly because he does not want to emphasize his source, as Rogers was a Dissenter and connected to early nineteenth-century radicalism.

73. Rogers, *The Pleasures of Memory*, vii–viii.

74. Peter T. Murphy points out that in Rogers's poem, memory, as a "vast reservoir, equal to the drain of all possible loss," "compensates us for the loss of the past, pure and simple." "Climbing Parnassus, and Falling Off: Rogers and *The Pleasures of Memory*," *Wordsworth Circle* 24, no. 3 (1993): 153.

75. Richmond, *Annals of the Poor*, 284–85.

76. Rogers was a banker and art connoisseur as well as a poet, a frequent diner at Dickens's home, and a supporter of the cause of reforming working conditions in factories. He was especially well known for his extraordinarily generous financial support to other writers. See Richard Garnett, "Rogers, Samuel (1763–1855)," rev. Paul Baines, in *Oxford Dictionary of National Biography* (Oxford: Oxford University Press, 2004–10), http://www.oxforddnb.com/view/article/23997 (accessed January 14, 2009).

77. On the larger cultural domain of Victorian practices of mourning and memorializing the dead, to which, I argue, *The Old Curiosity Shop* contributes a particular reading practice, see Matthew Campbell, Jacqueline M. Labbe, and Sally Shuttleworth, eds., *Memory and Memorials, 1789–1914: Literary and Cultural Perspectives* (London: Routledge, 2000), and Schor, *Bearing the Dead*.

78. Richmond, *Annals of the Poor*, 43.

79. Benedict, *Curiosity*, 1. For another important history of early modern curiosity and epistemology, see Lorraine Daston and Katharine Park, *Wonders and the Order of Nature, 1150–1750* (New York: Zone Books, 2001).

80. Benedict, *Curiosity*, 2–3.

81. For an alternative reading of curiosity in *The Old Curiosity Shop* as an omiscient narrative surveillance expressed in the narrator's relation to his characters, see Audre Jaffe, *Vanishing Points: Dickens, Narrative, and the Subject of Omniscience* (Berkeley: University of California Press, 1991), chap. 2.

82. Adorno, "An Address," 98.

83. These rationales include Quilp's own miscalculation in barring the gate to his possible rescuers, the didactic necessity that he be punished, and his violent death as the negative opposite of Nell's peaceful death. See the discussion of these deaths and the novel's "polarization" of Nell and Quilp in Garrett Stewart, *Dickens and the Trials of Imagination* (Cambridge, Mass.: Harvard University Press, 1974), 97–99.

84. David Hume, *A Treatise of Human Nature*, ed. P. H. Nidditch, 2nd ed. (Oxford: Oxford University Press, 1978), 70.

85. In a brief note, Malcolm Andrews has also suggested a relation between Dickens's use of contrast in the novel, "to a greater degree than in any of his other novels," and Rogers's reference, in his "Abstract" of *The Pleasures of Memory*, to the

power of contrast as an associating force. According to Rogers, "[By association] a picture directs our thoughts to the original: and, as cold and darkness suggest forcibly the ideas of heat and light, he, who feels the infirmities of age, dwells most on whatever reminds him of the vigour and vivacity of his youth." As Andrews points out, this passage also provides an associationist rationale for Master Humphrey's interest in Nell. "Dickens, Samuel Rogers, and *The Old Curiosity Shop*," *Notes and Queries* 18, no. 11 (1971): 410–11; Rogers, *Pleasures of Memory*, vii.

    86. See my discussions of Bacon and Hobbes on memory in Chapters 1 and 2.

    87. Horne, *A New Spirit of the Age*, 4.

4. The Pleasures of Memory, Part II: Epitaphic Reading and Cultural Memory

    1. Charles Dickens, *Oliver Twist*, ed. Peter Fairclough (London: Penguin, 1966), 34–35. All further references will appear in the text.

    2. John Manning, *Dickens on Education* (Toronto: University of Toronto Press, 1959), 94.

    3. Peter Ackroyd, *Dickens* (New York: HarperCollins, 1990), 257.

    4. Charles Dickens, *Nicholas Nickleby*, ed. Michael Slater (London: Penguin, 1986), 47. All further references will appear parenthetically in the text. For a facsimile edition of the novel as originally published in parts, see Charles Dickens, *The Life and Adventures of Nicholas Nickleby*, edited by Michael Slater, 2 vols. (Philadelphia: University of Pennsylvania Press, 1982).

    5. Amanda Claybaugh's observation in *The Novel of Purpose: Literature and Social Reform in the Anglo-American World* (Ithaca, N.Y.: Cornell University Press, 2007) that "Dickens intended his depiction of the schools to be entertaining and was astonished when they had a reformist effect" (53–54) overlooks Dickens's experience as an investigative reporter and the evidence of this trip to the Yorkshire schools prior to writing *Nicholas Nickleby*. However, she provides a convincing analysis of the significance of Dickens's interaction with United States social reform movements after his trip there in 1842 (see chap. 3).

    6. For the details of Dickens and Browne's trip to Yorkshire in late January and early February 1838, the circumstances of which are rendered in Nicholas's trip to Dotheboys Hall, see Ackroyd, *Dickens*, 249–52; and Michael Slater, "The Composition and Monthly Publication of *Nicholas Nickleby*," in Charles Dickens, *The Life and Adventures of Nicholas Nickleby*, ed. Slater, ix–xxvi.

    7. John M. L. Drew, *Dickens the Journalist* (London: Palgrave Macmillan, 2003), 25.

    8. Charles Dickens, *Sketches by Boz*, ed. Dennis Walder (London: Penguin, 1995), 251. "Thoughts about People" was first published in the *Evening Chronicle* on April 23, 1835.

    9. Ibid., 253.

    10. For a compelling reading of Dickens's development of these themes in *The Haunted Man and the Ghost's Bargain*, see Rosemarie Bodenheimer, "Knowing and Telling in Dickens's Retrospects," in *Knowing the Past: Victorian Literature and Culture*, ed. Suzy Anger (Ithaca, N.Y.: Cornell University Press, 2001), 215–33.

11. Defending himself against the imputation that Squeers was meant as a portrait of a particularly abusive schoolmaster whom he had met on his trip to Yorkshire, Dickens insists in the 1848 preface that "Mr Squeers is the representative of a class, and not of an individual" (*Nicholas Nickleby*, 50). For a collection of accounts by Victorians who had attended Yorkshire schools and wrote to confirm the substantial accuracy of Dickens's representation, see Slater, "The Composition and Monthly Publication of *Nicholas Nickleby*," xiv–xvii.

12. Manning, *Dickens on Education*, 87–88.

13. Ibid., 87–94.

14. Charles Dickens to Mrs. S. C. Hall, December 29, 1838, in ibid., 89.

15. T. P. Cooper, "Burials of Boys in the Delightful Village of Dotheboys," *Dickensian* 35 (1929), in Ackroyd, *Dickens*, 252. On the multiple graves of schoolboys in the Bowes village churchyard that Dickens visited, see also Slater, "The Composition and Monthly Publication of *Nicholas Nickleby*," xxiii–xxv.

16. Drew, *Dickens the Journalist*, 31.

17. On the resurrectionists and their clients in the 1830s, see Martin Fido, *Bodysnatchers: A History of the Resurrectionists, 1742–1832* (London: Weidenfeld and Nicolson, 1988), and Sarah Wise, *The Italian Boy: A Tale of Murder and Body Snatching in 1830s London* (New York: Metropolitan Books, 2004).

18. See also Albert D. Hutter, "The Novelist as Resurrectionist: Dickens and the Dilemma of Death," *Dickens Studies Annual* 12 (1983): 1–39.

19. John Locke, *An Essay Concerning Human Understanding*, ed. Peter H. Nidditch (Oxford: Clarendon Press, 1975), 152.

20. William Wordsworth, "Essays upon Epitaphs, 1" in *The Prose Works of William Wordsworth*, ed. W. J. B. Owen and Jane Worthington Smyser (Oxford: Clarendon Press, 1974), 2:57.

21. Legh Richmond, *Annals of the Poor* (London, 1828), 210.

22. Paul de Man investigates the trope of prosopopoeia in "Autobiography as De-facement," "Shelley Disfigured," and "Hypogram and Inscription," in *The Resistance to Theory* (Minneapolis: University of Minnesota Press, 1986).

23. The narrator's heightened rhetoric employs a style akin to Dickens's journalism. Many Victorian churchyards, both in cities and in the country, were overcrowded and situated in proximity to dwellings and thus were sources of contamination and illness. For several recent studies of Victorian burial practices and cemeteries, see Chris Brooks, *Mortal Remains: The History and Present State of the Victorian and Edwardian Cemetery* (Exeter, UK: Wheaton, 1989); Mary Elizabeth Hotz, *Literary Remains: Representations of Death and Burial in Victorian England* (Albany: SUNY Press, 2009); Pat Jalland, *Death in the Victorian Family* (Oxford: Oxford University Press, 1996); and John M. Landers, *Death and the Metropolis: Studies in the Demographic History of London (1670–1841)* (Cambridge: Cambridge University Press, 1992).

24. For two important recent analyses of representations of the urban crowd in nineteenth-century British literature, see John Plotz, *The Crowd: British Literature*

and Public Politics (Berkeley: University of California Press, 2000), and Richard Maxwell, *The Mysteries of Paris and London* (Charlottesville: University Press of Virginia, 1992). For a seminal treatment of Dickens's urban imagination, see also Alexander Welsh, *The City of Dickens* (Oxford: Clarendon Press, 1971).

25. A foundational work on rhetorical *copia* as practiced by Renaissance humanists is Desiderius Erasmus, *De Copia, On Copia of Words and Ideas*, trans. Donald B. King and H. David Rix (Milwaukee, Wis.: Marquette University Press, 1963).

26. William Hazlitt, "Remarks on the Systems of Hartley and Helvetius," in *Essays on the Principles of Human Action, on the Systems of Hartley and Helvetius, and on Abstract Ideas* (Bristol, UK: Thoemmes, 1990), 81.

27. Wordsworth, "Essays upon Epitaphs, 1," 57.

28. The enormous popularity of Little Nell has made her relationship to Victorian taste particularly interesting to literary critics. Nineteenth-century responses to Nell's story ranged from that of the American author Washington Irving, who praised its "exquisite pathos" and "moral sublimity," or the Scottish judge and literary critic Francis Jeffrey, who found that literature had produced "nothing so good as Nell since Cordelia," to Oscar Wilde's famous quip at the end of the century that one must have a heart of stone to read the death of Little Nell without laughing. George H. Ford sums up his review of these responses to the novel by pointing to Nell as the "inevitable whipping-girl of the anti-Dickensians, the principal drag upon the full critical acceptance of his art." *Dickens and His Readers: Aspects of Novel-Criticism since 1836* (Princeton, N.J.: Princeton University Press, 1955), 55–71. Fred Kaplan includes Little Nell along with Richardson's Clarissa and Fielding's Sophia as embodiments of philosophical sentimentality. *Sacred Tears: Sentimentality in Victorian Literature* (Princeton, N.J.: Princeton University Press, 1987), 16–17, 20–21, 32. Dennis Walder contends that Nell's story appealed to the "unsophisticated religious conceptions of ordinary people" and to a "level of belief not catered for by the religious periodicals." *Dickens and Religion* (London: Allen and Unwin, 1981), 82–90. Barry V. Qualls links Dickens's treatment of Nell as a "secular pilgrim" to the traditional emblems of the seventeenth-century Protestant tradition represented by Bunyan and Francis Quarles. *The Secular Pilgrims of Victorian Fiction: The Novel as Book of Life* (Cambridge: Cambridge University Press, 1982), 90–100. Alexander Welsh explains Dickens's treatment of Nell as part of a larger strategy of domesticating death itself along with the threats posed by the dislocation, dirt, disease, crowding, and other perceptible ills of the nineteenth-century city. *The City of Dickens* (Oxford: Clarendon Press, 1971), especially chaps. 7 and 12. Questioning twentieth-century critics' tendency to "look down upon [the] literary competence" of Victorian readers, Richard Walsh concludes that "*The Old Curiosity Shop* does not offer a realist mode of characterization *debased* by sentimentality, but romance characterization *dedicated* to sentimentality." "Why We Wept for Little Nell: Character and Emotional Involvement," *Narrative* 5, no. 3 (1997): 313–14.

29. Richmond, *Annals of the Poor*, 209.

30. Samuel F. Pickering Jr., *Moral Instruction and Fiction for Children, 1749–1820* (Athens: University of Georgia Press, 1993), 107.

31. Charles Dickens, *The Old Curiosity Shop*, ed. Angus Easson (London: Penguin, 1972), 503. All further references will appear parenthetically in the text.

32. David Hume, *Abstract of "A Treatise of Human Nature"* (1740), in David Hume, *A Treatise of Human Nature*, edited by P. H. Nidditch, 2nd ed. (Oxford: Oxford University Press, 1978), 662.

33. David Hume, *A Treatise of Human Nature*, ed. P. H. Nidditch, 2nd ed. (Oxford: Oxford University Press, 1978), 201.

34. Ibid., 259.

35. Ibid., 261–62.

36. Ibid., 635.

37. Walder argues that this scene offers a "representation of the belief that after death there is a resurrection," since the narrator alludes later to Nell's being in heaven (*Dickens and Religion*, 78). Richard Maxwell reads this vignette as suggesting that "all art aspires to the condition of the epitaph, which not only defines a person's life but defines it selectively, so that biography is the construction of a moral ideal" (*The Mysteries of Paris and London*, 188–89).

38. I am grateful to Thomas Recchio for helping me determine that it was George Cattermole who drew this illustration. See also Frederic G. Kitton, *Dickens and His Illustrators* (Amsterdam: S. Emmering, 1972).

39. Hannah More, *Practical Piety; or, The Influence of the Religion of the Heart on the Conduct of Life* (Philadelphia: American Sunday-School Union, 1876), 29–30.

40. The illustration of Nell's new serial reading habit fits Garrett Stewart's observation that the pictorial representation of reading "descends by one route or another from the representation of the religious Word." "Painting," Stewart argues, "often carries just this citational function with it into the secular scene of reading, where it is resituated within the whole range of adjacent genres that the scene of reading . . . thrives on incorporating." *The Look of Reading: Book, Painting, Text* (Chicago: University of Chicago Press, 2006), 33. Stewart's notion of the "implicit power of mental imaging" (36) represented in the tradition of painting scenes of reading also captures what I regard as being at stake, both cognitively and in relation to the history of modern media, in this episode from *The Old Curiosity Shop*.

41. For an illuminating analysis of the role of windows in framing virtual reality from Renaissance art to digital media, see Anne Friedberg, *The Virtual Window: From Alberti to Microsoft* (Cambridge, Mass.: MIT Press, 2006).

42. The original serial issue of *Master Humphrey's Clock* in which Nell's scene of reading in the gothic chapel was published was number 29, November 21, 1840, which included chapters 52 and 53. J. Don Vann, *Victorian Novels in Serial* (New York: Modern Language Association of America, 1985), 64.

43. The scene of Nell's reading in the chapel occurs in chapter 53, while her death is narrated in chapter 71, and described in chapter 72, which made up the penultimate weekly installment of the novel for January 30, 1841 (Vann, *Victorian Novels in Serial*, 64–65). At two chapters per weekly installment, this gap represents nine weekly installments.

44. Richard D. Altick, *The English Common Reader: A Social History of the Mass Reading Public, 1800–1900*, 2nd ed. (Chicago: University of Chicago Press, 1957), 151–52.

45. In the original serial edition of the novel published in *Bentley's Miscellany*, this passage is slightly different: "The boy stirred and smiled in his sleep, as though these marks of pity and compassion had awakened some pleasant dream of a love and affection he had never known; as a strain of gentle music, or the rippling of water in a silent place, or the odour of a flower, or even the mention of a familiar word, will sometimes call up sudden dim remembrances of scenes that never were, in this life, which vanish like a breath, and which some brief memory of a happier existence long gone by, would seem to have awakened, for no power of the human mind can ever recall them." *Oliver Twist*, ed. Philip Horne (London: Penguin, 2002), 238–39. In addition to breaking up the long sentence into several in his later revision for the three volume edition of 1838, Dickens seems to have placed greater emphasis on the involuntary nature of such recollections, while also allowing for the possibility of voluntary representations of such memory effects in his own narration.

46. The passage seems to invoke Wordsworth's "Ode: Intimations of Immortality." It also seems to allude to the "Radcliffean melancholy" that Adela Pinch identifies in Ann Radcliffe's *The Mysteries of Udolpho* (1794) as being "about recognizing clichés rather than experiencing the things to which the images refer," *Strange Fits of Passion: Epistemologies of Emotion, Hume to Austen* (Stanford, Calif.: Stanford University Press, 1996), 117.

47. I have quoted from the definition of *inopinatum* listed in the online rhetoric "Silva Rhetoricae" (http://humanities.byu.edu/rhetoric/silva.htm), written and designed by Gideon Burton of Brigham Young University (accessed January 22, 2009).

48. These could include such frequently reprinted works as Vicesimus Knox's *Elegant Extracts; or, Useful and Entertaining Piece of Poetry Selected for the Improvement of Youth in Speaking, Reading, Thinking, Composing; and in the Conduct of Life* (1784) and Anna Laetetia Barbauld's *The Female Speaker; or, Miscellaneous Pieces in Prose and Verse, Selected from the Best Writers, and Adapted to the Use of Young Women* (1811). On the importance of such anthologies within the history of reading practices, see J. Paul Hunter, *Before Novels: The Cultural Contexts of Eighteenth-Century English Fiction* (New York: Norton, 1990), chap. 3, and Leah Price, *The Anthology and the Rise of the Novel: From Richardson to George Eliot* (Cambridge: Cambridge University Press, 2000), chap. 2.

49. Dickens gave this speech at a banquet in his honor at Edinburgh. K. J. Fielding, ed., *The Speeches of Charles Dickens: A Complete Edition* (Oxford: Clarendon Press, 1960), 9.

50. John Kucich has argued that Nell's death serves as "an invitation to a common mourning and a corresponding sense of recovered community" by legitimating Victorian "desires for death by merging them with a positive cultural ideal."

"Death Worship among the Victorians: *The Old Curiosity Shop*," *PMLA* 95, no. 1 (1980): 69, 58.

51. Charles Dickens to John Forster, January [8?], 1841, in Dickens, *The Letters of Charles Dickens*, ed. Madeline House, Graham Storey, and Kathleen Tillotson, Pilgrim Edition (Oxford: Clarendon Press, 1965–2002), 2:181–82.

52. Fielding, *The Speeches of Charles Dickens*, 10.

53. Esther Schor argues, "While mourning was, during the Enlightenment, a figurative moral currency for the nation, it becomes in the Victorian period virtually a form of legal tender negotiable for 'respectability.' . . . The proffering of sympathy, in other words, no longer promotes the vitality of a moral economy within a community, but rather signifies an amassment of wealth sufficient to purchase social status." *Bearing the Dead: The British Culture of Mourning from the Enlightenment to Victoria* (Princeton, N.J.: Princeton University Press, 1994), 230–31.

54. Ibid., 3.

55. John Forster, *The Life of Charles Dickens* (London: J. M. Dent, 1966), 2:421–22.

56. Charles Dickens, *The Mystery of Edwin Drood*, ed. Steven Connor (London: J. M. Dent, 1996), 41.

57. Simon Eliot, "The Business of Victorian Publishing," in *The Cambridge Companion to the Victorian Novel*, ed. Deirdre David (Cambridge: Cambridge University Press, 2000), 44.

58. See Michael Cotsell, "The Stephen Family and Dickens's Circumlocution Office Satire," *Dickens Quarterly* 3 (1986): 175–78; George Holoch, "Consciousness and Society in 'Little Dorrit,'" *Victorian Studies* 21 (Spring 1978): 335–51; Roger D. Lund, "Genteel Fictions: Caricature and Satirical Design in *Little Dorrit*," *Dickens Studies Annual* 10 (1982): 45–65; Nancy Aycock Metz, "*Little Dorrit*'s London: Babylon Revisited," *Victorian Studies* 33 (Spring 1990): 465–86; William Meyers, "The Radicalism of 'Little Dorrit,'" in *Literature and Politics in the 19th Century*, ed. John Lucas (London: Methuen, 1971), 77–104; John R. Reed, "Confinement and Character in Dickens' Novels," *Dickens Studies Annual* 1 (1970): 41–54; Brian Rosenberg, *Little Dorrit's Shadows: Character and Contradiction in Dickens* (Columbia: University of Missouri Press, 1996); Sambudha Sen, "*Bleak House* and *Little Dorrit*: The Radical Heritage," *English Literary History* 65 (1998): 945–70; Michael Squires, "The Structure of Dickens's Imagination in *Little Dorrit*," *Texas Studies in Literature and Language* 30 (1988): 49–64; Wenying Xu, "The Opium Trade and *Little Dorrit*: A Case of Reading Silences," *Victorian Literature and Culture* 25, no. 1 (1997): 53–66. Particularly illuminating on the relationship between the plot of *Little Dorrit* and dramatic events in Dickens's personal life is David Payne, *The Reenchantment of Nineteenth-Century Fiction: Dickens, Thackeray, George Eliot, and Serialization* (Basingstoke, UK: Palgrave Macmillan, 2005), chap. 3.

59. In designating *Little Dorrit* a novel "about society in its very essence," Lionel Trilling contends that the prison "is an actuality before it is ever a symbol; its connection with the will is real, it is the practical instrument for the negation of man's

will which the will of society has contrived," *Sincerity and Authenticity* (Cambridge, Mass.: Harvard University Press, 1972), 147.

60. Given that the social constitution of mind and regulated freedom of thought also appear as operative assumptions within Dickensian novels through their uses of associationist theory to theorize reading, society cannot be construed simply as an oppressive force external to the individual mind. The novel's depiction of the institutionalizing disciplinary modernity characterized by Michel Foucault in *Discipline and Punish: The Birth of the Prison*, trans. Alan Sheridan (New York: Vintage, 1979) suggests that rather than reading the prison metaphor as representing the novel itself, we should read *Little Dorrit* as a self-consciously analytical passageway through a prison-like institutional culture.

61. Charles Dickens, *Little Dorrit*, ed. Stephen Wall and Helen Small (London: Penguin, 1998), 33. All further references will appear in the text.

62. [E. B. Hamley], "Remonstrance with Dickens," *Blackwood's Edinburgh Magazine*, April 1857, 490–503, in Philip Collins, ed., *Dickens: The Critical Heritage* (New York: Barnes & Noble, 1971), 361. James Fitzjames Stephen also published a scathing critique of Dickens's representation of government as the Circumlocution Office in the *Edinburgh Review*, July 1857, 124–56, in Collins, *Dickens: The Critical Heritage*, 366–77. Despite these criticisms, *Little Dorrit* was one of Dickens's most popular novels, having sold approximately 84,240 copies by the time of Dickens's death in 1870. Wall and Small eds., *Little Dorrit*, xxv.

63. Charles Dickens, speech to the Administrative Reform Association, June 27, 1855, in Fielding, *The Speeches of Charles Dickens*, 200–201.

64. Charles Dickens, "A Preliminary Word," *Household Words*, March 30, 1850, in *The Amusements of the People and Other Papers: Reports, Essays, and Reviews, 1834–51*, ed. Michael Slater, Dent Uniform Edition of Dickens' Journalism (Columbus: Ohio State University Press, 1996), 177.

65. In this respect, since the familial metaphors related to paternalism are so signally hollow in the novel, *Little Dorrit* participates in what literary scholar Catherine Gallagher has called "the rhetoric of domestic ideology, in which the family and society are metonymically, rather than metaphorically, related." *The Industrial Reformation of English Fiction, 1832–1867* (Chicago: University of Chicago Press, 1985), 129.

66. See my more critical analysis of these elements of the novel in "Domestic Fictions: Feminine Deference and Maternal Shadow Labor in Dickens' *Little Dorrit*," *Dickens Studies Annual* 18 (1990): 243–54. On the central role of daughters and doubts about patriarchal authority in Dickens's novels, see Hilary M. Schor, *Dickens and the Daughter of the House* (Cambridge: Cambridge University Press, 1999).

67. On English evangelical Calvinists as "stern and gloomy enthusiasts," see Charles Dickens, *Sunday under Three Heads*, in *Sketches by Boz and Other Early Papers, 1833–39*, ed. Michael Slater, Dent Uniform Edition of Dickens' Journalism (Columbus: Ohio State University Press, 1994), 491–92.

68. Stefan Collini, *Public Moralists: Political Thought and Intellectual Life in Britain, 1850–1930* (Oxford: Clarendon Press, 1991), 63. Drawing attention to its longevity,

Collini also remarks that "the project of rebutting systematic egoism had arguably been on the agenda of English and Scottish moral philosophy since the time of Hobbes and certainly since Mandeville" (66–67).

69. In her analysis of Dickens's explorations of cosmopolitanism in *Little Dorrit*, Amanda Anderson argues of Miss Wade and the novel's other "suspicious social critics" that their "haunting presence . . . and the highlighted myopia and confusion of the sympathetic characters, seriously impedes any reading of this novel for a reconstituted modest circle of duty." She therefore dismisses Dickens's characterology as epistemologically faulty and ethically incomplete: "While Dickens's wider vision takes in structural forces that are lost to view in many novels of the period, his characterology largely remains truncated and reductively moralizing: he cannot imagine any sustained and positive dialectical relation between cultivated suspicion and ethical practice." *The Powers of Distance: Cosmopolitanism and the Cultivation of Detachment* (Princeton, N.J.: Princeton University Press, 2001), 89–90. Anderson's critique seems to echo George Eliot's and G. H. Lewes's critiques of Dickens, which I discuss in Chapter 6.

70. Francis Bacon, *The New Organon*, ed. Lisa Jardine and Michael Silverthorne (Cambridge: Cambridge University Press, 2000), 79.

71. Such skepticism was probably not adopted by many Victorian readers, however. For an analysis of the role of skepticism in relation to materialism and fetishism, focusing on Dickens's *Great Expectations*, see Catherine Gallagher's "The Novel and Other Discourses of Suspended Disbelief," the sixth chapter of her publication coauthored with Stephen Greenblatt, *Practicing New Historicism* (Chicago: University of Chicago Press, 2000). Andrew H. Miller also offers a compelling analysis of the forms of skepticism that were represented as a series of obstacles, or alternatives, to the Victorian pursuit of moral perfectionism in *The Burdens of Perfection: On Ethics and Reading in Nineteenth-Century British Literature* (Ithaca, N.Y.: Cornell University Press, 2008).

72. Thompson writes of the similarity between the early nineteenth-century Methodists' and Radicals' intellectual practices of moral seriousness, and the differences in their ultimate goals: "There was a profound difference between disciplines recommended for the salvation of one's soul, and the same disciplines recommended as means to the salvation of a class. The Radical and free-thinking artisan was at his most earnest in his belief in the *active* duties of citizenship." *The Making of the English Working Class* (New York: Vintage, 1966), 743. Nineteenth-century Methodism, however, does not have to be read as advocating passivity, as Thompson implies.

73. Henry Mayhew, *What to Teach and How to Teach It: So That the Child May Become a Wise and Good Man* (London: William Smith, 1842), 2. All further references will appear in the text. In her biography of Mayhew, Anne Humpherys states that *What to Teach* is an unfinished work but does not explain further. See also Humpherys's discussion of Mayhew's books for children in *Henry Mayhew* (Boston: Twayne, 1984), 55–67.

74. On the history of communication theory and the emergence of communications as a modern discipline in the twentieth century, see John Durham Peters, *Speaking Into the Air: A History of the Idea of Communication* (Chicago: University of Chicago Press, 1999).

5. Learning by Heart in Our Mutual Friend

1. On the role of literacy among the array of character traits that both Liberal and Tory party leaders deemed essential to the gradual inclusion of a certain measure of working men in the franchise, see K. Theodore Hoppen, *The Mid-Victorian Generation, 1846–1886* (Oxford: Clarendon Press, 1998), 239, and Patrick Joyce, *Democratic Subjects: The Self and the Social in Nineteenth-Century England* (Cambridge: Cambridge University Press, 1994).

2. *Our Mutual Friend*'s investigation of literacy should, then, be included in Dickens's writing of autoethnography, as delineated in James Buzard's illuminating reading of *Bleak House* in *Disorienting Fiction: The Autoethnographic Work of Nineteenth-Century British Novels* (Princeton, N.J.: Princeton University Press, 2005), chap. 5.

3. Charles Dickens, *Our Mutual Friend*, ed. Michael Cotsell (Oxford: Oxford University Press, 1989), 18. All further references will appear parenthetically in the text.

4. Many critics have discussed the themes of reading and literacy in *Our Mutual Friend*, including Richard D. Altick, "Education, Print, and Paper in *Our Mutual Friend*," in *Nineteenth-Century Literary Perspectives: Essays in Honor of Lionel Stevenson*, ed. Clyde de L. Ryals (Durham, N.C.: Duke University Press, 1974), 237–54; Robert S. Baker, "Imagination and Literacy in Dickens' *Our Mutual Friend*," *Criticism* 18 (Winter 1976): 57–72; Stanley Friedman, "The Motif of Reading in *Our Mutual Friend*," *Nineteenth-Century Fiction* 28, no. 1 (1973): 38–61; Rosemary Mudhenk, "The Education of the Reader in *Our Mutual Friend*," *Nineteenth-Century Fiction* 34, no. 1 (1979): 41–72; and Kenneth M. Sroka, "Dickens' Metafiction: Readers and Writers in *Oliver Twist, David Copperfield*, and *Our Mutual Friend*," *Dickens Studies Annual* 22 (1973): 35–65.

5. Charles Dickens, Speech at a Banquet in his Honour: Hartford [Connecticut], February 7, 1842, in K. J. Fielding, ed., *The Speeches of Charles Dickens: A Complete Edition* (Oxford: Clarendon Press, 1960), 24.

6. Henry Mayhew, *What to Teach and How to Teach It: So That the Child May Become a Wise and Good Man* (London: William Smith, 1842), 1, 5.

7. In his discussion of Dickens's uses of association psychology, Michael S. Kearns argues that for Dickens, "The heart remains a mysterious entity; it is linked by association to elements of the phenomenal world and exercises its power through this link. This was Dickens's new accommodation between association psychology's view of human development as continuous and the common experience of sudden changes and reversals, his adjustment between that psychology's insistence on the power of the external world over the life of the mind and the belief that inner

forces, collectively characterized as 'the heart,' can counteract the external world's power." *Metaphors of Mind in Fiction and Psychology* (Lexington: University Press of Kentucky, 1987), 159. To a greater degree than Kearns, I emphasize the transitional nature of internal and external aspects of experience in Dickens's associationism.

8. For a comprehensive survey of Dickens's representations of teachers and schooling, see Philip Collins, *Dickens and Education* (London: Macmillan, 1963).

9. Thomas Hobbes, *Leviathan, with Selected Variants from the Latin Edition of 1668*, ed. Edwin Curley (Indianapolis: Hackett, 1994), 46.

10. Ibid.

11. John Locke, *Some Thoughts Concerning Education* and *Of the Conduct of the Understanding*, ed. Ruth W. Grant and Nathan Tarcov (Indianapolis: Hackett, 1996), 126–29, 132–34.

12. John Locke, *An Essay Concerning Human Understanding*, ed. Peter H. Nidditch (Oxford: Clarendon Press, 1975), 394–95.

13. Maria Edgeworth and Richard Lovell Edgeworth, *Practical Education* (Boston: Samuel H. Parker, 1823), 221.

14. Ibid., 222.

15. Ibid.

16. *The Pickwick Papers* (1836–37) offers an early example of this concern with lower-class literacy in its depiction of Sam and Tony Weller's comical composition of an eloquent Valentine (chapter 33). Sam's ability to write shows that he has attained a more advanced level of literacy, since the teaching of reading in nineteenth-century schools for the poor did not always include instruction in writing. Although Sam and Wegg are moral opposites, they possess similar levels of literacy. While we find out that Sam has had to live on the streets for a short time (*The Pickwick Papers*, ed. Robert S. Patten, 290–91), we never find out in either novel how or when he and Wegg learned to read.

17. Charles Dickens, *Bleak House*, ed. Nicola Bradbury (London: Penguin, 1996), 233–34.

18. In his biography of Dickens, John Forster reports that among the notes in the Book of Memoranda that Dickens began to keep as he was finishing *Little Dorrit* in January 1857, there were lists of names from which Dickens selected some names for characters. One of the lists was entitled "Boys from Privy Council Education lists" and the name "Bradley" is included among these. *The Life of Charles Dickens*, ed. J. W. T. Ley (London: Cecil Palmer, 1928), 757. See also Joel Brattin, "Dickens' Creation of Bradley Headstone," *Dickens Studies Annual* 14 (1985): 147–65.

19. For a useful history of methods for teaching reading up to the nineteenth century, see Victor E. Neuburg, *Popular Education in Eighteenth Century England* (London: Woburn Press, 1971).

20. M. K. Ashby, *Joseph Ashby of Tysoe, 1859–1919: A Study of English Village Life* (Cambridge: Cambridge University Press, 1961), 16–17.

21. On Dickens's own involvement with the Ragged School movement, which took off in the 1840s, see Norris Pope, *Dickens and Charity* (New York: Columbia University Press, 1978), 152–99, and Philip Collins, "Dickens and the

Ragged Schools," *Dickensian* 55 [May 1959]: 94–109. While Dickens supported the efforts of the Ragged School teachers and founders through the 1840s and 1850s, Pope argues that "Dickens consistently viewed the ragged school movement as a prelude to more comprehensive educational and social reforms, and never as an alternative system of providing religious instruction along strictly evangelical lines" (*Dickens and Charity*, 164).

22. Ashby, *Joseph Ashby of Tysoe*, 17. On the effects of the syllabic method, see also Richard D. Altick: "As time went on, some attempt was made to have the child grasp the meaning of the individual words before him, but the way in which it was done discouraged far more incipient readers than it inspired. . . . The child was seldom urged to reflect on the total meaning of a sentence or paragraph, let alone allowed to take any pleasure in what he read. Instead there was the constant, nagging necessity of parsing, explaining derivations, searching a desperate memory for the fixed definition of this word and that, a definition modified at the pupil's peril." *The English Common Reader: A Social History of the Mass Reading Public, 1800–1900*, 2nd ed. (Chicago: University of Chicago Press, 1957), 151.

23. Altick, *The English Common Reader*, 19–21.

24. Ibid., 22–23.

25. In her fictionalized memoir of her childhood among farm laborers in 1880s Oxfordshire, Flora Thompson recalls almost exactly the same message from her rector's visits to her classroom: "The children must not lie or steal or be discontented or envious. God had placed them just where they were in the social order and given them their own especial work to do; to envy others or to try to change their own lot in life was a sin of which he hoped they would never be guilty." *Lark Rise* (London: Oxford University Press, 1939), 204–5. On elementary schooling in rural England, see also Pamela Horn, *Education in Rural England, 1800–1914* (New York: St. Martin's Press, 1978).

26. F. H. Spencer, *An Inspector's Testament* (London, 1938), 51, in David Vincent, *Literacy and Popular Culture: England, 1750–1914* (Cambridge: Cambridge University Press, 1989), 78.

27. David Hartley, *Observations on Man, His Frame, His Duty, and His Expectations* (Gainesville, Fla.: Scholars' Facsimiles and Reprints, 1966), 1:318–19.

28. W. B. Hodgson, "Exaggerated Estimates of Reading and Writing," *Transactions of the National Association for the Promotion of Social Science* (1867): 400, quoted in Vincent, *Literacy and Popular Culture*, 79.

29. H. C. Barnard, *A Short History of English Education from 1760–1944* (London: University of London Press, 1947), 122.

30. James Kay-Shuttleworth, *Four Periods of Public Education* (London: Longman, Green, Longman, and Roberts, 1862), 320. For a biography of Kay-Shuttleworth, see R. J. W. Selleck, *James Kay-Shuttleworth: Journey of an Outsider* (Essex, UK: Woburn Press, 1994).

31. Kay-Shuttleworth, *Four Periods*, 321.

32. For a detailed discussion of the object lesson method and its implementation in colonial Indian schools, see Parna Sengupta, "An Object Lesson in Colonial Pedagogy," *Comparative Studies in Society and History* 45 (2003): 96–121.

33. See Marx's discussion of the commodity in *Capital*, vol. 1 (1867), chapter 1. In Karl Marx, *Capital: A Critique of Political Economy*, trans. Ben Fowkes (London: Penguin, 1976), 125–77.

34. For an intellectual history of this correlation, see Albert O. Hirschman, *The Passions and the Interests: Political Arguments for Capitalism Before Its Triumph* (Princeton, N.J.: Princeton University Press, 1977).

35. Riderhood seems to have had the rudiments of a pauper school education and is just barely able to read; he can decipher Eugene's calling card by "spelling it out slowly" (150).

36. John Stuart Mill, *On Liberty*, ed. Elizabeth Rapaport (Indianapolis: Hackett, 1978), 57.

37. In his analysis of the relations among the circulation of commodities, housekeeping, and the work of writing in Dickens's *Our Mutual Friend*, Andrew Miller points out that Dickens himself followed a daily routine as precise and predictable as Mr. Podsnap's, and argues that "Dickens' relation to social institutions and their effects on individuals within them is as conflicted as his response to the material landscapes he sees those institutions producing." *Novels Behind Glass: Commodity Culture and Victorian Narrative* (Cambridge: Cambridge University Press, 1995), 128.

38. Ruth Bernard Yeazell has argued in relation to the physical signs of Podsnap's willed ignorance that "the recurrent 'flush' with which Podsnap sweeps away all supposed threats to his daughter Georgiana's innocence is the involuntary sign of the very consciousness he wishes to deny." "Podsnappery, Sexuality, and the English Novel," *Critical Inquiry* 9 (December 1982): 357.

39. Collins, *Dickens and Education*, 159, 168.

40. See Hoppen, *The Mid-Victorian Generation*, 242–53.

41. Charles Dickens to W. W. F. De Cerjat, January 1, 1867, in Dickens, *The Letters of Charles Dickens*, ed. Madeline House, Graham Storey, and Kathleen Tillotson, Pilgrim Edition (Oxford: Clarendon Press, 1965–2002), 11:292–93. For an account of the events of the Trades Societies demonstration, see George Barnett Smith, *The Life and Speeches of John Bright, M.P.* (London: Thomas C. Jack, 1886), 4:517–22.

42. Robert Lowe, it should be noted, vehemently opposed further electoral reform in a series of speeches in Parliament between 1865 and 1867. Historian James Epstein observes, "Lowe was demonized at reform meetings, but stood for an important Benthamite legacy [within the Liberal party]. Following the 1868 election, Gladstone named him Chancellor of the Exchequer." *In Practice: Studies in the Language and Culture of Popular Politics in Modern Britain* (Stanford, Calif.: Stanford University Press, 2003), 54.

43. In keeping with its position of religious neutrality, Parliament also funded Roman Catholic and Jewish schools.

44. See the "Report of the Commissioners Appointed to Inquire into Popular Education in England and Wales," vol. 1, *Parliamentary Papers* 21, no. 1 (1861).

45. *Hansard's Debates*, vol. 165, 3rd ser. (London: T. C. Hansard, 1862), 229.

46. Ibid., 230.

47. As Richard D. Altick has shown, the Revised Code's effect on pedagogy was that "a new premium was put on rote memorization." A school would lose two shillings, eightpence, for every student who failed to pass the examination. Thus, teachers were obliged to teach to the test, which in the case of the reading test usually meant spending the year drilling the students on the contents of one textbook, with the result that "the best child (assuming he was not struck mute on examination day) was the one who had memorized the whole book" (*English Common Reader*, 157).

48. "Report of the Commissioners," 159.

49. Matthew Arnold quotes these instructions in his "General Report for 1867," in *Reports on Elementary Schools, 1852–1882*, 2nd ed. (London: Eyre and Spottiswoode, 1910), 105.

50. Asher Tropp, *The School Teachers: The Growth of the Teaching Profession in England and Wales from 1800 to the Present Day* (London: William Heinemann, 1957), 31.

51. "Report of the Commissioners," 166, 149.

52. *Hansard's Debates*, 211, 212.

53. Ibid., 211.

54. "Report of the Commissioners," 162.

55. In justification of the Revised Code, Lowe asserted that the social effect of improving the schoolmasters' class status was "not foreseen by the authors of the plan." He argued that, given the teachers' expectations that Parliament assumed a "duty to maintain them in the 'social *status*' they now enjoy," "such a system, which induces persons to entertain these expectations, is one which we should do well, with all fairness and justice, to get rid of" (*Hansard's Debates*, 213). In his history of the professionalization of schoolmasters, Asher Tropp identifies both the concern with growing financial outlays on the part of Lowe and other Liberals such as Gladstone, who was chancellor of the Exchequer, and middle-class resentment of the way the state was fostering popular education while neglecting to support middle-class schooling, as further reasons for the Revised Code's undermining of the schoolmasters (*School Teachers*, 60). For a detailed political history of the Revised Code, and partial defense of Lowe's role in devising it, see D. W. Sylvester, *Robert Lowe and Education* (Cambridge: Cambridge University Press, 1974).

56. In a speech delivered on February 13, 1862, Lowe cited with undisguised disgust a document circulated on behalf of teachers in which they asserted that "our votes and influence are for the men who aid us in this conjuncture" (*Hansard's Debates*, 212).

57. "Report of the Commissioners," 131.

58. Mr. Wilkinson, an assistant commissioner, reports this sentiment on the part of teachers and relates it to their dissatisfaction with salary levels (cited in Lowe's February 13, 1862, speech in *Hansard's Debates*, 231).

59. "Report of the Commissioners," 159.

60. Lauren Goodlad has recently argued, "Bradley Headstone's radically destabilized body is the expression of Dickens's antipathy towards social engineering"

that "entails a pernicious blend of bureaucratic depersonalization and bourgeois arrogance." *Victorian Literature and the Victorian State: Character and Governance in a Liberal Society* (Baltimore: Johns Hopkins University Press, 2003), 176. Goodlad reads Bradley's plot in light of larger developments in Victorian liberal governance reflected in the Revised Code, in particular, "the stabilization of a mid-Victorian consensus in which the middle classes delegated political power to the upper-class elite in exchange for free rein over commercial enterprise." She explains that "In the wake of Chartism, commercial scandals, the Crimean debacle, rebellion in India, and the fall of the Sanitary Idea—to name just a few contemporary controversies—the ideal of a stable social hierarchy presided over by the 'disinterested' government of born-and-bred gentlemen had gained a wide currency. It is in this context that an early Victorian educational agenda that claimed to build working-class character was superseded by a mid-Victorian agenda that aimed to strengthen the governing credentials of the nation's elite through public school and university reform" (173). Equally present in the debates over the Revised Code and particularly visible in Lowe's role, however, were combined middle-class, Benthamite, and commercial agendas to impose market criteria of efficiency and utility on government and education.

61. For an influential reading of sexual politics and homosociality in *Our Mutual Friend*, see Eve Kosofsky Sedgwick, *Between Men: English Literature and Homosocial Desire* (New York: Columbia University Press, 1985), 161–79.

62. Kay-Shuttleworth, *Four Periods*, 617. In its efforts to severely restrict the government's potential treatment of schoolteachers as civil servants, the Revised Code directly contradicted the legislation following the 1855 Northcote-Trevelyan report, or the report "On the Organization of the Permanent Civil Service," to regularize admission into the civil service through examination. Unlike the schoolmasters and schoolmistresses, aspiring civil servants were typically from the middle and upper classes, and thus their professional aspirations and financial ties to the government were viewed as falling within the pale of the state's meritocracy. In an 1859 letter written to J. A. Langford, a Birmingham journalist, Dickens supported the schoolmasters' entitlement to a decent wage: "They have as good a right to be paid for their labour as the Working Man has to be paid for his; and they are not, in their degree, really better paid than he is." Dickens to J. A. Langford, Nov. 25, 1859, quoted in John Manning, *Dickens on Education* (Toronto: University of Toronto Press, 1959), 188.

63. Kay-Shuttleworth, *Four Periods*, 632–33.

64. For a contrasting argument about Dickens's uses of examination in *Our Mutual Friend* to support that novel's defense of authorship as professional expertise, see Cathy Shuman, *Pedagogical Economies: The Examination and the Victorian Literary Man* (Stanford, Calif.: Stanford University Press, 2000), chap. 4.

65. R. W. Rich cites a note folded into a copy of a pamphlet entitled "How Can the Church Educate the People," published by G. F. Mathison in 1844, from Mathison to a member of Parliament that states: "I confess that elementary day schools for little children who go to plow at 8, and always earn their bread in some

way at 12, have never appeared to me as great a panacea as to many others, for national wants. . . . I cannot help thinking, however, that Colleges, where select youths may be trained and loyalised, are now a real desideratum." *The Training of Teachers in England and Wales During the Nineteenth Century* (Cambridge: Cambridge University Press, 1933), 85.

66. Kay-Shuttleworth narrates the founding of Battersea Training College and describes its organization and curriculum in *Four Periods*, 387–431.

67. Ibid., 634.

68. Charles Dickens, "The Great Baby," *Household Words*, August 4, 1855, in *'Gone Astray' and Other Papers from "Household Words," 1851–59*, ed. Michael Slater, Dent Uniform Edition of Dickens' Journalism, London: J. M. Dent, 1999, 312–13.

69. In his editorial introduction to "The Great Baby," Michael Slater explains that Dickens wrote it in part to respond to what he saw as the interfering testimony by sabbatarian temperance campaigners at a parliamentary commission investigating the 1854 Sunday Beer Act, which had drastically limited the hours that pubs and beer-houses could stay open on Sundays; ibid., 310.

70. Ibid., 312–13.

71. Elaine Hadley argues, for example, "The Ballot Act [of 1872] hoped to mass-produce a new abstract space of privacy or, rather, mass-produce two abstract spaces of privacy—the [voting] booth itself and the evanescent liberal citizen, con-stituted by his cognitive abstraction, who was momentarily capable of embodying his citizenship through an abstracted interest in the national or imperial good." *Living Liberalism: Practical Citizenship in Mid-Victorian Britain* (Chicago: University of Chicago Press, 2010), 180–81.

72. Raymond Williams, "Dickens and Social Ideas," in *Dickens, 1970*, ed. Michael Slater (New York: Stein and May, 1970), 90.

73. Charles Dickens, speech, Birmingham and Midland Institute's annual inau-gural meeting, Birmingham, September, 27, 1869, in Fielding, *The Speeches of Charles Dickens*, 400–402.

74. Ibid., 403.

75. Ibid., 407.

76. See Fielding's editorial notes on the press reaction to the final lines from this speech, which, without the proper punctuation, seemed to suggest that Dickens was criticizing the current Liberal government and speaking against electoral reform, when he in fact had praised John Bright earlier in the speech (ibid., 408).

77. Ibid., 412.

78. Ibid., 410–12; H. T. Buckle, *History of Civilization in England* (New York: Longmans, Green and Company, 1902), vol. 3, 170.

79. This scene could also be classified as a version of Aristotelian *anagnorisis* because it involves ties of kinship or friendship. See Aristotle, *Poetics*, chaps. 10 and 11.

80. Harry Stone, ed., *Dickens' Working Notes for His Novels* (Chicago: University of Chicago Press, 1987), 343.

81. Kay-Shuttleworth, *Four Periods*, 608.

82. For a persuasive interpretation of Jenny Wren's linguistic artistry and its implications for Dickens's own views of art and imagination, see Garrett Stewart, *Dickens and the Trials of Imagination* (Cambridge, Mass.: Harvard University Press, 1974), 202–21.

83. Samuel Rogers, *The Pleasures of Memory with Other Poems* (Paris: Baudry's European Library, 1852), vii–viii.

84. See John B. Thompson's chapter 6 on the "re-mooring of tradition" in *The Media and Modernity: A Social Theory of the Media* (Stanford, Calif.: Stanford University Press, 1995).

85. Pam Morris presents the novel's series of dilemmas in a similar way: "Throughout the text of *Our Mutual Friend*, discontent (even hatred) with things as they are is registered in a desire for transformation, split between imaginative remaking and a tired escape from the need to struggle." *Dickens's Class Consciousness: A Marginal View* (London: Macmillan, 1991), 137.

86. George Orwell, *Dickens, Dali, and Others* (New York: Harcourt, Brace, 1963), 75.

87. This anti-hierarchical movement seems related to what Gauri Viswanathan analyzes as Dickens's elevation of marginal characters to importance in order to provide a model for religious tolerance in *Barnaby Rudge* (1841): "Dickens is too aware of the inherent contradictions in a project of religious tolerance founded on secular culture to look toward a leadership in a secular elite." *Outside the Fold: Conversion, Modernity, and Belief* (Princeton, N.J.: Princeton University Press, 1998), 25–26.

88. Charles Dickens, *David Copperfield*, ed. Trevor Blount (London: Penguin, 1966), 540–41.

89. For a reading of Dickens's uses of melodrama to attack the New Poor Law of 1834 in *Oliver Twist* as situated in the larger cultural transition from a status-based to a class-based social organization, see Elaine Hadley, *Melodramatic Tactics: Theatricalized Dissent in the English Marketplace, 1800–1885* (Stanford, Calif.: Stanford University Press, 1995), 77–132.

90. Charles Dickens, preface to *Little Dorrit*, ed. Stephen Wall and Helen Small (London: Penguin, 1998), 5.

91. Here I allude to M. M. Bakhtin's theory of the "ideological becoming" of the individual in "Discourse in the Novel," in *The Dialogic Imagination: Four Essays*, trans. Caryl Emerson and Michael Holquist, ed. Michael Holquist (Austin: University of Texas Press, 1981), 341–49.

6. Dickens's Laughter: School Reading and Democratic Literature, 1870–1940

1. Rick Rylance, *Victorian Psychology and British Culture, 1850–1880* (Oxford: Oxford University Press, 2000), 7.

2. George Eliot, "The Natural History of German Life," in *Selected Essays, Poems and Other Writings*, ed. A. S. Byatt and Nicholas Warren (London: Penguin, 1990), 107. All further references appear in the text.

3. On the histories of these disciplines, see Christopher Herbert, *Culture and Anomie: Ethnographic Imagination in the Nineteenth Century* (Chicago: University of

Chicago Press, 1991); George W. Stocking Jr., *Victorian Anthropology* (New York: Free Press, 1987); and Benedikt Stuchtey and Peter Wende, eds., *British and German Historiography, 1750–1950* (Oxford: Oxford University Press, 2000).

4. These are precisely the kind of managerial credentials of the expert witnesses on whom Charles Booth would rely for his seventeen-volume *Life and Labour of the People in London* (1889–1902); his sources of information on the life of the poor included visitors from the London School Board, who were charged to visit the homes of every family with school-aged children, as well as "poor-law officials, rent collectors, sanitary inspectors, factory inspectors, clergymen, the police, residents in settlement houses," and employers. Gertrude Himmelfarb, *Poverty and Compassion: The Moral Imagination of the Late Victorians* (New York: Knopf, 1991), 98–99.

5. See Dickens's preface to *Little Dorrit*, ed. Stephen Wall and Helen Small (London: Penguin, 1998), originally included as an afterword to the last serial number of the novel published in June 1857.

6. For two important recent analyses of the development of this detached liberal perspective in Victorian writing across philosophical, political, and literary genres, see Amanda Anderson, *The Powers of Distance: Cosmopolitanism and the Cultivation of Detachment* (Princeton, N.J.: Princeton University Press, 2001), and Elaine Hadley, *Living Liberalism: Practical Citizenship in Mid-Victorian Britain* (Chicago: University of Chicago Press, 2010).

7. Charles Dickens, speech to the Administrative Reform Association, June 27, 1855, in K. J. Fielding, ed., *The Speeches of Charles Dickens: A Complete Edition* (Oxford: Clarendon Press, 1960), 207.

8. G. H. Lewes, review of vol. 1 of Forster's *Life of Dickens*, *Fortnightly Review*, February 1872, 141–54, in Philip Collins, ed., *Dickens: The Critical Heritage* (New York: Barnes & Noble, 1971), 571. All further references are included in the text.

9. David Hume, *A Treatise of Human Nature*, ed. P. H. Nidditch, 2nd ed. (Oxford: Oxford University Press, 1978), 265. Hume describes mental causation as follows: "Experience is a principle, which instructs me in the several conjunctions of objects for the past. Habit is another principle, which determines me to expect the same for the future; and both of them conspiring to operate upon the imagination, make me form certain ideas in a more intense and lively manner, than others, which are not attended with the same advantages. Without this quality, by which the mind enlivens some ideas beyond others (which seemingly is so trivial, and so little founded on reason) we cou'd never assent to any argument, nor carry our view beyond those few objects, which are present to our senses."

10. Paul de Man, "Hypogram and Inscription," in *The Resistance to Theory* (Minneapolis: University of Minnesota Press, 1986), 49.

11. On critics' similar recasting of Byron's poetic genius as pathological after his death, see Dino Franco Felluga, *The Perversity of Poetry: Romantic Ideology and the Popular Male Poet of Genius* (Albany: SUNY Press, 2005), chap. 4.

12. De Man, "Hypogram and Inscription," in *The Resistance to Theory*, 49–50.

13. Q. D. Leavis, *Fiction and the Reading Public* (London: Pimlico, 2000), 156. In *Dickens the Novelist* (London: Penguin, 1970), written with F. R. Leavis, however, Q. D. Leavis participates in rehabilitating Dickens's standing among literary critics.

14. Nicholas Dames, *The Physiology of the Novel: Reading, Neural Science, and the Form of Victorian Fiction* (Oxford: Oxford University Press, 2007), 53.

15. Ibid., 55. Dames quotes from Bain's *The Emotions and the Will* (1899 edition).

16. Ibid.

17. Ibid., 41.

18. One could begin to explore the extensive literature on the emergence of psychology as a dominant modern disciplinary knowledge with Richard Sennett, *The Fall of Public Man: On the Social Psychology of Capitalism*, 2nd ed. (New York: Vintage, 1976); Philip Rieff, *The Triumph of the Therapeutic* (New York: Harper and Row, 1968); and Joel Pfister and Nancy Schnog, eds., *Inventing the Psychological: Toward a Cultural History of Emotional Life in America* (New Haven, Conn.: Yale University Press, 1996).

19. Adolphus William Ward, *Dickens* (London: Macmillan, 1906), 205.

20. Ibid., 211.

21. Ibid., 210.

22. Charles Dickens, *The Letters of Charles Dickens*, ed. Madeline House, Graham Storey, and Kathleen Tillotson, Pilgrim Edition (Oxford: Clarendon Press, 1965–2002), 7:10.

23. Ward, *Dickens*, 215.

24. Ibid., 216.

25. Ibid., 224.

26. [Mrs. Oliphant], "Charles Dickens," *Blackwood's Magazine*, June 1871, 673–95, in Collins, *Dickens: The Critical Heritage*, 559–68; Mowbray Morris, "Charles Dickens," *Fortnightly Review*, December 1, 1882, 762–79, in Collins, *Dickens: The Critical Heritage*, 599–611. See the discussion of these reviews in K. J. Fielding, "1870–1900: Forster and the Reaction," *Dickensian* 66 (1970): 85–100, and the collection of obituary tributes to Dickens and reviews of Forster's biography in Collins, *Dickens: The Critical Heritage*, 502–37, 565–88. Philip Waller discusses how critical "reservations" about Dickens's art were "eventually enshrined" by Leslie Stephen in his contribution on Dickens to the new *Dictionary of National Biography* in 1888. *Writers, Readers, and Reputations: Literary Life in Britain, 1870–1918* (Oxford: Oxford University Press, 2006), 195. Waller traces the critical reputations of numerous Victorian authors in chapter 5.

27. For a detailed account of the publication of these cheap editions that I discuss in this paragraph, see Robert L. Patten, *Charles Dickens and His Publishers* (Oxford: Clarendon Press, 1978), 327–30.

28. Ibid.; Anthony Trollope, "Novel-Reading. The Works of Charles Dickens. The Works of W. Makepeace Thackeray," *Nineteenth Century* 5, no. 23 (1879): 32–33. On the plethora of Chapman and Hall editions after Dickens's death, see also Waller, *Writers, Readers, and Reputations*, 194.

29. On Dent's Everyman Library, initiated in 1906, and other contemporaneous ventures to publish cheap series of literary classics in Britain, see Richard D. Altick,

Writers, Readers, and Occasions: Selected Essays on Victorian Literature and Life (Columbus: Ohio State University Press, 1989), 174–95, and Waller, *Writers, Readers, and Reputations*, 58–59. For a survey of American literary classics series, see discussions in Thomas Recchio, "'Charming and Sane': School Editions of *Cranford* in America, 1905–1914," *Victorian Studies* 45, no. 4 (2003): 604, and Lane Stiles, "Packaging Literature for the High Schools: From the Riverside Series to *Literature and Life*," in *Reading Books: Essays on the Material Text and Literature in America*, ed. Michele Moylan and Lane Stiles (Amherst: University of Massachusetts Press, 1996), 269 n. 21.

30. Patten, *Charles Dickens and His Publishers*, 331–32.

31. Charles Dickens, *A Christmas Carol and The Chimes*, ed. Hugh Reginald Haweis (London: George Routledge and Sons, 1886), 6.

32. Ibid.

33. Ibid.

34. Ibid. K. Theodore Hoppen notes the dramatic increase in numbers of voters under the 1884 Representation of the People Act: "In England and Wales the 2,618,453 voters of 1883 became 4,376,916. In Scotland numbers rose from 310,441 to 560,580, in Ireland . . . from 224,018 to 737,965." Hoppen points out, however, that only 62.2 percent of adult males could vote in England and Wales in 1891, while in Scotland and Ireland these numbers were in the fiftieth percentile; women, of course, remained without the vote. *The Mid-Victorian Generation, 1846–1886* (Oxford: Clarendon Press, 1998), 265–66.

35. Sir Henry Maine, *Popular Government* (1885), quoted in Hoppen, *The Mid-Victorian Generation*, 265.

36. J. C. Collins, *The Study of English Literature* (London, 1891) 147–48, in Chris Baldick, *The Social Mission of English Criticism, 1848–1932* (Oxford: Clarendon Press, 1983), 64–65.

37. Stephen Heathorn, *For Home, Country, and Race: Constructing Gender, Class, and Englishness in the Elementary School, 1880–1914* (Toronto: University of Toronto Press, 2000), 6–7. In this context, "the history presented to working-class children as a basis of their identity was largely emptied of any radical or 'populist' alternatives to a socially inclusive, yet functionalist and statist, view of the nation" (21).

38. Ibid., 222–23.

39. Margaret Mathieson, *The Preachers of Culture: A Study of English and Its Teachers* (Totowa, N.J.: Rowman and Littlefield, 1975), 52–53.

40. Heathorn, *For Home, Country, and Race*, 8.

41. J. M. Goldstrom, *The Social Content of Education, 1808–1870: A Study of the Working Class School Reader in England and Ireland* (Shannon: Irish University Press, 1972), chap. 3.

42. Goldstrom states that approximately £22,000 was spent on books, maps, and diagrams for use by approximately 1,048,851 registered schoolchildren in England and Wales in 1851, and £61,834 spent on such materials in 1859 for approximately 1,549,312 schoolchildren. Ibid., 141–45.

43. Heathorn, *For Home, Country, and Race*, 10–11.

44. Ibid., 14–15.

45. Ibid.

46. *Journal of Education*, July 1, 1891, 351; *Educational Times and Journal of the College of Preceptors*, January–December 1907, 277 (available on Google Books).

47. Stefan Collini, *Public Moralists: Political Thought and Intellectual Life in Britain, 1850–1930* (Oxford: Clarendon Press, 1991), 352. For an extended and compelling consideration of the role of the *OED*'s model of historical philology in creating an image of English authorship, see also Dennis Taylor, *Hardy's Literary Language and Victorian Philology* (Oxford: Clarendon Press, 1993).

48. Taylor provides these figures in *Hardy's Literary Language*, 124–25.

49. Altick documents the impressive sales figures for this series: "over 300,000 copies between 1878, when the first volumes, priced at 2*s*. 6*d*. were published, and 1887, when a reissue in monthly volumes at 1*s*. in paper, 1*s*. 6*d*. in cloth, was begun." *Writers, Readers, and Occasions*, 194.

50. Collini, *Public Moralists*, 355–57.

51. Charles Carpenter provides the publication information in *History of American Schoolbooks* (Philadelphia: University of Pennsylvania Press, 1963), 164. I have consulted an 1853 American edition. The book consists of lectures that Shaw gave as professor at the Imperial Alexander Lyceum of St. Petersburg, Russia.

52. Thomas B. Shaw, *Outlines of English Literature: A New American Edition. With A Sketch of American Literature by Henry B. Tuckerman* (Philadelphia: Blanchard and Lea, 1853), 388.

53. Ibid., 392.

54. William Spalding's 1853 textbook *The History of English Literature: With an Outline of the Origin and Growth of the English Language* (New York: D. Appleton, 1853) mentions Dickens briefly in his chapter on "The Nineteenth Century, 1830–1853," comparing Dickens favorably to Thackeray as the "founders of a new school of novel-writing" (401).

55. Henry Morley, *A First Sketch of English Literature*, 26th ed. (London: Cassell, 1890), 1062–63.

56. R. Shelton Mackenzie, *Life of Charles Dickens* (Philadelphia: T. B. Peterson & Brothers, 1870), 18. The dedication is dated August 1, 1870. I thank Thomas Recchio for bringing this book to my attention.

57. Ibid., 336.

58. Ibid., 317.

59. For other similar capsule biographies of Dickens in late nineteenth- and early twentieth-century literary histories, see William Vaughn Moody and Robert Morss Lovett, *A History of English Literature* (New York: Charles Scribner's Sons, 1906), 363–68; Henry S. Pancoast, *An Introduction to English Literature*, 3rd ed. (New York: Henry Holt, 1894), 558–60; Eva March Tappan, *A Short History of England's Literature* (Boston: Houghton Mifflin, 1905), 223–26. Repeating many of Lewes's criticisms of Dickens, George Saintsbury nevertheless praises him as one of the two most important early Victorian novelists, along with Thackeray, and singles out *The*

Pickwick Papers, David Copperfield, and *Great Expectations* as his masterpieces. *A Short History of English Literature* (London: Macmillan, 1898), 740–43.

60. Reuben Post Halleck, *History of English Literature* (New York: American Book, 1900), 436.

61. Ibid., 6.

62. See Jean Ferguson Carr, Stephen L. Carr, and Lucille M. Schultz, *Archives of Instruction: Nineteenth-Century Rhetorics, Readers, and Composition Books in the United States* (Carbondale: Southern Illinois University Press, 2005); Ruth Miller Elson, *Guardians of Tradition: American Schoolbooks of the Nineteenth Century* (Lincoln: University of Nebraska Press, 1964); Recchio, "Charming and Sane"; Stiles, "Packaging Literature for the High Schools"; and Richard L. Venezky with Carl F. Kaestle, "From McGuffey to Dick and Jane: Reading Textbooks," in *Print in Motion: The Expansion of Publishing and Reading in the United States, 1880–1940*, ed. Carl F. Kaestle and Janice A. Radway (Chapel Hill: American Antiquarian Society and University of North Carolina Press, 2009), 414–30.

63. Carr, Carr, and Schultz, *Archives of Instruction*, 84.

64. Carl F. Kaestle and Janice A. Radway, "A Framework for the History of Publishing and Reading in the United States," in Kaestle and Radway, *Print in Motion*, 15.

65. Ibid., 21.

66. Carr, Carr, and Schultz find that "across the [nineteenth] century . . . reading changed from *elocutionary*—from reading aloud, with attention to pronunciation, emphasis, and gesture—to *literary*, reading silently, with attention to meaning and interpretation" (*Archives of Instruction*, 115). This marked shift away from oral recitation and elocution as classroom methods and popular models for the uses of literacy in public speaking continued through the early decades of the twentieth century. By the time of the widely employed "Dick and Jane" series of the 1940s, Venezky and Kaestle conclude, "reading for meaning, not pleasure, [had] replaced reading for rhetorical expression." "From McGuffey to Dick and Jane," 418–20, 429.

67. Venezky and Kaestle, "From McGuffey to Dick and Jane," 423–24.

68. Ibid., 426. In his innovative study of the publication history of Elizabeth Gaskell's *Cranford* (1853) as an American school text during this period, Thomas Recchio has argued more specifically that the editors' prefaces promoted the novel as accomplishing a "moral eugenics" by constructing a "healthy and sane" Anglo-Saxon form of generic American "ethnic" identity within a demographic context of increasing ethic diversity resulting from repeated waves of immigration, primarily from southern Europe and Asia. "Charming and Sane," 598–600. See also Recchio's *Elizabeth Gaskell's "Cranford": A Publishing History* (Aldershot, UK: Ashgate, 2009).

69. Kaestle and Radway, "A Framework," 7.

70. Charles Dickens, *The Old Curiosity Shop*, ed. Angus Easson (London: Penguin, 1972), 363.

71. Ibid., 364.

72. Heathorn, *For Home, Country, and Race*, 146.

73. Stiles, "Packaging Literature for the High Schools," 255. Stiles points out that because many high school teachers lacked professional training in the early decades of the twentieth century, "the principal user of the text[book] was not the high school student but the high school teacher, who functioned as a proxy for [the textbook editor's] cultural authority in the classroom—as a privileged interpreter . . . of Anglo-Saxon tradition."

74. George S. Hillard, ed., *The Fifth Reader, for the Use of Public and Private Schools* (Boston: Brewer and Tileston, 1863); Emma J. Todd and W. B. Powell, *The Normal Course in Reading: Fifth Reader* (New York: Silver, Burdett, 1895); Ellen M. Cyr, *Cyr's Fourth Reader* (Boston: Ginn, 1898); Isabel Moore, *The Eaton Readers: Fourth Reader* (Chicago: Eaton, 1906); Isabel Moore, *The Eaton Readers: Fifth Reader* (Chicago: Eaton, 1906); Joseph H. Wade and Emma Sylvester, *The Language Readers: Fifth Reader* (Boston: Ginn, 1906); Kate F. Oswell and C. B. Gilbert, *The American School Readers: The Literary Reader for Higher Grades* (New York: Macmillan, 1912); William Iler Crane and William Henry Wheeler, *Wheeler's Graded Literary Readers, with Interpretations: An Eighth Reader* (Chicago: W. H. Wheeler, 1919). Notable in this group of readers is the large number of women authors, editors, or coeditors. Carr, Carr, and Schultz report that Dickens's "Two Views of Christmas" was included in Monroe's *Sixth Reader* (1872) and that McGuffey's *Sixth Reader* (1879) included an excerpt from Dickens's *Old Curiosity Shop* (*Archives of Instruction*, 113–14). They point out that school readers from this 1870s period tend to assert that they have not adapted the original literary works that they excerpt, and also "include pieces that challenge the efficacy of school instruction and suggest the importance instead of self-culture or immersion in nature" (ibid).

75. Stiles, "Packaging Literature for the High Schools," 257.

76. Crane and Wheeler, *Wheeler's Graded Literary Readers*, 154–55.

77. R. H. Horne, *A New Spirit of the Age*, 2nd ed., vol. 1 (London: Smith, Elder, 1844), 70–71.

78. A more detailed treatment of these educational materials than I can offer here would take into account the curricular mandates and local politics of the specific state education systems in which each textbook was used, as well as the educational credentials and training of the authors and editors, which are prominently displayed in each case on the title page. On the history and theory of teaching reading during this period, see also David E. Bartine, *Early English Reading Theory: Origins of Current Debates* (Columbia: University of South Carolina Press, 1989), and *Reading, Criticism, and Culture: Theory and Teaching in the United States and England, 1820–1950* (Columbia: University of South Carolina Press, 1989).

79. Such instructions suggest that textbooks may provide important evidence for the emergence or implementation of New Critical academic protocols of close reading in the public schools. On the role of the New Criticism in forming the literary canon, see John Guillory, *Cultural Capital: The Problem of Literary Canon Formation* (Chicago: University of Chicago Press, 1993), chap. 3.

80. Wheeler, *Wheeler's Graded Literary Readers*, 3–6.

81. Ibid., 104.

82. Guillory, *Cultural Capital*, 43.

83. Charles Dickens, *A Christmas Carol. Being a Ghost Story of Christmas*, ed. Albert F. Blaisdell (New York: Maynard, Merrill, 1892), 7–8. The text ends with questions on the reading such as "1. Give some facts in the early life of Dickens. . . . 10. Did Dickens have any special object in writing several of his stories? 11. What was the practical effect upon the abuses in question? 12. What can you say of the popularity of these novels? . . . 20. Some prominent traits in the character of Dickens. . . . 22. Have you any opinion to give on the future of his fame? (Cf. Ward's *Dickens*, Ch. 7). 23. Of the many artists who have illustrated Dickens, what ones do you prefer, and why?" (63–64). These questions are quite similar to a set on Edmund Spenser that Graff quotes from an 1857 British textbook by Charles Cleveland, *Compendium of English Literature*, in *Professing Literature: An Institutional History* (Chicago: University of Chicago Press, 2007), 39.

84. Graff, *Professing Literature*, 64.

85. Google Books has generated an extensive controversy over whether such universal access can or should be provided by a for-profit company that also depends on the holdings of academic libraries to source its digitizing project. For a Web site with extensive links to documents related to the ongoing legal and scholarly debate over Google Books, see "Google Books Bibliography" by Charles W. Bailey Jr., http://www.digital-scholarship.org/gbsb/gbsb.htm (accessed October 23, 2010).

86. Stiles reports that an abridged version of *A Tale of Two Cities* was included under the heading "Man and his Fellows" along with texts promoting democracy and humanitarianism by Woodrow Wilson, Theodore Roosevelt, and Robert Burns, in *Literature and Life*, a four-volume textbook first published by Scott Foresman in 1922 that was also one of the first modern English and American literature anthologies geared specifically for high schools. *Literature and Life* was characterized by its "layer after layer of biography, history, criticism, explication, formal analysis, appreciation, citizenship training, and composition and literacy instruction." "Packaging Literature for the High Schools," 250, 264, 270 n. 26.

87. Dora V. Smith, *Instruction in English*, Office of Education Bulletin No. 17, 1932, National Survey of Secondary Education, Monograph No. 20 (Washington, D.C.: U.S. Government Printing Office, 1933), 51–52. Smith supplies a graph of titles ranked in order of most common appearance in curricula and showing in what grade each work was taught. The top ten books on this list are as follows: Eliot's *Silas Marner*, Shakespeare's *Julius Caesar*, Tennyson's *Idylls of the King*, Scott's *Ivanhoe*, Dickens's *Tale of Two Cities*, Scott's *Lady of the Lake*, Coleridge's *Rime of the Ancient Mariner*, Stevenson's *Treasure Island*, Shakespeare's *Merchant of Venice*, and Lowell's *Vision of Sir Launfal*. The appearance at the top of the list of *Silas Marner*, the prominence of Scott, the prevalence of Romantic medievalism among the poetic works, and the appearance of only one text by an American author in the top ten all suggest that there are many more stories to be told about the images of English literature and Anglo-American (Anglo-Saxon) literary culture projected by these early twentieth-century curricula.

88. Ibid., 51–52.

89. Dora V. Smith, *Evaluating Instruction in Secondary School English: A Report of the New York Regents' Inquiry into the Character and Cost of Public Education in New York State*, English Monograph No. 11 (Chicago: National Council of Teachers of English, 1941), 59.

90. Ibid., 59–75. Beyond Dickens and George Eliot, the Victorian period is represented in these lists of high school reading by Charlotte Brontë's *Jane Eyre*, Hardy's *A Pair of Blue Eyes*, Stevenson's *The Black Arrow* and *Treasure Island*, and *The Sign of Four* by Conan Doyle.

91. On Houghton Mifflin's Riverside series, see Stiles, "Packaging Literature for the High Schools," 253, 258–59.

92. Edwin Percy Whipple, introduction to Charles Dickens, *The Personal History of David Copperfield* (Boston: Houghton Mifflin, 1894), 1:xxxi–xxxii.

93. Ibid.

94. A biographical essay on Dickens by Whipple was also reprinted in William Swinton's 1880 *Studies in English Literature* (New York: Harper and Brothers, 1888), a collection of selections by forty English and American authors, and advertised on its title page as including "definitions, notes, analyses, and glossary as a systematic aid to literary study." Swinton's preface recommends the textbook's use in normal schools and high schools "at the meeting point of literature and rhetoric" (iii). This anthology includes *A Christmas Carol* as Dickens's representative work. Charles Carpenter includes Swinton's text among an initial group of nineteenth-century textbooks published between 1850 and 1880 that were explicitly geared toward the study of literature as a separate subject in American schools. *History of American Schoolbooks* (Philadelphia: University of Pennsylvania Press, 1963), 162–65.

95. Henry Mayhew, *What to Teach and How to Teach It: So That the Child May Become a Wise and Good Man* (London: William Smith, 1842), 2.

96. Arlo Bates, "Edwin Percy Whipple," in Edwin Percy Whipple, *Charles Dickens: The Man and His Work* (Boston: Houghton Mifflin, 1912), 1:xv.

97. Ibid. For an analysis of critics' efforts circa 1850–1900 to frame reader response to the burgeoning periodical market by warning against the potentially "pathological" results of the "desultory" reading of serials, see Kelly J. Mays, "The Disease of Reading and Victorian Periodicals," in *Literature in the Marketplace: Nineteenth-Century British Publishing and Reading Practices*, ed. John O. Jordan and Robert L. Patten (Cambridge: Cambridge University Press, 1995), 165–94.

98. Janice A. Radway, *A Feeling for Books: The Book-of-the-Month-Club, Literary Taste, and Middle-Class Desire* (Chapel Hill: University of North Carolina Press, 1997), 284.

99. Ibid.

100. *Educational Times and Journal of College Preceptors*, January–December 1906, 408 (available on Google Books). I have also found a reference to a Black's edition of *David Copperfield*, suggesting that there were probably other novels by Dickens included in this series.

101. The Dickens Fellowship history can be found at http://www
.dickensfellowship.org.

102. See Waller's discussion of the early activities of the Dickens Fellowship in
Writers, Readers, and Reputations, 191–92.

103. Paul K. Saint-Amour, *The Copywrights: Intellectual Property and the Literary
Imagination* (Ithaca, N.Y.: Cornell University Press, 2003), 181.

104. Today, the two most likely candidates for inclusion in high school curricula
are still *A Tale of Two Cities*, but also the more socially critical late work *Great Expectations* (1860–61), suggesting that the early twentieth-century assimilationist project
of inculcating generic democratic allegiances in children shifted to a more self-critical, even postmodern, mode. Sandra Stotsky's recent survey of literary study in
United States high schools lists *Great Expectations* as the ninth most commonly
taught work of literature in grade 9. "Literary Study in Grades 9, 10, and 11: A
National Survey," *Forum: A Publication of the ALSCW* 4 (Spring 2010), 15. On *Great
Expectations* as a text that "anticipates" postmodernism, see Jay Clayton, *Charles
Dickens in Cyberspace: The Afterlife of the Nineteenth Century in Postmodern Culture*
(Oxford: Oxford University Press, 2003), chap. 6.

105. See Clayton, *Dickens in Cyberspace*.

106. [Henry James], review, *Nation*, December 21, 1865, in Collins, *Dickens: The
Critical Heritage*, 470.

107. Henry James, *A Small Boy and Others* (New York, 1913), in *Autobiographies*
(1956), 65–70, in Collins, *Dickens: The Critical Heritage*, 613–14.

108. Ibid., 65–70, 251, in Collins, *Dickens: The Critical Heritage*, 615.

109. Ibid., 65–70, 388, in Collins, *Dickens: The Critical Heritage*, 615.

110. George Gissing, "Dickens in Memory: A Personal View," *Literature*,
December 21, 1901, 572–73, in *Collected Works of George Gissing on Charles Dickens*,
vol. 1, *Essays, Introductions, and Reviews*, ed. Pierre Coustillas (Surrey, UK: Grayswood Press, 2004), 47–51. This essay was originally commissioned for a December
21, 1901, issue of the weekly journal *Literature* devoted to Dickens. Each issue of
this magazine included a high-quality reproduction of a photographic image on
heavy bond paper—a "Literature Portrait"—of a famous author, suitable for framing and collecting.

111. George Orwell, *Dickens, Dali, and Others* (New York: Harcourt, Brace:
1963), 57–58.

112. Ibid., 75.

113. F. R. Leavis, "The First Major Novel: *Dombey and Son*," in Leavis and
Leavis, *Dickens the Novelist*, 21–22.

114. G. K. Chesterton, *Charles Dickens: A Critical Study* (New York: Dodd,
Mead, 1911), 4. All further references appear in the text.

115. In his entry on "Democracy," Raymond Williams notes that "Aristotle
(*Politics*, IV, 4) wrote: 'a democracy is a state where the freemen and the poor, being
in the majority, are invested with the power of the state.' " *Keywords: A Vocabulary
of Culture and Society*, rev. ed. (New York: Oxford University Press, 1983), 93.

116. Charles Dickens, *The Mystery of Edwin Drood*, ed. Steven Connor (London: J. M. Dent, 1996), 35.

117. The possibility that global citizenship is implied in Dickens's personification of the English literature curriculum becomes more conceivable in light of Joseph R. Slaughter's groundbreaking analysis of the enlistment of the *Bildungsroman* in the formulation of modern definitions of human personality in the international law of human rights. Slaughter argues that "one of the primary carriers of human rights culture, the *Bildungsroman* has been a conspicuous literary companion on [globalization's] itineraries, traveling with missionaries, militaries, colonial administrators, and technical advisors—as the numerous allusions (both explicit and oblique) to *Great Expectations, Jane Eyre, Sentimental Education*, and *Wilhelm Meister's Apprenticeship* in contemporary postcolonial *Bildungsromane* attest." *Human Rights, Inc.: The World Novel, Narrative Form, and International Law* (New York: Fordham University Press, 2007), 123.

Afterword

1. Benedict Anderson, *Imagined Communities: Reflections on the Origin and Spread of Nationalism*, rev. ed. (London: Verso, 1991), 9–36.

2. Ibid., 26.

3. See Michel de Certeau, *The Practice of Everyday Life*, trans. Steven Rendall (Berkeley: University of California Press, 1984).

4. Guglielmo Cavallo and Roger Chartier, eds., *A History of Reading in the West*, trans. Lydia G. Cochrane (Amherst: University of Massachusetts Press, 1999), 34–35.

5. For an intriguing consideration of the contemporary survival of Dickens in popular culture, see Jay Clayton, *Dickens in Cyberspace: The Afterlife of the Nineteenth Century in Postmodern Culture* (Oxford: Oxford University Press, 2003).

6. Mark Poster, "Digital Networks and Citizenship," *PMLA* 117, no. 1 (2002): 101.

7. Ibid., 99. Poster's optimistic assessment of the Internet's impact on global political relations could be placed alongside investigations by psychologists of possible negative effects on the brain and behavior of excessive multitasking online, including increasing fragmentation of the user's attention, inability to focus on tasks requiring sustained thinking, decreasing face-to-face contact with others in favor of virtual contact through social networking, and even "net addiction." The two developments are not incompatible; that is, Internet communication could enhance new global political alliances while, on an everyday or workplace-driven basis, taking time away from more intimate relationships. For a recent discussion of research suggesting that technological multitasking may rewire the brain, see Matt Richtel, "Hooked on Gadgets, and Paying a Mental Price," *New York Times*, June 9, 2010.

8. Henry Mayhew, *What to Teach and How to Teach It: So That the Child May Become a Wise and Good Man* (London: William Smith, 1842), 3.

Bibliography

Sources Published Before 1900

Anon. "Article I." *British Quarterly Review*, April 1, 1869, 313–45.

Anon. *The Public Characters of 1798*. Dublin: J. Moore, 1799. (Google Books)

Anon. *A Schoolmaster's Difficulties, Abroad and at Home*. London: Longman, Brown, Green and Longmans, 1853.

Arbuckle, James. *Hibernicus's Letters*. Vol. 2. London, 1734.

Cowper, William, and Robert Southey. *The Works of William Cowper, Esq.: Comprising His Poems, Correspondence and Translations. With a Life of the Author by the Editor, Robert Southey*. Vol. 2. London: Baldwin and Cradock, 1836. (Google Books)

Craig, Asa Hollister. *New Common School Question Book: Comprising Questions and Answers on All Common School Studies*. New York: Hinds and Noble, 1897. (Google Books)

Cyr, Ellen M. *Cyr's Fourth Reader*. Boston: Ginn, 1898. (Google Books)

Dickens, Charles. *A Christmas Carol and The Chimes*. Edited by Hugh Reginald Haweis. London: George Routledge and Sons, 1886. (Google Books)

———. *A Christmas Carol. Being a Ghost Story of Christmas*. Abridged and edited by Albert F. Blaisdell. New York: Maynard, Merrill, 1892. (Google Books)

———. *The Personal History of David Copperfield*. 2 vols. Boston: Houghton Mifflin, 1894. (Google Books)

Dolby, George. *Charles Dickens as I Knew Him: The Story of the Reading Tours in Great Britain and America (1866–1870)*. Philadelphia: J. B. Lippincott, 1885.

Dunn, Henry. *Principles of Teaching; or, The Normal School Manual: Containing Practical Suggestions on the Government and Instruction of Children*. 10th ed. London, n.d.

Edgeworth, Maria, and Richard Lovell Edgeworth. *Practical Education*. Boston: Samuel H. Parker, 1823.

[Ellis], Sarah Stickney. "An Apology for Fiction." In *Pictures of Private Life*. Philadelphia: Carey, Lea, and Blanchard, 1833.

———. *Family Secrets; or, Hints to Those Who Would Make Home Happy*. London: Fisher, Son, 1841.

Fitzgerald, Percy. *The History of Pickwick*. London: Chapman and Hall, 1891.

Gissing, George. *Charles Dickens: A Critical Study*. London, 1898.

Grego, Joseph, ed. *Pictorial Pickwickiana: Charles Dickens and His Illustrators*. 2 vols. London: Chapman and Hall, 1899.

Hansard's Debates. Vol. 165. 3rd ser. London: T. C. Hansard, 1862.

Hillard, George S., ed. *The Fifth Reader, for the Use of Public and Private Schools.* Boston: Brewer and Tileston, 1863. (Google Books)

Horne, R. H., ed. *A New Spirit of the Age*. 2nd ed. Vol. 1. London: Smith, Elder, 1844.

Huxley, Thomas Henry. *Collected Essays*. Vol. 6, *Hume: With Helps to the Study of Berkeley*. London: Macmillan, 1894.

James, William. *The Principles of Psychology*. 2 vols. New York: Henry Holt and Company, 1890. (Google Books)

Kay-Shuttleworth, James. *Four Periods of Public Education*. London: Longman, Green, Longman, and Roberts, 1862.

Knight, Charles. *Passages from the Life of Charles Knight*. New York: G. P. Putnam's Sons, 1874. (Google Books)

Lorimer, James. *The Universities of Scotland: Past, Present, and Possible*. Edinburgh: W. P. Kennedy, 1854. (Google Books)

Mackenzie, R. Shelton. *Life of Charles Dickens*. Philadelphia: T. B. Peterson & Brothers, 1870.

Matthews, J. Brander. *The Theatres of Paris*. London: Sampson Low, Marston, Searle, & Rivington, 1880. (Google Books)

Mayhew, Henry. *What to Teach and How to Teach It: So That the Child May Become a Wise and Good Man*. London: William Smith, 1842. (Google Books)

Meiklejohn, J. M. D. *An Old Educational Reformer, Dr. Andrew Bell*. London, 1881.

More, Hannah. *Practical Piety; or, The Influence of the Religion of the Heart on the Conduct of Life*. Philadelphia: American Sunday-School Union, 1876.

————. *The Works of Hannah More, Complete in Seven Volumes*. Vol. 1, *The Repository Tales*. New York: Harper and Brothers, 1855.

Morley, Henry. *A First Sketch of English Literature*. 26th ed. London: Cassell, 1890. (Google Books)

Pancoast, Henry S. *An Introduction to English Literature*. 3rd ed. New York: Henry Holt, 1894. (Google Books)

Poole, John. *The Comic Sketch-Book; or, Sketches and Recollections*. London: Routledge, Warne, and Routledge, 1859. (Google Books)

Priestley, Joseph. *Introductory Essays to Hartley's Theory of the Human Mind, on the Principle of the Association of Ideas*. London, 1817.

"Report of the Commissioners Appointed to Inquire into Popular Education in England and Wales," vol. 1, *Parliamentary Papers* 21, no. 1 (1861).

Richmond, Legh. *Annals of the Poor*. London, 1828.

Rogers, Samuel. *The Pleasures of Memory with Other Poems*. Paris: Baudry's European Library, 1852.

Saintsbury, George. *A Short History of English Literature*. London: Macmillan, 1898. (Google Books)

Shaw, Thomas B. *Outlines of English Literature: A New American Edition. With A Sketch of American Literature by Henry B. Tuckerman*. Philadelphia: Blanchard and Lea, 1853. (Google Books)

Smith, George Barnett. *The Life and Speeches of John Bright, M.P.* Vol. 4. London: Thomas C. Jack, 1886. (Google Books)

Spalding, William. *The History of English Literature: With an Outline of the Origin and Growth of the English Language.* New York: D. Appleton, 1853. (Google Books)

Swinton, William. *Studies in English Literature.* New York: Harper and Brothers, 1888. (Google Books)

———. *Word-Analysis: A Graded Class-Book of English Derivative Words, with Practical Exercises in Spelling, Analyzing, Defining, Synonyms, and the Use of Words.* New York: Ivison, Blakeman, Taylor, 1873. (Google Books)

Taine, Hippolyte. "Charles Dickens: Son talent et ses oeuvres." *Revue des Deux Mondes*, February 1, 1856: 618–47.

Todd, Emma J., and W. B. Powell. *The Normal Course in Reading: Fifth Reader.* New York: Silver, Burdett, 1895. (Google Books)

Trollope, Anthony. "Novel-Reading. The Works of Charles Dickens. The Works of W. Makepeace Thackeray." *Nineteenth Century* 5, no. 3 (1879): 25–33.

Watts, Isaac. *Cheap Repository. Divine songs attempted in easy language for the use of children by I. Watts, D.D. To which are added, prayers for children.* [Bath], [between ca. 1795 and 1798?]. Gale Eighteenth Century Collections Online (accessed Oct. 15, 2010).

———. *The Improvement of the Mind, in Two Parts. Also, a Discourse on the Education of Youth and Remnants of Time Employed in Prose and Verse.* Bennington, Vt.: Anthony Haswell, 1807.

Sources Published After 1900

Aarsleff, Hans. "Locke's Influence." In *The Cambridge Companion to Locke*, edited by Vere Chappell, 252–89. Cambridge: Cambridge University Press, 1994.

Ackroyd, Peter. *Dickens.* New York: HarperCollins, 1990.

Adler, Hans, and Sabine Gross. "Adjusting the Frame: Comments on Cognitivism and Literature." *Poetics Today* 23, no. 2 (2002): 195–220.

Adorno, Theodor. "An Address on Charles Dickens's *The Old Curiosity Shop*." Translated by Michael Hollington. *Dickens Quarterly* 6, no. 3 (1989): 95–101.

———. "Rede über den *Raritätenladen* von Charles Dickens." In *Gesammelte Schriften*. Vol. 11, *Noten zur Literatur*, edited by Gretel Adorno and Rolf Tiedemann, 515–22. Frankfurt am Main: Suhrkamp, 1973.

Allen, James Smith. *In the Public Eye: A History of Reading in Modern France, 1800–1940.* Princeton, N.J.: Princeton University Press, 1991.

———. *Popular French Romanticism: Authors, Readers, and Books in the 19th Century.* Syracuse, N.Y.: Syracuse University Press, 1981.

Allingham, Philip V. "Samuel Rogers (1763–1855), Survivor from 'the Age of Sentiment.'" http://www.victorianweb.org/authors/rogers/bio.html (accessed May 21, 2008).

Altick, Richard D. "Education, Print, and Paper in *Our Mutual Friend*." In *Nineteenth-Century Literary Perspectives: Essays in Honor of Lionel Stevenson*, edited by Clyde de L. Ryals, 237–54. Durham, N.C.: Duke University Press, 1974.

————. *The English Common Reader: A Social History of the Mass Reading Public, 1800–1900*. 2nd ed. Chicago: University of Chicago Press, 1957.

————. *The Presence of the Present: Topics of the Day in the Victorian Novel*. Columbus: Ohio State University Press, 1991.

————. *Writers, Readers, and Occasions: Selected Essays on Victorian Literature and Life*. Columbus: Ohio State University Press, 1989.

Anderson, Amanda. *The Powers of Distance: Cosmopolitanism and the Cultivation of Detachment*. Princeton, N.J.: Princeton University Press, 2001.

Anderson, Benedict. *Imagined Communities: Reflections on the Origin and Spread of Nationalism*. Rev. ed. London: Verso, 1991.

Anderson, Olive. "The Janus Face of Mid-Nineteenth-Century English Radicalism: The Administrative Reform Association of 1855." *Victorian Studies* 8, no. 3 (1965): 231–42.

Anderson, Patricia. *The Printed Image and the Transformation of Popular Culture, 1790–1860*. Oxford: Clarendon Press, 1991.

Andrews, Malcolm. *Charles Dickens and His Performing Selves: Dickens and the Public Readings*. Oxford: Oxford University Press, 2006.

————. *Dickens and the Grown-Up Child*. Iowa City: University of Iowa Press, 1994.

————. "Dickens, Samuel Rogers, and *The Old Curiosity Shop*." *Notes and Queries* 18, no. 11 (1971): 410–11.

Armstrong, Nancy. *Desire and Domestic Fiction: A Political History of the Novel*. New York: Oxford University Press, 1987.

————. *Fiction in the Age of Photography: The Legacy of British Realism*. Cambridge, Mass.: Harvard University Press, 1999.

————. *How Novels Think: The Limits of Individualism from 1719–1900*. New York: Columbia University Press, 2006.

Arnold, Matthew. *Reports on Elementary Schools, 1852–1882*. 2nd ed. London: Eyre and Spottiswoode, 1910.

Ashby, M. K. *Joseph Ashby of Tysoe, 1859–1919: A Study of English Village Life*. Cambridge: Cambridge University Press, 1961.

Ashcraft, Richard, ed. *John Locke: Critical Assessments*. Vol. 2. London: Routledge, 1991.

Ashton, Owen, and Stephen Roberts. *The Victorian Working-Class Author*. London: Cassell, 1999.

Bacon, Alan. "English Literature Becomes a University Subject: King's College, London as Pioneer." *Victorian Studies* 29, no. 4 (1986): 591–612.

Bacon, Francis. *The Advancement of Learning*. Edited by Michael Kiernan. Oxford: Clarendon Press, 2000.

————. *The New Organon*. Edited by Lisa Jardine and Michael Silverthorne. Cambridge: Cambridge University Press, 2000.

Bailey, Charles W., Jr. "Google Books Bibliography." http://www.digital-scholarship.org/gbsb/gbsb.htm (accessed October 23, 2010).

Baker, Robert S. "Imagination and Literacy in Dickens' *Our Mutual Friend*." *Criticism* 18 (Winter 1976): 57–72.

Bakhtin, M. M. *The Dialogic Imagination: Four Essays.* Translated by Caryl Emerson and Michael Holquist. Edited by Michael Holquist. Austin: University of Texas Press, 1981.

Baldick, Chris. *The Social Mission of English Criticism, 1848–1932.* Oxford: Clarendon Press, 1983.

Barbauld, Anna Laetitia. "On the Origin and Progress of Novel-Writing." In *Early Women Critics, 1660–1820: An Anthology,* edited by the Folger Collective on Early Women Critics, 175–86. Bloomington: Indiana University Press, 1995.

Barnard, H. C. *A Short History of English Education, from 1760 to 1944.* London: University of London Press, 1947.

Barney, Richard A. *Plots of Enlightenment: Education and the Novel in Eighteenth-Century England.* Stanford, Calif.: Stanford University Press, 1999.

Barthes, Roland. *The Pleasure of the Text.* Translated by Richard Miller. New York: Hill and Wang, 1975.

Bartine, David E. *Early English Reading Theory: Origins of Current Debates.* Columbia: University of South Carolina Press, 1989.

———. *Reading, Criticism, and Culture: Theory and Teaching in the United States and England, 1820–1950.* Columbia: University of South Carolina Press, 1992.

Bartle, G. F. "Dunn, Henry (1801–1878)." In *Oxford Dictionary of National Biography.* Oxford: Oxford University Press, 2004–10. http://www.oxforddnb.com/view/article/38813 (accessed July 23, 2009).

Baucom, Ian. *Specters of the Atlantic: Finance Capital, Slavery, and the Philosophy of History.* Durham, N.C.: Duke University Press, 2005.

Beer, Gillan. *Darwin's Plots: Evolutionary Narrative in Darwin, George Eliot and Nineteenth-Century Fiction.* 2nd ed. Cambridge: Cambridge University Press, 2000.

Belchem, John. *Class, Party and the Political System in Britain, 1867–1914.* Oxford: Basil Blackwell, 1990.

Bender, John, and David E. Wellbery. "Rhetoricality: On the Modernist Return of Rhetoric." In *The Ends of Rhetoric: History, Theory, Practice,* edited by John Bender and David E. Wellbery, 3–39. Stanford, Calif.: Stanford University Press, 1990.

Benedict, Barbara M. *Curiosity: A Cultural History of Early Modern Inquiry.* Chicago: University of Chicago Press, 2001.

Bennett, Scott. "John Murray's Family Library and the Cheapening of Books in Early Nineteenth Century Britain." *Studies in Bibliography* 29 (1976): 139–66.

———. "Revolutions in Thought: Serial Publication and the Mass Market for Reading." In *The Victorian Periodical Press: Samplings and Soundings,* edited by Joanne Shattock and Michael Wolff, 225–57. Leicester, UK: Leicester University Press and University of Toronto Press, 1982.

Bennett, Tony. "Text, Readers, Reading Formations." *Literature and History* 9, no. 2 (1983): 3–17.

Bentham, Jeremy. *Chrestomathia.* Edited by M. J. Smith and W. H. Burston. Oxford: Clarendon Press, 1983.

———. *The Principles of Morals and Legislation.* New York: Hafner Press, 1948.

Berman, Carolyn Vellenga. " 'Awful Unknown Quantities': Addressing the Readers in *Hard Times.*" *Victorian Literature and Culture* 37, no. 2 (2009): 561–82.

Bevis, Matthew. *The Art of Eloquence: Byron, Dickens, Tennyson, Joyce.* Oxford: Oxford University Press, 2007.

———. "Dickens in Public." *Essays in Criticism* 51, no. 3 (2001): 330–52.

Biagini, Eugenio F. "Introduction: Citizenship, Liberty and Community." In *Citizenship and Community: Liberals, Radicals and Collective Identities in the British Isles, 1865–1931,* edited by Eugenio F. Biagini, 1–17. Cambridge: Cambridge University Press, 1996.

———. "Liberalism and Direct Democracy: John Stuart Mill and the Model of Ancient Athens." In *Citizenship and Community: Liberals, Radicals and Collective Identities in the British Isles, 1865–1931,* edited by Eugenio F. Biagini, 21–44. Cambridge: Cambridge University Press, 1996.

Bialostosky, Don H., and Lawrence D. Needham, eds. *Rhetorical Traditions and British Romantic Literature.* Bloomington: Indiana University Press, 1995.

Bodenheimer, Rosemarie. "Knowing and Telling in Dickens's Retrospects." In *Knowing the Past: Victorian Literature and Culture,* edited by Suzy Anger, 215–33. Ithaca, N.Y.: Cornell University Press, 2001.

———. *Knowing Dickens.* Ithaca, N.Y.: Cornell University Press, 2007.

Bolter, Jay David, and Richard Grusin. *Remediation: Understanding New Media.* Cambridge, Mass.: MIT Press, 2000.

Booth, Wayne. *The Rhetoric of Fiction.* 2nd ed. Chicago: University of Chicago Press, 1983.

Bourdieu, Pierre. *Distinction: A Social Critique of the Judgment of Taste.* Translated by Richard Nice. Cambridge, Mass.: Harvard University Press, 1984.

———. "The Forms of Capital." Translated by Richard Nice. In *Handbook of Theory and Research for the Sociology of Education,* edited by John G. Richardson, 241–58. New York: Greenwood Press, 1986.

———. *The Logic of Practice.* Translated by Richard Nice. Stanford, Calif.: Stanford University Press, 1990.

———. *The Rules of Art: Genesis and Structure of the Literary Field.* Translated by Susan Emanuel. Stanford, Calif.: Stanford University Press, 1996.

———. "Systems of Education and Systems of Thought." In *Schooling and Capitalism: A Sociological Reader,* edited by Roger Dale, Geoff Esland, and Madeleine MacDonald, 192–200. London: Routledge & Kegan Paul and Open University Press, 1976.

Bowen, John. *Other Dickens: Pickwick to Chuzzlewit.* Oxford: Oxford University Press, 2000.

Boyarin, Jonathan, ed. *The Ethnography of Reading.* Berkeley: University of California Press, 1993.

Bradley, Ian. *The Call to Seriousness: The Evangelical Impact on the Victorians.* London: Jonathan Cape, 1976.

Brake, Laurel, Bill Bell, and David Finkelstein, eds. *Nineteenth-Century Media and the Construction of Identities.* Basingstoke, UK: Palgrave Macmillan, 2000.

Brantlinger, Patrick. *The Reading Lesson: The Threat of Mass Literacy in Nineteenth-Century British Fiction*. Bloomington: Indiana University Press, 1998.

———. "A Short History of (Imperial) Benevolence." In *Burden or Benefit: Imperial Benevolence and Its Legacies*, edited by Helen Gilbert and Chris Tiffin, 13–28. Bloomington: Indiana University Press, 2008.

Brattin, Joel. "Dickens' Creation of Bradley Headstone." *Dickens Studies Annual* 14 (1985): 147–65.

Bromwich, David. *Hazlitt: The Mind of a Critic*. New Haven, Conn.: Yale University Press, 1999.

Brooks, Chris. *Mortal Remains: The History and Present State of the Victorian and Edwardian Cemetery*. Exeter, UK: Wheaton, 1989.

Brooks, Peter. *The Melodramatic Imagination: Balzac, Henry James, Melodrama, and the Mode of Excess*. New Haven, Conn.: Yale University Press, 1976.

Brown, Ford K. *Fathers of the Victorians: The Age of Wilberforce*. Cambridge: Cambridge University Press, 1961.

Buckle, Thomas Henry. *History of civilization in England: in three volumes*. New York: Longmans, Green and Company, 1902. (Google Books)

Burke, Edmund. *A Philosophical Enquiry into the Origin of Our Ideas of the Sublime and Beautiful*. Edited by David Womersley. London: Penguin, 1998.

Burston, W. H. *James Mill on Philosophy and Education*. London: University of London and Athlone Press, 1973.

Burton, Gideon. "Silva Rhetoricae." http://humanities.byu.edu/rhetoric/silva .htm (accessed January 22, 2009).

Butt, John, and Kathleen Tillotson. *Dickens at Work*. London: Methuen, 1957.

Buzard, James. *Disorienting Fiction: The Autoethnographic Work of Nineteenth-Century British Novels*. Princeton, N.J.: Princeton University Press, 2005.

Campbell, Matthew, Jacqueline M. Labbe, and Sally Shuttleworth, eds. *Memory and Memorials, 1789–1914: Literary and Cultural Perspectives*. London: Routledge, 2000.

Carlisle, Janice. "Spectacle as Government: Dickens and the Working-Class Audience." In *The Performance of Power: Theatrical Discourse and Politics*, edited by Sue-Ellen Case and Janelle Reinelt, 163–80. Iowa City: University of Iowa Press, 1991.

Carlyle, Thomas. *Selected Writings*. Edited by Alan Shelston. London: Penguin, 1971.

Carpenter, Charles. *History of American Schoolbooks*. Philadelphia: University of Pennsylvania Press, 1963.

Carr, Jean Ferguson, Stephen L. Carr, and Lucille M. Schultz. *Archives of Instruction: Nineteenth-Century Rhetorics, Readers, and Composition Books in the United States*. Carbondale: Southern Illinois University Press, 2005.

Carruthers, Mary J. *The Book of Memory: A Study of Memory in Medieval Culture*. Cambridge: Cambridge University Press, 1992.

Case, Sue-Ellen, and Janelle Reinelt, eds. *The Performance of Power: Theatrical Discourse and Politics*. Iowa City: University of Iowa Press, 1991.

Cavallo, Guglielmo, and Roger Chartier, eds. *A History of Reading in the West.* Translated by Lydia G. Cochrane. Amherst: University of Massachusetts Press, 1999.

Chadwick, Owen. *The Victorian Church. Part 1, 1829–48.* New York: Oxford University Press, 1966.

Chartier, Roger. *Forms and Meanings: Texts, Performances, and Audiences from Codex to Computer.* Philadelphia: University of Pennsylvania Press, 1995.

———. *Cultural History: Between Practices and Representations.* Translated by Lydia G. Cochrane. Ithaca, N.Y.: Cornell University Press, 1988.

Chesterton, G. K. *Charles Dickens: A Critical Study.* New York: Dodd, Mead, 1911. (Google Books)

Chittick, Kathryn. *Dickens in the 1830s.* Cambridge: Cambridge University Press, 1990.

Christensen, Jerome. *Coleridge's Blessed Machine of Language.* Ithaca, N.Y.: Cornell University Press, 1981.

Churchill, Winston. *The Celebrity: An Episode.* London: Macmillan, 1898. Reprint, Kessinger, 2003.

Claybaugh, Amanda. *The Novel of Purpose: Literature and Social Reform in the Anglo-American World.* Ithaca, N.Y.: Cornell University Press, 2007.

Clayton, Jay. *Charles Dickens in Cyberspace: The Afterlife of the Nineteenth Century in Postmodern Culture.* Oxford: Oxford University Press, 2003.

Cohen, Margaret. *The Sentimental Education of the Novel.* Princeton, N.J.: Princeton University Press, 1999.

Coleridge, Samuel Taylor. *Biographia Literaria; or, Biographical Sketches of My Literary Life and Opinions.* Edited by James Engell and W. Jackson Bate. Princeton, N.J.: Princeton University Press and Routledge and Kegan Paul, 1983.

Colley, Ann C. *Nostalgia and Recollection in Victorian Culture.* Basingstoke, UK: Macmillan, 1998.

Collini, Stefan. *Public Moralists: Political Thought and Intellectual Life in Britain, 1850–1930.* Oxford: Clarendon Press, 1991.

Collins, Philip. *Dickens and Education.* London: Macmillan, 1963.

———. "Dickens and the Ragged Schools." *Dickensian* 55 (1959): 94–109.

———, ed. *Dickens: The Critical Heritage.* New York: Barnes & Noble, 1971.

Cotsell, Michael. "The Stephen Family and Dickens's Circumlocution Office Satire." *Dickens Quarterly* 3 (1986): 175–78.

Cottom, Daniel. *Social Figures: George Eliot, Social History, and Literary Representation.* Minneapolis: University of Minnesota Press, 1987.

Craig, Cairns. "Coleridge, Hume, and the Chains of the Romantic Imagination." In *Scotland and the Borders of Romanticism,* edited by Leith Davis, Ian Duncan, and Janet Sorenson, 20–37. Cambridge: Cambridge University Press, 2004.

Crane, William Iler, and William Henry Wheeler. *Wheeler's Graded Literary Readers, with Interpretations: An Eighth Reader.* Chicago: W. H. Wheeler, 1919. (Google Books)

Crary, Jonathan. *Techniques of the Observer: On Vision and Modernity in the Nineteenth Century.* Cambridge, Mass.: MIT Press, 1990.

Crawford, Robert. *The Scottish Invention of English Literature.* Cambridge: Cambridge University Press, 1998.

Crowley, Sharon. *The Methodical Memory: Invention in Current-Traditional Rhetoric.* Carbondale: Southern Illinois University Press, 1990.

Cruse, Amy. *The Englishman and His Books in the Early Nineteenth Century.* London: George G. Harrap, 1930.

———. *The Victorians and Their Reading.* Boston: Houghton Mifflin, 1936.

Curtis, Gerard. "Dickens in the Visual Market." In Jordan and Patten, *Literature in the Marketplace,* 213–49.

———. *Visual Words: Art and the Material Book in Victorian England.* Aldershot, UK: Ashgate, 2002.

Dames, Nicholas. *Amnesiac Selves: Nostalgia, Forgetting, and British Fiction, 1818–1870.* Oxford: Oxford University Press, 2001.

———. *The Physiology of the Novel: Reading, Neural Science, and the Form of Victorian Fiction.* Oxford: Oxford University Press, 2007.

Darwin, Charles. *The Descent of Man, and Selection in Relation to Sex.* 2nd ed. New York: Prometheus Books, 1998.

Daston, Lorraine. "Historical Epistemology." In *Questions of Evidence: Proof, Practice, and Persuasion Across the Disciplines,* edited by James Chandler, Arnold I. Davidson, and Harry Harootunian, 282–89. Chicago: University of Chicago Press, 1994.

———. "Objectivity and the Escape from Perspective." *Social Studies of Science* 22, no. 4 (1992): 597–618.

Daston, Lorraine, and Katharine Park. *Wonders and the Order of Nature, 1150–1750.* New York: Zone Books, 2001.

David, Deirdre, ed. *The Cambridge Companion to the Victorian Novel.* Cambridge: Cambridge University Press, 2000.

Davidson, Cathy N., ed. *Reading in America: Literature and Social History.* Baltimore: Johns Hopkins University Press, 1989.

Davis, David Brion. *The Problem of Slavery in the Age of Revolution, 1770–1823.* New York: Oxford University Press, 1999.

De Certeau, Michel. *The Practice of Everyday Life.* Translated by Steven Rendall. Berkeley: University of California Press, 1984.

De Man, Paul. *Allegories of Reading: Figural Language in Rousseau, Nietzsche, Rilke and Proust.* New Haven, Conn.: Yale University Press, 1979.

———. *The Resistance to Theory.* Minneapolis: University of Minnesota Press, 1986.

Deleuze, Gilles. *Empiricism and Subjectivity: An Essay on Hume's Theory of Human Nature.* Translated by Constantin V. Boundas. New York: Columbia University Press, 1991.

Den Hartog, Dirk. *Dickens and Romantic Psychology: The Self in Time in Nineteenth-Century Literature.* London: Macmillan, 1987.

Derrida, Jacques. *The Gift of Death*. Translated by David Wills. Chicago: University of Chicago Press, 1995.

Desmond, Adrian, and James Moore. *Darwin's Sacred Cause: How a Hatred of Slavery Shaped Darwin's Views on Human Evolution*. Boston: Mifflin Harcourt, 2009.

DeVries, Duane. *Dickens's Apprentice Years: The Making of a Novelist*. New York: Harvester, 1976.

Dickens, Charles. *The Amusements of the People and Other Papers: Reports, Essays, and Reviews, 1834–51*. Edited by Michael Slater. Dent Uniform Edition of Dickens' Journalism. Columbus: Ohio State University Press, 1996.

———. *Bleak House*. Edited by Nicola Bradbury. London: Penguin, 1996.

———. *A Christmas Carol*. London: William Heinemann, 1906.

———. *David Copperfield*. Edited by Trevor Blount. London: Penguin, 1966.

———. *Dombey and Son*. Edited by Alan Horsman. New York: Oxford, 1966.

———. *Gone Astray and Other Papers from "Household Words," 1851–59*. Edited by Michael Slater. Dent Uniform Edition of Dickens' Journalism. London: J. M. Dent, 1999.

———. *Hard Times*. Edited by Graham Law. Toronto: Broadview, 1996.

———. *The Heart of Charles Dickens. As Revealed in His Letters to Angela Burdett-Coutts*. Edited by Edgar Johnson. New York: Duell, Sloan and Pierce, 1952.

———. *The Letters of Charles Dickens*. Edited by Madeline House, Graham Storey, and Kathleen Tillotson. Pilgrim Edition. 12 vols. Oxford: Clarendon Press, 1965–2002.

———. *The Life and Adventures of Nicholas Nickleby*. Edited by Michael Slater. 2 vols. Philadelphia: University of Pennsylvania Press, 1982.

———. *Little Dorrit*. Edited by Stephen Wall and Helen Small. London: Penguin, 1998.

———. *Martin Chuzzlewit*. Edited by P. N. Furbank. London: Penguin, 1968.

———. *Master Humphrey's Clock and A Child's History of England*. Oxford: Oxford University Press, 1991.

———. *The Mystery of Edwin Drood*. Edited by Steven Connor. London: J. M. Dent, 1996.

———. *Nicholas Nickleby*. Edited by Michael Slater. London: Penguin, 1986.

———. *The Old Curiosity Shop*. Edited by Angus Easson. London: Penguin, 1972.

———. *The Old Curiosity Shop*. Edited by Elizabeth M. Brennan. Oxford: Clarendon Press, 1997.

———. *Oliver Twist*. Edited by Peter Fairclough. London: Penguin, 1966.

———. *Oliver Twist*. Edited by Philip Horne. London: Penguin, 2002.

———. *Our Mutual Friend*. Edited by Michael Cotsell. Oxford: Oxford University Press, 1989.

———. *The Pickwick Papers*. Edited by Robert S. Patten. London: Penguin, 1972.

———. *The Pickwick Papers*. Edited by James Kinsley. Oxford: Clarendon Press, 1986.

———. *Sketches by Boz*. Edited by Dennis Walder. London: Penguin, 1995.

————. *Sketches by Boz and Other Early Papers, 1833–39*. Edited by Michael Slater. Dent Uniform Edition of Dickens' Journalism. Columbus: Ohio State University Press, 1994.

————. *The Uncommercial Traveller and Other Papers, 1859–70*. Edited by Michael Slater and John Drew. Dent Uniform Edition of Dickens' Journalism. Columbus: Ohio State University Press, 2000.

Draaisma, Douwe. *Metaphors of Memory: A History of Ideas about the Mind*. Translated by Paul Vincent. Cambridge: Cambridge University Press, 2000.

Drew, John M. L. *Dickens the Journalist*. London: Palgrave Macmillan, 2003.

Duncan, Ian. *Modern Romance and Transformations of the Novel: The Gothic, Scott, Dickens*. Cambridge: Cambridge University Press, 1992.

————. *Scott's Shadow: The Novel in Romantic Edinburgh*. Princeton, N.J.: Princeton University Press, 2007.

Eco, Umberto. *The Role of the Reader: Explorations in the Semiotics of Texts*. Bloomington: Indiana University Press, 1979.

Eigner, Edwin M., and George J. Worth. *Victorian Criticism of the Novel*. Cambridge: Cambridge University Press, 1985.

Elfenbein, Andrew. *Byron and the Victorians*. Cambridge: Cambridge University Press, 1995.

————. "Cognitive Science and the History of Reading." *PMLA* 121, no. 2 (2006): 484–502.

————. "Silver-Fork Byron and the Image of Regency England." In *Byromania: Portraits of the Artist in Nineteenth-and Twentieth-Century Culture*, edited by Frances Wilson, 77–92. London: Macmillan, 1999.

Eliot, George. "Leaves from a Note-Book." In *Essays of George Eliot*. Edited by Thomas Pinney. New York: Columbia University Press, 1963.

————. "The Natural History of German Life." *Selected Essays, Poems and Other Writings*, edited by A. S. Byatt and Nicholas Warren, 107–39. London: Penguin, 1990.

Eliot, Simon. "The Business of Victorian Publishing." In *The Cambridge Companion to the Victorian Novel*, edited by Deirdre David, 37–60. Cambridge: Cambridge University Press, 2000.

Elson, Ruth Miller. *Guardians of Tradition: American Schoolbooks of the Nineteenth Century*. Lincoln: University of Nebraska Press, 1964.

Engell, James. "The New Rhetoricians: Psychology, Semiotics, and Critical Theory." In *Psychology and Literature in the Eighteenth Century*, edited by Christopher Fox, 277–302. New York: AMS Press, 1987.

Epstein, James. *In Practice: Studies in the Language and Culture of Popular Politics in Modern Britain*. Stanford, Calif.: Stanford University Press, 2003.

Erasmus, Desiderius. *On Copia of Words and Ideas*. Translated by Donald B. King and H. David Rix. Milwaukee, Wis.: Marquette University Press, 1963.

Erickson, Lee. *The Economy of Literary Form: English Literature and the Industrialization of Publishing*. Baltimore: Johns Hopkins University Press, 1996.

Ezell, Margaret J. M. "John Locke's Images of Childhood." In *John Locke: Critical Assessments*, edited by Richard Ashcraft, 2:231–45. London: Routledge, 1991.

Felluga, Dino Franco. *The Perversity of Poetry: Romantic Ideology and the Popular Male Poet of Genius*. Albany: SUNY Press, 2005.

Feltes, N. N. *Modes of Production of Victorian Novels*. Chicago: University of Chicago Press, 1986.

Fido, Martin. *Bodysnatchers: A History of the Resurrectionists, 1742–1832*. London: Weidenfeld and Nicolson, 1988.

Fielding, K. J. "1870–1900: Forster and Reaction." *Dickensian* 66 (1970): 85–100.

———. "Dickens as a Speaker." In *The Speeches of Charles Dickens*, edited by K. J. Fielding, xix–xxiv. Oxford: Clarendon Press, 1960.

———, ed. *The Speeches of Charles Dickens: A Complete Edition*. Oxford: Clarendon Press, 1960.

Fielding, K. J., and Anne Smith. "*Hard Times* and the Factory Controversy: Dickens vs. Harriet Martineau." In *Dickens Centennial Essays*, edited by Ada Nisbet and Blake Nevius, 22–45. Berkeley: University of California Press, 1971.

Flint, Kate. *The Woman Reader, 1837–1914*. Oxford: Clarendon Press, 1993.

Fogelin, Robert J. "Hume's Skepticism." In *The Cambridge Companion to Hume*, edited by David Fate Norton, 90–116. Cambridge: Cambridge University Press, 1993.

Ford, George H. *Dickens and His Readers: Aspects of Novel-Criticism since 1836*. Princeton, N.J.: Princeton University Press, 1955.

Forster, John. *The Life of Charles Dickens*. Edited by J. W. T. Ley. London: Cecil Palmer, 1928.

———. *The Life of Charles Dickens*. 2 vols. London: J. M. Dent, 1966.

Foucault, Michel. *Discipline and Punish: The Birth of the Prison*. Translated by Alan Sheridan. New York: Vintage, 1979.

———. *The Foucault Effect: Studies in Governmentality*. Edited by Graham Burchell, Coline Gordon, and Peter Miller. Chicago: University of Chicago Press, 1991.

———. "The Masked Philosopher." In *Ethics: Subjectivity and Truth*, edited by Paul Rabinow, 321–28. Translated by Robert Hurley et al. New York: New Press, 1997.

———. *The Order of Things: An Archaeology of the Human Sciences*. New York: Random House, 1970.

Fox, Christopher, ed. *Psychology and Literature in the Eighteenth Century*. New York: AMS Press, 1987.

Freud, Sigmund. *The Standard Edition of the Complete Psychological Works of Sigmund Freud*. Vols. 4–5, *The Interpretation of Dreams*. Edited by James Strachey in collaboration with Anna Freud, assisted by Alix Strachey and Alan Tyson. Translated by James Strachey. London: Hogarth Press and Institute of Psycho-analysis, 1953–74.

Friedberg, Anne. *The Virtual Window: From Alberti to Microsoft*. Cambridge, Mass.: MIT Press, 2006.

Friedman, Stanley. "The Motif of Reading in *Our Mutual Friend*." *Nineteenth-Century Fiction* 28, no. 1 (1973): 38–61.

Gadamer, Hans-Georg. *Truth and Method*. Translated by Joel Weinsheimer and Donald G. Marshall. 2nd rev. ed. New York: Continuum, 1989.

Gallagher, Catherine. *The Industrial Reformation of English Fiction, 1832–1867*. Chicago: University of Chicago Press, 1985.

Gallagher, Catherine, and Stephen Greenblatt. *Practicing New Historicism*. Chicago: University of Chicago Press, 2000.

Garnett, Richard. "Rogers, Samuel (1763–1855)." Rev. Paul Baines. In *Oxford Dictionary of National Biography*. Oxford: Oxford University Press, 2004–10. http://www.oxforddnb.com/view/article/23997 (accessed January 14, 2009).

Genette, Gérard. *Figures of Literary Discourse*. Translated by Alan Sheridan. New York: Columbia University Press, 1982.

Georgas, Marilyn. "Little Nell and the Art of Holy Dying: Dickens and Jeremy Taylor." *Dickens Studies Annual* 20 (1991): 35–56.

Gillooly, Eileen. *Smile of Discontent: Humor, Gender, and Nineteenth-Century British Fiction*. New York: Columbia University Press, 1999.

Gissing, George. "Dickens in Memory: A Personal View." In *Collected Works of George Gissing on Charles Dickens*. Vol. 1, *Essays, Introductions, and Reviews*, edited by Pierre Coustillas, 45–51. Surrey, UK: Grayswood Press, 2004.

Gitelman, Lisa, and Geoffrey B. Pingree, eds. *New Media, 1740–1915*. Cambridge, Mass.: MIT Press, 2003.

Godwin, William. *Caleb Williams*. Edited by Maurice Hindle. London: Penguin, 1988.

Goldstrom, J. M. *The Social Content of Education, 1808–1870: A Study of the Working Class School Reader in England and Ireland*. Shannon, Ireland: Irish University Press, 1972.

Goodlad, Lauren M. E. *Victorian Literature and the Victorian State: Character and Governance in a Liberal Society*. Baltimore: Johns Hopkins University Press, 2003.

Gordon, John. *Physiology and the Literary Imagination: Romantic to Modern*. Gainesville: University Press of Florida, 2003.

Graff, Gerald. *Professing Literature: An Institutional History*. Chicago: University of Chicago Press, 2007.

Green, Laura Morgan. *Educating Women: Cultural Conflict and Victorian Literature*. Athens: Ohio University Press, 2001.

Gross, Daniel M. *The Secret History of Emotion: From Aristotle's Rhetoric to Modern Brain Science*. Chicago: University of Chicago Press, 2006.

Guillory, John. *Cultural Capital: The Problem of Literary Canon Formation*. Chicago: University of Chicago Press, 1993.

———. "Literary Study and the Modern System of the Disciplines." In *Disciplinarity at the Fin de Siècle*, edited by Amanda Anderson and Joseph Valente, 19–43. Princeton, N.J.: Princeton University Press, 2002.

———. "The Sokal Affair and the History of Criticism." *Critical Inquiry* 28 (Winter 2002): 470–508.

Habermas, Jürgen. *The Structural Transformation of the Public Sphere: An Inquiry into a Category of Bourgeois Society.* Translated by Thomas Burger and Frederick Lawrence. Cambridge, Mass.: MIT Press, 1989.

Hadley, Elaine. *Living Liberalism: Practical Citizenship in Mid-Victorian Britain.* Chicago: University of Chicago Press, 2010.

———. *Melodramatic Tactics: Theatricalized Dissent in the English Marketplace, 1800–1885.* Stanford, Calif.: Stanford University Press, 1995.

Halévy, Elie. *The Growth of Philosophic Radicalism.* Translated by Mary Morris. Boston: Beacon Press, 1955.

Hall, Catherine. *Civilizing Subjects: Metropole and Colony in the English Imagination, 1830–1867.* Chicago: University of Chicago Press, 2002.

Hall, Catherine, Keith McClelland, and Jane Rendall. *Defining the Victorian Nation: Class, Race, Gender and the British Reform Act of 1867.* Cambridge: Cambridge University Press, 2000.

Halleck, Reuben Post. *History of English Literature.* New York: American Book, 1900. (Google Books)

Hamer, Mary. *Writing by Numbers: Trollope's Serial Fiction.* Cambridge: Cambridge University Press, 1987.

Hart, F. Elizabeth. "The Epistemology of Cognitive Literary Studies." *Philosophy and Literature* 25, no. 2 (2001): 314–34.

Hartley, David. *Observations on Man, His Frame, His Duty, and His Expectations.* Gainesville, Fla.: Scholars' Facsimiles and Reprints, 1966.

Haskell, Thomas L. "Capitalism and the Origins of the Humanitarian Sensibility, Part I." *American Historical Review* 90, no. 2 (1985): 339–61.

———. "Capitalism and the Origins of the Humanitarian Sensibility, Part II." *American Historical Review* 90, no. 3 (1985): 547–66.

Hatfield, Gary. *The Natural and the Normative: Theories of Spatial Perception from Kant to Helmholtz.* Cambridge, Mass.: MIT Press, 1990.

Hawkins, Angus. "'Parliamentary Government' and Victorian Political Parties, c. 1830–c. 1880." *English Historical Review* 104, no. 412 (1989): 638–69.

Haywood, Ian. *The Revolution in Popular Literature: Print, Politics and the People, 1790–1860.* Cambridge: Cambridge University Press, 2004.

Hazlitt, William. "Remarks on the Systems of Hartley and Helvetius." In *Essays on the Principles of Human Action, on the Systems of Hartley and Helvetius, and on Abstract Ideas.* Bristol, UK: Thoemmes, 1990.

Heathorn, Stephen. *For Home, Country, and Race: Constructing Gender, Class, and Englishness in the Elementary School, 1880–1914.* Toronto: University of Toronto Press, 2000.

Herbert, Christopher. *Culture and Anomie: Ethnographic Imagination in the Nineteenth Century.* Chicago: University of Chicago Press, 1991.

———. *Victorian Relativity: Radical Thought and Scientific Discovery.* Chicago: University of Chicago Press, 2001.

Hilton, Boyd. *The Age of Atonement: The Influence of Evangelicalism on Social and Economic Thought.* Oxford: Clarendon Press, 1988.

Himmelfarb, Gertrude. *Poverty and Compassion: The Moral Imagination of the Late Victorians.* New York: Knopf, 1991.

Hinchliff, Peter, and John Prest. "Jowett, Benjamin (1817–1893)." In *Oxford Dictionary of National Biography.* Oxford: Oxford University Press, 2004–10. http://www.oxforddnb.com/view/article/15143 (accessed December 1, 2008).

Hirschman, Albert O. *The Passions and the Interests: Political Arguments for Capitalism Before Its Triumph.* Princeton, N.J: Princeton University Press, 1977.

"Historical resources for UK temperance movement at Institute of Alcohol Studies, Alliance House Foundation, London." http://historyofalcoholanddrugs .typepad.com/alcohol_and_drugs_history/2007/08/historical-reso.html (accessed October 11, 2010).

Hobbes, Thomas. *Leviathan, with Selected Variants from the Latin Edition of 1668.* Edited by Edwin Curley. Indianapolis: Hackett, 1994.

Holland, Norman N. *The Dynamics of Literary Response.* New York: Oxford University Press, 1968.

Hollingsworth, Keith. *The Newgate Novel, 1830–1847: Bulwer, Ainsworth, Dickens, and Thackeray.* Detroit: Wayne State University Press, 1963.

Hollington, Michael, trans. "An Address on Charles Dickens's *The Old Curiosity Shop.*" *Dickens Quarterly* 6, no. 3 (1989): 95–101.

———. "Adorno, Benjamin, and *The Old Curiosity Shop.*" *Dickens Quarterly* 6, no. 3 (1989): 87–95.

———. *Dickens and the Grotesque.* London: Croom Helm, 1984.

Holoch, George. "Consciousness and Society in 'Little Dorrit.'" *Victorian Studies* 21 (Spring 1978): 335–51.

Hoppen, K. Theodore. *The Mid-Victorian Generation, 1846–1886.* Oxford: Clarendon Press, 1998.

Horn, Pamela. *Education in Rural England 1800–1914.* New York: St. Martin's Press, 1978.

Hotz, Mary Elizabeth. *Literary Remains: Representations of Death and Burial in Victorian England.* Albany: SUNY Press, 2009.

Houghton, Walter E. "Periodical Literature and the Articulate Classes." In *The Victorian Periodical Press: Samplings and Soundings*, edited by Joanne Shattock and Michael Wolff, 3–27. Leicester, UK: Leicester University Press and University of Toronto Press, 1982.

Hughes, Linda K., and Michael Lund. *The Victorian Serial.* Charlottesville: University Press of Virginia, 1991.

Hume, David. "Abstract of 'A Treatise of Human Nature.'" In *A Treatise of Human Nature.* Edited by P. H. Nidditch. 2nd ed. Oxford: Oxford University Press, 1978, 640–62.

———. *Enquiries Concerning Human Understanding and Concerning the Principles of Morals.* Edited by L. A. Selby-Bigge and P. H. Nidditch. 3rd ed. Oxford: Clarendon Press, 1975.

———. *A Treatise of Human Nature.* Edited by P. H. Nidditch. 2nd ed. Oxford: Oxford University Press, 1978.

Humpherys, Anne. *Henry Mayhew.* Boston: Twayne, 1984.

Hung, Eva. "The Introduction of Dickens into China (1906–1960): A Case Study in Target Culture Reception." *Perspectives* 4, no. 1 (1996): 29–41.

Hunter, Ian. *Culture and Government: The Emergence of Literary Education.* Basingstoke, UK: Macmillan, 1988.

Hunter, J. Paul. *Before Novels: The Cultural Contexts of Eighteenth-Century Fiction.* New York: Norton, 1990.

Hutter, Albert D. "The Novelist as Resurrectionist: Dickens and the Dilemma of Death." *Dickens Studies Annual* 12 (1983): 1–39.

Inglis, Fred. "The Performance of Celebrity." Lecture delivered at the Humanities Institute, University of Connecticut, Storrs, April 3, 2003.

Iser, Wolfgang. *The Act of Reading: A Theory of Aesthetic Response.* Baltimore: Johns Hopkins University Press, 1978.

————. *The Implied Reader: Patterns of Communication in Prose Fiction from Bunyan to Beckett.* Baltimore: Johns Hopkins University Press, 1974.

Jaffe, Audrey. *Scenes of Sympathy: Identity and Representation in Victorian Fiction.* Ithaca, N.Y.: Cornell University Press, 2000.

————. *Vanishing Points: Dickens, Narrative, and the Subject of Omniscience.* Berkeley: University of California Press, 1991.

Jalland, Pat. *Death in the Victorian Family.* Oxford: Oxford University Press, 1996.

James, Louis. *Fiction for the Working Man, 1830–50.* London: Oxford University Press, 1963.

————. "Reynolds, George William MacArthur (1814–1879)." Edited by H. C. G. Matthew and Brian Harrison. In *Oxford Dictionary of National Biography.* Oxford: Oxford University Press, 2004–10.

Jauss, Hans Robert. *Aesthetic Experience and Literary Hermeneutics.* Minneapolis: University of Minnesota Press, 1982.

Jay, Elisabeth. *Religion of the Heart: Anglican Evangelicalism and the Nineteenth-Century Novel.* Oxford: Clarendon Press, 1979.

Johns, Adrian. *The Nature of the Book: Print and Knowledge in the Making.* Chicago: University of Chicago Press, 1998.

Johnson, Richard. " 'Really Useful Knowledge': Radical Education and Working-Class Culture, 1790–1848." In *Working-Class Culture: Studies in History and Theory,* edited by J. Clarke, C. Crichter, and R. Johnson, 75–102. New York: St. Martin's Press, 1970.

Jones, Catherine. *Literary Memory: Scott's Waverly Novels and the Psychology of Narrative.* Lewisburg, Pa.: Bucknell University Press, 2003.

Jones, Gareth Stedman. "Rethinking Chartism." In *Languages of Class: Studies in English Working Class History, 1832–1982.* Cambridge: Cambridge University Press, 1983.

Jordan, John O., and Robert L. Patten, eds. *Literature in the Marketplace: Nineteenth-Century British Publishing and Reading Practices.* Cambridge: Cambridge University Press, 1995.

Joyce, Patrick. *Democratic Subjects: The Self and the Social in Nineteenth-Century England*. Cambridge: Cambridge University Press, 1994.

———. *Visions of the People: Industrial England and the Question of Class, 1848–1914*. Cambridge: Cambridge University Press, 1991.

Kaestle, Carl F., and Janice A. Radway. "A Framework for the History of Publishing and Reading in the United States." In *Print in Motion: The Expansion of Publishing and Reading in the United States, 1880–1940*, edited by Carl F. Kaestle and Janice A. Radway, 7–21. Chapel Hill: American Antiquarian Society and University of North Carolina Press, 2009.

Kallich, Martin. *The Association of Ideas and Critical Theory in Eighteenth-Century England: A History of a Psychological Method in English Criticism*. Paris: Mouton, 1970.

Kaplan, Fred. *Sacred Tears: Sentimentality in Victorian Literature*. Princeton, N.J.: Princeton University Press, 1987.

Kearns, Michael S. *Metaphors of Mind in Fiction and Psychology*. Lexington: University Press of Kentucky, 1987.

Kent, Charles. *Charles Dickens as a Reader*. London: Chapman and Hall, 1872. Reprint, New York: Haskell House, 1973.

Kittler, Friedrich A. *Gramophone, Film, Typewriter*. Translated by Geoffrey Winthrop-Young and Michael Wutz. Stanford, Calif.: Stanford University Press, 1999.

———. *Discourse networks 1800/1900*. Translated by Michael Metteer with Chris Cullins. Stanford, Calif.: Stanford University Press, 1990.

Kitton, Frederic G. *Dickens and His Illustrators*. Amsterdam: S. Emmering, 1972.

Klancher, Jon P. *The Making of English Reading Audiences, 1790–1832*. Madison: University of Wisconsin Press, 1987.

Klein, D. B. *A History of Scientific Psychology: Its Origins and Philosophical Backgrounds*. New York: Basic Books, 1970.

Kostal, R. W. *A Jurisprudence of Power: Victorian Empire and the Rule of Law*. Oxford: Oxford University Press, 2005.

Kucich, John. "Death Worship Among the Victorians: *The Old Curiosity Shop*." *PMLA* 95, no. 1 (1980): 58–72.

———. *Imperial Masochism: British Fiction, Fantasy, and Social Class*. Princeton, N.J.: Princeton University Press, 2006.

———. *Repression in Victorian Fiction: Charlotte Brontë, George Eliot, and Charles Dickens*. Berkeley: University of California Press, 1987.

Lacan, Jacques. *Écrits: A Selection*. Translated by Alan Sheridan. 2nd ed. New York: Norton, 1977.

Landers, John M. *Death and the Metropolis: Studies in the Demographic History of London (1670–1841)*. Cambridge: Cambridge University Press, 1992.

Langbauer, Laurie. *Novels of Everyday Life: The Series in English Fiction, 1850–1930*. Ithaca, N.Y.: Cornell University Press, 1999.

Laqueur, Thomas. *Religion and Respectability: Sunday Schools and Working Class Culture, 1780–1850*. New Haven, Conn.: Yale University Press, 1976.

Law, Graham. *Indexes to Fiction in the "Illustrated London News" (1842–1901) and the "Graphic" (1869–1901).* Victorian Fiction Research Guides. http://www .canterbury.ac.uk/arts-humanities/Media/victorian-research fiction/Home.aspx (accessed December 2008).

———. *Serializing Fiction in the Victorian Press.* New York: Palgrave Macmillan, 2000.

Law, Jules David. *The Rhetoric of Empiricism: Language and Perception from Locke to I. A. Richards.* Ithaca, N.Y.: Cornell University Press, 1993.

Leavis, F. R., and Q. D. Leavis. *Dickens the Novelist.* London: Penguin, 1970.

Leavis, Q. D. *Fiction and the Reading Public.* London: Pimlico, 2000.

Ledger, Sally. *Dickens and the Popular Radical Imagination.* Cambridge: Cambridge University Press, 2007.

Levine, George. *Dying to Know: Scientific Epistemology and Narrative in Victorian England.* Chicago: University of Chicago Press, 2002.

Lewis, Donald M. *Lighten Their Darkness: The Evangelical Mission to Working-Class London, 1828–1860.* New York: Greenwood Press, 1986.

Locke, John. *An Essay Concerning Human Understanding.* Edited by Peter H. Nidditch. Oxford: Clarendon Press, 1975.

———. *Some Thoughts Concerning Education* and *Of the Conduct of the Understanding.* Edited by Ruth W. Grant and Nathan Tarcov. Indianapolis: Hackett, 1996.

Lorimer, Douglas A. *Colour, Class, and the Victorians: English Attitudes to the Negro in the Mid–Nineteenth Century.* New York: Holmes & Meier, 1978.

Losonsky, Michael. *Linguistic Turns in Modern Philosophy.* Cambridge: Cambridge University Press, 2006.

Lund, Michael. *Reading Thackeray.* Detroit: Wayne State University Press, 1988.

Lund, Roger D. "Genteel Fictions: Caricature and Satirical Design in *Little Dorrit.*" *Dickens Studies Annual* 10 (1982): 45–65.

Lynch, Deidre Shauna. *The Economy of Character: Novels, Market Culture, and the Business of Inner Meaning.* Chicago: University of Chicago Press, 1998.

Lyons, Martyn. "New Readers in the Nineteenth Century: Women, Children, Workers." In *A History of Reading in the West,* edited by Guglielmo Cavallo and Roger Chartier, 313–44. Translated by Lydia G. Cochrane. Amherst: University of Massachusetts Press, 1999.

———. *Readers and Society in Nineteenth-Century France: Workers, Women, Peasants.* Basingstoke, UK : Palgrave Macmillan, 2001.

———. *Reading Culture and Writing Practices in Nineteenth-Century France.* Toronto: University of Toronto Press, 2008.

MacFarlane, Harold. "The Value of a Dead Celebrity." *Cornhill Magazine,* March 1900: 367–71. (Google Books)

Mackie, J. L. *The Cement of the Universe: A Study of Causation.* Oxford: Clarendon Press, 1974.

MacPike, Loralee. " 'The Old Curiosity Shape': Changing Views of Little Nell, Part I." *Dickens Studies Newsletter* 12, no. 2 (1981): 33–38.

————. "'The Old Curiosity Shape': Changing Views of Little Nell, Part II." *Dickens Studies Newsletter* 12, no. 3 (1981): 70–76.

Manning, John. *Dickens on Education.* Toronto: University of Toronto Press, 1959.

Marcus, Steven. *Dickens: From Pickwick to Dombey.* New York: Basic Books, 1965.

————. "Language into Structure: Pickwick Revisited." *Daedalus* 101, no. 1 (1972): 183–202.

Marx, Karl. *Capital: A Critique of Political Economy.* Translated by Ben Fowkes. London: Penguin, 1976.

Mathieson, Margaret. *The Preachers of Culture: A Study of English and Its Teachers.* Totowa, N.J.: Rowman and Littlefield, 1975.

Matlock, Jann. *Scenes of Seduction: Prostitution, Hysteria, and Reading Difference in Nineteenth-Century France.* New York: Columbia University Press, 1994.

Maxwell, Richard. *The Mysteries of Paris and London.* Charlottesville: University Press of Virginia, 1992.

Mays, Kelly J. "The Disease of Reading and Victorian Periodicals." In Jordan and Patten, *Literature in the Marketplace,* 165–94.

McAleer, Joseph. *Popular Reading and Publishing in Britain, 1914–1950.* Oxford: Clarendon Press, 1992.

McDayter, Ghislaine. "Conjuring Byron: Byromania, Literary Commodification and the Birth of Celebrity." In *Byromania: Portraits of the Artist in Nineteenth- and Twentieth-Century Culture,* edited by Frances Wilson, 43–62. London: Macmillan, 1999.

McKeon, Michael. *The Origins of the English Novel, 1600–1740.* Baltimore: Johns Hopkins University Press, 1987.

————, ed. *Theory of the Novel: A Historical Approach.* Baltimore: Johns Hopkins University Press, 2000.

McLane, Maureen N. *Romanticism and the Human Sciences: Poetry, Population, and the Discourse of the Species.* Cambridge: Cambridge University Press, 2000.

McLaughlin, Kevin. *Writing in Parts: Imitation and Exchange in Nineteenth-Century Literature.* Stanford, Calif.: Stanford University Press, 1995.

McLuhan, Marshall. *Understanding Media: The Extensions of Man.* New York: McGraw-Hill, 1964.

Meisel, Joseph S. *Public Speech and the Culture of Public Life in the Age of Gladstone.* New York: Columbia University Press, 2001.

Mellor, Anne K., and Richard E. Matlak, eds. *British Literature, 1780–1830.* Fort Worth, Tex.: Harcourt Brace, 1996.

Metz, Nancy Aycock. "Little Dorrit's London: Babylon Revisited." *Victorian Studies* 33 (Spring 1990): 465–86.

Meyers, William. "The Radicalism of 'Little Dorrit.'" In *Literature and Politics in the 19th Century,* edited by John Lucas, 77–104. London: Methuen, 1971.

Mill, James. *Analysis of the Phenomena of the Human Mind.* Edited by Alexander Bain, Andrew Findlater, and George Grote. 2nd ed. 2 vols. New York: Augustus M. Kelley, 1967.

————. *Political Writings*. Edited by Terence Ball. Cambridge: Cambridge University Press, 1992.

Mill, John Stuart. *Autobiography*. Edited by John Robson. London: Penguin, 1989.

————. "On Genius." In *The Collected Works of John Stuart Mill*. Vol. 1, *Autobiography and Literary Essays*, edited by John M. Robson and Jack Stillinger, 327–39. Toronto: University of Toronto Press, 1981.

————. *On Liberty*. Edited by Elizabeth Rapaport. Indianapolis: Hackett, 1978.

Miller, Andrew H. *The Burdens of Perfection: On Ethics and Reading in Nineteenth-Century British Literature*. Ithaca, N.Y.: Cornell University Press, 2008.

————. *Novels Behind Glass: Commodity Culture and Victorian Narrative*. Cambridge: Cambridge University Press, 1995.

————. "The Specters of Dickens's Study." *Narrative* 5, no. 3 (1997): 322–41.

Miller, D. A. *The Novel and the Police*. Berkeley: University of California Press, 1988.

Miller, J. Hillis. "The Fiction of Realism: *Sketches by Boz, Oliver Twist,* and Cruikshank's Illustrations." In *Dickens Centennial Essays*, edited by Ada Nisbet and Blake Nevius, 85–153. Berkeley: University of California Press, 1971.

Miller, Thomas P. *The Formation of College English: Rhetoric and Belles Lettres in the British Cultural Provinces*. Pittsburgh: University of Pittsburgh Press, 1997.

Mole, Tom. *Byron's Romantic Celebrity: Industrial Culture and the Hermeneutic of Intimacy*. Basingstoke, UK: Palgrave Macmillan, 2007.

Moody, William Vaughn, and Robert Morss Lovett. *A History of English Literature*. New York: Charles Scribner's Sons, 1906. (Google Books)

Moore, Grace. "Swarmery and Bloodbaths: A Reconsideration of Dickens on Class and Race in the 1860s." *Dickens Studies Annual* 31 (2002): 175–202.

Moore, Isabel. *The Eaton Readers: Fifth Reader*. Chicago: Eaton, 1906. (Google Books).

————. *The Eaton Readers: Fourth Reader*. Chicago: Eaton, 1906. (Google Books)

Morgentaler, Goldie. *Dickens and Heredity: When Like Begets Like*. London: Macmillan, 2000.

Morris, Pam. *Dickens's Class Consciousness: A Marginal View*. London: Macmillan, 1991.

————. *Imagining Inclusive Society in Nineteenth-Century Novels: The Code of Sincerity in the Public Sphere*. Baltimore: Johns Hopkins University Press, 2004.

Mudhenk, Rosemary. "The Education of the Reader in *Our Mutual Friend*." *Nineteenth-Century Fiction* 34, no. 1 (1979): 41–72.

Munby, G. F. W. "Richmond, Legh (1772–1827)." Rev. Clare L. Taylor. In *Oxford Dictionary of National Biography*. Oxford: Oxford University Press, 2004–10.

Murphy, Peter T. "Climbing Parnassus, and Falling Off: Rogers and *The Pleasures of Memory*." *Wordsworth Circle* 24, no. 3 (1993): 151–55.

Myers, Mitzi. "Hannah More's Tracts for the Times: Social Fiction and Female Ideology." In *Fetter'd or Free? British Women Novelists, 1670–1815*, edited by Mary Anne Scholfield and Cecilia Macheski, 264–84. Athens: Ohio University Press, 1986.

Nardin, Jane. "Hannah More and the Problem of Poverty." *Texas Studies in Literature and Language* 43, no. 3 (2001): 267–84.

Neuburg, Victor E. *Popular Education in Eighteenth Century England*. London: Woburn Press, 1971.

———. *Popular Literature: A History and Guide*. London: Woburn Press, 1977.

Nisbet, Ada, and Blake Nevius, eds. *Dickens Centennial Essays*. Berkeley: University of California Press, 1971.

Nunokawa, Jeff. *The Afterlife of Property: Domestic Security and the Victorian Novel*. Princeton, N.J.: Princeton University Press, 1994.

Olsen, Richard. *The Emergence of the Social Sciences, 1642–1792*. New York: Twayne, 1993.

Orwell, George. *Dickens, Dali, and Others*. New York: Harcourt, Brace, 1963.

Oswell, Kate F., and C. B. Gilbert. *The American School Readers: The Literary Reader for Higher Grades*. New York: Macmillan, 1912. (Google Books)

Otis, Laura. *Organic Memory: History and the Body in the Late Nineteenth and Early Twentieth Centuries*. Lincoln: University of Nebraska Press, 1994.

Owen, Robert. *Robert Owen on Education*. Edited by Harold Silver. Cambridge: Cambridge University Press, 1969.

Palmer, D. J. *The Rise of English Studies*. London: Oxford University Press, 1965.

Patten, Robert L. *Charles Dickens and His Publishers*. Oxford: Clarendon Press, 1978.

———. "*Pickwick Papers* and the Development of Serial Fiction." *Rice University Studies* 61 (Winter 1975): 51–74.

———. "Serialized Retrospection in *The Pickwick Papers*." In Jordan and Patten, *Literature in the Marketplace*, 123–42.

Payne, David. *The Reenchantment of Nineteenth-Century Fiction: Dickens, Thackeray, George Eliot, and Serialization*. Basingstoke, UK: Palgrave Macmillan, 2005.

Paz, D. G. *Dickens and Barnaby Rudge*. Monmouth, UK: Merlin Press, 2006.

Pearson, Jacqueline. *Women's Reading in Britain, 1750–1835: A Dangerous Recreation*. Cambridge: Cambridge University Press, 1999.

Pedersen, Susan. "Hannah More Meets Simple Simon: Tracts, Chapbooks, and Popular Culture in Late Eighteenth-Century England." *Journal of British Studies* 25 (1986): 84–112.

Peters, John Durham. *Speaking into the Air: A History of the Idea of Communication*. Chicago: University of Chicago Press, 1999.

Pfister, Joel, and Nancy Schnog, eds. *Inventing the Psychological: Toward a Cultural History of Emotional Life in America*. New Haven, Conn.: Yale University Press, 1996.

Pickering, Samuel F., Jr. *John Locke and Children's Books in Eighteenth-Century England*. Knoxville: University of Tennessee Press, 1981.

———. *Moral Instruction and Fiction for Children, 1749–1820*. Athens: University of Georgia Press, 1993.

———. *The Moral Tradition in English Fiction, 1785–1850*. Hanover, N.H.: University Press of New England, 1976.

Pinch, Adela. *Strange Fits of Passion: Epistemologies of Emotion, Hume to Austen.* Stanford, Calif.: Stanford University Press, 1996.

Plotz, John. *The Crowd: British Literature and Public Politics.* Berkeley: University of California Press, 2000.

Poovey, Mary. "Forgotten Writers, Neglected Histories: Charles Reade and the Nineteenth Century Transformation of the British Literary Field." *ELH* 71 (2004): 433–53.

———. *Genres of the Credit Economy: Mediating Value in Eighteenth- and Nineteenth-Century Britain.* Chicago: University of Chicago Press, 2008.

———. *A History of the Modern Fact: Problems of Knowledge in the Sciences of Wealth and Society.* Chicago: University of Chicago Press, 1995.

———. *Making a Social Body: British Cultural Formation, 1830–1864.* Chicago: University of Chicago Press, 1995.

———. *Uneven Developments: The Ideological Work of Gender in Mid-Victorian England.* Chicago: University of Chicago Press, 1988.

Pope, Norris. *Dickens and Charity.* New York: Columbia University Press, 1978.

Poster, Mark. "Digital Networks and Citizenship." *PMLA* 117, no. 1 (2002): 98–116.

Powell, Margaret K., and Susanne F. Roberts. "Imperial Views, Colonial Subjects: Victorian Periodicals and the Empire: Images from an Exhibition, Sterling Memorial Library, Yale University, August–October 1999." http://www .library.yale.edu/~mpowell/victorianper.html#lh (accessed January 2009).

Price, Leah. *The Anthology and the Rise of the Novel: From Richardson to George Eliot.* Cambridge: Cambridge University Press, 2000.

———. "Introduction: Reading Matter." *PMLA* 121, no. 1 (2006): 9–16.

Priestly, Joseph. *Priestley's Writings on Philosophy, Science, and Politics.* Edited by John A. Passmore. New York: Collier Books, 1965.

Qualls, Barry. *The Secular Pilgrims of Victorian Fiction: The Novel as Book of Life.* Cambridge: Cambridge University Press, 1982.

Radway, Janice A. *A Feeling for Books: The Book-of-the-Month Club, Literary Taste, and Middle-Class Desire.* Chapel Hill: University of North Carolina Press, 1997.

Rancière, Jacques. *Hatred of Democracy.* Translated by Steve Corcoran. London: Verso, 2006.

Rauch, Alan. *Useful Knowledge: Victorians, Morality, and the March of Intellect.* Durham, N.C.: Duke University Press, 2001.

Raven, James, Helen Small, and Naomi Tadmor, eds. *The Practice and Representation of Reading in England.* Cambridge: Cambridge University Press, 1996.

Recchio, Thomas. "'Charming and Sane': School Editions of *Cranford* in America, 1905–1914." *Victorian Studies* 45, no. 4 (2003): 597–623.

———. *Elizabeth Gaskell's "Cranford": A Publishing History.* Aldershot, UK: Ashgate, 2009.

Reed, Edward S. *From Soul to Mind: The Emergence of Psychology from Erasmus Darwin to William James.* New Haven, Conn.: Yale University Press, 1997.

Reed, John R. "Confinement and Character in Dickens' Novels." *Dickens Studies Annual* 1 (1970): 41–54.

"Report of the Commissioners Appointed to Inquire into Popular Education in England and Wales," Vol. 1, *Parliamentary Papers* 21, no. 1 (1861).

Rich, R. W. *The Training of Teachers in England and Wales during the Nineteenth Century.* Cambridge: Cambridge University Press, 1933.

Richards, Graham. *Mental Machinery: The Origins and Consequences of Psychological Ideas, Part 1: 1600–1850.* Baltimore: Johns Hopkins University Press, 1992.

Richards, Robert J. *Darwin and the Emergence of Evolutionary Theories of Mind and Behavior.* Chicago: University of Chicago Press, 1987.

Richardson, Alan. *British Romanticism and the Science of Mind.* Cambridge: Cambridge University Press, 2001.

———. "Cognitive Science and the Future of Literary Studies." *Philosophy and Literature* 23 (1999): 157–73.

———. *Literature, Education, and Romanticism: Reading as Social Practice, 1780–1832.* Cambridge: Cambridge University Press, 1994.

Rieff, Philip. *The Triumph of the Therapeutic.* New York: Harper and Row, 1968.

Rose, Jonathan. *The Intellectual Life of the British Working Classes.* New Haven, Conn.: Yale University Press, 2001.

———. "Rereading the English Common Reader: A Preface to a History of Audiences." *Journal of the History of Ideas* 53, no. 1 (1992): 47–70.

Rosenberg, Brian. *Little Dorrit's Shadows: Character and Contradiction in Dickens.* Columbia: University of Missouri Press, 1996.

Rosman, Doreen M. *Evangelicals and Culture.* London: Croom Helm, 1984.

Ruth, Jennifer. *Making Professions: Labor, Value, and the Mid-Victorian Novel.* Columbus: Ohio State University Press, 2006.

Rylance, Rick. *Victorian Psychology and British Culture, 1850–1880.* Oxford: Oxford University Press, 2000.

Saffin, N. W. *Science, Religion, and Education in Britain, 1804–1904.* Victoria, Australia: Lowden, 1973.

Saint-Amour, Paul K. *The Copywrights: Intellectual Property and the Literary Imagination.* Ithaca, N.Y.: Cornell University Press, 2003.

Schad, John. *The Reader in the Dickensian Mirrors: Some New Language.* London: Macmillan, 1992.

Schlicke, Paul. *Dickens and Popular Entertainment.* London: Allen and Unwin, 1985.

———. "The True Pathos of *The Old Curiosity Shop.*" *Dickens Quarterly* 7, no. 1 (1990): 189–99.

Scholfield, Mary Anne, and Cecilia Macheski, eds. *Fetter'd or Free? British Women Novelists, 1670–1815.* Athens: Ohio University Press, 1986.

Schor, Esther. *Bearing the Dead: The British Culture of Mourning from the Enlightenment to Victoria.* Princeton, N.J.: Princeton University Press, 1994.

Schor, Hilary M. *Dickens and the Daughter of the House.* Cambridge: Cambridge University Press, 1999.

Sedgwick, Eve Kosofsky. *Between Men: English Literature and Homosocial Desire*. New York: Columbia University Press, 1985.

Selleck, R. J. W. *James Kay-Shuttleworth: Journey of an Outsider*. Essex, UK: Woburn Press, 1994.

Semmel, Bernard. *Jamaican Blood and Victorian Conscience: The Governor Eyre Controversy*. Boston: Houghton Mifflin, 1963.

Sen, Sambudha. "*Bleak House* and *Little Dorrit*: The Radical Heritage." *English Literary History* 65, no. 4 (1998): 945–70.

Sengupta, Parna. "An Object Lesson in Colonial Pedagogy." *Comparative Studies in Society and History* 45 (2003): 96–121.

Sennett, Richard. *The Fall of Public Man: On the Social Psychology of Capitalism*. 2nd ed. New York: Vintage, 1976.

Shattock, Joanne, and Michael Wolff, eds. *The Victorian Periodical Press: Samplings and Soundings*. Leicester, UK: Leicester University Press and University of Toronto Press, 1982.

Shillingsburg, Peter L. *Pegasus in Harness: Victorian Publishing and W. M. Thackeray*. Charlottesville: University of Virginia Press, 1992.

Shuman, Cathy. *Pedagogical Economies: The Examination and the Victorian Literary Man*. Stanford, Calif.: Stanford University Press, 2000.

Shuttleworth, Sally. *Charlotte Brontë and Victorian Psychology*. Cambridge: Cambridge University Press, 1996.

———. " 'The Malady of Thought': Embodied Memory in Victorian Psychology and the Novel." In *Memory and Memorials, 1789–1914: Literary and Cultural Perspectives*, edited by Matthew Campbell, Jacqueline M. Labbe, and Sally Shuttleworth, 46–59. London: Routledge, 2000.

Silver, Harold. *The Concept of Popular Education: A Study in Ideas and Social Movements in the Early Nineteenth Century*. London: MacGibbon & Kee, 1965.

Simon, Brian. *Studies in the History of Education, 1780–1870*. London: Lawrence & Wisehart, 1960.

Siskin, Clifford, and William Warner, eds. *This Is Enlightenment*. Chicago: University of Chicago Press, 2010.

Slater, Michael. *Charles Dickens*. New Haven, Conn.: Yale University Press, 2009.

Slaughter, Joseph R. *Human Rights, Inc.: The World Novel, Narrative Form, and International Law*. New York: Fordham University Press, 2007.

Small, Helen. *Love's Madness: Medicine, the Novel, and Female Insanity, 1800–1865*. Oxford: Oxford University Press, 1996.

———. "A Pulse of 124: Charles Dickens and a Pathology of the Mid-Victorian Reading Public." In *The Practice and Representation of Reading in England*, edited by James Raven, Helen Small, and Naomi Tadmor, 263–90. Cambridge: Cambridge University Press, 1996.

Smith, Dora V. *Evaluating Instruction in Secondary School English: A Report of the New York Regents' Inquiry into the Character and Cost of Public Education in New York State*. English Monograph No. 11. Chicago: National Council of Teachers of English, 1941.

————. *Instruction in English*. Office of Education Bulletin No. 17. 1932. National Survey of Secondary Education, Monograph No. 20. Washington, D.C.: U.S. Government Printing Office, 1933.

Smith, Jonathan. *Fact and Feeling: Baconian Science and the Nineteenth-Century Literary Imagination*. Madison: University of Wisconsin Press, 1994.

Smith, Sheila M. "John Overs to Charles Dickens: A Working-Man's Letter and Its Implications." *Victorian Studies* 18, no. 2 (1974): 195–217.

Solomon, Julie Robin. *Objectivity in the Making: Francis Bacon and the Politics of Inquiry*. Baltimore: Johns Hopkins University Press, 1998.

Spencer, Herbert. *The Principles of Psychology*. London: Longman, Brown, Green, and Longmans, 1855. Reprint, Westmead, UK: Gregg International, 1970.

Spinney, G. H. "Cheap Repository Tracts: Hazard and Marshall Edition." *Library*, 4th ser., 20, no. 3 (1939): 295–340.

Spring, David. "The Clapham Sect: Some Social and Political Aspects." *Victorian Studies* 5 (September 1961): 35–48.

Squires, Michael. "The Structure of Dickens's Imagination in *Little Dorrit*." *Texas Studies in Literature and Language* 30 (1988): 49–64.

Sroka, Kenneth M. "Dickens' Metafiction: Readers and Writers in *Oliver Twist*, *David Copperfield*, and *Our Mutual Friend*." *Dickens Studies Annual* 22 (1973): 35–65.

St Clair, William. "But What Did We Actually Read?" *Times Literary Supplement*, May 12, 2006.

————. *The Reading Nation in the Romantic Period*. Cambridge: Cambridge University Press, 2004.

Stepan, Nancy. *The Idea of Race in Science: Great Britain, 1800–1960*. London: Macmillan, 1982.

Stewart, Garrett. *Dear Reader: The Conscripted Audience in Nineteenth-Century British Fiction*. Baltimore: Johns Hopkins University Press, 1996.

————. *Dickens and the Trials of Imagination*. Cambridge, Mass.: Harvard University Press, 1974.

————. *The Look of Reading: Book, Painting, Text*. Chicago: University of Chicago Press, 2006.

Stiles, Lane. "Packaging Literature for the High Schools: From the Riverside Series to *Literature and Life*." In *Reading Books: Essays on the Material Text and Literature in America*, edited by Michele Moylan and Lane Stiles, 248–75. Amherst: University of Massachusetts Press, 1996.

Stocking, George W., Jr. *Victorian Anthropology*. New York: Free Press, 1987.

Stone, Harry, ed. *Dickens' Working Notes for His Novels*. Chicago: University of Chicago Press, 1987.

Stotsky, Sandra. "Literary Study in Grades 9, 10, and 11: A National Survey." *Forum: A Publication of the ALSCW* 4 (Spring 2010): 1–75.

Stott, Anne. *Hannah More: The First Victorian*. Oxford: Oxford University Press, 2003.

Stuchtey, Benedikt, and Peter Wende, eds. *British and German Historiography, 1750–1950*. Oxford: Oxford University Press, 2000.

Sucksmith, Harvey Peter. *The Narrative Art of Charles Dickens: The Rhetoric of Sympathy and Irony in His Novels*. Oxford: Clarendon Press, 1970.

Sutherland, John. *Victorian Fiction: Writers, Publishers, Readers*. New York: St. Martin's Press, 1995.

Sutton, John. *Philosophy and Memory Traces: Descartes to Connectionism*. Cambridge: Cambridge University Press, 1998.

Sylvester, D. W. *Robert Lowe and Education*. Cambridge: Cambridge University Press, 1974.

Tambling, Jeremy. *Dickens, Violence and the Modern State*. New York: St. Martin's Press, 1995.

Tappan, Eva March. *A Short History of England's Literature*. Boston: Houghton Mifflin, 1905. (Google Books)

Taylor, Dennis. *Hardy's Literary Language and Victorian Philology*. Oxford: Clarendon Press, 1993.

Taylor, Jenny Bourne, and Sally Shuttleworth, eds. *Embodied Selves: An Anthology of Psychological Texts, 1830–1890*. Oxford: Clarendon Press, 1998.

Terdiman, Richard. *Present Past: Modernity and the Memory Crisis*. Ithaca, N.Y.: Cornell University Press, 1993.

Tholfsen, Trygve R. "The Intellectual Origins of Mid-Victorian Stability." *Political Science Quarterly* 86, no. 1 (1971): 57–91.

Thomas, William. *The Philosophic Radicals: Nine Studies in Theory and Practice, 1817–1841*. Oxford: Clarendon Press, 1979.

Thompson, E. P. *The Making of the English Working Class*. New York: Vintage, 1966.

Thompson, Flora. *Lark Rise*. London: Oxford University Press, 1939.

Thompson, John B. *The Media and Modernity: A Social Theory of the Media*. Stanford, Calif.: Stanford University Press, 1995.

Thorburn, David, and Henry Jenkins, eds. *Rethinking Media Change: The Aesthetics of Transition*. Cambridge, Mass.: MIT Press, 2003.

Tompkins, Jane P., ed. *Reader-Response Criticism: From Formalism to Post-structuralism*. Baltimore: Johns Hopkins University Press, 1980.

Trilling, Lionel. *Sincerity and Authenticity*. Cambridge, Mass.: Harvard University Press, 1972.

Tropp, Asher. *The School Teachers: The Growth of the Teaching Profession in England and Wales from 1800 to the Present Day*. London: William Heinemann, 1957.

Turk, Christopher. *Coleridge and Mill: A Study of Influence*. Aldershot, UK: Avebury, 1988.

Turner, Mark W. *Trollope and the Magazines: Gendered Issues in Mid-Victorian Britain*. Basingstoke, UK: Macmillan, 2000.

Vann, J. Don. "The Early Success of *Pickwick*." *Publishing History* 2 (1977): 51–55.

———. *Victorian Novels in Serial*. New York: Modern Language Association of America, 1985.

Venezky, Richard L., with Carl F. Kaestle. "From McGuffey to Dick and Jane:
Reading Textbooks." In *Print in Motion: The Expansion of Publishing and Reading
in the United States, 1880–1940*, edited by Carl F. Kaestle and Janice A. Radway,
414–30. Chapel Hill: American Antiquarian Society and University of North
Carolina Press, 2009.

Vernant, Jean-Pierre. *Mortals and Immortals: Collected Essays.* Edited by Froma I.
Zeitlin. Princeton, N.J.: Princeton University Press, 1991.

Vernon, James. *Politics and the People: A Study in English Political Culture, c. 1815–
1867.* Cambridge: Cambridge University Press, 1993.

Vincent, David. *Literacy and Popular Culture: England, 1750–1914.* Cambridge:
Cambridge University Press, 1989.

Viswanathan, Gauri. *Masks of Conquest: Literary Study and British Rule in India.* New
York: Columbia University Press, 1989.

———. *Outside the Fold: Conversion, Modernity, and Belief.* Princeton, N.J.:
Princeton University Press, 1998.

Vlock, Deborah. *Dickens, Novel Reading, and the Victorian Popular Theatre.*
Cambridge: Cambridge University Press, 1998.

Vrettos, Athena. "Defining Habits: Dickens and the Psychology of Repetition."
Victorian Studies 42, no. 3 (1999–2000): 399–426.

Wade, Joseph H., and Emma Sylvester. *The Language Readers: Fifth Reader.* Boston:
Ginn, 1906. (Google Books)

Walder, Dennis. *Dickens and Religion.* London: Allen and Unwin, 1981.

Wall, Stephen, ed. *Charles Dickens: A Critical Anthology.* Harmondsworth, UK:
Penguin, 1970.

Waller, Philip. *Writers, Readers, and Reputations: Literary Life in Britain, 1870–1918.*
Oxford: Oxford University Press, 2006.

Walsh, Richard. "Why We Wept for Little Nell: Character and Emotional
Involvement." *Narrative* 5, no. 3 (1997): 306–21.

Ward, Adolphus William. *Dickens.* London: Macmillan, 1906.

Warren, Howard C. *A History of the Association Psychology.* New York: Charles
Scribner's Sons, 1967.

Waters, Catherine. *Commodity Culture in Dickens's "Household Words": The Social
Life of Goods.* Surrey, UK: Ashgate, 2008.

Watt, Ian. *The Rise of the Novel: Studies in Defoe, Richardson, and Fielding.* Berkeley:
University of California Press, 1957.

Weiss, Barbara. "Secret Pockets and Secret Breasts: *Little Dorrit* and the Commercial
Scandals of the Fifties." *Dickens Studies Annual* 10 (1982): 67–76.

Welsh, Alexander. *The City of Dickens.* Oxford: Clarendon Press, 1971.

———. *From Copyright to Copperfield: The Identity of Dickens.* Cambridge, Mass.:
Harvard University Press, 1987.

———. *George Eliot and Blackmail.* Cambridge, Mass.: Harvard University Press,
1985.

Whipple, Edwin Percy. *Charles Dickens: The Man and His Work.* 2 vols. Boston:
Houghton Mifflin, 1912. (Google Books)

Williams, Ioan, ed. *Novel and Romance, 1700–1800: A Documentary Record*. London: Routledge, 1970.

Williams, Raymond. "Dickens and Social Ideas." In *Dickens, 1970*, edited by Michael Slater, 77–98. New York: Stein and May, 1970.

———. *Keywords: A Vocabulary of Culture and Society*. Rev. ed. New York: Oxford University Press, 1983.

———. *The Long Revolution*. Harmondsworth, UK: Penguin, 1965.

———. *Marxism and Literature*. Oxford: Oxford University Press, 1977.

Williams, Stanley T. "The Founding of Main Street—IV: The Letters of Matthew Arnold." *North American Review* 216 (1922): 411–16. (Google Books)

Wilson, Frances, ed. *Byromania: Portraits of the Artist in Nineteenth- and Twentieth-Century Culture*. London: Macmillan, 1999.

Winter, Alison. *Mesmerized: Powers of Mind in Victorian Britain*. Chicago: University of Chicago Press, 1998.

Winter, Sarah. "Domestic Fictions: Feminine Deference and Maternal Shadow Labor in Dickens' *Little Dorrit*." *Dickens Studies Annual* 18 (1990): 243–54.

———. *Freud and the Institution of Psychoanalytic Knowledge*. Stanford, Calif.: Stanford University Press, 1999.

———. "Mental Culture: Liberal Pedagogy and the Emergence of Ethnographic Knowledge." *Victorian Studies* 41, no. 3 (1998): 427–54.

———. "The Novel and Prejudice." *Comparative Literature Studies* 46, no. 1 (2009): 76–102.

Wise, Sarah. *The Italian Boy: A Tale of Murder and Body Snatching in 1830s London*. New York: Metropolitan Books, 2004.

Woodmansee, Martha. *The Author, Art, and the Market: Rereading the History of Aesthetics*. New York: Columbia University Press, 1994.

Woolf, Virginia. *The Common Reader: First Series*. http://ebooks.adelaide.edu.au/w/woolf/virginia/w91c (accessed June 12, 2010).

Wordsworth, William. "Essays upon Epitaphs." In *The Prose Works of William Wordsworth*, edited by W. J. B. Owen and Jane Worthington Smyser. 2:43–119. Oxford: Clarendon Press, 1974.

———. *Selected Poems and Prefaces*. Edited by Jack Stillinger. Boston: Houghton Mifflin, 1965.

Wynne, Deborah. *The Sensation Novel and the Victorian Family Magazine*. New York: Palgrave Macmillan, 2001.

Xu, Wenying. "The Opium Trade and *Little Dorrit*: A Case of Reading Silences." *Victorian Literature and Culture* 25, no. 1 (1997): 53–66.

Yates, Francis A. *The Art of Memory*. London: Pimlico, 1992.

Yeazell, Ruth Bernard. "Podsnappery, Sexuality, and the English Novel." *Critical Inquiry* 9 (December 1982): 339–57.

Yeldham, Charlotte. *Margaret Gillies RWS, Unitarian Painter of Mind and Emotion 1803–1887*. Lewiston, N.Y.: Edwin Mellen Press, 1997.

Zangwill, I. *The Mantle of Elijah*. New York: Harper and Brothers, 1900. (Google Books)

Index

Aarsleff, Hans, 45

Ackroyd, Peter, 177

Addison, Joseph, 51

Administrative Reform Association, 7, 214, 331n16

Adorno, Theodor, 169, 378n50

Ainsworth, William Harrison, 88, 94, 363n48, 374n1

Alison, Archibald, 51

All the Year Round, 90, 97

Altick, Richard D., 24, 86, 100, 111, 113, 150, 203, 341–42n76

Amateurs, the (theater troupe), 79

analogy

associationist: between conventions and nature, 332n21; between failures of memory and social neglect, 179; between history and language, 278–79; linked to homology, 65–66, 355n98; between mental and social order, 49–50, 52; between reading and death, 199–201; between reading and experience, 25, 27, 34, 62–68, 123, 125, 175, 182, 204–6, 209, 226, 235, 238–39, 280–81, 313; between serial memory and serial fiction, 16; between transmission of knowledge and circulation of money, 229; as type of association, 66

Evangelical: between economic and spiritual profits, 150, 155–57; and typological uses, 174, 155, 377n42

in textbooks: between authorship and empire, 304. *See also* Hartley, David

Anderson, Benedict, 325

Andrews, Malcolm, 123

Arbuckle, James, 57

Aristotle, 406n13; Aristotelian literary theory, 129, 130, 396n79

Arnold, Matthew, 85, 228, 245

Arnold, Thomas, 87

arts of memory: and Dickens's oratory, 36–37; in Dickens's serial fiction, 118, 217–18, 238, 259–61; Francis Bacon and, 118, 348n25; and rhetoric, 35, 37, 67. *See also* mnemonics

Ashby, Joseph, 233–34, 236

Ashby, M. K., 102, 233

associationism, or the association of ideas: and connectionism, 42–43, 349n31; "crash" of, 76, 358n124; and critiques of, 72–74, 192, 277–85; and definitions, 16–18, 51, 42–44, 45–50, 51–54, 66–69, 115–16, 165–66, 174–75, 197; in Dickens's novels, xii, 13, 26–28, 33, 55, 66, 70–72, 113–20, 122–26, 148, 157, 162–63, 167–68, 171–72, 175–76, 179–80, 184–85, 188, 190–94, 196–201, 211–12, 216, 217, 218–22, 226, 228, 241–42, 243, 252, 253–54, 260, 267, 269, 297–98, 336–37n44, 358n122, 390–91n7; and doctrines, 15, 42, 44, 52, 53, 57, 63, 67, 73, 74, 75; and education, 17, 19, 34–35, 57–60, 68–72, 233–35; and empiricism, 34, 74, 77, 117, 123–24; and epistemology, 35, 48–49, 169, 171–72, 180, 193, 197,

437

feedback loop: and celebrity authorship,
3–4, 81, 105–6, 311; between Dickens's mind and reader's memory, xii,
14, 131–39, 280, 319; as methodological, 314, 322–24
"fictitious realities," 110, 117, 135, 144,
180, 206, 208, 259: and Mrs. Gamp,
122–27, 280–81. *See also* Overs,
John; Hume, David; realism; virtual,
the
Fielding, Henry, 102, 183–84
Ford, Richard, 86, 87, 111, 126–27, 133
forgetting: and the dead, 41–42, 168,
185–86, 188–91, 196–97, 201–2; as
disavowal, 215–17, 237–38, 248,
254; and learning, 63, 73, 76, 229,
236–37, 262; and solitary Londoners,
179–80, 183, 188, 193. *See also*
crowds; death; Podsnappery; topoi
Forster, John, 3–4, 79, 102–3, 111, 128–
31, 133, 136, 145, 168, 279, 286, 307,
308, 310, 311, 317
Foucault, Michel, 144, 148, 388n60
free public libraries, Britain, 22, 340n66
freedom of thought, 25, 33, 34–35, 78,
116, 144, 201, 318: and mental freedom, 32–34, 54, 328, 345–46n3. *See
also* associationism

Gaskell, Elizabeth, 90, 402n68
gentleman, 28, 33, 61, 82, 120, 154,
158–59, 230, 302: as democratic,
262–64, 265, 267, 268
Gerard, Alexander, 51
German Idealist philosophers, 74
gestures, 36, 256, 240–43, 371n161. *See
also* Podsnappery
Gillies, Margaret, 133, 373n185
Gissing, George, 273, 317–18, 378n49
Gladstone, William Ewart, 36, 101, 253,
320, 394n55
Godwin, William, 38, 53, 54, 55
Goldsmith, Oliver, 370n145

Google Books, 83, 306, 404n85
Gosse, Edmund, 291

Hadley, Elaine, 6, 11, 345–46n3,
356n108
Hall, James N., 307
Halleck, Reuben Post, 294
Hamilton, Sir William, 72
Hardy, Thomas, 405n90
Hartley, David, 25–26, 34, 43, 51–53,
54, 55, 57, 62–67, 69, 72, 73–74, 76,
235, 328, 349n31, 352n58, 358n124
Haweis, Rev. Hugh Reginald, 288–89
Haywood, Ian, 96, 97
Hazlitt, William, 38, 73–74, 192
Heathorn, Stephen, 289, 290, 299,
400n37
Helvétius, Claude-Adrien, 54, 58
Herbert, Christopher, 58–59
hermeneutics, 24
Hetherington, Henry, 59–60, 355n88
Hilton, Boyd, 155
historical psychology, 24–25, 344n82
history of reading, 4, 23–25, 325–27,
341n74; and cognitive literary stud-
ies, 344n83; and history of rhetoric,
347n9. *See also* book history
Hobbes, Thomas, 1, 15, 25, 35, 44–45,
47, 50, 82, 115–17, 118, 122, 169,
172, 228, 275, 370n145
Holmes, Oliver Wendell Sr., 297, 300
Holyoake, George, 60
Home, Henry (Lord Kames), 51
home: and homelessness, 120, 233; in
school readers, 297–99
Homer, 68
Horace, 19
Horne, R. H. (Richard Hengist), 131–
36, 174, 302, 380n66
Household Words, 25, 90, 97, 102–4, 128,
214, 250, 276, 300, 367–68n106
Hughes, Linda K., 99
humanitarianism, 319, 320–21: and authorship, 5, 80, 106, 130, 131–33,

Oxford University, 1, 37, 124, 285
Oxford English Dictionary, 82, 85, 291

Parliament, Great Britain, 21, 33, 37, 67,
97, 149, 224, 230, 233, 235, 239, 242,
249, 262, 331n16: and House of
Commons, 239, 246; legislation and
policies, 28, 190, 228, 235, 243, 244–
48, 249, 339n58, 378–79n52, 393n43,
396n69; members, 7, 33, 101–2, 251–
52. *See also* Newcastle Commission;
Revised Code; Second Reform Act
Patten, Robert L., 97, 287
patter, 121–23, 124, 371n56. *See also*
Matthews, Charles
pedagogy: and United States, 294–307,
310–11; Victorian, 12, 19, 23–24, 26,
38–39, 46, 56, 62–67, 68–70, 72, 76,
157–58, 186–87, 196, 202, 223, 228,
229–30, 233–38, 394n47. *See also* associationism; catechism; cram; Chrestomathic school; education;
English literature; learning to read;
Mayhew, Henry; monitorial
method; More, Hannah; school
readers; syllabic method
Penny Magazine, 91, 92–94, 95, 97, 103.
See also Knight, Charles
penny-dreadfuls, 90, 130, 289
periodicals, Victorian, 6–7, 11, 26, 81,
83, 86–99, 149–50, 180, 193, 219,
316, 365n73. *See also* serial fiction
Philosophical Radicals. *See* Utilitarians
pleasures of memory, the, xii, 26, 55,
179, 210, 251, 311: and childhood
reading, 140, 273, 315–19; and
death, 199–201, 206; and definitions
of, 4, 53, 66–67, 166, 168, 208, 218;
and Dickens's own, 166–67, 208;
and intellectual pleasure, 60, 98, 120;
and literature curriculum, 136, 270,
273, 299, 303, 312, 314; and modern
serial genres, 181–82, 183, 326–28; as
motive for reading, 67, 209; and

popular tastes, 4, 228, 259–60, 267,
270, 285, 309, 318; and reader reception, 2, 19, 20, 29, 46–47, 78, 99,
109, 126, 141, 143, 144, 180, 195,
206–7, 209, 226, 271, 314, 323; and
remediation, 258; and Victorian critics and publishers, 26, 94, 95–96, 99.
See also associationism; cultural
memory; curiosity; memory; Overs,
John; reading audiences; Rogers,
Samuel; serial fiction
Podsnappery, 28, 229, 230, 240–43, 247,
257, 262–64, 265, 266, 393n37,
393n38
political economy, 53, 54, 90, 109–10,
228, 236, 290: of reading, 23
Poole, John, 83–84
poor, the, 220: and altruism, 105, 217,
271, 276–77; and cultural participation, 8, 28, 226, 227–28, 262, 313;
and economic enterprises, 108, 231,
262, 270; and education, 21, 22, 34–
35, 60, 62, 71, 145, 150–51, 227, 230,
232–34, 237–38, 244–46, 249, 267,
289–90; and patriotism, 298–99; as
readers, 102, 146–47, 152–56, 158–
62, 164, 217, 287, 377n42. *See also*
Evangelicals; Dickens, Charles; literacy; pious reading; poverty; Ragged
Schools
Poovey, Mary, 96, 98, 99, 351n53
popular theater, 121–22, 126, 277. *See
also* melodrama
Poster, Mark, 327, 407n7
poverty: and pauper burial grounds,
189–90, 193; and Podsnappery, 240;
as social problem, 8, 27, 106, 118–20,
147, 154, 162, 227, 249, 276–78, 294,
312, 332n21, 378–79n52, 398n4. *See
also* Dickens, Charles; humanitarianism; poor, the
Priestley, Joseph, 38, 43–44, 51, 53, 69,
346–47n9, 349–50n35